American Literature and the Academy

The Roots, Growth, and Maturity of a Profession

Kermit Vanderbilt

American Literature and the Academy is the biography of an academic profession whose members have, as Kermit Vanderbilt writes, "helped to create for Americans a sense of our literary history and, within that growing literary tradition, our awareness of a private and national selfhood."

Vanderbilt traces the development of the study of American literature through discussions of anglophilia and anglophobia, literary-critical wars, the origin of university departments, curriculum development, textbooks and anthologies, graduate study and more. The early and later shapers of the idea of an American literature discussed by Vanderbilt include Samuel Knapp, Rufus Griswold, the Duyckinck brothers, Bryant, Cooper, Whittier, Emerson, Longfellow, Poe, Lowell, Melville, Moses Coit Tyler, C.F. Richardson, Barrett Wendell, W.P. Trent, Stuart Sherman, Carl Van Doren, and the insurgent young critics Bourne, Frank, Macy, Mencken, and Van Wyck Brooks.

Vanderbilt also covers the growth of politics, scholarship, and teaching in the American literature profession from 1921 to 1939. The names of Pattee, Quinn, Foerster, and Hubbell emerge in this analysis of the young profession's struggle to gain respectability.

During the Second World War, Matthiessen, Kazin, Brooks, Warren, and others helped to keep the humanities alive, while Robert Spiller and his team of editors and contributors were engaged in the same purpose as they produced the monumental *Literary History of the United States*. Vanderbilt provides an illuminating anal-

(continued on back flap)

American
Literature
and the
Academy

American Literature and the Academy

The Roots, Growth, and Maturity of a Profession

Kermit Vanderbilt

University of Pennsylvania Press
Philadelphia   1986

FRONTISPIECE: Commencement at the University of Pennsylvania, 1952.
(Courtesy of the University of Pennsylvania Archives)

This work was funded in part by the National Endowment for the Humanities Publications Program.

Library of Congress Cataloging-in-Publication Data

Vanderbilt, Kermit.
　American literature and the academy.

　Includes index.
　1. American literature—Study and teaching (Higher)—
United States—History.　2. Politics and education—
United States.　3. American literature—History and
criticism—Theory, etc.　4. Criticism—United States—
History.　5. College teachers—United States.
6. Americanists—United States.　7. Universities and
colleges—United States—History.　I. Title.
PS47.U6V36　1986　810'.7'1273　　86-11424
ISBN 0-8122-8031-8 (alk. paper)

Printed in the United States of America

TO MY MENTORS, Living and Deceased,
Who Taught American Literature at the
University of Minnesota after World War II

Contents

Book Three: Maturity

The *Literary History of the United States* and the
Academy in Wartime (1939–1948)

Illustrations

Book Three

1. F. O. Matthiessen (1902–1950)
2. Cleanth Brooks (1906–)
3. Robert Penn Warren (1905–)
4. Henry Nash Smith (1906–)
5. Robert E. Spiller (1896–)
6. Willard Thorp (1899–)
7. Henry S. Canby (1878–1961)
8. Thomas H. Johnson (1902–)
9. Stanley T. Williams (1888–1956)
10. Howard M. Jones (1892–1980)
11. Dixon Wecter (1906–1950)

Acknowledgments

The debts incurred while thinking about the subject of these chapters and eventually writing the present book are so considerable that I hardly know where to start the accounting. The distant beginnings are suggested in my dedication to the exceptional faculty at the University of Minnesota, where I was introduced to the advanced study of American literature during the years after World War II. Surely the profession whose origins and growth I am about to recount had reason to celebrate its maturity in the array of American literature professors who were gracing the postwar classrooms at Minnesota: Joseph Warren Beach, Bernard Bowron, Theodore Hornberger, Leo Marx, Tremaine McDowell, William Van O'Connor, Henry Nash Smith, and Leonard Unger. Equally outstanding were guest professors who came to Minnesota in the summer: Joe Lee Davis (Michigan), Alfred Kazin, Robert Spiller (Pennsylvania), Randall Stewart (Brown), George Whicher (Amherst), and others barely less distinguished. Also present were distinguished writers on the faculty whose creative work gave constant stimulus to our study of modern American literature—Saul Bellow, John Berryman, Louis Coxe, Allen Tate, and Robert Penn Warren.

More recent obligations begin with a fellowship from the John Simon Guggenheim Memorial Foundation that brought relief from a heavy teaching schedule and valuable support for travel, research, and writing. A Huntington Library Fellowship provided the leisure to read American literary histories in a setting of matchless intellectual camaraderie. The San Diego State University Foundation supported my work through a Faculty Research Grant-in-Aid. I am grateful, also, to Robert Detweiler, former dean of the College of Arts and Letters at San Diego State, for making available a research office in Love Library, along with a generous summer stipend while I was writing this book.

The assistance of many librarians and archivists, dearest allies of the research scholar, has been so generous and extensive that I hope they will accept my expression of gratitude and meager repayment in listing them and their institutions here. They include Daria D'Arienzo, Amherst College Library; Martha Mitchell, John Hay Library, Brown University; Daniel Luckenbill, University Archives, University of California, Los Angeles; Daniel Meyer, the Joseph Regenstein Library, University of

Chicago; Paul Palmer, Columbiana Collection, Low Memorial Library, Columbia University; Kenneth Cramer, Baker Library, Dartmouth College; Erma Whittington, Jay B. Hubbell Center, William R. Perkins Library, Duke University; Joan Glasser, Pusey Library, Harvard University; the entire staff of the Huntington Library, San Marino, California; Anne Gilliland, University Library, University of Illinois at Urbana-Champaign; Pat Schulte, John Dixon Library, the Lawrenceville School; Sandra Cherry, University Library, Louisiana State University; Mary Jo Pugh, Bentley Historical Library, University of Michigan; Lois Hendrickson, Walter Library, University of Minnesota; Elsie Thomas, the University Libraries, University of Nebraska at Lincoln; Jerry Cotton, Wilson Library, University of North Carolina at Chapel Hill; Cynthia Ahmann, Penn State Room, Fred Lewis Pattee Library, Pennsylvania State University; Neda Westlake, Rare Book Room, Van Pelt Library, University of Pennsylvania; Richard Ludwig, Rare Books and Manuscripts Room, Firestone Library, and Earle Coleman, Seeley G. Mudd Manuscript Library, Princeton University; Lee Milazzo, Office of University Archives, Southern Methodist University; Carolyn Davis, the George Arents Research Library, Syracuse University; William Richter, Barker Texas History Center, the General Libraries, University of Texas at Austin; Richard Engeman, Pacific Northwest Collection, University of Washington Libraries; Lawrence Dodd, Penrose Library, Whitman College; Bernard Schermetzler, Memorial Library, University of Wisconsin at Madison; Patricia Stark, Yale University Library; and the courteous staff of Love Library, San Diego State University.

Special thanks belong to Daniel Traister, curator of Special Collections, Van Pelt Library, University of Pennsylvania, for requesting that the original manuscript, a trilogy that has been condensed into the present volume, be deposited as part of the archives of the *Literary History of the United States*.

More personal obligations extend to various colleagues for their counsel and friendship over these many months. Warner Berthoff, Louis Budd, and Robert Spiller patiently and expertly read the entire manuscript and suggested valuable ways of improving (and shortening) it. George Arms, Glen Love, Richard Ruetten, and Donald Taylor lent their knowledge and encouragement at every stage of this study. From Robert and Nadine Skotheim, I received stimulation and insight from our long talks at Jackson Lake, Wyoming, in the summer of 1983. Near the end, I was fortunate to receive the considerate and talented services of Kathleen Robinson, Jo Mugnolo, and Zachary Simpson of the University of Pennsylvania Press. Finally, my thanks go to Janet Hamann, who relieved me at the typewriter and brought forth most of the final manuscript copy; and to my wife for sympathy and critical good sense over the years.

Introduction

The immediate impulse to write a book somewhat like the present one arose during the years of campus unrest when the country was engaged in the debacle in Vietnam. The subject would be the crisis in the humanities, with a special focus given to the impact of the war on my own profession, the teaching and scholarship of American literature. The role of the humanities in American social and industrial life, and in the education that prepares our young to participate in that life, had been argued, of course, over the previous hundred years. Into the 1950s and 1960s, we heard the fears expressed by the eloquent C. P. Snow and others over the schism between science and the humanities. Public support of study and research in the humanities lagged far behind endowments for the sciences. Then came the challenge of Russia's technological supremacy after they placed Sputnik into orbit, thus exacerbating the division between Snow's two cultures.

Even so, by 1965, the most serious trouble had not surfaced. Verbal scores on the Scholastic Aptitude Test for freshmen entering the academy had not yet markedly declined. Professors of American literature, in fact, published in that year a collection of papers from the recent convention of the National Council of Teachers of English. The articles glowed with professional confidence in the successful and unmistakably high cultural errand of teaching American literature in the nation's classrooms. The essays were edited by Lewis Leary of Columbia, who declared in the preface that "literature when fully revealed is perhaps also the most seminal and important element in the educative process. It is language come alive, most persuasively, most suggestively." The decisive effect of literary appreciation on the growth of individual selfhood was too obvious to require argument or explanation: "Beyond its private charm as self-revealing or self-satisfying discovery, literature has always been recognized for its power in extending self, of drawing the reader out of himself, even of becoming catharsis to self."[1]

Such paeans gave new meaning to the transcendent rewards enjoyed within the much-caricatured groves of academe. But there were also newer campus voices just beginning to be heard at Berkeley and elsewhere that intended to challenge the self-evident good and charm and power of the literary classics being taught by a smug professoriate. Repercussions of our growing involvement in Vietnam soon erupted on the American streets and campuses to fuel the new dissidence. College students whose lives seemed variously threatened by the "military–industrial complex" angrily started to question not only the political grounds of our official morality, but also the substance and structure of American education, which had helped to produce the nation's mainstream culture. The American academy, hallowed bastion of high culture and intellectual tradition, conservator of the wisdom and truth of the ages, began to tremble with the political rumblings of the young who, among other dissatisfactions, did not discover their liberal arts education to be especially liberal nor their humanities courses humane or (the new buzzword) relevant.

No less unsettling and novel were the reactions to the Vietnam crisis within the profession itself. In December 1968, at the convention in New York of the eighty-five-year-old Modern Language Association (MLA), the normally polite and conservatively orchestrated annual meeting of its thousands of professors turned into something closer to havoc and revolution. In the past, elderly members had arranged the program to hear each other and some of the favored young in the profession read papers on the transitive verb in Old High German or a new source for Longfellow's "Hiawatha." Or so the academic politics seemed to aspiring graduate students and untenured young professors who had gone to the convention to be interviewed for a job at what they termed the annual slave auction. But in 1968, just as their students were demanding contemporary relevance in the classrooms, these young instructors now voiced similar dissatisfaction with their own elders and the prevailing mode of operating at the official assembly of the profession. Tempers were heated by phrases on posters erected in the lobby of Hotel Americana over the objection of hotel guards:

WE DEMAND AN END TO AMERICA'S WAR ON VIETNAM
TO PROFESSIONAL IRRELEVANCE

JOIN US IN BUILDING A HUMANE PROFESSION IN A HUMANE NATION
A FREE UNIVERSITY IN A FREE SOCIETY

A few of the more insistent poster defenders were arrested when police arrived. At a stormy business meeting of the association on 29 December, insurgent members assembled a slim majority to pass four resolutions heavily charged with political commitments that (1) opposed governmental withholding of financial support to disruptive students, (2) favored withdrawal of all foreign troops from Vietnam, (3) opposed the military draft and any cooperation with it, and (4) condemned political harassment of radical writers, including Eldridge Cleaver, LeRoi Jones, Octavio Paz, and Carlos Fuentes.[2] (The next year, the business meeting was taken up with further radical issues, including the rights of women in the profession.)

That some of the most visible discontent within the MLA should have come in 1968 from the radical young in American literature was appropriate, as we shall discover in later chapters. And in the same regard, it was appropriately ironic that president-elect of the MLA for the following year, 1968–1969, was Henry Nash Smith, only the second American literature professor ever to hold that office. (Howard Mumford Jones, four years before, was the first.) A liberal-minded veteran of academic skirmishes, Smith turned out to be an ideal leader in a troubled time, and he did his best to mediate the demands of the various factions.

This talent was obvious in his valedictory address at Denver on 27 December 1969, when he remarked that "the intellectual and emotional disturbances that began with the 'silent vigil' in front of the lectern at the American Literature Section last year have made my term as president distinctly uncomfortable"; but perhaps the effect was also salutary, for "the militants have succeeded in waking us up." Smith addressed their two principal charges. First, the MLA, in the view of the militants, was "dominated by an Establishment, a self-perpetuating elite composed of academic politicians from a small number of 'prestige universities,'" while young professors and graduate students participated in the annual meetings mainly in "'a corral and auction block.'" Second, the young insurgents complained that the parent organization sponsored a scholarship and a spirit of education "corrupt because they serve a corrupt society," and the profession's own journal, *Publications of the Modern Language Association of America (PMLA)*, was therefore inevitably stodgy, socially irrelevant, and unreadable even for scholars. Smith concluded on a note eloquently conciliatory both to the traditionalists and social activists. He affirmed that "language and literature are the principal medium for the preservation and transmission of values in our society. Our profession makes us custodians of this medium, and we are therefore compelled to deal with the most intense intellectual conflicts of the contemporary world."[3]

Other professors of American literature in the MLA were similarly awakened to the new realities impinging on their previously well-ordered professional lives. After the disruptive sessions of 1968, and the silent vigil in front of the lectern at the American Literature Section to which Smith alluded, Professor John Gerber (Iowa), chairman of the section, proposed to his Advisory Council that the program topic for the next year might well be the overarching and thoroughly relevant question: "What do we think we're doing in teaching American literature?" For many years, professors of *English* literature in the MLA and the academy's English departments had politely doubted the comparative worth of our seemingly poor little rough-hewn body of American literature, and this resistance united the earlier champions of American literature scholarship with an underdog's defiant will and purpose. But Professor Gerber's question carried overtones now of professional concern and doubt within his own ranks. (Recall Professor Leary's buoyant assurances only three years before.)

Shortly thereafter, I began to realize more clearly the direction and shape of the chapters that follow. One modest way of understanding some part of the continuing plight of the humanities was to gain an historical perspective on where we in American literature teaching and scholarship had been and where we have arrived. Howard Mumford Jones, Robert E. Spiller, and Richard Ruland had considered important theoretical questions in American literature studies, and Spiller had also written several essays in which he recalled important events in our literary history and scholarship. But no one had written a sustained account of the struggle in the American academy to study and teach and define our native literature, and, before that academic mission, the long campaign on behalf of our national literary independence. Both movements were impeded by an American sense of cultural inferiority to England. Tracing the background, birth, and growth of this profession, the historian might remind present-day colleagues that pioneering professors of American literature had faced earlier frustrations, doubts, and sacrifices in times scarcely less difficult than our own.

The book was stalled by the usual obligations and harassments of the professor's life. But the delay by no means rendered the subject less timely, for a new climate in the academy presently threatened the humanities after the Vietnam involvement had ended. During this interval, other studies created a broad setting and some of the contexts for my own story. Among the most stimulating was Richard Ohmann's *English in America: A Radical View of the Profession* (1976). Ohmann, who helped disturb and partially reform the MLA establishment in 1968 and after, ranged among the larger political and social forces of reaction and capitalist accommodation implicit in the way the English language and literatures are taught and studied in the academy. (He edited the influential *College English* from 1966 to 1978.) He also argued that the bourgeois model governs professorial behavior all the way from local university departments to the competition and consolidation within the national MLA.

Realistically, Ohmann recognized, too, that by the mid-seventies, the spirit of alienation and rebellious activism that lately had fired the hopes of militants in the humanities had greatly slackened. The observation was easily verified here and there in the profession. Even during the final years of the war, new positions in literature faculties were disappearing. The maligned "auction block" at MLA meetings, where interviews had been plentiful, at any rate, in the late sixties, now went virtually out of business.[4] Soon the war ended, and many college students happily became materialistic once more. San Diego State University still boasted a healthy total of fifteen hundred English majors as late as 1974. Within a year, the figure was reduced by one-half. A degree in literature was not a good vocational choice, but a few years before, students were not concerned about lucrative employment. Teaching and debating the humanizing values and revolutionary ideas in literature, demanded so recently by idealistic American youth, was itself fast becoming an "irrelevant" classroom activity. Each new floating population of students on campus was in narcissistic pursuit of practical diplomas leading to a brand of self-fulfillment more or less scorned by the Vietnam generation.

How has this changing scene, with its rather bleak outlook for the profession in recent years, affected our American literature scholar-teachers? What seems a renewed assault on the integrity and usefulness of humanistic learning has generally reduced the morale of professors, old and young, in all literature fields at the time of this writing. Many of my older colleagues plan to retire early, and the younger ones all too frequently dream of retirement. This defection elicits sympathy, to be sure, but many professors have no one but themselves and their abdication from serious professionalism to blame for their sagging morale. In dread today lest they seem to America's youth stodgy and irrelevant by teaching their discipline with a conscious pride in its historical tradition, they have stampeded en masse, entire departments at a time, to satisfy the trends and tastes, the whims and "evaluations" of the inexperienced young. Historian John Higham has reminded us that a profession is "among other things, a body of individuals with a particular skill, who by co-operative action establish and maintain their own standards of achievement instead of obeying some external authority."[5]

Higham's definition, however, has been mocked by American literature professors who have introduced into the curriculum trivial literature courses barren of professional "standards of achievement" through the foolish hope that such offerings will be popular and well received by "some external authority." The result has usually been a loss of professional self-esteem with no compensating gain in popularity and respect for the humanities and American literature. The remedy for this current malady that I propose in the present book is a renewed appreciation of what has been achieved in the past when members of our profession enjoyed higher morale despite, or rather because of, their embattled campaign to build respect for America's authors and create standards of excellence in the study and teaching of our own literature.

*　*　*

This biography of an academic profession, from its nineteenth-century gestation, to its birth pains in the early years of this century, to the mature achievements up to 1948, becomes as well a many-faceted chapter in American cultural history. The Contents point to a story that embraces our early nationalistic pride, anglophilia and anglophobia, literary–critical wars, the rise of literary histories, the origin of university departments, curriculum development, textbooks and anthologies, graduate study, co-operative scholarship, professional societies and politics, and more. Nor do we want to ignore those moments when American literature professors have brought their scholarly commitments to bear on social questions in the public arena during times of national emergency. In short, this book ranges over a broad spectrum of issues and personalities to interest an academic audience at large and, it may be, many a general reader. More personally, of course, these pages will speak to the audience of professors of American literature who readily admit their unfamiliarity with the people and historic controversies that have shaped the study of our American authors. An older generation of professors will nod in recognition at the names Knapp, Griswold, Duyckinck, Wendell, Trent, Van Doren, Foerster, Parrington, Spiller, and Matthiessen. But to one who entered the academy during the past thirty years, many of these pioneers are merely names occasionally associated with a significant book or two from the dim past. In the pages to follow, the illuminating careers of these professors and other influential figures will be amply recounted, for the accumulated lives of the separate members quite obviously comprise the biography of a profession in all its necessary humanity.

The human dimension extends into the professional politics that permeate this history in the 1920s and after. This part of the story does not always flatter the illustrious participants. But it is inescapable if we are pursuing the larger and often painful truth about high-minded intellectuals whose democratic idealism may at times falter in practice. The family of American literature professors, from local departments to regional and national organizations, resembles other professions not only in the instances of wide mutual support among young and old, but also in the narrower competition, cronyism, and assumption of power that invade our human ranks. In the latter case, the militants of 1968 were neither the first nor the last to expose a self-perpetuating elite in the profession. An inexorable justice arrives, of course, when the elite grow into aging professors no longer self-perpetuating and feel the sting of being ignored on programs and having their work sharply rejected by younger editors and scholars among the rising generation who are, in their turn, vying with each other for the higher rungs of the academic ladder. All of these recurring varieties and completed cycles of Oedipal and sibling rivalry and antagonism surface in research on the history of a profession. I have tried to weigh them in the double perspective of remembered youth (the outsider) and acquired age (the insider).

In the case of private revelations discovered in extant correspondence or gained in interviews with some of the earlier survivors, I have tried to resist, as a biographer and historian, any inclination to expose lurid rivalry or gossipy antagonism merely for the sake of livelier reading. Similarly, as a critic I have avoided the occasional chance to make easy sport of some of these pioneers who struggled to interpret a growing corpus of national literature. T. S. Eliot has reminded us that we presume to know so much more than our forebears did—but they are also that which we know. The teachers, critics, and scholars we are about to meet have helped to create for Americans a sense of our literary history and, within that growing literary tradition (to echo Professor Leary at the beginning of this introduction), our awareness of a private and national selfhood.[6] And for the profession of

American literature scholar-teachers, this legacy is especially important in a time when many in the academy have begun to ask if indeed they have a calling any longer. These forerunners return all of us, young and old, to the roots, growth, and maturity of our vocation, to our reason for being in the American intellectual community.[7]

Book One   Roots

The *Cambridge History of American Literature* (1913–1921): Summing Up the First Century

Chapter 1

Prelude: Origins of the *CHAL*

Walt Whitman wrote in 1891, the year before his death, that "to have great heroic poetry we need great readers—a heroic appetite and audience." And rather glumly, he added, "Have we at present any such?" His own great audience, he felt, had never arrived, not even among the "savants," though he never had courted them. Whitman was not alone in suffering this neglect. American writers had only begun to be studied in the colleges, few histories of our infant literature had been attempted, and scholars interested in the study of our nation's authors had no sense of community within the academy.

The seeds for such a profession, however, had been sown for many decades and were taking root. By the turn of the century, a surge of national pride encouraged the study of American literature, and publishing houses soon competed for textbook authors to satisfy the new market. But entrepreneurial authorship does not create the esprit required to create a profession. A compelling occasion is needed to bring scholars together with the purpose of defining a shared field of interest and systematically exploring its riches. Such a moment arrived in the decade of World War I at Columbia University. There, the *Cambridge History of American Literature* (*CHAL*) was envisioned by three adventurous professors. The four volumes appeared in three epoch-making installments from 1917 to 1921. This monumental achievement by sixty American scholars bore convincing evidence that our indigenous literature (or at least a selective Anglo-Saxon portion of it) had a history worthy of challenging our best scholarly minds. The far-reaching influence of the *CHAL* on American letters will be recounted in later pages. But here we may consider, for the first time, the story of this unprecedented venture within the American academy, which not only produced our first large-scale, cooperative literary history, but also ushered in the distinctive profession of American literature scholarship.

✦   ✦   ✦

How and when the *CHAL* was undertaken at Columbia differs in the memory of the editors. John Erskine recalled in the late

1940s that it was perhaps in autumn of 1914 when publisher George Haven Putnam planned to bring out an American literary history in cooperation with Cambridge University. Putnam had asked William P. Trent, Erskine's colleague at Columbia, "to take charge of the planning and editing, with associates of his own selection." Trent had then invited as coeditors both Erskine and Carl Van Doren, Trent's former student and present colleague at Columbia. The three then agreed quickly on a fourth editor, Stuart P. Sherman, under whom Van Doren had studied as a graduate student at Illinois. Despite the Columbia majority, Erskine viewed the four-man board a fair regional mixture. Trent was originally a Southerner and Sherman a formidable representative of the Midwest by birth and subsequent return. "We might have added a fifth editor from the Far West," said Erskine, "if the Pacific Coast had not been so very far."[1]

In his autobiography, Carl Van Doren presents a slightly different version of the beginnings. Dissatisfied with the spate of textbooks masquerading as American literary histories, he was planning a history "to be written by many specialists and edited by Sherman, John Erskine my colleague at Columbia, and me." Meanwhile, George Putnam had asked Trent to edit an American literary history to be modeled after the current *Cambridge History of English Literature* (14 vols., 1907–17; Trent had contributed the chapter on Defoe to the *CHEL*). Aware that Van Doren was projecting a similar cooperative history, however, Trent invited his young colleague and protégé into the Putnam venture.[2]

In the journals he kept during this period, Van Doren recorded in more detail the true beginnings of the *CHAL*. In the entry on Friday, 21 February 1913, he mentioned a long talk with Erskine that included the notion of trying to bring Sherman to Columbia. Nothing was said about coediting a literary history. But a month later, we find this notation: "Just now I am ambitious to undertake a *Columbia History of American Literature* with Erskine and Sherman. A ripe ruddy trio who could make it a good work."[3] Three days later, he met in the afternoon with Erskine to discuss "my plan for the American literature on cooperative scheme which I had broached at lunch. He pleased but inclined to think Trent should be in. . . . Erskine and [George] Whicher planning a series of literary histories from various points of view, which they want time to consider the technical contributions and peculiarities of England." Clearly, the currents of literary history were very much in the air at Columbia and moving in several directions. Then in July came the exciting news to Van Doren, who was vacationing out of the city, that the Cambridge people wanted

Putnam to undertake an American literary history; Putnam had consulted with Trent, and Trent had credited Van Doren with having already planned such a work. Also, Trent had recommended Erskine and Sherman as coeditors. The next day, 27 July (Sunday), Van Doren noted, "I piddled all morning at plans for the Am lit—may God and Putnam grant we get it!" By the next Wednesday, Erskine wrote that "the deal has gone thru with Putnam, who now writes to the Cambridge people for details. Glory!" Two days later, after talking with Erskine, Van Doren wrote, "It looks as if Ward Waller & Trent will be the editors; Erskine, Sherman, and I will be the workers and advisory board."

The plans then lay somewhat dormant until 29 October 1913, when Van Doren mentions an afternoon meeting at the Columbia Faculty Club with Trent and Erskine to discuss a letter from Putnam "which seems to mean pretty surely that our plans for the Am lit now lack only the technical details and the contract." During the next two weeks, he met separately and jointly with Erskine and Trent, and Van Doren's days were consumed with sketching the history. According to his entry on Thursday evening, 13 November: "I typed the list of chapters for our Am lit and sent them to Professor Trent." Meanwhile, Sherman was invited to come aboard. On 18 September 1913, he wrote to Van Doren that he was feeling "very much honored," but suspecting he would be a "dubiously useful" editor from so great a distance. He also doubted that many of the younger generation were "qualified to write well of American authors and movements." Still, "the undertaking of this history should have a wholesome effect in stimulating interest in the 'national past.'"[4] In early 1914, Sherman joined his three coeditors for a conference in New York City to outline the work more completely and formulate general plans. By late March, a number of assignments had already gone out for the projected two-volume history.[5]

Such were the swift beginnings of this epochal literary history. Why, then, did the enterprise drag on until 1921 and balloon to an additional two volumes? One answer lies in the unexpected delays of producing the history in time of war. Even more, the editors had not calculated the enormity of defining and organizing the legacy of American writers. When the next cooperative literary history was being planned twenty-six years later on the eve of another world war, Robert Spiller and his colleagues had wisely learned their lessons from the experience of the *CHAL*. These earlier editors did not realize that by having neglected to establish for contributors a common theory of literary—historical evolution, aesthetic evaluation, and literary nationalism, the

CHAL could only advance haphazardly, its unity and scope never clearly envisioned. We ask, also, at this point if the four editors had brought to their task, by 1914, the credentials in American literature study necessary for this extensive scholarly adventure.

*   *   *

Relatively few members of the profession today, we suspect, could name the quartet who edited the *CHAL*. The three younger members went on to enjoy distinguished careers, while their senior colleague and titular editor-in-chief, William Peterfield Trent, was already a respected scholar. A Virginian by birth, Trent (1862–1939) received the B. Litt. (1883) and M.A. (1884) at the University of Virginia, where he also edited the *University Magazine*. He contributed poems to the journal, as well as literary essays on nineteenth-century English, but not American, writers. After a three-year interim of desultory reading in law and teaching at the prep-school level, he entered the Johns Hopkins Graduate School to study history and political science with Herbert G. Adams, Woodrow Wilson, and others.[6]

Though he never completed the Ph.D., Trent was offered a salary of $1,500 in 1888 to replace Greenough White at the University of the South in Sewanee, Tennessee. There he remained for twelve years before his permanent move to Columbia. He regarded himself a professor of history but was listed in the 1888–89 catalog at Sewanee as professor of English language and literature. In his first year, he offered a special course, mainly lectures, in American literature. The next year, he taught a course in modern English literature, this time merely appending some American writers out of Henry A. Beers's edition of *A Century of American Literature* (1878) in the final term of the course. Such was the usual mixed course in university "English" departments when American literature was deemed at all worthy of study in these years.

Without an academic reputation established in American literature, but always a prodigious worker, Trent accepted an invitation from Charles Dudley Warner to write the volume on William Gilmore Simms in the American Men of Letters series (after George W. Cable failed to deliver on the assignment). He gained wide notoriety, particularly in the South, when the monograph appeared in 1893. Unwilling to praise the cultural institutions of the prewar South and thereby flatter the shaky pride of postwar Southerners (and perhaps also to gain some small revenge for a lost patrimony owing to the war), Trent viewed Simms as a deprived victim of his sectional heritage. So extreme was the

Southern reaction that Trent's mother was snubbed by Richmond society; and in Simms's South Carolina, Trent felt his life to
be unsafe on the streets of Charleston.

While studying Simms's relations with various journals in the
South, Trent was moving toward his own venture in that field. He
founded the *Sewanee Review* in 1892 and was virtually a one-
man editorial board during the rest of the decade. Up to the eve
of the *CHAL*, he wrote more articles for the *Sewanee* than any
other contributor, ranging widely in modern literature and criticism.[7] Trent was also contributing articles to Eastern journals,
including *McClure's, Forum, Bookman,* and *Atlantic Monthly*—
a total of twenty-eight signed articles from 1895 to 1900—and
in these same years had edited two volumes of Poe for the Houghton Mifflin Riverside Literature Series, met Mark Twain and reviewed his *Joan of Arc,* and published for Scribner *The Authority
of Criticism* (1899) with his mildly critical "Mr. Howells and
Romanticism."

Trent owed much of this access to the literary and publishing
circles in the East to the kindness of Brander Matthews of Columbia, whom Trent had met not long after Matthews reviewed
the Simms book in the February 1893 *Cosmopolitan.* In 1895,
Trent had returned the favor with overweening praise for the "wit
and charm and sincerity" of Matthews the man, novelist, play-
wright, humorist, and professor, and in addition, for his unap-
preciated acumen as a critic.[8] It was Matthews, also, who helped
bring Trent to Columbia. In January 1900, Barnard College was
being more fully incorporated with Columbia and needed another
professor of English literature. Matthews, with Nicholas M. Butler
and Teddy Roosevelt (whom Trent had met after Roosevelt's review of the *Simms* in the *Atlantic*), presented Trent's name to Columbia president Seth Low. Trent visited the campus on 5 March
1900 and was elected to the professorship at $4,000, the salary to
be paid out of the funds at Barnard. On campus, he quickly became a presence, with his deep lecturing voice, Roman nose,
gray-red pointed beard, and cane (he never told his colleagues of
a congenital club foot). He also possessed a volatile temper. Altogether, he seemed larger than his five feet ten inches.

The most important scholarly preparation for his later editorial
role with the *CHAL* began in 1898. On 6 April, Edmund Gosse
invited Trent, then at *Sewanee,* to write the volume on American
literature for Appleton's Short Histories of the Literature of the
World. After the many interruptions of his other duties, together
with the major change of his academic residence, Trent completed in 1902 the manuscript of *A History of American Lit-*

erature, 1607–1865. It appeared in 1903, the year in which he also published two works in American history and edited a volume of Spenser. In 1904, he added to his literary history a chapter on American literature from 1866 to the present (and then condensed the volume into a school textbook, *A Brief History of American Literature,* for Appleton's Twentieth Century Text Books series). For this additional chapter, he drew on a recent essay for the Chicago *Dial* twentieth-anniversary issue. With characteristic energy and inclusiveness, he had considered 150 living writers, recognized a "distinct ascent" in our national literature from Charles Brockden Brown to the era of Howells, and, though regretting the absence of authoritative literary criticism in America, was cheered by the belated recognition of Poe and Whitman.[9]

This literary history notwithstanding, in his first thirteen years at Columbia to the inception of the *CHAL,* Trent was not known chiefly as a specialist in American literature, though Ludwig Lewisohn, who took his Columbia M.A. in 1903, credits Trent in the preface of *Expression in America* (1932) for the early inspiration of a seminar in American literature. But Trent mainly taught English literature, with his greatest energies reserved for Milton and Defoe. He also edited Thackeray as well as Spenser. Some knew him as America's authority on Balzac. In 1912, after seven years of work on Defoe and a manuscript of three thousand pages, he wrote the twenty-three-page chapter on Defoe for the *CHEL.* In 1908, he gave the address at Columbia's Milton Tercentenary and began preparations for the monumental *Columbia Milton,* the eighteen-volume edition that was finally completed in the 1930s. Where, we ask, were there inclination, time, and energy for Trent to concern himself with American literary history?

Yet he continued to write on American literature and edited numerous volumes on American writers. In 1901, he joined brother-in-law Benjamin Wells to edit the three-volume *Colonial Prose and Poetry* for Crowell. Other editions on American writers followed: Melville's *Typee* in Heath's Home and School Classics series (1902), a preface for his student Ludwig Lewisohn's edition of Crevecoeur's *Letters of an American Farmer* (1904), *Southern Writers* (1905), and *The Best American Tales* (1907) with John B. Henneman. In 1903, he began a biography of Poe that he never finished; but he gave the manuscript to former student T. O. Mabbott, who used and quoted from it in an edition of *Tamerlane* (1941). Trent was guest speaker at the Poe Centenary Celebration in Baltimore in 1909. His University of Illinois Class Day lecture on Longfellow in 1907 (at the invitation of a fourth-year student, Carl Van Doren, who was, however, too shy to meet

Trent when he appeared) was included in *Longfellow and Other Essays* (1910) and formed a basis for Trent's Longfellow chapter in the *CHAL*. Small wonder that in the midst of this productive career Trent became the victim of physical and nervous disorders. In 1911, and again in 1915, he suffered a nervous collapse, the latter one partly the result, we shall see, of political as well as literary stimuli, as pressures of World War I added to the burdens of the *CHAL*. Before his first collapse, he was mentor to Jay B. Hubbell, a University Scholar who studied with Trent from 1909 to 1910 after two years at Harvard. Hubbell's resounding tribute to Trent seems plausible in view of the achievements just sketched: "He did more than any scholar of his generation for the study of American literature."[10]

✱   ✱   ✱

For John Erskine (1879–1951) as for Trent, American literature was a field of secondary scholarly interest. He was known at Columbia as a forceful and charming, if opinionated, teacher of the Elizabethan and seventeenth-century English lyric poets. An aesthete par excellence, he wrote the music for his 1900-class show at Columbia and, later in life, earned some fame as a concert pianist. At Amherst, where he taught for six years after his Ph.D. from Columbia in 1903 (he had been one of Trent's early students), Erskine encouraged his classes to read literature for pure joy and as a preparation for life. "How well read a graduate would be who knew all of Shakespeare, the 'Fairie Queene,' 'Paradise Lost,' and the novels of Scott, Dickens, and Thackeray!" he wrote in 1908.[11]

When Erskine joined the faculty at Columbia the following year, he held almost no claim to the role he would presently assume as one of the shapers of a massive literary history of the United States. He had, however, been seriously reading several American writers just before on visits to the Amherst library. Essays on six of these writers appeared in *Leading American Novelists* (1910)—Brown, Cooper, Simms (with acknowledgment of Trent's monograph), Hawthorne (acknowledging the study of his Columbia teacher, George Woodberry), Stowe, and Harte. As we expect, Melville was absent, as were moderns like Howells, James, and Mark Twain. Erskine admitted also his debts to W. C. Brownell's *American Prose Masters* (1909) and Lillie D. Loshe's *The Early American Novel* (1907, her dissertation with Trent) and cheerfully owned that his final judgments came from "the opinion of the best critics of to-day, rather than my own impression" (p. vii). Still, these initial studies were personally fruitful.

Out of the rather perfunctory and overly long recitals of the authors' lives and subject matter, Erskine derived some of his chapters two years later for *Great Writers in America,* coauthored with the indefatigable Trent in Holt's Home University Library of Modern Knowledge, for which Trent was general editor. Erskine wrote on Brown in chapter 1; all of chapters 3–6—Cooper, Hawthorne, Poe, and the Transcendentalists; and 10–12, on Stowe, Whitman, Harte, and Mark Twain. Trent's pages dealt with Franklin, Irving, Bryant, the New England poets and, given his interests in history, Webster, Lincoln, and the historians.[12]

Though he was incapable of the prodigious industry apparent in Trent's scholarship, Erskine was advancing in his own way, then, toward a command of his American subjects. One example is the treatment of Hawthorne. In 1910, he defined Hawthorne's literary voice as the subjective, inward spirit of Puritanism; but Hawthorne overlooked the active and cheerful elements of Puritan experience. In 1912, Erskine added a component in the shaping of Hawthorne's literary imagination, the stimulus of transcendentalism, though Erskine viewed this influence as mainly a reinforcement of Hawthorne's earlier Puritan inwardness, a focus on the inner self as reflector of impulses received from the physical world. A third stage occurred in the chapter on Hawthorne in the *CHAL,* where Erskine interpreted the Emersonian influence on Hawthorne more broadly. This time, Erskine saw in Hawthorne ambivalent responses to such doctrines as self-reliance and compensation, and these reactions help to explain the spirit and meaning in much of the fiction. Coincidentally, F. O. Matthiessen elaborated this Emersonian stimulus in *American Renaissance* (1941), though he paid his respects not to Erskine's chapter in the *CHAL* but to Woodberry's *Hawthorne* (1902), which had been Erskine's earlier source as well. Erskine, in fact, had gone beyond Woodberry in exploring Hawthorne's problem with Emerson. In view of the country-cousin relationship of American literature in university English departments, Erskine deserves respect for these substantial forays into a field outside his Elizabethan specialty. He was more than marginally qualified to join his Columbia colleagues in their new adventure.

✦   ✦   ✦

Stuart Pratt Sherman (1881–1926) was Erskine's junior by two years and Trent's by twenty. He became the best known of the four editors, an incisive and trenchant critic with a masterly style honed for literary combat in subsequent years when he entered the ranks of the New Humanists and clashed with H. L. Mencken.

Born in Iowa, he lived in the Far West as a child and then came back to his grandfather's New England, where he was a prize student and budding poet at Williams College. In 1903, he received from Williams a three-year graduate scholarship to Harvard carrying an annual stipend of five hundred dollars. (Harvard supplemented it in his second and third years.) There he learned his composition in Dean Briggs's English 12, studied with George L. Kittredge, Barrett Wendell, and Irving Babbitt, wrote his dissertation on the dramas of John Ford, and barely endured the new philological approach to literature. But as Carl Van Doren later put it, "once done with Harvard, he bludgeoned its manner of literary study till the welkin shook."[13] He was profoundly influenced by Babbitt, however, and through this favorite of his professors he met Paul Elmer More and contributed to the *Nation* when More was editor (1909–14).

Sherman accepted his first teaching position at Northwestern in 1906 and then moved to his second—and final—academic address at nearby University of Illinois in 1907. There he soon met and greatly stimulated the young graduate student Carl Van Doren. The next year, Van Doren departed on a scholarship to Columbia. Sherman remained at Illinois for eighteen years until he returned to the East to become literary editor of the *New York Herald Tribune* in a brilliant and exhausting new career that ended shockingly in his early death by drowning in 1926.

When Van Doren and Erskine were conceiving the *CHAL* in 1913, Sherman came to mind as the man Van Doren could fully respect as a coeditor. But Sherman's credentials in American literary history and criticism at the time, inferred from his pieces on contemporary literature in *Nation* and elsewhere, are far less obvious than Trent's or even Erskine's. Mark Van Doren, Carl's brother, was a student of Sherman's at Illinois and hailed him as "the finest teacher I was ever to know," but the classes were in English, not American, literature. Typical of curricula at the time, Sherman's course in prose writers of the nineteenth century, in the younger Van Doren's words, included "Carlyle, Arnold, and Newman, with side glances across the Atlantic at Emerson and Thoreau."[14] Sherman eventually wrote the chapters on Franklin and Mark Twain in the *CHAL*, and these superior pages became his strongest contribution to the history. As an editor, he was "at too great a distance," as Erskine recalled in his memoirs. "Our collaboration was by mail; in other words, we three at Columbia made the urgent decisions and asked Sherman's opinion afterward."[15]

*   *   *

Carl Van Doren was the youngest and, as it turned out, fittingly, the hardest working of the quartet of editors. Born in 1885, he attended the University of Illinois in his native state. Van Doren graduated in 1907 after distinguishing himself as a student of literature, a promising writer, and, like Trent, editor of his school's literary magazine. Curricula in American and English literature being limited, Van Doren noted in his autobiography that "on the whole I was self-taught in a university which gave me leisure and excuse to read." The effects appeared brilliantly when he once wrote, under pseudonyms, an entire issue of the campus journal—poems, stories, essays, and translations. At commencement, he was class poet.[16]

In his initial postgraduate year at Illinois, Van Doren became a disciple and friend of Sherman, just arrived and living on the next street. Van Doren's scholarship to Columbia in 1908 interrupted the relationship, though he joined Sherman in the summer of 1910 on a biking trip to literary sites in England. Of his three years as a graduate student at Columbia (1908–11), Van Doren recalled that this was a time when American literature was in the doldrums. (We remember the similar response to these years in Ezra Pound's *Hugh Selwyn Mauberley*.) He studied with Trent, his "favorite teacher and the noblest man I ever knew," and wrote his dissertation on the life of Thomas Love Peacock. After the degree came an appointment to the Columbia faculty. Always conscious of trends, Van Doren sensed the quickening of serious interest in past and present national literature and "set out to become a specialist in American literature," though his friends thought it an ill-advised pursuit of a dubious Cinderella. "Then came the sudden prosperity of Cinderella."[17]

Because Van Doren kept a diary of his early years at Columbia, he is a rewarding subject for a biographer of the profession. He allows the rare privilege of following the origins and growth of a noted scholar and professor of American literature. We enter the journal in early 1913, in the months just before Van Doren begins to consider, somewhat presumptuously, the creation of a massive literary history. There, we discover him reading, for a first time, James's *The American* and "The Turn of the Screw" and commenting on the latter, "powerful . . . . How can art go further? Such delicate suggestion and artistic cumulation of dread."[18] Van Doren has been reading, too, Albert Bigelow Paine's recent biography of Mark Twain and also seriously studying the fiction of O. Henry, from which labor he produces, in succeeding months, an ambitious article that the *Atlantic Monthly* rejects. On Saturday, 22 March 1913, comes the portentous entry on the notion of a literary history. But Van Doren's concerted reading does not fully commence until early 1914, when he embarks on an intensive study of the American novel to prepare his own contribution to the *CHAL*. With a bibliographical assist from his literary young wife Irita, Van Doren begins his study of the early American novel and Charles Brockden Brown.

By the end of January, Van Doren has turned to Melville. Hearing about the sale for $12.25 of a four-volume edition of Melville (no doubt Arthur Stedman's), he hurries down to Fifth Avenue on Wednesday, 28 January, and in the afternoon, "ate Typee alive." His self-education in American literature proceeds rapidly into February 1914. In an extension class at Columbia, Van Doren is offering Emerson, Longfellow, Thoreau, Lowell, Whitman, Parkman, and Mark Twain. At home, he is reading *The House of the Seven Gables* (14 February), *Moby-Dick* a first time (completed on 15 February), *White-Jacket* (begun 16 February and finished a week later), Henry Adams's biography of Randolph (22 February), Susannah Rowson's *Charlotte Temple* (2 March), and Brown's *Arthur Mervyn* (4 March). On 23 March, the editors decide that Van Doren should also write on Cooper. He puts off that reading until July. Meanwhile, on 3 April, he has bought Moses Coit Tyler's history of colonial literature and has also begun to read Simms's *The Yemassee*. And amid this springtime indoctrination into a new field of scholarship, he records, too, the time (and energy) consumed in reading themes, grading examinations, and handling editorial correspondence for the *CHAL*, not to mention the evenings devoted to social events.

Into the early summer of 1914, Van Doren is preparing to teach two summer courses—composition and American literature, but his heavy reading schedule does not abate. In June, it embraces Longstreet's *Georgia Scenes*, Brackenridge's *Modern Chivalry*, Tyler's literary history, Mark Twain's *Innocents Abroad*, Dunlap's biography of Brown, Fessenden's *Democracy Unveiled*, the Irving and Paulding *Salmagundi*, Bird's *Nick of the Woods*, plus the numbers of Brown's *Monthly Magazine* and Joseph Dennie's *Port Folio*. On 1 July, he arises at 5:30 A.M. to work on his chapter, but "it has no distinction, and I think of the smooth-slipping syllables of S.P.S. [Sherman]." The next day, he "rewrote all the account up to Brockden Brown." Meanwhile, Van Doren's American literature class overflows with ninety students ("American literature is popular"), and he plans to ask the department to hire Irita as his assistant. In July, he reads, consecutively, Cooper's *The Prairie*, Irving's *Bracebridge Hall*, Cooper's *The Pilot*, Mary Phillips's *Cooper*, and then Cooper's *Precaution*, *The Pioneers*, and *Lionel*

Lincoln; and he nearly completes his Brown bibliography. To the diary comment for Sunday morning, 26 July 1914, university professors everywhere will nod understandingly: "worked painfully on my chapter and found it so dreadfully hard. I hardly see how I am ever to do these chapters, with all the savage work on my back. The S.S. [summer session] is really very wearing."

Before the end of 1914, Van Doren has completed the pioneering "model bibliography of Melville" (Sherman's praise).[19] By January (1915), he is still struggling with the Cooper chapter. Amid professional interruptions, he continues to read Cooper into March. On 24 May 1915, he is finally able to note that "I gave the last touches to Cooper." And not a moment too soon, for the other *CHAL* contributors have begun to flood his desk with manuscripts. Yet Van Doren is unable to resist still another grandiose assignment, one that also lies well beyond his current expertise. He presently signs a contract with Macmillan to write a 100,000-word volume on American fiction. Presumably, there is not a deadline, for his pioneering *The American Novel* (1921) will appear late in the prolonged travails of the *CHAL*.

Given to a lifelong and immodest scholarly overreaching, Van Doren was also refreshingly self-debasing when he owned, in his later memoirs, to a consistent weakness as a critic and literary historian: He was deficient in theory.[20] The admission returns us to the planning stages of the *CHAL* and the issues in literary history that faced Van Doren and his coeditors. We join them as they begin, in 1914, to make chapter assignments and gradually comprehend some part of a century of literary scholarship bearing on three centuries of literary creation in America.

Chapter 2

Organizing the *CHAL* Team

Before the contract with Putnam was signed, the *CHAL* editors were already planning to recruit the best minds currently engaged in American literature studies. We find Van Doren, Erskine, and Trent holding conferences at the Faculty Club at Columbia while Sherman, feeling "dubiously useful" back at Illinois, was suggesting contributors and pondering what his own instant expertise might possibly entail—perhaps Franklin, Paine, Thoreau, Hawthorne, Mark Twain, and even O. Henry.[1] The most detailed information on the preliminary organization of the contents and the team lies, once more, in the journals of Van Doren. With the new year of 1914, the history had begun to dominate his waking hours. On Friday, 2 January: lunch with Erskine and "worked on our plans for the Am Lit." Later in the library, he bumped into George Whicher, who had heard about the plans from Trent. On 6 January: happened onto Trent in the library and went to his house at 5:00 P.M. to discuss the two-volume history, now seemingly a sure thing with Putnam. Van Doren gives no indication if these early discussions touched on theory and structure of the *CHAL,* though years later he wrote that Trent's "masterly design was its foundation."[2] (Critics then and later, we shall see, were not so impressed with that design.)

Soliciting the contributors in 1914 was a task that the three Columbia editors performed with moderate success despite their less-than-coordinated procedures. When the earliest authors had been secured, Van Doren apparently assumed the responsibility of "outlining the chapters in detail [and] explaining them to the specialists," duties fit, as he later said, for "the most interested and the youngest of the editors." He also "[brought] the material together, fitting the parts into the total scheme," though Trent's biographer insisted that the senior editor was present at every stage of the unfolding history.[3] Trent, to be sure, was to make the most of his previous editorial and academic connections; and he had already grappled with the difficulties of organization and substance in his own volume of American literary history. But this time, his hot temper soon led to estrangement with Putnam, and Van Doren was left to manage the greater burden of editorial chores, small and large. On 21 January 1914, for example, he had met again with Trent to revise the outline and noted that he had typed up the changes and sent them in a memorandum to the editors. Also by now, Putnam had figured the editorial remuneration at $750 for each of the two volumes, with $100 for clerical expenses.

Meanwhile, the chapter organization was sufficiently firm so that the editors could begin to gather their team of scholars and also to claim their own favorite authors. Van Doren, we have seen, had begun studying the early novel intensely. Sherman assumed the Irving chapter to be his and was even envisioning the New York Irving as the "hero and keynote of the history—thus dashing a little more cold water into the Frog Pond on Boston Common." (This, the lingering rancor of a disaffected Harvard man toward the Boston–Cambridge axis.)[4] Then came the first of the countless headaches in selecting the contributor team. Van Doren noted in his journal of 13 January 1914 (the same date that Sherman had written from Illinois to claim Irving): "Professor Trent told me he had to give the chapter on Irving to Mr. Putnam, whose father was Irving's great publisher. So be it. Now for [my working on] the American novel, till somebody wants it." Two days later, Sherman's letter arrived, "full of enthusiasm for Irving and American literature generally," to which Van Doren must now frame an apologetic answer.

In the weeks that followed, Van Doren recorded that the chapter on newspapers had gone to Frank Scott of Illinois (recommended by Sherman), W. B. Cairns of Wisconsin begged for time on a decision to write on periodicals and gift books (later accepted), political writers were offered to Allen Johnson of Yale (declined), historians to Carl Becker of Kansas (declined), Lowell to Irving Babbitt of Harvard (declined), and explorers to George Winship of the Harvard library (accepted). One completed chapter arrived, Henry Cabot Lodge's Webster, on which Van Doren commented (9 March): "surprisingly bad. Lord, why did we relax and ask him!"

During these preliminary stages, Sherman wrote again to Van Doren that he felt rather uselessly out of the editorial and business planning of the *CHAL* and offered the Columbia editors "a free chance to eliminate me at this point" at his Illinois outpost. In the meantime, he was working on Franklin and imagining a list of ideal contributors: Paul E. More on both Emerson and Thoreau, Brander Matthews on dramatic literature, Harvard gadfly George Santayana on some subject "which he wouldn't merely poke fun at," plus critic William C. Brownell (literary adviser at Scribners), Ferris Greenslet (editor-in-chief of Houghton Mifflin), Robert Herrick (Chicago), and in fact, qualified professors from as many separate colleges as possible to create widespread interest, and sales, for the history.[5]

Trent, on the other hand, was not merely imagining but actively soliciting contributors. On 29 March 1914, for example, he wrote to his friend Edwin Mims (professor of English at Vanderbilt), whom he had known since the *Sewanee* days, and asked for an essay on poets of the Civil War. (Mims had written in 1905 the American Men of Letters volume on Lanier.) Since this became the thirty-sixth chapter near the end of volume II, little more than midway through the eventual *CHAL*, we begin to realize that the Columbia editors were blessedly unaware of the huge task they had imperfectly envisioned for a two-volume history. Trent's letter to Mims showed that the editorial board was, at least, conceiving some of the finer details of these early solicited chapters:

> We propose to have one chapter in two sections deal with the poets of the Civil War. Professor W. D. Howe of Indiana has agreed to do the Northern poets—Brownell [et al.] in 4000 words. Will you be good enough to undertake the Southern poets—Timrod, Hayne, Randall, Ryan *et al.* in 6000 words? Fuller directions will be given later, should you accept, but I may say now that you would not treat extensively a man like Simms, whose main work was done before 1860, or a man like Lanier, whose main work was done after 1865. You would, however, carry men like Hayne, Ryan to their deaths, giving their biographies briefly and summarizing their work, but emphasizing their war poetry.

Trent added that the deadline was 1 January 1915. Compensation would be "very small," the same figure as with the *CHEL*—$2.50 per page.[6]

Since the greatest percentage of contributors, plus three of the four editors, were living in New York City, the correspondence that could help to enlarge an editorial history of the *CHAL* is relatively limited. Fortunately, Trent and Van Doren left the city in summer and, characteristically, brought along their scholarly work in progress. In these intervals away from Columbia, they kept in close correspondence with Erskine, other colleagues, and each other. Erskine wrote to Van Doren in June 1914 that assigning the Hawthorne chapter remained a problem; he had written to Trent, offering to write the chapter himself. He would also ask John S. Harrison of Kenyon to do the Emerson, and Walter B. Pitkin of Columbia the Thoreau.

Trent, meanwhile, was vacationing in Essex, New York, and wrote to Van Doren that Mims had agreed to do his chapter, as had C. Alphonso Smith of the Naval Academy ("Dialect Writers") and William McDonald, historian at Brown ("American Political Writing, 1760–1789"). U. B. Phillips (professor of history, University of Michigan) had also agreed to an assignment. (For whatever reason, it never appeared.) For the "Publicists and Orators, 1800–1850," a historian would be best. Had Van Doren written to A.C. McLaughlin of Chicago? St. G. L. Scoussat of Vanderbilt was another possibility, as were visitors at Columbia's "summer session contingent." (McLaughlin eventually wrote the chapter.) Hatcher Hughes, lecturer in English at Columbia, was, said Trent, another possible author for the history. (He never contributed.) Trent suggested that Van Doren try to complete the list of likely contributors with people outside the academy, a notion to which Sherman concurred.[7]

In July 1914, Paul Elmer More, like Trent, was vacationing at Essex and sent a note to Van Doren that he had agreed to Trent's invitation to write the Edwards chapter. He would also do the Emerson if the 1 January 1915 deadline could be moved to 1 July. But he would understand if the editors decided to solicit the Emerson chapter from someone else. Trent wrote to Van Doren some weeks later from Essex that More would be their man for Emerson and asked that Van Doren inform Erskine to suspend all negotiations with any other scholar. More, in turn, had suggested a young professor at Wisconsin, Norman Foerster, as a possible candidate for the Thoreau. As an editor of *Nation*, More had known him to be a fine reviewer for that journal. Foerster was eventually tapped for the "Later Poets," and the Thoreau went to Archibald MacMechan of Dalhousie, the only Canadian to contribute. Trent wondered if "the modern philosophers, James, *et al.*" should not go to either John Dewey (Columbia) or Oscar Firkins (Minnesota). This chapter on "Later Philosophy" was finally written by Morris Cohen of CCNY.[8]

By autumn of 1914, the editors were projecting the chapters that would soon require a further volume III and then IV, and we suspect that they had an inkling that their history might now be bursting its original limits. The projected manuscript deadline of 1 January 1915, they clearly discovered, had been too optimistic. Far-flung professors were bogged down in multiple academic duties that easily interfered with their writing deadlines. And then there were the defectors who must be replaced. Van Doren and Trent bore most of these editorial headaches, or so the extant documents suggest, though Erskine seemed to be quite active in the survey of prospective contributors and later took his turn at reading the manuscripts. More than thirty years afterward, he recalled that he persuaded his fellow editors to give the Whitman chapter to Leon Bazalgette, French author of the recent (1908) biography. Bazalgette "signed the contract enthusiastically." Erskine agreed to translate the chapter. But then Bazalgette was called into armed service for the duration.[9] For this aborted assignment, the editors then tapped one of their local specialists on Whitman, the young Emory Holloway of Adelphi. Erskine also persuaded Trent that George Woodberry, who had been a great influence on Erskine, be given carte blanche as a contributor, partly because Woodberry had been scarred by an internal fracas with President Butler, which led to Woodberry's resignation in 1904. Not to include Woodberry, Erskine argued, would lend the appearance of siding with Butler. Erskine and Trent then urged Woodberry to write the chapter on his old Harvard professor Lowell. He signed the contract and added emphatically, "I owe Lowell something." But he later pleaded a release due to ill health.[10] The editors fell back on still one more of their own, Ashley Thorndike of Columbia.

Erskine was also supporting his earlier classmates and students. Both William Ellery Leonard of Wisconsin ("Bryant and the Minor Poets") and Marion Tucker of Brooklyn Polytechnic Institute ("The Beginnings of Verse, 1610–1808") had been Erskine's classmates in Trent's graduate seminar at Columbia. George Hellman ("Later Essayists"), another fellow student, edited the *Literary Monthly* at Columbia. He later joined Erskine's staff at Beaune, France, during the war. George Whicher, en route to Amherst from Illinois in 1915, had studied under Erskine; he wrote chapters on "Early Essayists" and the later "Minor Humorists." And Percy Boynton of Chicago ("Patriotic Songs and Hymns") would presently direct the summer school at Chautauqua where Erskine then taught in the summer of 1916.[11]

Sherman's part in the history during late 1914 continued, as before, to be rather minimal. He was diligently shaping his chapter on Franklin, together with what he considered a fairly complete bibliography.[12] Meanwhile, Trent and Van Doren were hoping to nail down some final assignments. Particularly pressing was the need for a scholar to write the early "The Puritan Divines, 1620–1720," chapter 3. Trent wrote Van Doren that he was unable to come up with a suitable name. What about E. W. Emerson, who had recently completed the edition of his father's journals? Or Edwin D. Mead? (Mead, an author and lecturer, had written *The Influence of Emerson* in 1903.)[13] The literary adviser at Macmillan then told Van Doren that Vernon Parrington of the University of Washington had proposed to that publisher a literary history. (Presently titled *The Democratic Spirit in American Letters*, this was an early version of *Main Currents in American Thought*.) On 16 January 1915, Van Doren wrote to Parrington for a copy of the pages "which deal with the Puritan Divines to the death of Cotton Mather." Parrington obliged, and on 12 February, Van Doren asked him to write the *CHAL* chapter. In accepting the honor, Parrington complained, however, that to complete the assignment in twenty-five pages would not be easy. Van Doren understood, but, as he said to Parrington on 31 March, space was at a premium, and "it is simply impossible to undertake the culture history which we should like." Van Doren added to the future author of *Main Currents* that such a full-scale history "should certainly be done, sometime, by some-one."[14] At the same time, Van Doren had also written to V. L. O. Chittick at the University of Washington. (Chittick wrote his dissertation on Thomas Chandler Haliburton—"Sam Slick"—at Columbia with Van Doren.) Chittick confirmed that Parrington was the best man available on the Puritans.[15]

On the last day of 1914—the day before the nominal deadline for manuscripts—Trent sent a note to Van Doren asking him to drop in at 5:00 P.M. to pick up two chapters "and discuss some methods I have thought of for safeguarding mss and for revising them." He also wanted to know "where we are" and "arrange for a 'prodding letter' to contributors," since Putnam was itchy to begin typesetting. But even Van Doren was struggling tardily with his Cooper. Other *CHAL* professors were sidetracked in the academy with other responsibilities and obviously awaiting the next summer vacation for a chance to return to their chapters. Among those currently at work, More wrote to Van Doren about problems with his Edwards manuscript (4 and 5 January 1915), and William Ellery Leonard acknowledged with thanks the specifications for his chapter on the poets; he also hoped that a graduate student could be found to compile his bibliography (24 January 1915).

Perhaps the most serious threat to the entire *CHAL* undertaking occurred in these early weeks of 1915, and it highlights one of the prominent aspects of academic life: the activism of the professor during periods of national stress. Trent's strenuous anglophobia in response to the current World War had now erupted. Van Doren's diary for 18 February mentions lunch with Erskine and Trent, where Trent produced his poem, "Germany, 1915," which he planned to print in a private edition of fifty copies. Fifteen years before, he had written anti-imperialist poetry against his nation's role in the Spanish-American War. Currently, he viewed the British as the imperialists, and his vigorous stance had already strained relations with Brander Matthews, a forceful anglophile. A few weeks passed, and Trent then went public. He published his thirty-four-line poem in the New York *Staats-Zeitung*. His pro-German sentiments were reprinted in the *New York Times* (7 March 1915) and the *Literary Digest*. (Lines in praise of Germany included "Wise in peace, great in war / . . . This stark, consummate might / Is girt with adamantine right—") George Haven Putnam's letters assailing Germany, Trent was well aware, had been appearing prominently in the New York press, and Trent could hardly have been surprised that the Putnam brothers would not be kindly disposed to his poetic sympathies. A short interval of polite tolerance followed, perhaps as the Putnams huddled to discuss the fate of the *CHAL*. Then on 11 May 1915, Van Doren described their response, which took the form of an "insulting letter from Irving Putnam" that had left Trent in a rage and his wife in tears, while Van Doren counseled "utter silence" from his revered mentor. The result was that Trent refused to deal directly with Putnam thereafter, and even more editorial labors descended on Van Doren. Perhaps not coincidentally, George Putnam, the day before Irving's letter to Trent, had written an "open letter" to President Wilson protesting the recent sinking of the Lusitania and sneered at the excuse by the *Staats-Zeitung* that Germany had amply warned the United States of such risk in the Atlantic.[16]

Trent went even further by joining with William Jennings Bryan, David Starr Jordan, and others to urge U.S. neutrality. The reverberations were at once far reaching and jeopardized Trent's academic career. His name soon appeared on the U.S. Senate's enemy list. Schools threatened to abandon his textbooks. At Columbia, he became estranged from the faculty to such a degree, in fact, that he drafted a letter of resignation. Erskine convinced him to destroy the letter. His physical and emotional health, always precarious in the previous four years, briefly collapsed, and he would be permanently impaired by the effects of these wartime skirmishes.[17] But he was too crusty to relent and spare himself. In a letter to Van Doren during the summer, he mentioned that he was trying to write more poetry. The summer heat had been discouraging his muse, "but perhaps something inspiring will happen soon—something like Woodrow Wilson's bursting through the spontaneous combustion of his own humanity, or Brander Matthews's learning the German alphabet—and then I'll break into the columns of the *New York Times* with a Paean dedicated to George Haven Putnam. Look for it!"[18] In a subsequent chapter, I return to the war years and their relation to American literature study.

Trent's frustrations aside, the summer of 1915 became a period of humming activity for the *CHAL*. Leonard's chapter on Bryant et al. arrived for editorial scrutiny. Erskine wrote from the Columbia summer session to Van Doren at West Cornwall, Connecticut, that Trent had received the agreement of George Hellman to do the later essayists, and would Van Doren please give Hellman the necessary details on that chapter? Also, George H. Palmer (Harvard, emeritus) had refused the Longfellow chapter, and could Van Doren think of a substitute? Apparently Van Doren suggested Raymond M. Alden (Stanford), for Erskine wrote again that he and Trent agreed to that name, and Erskine would ask Alden. Would Van Doren write to Hellman about doing the Thoreau bibliography (for MacMechan's chapter)? In August, Trent told Van Doren that the first six chapters would be en route, for he and Erskine had read them "carefully"; but "there are a good many things to be done before they can go the printer. . . . The other chapters I'll keep." Sherman's Franklin and Parrington's Divines "need little," Trent noted, but he and Erskine had serious doubts about More's Edwards. George Winship's Explorers also bothered Trent because it was the crucial opening chapter and remained unsatisfactory. Could Van Doren work on it? A week later, Erskine sent the chapter on the early dramatists by Arthur H. Quinn (Pennsylvania) to Van Doren with the judgment that "barring punctuation, [it] seems mighty good. . . . After going over the other chapters in detail, one is in the right frame of mind to appreciate the solidity of Quinn's."[19]

In early September 1915, Trent wrote from Northampton, Massachusetts, to advise Van Doren not to go to the printer with the early chapters until all three Columbia editors could have a session together. He suggested that Van Doren try some surgery on the "Colonial Newspapers and Magazines" by Elizabeth Cook (Columbia), and Trent would presently see John Bassett at Smith about changes in his chapter 2 on early historians. Trent wrote again the next week to report that Erskine said Alden would not take the Longfellow chapter. Erskine suggested Stark Young, just arrived at Amherst from the University of Texas. But Trent felt that Young might be a bit overpowering, amid the others, and wondered if the venerable Frank B. Sanborn, the old schoolmaster and Concord biographer, would not be the man for the Longfellow assignment. Or perhaps Trent should write the chapter after all. He, at least, would not be tempted to "running Long-fellow down." And if the Poe chapter were still open, Trent knew that Killis Campbell (University of Texas) had made some recent findings in Poe biography and would be a good choice. (Trent's own work in Poe qualified him, but he was content to let the chapter go to Campbell.) As to More's Edwards, on which Erskine had expressed serious reservations, Trent commented in his finest vein of trenchant irony and candor:

> Personally I do not give a _____ for anyone's philosophy, not even my own, hence I am probably not well qualified in philosophic eyes to judge the chapter. Between us, I always find More's criticism wanting in certain respects, and I think this chapter hardly his best, but I am not sure that it will be worth while to ask him to revise it except in small details.[20]

Two days later, Van Doren received Erskine's response to Trent's recent suggestions. Erskine hoped that Trent, and not the elderly Sanborn, would write the Longfellow: "Senility need not be pre-arranged in a work of this sort." Also, he suspected (rightly) that Trent was not troubled enough by More's condescension toward Edwards, and Erskine elaborated to Van Doren: "Here's just the place where Brander's [that is, Matthews] championing of Ameri-can thought should come in. If Edwards gets patronized in this priggish way, what should be done to smaller men?" More's chap-ter was, consequently, sent to a predictably sympathetic Sher-man, and Van Doren had the reply in late October. Was More unjust? No, said Sherman; he was good on Edwards's intellectual vigor, integrity, mysticism, and poetic leanings. Perhaps the human relationships were slighted, however. Should there be a paragraph on influence? Yes, for More left Edwards as somewhat a "wreck on the remote sands of time," and a comment on his effect on subsequent thought and the "moral consciousness of New England would make him more of a *figure* in the literary history." More's handling of Edwards on evil, Erskine had noted in the margin, was "childish—the problem no longer exists in this form." True, said Sherman, but that was More's point, too.[21]

The progress of chapter 5, the eighteenth-century "Philoso-phers and Divines" by Woodbridge Riley (Vassar), can be traced with gratifying fullness in the Van Doren correspondence. Writ-ing in August 1915 from Siasconset, Massachusetts, Riley in-formed Van Doren that the chapter was complete except for Samuel Johnson and he had left behind at Vassar his notes on Johnson. Would a 1 October deadline be allowed? He had written three thousand words on the New Light controversy in Chauncey, Mayhew, and Whitefield, plus another thirty-five hundred words on Woolman, which he hoped to trim. He would aim at two thousand words on Johnson, whom he had treated in his previous books, for a total chapter of eight thousand words. In mid-October, having missed his deadline, he promised to have his chapter typed within the week. In early December, he mailed the forty-four-page manuscript of six thousand words. But he would need another month, and a trip to the New York City libraries, to make his bibliography "anything like those appaling [*sic*] lists in the English [*CHEL*] volume."[22]

In early 1916, the history finally began to approach the publishing stage that the editors had hoped to reach a full year before. Van Doren recorded in his diary the continuing routine of an editor's life. 6 January: early chapters were on hand "which simply must go to press within a week or so." 11 January : "slaving at editorial corrections, stupid contributor's blunders." 17 January: had sent off a "flock of letters" to contributors and planned to tie up the first chapters for the printer tomorrow. Then came an offer as headmaster of the Brearly School for girls in the city, at a salary of seven thousand dollars, and Trent urged him to accept. The higher salary would enable him to buy more time. (Van Doren soon took the post and remained there over the next three years.) On Sunday morning, 12 March, he was reading the first *CHAL* proofs and corresponding with authors. Three days later, his assignment was George H. Putnam's own essay on Irving, "surely one of the worst essays ever written by the hand of man or publisher." During the next two weeks, he devoted virtually all of his spare time, even into the early morning hours, to the "drudgery of proof," including the worry over extended bibliographies ("almost every man has more bibliography than chapter"). And he was completing his own proofs on Brown and Cooper. He commented on 22 March about his "grouchy toil": "I thus pay for being the youngest of the editors"; then he wickedly thought of the prospective job at Brearly: "But how will it be when I am the highest paid of all them?"

In the meantime, Trent had returned some of the proofs with his stylistic corrections, including the tart comment on Bassett's essay on the early historians, "I think we may as well make up our minds that *sheer wooden* style, as particularly in Chap. II, must be improved when possible."[23] On 13 April, Van Doren recorded a solid day of work to that same end, "mostly trying to put Ruth Putnam's horrid chapter on Prescott-Motley into English." (She was the sister of George and Irving.) Trent added his own burden on 13 May: "Here is the Longfellow—I cannot say 'effu-sion,' because it *dribbled* rather than *poured* itself out. Make any changes you will, & believe me to be / Yours wearied of literary criticism."

A sampling of the correspondence in the summer of 1916 clearly shows how Van Doren was saddled with the ultimate edi-torial duties. Trent continued to read galleys and advise Van Doren how best to deal with Putnam in Trent's stead. In June, he recommended that Van Doren tell Putnam not to destroy the gal-leys at once. "This insures us," he wrote, "in case we should encounter an obstreperous chap who should declare that some-thing in the pages had not been in the galleys." (Trent also ad-vised against sending page proofs to authors unless their galleys happened to be much revised.) Preserving galleys "may also be a protection against our printers," he noted.[24] Also in June, Erskine wrote from Cresco, Pennsylvania, on stationery now bearing the *CHAL* letterhead, and gleefully began, "I seize on the oppor-tunity to use this blessed paper!" He was sending some proofs to Van Doren by way of Trent, reported that Quinn wanted his chapter and bibliography proofs back for revisions ("The Early Drama"), and regretted that his own Hawthorne chapter was so long in coming. "I have had the chapter sketched for some time, but it's pretty rotten," he reported, but thanks to the prodding of Van Doren's recent card, he would put it into shape and send it to his sister in New York City for typing. He next departed for three weeks of teaching at Percy Boynton's Chautauqua summer ses-sion. Subsequently, he managed to finish the Hawthorne essay and wrote in defense of his tardy mailing: "The ideas, I thought, would be novel and would set people thinking provided they were properly expressed." The bibliography was another matter, and he asked Van Doren, "Have you a copy of that schedule of in-structions by you?" In late August, he wrote again for advice on bibliographical items and finally sent off the copy in September with the request that Van Doren alter it in any way he deemed fit; and Erskine would add any final sources when galleys arrived.[25]

Other contributors who corresponded with the harassed Van Doren in summer of 1916 included, once again, the disorderly Woodbridge Riley, who wrote in July from Cape May, New Jersey, that his bibliography on Woolman could not be completed un-til he returned to Vassar in September "unless I make a special trip to Philadelphia." And then there was publisher-contributor George Putnam, who returned his galleys on Irving and clearly was irritated that his wartime adversary Trent had corrected a factual error: Putnam had been following Pierre Irving's biography and had not been privileged to see, as Trent had, the manuscript of Irving's diary. More headaches came by way of William Ellery Leonard. From New York City, he wrote that his proofs had apparently gone astray somewhere between New York and Wisconsin. (He finally did receive them.)[26] Trent, it seems, would not have grieved if the proofs had remained lost. After sending Leonard's chapter and all the others to Erskine in July, he had written to Van Doren on 7 July:

> In the main they strike me as excellent—especially yours, which "Do you proud." It's the best treatment of the subject I know of—particularly the Cooper. L.[eonard] has buried himself & Bryant in the depths of his own complexity, but such things will happen. My own Longfellow is sufficiently *simple sine plica*—it didn't cause much knitting of the brows to write!—to balance it!

In the middle of this hectic summer of editorial work, Van Doren decided, rather foolishly, to complete a novel of his own, titled *Convictions*. During the final week of September, he noted in his diary that he had finished it and was preparing (1) to return to New York City to a new apartment, (2) to begin his new headmastership at Brearly, and (3) to teach an overflow class in American fiction at Columbia. Not least, he must soon deal with Major Putnam, who had recently been concerned over the growing bulk of the history and had been goading Van Doren with the economic need of keeping the twin volumes to a marketable size. Van Doren relayed Putnam's worries to Trent and received a letter of advice from Northampton (dated 23 September) on how to deal with the publisher on any changes in format. Shortening the bibliographies, Trent suggested, would hardly be the way to reduce the volume:

> [D]escribe your work already done in the way of cutting out useless bibliographical items, and point to the fact that further bleeding will necessitate consultation with authors—with the delay incident to negotiations with that irascible tribe, only less detestable to G. H. P. than the Germans—and also that the greater demand for bibliographies made by Americans as compared with British scholars must be considered.

(The bibliographies turned out to be enormously valuable to American scholars, as Trent knew they would be. But they also made necessary four volumes, rather than two, and comprised nearly one-half of the fourteen hundred pages of the total history.) Trent went on to entertain three publishing options for Van Doren to present to Putnam:

(1) Three volumes instead of *two*—in which case American sales would probably make up for some loss in English sales. (2) Frank acceptance of [two] thicker volumes. (3) Two separate two-vol. editions, similar in text, but varying in bibliographies—the English edition being much cut down.

Trent suggested that Van Doren consult with Erskine and then arrange a meeting with Putnam. On 17 October 1916, Van Doren noted somewhat belatedly in his diary (which, unfortunately for us, he soon discontinued) that five days before, "I saw Mr. Putnam and we agreed to issue the *CHAL* in 3 vols., as it should be. The whole text is now set up." The eventual text would, however, still burgeon to many more chapters.

Still another year passed before the first volume at last appeared. In February 1917, Putnam sent payment to Trent for services of the editorial board, contracted at fifteen hundred dollars for a two-volume history, and Trent then mailed separate checks to each editor. (Contributors, it will be recalled, were to receive $2.50 per page on publication.) Putnam also granted fifty dollars for postage, which sum Trent turned over to Van Doren. Some months later, Putnam agreed to pay additionally, either to the chapter authors or their assistants, for the extensive bibliographies.[27] Page proofs, meanwhile, were still being revised in spring of 1917. By early May, the first volume seemed to be completed, or so W. E. Leonard was given to believe when he sent Van Doren his congratulations. The editors were now passing around drafts of the preface. But even in late June, the publishers were unsatisfied. Two of Putnam's editors suggested changes in Sherman's prose in the Franklin chapter. Van Doren wrote impatiently to Trent, "It seem [sic] to me that they have been frightened by a few sharp touches inseparable from Sherman's style, which I do not think inferior to that of either of the gentlemen [Putnam editors] in question."[28]

Editorial work in the summer of 1917 continued on volume II, while more contributors were recruited for the later chapters. At long last, in late autumn, Van Doren received from George H. Putnam a copy of volume I and the compliment that the contributors to the *CHAL* had been chosen with "excellent judgment (to be modest I imagine I ought to make one exception to this statement)." The editors, it will be recalled, had earlier concurred to Putnam's modest exception in the parentheses.[29]

Before considering the individual chapters and the critical reception of volume I, and the further contents, which enlarged to
a four-volume history not to be completed until 1921, we may
turn at this moment to the preface to volume I. In it, the editors
defined the enterprise that was about to meet the light of public
scrutiny and effectively give birth to an academic profession.
While they did not give us a prefatory explanation of literary or
historical principles (none, as we have noticed, seem to have
been formulated), they did acknowledge six milestones in American literature study in the previous century that had decisively
influenced the *CHAL*. In the next several chapters, it will be
rewarding to appreciate these origins of an unprecedented
American literary history and the correlative roots of a scholarly
profession.

Chapter 3

Preface to Volume I:
Trailblazers in the Nationalist Era
of Samuel Knapp

In their preface to the first volume (1 June 1917), the *CHAL* editors pay respects to their chief forerunners—Samuel Knapp, Rufus Griswold, Evert and George Duyckinck, Moses Coit Tyler, Charles F. Richardson, and Barrett Wendell—who conveniently become, for us, the centers, respectively, of the next six chapters, which pursue the study of American literature to its origins in the previous century. The first of these, Samuel Knapp, was the author of *Lectures on American Literature* in 1829. Knapp's pioneering history, claim the editors, was important in four ways. He traced our literary history "'back to the previous age of heroick virtue and gigantick labours'" (I, iv) before the vaunted period of national revolution. Knapp thereby recovered colonial writing as a necessary component of American literature. Second, he entered the school textbook market—a besetting commercial sin of American literary scholars "from his day to ours" (I, iv). Why the commercially minded *CHAL* editors reacted to this activity is not clear, but it profitably opens the door to our considering the state of American literature in the early American colleges. Third, Knapp reminded us that local pride, ever since Cotton Mather, had tainted our literature with a marked provincialism—in a young country an understandable, though nationally divisive, state of mind. Finally, Knapp entered the post-Revolution crusade for an autochthonous national literature.

The four emphases in the *CHAL* preface are perceptive. Knapp, first of all, does, indeed, throw a floodlight on America's colonial writing. Dividing his two hundred years of history into four equal periods, for "more easily managing my subject" rather than from any theory of literary causation, Knapp then grants to colonial writers, in effect, a deserving three-fourths of America's literary history.[1] After Lecture I, an historical sketch of the English language (which he terms the colonists' only British inheritance, p. 9), Knapp devotes nine of his remaining fourteen lectures to his four periods. Four of these lectures treat the pre-Revolutionary writers. Predictably, Knapp has a rather weak grasp of aesthetic values among the figures he has studied. He rightly emphasizes the literary influence of the Bible and almanacs, but he clearly regards literature as a record of the life of the mind, including political and scientific thought, rather than a form of distinctly expressive art. Yet Knapp has moments of aesthetic discrimination. He distinguishes, in Jonathan Edwards senior, the "strength and depth" of *Freedom of Will* despite the "obscure and involved" parts, and praises the son whose writings are at least "more lucid than his father's" (pp. 82–83). When Knapp, in his best form as a contemporary spread-eagle orator, lectures on the style of Cotton Mather, we shall not find again until Moses Coit Tyler or Vernon Louis Parrington a scholar who exudes such delight in writing literary history:

> Whenever [Cotton Mather] attempted to spread before the public his own thought, there came rushing to his memory ten thousand thoughts of other men; probably not so good as his own, but which, from the pride of learning, must be used. These thoughts often dazzled his own vision, and obscured or misled his understanding. Thus the children of his own brain were bedizzened with the flaming colours of all costumes, and were half-smothered in the tatters of outlandish wardrobes. His logick was often overlaid by illustration, and the force of his eloquence lost by vanity, quaintness, and punning. Acquainted with the pure fountains of classical literature, and often refreshed with copious draughts from them, he feared his piety might be questioned by having this generally known; and therefore he drew his quotations, and in fact, formed his taste, from the literature of scholastick divinity; forgetting, that some waters may be fit to bathe in, which might be deleterious to drink. (p. 60)

Thus inspired by Mather, even at the moment of rebuking him, Knapp obviously enjoyed these flourishes of allusion, imagery, and rhetoric. Indeed, the vigor of American eloquence was his subject in Lecture XII. The *CHAL* editors are no doubt justified in seeing him as something less than a disinterested scholar and perhaps an occasional pitchman for the share of the school market where literature served as handmaid to rhetoric, oratory, and history.[2] A lawyer and noted orator (with Daniel Webster, he eulogized Adams and Jefferson at Boston in 1826), Knapp was also an itinerant journalist. He was editing the *National Journal* in Washington, D.C., when he advertised in that journal, late in

1828, his "panoramic . . . history of the American mind, and the productions of that mind."[3] The "history" was, expectably for Knapp, not studies but lectures. No evidence remains, however, that any were delivered publicly, something difficult to believe in view of Knapp's restless opportunism. In his preface directed to teachers, parents, and a nation already proud of its public schools, he urged that America's (and Samuel Knapp's) literary history become an integral part of the school curriculum. "You will struggle in vain to make American history well understood by your pupils," he warned the "priesthood" of instructors, "unless biographical sketches, anecdotes, and literary selections are mingled with the mass of general facts" (p. 4).

Knapp's intended market was very likely the secondary school, an audience later to be widely exploited, with the colleges, after the Civil War. A sufficiently remunerative school trade existed even in these early years of our national period. According to publisher S. G. Goodrich, author of 120 immensely lucrative books for children (his first Peter Parley stories, mixing "amusement and instruction," appeared in 1827), school books in 1820 represented one-third of the $2,500,000 book-publishing trade in America. By 1830, income from school books had increased by a third, to $1,100,000 in a national book market of $3,500,000. By 1850, the school trade had ballooned by 500 per cent, and unlike a half-century earlier when England dominated the American market, it was exclusively an American enterprise. To be sure, the books specifically on American literature and history shared only a meager part of these earnings in comparison with school geographies, McGuffey Readers, and the millions of Webster spelling books. But Knapp accurately sensed the imminent school market for American history, and literary history, in the 1830s. The quality of both school books and the entire common-school system was about to improve markedly under the decisive influence of Horace Mann, Henry Barnard, and others.[4]

Knapp aimed, no doubt, at an advanced audience, also, for his *Lectures* "in a cheap and proper edition" (p. 287), but such a readership would not have been vast in the higher reaches of American education. Although the number of American colleges doubled between 1820 and 1835, to a total of seventy-nine, American literature had scarcely entered the curriculum. Nor had England's writers, for that matter. Conventional minds dominated the American university before the Civil War. French, German, and Spanish languages, all important to commerce, had been studied since the turn of the century. Some American history was necessary to ensure patriotism. And the sciences were honored. (When English literature later entered the curricula, professors defensively stressed the *facts* of literary history and philology.)[5] Here and there, some American literature was allowed to grace the courses in oratory and rhetoric. In 1826, for example, one John Frost of Boston published his *Class Book of American Literature* and claimed it to be the first textbook of purely American literature. In its 312 pages, however, the brief passages and 144 lessons were designed not to foster literary appreciation but to advance the student's patriotism and liven his gifts of elocution.[6]

In 1828, when Knapp advertised his book, only Amherst seemed to have offered a course that gave specific attention to American literature as a subject for college study. From 1827 to 1829, the catalog announced Lectures in English and American Literature. The American portion of the lectures was given by Nathan W. Fiske, professor of belles lettres and father of Helen Hunt Jackson. In 1848, Middlebury College's Reverend James Meacham offered two courses, Critiques on the British and American Classics for third-term juniors and Analysis of American Orators for third-term seniors. Middlebury has never dropped American literature since 1848, thereby ranking as our college with the longest continuous tradition of teaching American literature. Also in the 1840s, apparently during one year (1841–42), Marietta College in Ohio offered American literature as an adjunct course to history, politics, and eloquence.[7]

Despite the surge of literary nationalism that carried into the 1830s and 1840s, American colleges remained generally hidebound in their resistance to modern literatures. But American publishers in the 1840s were beginning to test the waters, and Harpers ventured a fairly successful textbook, J. R. Boyd's *Elements of Rhetoric and Literary Criticism* (1845), designed (according to its elaborate subtitle) "with Copious Practical Exercises and Examples. For the Use of Common Schools and Academies. Including, also, a Succinct History of the English Language, and of British and American Literature to the Present Times." Boyd was a Presbyterian minister at New York's Hamilton College, and his American section reveals strong borrowings from Samuel Kettell and Rufus Griswold (figures we meet in the next chapter), along with the contemporary critical emphasis on the moral purity inherent in our best American writers. After three years, Boyd had enjoyed six reprintings.[8] How much of these sales were from the college trade, Hamilton College and beyond, has not been determined.

Knapp's quest for schoolbook profits came some twenty years

too early. (He had tried again in 1832, with emphasis on English writers, in *Advice on the Pursuits of Literature*.) In the later 1840s appeared the classic best seller that was to dominate the college trade for thirty years. This was Englishman Thomas Budd Shaw's *Outlines of English Literature*, written originally for his students in the Imperial Alexander Lyceum in St. Petersburg. The English editions of 1846 and 1849 (Murray) quickly sold out. The *Outlines* were then reissued as "a new American edition" in 1852 (Philadelphia: Blanchard and Lee), to include Henry Tuckerman's terminal "Sketch of American Literature" (pp. 433–89). Even the American publisher obviously was banking on a school-trade interest chiefly in English, not American, writers. Consistent with modern practice, the Shaw best seller was revised after Shaw's death in 1862 to vie with upstart competitors. Retitled *A Complete Manual of English Literature* in 1864, it was revised by William Smith, examiner at the University of London, and issued in the series of Murray's Student Manuals. In the New York edition (Sheldon and Co., 1867), it included Tuckerman's "Sketch of American Literature," to which we shall return.

✦   ✦   ✦

The *CHAL* editors, in their prefatory comments on the significance of Knapp's *Lectures,* also cited the penchant of the nineteenth-century historian (and indeed an eighteenth-century Cotton Mather) "to magnify the achievements of one's own parish at the expense of the rest of the country" (I, v). Since the editors, we have already noticed, were not infected with a bias in favor of New England, they (and Trent in particular) would not be impressed that Knapp slighted the South's earlier writers while New England's received two-thirds of his space. This provincial charge against Knapp (Dartmouth class of 1804) was made rather obliquely; the editors would soon direct it unmistakably against Barrett Wendell. At present, they asserted that local pride may be "a useful passion" and "more or less justifiable" for literary growth in isolated colonies or again in latter-day "'local colorists'" and the regional "school" within "a country of a hundred million inhabitants." But regional prejudice "is not conducive to the production of a quite unbiassed history of American literature" (I, v–vi).

They were slightly harsher with Knapp for his lapses into "national pride . . . a profound bias in favor of the autochthonous" (I, vi). His defensive pride and profound bias were understandable when we return to the 1820s and recall the infamous taunt

Sydney Smith had delivered in the *Edinburgh Review* at the beginning of the decade: "In the four quarters of the globe, who reads an American book?"[9] Knapp spoke for many an incensed and patriotic American—critics, magazine editors, and assorted literary folk—when he wrote in his preface of November 1829, "you are aware that it has been said by foreigners, and often repeated, that there was no such thing as American literature." He then chided his diffident countrymen who had assented to this criticism and too easily underestimated both the "great epoch" of the Revolution and the colonial years of "heroick virtue and gigantick labours."[10]

Surveying the literature on hand in 1829, Knapp took his opportunities where he found them to offer his encomiums to earlier American writers. He divided the first two centuries into four arbitrary fifty-year periods, reserving most of his pride for prose writers of the fourth, or revolutionary, period. John Adams was "at all times, a bold straight-forward writer" (p. 92) and Dr. Samuel Cooper seemed "remarkable for perspecuity and elegance" (p. 92). Judge Breckenridge of Philadelphia was more than the equal of Pericles as a eulogist of the war dead: "The American orator is more impassioned than his great prototype of Athens; his language glows with more warmth; there was less ambition in his strain of eloquence, and more of humanity than the orator of Athens allowed in his philosophy" (p. 105). George Washington "never suffered a sentiment to come from his pen negligently written; all was worked into ease and dignity" (p. 107). The Declaration of Independence bore "the calm language of enduring philosophy and patriotism, without one particle of rage or vengeance, but still strong, clear, bold, and impressive" (p. 103). And of the Federalist papers as literature, Knapp concluded: "Such was the correctness and beauty of the style of these numbers, that by them the taste of the country was refined" (p. 112).

In Lecture VIII, Knapp ventured into the national period, especially praising Washington Irving and biographers Aaron Bancroft (on Washington) and William Dunlap (Charles Brockden Brown). As an editor, Knapp was naturally effusive about the rise of American journalism. Our newspapers "surpass [those of] all other countries" (p. 135), Joseph Dennie's *Port Folio* (1801–12) rivaled its British counterparts, and the *North American Review* (founded 1815) was "a well conducted journal," every bit the equal of the notoriously anti-American *Edinburgh Review* (p. 137). Deserving quotation in full is Knapp's assessment of a widespread cultural *naissance* in America:

The literature of our country is increasing with a most astonishing rapidity; and knowledge is pouring upon us in its lesser and greater streams from all parts of the land; besides weekly and monthly magazines, which are profusely scattered throughout all our territories, we have several journals in medicine and law; and six established quarterly reviews, extensively read, and well supported. The editors of these quarterly works are pursuing a wise course, in repelling the attacks which have been made upon our literature, rather by exhibiting fine specimens of thought and taste in composition, than by retort and vituperation. (p. 138)

In his two succeeding lectures, Knapp then exhibited his own selected "fine specimens of thought and taste" among the pre- and post-Revolutionary American poets. Among the colonial poets, poetasters, and "village elegists" (*CHAL* editors' term for figures whom anthologists of Knapp's time had corralled into "pretentious" collections, p. vi), the following gained Knapp's approval, usually with illustrative quotation: John Cotton, Peter Bulkeley, John Norton, Benjamin Woodbridge, Governor Bradford, Roger Williams, Michael Wigglesworth, and Thomas Godfrey. Franklin's verses were mentioned but not quoted.

Versifiers since the Revolution—Robert Treat Paine, Charles Prentiss, and John Lathrop—received Knapp's comparative ranking. Connecticut Wits Joel Barlow and Timothy Dwight were duly quoted. William Clifton he judged the equal of Dryden and Pope. Among the living, he rated Freneau worthy but inconsistent, while John Trumbull's *M'Fingal* was "in many things, superiour" to his Hudibrastic model (p. 164). "I have no hesitation in saying," Knapp concluded, "that we abound in good poets, whose writings will remain to make up the literature of a future age . . ." (p. 187). And in a rapture over American geography, anticipating Whitman (and quoted with amusement by the editors of *CHAL*), Knapp measured our Potomac and Missouri rivers favorably against the classic Avon, Tiber, or Ilissus. He then envisioned the great American audiences who would encourage great poets to come: "Whenever a nation wills it, prodigies are born. Admiration and patronage create myriads who struggle for mastery, and for the olympick crown. Encourage the game, and the victors will come" (p. 189).

Knapp's voice, of course, was no more than representative of our literary enthusiasts in the early national period. Neither was he the first nor, with Emerson's lectures and essays imminent, the most eloquent. The impulse for an autochthonous literature generally free of slavish influence from the courtly muses of England and Europe had already appeared in such post-

Revolutionary ventures as Matthew Carey's *American Museum* (1787–92), which reserved space at the end of every issue for the works of the emerging Philip Freneau, William Smith, the Connecticut Wits, and miscellaneous rhymesters. (These journals, together with American anthologies of the period, will be discussed in the next chapter). Writers of the 1780s and 1790s now expressed their national pride by appropriating American subject matter. "A Native Bard, a native scene displays"—so began William Dunlap's prologue to the American tragedy of *André* (1789). Authors like Freneau, Joel Barlow, Royall Tyler, Timothy Dwight, and C. B. Brown also wrote instructive prefaces to their works, alerting readers and theater audiences to a healthy growth of literacy, belles lettres, and indigenous romance in an otherwise workaday new nation. At the turn of the century, hundreds of newspapers in the country were debating American questions of law, fashion, slavery, alcohol, and occasionally literature, even though expressive literature itself had lost some of its post-Revolutionary spirit and impetus.

Neither was the fever of nationalism always at a peak level in the reign of Jefferson, we are reminded in the cautious and caustic utterances of a Boston Federalist like Fisher Ames. He was looking in vain for any "great original work of genius" or, indeed, even one first-rate poet amid our rampant Jeffersonian democracy. From his jaundiced viewpoint, Americans were driven by a love of commerce, property, and luxury, not by letters and poetry. But perhaps this wealth would one day create "literary leisure" and at least a minority of the affluent and "eminently learned" citizens might encourage "some men of genius who will be admired and imitated."[11]

After the War of 1812 came a new period for inward-looking nationalists. In journalism, it was heralded by the appearance of the *North American Review* in 1815, to be followed, says W. B. Cairns, by roughly sixty-eight "purely literary" journals up to 1833.[12] In the early years, the *Review* was often as reserved as Fisher Ames in offering its plaudits to native authors, much to the displeasure of the more fervent champions of a national literature. William Tudor, E. T. Channing, and other editors and reviewers sensed their historic opportunity to assess and guide the emerging American mind and imagination. In the generous expanse of virtually every issue, the scholarly critics of the *Review* educated subscribers on the issues of literary nationalism. The subject was invariably treated in Phi Beta Kappa lectures, long before Emerson's celebrated address on cultural nationalism, "The American Scholar" (1837), and the *Review* faithfully printed many of these orations. In fact, a particularly revealing Phi Beta Kappa address had been delivered at Harvard as early as 1809 by the Reverend Joseph Stevens Buckminster. He viewed the revolutionary times harmful to sober learning in America and a reason for the slow growth of a national literature. But signs of a flowering were in the air: "The genius of our literature begins to show symptoms of vigour, and . . . the spirit of criticism begins to plume itself." [13]

In the *North American*'s maiden year appeared a Phi Beta Kappa address on national literature by William Tudor, together with two essays by Walter Channing (physician-brother of E. T. and William Ellery the elder). In his address to the society at Harvard, Tudor refuted the alleged absence of native themes and subjects for American poets. He argued the wealth of colonial experience, climaxed by the Revolution, and pronounced this history rich in materials awaiting an epic treatment by the young nation. Likewise accessible to our native bards were American forests, waterfalls, and wildlife, as well as the character and history of Indian aborigines—their eloquence, their former glory, and the dramatic fall of the Five Nations. [14]

Walter Channing began both of his essays by agreeing to England's low assessment of American writers. But he chided his countrymen for assuming that our present inferiority in literature could be improved through imitating English models. (Walter Scott's *Guy Mannering*, coincidentally, was being serialized in this same issue.) Special advantages for American writers lay in our geography and institutions, the Indian oral tradition, and the American vigor of our shared English language. From these sources was certain to emerge a national character. In his second essay, Channing again acknowledged and then sought the reasons for our "literary delinquency." Our chief error, he repeated, was a lingering colonial mentality, a dependence on, and lazy satisfaction with, the imported English product. And we compounded this dependency with two erroneous, and related, assumptions that defeated original creativity: the belief that our market for literature was already brimful and that the profession of writing could not thrive in America. Channing admitted to some genuine handicaps in our limited past and materialistic present. Yet many English writers did not rely on England's far richer historical past, and they, too, were living in a distinctly materialistic society. Channing concluded that we must begin to envision the wealth available in our history, in the political, social, religious, and literary components of American life and character. And he looked to the future for anthologies and biographies that would acquaint us with our American poets. This essay, appearing in tandem with Tudor's Phi Beta Kappa address, concluded an auspicious opening year for the *Review,* whose longevity and prestige would be unrivaled far into the present century.[15]

The next year, the *Review* published a plea for American originality in literature by Walter's brother, assistant editor E. T. Channing. He, too, opposed our imitation of foreign customs and literary classics and urged a literary absorption of American institutions, habits, and geography—our mountains, plains, and seascapes: "The literature of a country is just as domestick and individual as its character or political institutions. Its charm is its nativeness."[16] In the next month, Boston lawyer Francis C. Gray gave the annual Phi Beta Kappa address, and the *Review* dutifully published the speech in the September issue. Like many others, Gray did not praise the American writer ("we cannot boast one worthy of immortality") but, instead, inquired into the conditions adverse to our cultural growth that required diagnosis and remedy. Commercial enterprise and prosperity, together with a preoccupation with politics and the military, had beckoned the citizenry away from learning and literature and slowed the creation of libraries and a truly distinguished public-school system. Gray concluded, however, with a customary pep talk: Persevere! Seek cultural excellence, private virtue, and opportunities for service![17]

Presently entering the debate over a national literature was William Cullen Bryant. Smarting from the uninformed and "unmerited contumely" of English critics writing on American literary efforts, Bryant argued in the *Review* that these extreme responses were, unfortunately, being answered in America by equally extreme and indiscriminate boasting. Both were injuring the cause of badly needed literary standards. Bryant's remarks appeared in a critique of *An Essay on American Poetry* by Solyman Brown (1818). Bryant displayed the balanced standards he was advocating and visited both praise and blame on the Connecticut Wits, but scoring them in particular for their "artificial elevation of style" in unhappy imitation of English rhymers. He judged William Clifton a superior poet whose promise was cut short by early death. St. John Honeywood was the victim of undeserved neglect. Robert Treat Paine was given to both an unduly epigrammatic and a "false sublime" manner in his "fine but misguided genius." Bryant closed with a fairly high estimate of American taste in 1818. Though he warned our poets against their weakness for the English example, he praised American readers who, he was satisfied, were growing in literary acumen and becoming the audience that would inspire the poets to come.[18]

Bryant was followed by our chief literary diplomat of the time, Washington Irving, and his earlier coauthor James Kirke Paulding. In the *Sketch Book,* Irving submitted two essays designed to build a rapprochement with old England. In "An Author's Account of Himself," he nicely blended a national pride in our native landscape with homage to Europe's richer culture and history, though he gently prodded self-important English travelers who preferred to view the American as a mythic degradation of Western man. More elaborately in "English Writers on America," he advocated mutual understanding and respect. He rebuked the crass English visitors who berated the crass American in their reports to gullible readers back home. To his countrymen, Irving counseled generosity and tolerance, in keeping with the best American tradition, and also asked them to realize that England, after all, was not so bad a model from which to learn something in the way of manners, thought, and morality.[19]

Paulding, Irving's coeditor of the first papers in *Salmagundi* (1807–8), returned to publish a new series in 1819 and 1820. One subject, national literature, was inevitable, as was, too, perhaps, the lack of any new wrinkle on the subject. Paulding repeated the two-pronged argument that we should reduce our "servile imitation" of Europe at the same time that we cultivate the rich soil of our new-world garden. In "the race of literary glory," we had forgotten that genuine romance, natural wonders, and a varied humanity lie all about us; and we looked to Europe for romantic-Gothic trappings of wonderment and the supernatural. "We have cherished a habit of looking to other nations for examples of every kind," he complained, "and debased the genius of this new world by making it the ape and the tributary of the old."[20]

And so the campaign advanced from year to year, at times graced by a novel insight (mercifully) or a new rhetorical strategy to relieve the sameness of the arguments. Briefly to cite one example annually into the middle 1820s, we have, in 1821, historian John G. Palfrey's didactic close to a review article on the narrative poem *Yamoyden* by James W. Eastburn, a New York preacher. Not only was this seventeenth-century New England saga about a Nipnet Indian, who wins the love of a Christian woman and adopts her religion, a worthy American poem, but even more, said Palfrey (echoing Paulding), "We are glad that somebody has at last found out the unequalled fitness of our early history for the purposes of a work of fiction [that is, imagination]." In our past are heroic figures participating in the excitement of American religious, political, and military history. And adjacent to this white civilization is the American savage, fierce and eloquent amid the "rude grandeur of nature."[21]

Further south, the concern over a national literature was also alive. In 1822, Virginian George Tucker collected among his essays an assessment, "On American Literature," written a number of years before but still, to its author, in no need of revision. It could have been co-authored with Sydney Smith, whose recent estimate of our literature was echoed by Tucker in the central question, Why is our literary product inferior to that of Europe, England, and even Ireland? Tucker dismissed any theory that we were deficient in physical vigor or intellectual endowment (alluded to previously by Irving). But rather than answer to our literary inferiority, Tucker framed some further questions. Do we lack proper intellectual training? Or the stimulus of libraries and museums? Or capable professors? Or the leisure that allows our native genius to mature? Or great audiences? Or a proper literary center? In other fields, we have demonstrated, for example, political eloquence, medical skill, scientific inventiveness (vide Franklin), and a talent, European-trained to be sure, in painting. Perhaps, he implied, we shall follow the late example of Scotland, where the national culture was just now reaching maturity, so that it nourished the literary genius.[22]

In Philadelphia the next year, Charles J. Ingersoll addressed the American Philosophical Society on the same questions concerning the maturity of American mind and culture. In the main, he seemed content that we had advanced the useful arts and the sciences to a high degree in the civilized world, chiefly because we had established a system and spirit of mass education over the past two centuries that were unequaled in any society of Europe. Three thousand students matriculated in our colleges annually. Though our literature still lagged behind England's, American poetry was on the rise. Our respect for the life of the mind was also reflected by the two to three millions of dollars spent in book publishing each year, by the proliferation of learned journals, and especially by the high critical office assumed by the *North American Review* (circulation 4,000), a periodical unrivaled in Britain while it "superintends with ability the literature and science of America."[23]

And, indeed, that voice emanating from the *Review* continued to superintend the debate over an infant national literature.

On 26 August 1824, former editor Edward Everett, professor of Greek literature at Harvard, delivered his Phi Beta Kappa address at Cambridge, "The Circumstances Favorable to the Progress of Literature in America." The minister in Everett organized a three-part speech transparent in purpose and movement, while the public-minded orator invoked history and democracy to buttress his case for a national literature. (A few months later, he served his first term in Congress.) The first circumstance favorable to the literary character of our citizenry, said Everett, was the "equable diffusion of rights and privileges," which had brought an "astonishing development of intellectual energy." (No decline of Western man here.) Such intellectual ferment, rather than courtly patronage, truly advanced an infant national literature. Second, our ample nation was firmly united in a single government, language, and character, all nurturing a high common intelligence and literature. Finally, our dynamic growth in population was producing a wider audience, which served as a boon to literary ambition. Or in Everett's flowery style,

> The writer, by whom the noble features of our scenery shall be sketched with a glowing pencil, the traits of our romantic early history gathered up with filial zeal, and the peculiarities of our character delineated with delicate perception, cannot mount so rapidly to success, but that ten years will add new millions to the numbers of his readers.

On this resounding note, the oratorical Everett announced that all the ages past were voices now exhorting us on. Inevitably, he then intoned Berkeley's lines on "Westward the course of Empire," as so many others would also in the expansionist oratory to come.[24]

The month after Everett was instructing his American scholars at Harvard, another advocate of American literature, John Neal, was edifying an English audience in *Blackwood's* with a series of essays on our literary history. Neal, as we have come to know him, was an irrepressible egotist and scribbler. While Knapp would soon draw on painstaking research in American libraries and collections, Neal wrote these "American Writers" chapters from memory. Born in Maine some thirty years earlier, he was first a Yankee merchant and lawyer before turning exclusively to writing. As a member of the Delphian literary club of Baltimore, he edited their monthly *Portico* (1816–18), which echoed the older *Port Folio* and *Niles' Weekly Register* in militant support of a new literary nationalism after the War of 1812.[25] After arriving in England in January 1824, Neal was at a dinner when Sydney Smith's question four years earlier—Who reads an American book?—was echoed among the guests. He elected to answer it in *Blackwood's*, "the cleverest, the sauciest, and the most unprincipled of all our calumniators."[26]

Neal's five installments appeared from September 1824 to February 1825. He discussed the authors alphabetically, from John Q. Adams to W. E. Wyatt. Each issue (save number 4) was signed "X.Y.Z.," whom Neal introduced in the initial chapter as a judicious Englishman who wished to view impartially the currently wild claims and criticisms of America's meager, miscellaneous, and questionably original literature. "Give the Americans fair play," he urged, for they own ten times more of good authors than the English are aware, including three true originals—Paulding, John Neal (!), and C. B. Brown. Neal then dealt frank praise or censure to his writers, whether Bryant, E. T. Channing, or whomever. His sketches were frequently no more than a scant paragraph, casually sprinkled with a misspelling here and misinformation there. Some of these errors, he promptly acknowledged in the second installment, must be assigned to his writing from memory. He reaffirmed the critical attitude needed on both sides of the Atlantic: American writers should be regarded without undue flattery, apology, or ridicule. In his sketches this time, and in the succeeding chapters, he granted extensive treatment to authors like Brown (but not Cooper), Franklin, and Irving, as well as lesser figures like Alston [*sic*] and Alexander Everett (brother of Edward). The fifth, or final, chapter was memorable for Neal's discussion of John Neal, complete with privileged information gained from this absurdly candid fellow who reputedly had belittled as "adventurous, impudent, strange, foolish" his own literary contributions.

Neal's series was popular and widely quoted. He went on to publish in other British periodicals and then returned to America to write four novels before the decade ended. A magazine editor for a time, Neal then resumed the practice of law in Maine, received an honorary degree in 1836 from Bowdoin, wrote several dime novels in the sixties, and died an octogenarian in 1879. It is pleasant to imagine the amusement with which this self-ironic egotist might have read Lowell's verdict in "A Fable for Critics" (1848):

> There swaggers John Neal, who has wasted in Maine
> The sinews and cords of his pugilist brain,

Who might have been poet, but that, in its stead, he
Preferred to believe that he was so already;
Too hasty to wait till Art's ripe fruit sh'd drop,
He must pelt down an unripe and colicky crop;

. . . .

A man who's made less than he might have, because
He always has thought himself more than he was.[27]

Meanwhile, on the native scene in 1825, Bryant was amplify-
ing his earlier views on a national literature when he lectured on
poetry at the New York Athenaeum shortly after settling in New
York City. For his third of the four lectures, "On Poetry in Its Relation to Our Age and Country," he addressed the familiar charges
that his countrymen were nonpoetic and their nation wanting in
"romance either in our character, our history, or our condition of
society." He granted that our writers possessed no American mythology on which to build their fables. But mythology for the
Greeks and Romans had, in fact, produced the adverse effect of
destroying a mystery of things by rendering them familiar and
explainable. Americans, on the other hand, were starting anew
and responding directly to "creatures and things of God's universe." If we lacked native superstitions and legends, we could,
said Bryant (thinking of Irving?), judiciously incorporate foreign
materials. Our poets were doubly advantaged. First, the somewhat trying conditions at home actually served as a spur to poetry (as Bryant himself had learned during his earlier conflict
between poetry and a practical vocation). Second, an advanced
literature abroad provided matter out of which the native genius
could build the fabric of an American poetic art. Too, we were
blessed with an English language admirably flexible for describing the practical and ideal experiences of America. Therefore,
the materials as well as opportunities for poetry amply existed in
these states, Bryant concluded in a refreshingly original and adventurous essay.[28]

Young Longfellow, at age eighteen, was delivering the graduate's oration at Bowdoin in this same year. His speech, "Our Native Writers," reads like an intelligent student's clear paraphrase
of the arguments his elders had been disseminating in print and
in lecture rooms. Our national literature will carry the spirit of
"our free political institutions." Helped by "liberal patronage,"
once we have advanced beyond the present phase of practical enterprise, our committed authors will create a literature not from
the dust of libraries and allusions echoed from the classics of old,
but in a manner free and alive, formed out of the stuff of native

chronicles and nourished on the "hills and vales, on the woods and waters of New England." (The regional emphasis was perhaps obligatory on this occasion.) Meanwhile, of course, we must make the most of "our literary allegiance to Old England."[29]

James Fenimore Cooper, too, was presently making public his opinions on the matter of a national literature. They took the form of his instructive, and corrective, *Notions of the Americans, Picked up by a Traveling Bachelor.*[30] His foreign point of view and covert purpose were similar to Neal's. In Letter XXIII, Cooper's English bachelor-narrator reported on the meager literature and arts in the United States. To a degree, this initial attitude was Cooper's ploy to draw foreign readers into a favorable mood to hear a presumably routine belittling of literary efforts in the new republic. His narrator confirmed that America, especially among her professional classes, did enjoy a certain intellectual and literary life, thanks to her English inheritance. But he then reversed course and assailed his countrymen (the English) for their snobbish, dishonest, jealous, and possibly damaging views of America's infant culture: "There are many theories entertained as to the effect produced in this country by the falsehoods and jealous calumnies which have been undeniably uttered in the mother country, by means of the press, concerning her republican descendant" (II, 131). He then observed that the American, however, no longer felt hypersensitive or deferential to British opinions, because their ridiculous absurdities had been self-defeating and were now derided in America. "By all that I can learn," he concluded, "twenty years ago, the Americans were, perhaps, far too much disposed to receive the opinions and to adopt the prejudices of their relatives; whereas, I think it very apparent that they are now beginning to receive them with singular distrust" (ibid.). Cooper's reasonable tone belied his own irritation over recent books from abroad: Adam Hodgson's *Letters from North America* (1824) and John F. De Roos's *Personal Narrative of Travels in the United States and Canada* (1827).[31]

More valuable than his comments on British-American rivalry were Cooper's citing two powerful obstacles to the rise of a national literature. First was lack of "pecuniary support" (II, 140) for native talent. In the absence of international copyrights, American publishers could reprint English works without remuneration. Second, Cooper made an important critique of his nation's "poverty of materials" and her lackluster uniformity, her ordinariness:

There are no annals for the historian; no follies (beyond the most vulgar and commonplace) for the satirist; no manners for the dramatist; no obscure fictions for the writer of romance; no gross and hardy offenses against decorum for the moralist; nor any of the rich artificial auxiliaries of poetry. (II, 142)

This argument over America's lack of social complexity and rich historical associations would, of course, receive various echoings among native romancers to come, culminating in Hawthorne's well-known litany of American deprivations in the preface to *The Marble Faun* (1860) and the equally famous supplemental list in Henry James's *Hawthorne* (1879).

Still, Cooper's traveling English bachelor recognized the favorable signs of an infant national literature. Charles Brockden Brown had distinguished himself "for power and comprehensiveness of thought" and Irving "for a quality (humor) that has been denied his countrymen." Regional experiences, themes, and manners gave promise of original American opportunities for native writers. Finally, he closed his "letter" with the prediction that an original literature was imminent: "The impulses of talent and intelligence are bearing down a thousand obstacles. I think the new works will increase rapidly, and that they are destined to produce a powerful influence on the world" (II, 145, 146, and 151).

Three more noteworthy essays by major figures round out these early polemics over literary nationalism in and out of the work of Samuel Knapp.[32] Noah Webster published his *American Dictionary* in 1828, with a justifying preface wherein he explained that our government, laws, customs, and institutions were different from England's and therefore had necessitated a special American vocabulary. At times, even the words we shared with England possessed a different meaning over there. As to our literature, the best authors had preserved the English idiom while they spiced it with American colloquialisms. In his *Dissertations on the English Language* some forty years earlier, Webster argued for a "purity" and uniformity of language in America, especially in written public documents, that would help to unite the spirit of the nation. Such uniformity, as in spelling and pronunciation, should be gained, however, through a flexible and descriptive approach to language in our schools rather than from a prescriptive imitation of the English tongue, where the language, in fact, was not consistent anyway.[33] Webster's statements on American English would grow more significant in later years of the century when anglophiles in the academy argued that our literature, because written in a shared language, was essentially British.

From Boston in 1829, a prolific young poet and budding editor barely twenty, John Greenleaf Whittier, was also meditating on the nation's literature for his weekly, *The American Manufacturer*. This imitator of Burns, Scott, and Byron inquired into the "want of strength and boldness" in American poets that prevented their becoming an American Byron or Milton. They enjoyed, after all, the incomparable advantages of democratic freedom in a national landscape sublimely congenial to poetic inspiration: "It is the nature of Freedom to elevate the soul and mature its lofty purposes. They have looked upon Nature in her exceeding sublimity—the giant cataract—the kingly river—the mountain soaring under a tropic sky to the regions of eternal winter." Whittier put his finger on what, to him, was causing a patent mediocrity in the aspiration of our poets. They lacked courageous, candid, independent literary journals in which the critics might discourage rather than applaud the pleasant tameness and "imbecility of our poetry." Since our poets were published and lauded for their "light flashes of fancy—the tinsel and drapery of poetry, without the substance," why should they pursue the "darker and ruder pilgrimage"? [34]

And last, in 1830, William Ellery Channing followed the example of his two younger brothers and set forth his own views on literary nationalism. They came in a belated response to Ingersoll's "Influence of America on the Mind," which we glanced at several pages ago. The gentle Unitarian did not directly lock horns with his adversary, but used Ingersoll's *Discourse* as a point of departure to discuss "the importance and means of a National Literature." In implicit contrast to Ingersoll, he emphasized the more spiritually benign, rather than pragmatic, influences that the new-world experience should be engendering in the American mind and that our greatest writers must express.

Channing may have been rather irked by Ingersoll's treating as an afterthought the role of the church in American life. Also, while he praised the superior "diffusion of elementary knowledge" in our democracy, echoing but not citing Ingersoll, Channing somewhat sternly viewed that popular instruction to be quite superficial and our satisfaction in it an impediment to the growth of strenuous thought and "a commanding literature." He recited the familiar causes for America's previously slow progress in expressing the national mind. They included the priorities we had placed (and Ingersoll had endorsed?) on "useful knowledge." Contributing also had been our youthfulness, the exigencies of pioneering, and the assumption, fatal to artistic excellence, that we could import "profound, extensive, and elegant literature." Channing then encouraged an American spirit of self-formation, at once energized by, and resistant to, foreign literary influences, so that we might create "a literature to counteract," while we "use wisely the literature which we import." Finally were the bright prospects for such a literature. Though we did not as yet possess the libraries, universities, and other appurtenances of the cultures of Europe, we owned the superior basis for a humane society and government that would benefit our literature: "Man is the great subject of literature, and juster and profounder views of man may be expected here, than elsewhere." Lacking traditions, we were free of oppressive political and religious institutions. Channing anticipated Emerson and the Transcendentalists with his conviction that "our chief hopes of an improved literature rest on our hopes of an improved religion," a joyous universal spirit that "opens the eye to beauty and the heart to love." And with Knapp, he believed that enlightened patronage—in the great public and in our advancing schools and universities—would open the doors to a great national literature. "It will come if called for." [35]

And great American literature was called for in the best remembered of all the Phi Beta Kappa addresses when Emerson addressed the audience at Harvard on 31 August 1837. "The American Scholar," together with the corollary "Self-Reliance" and "The Poet," totally summed up the argument for literary nationalism voiced by his predecessors. The self-relying "man thinking" in America would create a new-world culture out of the immediate influences of nature, books, and action. And through organic expression of their American experience, our writers would no longer suffer a disjunction between native materials and themes on the one hand and English literary forms and traditions on the other. Inspiration would arrive not from the "courtly muses of Europe," but from the freer rhythms of American life recreated in an original "metre-making argument." In 1855, Walt Whitman sealed the Emersonian edict with the Preface and organically formed poems of *Leaves of Grass*.

So, of course, goes the party line in every well-informed literary classroom in America. Professors will do no injustice to Emerson and Whitman, however, by recalling that the two were latecomers to the transoceanic debate that had raged virtually without interruption since the opening years of the national period. If "The American Scholar" was, in the words of Oliver Wendell Holmes, Sr., "our Intellectual Declaration of Independence," many an earlier orator and essayist had contributed their own rough draft to the final Emersonian document. When scholars in the academy later pursued the nationalistic assumptions of an American literary tradition, they would discover the origins of that inquiry in the years of Samuel Knapp and his contemporaries.

Chapter 4

Rufus W. Griswold and the Collectors' Marketplace

The *CHAL* editors cite, after Samuel Knapp's *Lectures*, two other landmark efforts in the prewar period, Rufus Wilmot Griswold's *Prose Writers of America* (1847) and the two-volume *Cyclopaedia of American Literature* (1855) by Evert A. and George L. Duyckinck. Conveniently for our chronicle, Griswold and the Duyckincks help to complete the early story of American literary nationalism, touching both the commercial outlets for a native literature and the spirited literary polemics waged in the decades just before the Civil War. In the *CHAL* preface, the editors praise Griswold for his admirable sense of an original American literature, and they bid us remember him as the judicious and forward-looking editor of poets and prose writers from America's previous fifty years. His anthologies help us realize the mounting excitement felt at a time when authors could begin to believe that a sizable audience was taking American literature seriously and encouraging writers to flourish. It hardly needs saying that American literary creation, and the serious study of it, would have been drastically retarded without the services of Griswold and other editors who cultivated an interest and pride in our infant literature.

Today, Griswold is best remembered as an unreliable and vindictive editor of Poe, as well as the collector who, according to Lowell in "A Fable for Critics," had acquired a reputation by editing and exploiting the cacophonous outpourings of our earliest literary warblers:

> "But stay, here comes Tityrus Griswold, and leads on
> The flocks whom he first plucks alive, and then feeds on—
> A loud-cackling swarm, in whose feathers warm-drest,
> He goes for as perfect a—swan as the rest." [1]

More appreciative was the judgment of publisher Samuel Goodrich that the swelling audience for an American literature was mainly owing to "the enlightened and patriotic labors of Dr.

Griswold, who may be considered as the first and most influential of our authors in cultivating a respect for our own literature."[2]

In the 1830s and 1840s, the long shadow of England, as Emerson was complaining, still impeded original attempts in American prose and verse. The English skylark and nightingale presumably soared more gracefully and sang more melodiously than American birds. Griswold helped draw attention away from the English and toward the American scene and literature (though he cheerfully tallied his editorial profits from anthologies of English songsters, too). Between 1841 and 1854, he produced more than a score of collections, and in such efforts, together with his work as an interim editor of *Graham's* (displacing Poe), Griswold befriended many of our authors and gave them a wide public hearing.

Griswold's early *Poets and Poetry of America* (1842) was a handsomely designed, octavo-sized volume with frontispiece portraits of Longfellow, Bryant, Richard H. Dana (the elder), Fitz-Greene Halleck, and Charles Sprague. In his prefatory comments, Griswold urged the usual liberation from abject imitation of English poetry by seizing the opportunities provided in American history and geography. And he called for government support of American writers through subsidy and copyright law. A licensed preacher and doctor of divinity (the exact origin of these religious credits remains uncertain), Griswold lauded American poetry for its "moral purity" and added the prayer, "May it so remain forever" (p. vi), thereby lending his considerable influence to the obligatory Victorian flavor of a future American literature. The historical introduction and poetic selections revealed Griswold's considerable reliance on Samuel Kettell's earlier collection (1829). The selections were preceded by a sketch of each author, arranged chronologically by date of birth. Griswold acknowledged a wide correspondence with American authors, had secured poems in manuscript or print from the authors, and solicited the aid of such figures as William G. Simms, E. P. Whipple, and James T. Fields. In addition, said Griswold, he had accounted for five hundred volumes in his research. Usually judicious in his excerpts of ninety-one poets in these 468 pages, Griswold was, at times, given to favoritism. His friend Charles Fenno Hoffman was represented by forty-five poems in twelve pages, Poe by three in two pages. Well publicized and reviewed (Poe reviewed the volume favorably in *Graham's*, though he later reversed his approval), Griswold's *Poets* received three printings in the first year. By his death in 1857, Griswold had carried the book through sixteen editions and expanded the contents to represent 146 poets in 621 pages. (In 1849, he had removed the women poets into the separate *Female Poets of America,* which enjoyed its own popularity.)

Griswold's *Prose Writers of America* (1847) appeared at the height of the literary wars raging in the journals of the 1840s. But this lively controversy, together with Griswold's own volume, was possible only because many a national-minded editor had earlier published scores of American authors. The earliest attempt, as Griswold himself noted, was by the Loyalist printer, James Rivington, in 1773. He advertised for contributions to *A Collection of Poems by the Favorites of the Muses in America.* In 1791, Mathew Carey issued two volumes of mixed poetry: *The Beauties of Poetry, British and American.* But credit for the first authentic anthology of exclusively American poetry probably goes to Elihu Smith. In 1793, he published *American Poems,* the first, Smith hoped, in a series of such volumes. Included in his 304 pages of selected and original poems were offerings by Freneau, Dunlap, the Hartford Wits (of whom Smith was a lesser member), and poets from Boston to Philadelphia. The following year, a competing volume by Mathew Carey, *The Columbian Muse,* was a virtual plagiarism of Smith's edited selections, featuring most of the same poets. (The Wits' Joel Barlow was featured in the frontispiece.) Carey's volume of 224 pages ended any further venture by Smith and, in fact, appears to have saturated whatever market awaited these earliest collections of American verse.

The literary and commercial interest in native authors encouraged a flurry of journalistic enterprise in the early national period. Some twenty-seven new magazines, dedicated at least in part to promoting an American literature, sprang up between the Revolution and 1795. Two of these, both published in Philadelphia, deserve mention here: the *American Museum* (1787–92), edited by Mathew Carey; and perhaps more important, the *Columbian Magazine; or Monthly Miscellany* (1786–90 and continued as the *Universal Asylum* to 1792), edited by Carey and others and modeled after the English miscellany, *Gentleman's Magazine.* The *Columbian* was apparently the first American magazine to solicit original material and pay its authors, though a steady supply of contributors was not easily discovered. Still, during its tenure of six years and four months, the *Columbian* received the fiction of C. B. Brown (though editors objected on moral grounds to the novel); the poetry of various hands in a section grandly titled "The Columbian Parnassiad"; various first printings of Franklin's papers; and the work of Jeremy Belknap,

Benjamin Rush, and Noah Webster. The editors celebrated the American muse in selections on native geography, the Indians, the American past, and national character, but the English spirit and example of Addison, Richardson, Ossian, and others also permeated these pages. The Postal Act of 1792 established fatally high rates and contributed to the journal's demise. But in its short lifetime, the *Columbian* enjoyed the largest circulation of the century and was surpassed only in 1801 when Joseph Dennie sold two thousand copies of his new *Port Folio*. By comparison, the *North American Review,* which was proper successor to the *Monthly Anthology; or, Magazine of Polite Literature* (1803–11), claimed a circulation of only six hundred after five years—less than one-half the *Columbian*'s sales in 1790.[3]

In the 1820s came a renewed impulse for collections of American writers, including even a volume published in London and another in Glasgow. In this country, the most famous, or infamous, were published by Samuel Goodrich and edited by George B. Cheever and Samuel Kettell. Cheever's *The American Common-Place Book of Prose* (1828) and *The American Common-Place Book of Poetry* (the latter published in Boston not by Goodrich but Carter, Hendee, and Babcock, 1831) were sitting targets for critical punsters like Poe, who observed that "common-place" these books assuredly were. Kettell's *Specimens of American Poetry with Critical and Biographical Notes* (1829) in three volumes was, in its turn, soon dubbed "Goodrich's Kettle of Poetry."

Cheever's *Prose* included some seventy writers in his 468 pages. In his preface, he described his purpose to provide the busy American reader with essays and prose excerpts that would instill a "vivid admiration of nature and of human excellence" (p. 4). Cheever hoped the schools might find the book useful in "enlarging the intelligence, and disciplining the taste, of the rising minds, which, in their subsequent advancement, are to influence the literary estimation of their country" (p. 4). Snippets from Cooper and Irving competed with Cheever's six dozen other writers, among whom the Rev. Joseph Buckminster was amply represented. The extracts were given theme titles, with no dates of publication. An interesting concession to the vogue of the romantic savage was Cheever's printing of three speeches by Indian orators. Like other anthologists of the age, Cheever eschewed aesthetic criteria but to no apparent loss of sales. The book went through at least three editions.

Even more successful was Cheever's poetry collection three years later, in spite of a prefatory apology that American poets were inferior to her prose writers (p. 3). This volume enjoyed twenty-four printings in various editions over the next forty-five years. With his competitors, Cheever emphasized, above all, the moral tone, even the "spirit of the Bible," characteristic of American poetry, which gave it an appeal not merely to the "cultivated imagination" but also to the "religious mind." All his selections, Cheever assured the reader, possessed "the purest moral character," and he sent them forth with the injunction to "please and do good" (pp. 4–6). The original edition of 405 pages gave favored status (by poems represented) to Bryant (23) and W. H. Dana the elder (17), but John Pierpont (16), James G. Percival (15), John G. Brainard (15), Carlos Wilcox (14), N. P. Willis (13), and Mrs. Sigourney (13) were also favorites of the editor. His occasional notes to certain poets offered a bit of biography (Wilcox, p. 45n), urged the spirit of abolitionism (William L. Garrison, p. 57n), or commended particular lines of beautiful sentiment (Dana, p. 80n).

More gifted as a compiler of American poetry was one-time schoolteacher Samuel Kettell, eulogized at his death in 1855 by his sponsor Samuel Goodrich as "a man of genius" endowed with historical and linguistic gifts and blessed also with "a genial humor, a playful though grotesque wit, and withal, a kind, gentle, truthful heart."[4] This praise appears the more generous when we realize that Goodrich invested in one hundred rare books to help Kettell prepare *Specimens of American Poetry* and suffered a personal loss of fifteen hundred dollars in the failure of Kettell's mission.

Kettell plainly stated that mission in the preface to his three volumes, to "do something for the cause of American literature" by assembling, with the usual difficulties of the pioneering collector, such materials, whether of intrinsic merit as belles lettres or not, that would enable readers to trace "the general history of letters, and their connexion with the development of the moral and intellectual character of a people." He hailed "a national spirit in letters" emerging since Sydney Smith's vicious insinuation of our literary poverty nine years before. But Kettell affirmed that literary works of value had also existed before "Irving and Cooper and Pierpont and Percival" from writers either original or wisely imitative. Kettell then gathered in three volumes 189 poets, chronologically arranged from Cotton Mather to Whittier. (He omitted poet-dramatists, since he knew that William Dunlap was writing his *History of the American Theatre*. However, this work, published in 1832 and dedicated to Cooper, turned out less a study of literature than a volume of gossip and reminiscence.)

In an introduction that reads intelligently even today, Kettell sketched our poetical literature before Cotton Mather, gave extended treatment to Anne Bradstreet, and prepared the readers for many of the selections he would include in his capacious volumes. This opening essay also revealed the considerable sifting Kettell had undertaken, as did his appendix, titled "Catalogue of American Poetry" (III, 377–406), a chronological list of the many books and items he had studied in an incredibly few months. Clearly, Kettell does not deserve the reputation of a literary hack.

Kettell's reviewers, however, did not recognize any major critical ability in his ferreting out these poets who seemed, after all, deplorably fifth-rate and worse. Perhaps most illuminating is the review by S. A. Eliot in the *North American Review*. Eliot's comments perfectly mirrored the skepticism of the *Review* in this early phase of literary nationalism. Contrary to Kettell's view, Eliot asserted that the colonial period was *not* an age of poetry and we were foolish to claim otherwise; that exposing bad American poetry was worse than printing none at all (for example, the *Bay Psalm Book* and Cotton Mather's puns); and had Kettell possessed valid aesthetic taste, he would have given us one volume of poetry, not three. Still, Eliot was encouraged to see (1) how pure and unblushing was the poetic experience in America, (2) how many poets were women, and (3) how many walks of life were contributing to a national literature. Finally, Eliot praised Kettell's large and significant appendix-bibliography.[5]

Equally judicious but more devastating was Robert Walsh's critique of Kettell's selection of poets and verses, together with his careless errors of fact. Goodrich attributed to this recital of Kettell's blunders the lasting critical damage and financial disaster of the *Specimens*. But from the perspective of the middle 1850s, Goodrich also assessed Kettell's value to his successors Griswold and the Duyckincks (of whom, it might be noted, the Duyckinck brothers were the more open-handed in acknowledging the importance of Kettell's pioneering). In Goodrich's words, these later compilers—and borrowers—"have found in the mine wrought so abortively by Mr. Kettell, both gold and glory."[6]

Goodrich also knew that the success of a Griswold in the 1840s resulted from considerably more interest in American literature than Kettell had promoted. Indeed, the Age of Annuals, as Goodrich dubbed it, began just before Kettell and lasted well into the flush years enjoyed by Griswold. After Carey and Lea's annual collection, *Atlantic Souvenir,* begun as a Christmas and New Year's offering in 1825 to 1826, came Elam Bliss's *The Talisman* (New York, 1827), followed by Goodrich's own *The Token* (Boston,

1828). In all but one of its fifteen years of life, *The Token* was edited by Goodrich (N. P. Willis was editor in 1829) and became a major influence in American literature. Goodrich combined it with the *Atlantic Souvenir* in 1833 and published, in the 1837 annual alone, eight of Hawthorne's tales. In addition to carrying early efforts of Hawthorne, Longfellow, and many lesser authors, Goodrich's *The Token,* like its dozens of competitors (named, more exotically, after flowers and jewels) created a public taste for the elegantly designed, steel-engraved volumes that were presently gracing the parlors and boudoirs of America.

The age of annuals and gift books is also remembered today as the era of *Godey's Lady's Book,* a magazine of literature and fashion founded in 1837 by Philadelphian Louis A. Godey when he merged the *Lady's Book* (since 1820) with the Boston *Ladies Magazine* (founded in 1828). Godey retained his Boston editor, the prolific Sarah J. Hale, to run the new journal, and a successful business it became. In 1860, circulation was 150,000 and Godey was now a millionaire. By 1841, "edited solely by ladies," *Godey's* was already growing into a distinguished literary journal, and five years later, it was to enjoy the celebrity attending the appearance of Poe's controversial series, "The New York Literati." Not contributors like Poe, however, but Mrs. Hale and her intelligent women gave the journal the success it achieved. Not only in its editorial board was *Godey's* largely a woman's affair, but also in the female artists and authors that Mrs. Hale engaged during its most profitable years. *Godey's* was the elegant mother of many an inferior glamour magazine to come. Little wonder that Kettell's rather pedagogical trio of volumes, unattractively printed and lacking illustrations, were never fit to compete in the marketplace with *Godey's* or with the unending spate of expensively bound and illustrated gift books. The immense popularity of these publications continued through the subsequent decades to a total of well over a thousand volumes. Goodrich claimed, however, that he never made money in this market and regretted the time he had expended in it. But he was satisfied that these volumes had wrought a certain welcome revolution in the public taste for books and a native literature in America.[7]

By 1840, publishers in Boston, New York, and Philadelphia seem to have sensed that the public was ready to welcome the more serious anthology. William Cullen Bryant, who had co-edited the annual, *The Talisman,* from 1828 to 1830, included eighty poets, but no "amatory poems and drinking songs"— again, the moral-American emphasis—in his *Selections from the American Poets* (1840, p. iii). George P. Morris published close to two hundred poets in his *American Melodies* (1840), a collection of verse largely from his *New York Mirror*. And a third New York journalist (and a bookseller), John Keese, strangely arguing the need for his collection of poems because "we have left our pearls unstrung" (p. 10), published his 284 pages of *The Poets of America* (1839 and 1840). Inevitably, compilers with state and regional pride were also exploiting the fever for an original American literature. Anne C. Lynch's *The Rhode Island Book: Selections in Prose and Verse, from the Writings of Rhode Island Citizens* (1841) is a typical instance. She garnered 348 pages of literary effort from the land of Roger Williams, which, as her preface proudly announced, was the first experience in the history of the race where a state had been "founded on the broad principles of spiritual freedom" (p. vii). Yet here was only a fraction of Rhode Island's literary riches, she teased the readers; perhaps in another year, they would be eager for still another collection. Neighboring Connecticut was not to be outdone. The Rev. Charles W. Everest's *The Poets of Connecticut* (1843) was superior to other state collections, said the editor, for this one was soundly organized (historically by birth of the poets) and enriched with biographical sketches. Selection had required that the poets' birth be in Connecticut—thereby excluding Timothy and Theodore Dwight—and thence had been guided by Everest's poetic taste. Everest was more fortunate in his poets than most compilers of local talent. John Trumbull, Lemuel Hopkins, David Humphreys, Joel Barlow, Richard Alsop, Fitz-Greene Halleck, and James Percival all belonged to Connecticut through birth.

Everest went on to edit annuals with characteristic names— *The Hare-Bell: A Token of Friendship, The Memento: A Gift of Friendship,* and *The Primrose: A Gift of Friendship.* But he was never a match for Rufus W. Griswold. Similarly schooled in the marketplace of annuals and gift books, Griswold was superbly qualified to satisfy the nation's growing appetite for attractive books that proudly featured America's very own literary product and genius. Griswold's *Prose Writers of America* (1847), though it was less popular (only four editions) than his *Poets,* is a more authoritative work and also more significant, as it becomes one of the culminating events in the movement for an indigenous American literature in the 1830s and 1840s. Griswold had compiled a half-dozen more collections since the *Poets* when he now turned to the *Prose Writers.* As before, he sought help and advice from literary acquaintances—Horace Greeley, E. P. Whipple, John Neal (who probably wrote his own sketch therein), and others.[8] The result was 552 pages treating seventy-one prose figures, only a minority of them writers of fiction. The contents ostensibly supported a native pride in the American literary achievement of Emerson, Cooper, Irving, Franklin, Edwards, and others. But as Perry Miller observed, Griswold also provided "a sly, a casuistical and brazen demonstration that the tradition of American prose is at bottom conservative, is Whiggish, and that the Duyckinck connection have [*sic*] been wrong from the beginning."[9] In the next chapter, we shall understand the Duyckinck connection more fully, within and beyond some of Griswold's omissions (for example, Thomas Paine and Herman Melville) and unflattering criticism (of William G. Simms and Cornelius Matthews).

The *Prose Writers* is of most interest today for Griswold's significant assessment of American literature in his introductory essay, "The Intellectual History, Condition, and Prospects of the Country." He appeared at the outset to continue the all-out championing of literary nationalism that had engaged Samuel Knapp eighteen years before. Griswold repeated the predictable list of disadvantages American writers had suffered: the absence of international copyright protection, the national diffidence toward "*Americanism,* in thought or expression," and the admiration for the American writer if he had been first approved across the seas. Griswold then ranked our theological writers among the best in the world, praised the merit of the Revolutionary authors, the great ability of our writers on jurisprudence, and the native achievement in oratory, archeology, oriental and classical learning, philology (with plaudits to Noah Webster), physical sciences, and journalism. Though Griswold would presently minimize native fiction in his excerpts, he wanted it known that in his library resided more than seven hundred volumes. Receiving his laurels in fiction were C. B. Brown, Paulding, Timothy Flint, and the conservative, anti-romantic aspect of Cooper, who "has written above the popular taste, in avoiding the sickly sentimentalism which commends to shop-boys and chamber-maids one half the transatlantic novels of this age." Poe, though criticized for an absence of humor, received generally favorable treatment with John P. Kennedy, Robert M. Bird, Irving, Dana the elder, Hawthorne, and N. P. Willis. Griswold concluded that we were inevitably advancing in American letters toward a contribution to Goethe's ideal of a literature of the world.

Lying within Griswold's introductory remarks was an undercurrent of what the *CHAL* editors regarded as judicious reservations, but which we can now recognize to be covert antagonisms arising from the heated literary politics of the decade. First were his presumably common-sense literary judgments. Griswold offered the seemingly harmless observation that our literature will be American through a native *spirit* rather than an exclusively local subject matter. He then commented that the South, except when piqued by Northern stimulus, had "done comparatively nothing in the fields of intellectual exertion." And some pages later, he reserved for that region's author and journalist, William Gilmore Simms, the harshest verdict of the entire essay: "Though occasionally correct, animated and powerful, his style is too frequently abrupt, careless, and harsh." Griswold then viciously accomplished the ungracious effect that he claimed to deplore in Simms. The partisan Simms failed to realize, said the Rev. Mr. Griswold, that the "literary class should [aim] to civilize mankind, to soften asperities, to abolish prejudices, to extend the dominion of gentleness." This criticism of Simms, taken together with Griswold's general emphasis on high-minded morality and a need for elite rather than popular college education in America, adds up to a conservative Whig's implicit counterstatement to the program of the Duyckincks and other members of the Young America movement in literature, journalism, and politics. Griswold well knew that he was ruffling some feathers, and he expected less than unanimous acclaim for his judgments in *Prose Writers* but, as he wrote on 7 March 1847 to publisher James T. Fields, the critical reception became far worse than he expected.[10]

The most punishing review, however, had not yet appeared. Two weeks later, in his *Literary World,* Evert Duyckinck, who had been treated cordially enough in Griswold's pages, wrote a totally negative critique of *Prose Writers.* As a critic, said Duyckinck, Griswold presented simplistic judgments and held only two ideas, both derivative and tiresomely repeated—the program of literary nationalism and the inadequacy of copyright protection. Nor was Griswold an adequate historian, so that *Prose Writers* became neither a historian's compendium nor a critic's judicious selection of American literature. The reader, said Duyckinck, "is at one moment starved by a dry catalogue; at another, inflated by a windy disquisition with little profit any way." The compilation of snippets was "chaffy, meagre, and unprofitable"; the style was marred by "inelegant expressions"; and the pages generally were filled with printer's errors, self-contradictions, and (Duyckinck repeated) an "arid catalogue-ing," than which "nothing can be more painful to the eye or grievous to the soul." Equally unfortunate, Griswold's prejudice, or ignorance, had led him to slight the Southern writers (only 20 percent of the contents) as well as such figures as Albert Gallatin, James Kent, Thomas Paine, and Herman Melville. A slight of a different kind was palpable in the "coarse and illiberal treatment" of Cornelius Matthews. Duyckinck averred that he would not refute the charges; but he then proceeded to defend and praise Matthews. Duyckinck concluded that "a critical history of the literature" of America remained to be written, with an outlook benefited by better materials and a more affirmative attitude than Griswold had displayed "in this big and little book."[11] When the Duyckincks published the *Cyclopaedia of American Literature* nine years later, Griswold gained a Thyestean revenge in his retaliatory review and brought to a close an era of stimulating literary publishing and controversy in prewar America. To that controversy we now turn.

Chapter 5

The Duyckincks among the Young Americans, the Knickerbockers, and Others

The critical history of American literature that Evert Duyckinck called for in the review of Griswold's *Prose Writers of America* did not issue from Duyckinck's pen. But he contributed (with brother George) essential background preparations for that eventual history that would be written in the academy. As the editors of the *CHAL* rightly state with regard to a third major event in nineteenth-century pioneering scholarship, the Duyckinck brothers' *Cyclopaedia of American Literature* (1855) first made available "in something like adequate measure and proportion, materials for the study of our literature . . ." (I, viii). The *Cyclopaedia*, in two outsized volumes, stands today as a properly monumental climax of the pre–Civil War effort to comprehend and support a flowering national literature. And the critical wars that the Duyckincks and their allies waged during that flowering (from Poe to Lowell to Melville and to others) gave to the profession of American literature study the earliest example of acute and spirited literary criticism in America.

The three decades before the war have usually come down to us through the successive distillations of literary historians and critics as the Age of Emerson. The oracle of Concord did express the common national aspirations of an entire literary epoch, and, moreover, he gave this indigenous program the impressive universal sanction of a transcendental metaphysic. But vital goings-on were also happening elsewhere, above all in New York among the Young Americans, the Knickerbocker Set, and other journalists and literary activists who were waging what Perry Miller has called a "war of words and wits," generating a new excitement and enthusiasm for literary expression, study, and criticism just before midcentury.

The central figure in many of these encounters was Evert Duyckinck. When he cut to ribbons Griswold's *Prose Writers of America* in his own *Literary World* in 1847, Duyckinck had finally gained an editorial position of power to voice his opinions on American literature. The significant career of this authentic Dutch New Yorker and generally urbane and congenial booster of a native literature began some eleven years earlier. In the spring of 1836, as Emerson was readying his demands for an original American literature, Duyckinck (just graduated from Columbia College) and a small circle of friends in New York, including thirteen-year-old brother George, were holding meetings of the Tetractys Club with a purpose comparable to Emerson's. Like various professional literary clubs that had formed in the previous decades in New York, Boston, Philadelphia, and other eastern locales, the Tetractys Club helped to articulate and strengthen the movement for an American literature. Presently joining the group was Cornelius Mathews, the helplessly verbose and intemperate lawyer-turned-author to whom the gentle Evert would remain fiercely loyal through the years ahead despite the peril of such friendship to his own professional life. (Duyckinck's adverse review of Griswold's *Prose Wirters* may have been motivated in part by Duyckinck's having prepared the biographical sketch of friend Mathews, from which Griswold had deleted Duyckinck's words of praise.)

Mathews urged the club to take up the banner of literary Americanism, to ally themselves with democratic politics, and dub themselves the Young Americans. In December 1840, the club established the *Arcturus*. Until its demise in May 1842, this monthly published Hawthorne, Longfellow, and Lowell and aimed at an American stance in literary criticism. More exactly, the club offered a progressive version of the American verities of equality, freedom, and brotherhood to celebrate the "democratic genius" in literature. Its principles leaned to the utilitarian and non-aesthetic, to "a New Literature to fit the New Man in the New Age."[1]

After the *Arcturus* ceased publication in 1842—Poe later called it one of the best-edited magazines yet to appear in America— Evert Duyckinck sought further allies and, in particular, a new journalistic platform. It came to him when John L. O'Sullivan, founder of the *Democratic Review* in 1837, established the New York *Morning News* in 1844. Duyckinck became literary editor of the *News* and also helped guide the older *Review*. He then brought in fellow Young Americans Mathews and W. A. Jones. In the months that followed, Duyckinck had the satisfaction of seeing various careers advanced in the *Democratic Review:* Thoreau, Hawthorne, Horatio Greenough, Lowell, Whittier, and others.

The *Review* touted Simms and published Poe's *Marginalia*. In addition, Duyckinck extended his influence into the larger publishing world, becoming editor of Wiley and Putnam's Library of Choice Reading in 1845. Over the next two years, he brought forth, in The Library of American Books division of these editions, the work of Hawthorne, Poe, Simms, Mrs. Kirkland, Margaret Fuller, Melville, and various others.

O'Sullivan turned out to be less than the ideal ally for the Young Americans. Politically, he was an advocate of free trade. He also opposed the copyright and particularly disliked its bellicose advocate, Cornelius Mathews. So while Duyckinck became official literary editor of the *Democratic Review* in April 1845, the Young Americans were still looking for their own journal to express a liberal–political program for American literature. The opportunity arrived when Appleton, with Wiley and Putnam, agreed in January 1847 to finance the *Literary World* and hand over the controls to Duyckinck—with Putnam's proviso that the obnoxious and erratic Mathews have no connection with the journal. Nevertheless, the kindly Evert could not abandon his friend and gave Mathews an assignment in the maiden issue. Within weeks, Duyckinck was out and Charles Fenno Hoffman in. In October of the following year, Hoffman departed with a mental illness, and the Duyckinck brothers became official owners of the *Literary World*. The irony is that they had come by this long-needed journal a trifle late. The war of words and wits over the form and spirit of an American literature was beginning to run out of ammunition on both sides after more than ten years of vital debate between the Young Americans and their Knickerbocker adversaries.

We can retrace the literary warfare to its local origins. In 1834, two years before Duyckinck and his New York friends would first gather to discuss their mutual tastes in a democratic literature, Lewis Gaylord Clark had purchased the year-old *Knickerbocker* magazine and began to attract to his editor's "table" New York gentlemen of like (that is, Whiggish) interests in literature and society. By 1840, says Perry Miller, Clark had made the *Knickerbocker* "the most influential literary organ in America."[2] Something of a New York answer to Boston's *North American Review* but without the Harvard style of scholarly Unitarianism (they leaned to the urbane and Episcopal), the *Knickerbocker* and its circle espoused the universal over the national and insisted that our identity was essentially English. To their fondness for Byron and Scott, they joined Dickens and the later Wordsworth. In

"The Editor's Table," Clark was the cultivated gentleman offering opinions on topics from social drinking to behavior of children, or providing glimpses of New York life, or describing autumn in the country.[3]

But the journal had a strenuous mission as well. With contributors like New England defectors Henry Cary ("John Waters") and Charles F. Briggs ("Harry Franco"), Clark and the *Knickerbocker* took on the Young Americans and their various advocates, and literary controversy in New York continued almost nonstop for well over a decade. When the *Knickerbocker* insulted the work of southerner Simms, the cause of the *Southern Literary Messenger* became the cause of the Young Americans. Duyckinck's *Democratic Review* proceeded to praise, and overpraise, Simms. It also published Poe after he had insulted a Knickerbocker in *Graham's* and Clark specifically in *New World*. With Poe, the alliances in these journalistic battles become somewhat inconsistent. For when the Whiggish *American Review* was founded in late 1844 to counter the *Democratic Review,* editor George Colton, a cousin to the Knickerbocker Clark, proudly published Poe's "The Raven" in the second issue. In 1845, Knickerbocker Charles Briggs brought the temperamental Poe into the editorship of the *Broadway Journal* to stimulate sales even at the expense of Poe's embarrassing opinions. True to form, Poe waged further editorial combat with Briggs's own allies. The *Broadway Journal* died on his hands after scarcely a half year. Poe then secured space in *Godey's Lady's Book* later in 1846 to release his venom against Briggs, Clark, and company. In 1847, the journalistic wars continued without Poe, thanks in part to Mathews's *Yankee Doodle*, which joined battle against the *American Review* and the *Knickerbocker,* though its lifetime amounted to a mere three months. Of special interest among its diatribes is Duyckinck's reply to the hostile reception in the *American Review* of *Omoo* and his Young American recruit, Herman Melville.

Before Melville arrived on this lively scene, many of his literary seniors had entered the fray, purposefully or incidentally. Cooper and Bryant continued into the 1830s their earlier effort to define the national genius but also to correct misguided notions and attitudes entertained by their countrymen. Bryant, whose son-in-law Parke Godwin was one of Duyckinck's Young Americans, defended Cooper after *Home as Found* (1838) was criticized as an anti-American book that would give us a poor image abroad. Bryant wrote "Sensitiveness to Foreign Opinion" in his New York *Evening Post* (11 January 1839) and lamented our pitiable deference to "the superior judgment of the Old World." For all our national boasting, we not only were looking across the ocean for corroborative opinion that our books were worthy but in fact were seeking foreign opinion first.[4]

Poe, too, wrote in the 1830s ruing our low self-esteem. He was equally irritated by American critics for their "indiscriminate puffing of good, bad, and indifferent" in order to serve our "inordinate vanities and misapplied patriotism." The outburst appeared in 1836 and was prompted by recent books of poetry by Joseph Rodman Drake and Fitz-Greene Halleck, which were destined, he had no doubt, for great popular applause. America had some good poets who should be recognized, said Poe, but Drake and Halleck were not among them.[5] When Poe presently came north, he continued to argue for, and exhibit in his own columns, a responsible criticism of our own authors. He observed that when American publishers did take a chance with the American literary product, forsaking the advantages of printing English books at no copyright expense, our readers then snubbed the result until the work were "dubbed 'readable' by some illiterate Cockney critic . . . any anonymous sub-sub-editor of the 'Spectator,' the 'Athenaeum,' or the London 'Punch.'" The remarks came in his "Marginalia" for the *Broadway Journal* he was editing at the time (vol. 2, 4 October 1845, pp. 199–200). He reiterated other issues in the campaign for an American literature: that an American *spirit* rather than American *themes* gave the evidence of a national literature, that the Young Americans' egalitarian politics were essential to that spirit, and that American writers favored by the British were those who implicitly despised the democratic idea. When the occasion required it, Poe could become the momentary foe of the aristocracy.

Poe was not, of course, disposed to praise every product of the new American spirit. He was less than charitable in his estimate of the anthologies reviewed in the preceding chapter. Kettell's *Specimens*, Poe noted in 1842, were largely "doggerel" and "specimens of nothing but the ignorance and ill taste of the compiler." Cheever's *Common-Place* collection of poetry was "exceedingly commonplace," said Poe in 1842 and again in 1846. Keese showed better taste and knowledge than Morris and Bryant, though like Kettell, all failed to advance a "distinct view" of American poetry. But toward Griswold's *Poets*, Poe was notably complimentary in 1842, granting the book high praise in both *Graham's* and the *Boston Miscellany* as the most judicious collection of all. Poe called it "the most important addition which our literature has for many years received."[6]

The next year, Poe earned the lasting enmity of Griswold, who would become his posthumous editor. In his 1842 review, Poe had politely demurred regarding some of Griswold's poets, as well as his slightly favoring New England writers (though Lowell deserved more space, said Poe, and Holmes different selections). But in 1843, with Griswold having replaced him as the critical voice of *Graham's,* Poe may have been involved in writing a second review of *Poets* and its editor. This anonymous diatribe now pronounced Griswold a mediocrity, a plagiarizer (of Poe's definition of poetry), a critic whose judgment was "worthless" in *Poets* as well as in *Graham's* (now a journal of "trashy literary character" that previously enjoyed a "brilliant career . . . under Mr. Poe's care"). Griswold's biographical sketches "are miserably written," and the poets not included (their names supplied) could be grateful, "for if ever such a thing as literary ruin existed, or exists, nine-tenths of the *Poets* (!) of America are ruined forever by the praise of Mr. Griswold!"[7] To his credit, Poe in 1847 set personal irritations aside and gave a fair-minded estimate of Griswold's *Prose Writers,* terming it his best work, for Griswold appeared a "better judge of fact than of fancy."[8]

Poe himself had toyed with the notion of interpreting, in some fashion, America's literary past and present. What he did accomplish to that end appeared in six issues of the Philadelphia *Godey's Lady's Book,* from May to October 1846. He sketched thirty-eight writers in "The Literati of New York City," and the rather slipshod preparation is manifest in his explanatory subtitle: "Some Honest Opinions at Random Respecting Their Autorial Merit, with Occasional Words of Personality." Why Poe wrote some of these perfunctory sketches of harmlessly bland figures is anyone's guess, though they may have camouflaged a devilish intention to practice some selective character defamation and critical target shooting. The portraits of the Knickerbockers' Lewis Clark and Charles Briggs were particularly mischievous, not to say venomous. Clark had ridiculed Poe and the *Southern Literary Messenger* as "quacky" ten years before. Later, the two had locked horns in print over Poe's contention of disunity and plagiarism in Longfellow, the darling of the Knickerbockers and the *North American Review.* By 1846, with the failed *Broadway Journal* no longer available to him, Poe was a defenseless target for the barbs of Clark and his *Knickerbocker* allies. Poe's retaliation, we guess, appeared in these sketches in *Godey's.*

The first installment carried the sketch of Briggs, and Clark, in the *Knickerbocker,* immediately termed it "*ludicrously* untrue." Poe described Briggs as an imitative writer who "carries the simplicity of Smollett to insipidity, and his picturesque lowlife is made to degenerate into sheer vulgarity." Briggs's criticism, moreover, was a farce: "Mr. Briggs has never composed in his life three consecutive sentences of grammatical English. He is grossly uneducated." Lest Poe seem traitorous to his recent colleague at the *Broadway Journal,* he announced that their settled tastes in art were openly and radically at variance. As to Briggs's character, Poe conceded a measure of humor and warmth, but the man was also pretentious, garrulous, vacillating, and devious.

Though Clark rushed into print at once to defend his fellow Knickerbocker, Briggs prepared a more elaborate retort that appeared in serialization within a year, "Trippings of Tom Pepper," an ill-concealed satire of Poe. And like Clark, Briggs continued well after Poe's death to perpetuate a legend of Poe's treachery to friends and his unscrupulous ambition as an author.

The sketch of Clark came in the next-to-last number in *Godey's.* Clark had been waiting for it with pent-up wrath, and Poe did not disappoint the expectation. The editorial scraps from the *Knickerbocker* editor's table, said Poe, were "a little Boweryish" in tone. If Clark's style had any merit, vigor, force, or impressiveness were scarcely the words for it, and since "the editor has no precise character, the magazine, as a matter of course, can have none." It could once boast such contributors as Irving, Paulding, Bryant, and Neal, but no longer; and even in its most vital years "some incomprehensible *incubus* has seemed always to set heavily upon it, and it has never succeeded in attaining *position* among intelligent or educated readers." Hence the rather unfortunate subscription of perhaps fifteen hundred copies. The figure, as Poe surely knew, was closer to five thousand, and these readers were treated in the next issue to Clark's scurrilous reply, wherein Poe was exposed as an unprincipled hack and foul-mouthed inebriate.

Meanwhile, Poe had prepared a parting shot in the October issue of *Godey's.* It came as a needling digression within a sketch of Charles Fenno Hoffman:

> Mr. Hoffman was the original editor of "The Knickerbocker Magazine," and gave it while under his control a tone and character, the weight of which may be best estimated by the consideration that the work thence received an impetus which has sufficed to bear it on alive, although tottering, month after month, through even that dense region of unmitigated and unmitigable fog—that dreary realm of outer darkness, of utter and inconceivable dunderheadism, over which has so long ruled King Log the Second, in the august person of one Lewis Gaylord Clark.

Clark's response to this extraordinary insult, if known, would best be left unprinted. But he was to have the final victory. Poe

was presently in his grave, and Clark's friend Griswold immediately edited, and tampered with, Poe's letters and works. Poe's
sketch of Briggs, for one, Griswold recast with new comments
added and unfavorable sentences deleted. Clark then reviewed
the results of Griswold's work that were damaging to Poe and
supplied further posthumous malignings of his own.[9]

Poe enjoyed restful and appreciative moments as well in his literati portraits and none more so than in a sketch for the third
issue. That his complimentary tone was reserved for the leader of
the rival Young Americans would not have been lost on Clark.
Evert Duyckinck had recently cited Poe's imaginative and critical
powers, and Poe fully returned the compliment. He graciously
commended Duyckinck for the ease, originality, and force of his
"Felix Merry" essays and for his editorial acumen, first in the
Arcturus and later in Wiley and Putnam's Library of Choice
Reading. (In 1845, Duyckinck had printed separate volumes of
Poe's tales and poems in the companion Library of American
Books.) Poe's portrait of the personal Duyckinck echoed other
living tributes to the man:

> In character he is remarkable, distinguished for the *bonhomie* of
> his manner, his simplicity, and single-mindedness, his active benefi-
> cence, his hatred of wrong done even to any enemy, and especially
> for an almost Quixotic fidelity to his friends. He seems in perpetual
> good humor with all things, and I have no doubt that in his secret
> heart he is an optimist.[10]

Another member of Duyckinck's circle who prominently cam-
paigned for a national literature was William Gilmore Simms, one
of Griswold's targets in the *Prose Writers,* mentioned earlier. A
contributor to the *Knickerbocker* in the late 1830s, Simms had a
falling out with Clark over Simms's Young America sentiments in
Magnolia, which Simms edited from April 1841 to June 1842.
By the summer of 1843, he had met Evert Duyckinck and become a bona fide Young American. In 1844, Simms was editor of
the *Southern and Western Magazine* and opened its pages at
once to Mathews and Duyckinck. But after twelve issues, the
magazine died in December 1845. By then, however, the cordial
Duyckinck had made New York a hospitable place for Simms.
Less can be said for Clark's offices, and Simms by that time had
developed a fierce dislike for the Knickerbocker. The heated tempers flaring in these literary rivalries can be gauged by the epithets Simms fashioned for Clark in correspondence to friends in
1845 and after: "that wretched cur and scoundrel"; a "dirty,

crawling creeping creature"; "a creature to be kicked or spit upon[,] not argued with or spoken to"; "a liar"; "a dirty rascal"; and "that miserable skunk."[11]

In 1845, Duyckinck published a volume of Simms's stories in the Wiley and Putnam Library of American Books. And more centrally for our story, he solicited two volumes of Simms's critical meditations on American literature. *Views and Reviews,* first series, appeared in 1846, followed by a second series in 1847. The first volume has the greater significance today, especially with Simms's "Americanism in Literature," a document of the literary controversy of the age that nicely embodied many of the arguments of Young America. Simms repeated that a truly American literature had suffered from our writers' deference to European models, tastes, ideas, and critical praise or blame. But native landscape, society, and history were shaping an authentic American mind and art, aided by our release from practical labor and the "conquest of a savage empire." Our democratic freedoms would produce a more vigorous literature than was formerly sponsored by aristocratic despotisms. The Southerner in Simms did produce one unhackneyed observation: Though the restless mobility of Americans into the interior had made difficult a distinctive formation of American character and taste, American literature should not be controlled from a dominant center. Regional variety would generate a salutary atmosphere of competition and free enterprise.[12]

As we expect, Simms's views received a cold reception in conservative quarters. In the October 1846 *North American Review,* Cornelius Felton complained of the general absence of aesthetic taste and historical vision, together with the "extravagant nationality," in Simms's ill-conceived essays. Thus spoke Harvard's professor of Greek. The next month, Clark's *Knickerbocker* quoted Felton with cordial agreement. Young America countered in 1847, both in Mathews' *Yankee Doodle* and Duyckinck's *Literary World,* spiritedly endorsing Simms's echoing of their literary nationalism.[13]

New England was being heard from in and out of the pages of Emerson and the *North American Review* on the campaign for an American literature. Beyond her services for the *Dial,* Margaret Fuller had reviewed writers like Hawthorne and Longfellow in essays for Horace Greeley's New York *Daily-Tribune* that amounted to an incisive criticism of the American literary scene. Though she looked to future vistas of literary fulfillment, Fuller recognized several of our writers as already creating a distinguished literature. She quoted Simms's recent *Views and*

Reviews in praise of Cooper, and she lauded William H. Prescott, George Bancroft, William E. Channing the elder, Emerson, Bryant, and even Cornelius Mathews, whose verses, she noted, were "unpardonably rough and rugged" but poetry nevertheless. America would soon find a voice more free and vigorous than cramped and insular old England's, expressing "a genius wide and full as our rivers, flowery, luxuriant, and impassioned as our vast prairies, rooted in strength as the rocks on which the Puritan fathers landed." That spirit, however, was not yet heard in poets like Lowell ("his verse is stereotyped; his thought sounds no depth") or Longfellow ("artificial and imitative"). Such observations, obviously so congenial to Young America tastes, Fuller gathered into a volume that Duyckinck gratefully published (1846) in his Library of American Books.[14]

Lowell and Longfellow, too, were having their say in the 1840s, and in them we gain, for a first time, a semblance of the direct responsibility of the academy (Harvard) to criticize and shape the idea of American literature and even a recognizable literary canon. To be sure, no course in American literature existed at Harvard. Longfellow was Smith Professor of Modern Languages (1836–54), to be succeeded by Lowell, while Holmes presently (after 1847) was a professor in the medical school. But the Cambridge Poets, with their Harvard colleagues, created a scholarly milieu, and the *North American Review,* as it had been from the start, continued to be the organ of Harvard literary opinion. Lowell and Longfellow also made their presence felt among the literati of New York. Though Lowell was offended by Mathews, he seemed to Duyckinck a Young American under the skin.[15] Lowell contributed to the liberal *Democratic Review,* urged in his essay on Poe for *Graham's* the need for an American criticism to guide the young literature, and boasted to Knickerbocker's "Harry Franco" Briggs in 1848, after the initial *Biglow Papers* appeared, that "I am the first poet who has endeavored to express the American Idea."[16] More accurately, he was the first poet and critic who *succeeded* in expressing the American Idea (as Poe did not) in all of its foreign and domestic complexity.

One result of Lowell's range is that neither liberal nor conservative advocates knew how to claim him. By 1847, the task was not growing any easier. Late in that year, Lowell began to write the verse sketches of "A Fable for Critics," his own spirited caricatures of New York's literati (as well as New England's), which are saturated with outrageous rhymes and puns and consistently quotable and incisive as Poe's sketches in *Godey's* the year before generally are not. Beyond the acute judgments of individual writers are Lowell's larger estimates and telling asides that sum up the creative ferment and critical antagonisms astir in this springtime period of literature and criticism in America.

Though his comments most prominently excerpted today treated the major figures—Emerson, Bryant, Whittier, Hawthorne, Cooper, Poe ("three fifths of him genius and two fifths sheer fudge"), Longfellow, Irving, and Holmes—Lowell also knew the supporting cast serving American literary ambitions in the politics and journalism of the 1840s. Heading the long parade of established authors and would-be literary celebrities marching before Lowell's long-suffering Apollo were, in fact, our Young America leaders, Evert Duyckinck and Cornelius Mathews. Duyckinck was rather kindly portrayed as the indulgent promoter of his self-serving and distinctly paranoid friend. Duyckinck and fellow townsmen had also been too indulgent in their estimate of New York as the literary center of America. "What news," asked Apollo, addressing Duyckinck,

> "What news from that suburb of London and Paris
> Which latterly makes such shrill claims to monopolize
> The credit of being the New World's metropolis?"

Mathews served as the inevitable butt of Apollo's (and Lowell's) satire and scorn. Obsequiously marching several steps behind Duyckinck, this "small man in glasses" was full of vituperation against his countless enemies, British and domestic, and yet, as Apollo viewed it, he delighted in "displaying his critical crosses." Ever conciliatory, Duyckinck agreed with Apollo's judgment but then pressed on him a book by Mathews (no doubt, *Big Abel*, published in Duyckinck's Library of American Books in 1845, and promptly ridiculed by Clark in the *Knickerbocker*). Duyckinck assured Apollo space in the next *Democratic Review* for a critical appreciation of Mathews. Apollo replied that Duyckinck had already sent him forty-three copies of this book, and "'I've forty-two left, standing all side by side / (The man who accepted that one copy died).'" Apollo then hit on a plan to empty his shelves of all such books. He would advance "'a criminal code both humane and effectual. . . . I propose to shut up every doer of wrong / With these desperate books,'" while Mathews's new journal would be only lesser punishment for all "'petty thieves.'" They

> "Shall peruse Yankee Doodle a blank term of years,—
> That American Punch, like the English, no doubt,—
> Just the sugar and lemons and spirit left out."

Lowell/Apollo included Margaret Fuller's writings in these proposed criminal penalties, and her contribution would be the most brutal: "'Let murderers be shut, to grow wiser and cooler, / At hard labor for life on the works of Miss ———.'" Probably aware of, and smarting from, her recent criticism of his own work, Lowell presently unleashed a wickedly clever attack on a transcendental writer and editor, one tiresome "Miranda," clearly Miss Fuller, who then prompted him to a lengthy "'digression on bores.'" Her recent criticism of Lowell as a mind that "sounds no depth" was twice echoed in the fable. First, Miranda proudly claimed to have introduced Americans to authors whose works sound a depth. Apollo then commented, in an aside, on her writings: "'(Which, as she in her own happy manner has said, / Sound a depth, for 't is one of the functions of lead).'" When Miranda returned in the poem to resume more tedious discourse, Lowell rapidly closed his fable:

> Apollo at once seized his gloves, cane, and hat,
> And, seeing the place getting rapidly cleared,
> I too snatched my notes and forthwith disappeared.

Lowell was obviously not the poet-critic with whom one cared to be at odds. Following Duyckinck, Mathews, and Fuller in the earlier procession came Griswold with his endless flock of cackling versifiers. Other minor figures swelled the progress—John Neal and N. P. Willis, though Lowell had smaller grievance with them, and none at all with "Harry Franco" Briggs (who read the rough-draft installments and to whom the "Fable" is inscribed). Simms may be present in the anonymous horde of "'American Bulwers, Disraelis, and Scotts.'" While variously memorializing his major and lesser contemporaries, Lowell digressed into some tart judgments on the general American sensitiveness to foreign opinion and our critics' defensive puffery of native authors. His Apollo rebuked us for a foolish deference to England:

> "You steal Englishmen's books and think Englishmen's thought,
> With their salt on her tail your wild eagle is caught;
> Your literature suits its each whisper and motion
> To what will be thought of it over the ocean."

So much for the conservative anglophiles among us. At the same time, however, our liberal champions of nationalism indulged in an overcompensating and inflated Yankee rhetoric on behalf of native bards (comically estimated in Lowell's opening "candid remarks" at ten thousand who are judged "*lofty* and *true*" by the critics and a full thirty thousand "*full of promise* and *pleasing*"):

> "What puff the strained sails of your praise will you furl, if
> The calmest degree that you know is superlative?
>
> .   .   .   .
>
> I would merely observe that you've taken to giving
> The puffs that belong to the dead to the living." [17]

G. P. Putnam brought out Lowell's jeu d'esprit in 1848, and the public response seemed encouraging when the one thousand copies of the first edition were immediately sold. But activity slackened thereafter, and a mere three thousand copies of the matchless fable comprised the total sales. The literary wars obviously were cooling down by then, although Briggs, editor of the new *Holden's Dollar Magazine,* and Clark in the *Knickerbocker* eagerly reviewed the book—and pointedly quoted, of course, the segments on Mathews and Duyckinck.

Lowell kept his hand in the next year with a review of Longfellow's *Kavanagh* (1849), which had particularly attracted his attention by raising the question of a national literature. After Longfellow's student oration on the subject while at Bowdoin, he kept an eye on the nationalist movement and was no stranger to the activities of Duyckinck and the Young Americans. Their liberal sympathies in the *Democratic Review* were, to him, a "loco-foco politico-literary system." [18] He shared with his fellow Harvard contributors to the *North American Review* the conservative view of a universal rather than national criterion of an American literature. In 1842, while writing on Heine, Longfellow attacked "young America, which mocks the elder prophets" in its nationalist program. [19]

Longfellow's best-known challenge to the Duyckinck program came several years after, in chapter 20 of *Kavanagh.* There, Longfellow's dreamy hero Churchill, a teacher laboring to write a romance, was set upon by a Mr. Hathaway, who had read Churchill's work in the periodicals and wanted his help in establishing a new magazine "in order to raise the character of American literature." Hathaway anticipated a national literature "commensurate with Niagara, and the Alleghanies [*sic*], and the Great Lakes." Churchill appeared to speak for Longfellow and the *North American Review* when he questioned this geographical determinism: "'A man will not necessarily be a great poet because he lives near a great mountain. Nor, being a poet, will he necessarily write better poems than another, because he lives nearer Niagara.'"

Switzerland, after all, had produced no great poet. The poets' roots might grow in national soil "but their branches wave in the unpatriotic air." Churchill then argued our inevitably English traits and sympathies and literary continuities. Moreover, the "'savage and wild'" aspects of the alleged American genius would not automatically issue in literary art, which must arrive, instead, through "'culture and intellectual refinement.'" We can question, of course, how much authority Longfellow meant to attribute to his hero, who showed an undisciplined will and purpose, plus a romancer's blindness to Alice Archer's unrequited love for him. Yet Churchill's remarks on a national literature, taken together, were familiar enough echoes from Craigie House and official Cambridge.[20]

Longfellow's neighbor down the street, Lowell, once more reinforced the argument in the July 1849 *North American Review* when, as Perry Miller believes, Lowell reviewed *Kavanagh* with a purpose "to vent the spleen he had for years treasured up against Cornelius Mathews." In his twenty-page review, Lowell granted only the last four pages to *Kavanagh* itself. In the rest of the space, he addressed the larger question of an American literature touched off by the Churchill–Hathaway conversation. The running head on the odd-numbered pages of the review read "Nationality in Literature." Lowell supported Longfellow's implicit satire of the Young Americans. Lowell spoofed their argument for an environmentally determined American genius: "Since it seems to be so generally conceded, that the form of an author's work is entirely determined by the shape of his skull, and that in turn by the peculiar configuration of his native territory," perhaps the critic should judge the author's work by its fidelity to his topography, be it sublime, flat, or whatever. But more seriously, we are the sons and transplants of England's culture, without as yet an American history, national folklore, mythic or epic past; and we should therefore realize how slight a repository of literary material can be mined from Americanism as opposed to the claims of universal, common humanity. The ideal of the American literary imagination, Lowell concluded, will be a synthesis of traditional material with a new-world perspective, even as Shakespeare borrowed the Athenian subject and gave it Elizabethan-English life. The New York Whigs joyfully quoted from the review at once in the wake of, and in irritation with, the Young Americans' pride in their captive new author, Melville, and the presumed originality of his recent *Mardi*.[21]

Melville had met Duyckinck some time in mid-1846 after Duyckinck had read *Typee* without enthusiasm but had agreed to include it in his American Library series. Then came the success of *Typee*, and the Young Americans eagerly touted Melville as the living example of their native-born genius, even though the South Sea romance had raised embarrassing issues of sound morality and factual authenticity. Duyckinck also helped Melville get his *Omoo* published and opened his huge private library to Melville, an omnivorous reader. Duyckinck received an advanced copy of *Mardi* from Harper in 1849 for publication in the *Literary World,* and, climactically for our literature, after *Mardi, Redburn,* and *White-Jacket,* Duyckinck arranged the historic introduction of Melville to Hawthorne in summer of 1850.

The details of that meeting in the Berkshires, where both men were living that summer, are too well known to recount here (though we easily forget that the party included not only the Duyckinck brothers, but also Holmes and the ubiquitous Cornelius Mathews). Well known, too, is the fact that Duyckinck had recently sent Melville a copy of Hawthorne's *Mosses from an Old Manse* (1847) and that Melville's anonymous review, "Hawthorne and His Mosses," appeared after the meeting, in Duyckinck's *Literary World*. Years before, Duyckinck had championed Hawthorne, a fellow Democrat, and though a New Englander, clearly a writer in the mold of Young America. Hawthorne, in fact, was publishing his tales wherever he could find an outlet, including even Clark's *Knickerbocker.* But to Duyckinck, writing in the *Arcturus* (May 1841), Hawthorne was Young America's kind of writer, "the most original, the one least indebted to foreign models or literary precedents of any kind, and as the reward of his genius, he is the least known to the public."[22]

In "Hawthorne and His Mosses," Melville obligingly supported Duyckinck's cause and echoed the rhetoric of American literary nationalism ever since Sydney Smith's suggestion of its nonexistence thirty years before. Melville remarked not only on Hawthorne's fiction but also on the entire sweep of an original literature, as American Shakespeares were now "being born on the banks of the Ohio." He then applied some reverse English on Smith's famous insult by predicting that "the day will come when you shall say, Who reads a book by an Englishman that is a modern?" The following week, he amplified the anti-British sentiment. "We want no American Goldsmiths: nay, we want no American Miltons." Indeed, "England, after all, is in many things alien to us. China has more bonds of real love for us than she." Therefore, America should realize that "the world is as young today as when it was created" and should "prize and cherish" her own writers. This was not to say that such affection should become an uncritical doting and blurbing; in fact, we badly wanted a "just and discriminating criticism," said Melville, echoing Lowell and Poe, as well as Whittier's comment in 1829. In a parting judgment, with a delayed jolt that Ezra Pound would have relished, Melville appraised American literary criticism: "There are hardly five critics in America; and several of them are asleep." As to Hawthorne's native genius, Melville predictably singled out the conditioning effects of liberal democracy and American nature. Here was "a man who is bound to carry republican progressiveness into Literature as well as into Life"; and aiding that deeply liberal-American result, "the smell of your beeches and hemlocks is upon him; your own broad prairies are in his soul; and if you travel away inland into his deep and noble nature, you will hear the far roar of his Niagara."[23]

Afterward, Melville recast *Moby-Dick* into Ahab's story and, in 1851, dedicated the work to Hawthorne in appreciation of his stimulus and in "admiration for his genius." But Melville was slipping from the Duyckinck fold and, with *Pierre* (in Book XVII), declared his separation from Young America in literature. Elsewhere, the world of the Young Americans was also falling apart. Mathews's *Yankee Doodle* had failed in October 1847, after scarcely three months of life and despite the contributions of Melville. The *Weekly Mirror,* which the Young Americans had purchased in May from Hiram Fuller (of the enemy camp) and retitled *American Literary Gazette,* had an even shorter life. But the *Literary World,* launched in 1847, seemed robust and thriving at the end of the decade. Even so, tempers were cooling and exhaustion setting in. The Young Americans' oldest journal, the *Democratic Review,* was in failing health and expired in September 1853; the *Literary World* followed suit in December. A new era, in short, had begun. *Harper's New Monthly* (June 1850) and *Putnam's* (January 1853) now published Melville. And on the demise of *Putnam's* in 1856, Boston reasserted its leadership in American letters with the founding of the *Atlantic Monthly* in 1857.

One literary figure had emerged on the scene, however, to rebuild for a time a liberal Boston–New York axis. Walt Whitman was carrying the works of Emerson to work in his carpenter's lunch container in 1854, and the next year, when his simmering had been brought to a boil by the "master," he prefaced the first edition of *Leaves of Grass* with plentiful helpings of New England transcendentalism and the poetic doctrines of Emerson. But this familiar story has a distinctly New York component as well. When his editorship of the *Brooklyn Eagle* began in March

1846, Whitman had embraced the cause of Duyckinck's Young Americans (his editorial in July 1846 was titled "Home Literature"). The stout Americanism of his 1855 preface to *Leaves of Grass,* properly speaking, blended Young American democracy with the native and universal bardic emphasis Whitman was lately appreciating in Emerson. The close parallels with Emerson's essay on "The Poet" in 1844 are too well known to need demonstration. But over the next ten years amid the New York battle of words and wits, this immediate literary and political ferment could only awaken the national–democratic instincts of a Whitman. And in 1855, he rhapsodized on the unique opportunities of the American poet in Nature's nation (Perry Miller's coinage): "His spirit responds to his country's spirit. . . . He incarnates its geography and natural life and rivers and lakes" (and the roll call of states followed, with their natural and human variety). The inspiration and the rhetoric here could be claimed equally among followers of Emerson and Evert Duyckinck.

And to that New York gentleman, we return for a dramatic close to this crowded chapter of American literary controversy. As Whitman was preparing to enter the scene on one side of New York, with an epic performance, Evert Duyckinck, with helpful brother George, was effectively departing the scene, but not without a last, and similarly monumental, gift to American letters. Through most of 1854 and 1855, the brothers Duyckinck labored at the two-volume *Cyclopaedia of American Literature.* The range and meticulous detail of their research is astonishing in view of the difficulties of access, communication, and travel that they overcame in so brief a time. Aside from the resources of their immense private library (seventeen thousand volumes), they visited public libraries up and down the Atlantic coast; inspected private collections of John Carter Brown, George Ticknor, James Lenox, and George Bancroft; and solicited the help of individuals North and South—Irving, Henry T. Tuckerman, John Esten Cooke, Simms, and others. Too, there were the predecessors whom they faithfully comprehended: Elihu Smith, Mathew Carey, Kettell, Everest, and Griswold, together with the model provided by Robert Chambers's two-volume *Cyclopaedia of English Literature* a decade before and the several geographical dictionaries and bibliographies already assembled to satisfy America's growing hunger for information and self-culture.[24]

In their more than fourteen hundred pages, the Duyckincks ordered more than 550 authors mainly by date of birth, tried to represent fairly the literary output and regional "cultivation" of South and West (as Evert felt Griswold did not), and confessed to

an historical more than critical purpose (pp. v–vii). They reproduced over two hundred pictures and four hundred auto-
graphs, so that the *Cyclopaedia* becomes, for their time and ours,
a generously illustrated reference work. It is also generous in
spirit, bearing the considerate humanity of the Duyckincks as
they treated scores of American writers from colonial times to the
present and selected representative portions from the writings.

If any rancor survived from the recent literary battles, it may
be inferred from allotments of space—relatively little to Griswold,
rather ample to Melville. (To their credit, the Duyckincks recognized, as few early critics did, that *Moby-Dick* was Melville's "most
dramatic and imaginative" work, II, 373.) From Cotton Mather to
Margaret Fuller to Hawthorne and the Cambridge poets, New
England was duly honored, while Clark's Knickerbocker circle received virtually the same impartial consideration as Young America's "Centurion" and Duyckinck's troublesome friend, Cornelius
Mathews. This spirit of tolerance the Duyckincks also bade their
readers and critics reserve on behalf of the *Cyclopaedia's* weary
compilers: "In conclusion, we may, we trust, ask a generous and
kindly consideration for a work of much difficulty. Inequalities
and short-comings may, doubtless, be discovered in it" (p. x).

Shortcomings were indeed to be discovered in it. Griswold reviewed the work in the New York *Herald* of 13 February 1856.
Fatally ill (he died the next year), he still possessed the scholarly
energy, fired by a memory poisoned from Evert Duyckinck's review of the *Prose Writers* nine years earlier, to compose what
Perry Miller terms "the most destructive review of all American
history." [25] On matters of judgment and taste, of course, Griswold
could only argue his private preferences against the Duyckincks'.
He would have given less space to George Berkeley, Thomas
Paine, and Crevecoeur (author of "a feeble work about the common life of the American people"), more to Jonathan Edwards
and Joseph Dennie, and none to authors who never wrote a line
on American soil or never set foot here. Griswold would have included a Peter Zenger and Henry James, Sr., and the general
areas of journalism, book publication, and education (especially
the common schools). But the Duyckincks' ignorance, not their
taste, was Griswold's central target, and he listed, by states, the
figures who were apparently unknown to the compilers—a full
six pages' worth! Griswold also gave scores of examples of "bungling and incomprehensible sentences" in the graceless, even
ungrammatical, writing. But even more devastating, he submitted by the page-full errors of literary, historical, and biographical fact from colonial and revolutionary times to the recent

past. (We are at a loss to explain how the Duyckincks could have forgotten that the *Broadway Journal* was founded in 1845 by Briggs and Watson, not Briggs and Poe.)

And so Griswold had finally exacted his revenge, in spades. Evert Duyckinck never again made any pretensions to scholarship, though the *Cyclopaedia* went through two expanded editions before his death in 1879, and he did assist in the revision in 1866. (George had died three years before at a young forty.) The second revision, in the 1870s, was accomplished by M. Laird Simons. Griswold was unquestionably the better scholar, though his name now survives in infamy for his irresponsible editing of Poe (and for those who know this subsequent review, Griswold's savaging of Duyckinck). Duyckinck, on the other hand, remains in our literary history the beneficent gentleman, devoted bibliophile, faithful friend to the self-advertising Mathews, and champion of the struggling young Melville. Men as diverse as Poe and Samuel Goodrich recognized Duyckinck's invaluable services to American letters. Scholar Henry T. Tuckerman reviewed the *Cyclopaedia* in the *North American Review* two months after Griswold's hatchet performance and roundly praised the "disinterested sympathy with literature for its own sake, a patient accuracy, and an even, sensible, well-considered plan, that does credit to the good taste and intellectual integrity of the authors." Typically, the review mentioned the discernibly "true instinct of the gentleman" present in the discussion of living authors.[26] Neither could Knickerbocker antagonists dislike Evert Duyckinck. Even Lowell's querulous Apollo grew cordial in Duyckinck's presence: "I'm happy to meet / With a scholar so ripe, and a critic so neat, / Who through Grub Street the soul of a gentleman carries."

To later generations as well, the Duyckincks' huge *Cyclopaedia* stands out as a generous example of humane scholarship of the first order. More immediately in the postwar decades, it became a reference source invaluable to literary scholars in the academy who would soon write our first American literary histories.

Chapter 6

Moses Coit Tyler and the
Rise of American Literary History

After acknowledging the Duyckincks' *Cyclopaedia,* the *CHAL* editors leap two decades to the postwar literary history of the pioneering Moses Coit Tyler. "Notable and still unsurpassed" (I, viii) is their acclaim for Tyler's histories of colonial and Revolutionary War literature. And unsurpassed in several respects these four volumes remain to this day. A diligent scholar and superb stylist, Tyler arrived on the stage of widening American literature studies in the fullness of time. In the earlier decades, the central arguments on American writing had been, Is it "American"? and, Is it "literature"? Tyler addressed both questions and now asked, as well, if this literature possessed a substantial and traceable history.

Because he was committed to literary and democratic American values similar to those of Evert Duyckinck's Young Americans, Tyler nicely continued the critical and moral expectations of those prewar literary nationalists. We are fortunate, too, that this first important literary history returned to the very roots of American life and imaginative expression in the new world. In a further continuity with the Duyckincks, Tyler advanced their interest in literary history as biography but with a critical discrimination absent in the *Cyclopaedia* as well as in the indiscriminate bulk of the prewar anthologies of America's literary "specimens." He also brought to these growing resources a high degree of the gifts he admired in the ideal historian, the passion for "truth, fairness, and lucidity" uttered with a "nobility of expression."[1] Finally, Tyler was blessed by a further circumstance of time: The study of American writers was now entering the college classroom in the 1870s and providing for the scholarly professor an opportunity and stimulus to compose lectures that could be translated into the chapters of a sustained literary history. More commercially, the professor might prepare textbook manuals for the classroom—an activity with which Tyler was also familiar. We may well dub Tyler founding father of our scholarly profession, mindful that he inherited much of the legacy traced in the past three chapters.

When the Duyckinck *Cyclopaedia* appeared in late 1855, Tyler was in his third year at Yale. We suspect that Duyckinck soon became a part of his voracious library reading. (For his colonial literary history in 1878, Tyler used the enlarged 1875 edition of the *Cyclopaedia,* prepared by M. Laird Simons.) Other resources for American literature study were accumulating through the 1850s and 1860s, but at Yale, as at other American universities, including Michigan, where Tyler spent his freshman year close to home—his family, originally from Connecticut, had moved to Detroit—no place had been reserved in the curriculum for American literature. Indeed, no English department existed at all. As in earlier years, modern literature reached university classrooms mainly as it was spirited into courses in oratory and rhetoric.[2] At Yale with Tyler was Andrew Dickson White (later the first president of Cornell), who remembered the early 1850s to be a time of deadly rote learning of Greek and Latin grammar, while the aesthetic charm of the ancients was totally ignored. Students knew that exciting literature was being written in America and England, but none of it penetrated the ivy-covered walls of Yale University. "Our only resource, in this field," said White, was "the popular lecture courses in the town each winter," and "of these, that which made the greatest impression upon me was by Ralph Waldo Emerson."[3]

Tyler himself became more interested in oratory than literature at Yale, and after the example of Henry Ward Beecher, he was attracted to liberal theology and abolitionism as well. Following short terms at Yale Divinity School and Calvin Stowe's Seminary at Andover, Massachusetts, Tyler served three years as a Congregational minister in upper New York State before his health declined. He then moved to wartime Boston, where he met Emerson and the great abolitionist orators, William Lloyd Garrison, Wendell Phillips, and Frederick Douglass. But Boston offered Tyler no future. In April 1863, he sailed to England as a salesman for a company whose product was a health program termed musical gymnastics. The assignment seems curious, but presently it begins to appear providential. In his speeches to English schools and social clubs, Tyler inevitably branched out to the one subject the English were forever dubious and inquisitive about—the quality of life and culture in America. In late 1864, Tyler was lecturing on "American Humor," "The Pilgrim Fathers," and "American Oratory." A new career was beckoning. In his diary of 1865, he proposed to write six or eight chapters for a "purely literary audience" on the history of American literature. Returning to the United States, Tyler received and accepted in August 1867 a professorship of rhetoric and English literature at fifteen hundred dollars a year at the University of Michigan. Eleven years later, he published his two-volume history of colonial literature, and as he asserted with high hopes in the preface, this was but a part of his intention "to write the history of American literature from the earliest English settlements in this country, down to the present time," a history he was never to complete. Nor had the road to Tyler's colonial achievement been smooth, given the postwar status of American literature study in the nation's universities and, in particular, at a Midwestern school like Michigan.[4]

In 1867, when Tyler began his teaching career, American literature still remained a stranger to the college curriculum. For all the preliminary labors of Neal, Knapp, Kettell, Griswold, and the Duyckincks, plus the vigorous debate over literary nationalism in prewar journals at home and in England, and the steady growth of public, private, and self education, the colleges remained delinquent in the study of even the major writers who were being advanced in the name of a distinctive American literature. The backwardness is not surprising, of course, when we reflect that the university world has long been one of the hardrock bastions of conservatism and resistance to change in American life and institutions. The chief intellectual basis for literary study had long been established by 1870: The more remote in time the subject, the more suitable it was for lecture, recitations, and examination. In the American university classroom, classical authors, yes, and older British authors, perhaps; living authors, no. Even beyond the turn of the century, the American professor was asking how one lectured and examined students on a contemporary work of literature in which the older rhetoric and newer philology played no explanatory role.

Still, certain events of the Civil War years and just after were affecting literary study in the colleges, however slowly. The Morrill Act (1862) increased the number of state universities through federal land grants, perhaps loosening, thereby, the hold of conservative elitism in higher education enjoyed by the older universities along the Atlantic seaboard. This is not to say that the Morrill Act gave the humanities a special advantage. They have never received high priority in the state universities, as Professor Fred L. Pattee sadly learned early at Penn State and teachers of literature at these tax-supported institutions up to the present continue to realize.[5] Perhaps the Civil War did create the conditions for a somewhat more united American consciousness that aided the pursuit and study of a national literature. In the post-war era, too, innovative minds like President Eliot of Harvard inaugurated the elective system that soon relieved students from a prescribed curriculum of classical authors and, presently, from the new Germanized linguistic study of foreign literatures.

For a more detailed estimate of the progress American literature study was making in the academy, we return to John S. Lewis's scholarly survey. He reports that by 1870, sixty-three colleges on his list were offering a course in the English authors, usually as lectures to seniors, and this interest boded well for the study of American authors. During the decade, twenty-six colleges specified some American literature among the English courses, with twenty-three of that number prescribing Thomas Shaw's *Outlines of English Literature* with Henry T. Tuckerman's appended "Sketch of American Literature." (Shaw's manual, revised by other hands after his death in 1862, went through some fifteen postwar editions before the end of the century.) College interest in American literature during the seventies can be detected as well in the American topics among student prize essays at Hamilton and Hobart, while a bachelor's thesis at California (Berkeley) in 1875 treated California literature. Attention to American literature was heightened after the war, too, by the appearance of American writers on the faculties of Cornell (George W. Curtis, Bayard Taylor), California (Edward R. Sill), Johns Hopkins (Sidney Lanier), Harvard (W. D. Howells), and elsewhere. Richard Watson Gilder of Scribner's appeared on the campuses of Wesleyan and Wells and spoke to the women about a new alliance possible between the American writer and the academy, especially as women graduates increasingly joined the ranks of authors and influential taste-makers.

Still, by 1880, only fourteen colleges were offering American literature specifically in their curriculum. The powerful rise of linguistic study, especially after Johns Hopkins was founded in 1876, was ambiguously helpful. Under President Gilman, that university did give the first real impetus to graduate study of literature in America. But the Germanized, philological approach was itself of little benefit to the study of American authors on any level. In sum, the progress of American literature within the curriculum of the academy in the 1870s may be characterized as a change from almost nothing to at least something, the attainment, as our authority puts it, of a decent toehold for the new discipline.[6]

Roughly sketched, this is the American university scene that Tyler entered after he returned from England to begin a discontinuous fourteen-year term at Michigan (he resigned in 1872, then returned in 1874, and, in 1881, moved to Cornell). Skillful at lecturing, thanks to his earlier stint in the pulpit and the subsequent years of public speaking in England, Tyler was decently prepared to teach elocution and rhetoric. In his fifth year, he planned to teach what would have been the first college course in American literature. But he had grown frustrated intellectually at his Midwestern campus. He resigned to become literary editor in New York for the *Christian Union,* currently under the guidance of the idol of his college days, Henry Ward Beecher. During this editorial interim (less than two years, though Tyler's contract called for three), his most notable writing, for our purposes, was the unsigned reviews of John Seely Hart's *A Manual of American Literature: A Textbook for Schools and Colleges* (1873) and Francis H. Underwood's *A Hand-Book of English Literature: American Authors* (1873). Both may have spurred Tyler, in different ways, to reconsider his aborted career as a teacher and scholar of American literature.

Hart (1810–1877) was Tyler's counterpart at Princeton, a professor of rhetoric and English language, and by coincidence, Hart was planning his own initial American literature course in the same year as Tyler's. With Tyler's defection from Michigan, Hart in 1872 appears to have taught "the first definite course in American literature in any major American university."[7] Hart was not a newcomer to American literature or the school trade. He proudly referred in the preface of his *Manual* to his 1844 *Class Book of Poetry* and a companion for prose, which helped to begin the systematic study of English literature. In 1853, four years after Griswold, Hart brought out his own *Female Poets of America* (208 women were included in the 619 pages of his *Manual of American Literature*). Before coming to Princeton after the war, he had been an administrator in the New Jersey schools and recognized the struggle to gain a place for the study of English and American literatures in higher education. Satisfied that his class books had stimulated the study of English literature, Hart hoped in 1872 that his *Manual of American Literature* would inspire a "full and adequate treatment of the literature of our own country" (p. viii).

For his manual of sketches, Hart recorded his debts to Austin Allibone's *Critical Dictionary of English Literature and British and American Authors* (1858–71, three vols.) and to Griswold and the Duyckincks; but Hart also insisted that he was original in conception, form, structure, and material. He did, in fact, approximate a scheme of literary history. Hart provided brief

historical introductions to each of his five chapters, which he arranged chronologically into colonial and Revolutionary eras, followed by periods dated from 1800 to 1820, 1830 to 1850, and
1850 to the present. These three nineteenth-century chapters
were subdivided into poetry, fiction, and miscellaneous prose in
the fields of science, political economy, history, theology, and so
on. Important writers received not only a biographical summary
but also a prose or poetry selection or excerpt. Melville's best
works, said Hart, were *Typee* and *Redburn;* he did not mention
Moby-Dick. Whitman, though an iconoclast, was nevertheless
a genius. Howells's recent early work was honored with three
quotations from reviewers. We may infer something of Hart's
own American literature course at Princeton from his advice
to teachers (pp. xxiii–xxiv) that they use the manual not for
class recitations and student memory work but as a class reference text. Hart suggested that teachers treat fully one major
nineteenth-century author in each of the chapter sections and
then use independent judgment on how many of the indicated
minor authors to include. From 1873 to 1874, Hart's course was
required of Princeton seniors all three terms and was one of
seven required literature classes. The course, however, was
dropped in 1876. No doubt Hart's retirement in 1874 hastened its
demise. He died in 1877.[8]

Tyler welcomed Hart's *Manual of American Literature* in the
March 1873 *Christian Union* despite the factual errors and certain idiosyncratic judgments. He echoed Hart's call for a sustained appreciation of our own literature. Even by the 1870s,
American literature required a defense against the resident anglophiles. "American people are beginning to realize that their
own native writers have at least occasional claims to notice," said
Tyler wryly, and then added without irony, "there is something
morbid and degrading in the passion with which we have wor-
shiped exotic models in letters and have despised our own."
(Lowell had recently regretted this same lingering diffidence,
which encouraged the annoying condescension of foreigners,
though he was confident that the late war had also sobered and
matured the nation.)[9] Tyler's review of Underwood's *Hand-Book*
several months later also suggests that the pedagogue and scholar
were still alive within the literary journalist. Tyler applauded this
second handbook for its textbook virtues of clarity, taste, and
verve, praise intimating that Tyler might be conceiving a manual
of his own. (In 1879, he reconstructed Henry Morley's *A Manual
of English Literature* [1873] for the American classroom but be-
grudged the time and labor expended on this unrewarding task.)

More significant was Tyler's objection to Underwood's dismissal of American writers before Franklin, so that "the opportunity is lost of recalling to our memory forgotten names, and of furnishing to us some taste of literary productions which lie beyond ordinary reach." Similarly in the preceding review, Tyler had been concerned over our abandonment of colonial writers and hoped that Hart's *Manual* might "stimulate to the re-issue of early American books now out of print, and very difficult to access in any form." The journalist in Tyler was obviously giving way to the literary historian of our colonial writers.[10]

Indeed, Tyler's journalistic work in the months to follow was becoming more unsatisfying (Beecher, for example, never entered Tyler's name on any of the contributions). In the autumn of 1874, the University of Michigan regents made a precedent-shattering decision and rehired him. His previous salary of $1,500 at the university had risen, as a journalist in New York, to $3,500. Michigan recalled him at $2,500. Tyler returned to his earlier purpose and offered his American literature course to the seniors at Michigan in the year after rejoining the faculty. He was also, by 1875, well along in the scholarship for his projected history of American literature. The teaching and scholarship, says Fred Pattee, were expertly united during the lectures in his literature classes.[11]

Tyler had already intensified his study of American literary history in New York when his enthusiasm for journalism was declining. He happily devoted his mornings to the holdings of the New York Historical Society and the Astor Library. At the same time, Tyler was realizing the difficulties of research in the colonial period and mused on the benefits American scholars would derive from an early American text society. He was about to resign himself to writing a literary history that would have to begin in 1783.[12] When Tyler's research later carried him to the richer holdings in the Boston area, including the invaluable manuscripts and publications of the Massachusetts Historical Society and their reprints of colonial works originally published in England, he possessed the materials needed for a sufficiently crowded story of the colonial period—ultimately two volumes' worth. But the going was slow after his return to Michigan, and Tyler chafed under the interrupting delays of receiving necessary books from the East. He pleaded with George H. Putnam, his patient publisher-to-be, to hunt out friends who might own rare books of Americana and be willing to lend them to Tyler. The library at his alma mater, Yale, was especially accommodating in "the loan," as he put it, "of needed books to my distant home."[13] It will not do,

however, to exaggerate Tyler's lonely, originating scholarship. He
plainly acknowledged in footnotes an obligation to Knapp, Kettell,
Griswold, the Duyckincks, and many others who had already labored to prepare the ground for our first qualified literary historian. Nor was their work buried in Eastern archives. Tyler, that is
to say, was by no means a solitary Ishmael groping along in a
largely uncharted wilderness.

By 1870, there was a decent supply of encyclopaedias, dictionaries, and bibliographies of American literature. Tyler used
Allibone's *Critical Dictionary,* and we suppose that he inspected
historian Francis B. Drake's *Dictionary of American Biography*
(1871), well stocked, by the author's count, with nearly ten thousand entries. Doubtless Tyler used as a reference, too, Nickolaus
Trübner's superb *Bibliographical Guide to American Literature:
Being a Classified List of Books, in All Departments of Literature
and Sciences, Published in the United States of America During
the Last Forty Years* (1855, enlarged 1859). Supplementing
Trübner was Orville A. Roorbach's massive *Bibliotheca Americana: Catalog of American Publications, Including Reprints and
Original Works,* from 1820 to 1852 and thence to 1861 (published by himself, 1852–61, four vols.). In the 1860s, James Kelly
added two volumes to Roorbach with *The American Catalog of
Books,* Frederick Leypoldt continued Kelly's work into the 1870s,
and other hands compiled later volumes. Joseph Sabin, after nineteen years of research and classifying, published his first volume
of *A Dictionary of Books Relating to America from Its Discovery
to the Present Time* in 1868. For colonial literary history, Tyler
would have had the benefit of Sabin's first seven volumes, to
"Hall." Tyler was, in addition, almost certainly familiar with
Charles D. Cleveland's *Compendium of American Literature*
(1858), a college favorite in postwar years; surely Tyler would have
liked the generous space given Henry W. Beecher, though not
Cleveland's having ignored colonial writers.

Published selections of American writers also had continued
to proliferate. Besides the collections from Eastern states, an
awakened pride in regional authorship was spawning anthologies elsewhere, the bards either locally born or transplanted. We
noticed earlier the Rhode Island collection of Anne C. Lynch
(1841) and Charles W. Everest's *Poets of Connecticut* (1843, and
in a sixth edition by 1864). Others included William D. Gallagher,
Selections from the Poetical Literature of the West (1841) and
William T. Coggeshall, *The Poets and Poetry of the West* (1860).
During the war years, publication of such collections, and most
writings, slowed to a trickle. In 1865, Henry C. Murphy pub-

lished his *Anthology of New Netherland,* translations with accompanying sketches, which Tyler acknowledged in his chapter on the middle colonies (p. 439n). From the postwar South now came James W. Davidson, *The Living Writers of the South* (1869) and Ida Raymond (Mary T. Tardy), *Southland [Female] Writers* (1870, two vols.). In the early 1870s, two anthologies easily missed in the more prominent company of Hart and Underwood were Noble K. Royse, *A Manual of American Literature Designed for the Use of Schools of Advanced Grades* (1872); and more important, Benjamin N. Martin (professor of the City University of New York), *Choice Specimens of American Literature* (1871), a collection of more than 260 authors designed as an illustrative companion to Tuckerman's "Sketch of American Literature" in Shaw's *Outlines of English Literature.*[14]

Two other collections after the war are of special interest, highlighting as they do the bookseller's bid to cash in on centennial pride. William J. Linton's *Poetry of America* (London, 1878) celebrated the centenary with (as expressed in his subtitle) *Selections from One Hundred American Poets from 1776 to 1876.* Linton acknowledged collections from Kettell to Griswold to Richard H. Stoddard (who revised and enlarged Griswold's *Poets and Poetry* in 1872) but claimed precedence for offering the "first fair and comprehensive sample of American Poetry given to the old country" (p. ix). William M. Rossetti, America's literary advocate in the British Isles, had recently published *American Poems* (1872), though his book, said Linton, was less than representative (it was, however, 512 pages to Linton's 387). Rossetti and Linton were appealing to the same new-world curiosity that Tyler had met with in England. Unlike Tyler, Linton regarded colonial poetry, despite his generous excerpts, to be of little merit. Two other features of the book were his pointed omission of the religious poetry that earlier nationalists had considered deeply American and his back-of-the-bus inclusion of "some specimens of negro melody" in the final pages (379–87). More important to literary study in higher education was Henry A. Beers's modest centennial collection, *A Century of American Literature, 1776–1876* (1878). Adopted in the Chautauqua home study courses, Beers's book was popular for several decades among those professors (William P. Trent was one) who appended some American writers to their course in modern English literature.

A number of beginnings had been realized also in the writing of American literary history before Tyler began his work. The historical interest was always present, of course, in the anthologists and encyclopaedists whom he knew and acknowledged, including Hart and Underwood. The sketch of American literature in the ninth edition of the *Britannica* (1875), written by John Nichol, University of Glasgow, was cited by Tyler in his discussion of *The Bay Psalm Book* (p. 237).[15] A fair number of historical introductions had appeared earlier in the century in the works we have looked at in previous chapters. A rather ambitious series of articles was projected by the London *Athenaeum* in 1833, to be written by the Rev. Timothy Flint (Harvard class of 1800), who had just completed his book on Daniel Boone and recent novels on the romantic West. But financial arrangements were delayed, and Flint departed on still another trip into the western frontier. In early 1835, Nathaniel P. Willis, the American subeditor for the English *Athenaeum*, wrote four anonymous sketches on "Literature of the Nineteenth Century: America," announcing at the outset that he hoped to convince Englishmen that a definable American literature existed. Well-educated (Yale, 1827), well-traveled, and experienced in the world of contemporary journalism as a gifted editor for Samuel Goodrich, Willis was by then a rising young essayist, and he did acquaint his readers of the *Athenaeum* with the principal American writers. But his essays, taken together, become a parade of opinionated aesthetic pronouncements with very little sense of an evolving literary history. He acclaimed the work of writers who eventually had very little influence on the shape of our literature—Dana, Percival, Drake, Halleck, and some of the minor writers of fiction—while he repeated the clichés about the "pure and healthy moral feeling" resident in distinctly American poetry, as well as the shaping force of American nature that would determine a new era in our literature.[16]

Flint, meanwhile, reappeared and gave the *Athenaeum,* several months later, the first in a series of eleven "Sketches of the Literature of the United States." A part of his shaping outlook had appeared in an article for *Knickerbocker* in September 1833 (II, 161–70), where he discussed "Obstacles to American Literature," summing up the routine arguments of the previous decades. In the *Athenaeum* pieces, Flint, unlike Willis, did try to order his "Sketches" into a literary history and carve out distinguishable periods and trends. Flint located three epochs. His immigrant phase underlined the role of the classics in Virginia, and the Bible and dark wilderness as the influences on Puritan New England. The native period was hardly a time of liberation, despite the rise of colleges, since religious, and then political, ideas tyrannized creative expression. But in the national era, Flint's writers began to exhibit the promise of an American genius expressing itself in our literature. Flint was not quite able to demonstrate this new nationalism. No doubt to his chagrin, the *Athenaeum* deleted in this third period his discussions of writers who had already appeared in Willis's sketches.[17]

Perhaps the most remarkable occurrence in prewar American literary history was a volume by Philarète Chasles: *Anglo-American Literature and Manners* (translated and abridged for American readers by Donald McLeod, 1852). Many European studies of American literature in the century to come will be of too little consequence in the American academy to warrant attention in these pages, but this study is an exception. Chasles, a distinguished critic and lecturer at the College of France, had earlier impressed the Duyckincks with a perceptive article on Melville that appeared the *Revue des Deux Mondes* in 1849. The Duyckincks ran a translation in the *Literary World* on 4 and 11 August. Chasles's appreciative chapter on Melville in his literary history becomes the highlight of the book and another embarrassing instance of the neglected American author receiving his first extended appreciation abroad. For Chasles, Melville's "ornate" style and "florid descriptions," together with his penchant for hyperbole, were part of a distinctively American creative spirit "hardy, violent, and brusque, with a tendency to the terrible, the interesting, the unforeseen" (pp. 118–19). Chasles's opinions on other American writers within his vaguely defined three periods of American literary history carry the ring of original, if sometimes idiosyncratic, conviction.

Also in 1852 came Henry T. Tuckerman's school manual "Sketch of American Literature" appended to Shaw's *Outlines of English Literature*. Written in the starch-collared prose that gave rise to the term Tuckermanity, the sketch was an old-fashioned blend of literary history and moral precept that American students of an earlier time were obliged to endure. Tuckerman came to this seriousness by way of the Boston Latin School and Harvard College, though he was an urbane and well-traveled friend to Irving and Halleck, a minor poet, and briefly in the 1840s, an editor of the *Boston Miscellany*. Tuckerman died in 1872, and Evert Duyckinck, whose *Cyclopaedia* Tuckerman had cordially reviewed in 1856 (after Griswold's insulting attack), commemorated Tuckerman's career in a *Memorial* essay.

The historical sketch of 1852 was characteristically workmanlike. Tuckerman shaped his account in three chapters and prefaced each with a topical summary. The first treated the development of native prose from colonial days to the time of then-current historian, Francis Parkman. These were American authors who served the causes of religion, politics, journalism, and education. Chapter 2 was devoted to belles lettres from Franklin to Hawthorne, and Tuckerman (no doubt in cooperation with Shaw's section of the book) frequently aligned the qualities of our authors to those of English writers. In chapter 3, he described the history of our poetry from Freneau to the Cambridge poets, all his figures receiving one paragraph. Then came Bryant, who was given the final seven pages and the accolade of "the best representative of American poetry" for his "felicitous use of native materials, as well as in the religious sentiment and love of freedom, united with skill as an artist . . ." (p. 482). In 1867, a two-page addendum, presumably by Tuckerman, named the writers who had died since 1852 and listed, with an occasional epithet, some of the new lights of our literature, including Thoreau, James Parton, and William D. Howell [*sic*].[18]

Tyler, then, was not a solitary struggler bereft of precedent and example as we return to him in the early 1870s reading diligently in American history and literature during his tenure with the *Christian Examiner* in New York. His American literary history, however, was yet to be envisioned in clear design. The published writings and reference works available to him in the New York libraries, along with the original manuscripts and documents, occasionally must have shaken him into realizing the enormity of his subject. Fortunately, Tyler's work gained impetus and direction after he met and began his association with George H. Putnam. In 1875, after Tyler returned to Michigan, Putnam asked him to prepare a manual specifically for American literature and pointedly said that he did not want a suffix to a manual of English literature. (He was doubtless thinking of Tuckerman's annex to Shaw, as well as planning to enter into school-trade competition with Hart's American *Manual*.) Tyler responded that he preferred to write a scholarly survey of the literature and perhaps even capitalize on the upcoming centennial enthusiasm of 1876. Putnam agreed. But during the year, Tyler's writing was impeded by various professorial duties and the absence of needed books at Michigan.

By the end of February 1876, Tyler had written essays on only Anne Bradstreet and Nathaniel Ward. A month later, Tyler wrote Putnam about the unforeseen hardships. Unlike his colleagues in English literature, Tyler was unable to lean on pioneers in the field, especially for the colonial period. He slowly acquired some of the necessary books for the Michigan library. But he would certainly miss the centennial deadline, and he offered to dissolve the contract. Putnam replied that he was willing to wait for Tyler's survey.[19] Another year passed. In the summer of 1877, Tyler visited the special collections in the East, presumably those he acknowledged in his preface: the Boston Public Library, the Boston Athenaeum, the John Carter Brown collections at Providence, the Pennsylvania Historical Society, and the Library of Congress. He now called his survey the "History of Colonial American Literature." Fourteen months later, Tyler delivered final chapter 18 to the press. Putnam wanted the history in one volume; Tyler held out for two. Both volumes appeared in November 1878.[20]

Nearly twenty years passed until Tyler published the two-volume *Literary History of the American Revolution* that continued, and completed, his achievement in American literary history. (He died in 1900, three years afterward.) Tyler's move to Cornell in 1881 as the first Professor of American History in America had interrupted the momentum of his literary history.[21] Other labors siphoned his time and energy away from the studies of the Revolutionary period. He was ordained an Episcopal priest in 1883. The next year, he helped establish the American Historical Association. Distracting, too, were incidents of faculty unrest at Cornell, compounded by Tyler's intermittently poor health after middle age. But this is moving ahead of our story in the 1870s.

In their tribute to Tyler's achievement in literary history, the *CHAL* editors hoped to follow his spirit and manner as they pursued the subject up to their own time. Dozens of would-be American literary historians had already presumed to follow in Tyler's wake during the years after his colonial history appeared. Yet Tyler does indeed surpass them all and remain, perhaps with only our later Parrington, the historian of American literature whose work can be termed classic by virtue of its integrity and brilliance of vision and style. Tyler is the Homer of our literary history not only for his early example but also because he returns to the dawn of American writing and reenacts much of that history in all its vividness and excitement.

As a pioneering literary historian, Tyler also has his failings. Rather than patronize him and overlook these understandable shortcomings, we shall profit by putting Tyler to the same test that will be administered to his many successors in the academy. The staple issues for the literary historiographer, as for the literary historian, lie in the utterly basic questions: How do we define and explore the obvious terms American, literary, and history? The *American* aspects include the conception of new-world literary devices and cultural themes (including ideas, subjects, myths, indigenous and archetypal characters) leading to a national ethos—with attention to possible foreign influence on the home-grown creations and to even a priori or universal considerations beyond Tainean matters of race, epoch, and milieu. The literary aspects involve, after a framing definition of literature itself, an explanation of distinctive periods, movements, and schools; a definition of genres, subgenres, and modes; the structure of themes; explication of substance into appropriate form; and critical judgments that ultimately establish a "canon" of American literary works.

The historical inquiry turns to the evolution, flowering, and continuity or decline of periods, genres, modes, and themes as they are affected by American and international influences. Additionally, the historiographer responds to the literary craft in the history itself, to the historian's narrative voice, tone, creation of historical setting and happening, the portraits of individual and representative figures, and explanatory patterns of metaphor and imagery. Obviously, a fully documented analysis of our dozens of literary histories cannot be undertaken in the present book. But among the most important volumes, Tyler's work, above all, deserves a generous hearing.

Tyler began his literary history of the American colonies with an arresting nonliterary comment: "There is but one thing more interesting than the *intellectual* history of a man, and that is the *intellectual* history of a nation" (p. 5, italics added). Prefigured here were several of the significant features of the two volumes that followed. Tyler would shape his history primarily with ideas rather than aesthetic forms and their evolution. He tried to discover the advancing expression of an American mind and spirit. And he searched for that national expression largely through the collective history of individual writers, a procedure that, despite obvious limitations, became in his hands a stunning advance over previous literary-historical sketches. In his preface, Tyler seemed alert to the pitfalls of his predecessors, discussed in our previous pages, who assembled their biographical dictionaries or volumes of specimens with little or no aesthetic principles of selection and discrimination. Tyler assured his readers that he had exercised in his history "a most anxious judgment" to ensure a completeness in his selected writers and documents. This completeness was undertaken, however, with due regard for "appreciable literary merit." He added that some selections would cast "helpful light upon the evolution of thought and of style in America" (p. xii). Presumably, then, Tyler meant to trace a history of colonial style on a parallel course with the evolution of colonial thought and locate both, causally, within a distinctive American setting.

Mindful that his chief assignment as a historian was literary, Tyler usually tried to illustrate the aesthetic values in his writers. His usual procedure was to describe, excerpt, and judge their chief writings. He quoted liberally, as he explained in his preface, to "give freely, and with as much discrimination as I possess, such portions of our [largely inaccessible] early literature as may form a terse anthology of it" so that readers might "verify my statements" (p. xiv). Though Tyler's excerpts were sometimes unnecessarily long and his literary judgments usually impressionistic and peremptory, lacking the sophisticated precision of today's critical analysis in matters of diction and functional syntax or imagery, he was sufficiently attentive to his aesthetic mission. He noticed in his excerpts from John Smith the "easy and delightful strokes of imagery, quaint humor, shrewdness, and a sort of rough unconscious grace" (p. 27). The Rev. Alexander Whitaker of Virginia employed the "diction of an earnest, simpleminded, scholarly man" (p. 42); William Wood's *New England's Prospect* displayed an "easy command of the words that are at once nicely, concisely, and poetically descriptive" (p. 152); Mary Rowlandson's narrative of her Indian captivity was admirable in its "diction—the pure, idiomatic and sinewy English of a cultivated American matron" (p. 380); and Hugh Jones wrote "in a plain, positive style just sufficiently tinctured with the gentlemanly egotism of a Virginian and a Churchman" (p. 495). Jonathan Edwards's theological power owed much to his literary "minuteness of imaginative detail—bringing forward each element in the case one by one; so that drop by drop of the molten metal, of the scalding oil, fell steadily upon the same spot, till the victim cried out in shrieks and ululations of agony" (p. 425).

Like the best of old-fashioned impressionist critics, Tyler gained his authority here from his own unmistakable ability to write as well as the authors he praised. This praise commands our belief, too, because elsewhere he acridly dismissed inferior writings as "sad rubbish," "miserable stuff," "poems not absolutely indispensable to the world's continued existence," or verses that "scarcely rise to the puerile" and even "approach the idiotic." (We may question, of course, why the literary historian can even afford to consider the sad rubbish or puerile article in his crowded pages.)

Despite the *CHAL* editors and others who have admired Tyler's historical talents, he does not stand up particularly well to close scrutiny as an historian of literature itself. Though he intended to trace the evolution of style and relate it to the evolution of thought, Tyler was not notably successful in clarifying the separate origin, growth, and influence of either style or ideas in American literature, let alone their organic relationship to each other. For example, he traced style in our earliest literature to its "splendid parentage—the written speech of England," a fortunate birth epoch arising "at the very time when the firmament of English literature was all ablaze with the light of her full-orbed and most wonderful writers . . ." (p. 11). He then savored the racy and Elizabethan idiom of seventeenth-century colonial writers. The English influence on style and manner continued in the next century. Benjamin Colman's sermons were "fluent, polished, modern in tone, Addisonian" (p. 411); the cadences of Mather Byles, Popean (p. 429); and the learning, humor, and sonority of Samuel Sewall "of the quality of Sir Thomas Browne" (p. 374). But such treatment of transoceanic literary parallels and influence was, by modern standards, quite offhand. So, too, were suggested home-grown literary relationships. Tyler compared George Alsop's *A Character of the Province of Maryland* (1666) with Nathaniel Ward's *The Simple Cobbler of Agawam* (1647) on the mere basis of "mirthful, grotesque, and slashing energy" (p. 58) rather than considering the development of a genre. Tyler pronounced Nathaniel Ames's almanac better in most respects than Franklin's (p. 365). But the two were not critically compared. Franklin, in fact, was not discussed until Tyler's Revolutionary War volumes, thereby leaving an irreparable vacuum in the pre-Revolutionary periods and a literary history that Franklin vitally influenced and was influenced by.

Without a firmer analysis of English and autochthonous elements and effects in the literary work, Tyler was at a disadvantage when he confronted the decades-old controversy over literary nationalism—the question of precisely what was distinctly American in our writers. The intricacies of such definition did occur to him from the outset. With John Smith, how could one classify this English soldier of fortune an American author? Tyler decided that "while nearly all of [Smith's] books have a leading reference to America, only three of them were written during the period of his residence as a colonist in America. Only these three, therefore, can be claimed by us as belonging to the literature of our country" (p. 19). Was a necessary impulse from the new world, however briefly received, at play in these three works? Tyler did not say. He next implied a link among John Milton, Smith, and the American colonial spirit: In 1608, Smith's

A True Relation of Virginia ("the earliest of American writings") went on sale in London at a book shop a few steps from the birth-place of Milton, who would become a great exponent of political and religious freedom. Obviously, no causal importance, literary or intellectual or American, can be derived in either direction from this pairing of incidents. Nor did Tyler press for any. But he built from the suggestion a case that Smith's writing, as in his remarkable letter to the London stockholders, sounded the uniquely American spirit of freedom, "a note of unsubmissive-ness . . . a premonitory symptom of the Declaration of Indepen-dence" (p. 27). As to Smith's literary gifts, Tyler referred to his Elizabethan "Hotspur rhetoric" at one time but at another, to an English literary spirit and style quickened and transformed by the American atmosphere, "the sweet air, the rich soil, the waters, the mountains, in all the large and majestic framework of nature in the new world" (p. 27)—Tyler here echoing the familiar strains of "Nature's nation" that we heard in the previous debates over literary nationalism.

Tyler's conceptual difficulties were prefigured in these early pages on Smith. What was the peculiarly American genius in co-lonial literature and thought, what forces brought it into play, and what were the stages of its development? Tyler's preliminary an-swers were not so much articulated as expressively dramatized in his portrait of Smith. Here was the new-world pioneer, Tyler's admired man of thought and action, a naturalized type who would reappear in other dominant figures to come. Smith was an emerging composite of Tyler's ideal colonist, bold, idealistic, and fair-minded, who finally arose as the freedom fighter of 1776. As Tyler pursued this gradually realized American, he established as well a persistently liberal point of view from Smith on forward. Though Tyler did not cling to this bias as doggedly as Parrington would (Tyler admired more fully than Parrington the Puritans' mental toughness as dissenters and pointed out their commend-able ardor for what might be over what is), this liberal focus and tone gave Tyler's volumes a semblance of consistent and reasoned historical evolution.

Under closer inspection, we find discrepancies and contradic-tions in Tyler's causal treatment of Smith and his colonial con-temporaries. Because they were heroic, Tyler's Elizabethan men of action and thought were not limited by their American wilder-ness environment. His New England Puritans, too, were tough-minded individualists who conquered their environment and gave private and public shape to their search for freedom, "men who carried keen brains and despotic consciences throbbing in bodies toughened by toil. . . . At once a grim happiness began to sprout up out of the sturdy *freedom* and thrift *which they made for themselves here"* (p. 95, italics added). These same men founded Harvard College and "made arrangements by which *even in that wilderness* their young men could at once enter upon the study of Aristotle and Thucydides, of Horace and Tacitus, and the Hebrew Bible" (p. 87, italics added).

A decade earlier, George Sandys completed his translation of Ovid amid, and in spite of, the Indian-plagued forests of Virginia, though Tyler curiously hailed the translation a product of national literature, "the first utterance of the conscious literary spirit, articulated in America" (p. 48). Nathaniel Ward was also viewed by Tyler as a free spirit, writing with an original linguistic energy: "The first accents of literary speech in the American forests, seem not to have been provincial, but free, fearless, natural, . . . the English language spontaneously, forcefully [written] like honest men" (p. 207). Here Tyler stumbled into an additional ambiguity: Did the free, natural forests of America embody the very absence of an influencing environment or were they the causal force of a "literary speech . . . free, fearless, natural"?

At other times, Tyler quite clearly found a cause–effect relationship between his heroes' self-expression and the American environment. In John Hammond's *Leah and Rachel* (1656), "indeed, is American talk. Here certainly, in these brusque sentences, do we find a literature smacking of American soil and smelling of American air" (p. 56). The brilliant, English-educated Francis Higginson scarcely arrived on the shores of Massachusetts when all his pages, according to Tyler, "are full of sunshine, and the fragrance of flowers, and the gladness of nature in New England during the balmy season in which he came to it" (pp. 146–47). In general, Tyler credited New England writers with a literature superior to Virginia's because the northern colony nurtured "a great throng of writers, nearly all of whom took root in her soil" (p. 71). Also, the determining geography of Virginia—the river arteries creating small, isolated settlements—impeded the growth of the closely knit community enjoyed in New England. Rather than heightening the new-world freedom and growth of the American individual in Virginia, this absence of social community hindered education and book production. The result: "no literary class, and almost no literature" (p. 80).

And yet Tyler's American writers were, at other times, free, rugged spirits, individuals who distinguished themselves above and apart from social forces, writing without self-conscious literary origins and the civilized refinement of a literary class. On John Mason's *The History of the Pequot War* (1677): "We like his bluff narrative all the more because the varnish was left off" (p. 128). Edward Johnson's history of early New England was "crude enough in thought and style," and yet "its very faults of diction," its zeal, simplicity, and honesty "make it most authentic and a priceless memorial of American character and life in the heroic epoch of our earliest men" (p. 123). Even Governor Winthrop could be seen as the admirable possessor of "a stately unconscious eloquence. He was no artist, only a thinker and doer. Of course he never aimed at effect" (p. 114).

Tyler had an easier time with his national thought, style, and character when he arrived at his second literary period. The first generation of heroic Englishmen, and the troublesome questions of mother-country influence, now receded from the colonial scene, and Tyler could point the history toward the eighteenth-century community, where the revolutionary and democratic new-world spirit was more clearly defined. The second period of Tyler's literary history began with 1676, although no aesthetic event precipitated for him any shift in literary activity in that year. Instead, Bacon's rebellion in Virginia and King Philip's war in New England occurred contemporaneously to give unmistakable portents of a distinctively national independence of spirit.

Tyler then contrived a link between this quickened spirit in 1676 and a shift in literary expression. A home-grown generation was now producing "the earliest literary results flowing from the reactions of life in the new world upon an intellectual culture that was itself formed in the new world" (p. 261). The generalization does not hold, of course, for various colonies to the south of New England. Tyler did not escape the biases of a man born and educated in Connecticut; neither the middle colonies nor the South received more than a half-hearted chapter each, and Tyler found little in the way of identifiable American literary community there. Eighteenth-century forces of enlightenment soon predominated—in journalism, in new colleges, in studies of the physical sciences—and figures of an early Jeffersonian mould were replacing the more autonomous colonial individualists in the parade of Tyler's American heroes. Emerging was the clear outline of the national type: John Wise (the "first great American democrat," p. 359), Benjamin Colman ("his personal breadth burst the hoops of his creed," p. 409), and William Penn ("through every turnpike in [his] province, ideas travelled toll-free," p. 457).

As Tyler drew the history of colonial American literature to a close in the political year of 1765, he appeared to relax in the knowledge that his vexing colonial definitions were behind him. A national "American" spirit, unique, identifiable, and united, now seemed fully to have formed in the hearts of his liberal-representative colonialists. In his subsequent two volumes on the Revolutionary literature, Tyler easily harmonized the intellectual, the literary, and the national aspects, as well as the conflict of heroic freedom of mind and imagination with environmental causation. They merged now in the all-absorbing issues of a united struggle for American independence.

Despite lapses in definition and method, Tyler gains the allegiance of his readers in large measure because of the compelling force of his prose style. In his diary during the first year at Michigan, Tyler had asked, "Am I to be a literary artist?" and concluded that he would use his "powers of style both with tongue and pen to help American civilization to be a success."[22] In his colonial history, Tyler displayed a novelist's skill in creating a distinctive voice and tone, a consistent point of view, a sense of dramatic scene and conflict, and a technique of portraiture that brought into full play his vigorous, imagistic style.[23]

The narrative tone and critical point of view were unmistakably liberal, humanitarian, and democratic, the voice of one who opposed bigotry, repression, and superstition in all their guises. Tyler vented his feelings on these matters, however, in humor and irony more often than in explicit and sententious argument. On racism, he presented the colonists' fascination and puzzlement over the benighted aborigines and then dryly placed this bemused intolerance in historical perspective: "To us, of course, the American Indian is no longer a mysterious or even an interesting personage—he is simply a fierce dull biped standing in our way" (p. 9). Of the redoubtable John Cotton, that "unmitred pope of a pope-hating commonwealth," Tyler recalled the more liberal Roger Williams's subdued smile over this older Puritan's assumed infallibility, and Tyler then went Williams one better: "It was, of course, rather strange that the Almighty should permit such a man to die" (pp. 184–85). Yet Tyler also praised the "great intellectual poise, agility, and self-command" in this unrelenting Puritan worthy. The same ambivalent response extended to the dynasty of the Mathers, who exhibited enormous intellectual endowments yet were grotesquely careless when it came to a critical inspection of historical truth. Increase welcomed with a "palpable eagerness . . . from any quarter of the earth or sea or sky, any messenger whatever, who might be seen hurrying toward Boston with his mouth full of marvels" (p. 323). His son Cotton urged on the younger ministers "the need of mastering the lessons of history, and yet to be on [their] guard against the falsehoods of history," to which counsel Tyler wryly observed that here was "a theme on which Cotton Mather had an uncommon right to speak" (p. 333).

Consistently novelistic, beyond tone and point of view, was Tyler's creation of historical setting and dramatic scene. We embark from the Isle of Wight in the company of John Winthrop and share his reactions on the voyage westward. At Jamestown, after the Indian massacre in spring of 1622, we experience the aftermath in all the disarray that met the eyes of George Sandys, the gentle poet and government official, in his "overcrowded camp of half-fed but frenzied hunters, hunting only for red men with rifle and bloodhound." Pivotal moments in Tyler's literary history, such as Bacon's rebellion in 1676, turn out to be only faintly of literary significance; we are aware, instead, of the literary power with which Tyler rendered them. Few readers will forget Tyler's "somewhat dramatic scene" that introduces us to the seventy-year-old Rev. Mather Byles, the "distinguished and powerful divine, but an incorrigible Tory," who, like Mark Twain's Colonel Sherburn, confronted a mob of his (Revolutionary) accusers and contemptuously vanquished them: "The insulted pastor arose, indignation darkening all his face and giving dreadful resonance to his voice, and thundered out—'Tis false; 'tis false; 'tis false; and the church of Christ in Hollis Street knows that 'tis false'" (p. 428).

Equally lively are Tyler's finely drawn portraits of the many colonial writers he admired. Tyler's technique here was first to frame the writer and his career in a single paragraph or, indeed, in a single, monumental sentence of capsulating and qualifying phrases that enclosed, tinted, and shaded the portrait. Tyler then set his writer into motion, giving the dynamic shape and color of a life that had itself been expressed by purposeful action, thought, and energy of language. Here, Tyler also enlisted the appropriate imagery of heroic adventure. The reader who would savor this technique at its best should turn to Tyler's initial framing of John Smith (p. 17), John Pory (p. 43), Daniel Gookin (p. 131), Thomas Shepard (p. 179), Roger Wolcott (p. 297), William Douglass (p. 391), Benjamin Colman (p. 409), William Livingston (p. 452), and, above all, Roger Williams (pp. 208–9).[24] The portraits of these figures and others pass before the reader one by one as the history of individual men, which, multiplied, becomes Tyler's collective history of a colonial nation and its literary expression.

The continuous pageant is further enlivened by Tyler's consistently colorful imagery of adventure. He viewed his colonial writ-

ers as daring idealists who created in their lives and books the
drama and excitement of a perilous mission across the ocean and
over the land. Many were decked out in the classic Elizabethan
trappings of the soldierly poet-philosopher. Or they were new-
world Argonauts pursuing their ideal quest in Virginia (p. 45)
and again in New England (p. 144), though Puritans were the
more intensely conscious of the unprecedented "sacred opportunity" within their "grim battle" (p. 88). Individual writers
who gained from Tyler the strenuous epithet or military stripe
were the Rev. Samuel Willard—"a theological drill-sergeant"
(p. 406)—and Colonel Benjamin Church, the "scarred and
ancient paladin of the New England bush-whackers" (p. 382).
Increase Mather, armed with the weapon of his prodigious learning, "could march into his pulpit with confident tread" (p. 320),
while Mather Byles "smote men with the sword of their own accepted ideas" (p. 430). Enrobed with the Puritan's intolerance of
false religions, "John Norton, with the devout frankness of a
Spanish inquisitor, declared that for the putting down of error,
'the holy tactics of the civil sword should be employed'" (p. 94).
Cotton Mather, conscientious and vain, was his own inquisitor,
"stretched, every moment of his life, on the rack of ostentatious
exertion, intellectual and religious" (p. 325). The appearance of
his *Magnalia* was as the launching of a man-of-war, with admirers in attendance "who stood about and huzzaed, as the huge
and dreadful hulk glided down the well-greased stocks into the
sea" (p. 292).

Tyler took similar relish in the written style of his adventurous
author-heroes. Edward Johnson "handled the pen as he did the
sword and the broadaxe—to accomplish something with it"
(p. 119). Peter Bulkley "gives the impression of an athletic, patient, and orderly intellect. Every advance along the page is made
with the tread of logical victory. No unsubdued enemies are left
in the rear" (p. 188). William Hubbard's pages "almost quiver
with fury against the Indians, and are strewn with words that
seem to weary the vocabulary of execration and contempt"
(p. 378). Tyler admired the vigor of even an intolerant adversary's
prose style, as here with Hubbard, and again when Tyler responded to Ward's *The Simple Cobbler,* "a tremendous partisan
pamphlet, intensely vital yet, full of fire, wit, whim, eloquence,
sarcasm, invective, patriotism, bigotry" (pp. 198–99). Tyler recalled that the unpublished manuscripts of another feisty Puritan, Charles Chauncey, ended up on the floor of a pie maker's
oven, and "thus the eloquence and valuable writings of Charles
Chauncey were gradually used up, their numerous Hebrew and

Greek quotations, and their peppery Calvinism doubtless adding an unwonted relish and indigestibility to the pies under which they were laid" (p. 195).

Tyler was not so evenhanded at other times, and a brief sampling of his light imagery reveals some of the bias. On one hand were writers he admired. Virginia's Alexander Whitaker was the "true missionary for Christ" who carried "the true and beautiful light of his message . . . everywhere, across plantation and through wilderness, into the colonists' hut and the wigwam of the savage" (p. 41); or John Wise, who anticipated the liberal democratic principles of the Revolution with "prophetic clearness" (p. 359); or Roger Williams, who invoked the "'Father of Lights'" (pp. 220, 226) and conceived his truths in many a "luminous comparison" (p. 225). Tyler then presented the Puritans who viewed life as through an inquisitorial smoked glass darkly, eager to consign Williams's pages to the "flames of a Presbyterian auto-da-fé" (p. 218). The elder Mather wanted a similar fate granted Robert Calef's rational inquiry into the Mathers' wonders of the invisible world, but "its peculiar power could not be stifled by a hangman's smudge" (p. 343). Thomas Hooker's pages "gleam and blaze with the flashes of threatened hell-fire" and emitted the familiar Calvinist smudge: "His ink has even yet a smell of theological sulpher in it" (p. 173). John Cotton lived in the same brimstone-polluted atmosphere as he pondered "the science of God and man as seen through the dun goggles of John Calvin" (p. 183). Some Puritans could peer through the dun goggles more successfully than others, and Solomon Stoddard was one: "Persons enveloped in various sorts of theological and ethical fog, were much inclined to depend on his superior eyesight." In particular, Stoddard's Calvinist vision was never impaired by unpuritanly long hair, for as Tyler noted, he eloquently recited for Puritan males chapter and verse on the special abomination of tonsorial neglect (pp. 407–8).

Finally, Tyler used water imagery to suggest an origin, flow, and evolution of literature in the new land. Here imagery almost totally replaced literary-historical analysis. "The first lispings of American literature," he wrote, "were heard along the sands of the Chesapeake and near the gurgling tides of the James River"—no more than an imagistic pass here at discussing origin and flow in colonial writing. In a rare moment when he considered the evolution of a genre, say historical writing, Tyler broke forth again in water imagery that did not quite conceal the absence of a rigorous examination of the documents. Nathaniel Morton's *New England's Memorial* (1669) sputtered in the years after Bradford's and Winslow's histories closed (1646 and 1649) because Morton, said Tyler, "deprived of the copious currents of their assistance, dwindles into a mere rill of obituary notices. . . . Henceforward they who wish to seek our earliest history at its headwaters will of course pass by Nathaniel Morton, and draw from the same limpid and sweet well-spring that he drew from" (pp. 110–11).

For his transition into a second literary period in 1676, Tyler lulled his reader again with water imagery in place of logical summary and analysis. And he closed his history at 1765 with a similar stroke of rhetoric: "Henceforward American literature flows in one great, common stream, and not in petty rills of geographical discrimination" (p. 538). The flow and ease of this final image probably revealed, at least, the relief and pleasure Tyler must have felt in the consummation of his difficult narrative of colonial literary effort. He could now envision his next period, the simpler and more manageable Revolutionary era where he would encounter a "literature of one multitudinous people, variegated, indeed, in personal traits, but single in its commanding ideas and in its national destinies" (p. 538). Before that two-volume achievement greeted the academy in 1897, however, came two decades of accelerating interest in the study of American literature and, for a first time, the quickening of a professional identity among teachers and scholars in modern languages and literatures. That varied activity becomes our next subject.

Chapter 7

Charles F. Richardson and the Ferment of the Eighties

The *CHAL* editors move next, in their retrospective obligations, to Charles F. Richardson's two-volume *American Literature, 1607–1885*. Written also for Putnam, it became the most significant study within the academy after Tyler's colonial history.[1] Despite their debts to Richardson, the editors regret that he should have taken a route different from Tyler's, away from "historical enquiry and elucidation" and toward a "leading purpose" of "aesthetic judgment" (I, viii). The comment somewhat misleads a reader unfamiliar with Tyler's own very marked aesthetic judgments. More to the point, the *CHAL* editors then recognize a Victorian-tinged moralism in Richardson's fondness for the prewar era, but they do not see that such enthusiasm radically modified "aesthetic judgment" in the history. Richardson was applying moralistic criteria to rebuke the new realists and champion earlier fiction at the same instant that Howells, in the "Editor's Study" of *Harper's Monthly,* was advancing contrary arguments against the older romanticism. Nor did Richardson's proclaiming an aesthetic basis for winnowing our authors lead him to discover any alliance with Henry James and the aesthetic emphasis of his incisive essay on "The Art of Fiction" (1884). Richardson, in short, was an early example of the professor whom Mencken and others would presently assail for his inability to respond to modern voices in literature and criticism.

What Richardson did respond to in the 1880s was the modern scholarship vital to a literary historian. One event of the first importance was the launching of the American Men of Letters series by Charles Dudley Warner. Available to Richardson and partly cited by him were an impressive array in the eighties: Warner's own book on Irving (1881), O. B. Frothingham's George Ripley (1882), Frank B. Sanborn's Thoreau (1882—a special favorite of Richardson's), Thomas R. Lounsbury's Cooper (1883), O. W. Holmes's Emerson (1884), Thomas W. Higginson's Margaret Fuller (1884), George Woodberry's Poe (1885), and Henry

A. Beers's N. P. Willis (1885). As in so much of American scholarship before the *CHAL,* the inspiration here was British; John Morley's English Men of Letters series had begun in 1878.

The acceleration of intellectual and critical activity in the eighties also brought into being the Modern Language Association (MLA), of which Richardson was an early member but never, it seems, a participant in the annual meetings. In December 1883, forty teachers, led by A. Marshall Elliott of Johns Hopkins, met at Columbia College to organize fellow professors and demand (in the words of the forty-second president, John Livingston Lowes) "a place in the sun for Modern Languages in a field preëmpted and for centuries held by the Classics." At the next annual meeting, the MLA had 127 members, adopted a constitution, and heard fourteen papers on modern languages and literature.[2] The group immediately founded its own journal, *Publications of the Modern Language Association of America* (*PMLA*), to encourage scholarship and print the transactions of the society. Franklin Carter, president of Williams College, was elected the first president of the association (1884–86), and Elliott became the first long-term secretary (1884–92).

This movement away from a classical curriculum was chiefly a postwar phenomenon, and the MLA was organized, in the spirit of Matthew Arnold, to avoid a provincial state of mind in the academy. Through annual meetings, the teacher-scholars would gain wider professional stimulus and purpose, and the issues of *PMLA* would establish both the standards and the spirit of disciplined research and dedicated teaching. This is not to say that gestures and arguments on behalf of the modern languages had not been evident before the Civil War. In the North, Harvard had led the way, hiring a tutor in French as early as 1806. The Smith Professorship in French and Spanish began in 1816. German was taught at Harvard by 1830. In the South, three professors apparently were teaching modern languages before the war. In England, as Lionel Trilling notes, Matthew Arnold's inaugural address as Oxford Professor of Poetry in 1857, "On the Modern Element in Literature," may be said "to have established the teaching of English as an academic profession." And during our Civil War, the Early English Text Society (1864) was belatedly formed in England. (As late as 1891, however, British proponents of their own literature were still trying to advance the subject in the classics-oriented universities at home.)[3] After the war in this country, important dates include 1869 (forming of the American Philological Association) and 1876, the founding of Johns Hopkins and graduate education, mentioned in the preceding chapter. In

1878, the Johns Hopkins University Press was established and by 1886 was publishing five academic journals, including the *American Journal of Philology* (1880) and *Modern Language Notes* (1886), all a part of President Gilman's vision of an outstanding modern university.[4]

That American literature was largely or totally ignored in the arguments against a classics-centered curriculum is unsurprising. English and other modern languages and literatures first had to gain academic respectability before the fledgling American literature courses might command their own recognition. But after the MLA formed, philological science came to dominate American linguistics and literary—though not American literature—scholarship (with occasional objections from aesthetic and critical opponents of Germanized pedantry) even into the 1920s when, as we shall see (Chapter 13), the impatient and rebellious American Literature Group formed within the parent organization.

For the first three decades of the MLA, as we gather in a perusal of *PMLA*, scholars and teachers of American literature were gaining very little sense of a common profession at the annual meetings of the national and regional groups or in the pages of the association's journal. Papers and articles on English language and literature until 1920 were, naturally, of more than peripheral interest to the American literature teacher. But American literature itself made a poor showing, perhaps all the more disappointing because at an early meeting, in 1887, considerable attention was directed to a paper titled "American Literature in the Classroom" by Albert M. Smyth, teacher of English at Central High School, Philadelphia. The first volume of Richardson's literary history had recently appeared, but Smyth pronounced it (and Tyler's history) to be of little use as a classroom text. Nor were there, said he, any well-patterned and interpretive textbooks on the market, though Tuckerman and Whipple were helpful critics of American literature and virtually alone in the field. American literature deserved more attention in secondary and higher education, Smyth wrote, because unlike English literature, American "admits of a complete severance of literature from philology" and thus could encourage the critical faculties of the student. In a discussion period, Professors James W. Bright and Henry Wood of philology-oriented Johns Hopkins conceded that, yes, American literature was a worthy subject. A. H. Tolman remarked that Ripon College did not offer it, but one did apprise students there of the best magazines on their country's literature.[5]

Thereafter, the MLA meetings, and the pages of *PMLA*, greeted only rarely a paper or article on the American writer: Lanier, Timrod, and Joel C. Harris in the 1890s; an article in 1904 on E. T. A. Hoffman's influence on Poe; and in the second decade of the new century, three pieces on Poe by Killis Campbell. Henry James received unfriendly treatment in one article of 1912, as did Whitman (from Norman Foerster) in 1916. Longfellow fared a trifle better, chiefly in that he was susceptible of studies in European sources and influence. With a very few additional items, the list is completed. This discouraging record is thrown into dramatic relief by the contrasting success of the scholarship in American history and the hospitality of that profession's *American Historical Review* (1895). As John Higham explains it:

> By the beginning of the twentieth century American universities conventionally taught ancient, European, and American history; and the first task of research was to establish a sound basis of scholarship within those fields. The earliest efforts of professional scholars were concentrated overwhelmingly in American history, for which original sources were most accessible and patriotic motives strong. Almost nine-tenths of the historical dissertations written in American universities in the Eighties and Nineties dealt with native subjects. . . . In the early years most of the contributors to the *American Historical Review* wrote about American history, which still received as late as the 1920's slightly more space than European history. The period from 1900 to World War I, however, marked the emergence of outstanding professional scholars in the principal non-American fields.[6]

We can add that "original sources were most accessible and patriotic motives strong" for studying our native literature as well as history. Unfortunately, as we have seen, the untimely philological approach to modern literatures encouraged study of older English, not American, literature. Hence the imbalance in our English faculties. These American professors of English literature bore the cultural inferiority complex of the anglophile; and ironically, their betters at Oxford and Cambridge were still bearing, in their turn, as we have noted, their own feelings of cultural inferiority to the older Greek and Latin literatures. American historians were happily removed from these circumstances and could thrive on America's superior political sense of new-world independence from old England and older Europe.

We anticipate greater hospitality to American literature in the two early regional societies. The Central Division of the MLA was organized in December 1895 at the University of Chicago, after professors at Kansas, Nebraska, and Iowa complained that

Eastern MLA meetings were too difficult to attend. In subsequent meetings until 1923, when members agreed in Ann Arbor to suspend activities, this regional society, it turned out, allowed many a year to pass with no papers whatsoever on American literature. In the Far West, the Philological Association of the Pacific Coast (PAPC) held its organizational meeting in 1899 in San Francisco, with seventy charter members. When *PMLA,* in 1918, began to print PAPC proceedings, we look for a Western embracement of regional and national writers. In the first three years of these records, however, only one paper in American literature appears, Regis Michaud's "French Sources of Emerson."[7]

Another sign of the minimal attention paid American literature in the early decades of the MLA can be inferred from the annual address of respective presidents, as printed in *PMLA*. We search without success for a single presidential speech, or even portion thereof, devoted to the subject of American literature study. Returning to the 1880s, when our literature's own James Russell Lowell became the second president of MLA (1887–91), we might expect at least a witty tooting of his own horn in support of the national literature he and others had created in his lifetime. Indeed, Horace Scudder, presently to become Lowell's posthumous editor and biographer, had recently prompted that support in the *Atlantic Monthly* when he argued the primary need among our youth to study the literary classics, by which Scudder meant *American* classics.[8]

But the former professor of modern languages at Harvard was not about to advocate the academic study of American literature. We noticed in the preceding chapter that Lowell disliked the American servility that produced a condescension among foreigners. But that irritation did not move him to adopt a defensive literary nationalism. Lowell had never been an enthusiast of much that America had produced in the world's literature, and he was not at all disposed to become one in his old age. In his address prepared for the association's meeting at Harvard, Lowell teased his alma mater for the curriculum in Greek and Latin that was so religiously honored in his student years; and he was pleased by the progress of America's studies in the modern languages. Consistent in his dislike for tightly disciplined work, Lowell viewed philology as a preparation for, but finally separate from, literary appreciation. The true end of culture, he announced, was to give the mind pleasure and play beyond exercise and discipline. On the role of American literature in the university amid this modern literary study, Lowell had nothing to say.[9]

Lowell and MLA colleagues notwithstanding, American literature study in the academy did make some modest progress in the eighties. At least forty-five colleges taught American authors now, says John S. Lewis, and compared to the six distinct courses in American literature taught in the 1870s, there was now a gain of twenty-three in the 1880s. This increase was not unaccompanied by setbacks here and there. Eleven of the twenty-six colleges offering American literature in one guise or another in the previous decade had now dropped the authors, in some cases because the single professor offering the course had died or resigned or because the new philology was crowding American writers out of the curriculum. (The postwar professor of literature was more likely to have a German, or Germanized, Ph.D. than, as before, a D.D.)[10]

On individual campuses, Dartmouth was breaking the ground for a new day at the beginning of the 1880s, as Edwin D. Sanborn, professor of belles lettres, offered the first course in American literature at that college from 1880 to 1882. He was succeeded in the Winckley Chair of English by Richardson, who gave a three-hour elective course in American literature for seniors. Richardson's two-volume history, which we will turn to in a moment, grew from this course. Fred Pattee recalled that the classroom lectures he attended in 1888 were recognizable in the pages of volume II the following year.[11] To the south, Kate Sanborn (daughter of Richardson's predecessor at Dartmouth) established a course at Smith College in 1880 titled "Lectures on American Literature." In 1886, Wellesley offered its first course, taught by Louise M. Hodgkins, and the following year, Mt. Holyoke followed suit. In the late 1880s, Brown also began to allow American authors into the English curriculum; and Brown has the distinction of granting the first titled professorship when, in 1897, Lorenzo Sears became Associate Professor of American Literature. But other leading universities in the East were not leading the way, and through the 1880s, American authors were still not welcomed into the classroom at Harvard, Yale, Columbia, Johns Hopkins, Princeton, Pennsylvania, and North Carolina. New York University offered a course in 1885, dropped it in 1888, and did not revive an American offering until 1914.[12]

Colleges in the West, less mired in tradition, were opening their classrooms to American authors, even though we saw little evidence of such interest in the subsequent meetings of the regional societies. At Wisconsin from 1882 to 1883, one of the six literature courses was a junior–senior elective, "Study of English masterpieces—American Prose Writers," offered by John C. Freeman. Indiana listed an American literature course the same year.

Later in the decade, courses appeared at Notre Dame (1887) and Iowa (1888, resuming a class given from 1872 to 1879). Vanderbilt in 1888 offered "Lectures on American Literature" and used Stedman's *Poets of America* and collections of Emerson and Lowell as textbooks. At neighboring University of the South, Greenough White (Trent's predecessor) also had been introducing students to American authors. Other schools reporting American literature on their campuses include Nebraska (1882) and Luther College in Iowa (1884). Luther's was not a separate course, but readings for freshman composition, the textbook being William Swinton's *Seven American Classics* (1880), with selections from Irving, Cooper, Bryant, Hawthorne, Longfellow, Whittier, and Holmes. In the Far West, the University of Southern California offered a course in 1889, dropped it in 1893, and returned it to the curriculum in 1899. Among these far-flung beginnings, the courses varied from survey, period, or regional offerings to the individual author, groups of authors, or the separate course in prose or poetry. Notably missing were genre courses in the novel, short story, and drama.[13]

This classroom activity did not as yet affect the textbook market dramatically, though the old-style manuals or outlines by Shaw, Underwood, and Hart very soon would be challenged by an outpouring of anthologies and literary–history handbooks in the 1890s and onward into the next dozen years of the new century. Richard H. Stoddard's enlarged edition of Griswold's *The Poets and Poetry of America* (1872) had already pointed the new direction of the generous anthology, and a high standard for the new textbook was created by E. C. Stedman's critical commentary in the milestone *Poets of America* (1885). Stedman's was the first serious overview of American poetry, and his textbook marginal notations, familiarly old-fashioned and helpful, no doubt contributed to its immediate popularity in the school market. Twelve editions appeared by the early 1890s.

Professional men of letters like Stoddard and Stedman presently would be forced to compete with university professors in the college and high school textbook market. But as the eighties came to an end, Stedman fattened his earnings in a more sizable venture. He joined literary journalist Ellen Mackay Hutchinson in the landmark edition of *A Library of American Literature* (1889–90) in eleven volumes. Promoted as a home reader and a national gallery of our literature to enlarge the sales, it was brought out by Mark Twain's publishing company, Charles L. Webster. In the preface, the editors alerted the reader that this was not a new version of the Duyckinck-style cyclopedia, designed chiefly for students; instead, it was an anthology of writings chosen for "popular use and enjoyment . . . without note or comment, leaving to others the field of critical review." Even so, they followed the Duyckincks' chronological arrangement of authors by date of birth; there was biographical comment, though it was assembled at the end of volume 11; and the editors had kept a scholarly eye on Moses Coit Tyler, among others: Their colonial volumes 1 and 2 divided, like Tyler's, at 1676. Barrett Wendell considered it invaluable to the literary historian. It was widely advertised, cordially reviewed by professional admirers of Mark Twain, and destined to appear as recommended reading in high school and college textbooks over the next four decades.

No doubt impelled by this gradually deepening interest in American literature among the nation's colleges and publishers in the eighties, Charles F. Richardson at Dartmouth set out to write the first large-scale literary history from the beginnings to the present. Tyler was in Europe on sabbatical leave from Cornell during early 1889 when he saw a notice by his publisher, Putnam, heralding Richardson's completed two-volume work. The advertisement spurred Tyler to return to work on his Revolutionary literature volumes, by then ten frustrated years in the making and eight more to go before publication.[14] Had Tyler sampled this recent contribution to literary history, he may not have felt the pressure of serious competition in his trade. Richardson's treatment of our nation's literature, within and beyond Tyler's colonial and Revolutionary periods, was different in conception and, by comparison with Tyler, notably drab in spirit and style. Even so, it is indispensable to any appreciation of American literary historiography. Beyond the issues of history and nationalism, it is a valuable revelation of how an American professor was responding to the aesthetic ideas of the time, including the controversy generated outside the academy by such "realists" as James and Howells.

Like Tyler, Richardson (1851–1913) was born and educated in New England. He graduated from Dartmouth in 1871, and after a decade in journalism, he joined the faculty of his alma mater in 1882. During the next three decades, Richardson became a familiar campus character. In the classroom, the men of Dartmouth soon realized that behind his "gorgon stare" lay a "perennial sweetness" and a contagious love of literature. Outside the classroom, his tall, lean figure was exaggerated by the tiny dog he was fond of walking about campus. Known affectionately among students as "Clothespins," Richardson was the inevitable subject of their humorous cartoons. On his death two years after retirement in 1911, Richardson was eulogized by President Nichols: "The college has never had a more inspiring teacher. No one has ever given to more men a love of the best things in literature and an appreciation of its deep messages." To the present day, in the Class of 1902 Room of Baker Library hangs the large portrait of "The Immortal Clothespins," preserving after a century the figure of one of the best loved men ever to teach American literature on that campus.[15]

Richardson's chief pretentions as a scholar, before he joined the Dartmouth faculty, lay in *A Primer of American Literature* (1878), a miniature volume (4½ by 6 inches) of 117 pages, with equally miniature commentaries on some one hundred writers. To mark literary periods, Richardson had appropriated pivotal war years—1775, 1812, and 1861—without arguing their significance in literary history. Perhaps intended as a handbook for students and a pocket-sized digest for travelers, the volume must have had little scholarly value to the classroom professor or even to its author, though it probably convinced Dartmouth authorities that Richardson might become a devoted teacher of literature. If so, he more than satisfied their hopes. As an advancing scholar, Richardson seems to have ignored much of his *Primer,* and he presently went on to give the world, in the commemorative words of his student Pattee, "the first systematic presentation of American literary history" a decade later.[16]

In the introduction to volume I of his history, Richardson established a polemical, transoceanic perspective of American literature. He charged that European and English critics had recently praised American fiction as irresponsibly as they had earlier denounced our literature. (Novelists Howells and James, who were at odds with these critics, could have questioned how widely in recent criticism of fiction Richardson had been reading.) The time had come, Richardson suggested, when we subject our native writers to the same unrelenting aesthetic standards we apply to literature in any age and country, and he made ready to do so.

Presumably, Richardson had Tyler's work, at least, in mind when he conceded that colonial writers, particularly the Puritans, were "direct precursors and the actual founders of most that is good in American letters" (xvii). But he then observed that when we applied aesthetic criteria to the works of these precursors, very few could be admitted into the halls of great literature. Implying that his selectivity would be strenuous (and necessarily so to include a crowded century of writing beyond Tyler's colonial writers), Richardson stated, "The history of literature is one thing, bibliography is quite another thing." The time had come to argue a canon of American literature—"We have had enough description; we want analysis"—and in the process, the "older American books" (that is, those written before the current century) would get no special favors from him through any allowances for immaturity, patriotism, or environmental hardship. The even-handed literary historian should pose eight internal and external considerations as he approached the writers: to inquire into the author's aim, method, relation to other native writers, influence on them, debt to English literature, "intrinsic success," probable future rank, and the general effects of tides in literary taste. Richardson did not promise that he would absolutely pursue these problems. In fact, he did not consistently do so.

He separated his two volumes into American mind and belles lettres, subtitled *The Development of American Thought* and *American Poetry and Fiction,* respectively. Despite his introductory remarks, then, the avowedly aesthetic Richardson assumed the robes of an intellectual historian for an entire volume. But he implied that he would submit ideas to aesthetic evaluation, for in chapter 1, "The Race-Elements in American Literature," he defined literature as "the written record of *valuable thought,* having other than *merely practical* purpose" (I, 1, italics added). Though Richardson had already minimized environmental considerations for the literary historian, he suggested a quasi-Tainean causality for the evolution of literature: "Behind literature is race; behind race, climate and environment" (I, 1). Richardson defined the problem of nationalism environmentally as well and plainly entered a pervasive Anglo-Saxon bias: "The history of American literature is the history of the literature of the part of the English people, under new geographical and political conditions, within the present limits of the United States" (I, 1).

Richardson now tried to make some sense of colonial literature, but his presuppositions served quite haphazardly. He wavered, like Tyler, in the treatment of the American environment as a decisive influence on the early literary product. At times, Richardson viewed the colonists to be men of intrinsically stalwart character who brought with them from the old world the moral virtues favorable to the development of a distinguished native literature. The Dutch, Swedes, and Friends possessed the character, thrift, "rectitude of purpose," and political goals on which the foundations of literature could be built (I, 23). The Massachusetts colonists influenced literary development even more powerfully than the Friends, however, because of more favorably inborn, racial characteristics; the Friends lacked the

Saxon aggressive, positive moral attributes of the New England Puritan. In general, Richardson credited the colonial immigrant with a penchant for living in peace, and this character trait encouraged a respect for the life of the mind, which in turn encouraged the growth of literature. When the impulse to war had arisen in the land, the genuine American spirit had been subverted and literary expression suffered. Wars, Richardson believed, "have done little for American literature; peace has done much, and will do more" (I, 45, 47). In his *Primer* of 1878, the three major wars had marked separate eras in our literature; and subsequent literary scholars have argued that war has stimulated new periods of vital creativity for American writers. Richardson, however, elected not to examine this fruitful concept or indicate any progress of his thinking since 1878.

Early in his second chapter, "The New Environment of the Saxon Mind," Richardson reiterated the autonomy of colonial imagination, selfhood, and race; and he now emphatically ruled out geographical determinism: "Climate does not make character; still less does it produce literature" (I, 37). He also noted that a class of readers (presumably Anglo-Saxon) soon sprang up farther west, even though the materialistic hurry of American life should have militated against this interest and growth in literature. With Tyler, as well as several literary historians in years to come, Richardson viewed the frontier expanse as a free, spacious arena that did not constitute a determining environment.

Richardson began to display some distressing uncertainties when he raised the question of how a distinctly national American literature had, then, come into being. He resorted to certain older assumptions about the environmental influence of colonial America. The imperatives of economics and political survival in the new-world wilderness began to create a new man, a national type, an emerging national unity, and thus the conditions for an American literature (I, 43). But the going was slow, since the colonists lived in a land barren of historical and aesthetic associations. Literature "suffers in an environment which is crude and raw" (I, 50). Out of these conditions, Richardson did not quite know how to explain the rise of a postcolonial literature. We merely sense that Madison's *Federalist* pages pulsate not only with their "Johnsonian English" but also with a new-world, revolutionary idiom "already feeling the breath of a fresher day, a stirring with the intense purpose which pushed the Americans forward" (I, 198). And Irving demonstrated to readers at home and abroad that "good literature could spring from native soil" (I, 264). Though later urban America had adversely affected our

writers, driving some of them into European exile, Richardson
asserted that America had been a largely congenial setting for
the immigrant (Saxon) imagination: "American literature may be
described as *isolated inheritance, working freshly*" (I, 53).

From his theory of the superior Saxon race, only incidentally
transformed in the new world, Richardson ascribed an elitist
cast to the best in American literature. In this country, as in all
nations, the best and most characteristic expression came out of
the "middle and higher social classes. The peasant's world, the
voice of Robert Burns, is a rarity" (I, 55). At the New England
fountainhead of our literature, the Puritan writers were "representatives of old families" (I, 54). Richardson summed up his
puzzlements over causal origin and development in matters of
race, environment, political purpose, and social class by presenting the reader with a definition of our literature cloaked in the
rhetoric of elegant vagueness and paradox: "American literature
is the literature of a cultured and genuine Democracy, a sort of
Saxon-Greek renaissance in the New World; a liberty that is as
far removed from anarchy as it is from despotism" (I, 61).

After 177 pages of his literary history, Richardson announced,
"Thus far we have found not one American book of the first literary rank"; and some 150 pages later, "We had scarcely any literature at all when Emerson began to write." In all of volume I, only
the essays of Irving and Holmes unequivocally satisfied what
Richardson now and again fashioned as workable criteria of *aesthetic* value. Often enough, his pages repay our rereading in that
we discover on what the professor one century ago tried to base
what he assumed to be aesthetic judgments of literature proper.
One was the touchstone of English literature. Such comparisons
could, but did not, tempt Richardson to ask serious questions of
literary–historical influence. Instead, he invoked the English
author seemingly to humble American readers and particularly
the literary nationalists whose "fulsome puffery" of our inferior
colonial literature had been especially misguided (I, 40). Cotton
Mather, for example, "in talk . . . was a sort of lesser Johnson or
Coleridge; in literature a Puritan Burton, without his wit" (I,
132). Franklin was not the equal of Defoe. Most of his writings
"measured by the tests of English literature between 1725 and
1775 . . . are commonplace" (I, 159, 170). Madison's *Federalist*
paper XIV, however, drew Richardson's praise for its Johnsonian
English, as did Washington's "Farewell Address" and first inaugural speech (I, 198, 204).

When Richardson set down his aesthetic verdicts apart from
the contrast or corroboration of English literary example, he be-

came the distinctly old-fashioned critic who eschews any argued analysis of whatever evidence he deigns to submit. We are told, for example, that John Smith belonged to neither America nor literature. We then receive two and one-half pages of uninterrupted quotation—a "fair example of Smith's method and style"—with all of his literary characteristics and deficiencies supposedly self-evident (I, 69). Bradford's was a "better English style," though the literary merit of his and Winthrop's histories was inferior somehow (I, 72, 75). Timothy Dwight's *Travels* contained some interesting descriptions; however, "the 'literature of travel' barely belongs to literature at all" (I, 148). In John Woolman's *Journal*, one sensed a "purer literary style" than in David Brainerd's *Diary* (did Richardson recall the Englishman Charles Lamb's praise of Woolman?), and the reader was then assigned the labor of discovering that purity for himself within an extended quotation from Woolman. Franklin achieved "inherent literary merit" only in his *Autobiography,* the papers on electricity, and the *Almanac,* though in this last instance we are invited to know, without knowing why, that the almanac is scarcely a literary genre (I, 159, 160). We are also informed that Jefferson's style was "plain but sonorous," John Adams's was "picturesque" (he "could turn a phrase neatly"), Fisher Ames's was "quiet, and evidently elaborated with much care," John Calhoun's freighted with "rhetorical beauties" (I, 195, 205, 209, 228). Thoreau was inferior to Emerson, though he described the heart of nature "in simple, true, poetic, eloquent words"; but there was more "largeness and light" in Whitman (I, 385, 387).

In the final chapter of volume I, "Borderlands of American Literature," Mark Twain, who rated no mention in the fiction chapters of volume II, here was lumped with other would-be humorists whose works were dismissed by Richardson as vaguely inadequate to their literary mode: "Humor . . . must coexist with literary qualities, and must usually be joined with such pathos as one finds in Lamb, Hood, Irving, or Holmes" (I, 521). Moses Coit Tyler, of course, was scarcely more effective or modern in his literary explication, but he possessed one talent in far stronger degree than Richardson—a commanding, colorful style that bewitches the reader into accepting the peremptory literary judgment.

Richardson's first volume was not widely reviewed in the major journals of serious criticism. The reviewer for the *Nation* termed the volume a "useful larger manual." He liked Richardson's aesthetic criterion but wondered, then, why admittedly inferior books received so much space. On the individual writers, Richardson was rebuked for dismissing the humorists and Mark Twain. J. J. Halsey reviewed the book for the Chicago *Dial*. He located major weaknesses of perspective, in both excessive space granted the first two centuries and the separation of literature from its political, social, and economic causes. Some of Richardson's best pages were on Irving ("fresh"), Emerson ("strong"), and the political prose of Everett and Lincoln. If Richardson waited for something better from the *Atlantic*, he was not to find it in their June issue. The critic echoed the *Nation*, terming the history a "manual of American literature" useful in the schools. Richardson was praised as a "very honest" writer whose universal aesthetic was refreshing; but "it is a matter for regret that a critic of such excellent purposes should not be equally well endowed with abilities." He lacked "originality and force," and had ensured a "dullness" for this first volume by moving the poetry and fiction into a separate volume II.[17] In view of this tepid reception, Putnam was forced to reach into the more favorable newspaper reviews to advertise this first volume. From the *Hartford Post*: "A book that is a credit to the writer and to the nation, and which has a grand future"; from the *Boston Globe*: "It is the most thoughtful and suggestive work on American literature that has been published"; from the *New York World*: "It is a book of great learning, and the author has approached his task in the spirit of a true critic—wise, philosophical, and just."[18]

What awaited the reader of 1889 in Richardson's second volume were seven chapters on American poetry and five on fiction, the belles lettres we expected him to have arrived at some hundreds of pages earlier. In his first two chapters on the poetry, Richardson surveyed all the poets deserving mention before Longfellow (and some who did not). He granted separate essays to Longfellow, Poe, and Emerson; grouped Whittier, Lowell, and Holmes as "Poets of Freedom and Culture"; and in a final chapter, touched the postwar generation—Whitman, Lanier, Timrod, Taylor, R. H. Stoddard, Stedman, and some few others.

Viewing Richardson first as a critic and historian of American poetry, we are not surprised, after volume I, that he failed to enunciate or clearly imply the definition and evolution of periods, genres, modes, and metrics, or the aesthetic principles with which he judged literary excellence. His criteria were, at times, once more vaguely Saxon and universal. Longfellow had been recognized in America and "other great Teutonic countries" as our national poet, and his work possessed "universal interest which is a mark of true literary achievement" (II, 50, 51). At other times, Richardson seemed closer to Henry James's impressionist dictum that the writer receive and register an immediate response to the vivid "color of life." Here, he administered the obscure test of "spontaneity" and "vividness," noting their absence in Whitman, Lanier, and many Civil War poets, though not in Hayne, Timrod, and Stedman (II, 229, 232, 259).

The most important critical principle that Richardson seemed at first to adopt for his literary evaluations was that of organic expression, what Emerson had demanded as a "metre-making argument" for a new American poetry that would successfully wed new form with new experience. On his opening page, Richardson just barely implied the Emersonian formula in a definition of poetry more clearly indebted to Poe: "Poetry is the rhythmical expression of beauty or imagination," he wrote (substituting "expression" for Poe's "creation"), and in significant apposition, Richardson added that such expression is "the verbal utterance of the ideal." He linked the poetic idea more emphatically to its necessary form later when he wrote that in Poe "the artistic act fitly follows the artistic thought" (II, 102). For Richardson, poetry morally and artistically stood, therefore, as "the highest and most permanent form of literature" (II, 1), and we may expect him later in his treatment of fiction to observe this assumed hierarchy of literary forms.

The organic principle served Richardson unevenly as an instrument of aesthetic evaluaton. He stumbled over his nineteenth-century moralistic demand for "valuable thought," now become the poetic expression of the "ideal," and so he abandoned the functional principle of aesthetic fitness of technique to content that he so plainly had stated in the case of Poe. Even in Poe, expectably, Richardson ignored literary form and disapproved of content. Or he criticized the "unduly physical and material" in Whitman and then complained that Whitman's technique failed to express ethereal and "rhythmical beauty" (II, 276). Technique should accommodate the poet's vision, but that vision must also be ideal. At other times, Richardson endorsed the vision of Longfellow ("tender, sweet, and human") and then lapsed into idle and separate enjoyment of the poet's "best hexameters," which had a "genuine musical beauty of their own" (II, 75). The chapter on Emerson might have been the crowning test of Richardson's basically Emersonian aesthetic; and in fact, he did quote "The Snow-Storm" as an "apt union of words and thought" (though no critical analysis followed). But Emerson's unorthodox thought, scorned by Richardson in volume I, presumably was made even less acceptable, rather than given proper expression, by his unorthodox metrics: The unruly Emerson's unruly "form and finish" reached a point where he "almost defies the laws of poetics" (II, 141, 157, 170).

On the development of American poetry, Richardson offered little in the way of historical theory. He invoked, inevitably, an English and European tradition. Bryant was an American Gray in his "thoughtfulness and serenity" rather than a Milton, Burns, Browning, or Goethe: "Intense power was not his, nor broad creative range, nor soaring vision" (II, 40). Emerson, too, was ranked against writers abroad, while Longfellow's *Hiawatha* rivaled *Beowulf* and the *Song of Roland*. For indigenous evolution and influence, Richardson offered little more than the smokescreen of an occasional metaphor. "A new land needs many a little builder before its cathedrals rise in the world's view" was his gesture toward an historical bridge between early poets and the chapter on Longfellow (II, 31). As to literary periods, Richardson implied, without historical or critical analysis, that the thematic concerns of "freedom and culture" largely shaped the prewar era. The postwar chapter, "Tones and Tendencies of American Verse," gave no clue to what might characterize the period.

After his seven chapters on poetry, Richardson required but five more to survey the supposedly inferior art of fiction and to single out the few Americans who were worthy practitioners of fictional genres. As before, he avoided biographical and historical contexts, praised Saxon characteristics, and relied once more on a quasi-organic formula of artistic expression, again emphasizing that the writers' ideas should be suitably elevated. In fact, Richardson shifted the internal emphasis to moral substance more strongly than in the poetry chapters, since fiction, for him, did not rival the rhythmical higher art of poetry (II, 283). He rephrased for fiction the requisite of ideal and valuable thought: Like poetry, the best fiction must be "complete" as it delineated "life . . . [to] include the body, mind, and soul of man, in his journey from the infinite to the infinite" (II, 282). With this preliminary ruling, Richardson could dispatch the architects of realism whose finite vision and moral content were limited in range and less than wholesome. He posed the Jamesian question, "Which is the more important, the thing told or the way of telling it?" But Richardson replied, "The former; because all art is grounded on the necessity that the subject should have some reason for existence or delineation" (II, 439). The worthy subject embraced the immortal soul of man, and presumably this moral content made American literature properly Saxon and universal. Cooper's was an "honest Saxon soul," Hawthorne's art expressed his region's Anglo-Saxon ethics, which, to Richardson, elevated it into the company of universal literature. Richardson discovered the same universal interest in the wholesome pages of even local colorists Bret Harte, Mary N. Murfree, and George W. Cable (II, 322, 339, 426). The narrow subject of the realists, by contrast, had rightly given them "a somewhat limited minority" of American and English, that is, Anglo-Saxon, readers (II, 441).

Indigenous influences, historical continuity or change, and clues to aesthetic power eluded Richardson in American fiction as they did in American poetry. Indeed, the chief distinction of volume II was, and remains, that it completed our first full-scale literary history conceived from the beginnings to the modernism of Richardson's own present. In his postwar time, this unprecedented scope was appreciated, at least, by the critic of the *Nation.* In the lesser parts, though, he judged Richardson's work noticeably inferior to Tyler's colonial history, Stedman's recent *Poets of America,* and the monographs in Warner's American Men of Letters. To the critic for the *Dial,* the only other serious journal to review the second volume, Richardson's achievement was stimulating and his thought "vigorous, independent, aggressive." But the shortcomings were equally apparent. In style and acumen, he was deemed inferior to Stedman as a critic of poetry, and Richardson's treatment of living authors was "too oracular and too patronizing."[19] The *Atlantic* totally ignored the appearance of the second volume. Compensation arrived, however, from other quarters. In 1890, Stedman and Hutchinson filled a half-dozen pages of *Library of American Literature* (volume 11) with a portion of Richardson's appreciation of Hawthorne. And both Richardson's *Primer* and literary history brought gratifying returns in the marketplace. In 1883, he had added twelve pictures of authors in the *Primer* and, in 1893, an appendix of portraits and homes of eight authors. More than seventy-six thousand copies were sold in a dozen printings by 1896, and Richardson had rewritten nary a page. The literary history went into eight more printings by 1910, including popular and student editions of the two volumes as one.

A century later, with subsequent histories at hand, Richardson's groping for principles, definitions, and judgments finally deserves our sympathy, just as his daring to comprehend our entire literary history merits our respect and gratitude. The wide range of problems he addressed (and others that he ignored) have never been adequately solved by literary historians and critics who have come after him. Not until the 1920s did members of the profession reinterpret American literature in a fashion that would define, with any sophistication, the history of American genres and modes. Richardson's inarticulate commentary on the literary text represented the state of literary analysis and judgment in the American academy well into the 1940s, and not until the heirs of F. O. Matthiessen in the 1950s did we see aesthetic considerations properly intersected with the historical in our literary scholarship. What influence Richardson could claim in his time appears ambiguous at best. The *London Daily News* closed a review of the completed history with the advice, in Tyler's words, that American literature "is still so young it would be better for us to add to it than to be writing histories of it."[20] Richardson's would-be successors were deaf to any such counsel. At the end of the eighties, his ambitious example, and perhaps his obvious weaknesses, seem to have emboldened dozens of American professors who, for better or worse, soon embarked on their own literary histories. That intimidating bulk of scholarship, together with other new pursuits in the study of American literature, can hardly be compressed into a single essay. But such will be the effort in the following chapter.

Chapter 8

Barrett Wendell in a Turn-of-the-Century Harvest

The *CHAL* editors complete their prefatory survey of nineteenth-century American literature study by devoting a paragraph to the *Literary History of America* (1900) by Harvard's Barrett Wendell. They term Wendell's history interesting but quarrel with it on two counts. Like Richardson, Wendell had "the somewhat restricted point of view" that no distinguished literary expression in America occurred until the nineteenth century. Second, Wendell was a near-sighted New England chauvinist, rather anachronistically imbued with the elite "spirit of Cotton Mather" (he published a monograph on Mather in 1891) and unable to see that any literature worth the attention of a literary critic and historian had been written outside his region in the current century: "The total effect of the narrative is an impression that the literary history of America is essentially a history of the birth, the renaissance, and the decline of New England" (I, ix). William Dean Howells, in fact, had reviewed Wendell's "priggish and patronizing" book and proposed the title, "A Study of New England Authorship in Its Rise and Decline, with Some Glances at American Literature." More acidly, Fred L. Pattee later suggested it be called "A Literary History of Harvard University, with Incidental Glimpses of the Minor Writers of America."[1]

Wendell invited such jibes during and after his famous career at Harvard. He loved to overstate, tease, and goad, to play the gentlemanly snob born too late in a democratic society scornful of individual excellence. But he was also an important force in the growing reception of American literature as a subject deserving scholarly study in the 1890s. When his literary history appeared just after the decade ended, the country was put on notice that Harvard, still in the glow of its golden age of celebrated professors and living emeriti, had at last taken American literature seriously.[2]

Wendell was in his middle twenties in 1880 when he accepted an instructorship in English at Harvard. Boston born, he had lived several boyhood years in New York City where his father, a businessman, had moved the family in 1863. Wendell never harbored any fondness for the size and bustle of New York. Following two trips to Europe, fateful for his later literary preferences and cultural criticism, Wendell returned to New England, became a Harvard man active in campus drama and journalism, and a student of Dante with James Russell Lowell. After graduation in 1877, Wendell studied law, a profession for which he was apparently as unfit as Henry James. After Wendell failed the Massachusetts bar examinations in 1880, he gratefully took a position on the faculty at Harvard as composition assistant to his former professor Adams Sherman Hill.

In an era of the Germanized Ph.D., Wendell with his mere B.A. was, and knew himself to be, suspect as a literary scholar. His tenure at Harvard was uncertain and promotions slow—to assistant professor after eight years, to professor after eighteen. Chiefly an instructor of rhetoric and English literature, he turned in the early 1890s to the American field. His monograph on Cotton Mather appeared in the Dodd, Mead Makers of America series in 1891, and two years later came *Stelligeri,* essays on the Puritans, Whittier, and Lowell, together with an extended sketch for a history of American literature. Four years passed before Wendell, now chairman of the department, offered English 20, "Research in the Literary History of America," followed in 1898 by English 33, "Literary History of America," which he taught regularly until retirement in 1917.

Wendell called important attention to American literature study as much through his famous classroom manner as from his scholarly matter. *CHAL* editor Stuart Sherman, at Harvard after the turn of the century, recalled the striking impression Wendell made on his students:

> He entered the lecture room with a cane, in a cut-away coat and spats, with the air of the Anglicized Boston man of letters who had crossed the Charles to speak to the boys about life. As he proceeded to his desk we noticed that his hair was parted down the back of his head to the collar. He plucked his glasses from their hook, somewhere about his waistcoat, and diddling them on the end of his forefinger, began to speak in his highly mannered voice, with frequent breaks into falsetto.[3]

M. A. De Wolfe Howe, whose book on Wendell in 1924 had prompted Sherman's recollection, remembered that Wendell's classroom appearance and manner had been fully cultivated by the middle 1880s:

[He was] well-proportioned of figure, of moderate height, shapely of head, tawny-bearded, with quick blue eyes, alert and responsive in person encounter, the man of the world rather than the professor in general appearance. Ready of tongue, addicted to repartee, he expressed himself in a staccato and much-inflected speech that was eminently his own—not the utterance of Oxford, yet much more English in its effect than American. Add to this characteristic such an easily imitable habit as the twirling of a watch-chain while addressing an audience, and it is no wonder that Barrett Wendell offered an irresistible temptation to the mimic in successive generations.[4]

Howe's book also awakened the student memories of Walter P. Eaton, who recalled that his classmates busily jotted notes on "the patter of wit and comment, the jokes, the obscenity sometimes, the flashes of insight and aesthetic appreciation, the skillfully turned epigrams."[5] Wendell's mission in the Harvard classroom was not unlike that of his influential teacher and then colleague in the fine arts, Charles Eliot Norton. Both meant to prepare the student to lead as culturally elevated a life as is possible in a democratically ruled society. Each hoped to instill in the individual student a discriminating taste, high moral character, a questioning mind, and a striving for private excellence. Both used the technique of frankly outspoken judgment, at times verging on overstatement, sarcasm, and irony, to shock the complacent student, pique his interest, and start him on the road to critical thinking. With the industrious student in pursuit of such excellence, Wendell was unstintingly helpful, the soul of kindness. To the conniving or the deadbeat student, he seemed cruelly demanding. He required daily themes of a half-page, his colleague George Santayana remembered, which asked the student to describe how he *felt* about that day's reading—an encouragement of literacy in America, said Santayana, as well as evidence that his free-spirited colleague was more the "sentimentalist" than the intellectual ("his books were not worth writing").[6]

The Harvard student uninspired by Wendell had a sympathetic ally in Fred L. Pattee. In 1910, at age forty-seven, he visited Harvard on sabbatical from Penn State and audited the lectures of Wendell and George L. Kittredge. He came away "bored rather than inspired. Everywhere education [was] by the pouring-in process, the students sitting as passive buckets."[7] Pattee may have been partly indulging himself in the already familiar academic game of "sticking it" to a Harvard professor. Still, it is a tribute to Wendell that Pattee, at Penn State since 1894, should have devoted part of a sabbatical sixteen years later to this deferential pilgrimage to Wendell's precincts at Harvard Yard.

For his part, Pattee had earned his B.A. (class of 1888) and M.A. at Dartmouth, where, as noted in the preceding chapter, he attended Richardson's lectures in American literature. We find Pattee now in the nineties on the way to his own eminence. In 1895, he inaugurated the first American literature course at Penn State. And joining Pattee, Richardson, and Wendell in the decade were many more ranking scholars who we discover were now making a place for our literature in the curricula on the campuses around the nation.

In New England were Katherine Lee Bates (Wellesley), David L. Maulsby (Tufts), Lorenzo Sears (by 1897, Associate Professor of American Literature at Brown), and William Lyon Phelps (Yale). Down the coast were Brander Matthews (Columbia), Samuel M. Shute (George Washington), Robert A. Armstrong (West Virginia), and Charles W. Kent (Virginia). Killis Campbell had come to Texas. In the Midwest were Lemuel S. Potwin (Western Reserve), William B. Cairns (Wisconsin), Oscar Triggs (Chicago), and Charles W. Pearson (Northwestern). Isaac Demmon was still teaching at Michigan. Young Vernon Parrington arrived at Oklahoma in 1899, though his services to American literature had not yet begun. In the Far West, Alphonso G. Newcomer was teaching American authors at Stanford.

Many lesser names and institutions had begun to introduce American literature courses in recently established English departments, fifty by John S. Lewis's count, while twenty more were continuing courses inaugurated before the nineties. These were usually survey courses, requiring primary reading of the authors and frequently a text in literary history. The historical approach, however, seemed not to predominate in the college classroom. A sampling of college catalogs shows that on the undergraduate level, the professors meant to emphasize aesthetic values more strongly than facts and were not featuring writers important in American political, economic, or social history. (Lewis cites a variety of regional catalogs, including Tufts, Middlebury, CCNY, University of Richmond, Western Reserve, Illinois, University of North Dakota, University of Missouri, and University of Oregon.) How far English philology, powerful at Johns Hopkins and less so at Harvard, might have been adversely affecting the overall study of American literature is not easy to determine.[8]

Nor is it yet clear how the literary, political, and social nineties impinged on the American academy. During these final years of the century came a critical and emotional stock-taking of America's traditional values. The influx of foreign-born led to a movement to restrict immigration and may have helped revive the old debate over Americanism in literature, which now betrayed Anglo-Saxon anxieties discoverable in the recent histories of Richardson, Wendell, and even the liberal-minded Moses Coit Tyler. Shortly before his death, Whitman was invited to comment on the subject in the *North American Review,* no less. He reiterated his conclusions of "Democratic Vistas" two decades before: We still lacked an American national literature to express the high moral spirit of the new world. American literature should reflect our dominant characteristics of "Good-Nature, Decorum, and Intelligence"; but at present, the states and their authors were in a slump, deficient in a sense of "Patriotism, Nationality, Ensemble," though not, unfortunately, "braggadocio."

Journalist Henry C. Vedder was more optimistic in his assessment, *American Writers of Today* (1894). Bradford Torrey in the *Atlantic Monthly,* however, was closer to Whitman's feeling that the "American idea" was only slowly evolving and we remained a country finding expression in men of action rather than poets and philosophers. M. A. De Wolfe Howe's elegiac *American Bookmen* (1898), a volume generously illustrated for a popular audience, invoked "Americanism" as it had been expressed by our writers whose reputations were made in the prewar years. Donald G. Mitchell's *American Lands and Letters* (1897, 1899) also courted the general reader by carrying even more illustrations of our literary creators. He, too, appealed to a proud Americanism, and he instructively italicized the patriotism to be heard in our older mainstream writers like Hawthorne. Hamilton W. Mabie, writing in the *Forum,* also extolled the courage and purpose of earlier times, while he sensed a lack of conviction and "elemental power" in the literature of the past two decades, for all the modern accomplishment in form and style. America needed "a literature which shall speak to and for the consciousness of the nation." For the *Atlantic,* Charles Johnston recognized the power and vitality, but not the charm, color, mystery, and tradition of European literature, in our postwar Mark Twain, Cable, Harte, Frederic, and others. Charles L. Moore variously echoed most of these critics in a twenty-five-year backward glance for the *Dial.* Fact had triumphed over imagination in America and politics over religion. He repeated Whitman's critique: "We are industrial, we are commercial, but we are not religious or artistic"; but Moore did not temper the judgment with Whitman's saving optimism. Finally, we have Professor Oscar L. Triggs (Chicago) taking exception to Stedman's high estimate of our national expression in poetry, phrased in the introduction of his *American*

Anthology (1900). Stedman's collection itself, said Triggs, actually "betokens the inadequacy of poetic literature to sustain a large and vigorous modern national life; it denotes the transfer of power from the Sayer to the Doer."[9]

Elsewhere in the 1890s, our national self-consciousness was being heightened by troubled involvement in Venezuela and Cuba and by a new awareness of the "other America" with its urban poor, the greed and corruption of a new corporate industry, and the unsettled politics and economy of the New West, the Old South, and elsewhere. How did this world outside, along with the ferment of literary creation in the 1880s and 1890s, penetrate the halls of learning and affect public and academic support of American literature study? The available evidence is skimpy and unclear. The deaths of Emerson and Longfellow in the 1880s, and then of Lowell (1891), Whittier (1892), and Holmes (1894) appear to have deepened a sense that an era had ended and could begin to be duly assessed. In fact, Newton M. Hall (Iowa College) in 1892 called for just such appraisal in the colleges. Our first great cycle of literature was now over, he wrote, and our literature was a justifiable subject in the academy. Besides having sufficient scope, it was more vital to our students than classical or earlier English literature, for within our works lay the national democratic ideal and the strong morality of American life and character. Such study would deepen the student's cultural experience without breeding chauvinism or provincialism, for our literature ultimately possessed a broad universality. Hall's pedagogical essay, devoted exclusively to American literature, is a rarity in the 1890s and, in fact, very few companion articles would appear even during the next twenty-five years.[10]

Such assessment was partly under way at the graduate-school level. Thirteen universities listed graduate offerings in American literature during the decade, with the University of Virginia possibly giving the first course toward the Ph.D. in the year 1891–92.[11] The first doctoral dissertation in American literature has been officially credited to Oliver F. Emerson at Cornell, though the subject was actually linguistic, "The Ithaca Dialect: A Study of Present English." J. C. A. Schumacker wrote on "Sources of Longfellow's Poetry" in 1894 at Yale, and William B. Cairns's dissertation at Wisconsin in 1897 was "On the Development of American Literature, 1815–1833, with Especial Reference to Periodicals," the study we profited from in an earlier chapter. Also in 1897, Samuel E. Forman was awarded the Ph.D. at Johns Hopkins for "The Political Activities of Philip Freneau."[12] These were dissertations written within a doctoral program weighted toward English literary study and (especially at Johns Hopkins) philology. One graduate student, however, appeared to be specializing in American literature under Richardson at Dartmouth in 1895.[13]

To gauge this scholarly activity in American literature at the graduate level from a larger perspective, we can return to John Higham's reminder, in the preceding chapter, that many dissertations in American history were being written in the eighties and nineties. In all disciplines by 1900, roughly 250 doctorates had been awarded in some fifty of the country's 150 universities that had begun, after 1876, to develop graduate programs and faculty. Bernard Berelson nicely sums up this educational revolution from college to university in American higher education:

> In 1876 the college was at the top of the educational program with a largely ministerial faculty, a classical and tradition-centered curriculum, a recitative class session, a small student body highly selected for gentility and social status, an unearned Master's given to alumni for good behavior after graduation; and serious advanced students went abroad. By 1900, in a short twenty-five years, the university was firmly established in America and was leading the educational parade with its professional character, its utilitarianism and community-centered program, its stress on advancing learning, its new subjects of study, its seminars and laboratories and dissertations, its growing attraction for a new class of students—all capped by the earned Ph.D.[14]

But the stern fact remains that scarcely a dozen, or less than 10 percent, of these universities had developed graduate programs in American literature by 1900, and only four Ph.D.s had emerged in the field.

This slow progress of American literature study at the graduate level and below was related to the slightly better fortunes of English literature in the college curriculum. The joint campaign went forward in the 1890s at the annual sessions and in the publications of the Modern Language Association, with a public assist from two journals, the Chicago *Dial* and William P. Trent's new *Sewanee Review*. William Morton Payne, editor of the *Dial*, placed himself on the side of modern literature in the debate over classical studies versus modern, though his distaste for philology, science, and factuality in the study of literature may have upset the conservative members of the MLA. In 1894, he solicited for the *Dial* eighteen articles from the nation's professors of English. The following year, he published them, together with two more (from Johns Hopkins and Minnesota) and several pertinent

communications in the *Dial,* as *English in American Universities.* Though of greater interest to the chronicler of English
literature studies, the collection sheds light on American literature as well.

Wendell wrote the description of Harvard's English department of twenty members and the nine full-year courses and seventeen half-courses. He did not comment, however, on American
literature offerings. At Yale, Albert S. Cook (MLA president in
1897) reported that among the nineteen hours of English per
week given by five professors, he taught a two-hour course on selected American authors for juniors and seniors in the second
semester. Brander Matthews could not determine precisely how
many hours at Columbia, taught by himself and four colleagues
(plus assistants) in the department, could be designated English
courses. He taught a year-long course in American literature two
hours a week, with primary readings and no textbook. At Cornell, Hiram Corson spirited some Emerson and Lowell into a
course in nineteenth-century English prose. Chicago's English
department was the university's largest, with twelve members
giving forty-eight English courses from 1893 to 1894 to an enrollment of more than one thousand students, fifty-one of them
on the graduate level. Oscar Triggs taught American Literature
in Outline to undergraduates. Stanford reported that three hours
throughout the year were given to the history of American literature, the representative authors being taught, we gather, by
Alphonso Newcomer, though he was mentioned for only courses
in Homer and Dante.

The pedagogical clash in the ranks of modern literature teachers was unmistakably present in Payne's book through the contrasting attitude of Katherine Lee Bates at Wellesley and Johns
Hopkins's James W. Bright (currently secretary of MLA until
1902 and then its president). Bates championed the teaching of
literature as an art, free of the tyranny of Germany and Oxford.
Bright described, without apology, the rigorous philological and
historical method reigning in his department.

At the University of the South in Sewanee, Tennessee, W. P.
Trent also advanced the cause of modern English literature by
publishing reviews of scholarship and articles on curricula and
pedagogy in the *Sewanee Review.* In 1893, Henry E. Shepherd,
president of the College of Charleston and director of a summer
school of English, wrote two related essays on the debate over
philology and aesthetic appreciation. In the first, he criticized
the "exclusive devotion to a hard verbal discipline, a cold, fastidious exegesis of language" that had descended on literary studies

in the past twenty-five years, and he bemoaned that *PMLA* had been widely encouraging such scholarship. He praised Harvard as a major institution that had resisted the Germanic invasion. In the second article, Shepherd described how his college had reconciled the philological approach with the aesthetic. In a three-year literary program, students were introduced to philology in the first semester and history of the language the second; but linguistic and aesthetic emphases were integrated. From this disciplinary basis, they proceeded in the second and third years to a well-prepared reading of the English classics.

The next year, John B. Henneman of nearby University of Tennessee wrote in the *Sewanee* a history of the work in English at Southern universities, tracing the study of Anglo-Saxon back to Virginia under the enlightened influence of Jefferson in 1825. Henneman eleborated on this sketch in Payne's collection of essays just mentioned and was proud to list the Southern colleges that, virtually from their inception in the current century, established programs in English. Another article printed by Trent also illuminated the transitional condition of English study as the classical tradition, however, refused to die. W. H. McKellar observed that teaching the classics acquainted the student with the rules of grammar, but such translating did not promote either compositional style or appreciation of literature in English. As to the teaching of literature, he advised against systems and proposed that teachers encourage the students' aesthetic response to the entire work in advance of dissection and analysis. In particular, he opposed the dulling effect of the current textbooks.[15]

McKellar was alluding to a textbook market that publishing houses eagerly pursued during the next two decades. These volumes, designed in many instances to accommodate both the secondary-school and college classrooms, divide into three categories—anthologies, literary-history textbooks, and some combination of the two. Men of letters like Horace Scudder and E. C. Stedman fashioned early anthologies. Scudder prepared volumes of American poetry and prose in the Riverside Literature Series of Houghton Mifflin in the early 1890s, and second editions followed almost at once. Stedman's 885-page *An American Anthology* (1900), issued as a companion to his critical *Poets of America* (1885), went to a seventh impression within months. The combination anthology–history text was also an early labor of the nonacademic professional writers, the *American Literature* (1891) by Julian Hawthorne and Leonard Lemmon being a favorite in the colleges.

But university professors also sought their share of the school trade. Henry Beers of Yale entered, or rather reentered, the market with an anthology plus commentary in 1891, and his book was followed with more of the same by academic colleagues F. V. N. Painter of Roanoke College (*Introduction to American Literature*, 1897), Minnesota's Richard E. Burton (*Literary Leaders of America*, 1903), and others. In the case of the strictly literary history designed or appropriated as a textbook, the teaching profession largely had its way. Some of these studies were by Selden L. Whitcomb of Iowa College (1894); Brander Matthews of Columbia (1896); Fred Pattee of Penn State (1896); Katherine Lee Bates of Wellesley (1897); Moses Coit Tyler, then at Cornell (1897); Walter Bronson of Brown (1900); Alphonso Newcomer of Stanford (1901); Trent of Columbia (1903); and numerous others up to Wisconsin's W. B. Cairns and his work in 1912, which seems to have marked a point of exhaustion for these single-author flights and signaled the need for the large-scale, cooperative enterprise of the *CHAL*.[16]

The 1890s, then, was a fertile decade for writing American literary histories, whether incidentally or primarily for use as textbooks, and we should reserve several pages to the most distinguished authors, apart from Wendell. These were Beers, Matthews (who, we have seen, pointedly avoided using a textbook in his own American literature class), Bronson, and Tyler. In 1891, Beers reissued his *An Outline Sketch of American Literature* (1887) as *Initial Studies in American Letters,* intended, like the selections in his earlier *A Century of American Literature* (1878), for Chautauqua home-study courses. After some two hundred pages of history, written in a graceful style, with an occasional turn of metaphor, he appended sixty pages of literary examples. The main text, he announced in the preface, was chiefly a history of belles lettres.

As in the other literary histories of the time, however, Beers offered no remarkable sense of distinctively literary periods despite his presumed aesthetic approach, the only suspense for the reader, perhaps, lying in how Beers would elect to skew the familiar political eras. His "Revolutionary Period" was from 1765 to 1815, followed by "National Expansion to 1837," three separate chapters for 1837 to 1861 on Concord, Cambridge, and "Literature in the Cities," and a concluding "Literature Since 1861," which he admitted to be too recent for him to elucidate successfully. Like others, Beers admired Tyler at the same time that he moved swiftly past the colonial writers. Typical of his contemporaries, also, Beers tossed off a predictable judgment here and there and justified the critical verdict by presenting, at most, an unexplicated quotation or two from the literary work.

Five years later came Brander Matthews's *An Introduction to the Study of American Literature* (1896), at best an average contribution to the progress of American literature study. Undoubtedly, Matthews helped to bring native authors into the classroom with this appealingly illustrated textbook. Fred L. Pattee, whose own successful American literary history textbook appeared and was jointly reviewed with Matthews's in 1896, testified to the hungry market the publishers had discovered for these books. Both he and Matthews finally sold some quarter of a million copies.[17]

Matthews may have impeded the cause of American literature, as well, by showing a conventional deference to English letters, an unrelenting stance that he maintained even into the 1920s (he died in 1929). In his introductory chapter, he repeated the anglophile's linguistic definition that "the record of the life of the peoples using the English language is English literature," though he deemed it best to call the writings of the British Isles British literature, reserving for English literature the larger corpus of British, American, Canadian, and Australian writings (pp. 10, 12). Almost as a conciliatory gesture, he granted that American conditions had, of course, created a somewhat distinctive life and literature. (As president of MLA in the year 1910–11, he gave a diplomatically broad address on "The Economic Interpretation of Literary History.")

Matching his bland Toryism was Matthews's comfortable bundle of easy assumptions and clichés, presented in an accomplished style that implied an unflappable certainty of judgment as he moved through single-chapter treatments of the major authors. Dubious figures like Melville and Whitman received mention in a penultimate chapter, "Other Writers," with *Typee* cited as Melville's not-quite-fictional and only remembered work, while Whitman was rather embarrassingly praised for his popular Lincoln poem: "No one of the many tributes to Lincoln, not even Lowell's noble eulogy, is more deeply charged with exalted feeling than Whitman's 'O Captain, My Captain'" (p. 225). Matthews's definition of literature was a mixture of cultural-history criteria and a nonelitist impressionism—the record of the thoughts, feelings, and actions of a people "so skillfully made as to give pleasure to the reader" (p. 9). He avoided any controversy over contemporary literature by neither discussing nor even naming any living writer in the text. Even the study questions were nonargumentative: "What is the distinguishing characteristic of American literature?" The expected answer: expression of the dignity of a free and equal citizenry (p. 14).

Walter C. Bronson's *A Short History of American Literature* (1900) was D. C. Heath's entry for a part of the school market, and it was successful enough to be revised and enlarged in a 1919 edition. Bronson admitted to somewhat more than textbook aspirations, hoping that his footnotes and bibliography would qualify the volume also as a reference work (that is, attractive to the nation's libraries as well as classrooms) and draw attention to his scholarship beyond Moses Coit Tyler through study in the local John Carter Brown library holdings in poetry of the early republic. Bronson professed only a casual periodization of American literary history, rightly so as it turned out. After the colonial and Revolutionary eras, he settled for a "Republic" period from 1789 to 1900 (subdivided into "National Beginnings," 1789 to 1815; "Golden Age," 1815 to 1870; and the literature since 1870). He viewed Americans to be members of the English and ancillary races and, like Matthews, regarded American literature an unequal branch of the literature of England. Before the period discussions, Bronson paralleled American history dates to contemporary events in England and reminded the student which great English authors were writing at the time.

Before turning to Wendell's far superior literary history in the same year, we cannot pass by the great publishing event for American literature scholarship in 1897. Three years before his death, Moses Coit Tyler had at last completed his two-volume *Literary History of the American Revolution*. Even in a chapter as crowded as the present one, this achievement must be honored, if ever too briefly. Tyler rehearsed these chapters in his classroom lectures—in history—during his final period at Cornell. Perhaps the effects drifted across to the literature department, for in the year the book came out, Fred L. Pattee remarked, "His college caught up with him and added to its curriculum an unattached course in the history of American literature." [18]

Tyler's road to this last major work had been long and exhausting. More than seventeen years had passed since 7 August 1879, when he began to study the Revolutionary period in earnest, though still weary almost a year after publication of the colonial volumes. By spring of 1880, he had read many figures of, and beyond, the Revolution, for a history he had projected from 1765 to 1815. His progress then slowed. More than four years later (9 September 1884), he read to the newly created American Historical Association "The Influence of Thomas Paine on the

Popular Resolution for Independence." But in 1886, Tyler was depressed that the history was so burdensome. So he set to work on the less formidable monograph of Patrick Henry in April and completed it the next year for J. T. Morse's American Statesmen Series (Houghton Mifflin). Tyler's creative mood for the history returned in late 1887, but the next year, he went to Europe on a rest sabbatical. In May 1889, however, he was happily engaged in research in London on Bishop Berkeley.

After returning to Cornell, Tyler suffered the disruption of faculty unrest, soon compounded by periods of poor health. By 18 April 1893, the first four of an eventual thirty-nine chapters were in final draft. In July, he was completing chapter 8 (on Francis Hopkinson). Then came the salutary decision to write the literary history of only the Revolution, and Tyler changed his terminal date from 1815 to 1783. In 1895, the unused notes on the Connecticut Wits Theodore Dwight and Joel Barlow, plus the earlier research on Bishop Berkeley, became *Three Men of Letters*. Finally, Tyler pruned superfluous figures, reducing his list of 203 names to 97 and subsequently to 49. The remaining chapters rapidly took shape, and in November 1896, all thirty-nine weighed a hefty nineteen pounds when they arrived in the offices of G. P. Putnam.[19]

On 24 January 1897, Tyler wrote his preface to volume I (1763–1776) of the *Literary History of the American Revolution* (hereafter *LHAR*, with pages given in parentheses), these first twenty-three chapters appearing while the sixteen of volume II (1776–1783) were still being printed. With a certainty of expressed purpose that belies his seventeen years of struggling conception, undetermined scope, and painful composition, Tyler described his "inward history" to be a revelation of "the soul, rather than the body, of the American Revolution" created by Revolutionist *and* Loyalist "penmen," and through this tolerant hearing of both parties, he hoped to diminish the "race feud" still alive between American and English partisans. (He did not comment on our Anglo-Saxon nativism and prejudices against European newcomers in the 1880s and 1890s that were displacing traditional anglophobia with racial animus of a different stripe.)

Tyler traced three developments in both camps that were shaped by similar political pressures. The first movement, filled with the growing anxiety over a split with England, carried to the spring day of 1775 at Lexington and Concord; from then until early summer of 1776, loyalty to England seemed increasingly doubtful among Whigs and increasingly dangerous for Tories; and from the Declaration to 1783, the Whigs supported the integrity of separation and war while the Tories opposed it with equal vehemence and satire. This third phase occupied Tyler's volume II, though he explained in that preface that he inevitably moved forward and back across the artificial boundary of 1776 to gain a comprehensive history of the literature in its several aspects on both American sides. He dealt in fact with nine groups of writings: letters; state papers; oral addresses, secular or sacred; political essays, especially the pamphlet; political satires in prose or verse; popular lyrics and songs; miscellaneous humor in verse and prose; dramatic works, mainly in verse; and prose narratives of Revolutionary experiences.

And so at the end of a century charged, from time to time, with literary nationalism that was long on rhetoric and short on judicious assessment, Tyler concentrated on our final writers of the colonial era and forsook another century of his projected survey in order to deliver a two-volume verdict on these unlikely two decades in our literary history. Many years would pass before we enjoyed another literary historian with Tyler's scholarly thoroughness and exuberant style. To the present day, no one has surpassed his intensity of focus on a restricted period of American writing. He traced the roots and exact phases of Loyalist literary activity and enforced silence. He located the English and French influences on genres and modes practiced by Whigs and Tories alike, noticed Crevecoeur's reciprocal influence on English writers, and marked the distinctly American origins of verse drama, a prison literature, and the general (as distinguished from parochial) historical writing inspired "under the fires of a common danger" (I, 384). Judging the leaders of a forthcoming national literature, Tyler was particularly eloquent on our "first American poet of Democracy," Philip Freneau (II, 274). What distinguished true poetry in Freneau, however, or all literature in the aesthetic sense, became, once more, the least satisfactory of Tyler's literary–historical explanations. Even so, his commanding narrative voice and vivid creation of setting, dramatic happening, character, and functional style (especially the military and atmospheric imagery) could again disarm the readers at the very moment they might charge him with conceptual vagueness or scanty analysis.

Tyler's verbal gusto, however, was soon weakened by poor health, and he died on Friday, 28 December 1900. Cornell colleague George L. Burr fittingly remarked that anyone who read Tyler's books had come to know the man within the scholar through his style and the tone of his richly human authorial voice—generous, sympathetic, ironic, companionable, whimsical, austere, reverent, and truthful.[20] Among the readers who had drawn inspiration from Tyler, even to the final pages of the recent *LHAR,* was Barrett Wendell, and to his work we now return.

✷   ✷   ✷

In the year of Tyler's death, Wendell published the full-length literary history that Tyler had aspired to write. But Wendell's spirit seems, at first, closer to Bronson and his version of American literary inferiority, published also in 1900. True to form, Wendell disguised his underlying streak of stubborn Americanness. He was more fully immersed in the life of the 1890s than his aloof cane and spats appearance in Harvard Yard might have suggested to collegues and mimicking students. He traveled to the Chicago World's Fair in 1893, returned from an extended trip to Italy and the Middle East in the year 1894–95, and despite his pose of feeling out of it in America, Wendell was worrying over the unsettled conditions on the national scene (he gave his qualified support to McKinley over Bryan in 1896). In 1897, Wendell introduced Harvard students to American literary history and continued the instruction for twenty more years. In 1898, he finally received promotion to full professor. Perhaps from this moment, he gained the necessary confidence and self-esteem to assert himself as a scholar.

During the next dozen years, Wendell published books on American and English literature, on life in contemporary France, on problems of education and social classes in America, and also lectured at the universities of California, Cambridge, and the Sorbonne. His final ten years, to his death in 1921, were filled with honors at home and abroad. Expectably through it all, Wendell protested the alien times and bemoaned his outcast state.

This productive era truly began with the work on which Wendell's scholarly reputation has now come to rest, his *Literary History of America* (hereafter, the *LHA*). His extant correspondence in the 1890s is sparse, leaving the genesis of the *LHA* a matter of speculation and inference. In a letter to Sir Robert White-Thomson, an English friend whom Wendell met many years before in Europe while recovering from a nervous breakdown during his freshman year at Harvard, he wrote on 14 August 1899: "I am writing very constantly this summer on a *Literary History of America,* which I think I have mentioned to you before. A publisher wanted the book; and I agreed to write it some time ago." The publisher was Scribner, who had issued *Stelligeri* in 1893. We may safely guess that Wendell's long sketch of

American literary history in that collection inspired Scribner to bring Wendell into the expanding market of history textbooks in American literature. This writing on demand, said Wendell, was not going easily in 1899 and was in fact "so arduous and tedious that I am trying to make a resolve never to write a line to order again." He expected to have the history blocked out in a month and to that end was dictating copy to a stenographer—an approach of mixed blessings: "One gets ahead at a tremendous rate; but in such appalling style that pretty much every sentence must be recast."[21]

These difficulties of composition must have been somewhat eased by Wendell's recent classroom preparations in American authors and also by the burgeoning studies in American literature that he acknowledged in the "Authorities and References" section of the *LHA*. This ample bibliography was itself a valuable reflection of the scholarship that had accrued by 1900. Ever diffident about his academic qualifications (though perhaps at times the more opinionated because of it), Wendell was an eclectic scholar, grateful to his sources, which included the Griswold anthologies, the biographical encyclopedias of Jared Sparks and the Duyckincks, the postwar literary histories of Tyler and Richardson and several others, Stedman's *Poets of America,* and the many monographs in the American Men of Letters series. He cited the American Men of Letters volumes in the 1880s, mentioned in the previous chapter, together with the new ones of the 1890s: Simms (W. P. Trent, 1892), Curtis (Edward Cary, 1894), Bayard Taylor (Albert H. Smyth, 1896), and Stowe (Mrs. J. T. Fields, 1897).

Wendell also had consulted the English Great Writers series, including Richard Garnett's Emerson (1888), WIlliam J. Linton's Whittier (1893), and Eric S. Robertson's Longfellow (1887). Nor did Wendell overlook James's *Hawthorne* (1879) in the English Men of Letters series. He also acknowledged the invaluable Riverside editions of American authors, without which our literature studies, including the *CHAL,* would have been longer in coming. By 1900, he had availed himself of these handsome multivolume primary editions of Stowe, Lowell, Everett, Thoreau, Emerson, Whittier, Longfellow, Holmes, and Hawthorne. In addition, Stone and Kimball in Chicago had issued the ten-volume edition of Poe (editors Stedman and Woodberry) in 1895. Valuable also to Wendell was the *Library of American Literature* (1889–90) of Stedman and Hutchinson, previously discussed. A last publication of great regional significance came too late for Wendell, though he would have had little use for it, the *Library of Southern Literature,* by various scholars of the South from 1908 to 1913, a work the four editors of the *CHAL* pronounced indispensable to their new synthesis of American literary history (I, xi).

Wendell admired Tyler (he cited, in particular, the recent pages on the Loyalists, Freneau, and the Declaration) but followed the lead of Richardson by avowing in the introduction of *LHA* that the only "literature of any importance" in America had appeared since 1800. Consequently, Wendell devoted 70 percent of the history to the nineteenth century. The earlier writing, though not "pure" literature, became the necessary basis in New England for a nineteenth-century "renaissance" (Wendell's own coinage) of various colonials—Cotton Mather, Edwards, and some few others. These earlier sections of the *LHA,* though truncated, help us understand an evolving historiography for American literature. Wendell established here, directly and implicitly, his assumptions as a literary critic and historian of American writing.

Wendell's announced approach as an historian differed from Richardson's, for Wendell stated that we must know how the writer, even the individual genius, has lived through the vicissitudes of his time if we are to understand his literary work. Wendell's attention to race, moment, and milieu in America apparently owed something to Hippolyte Taine here, and in *The France of Today* (1907), Wendell explicitly praised Taine for his precision and suggestiveness. Wendell, though, was quite rudimentary in relating the writer's life and times to his work. He did not uncover from biography any startling subtleties of meaning in the literary text, and several times—with Poe, Hawthorne, and Whitman—Wendell explicitly denied biography to be of value in explaining their literary art. As to overall design, Wendell's literary history carried the earmarks of the rather apathetic blocking out he mentioned in the summer of 1899, his treatment of periods, genres, modes, and influences being, in the main, quite predictable and derivative.

His walled-in century periods notwithstanding, Wendell propounded a cyclical theory of "the growth, development, and decline of all literature and all fine art whatsoever." He drew on Shakespeare and the English Renaissance (and from his own *Shakspere,* published by Scribner in 1894) to advance the idea that the rebel artists help create a literary era and foster experiment and innovation that, in turn, lead to a "freshly established tradition." This tradition is both support and anathema to the individual talent as the new cycle begins. Later, the creative imagination grows placid and languorous amid the ripeness of the reigning literary tradition. The period winds down, and the world awaits a new cycle of creative energy.

How well did this cyclical hypothesis clarify the course of American literature? Wendell accommodated our native literature to his formula by arguing that American literature properly exists in only the early nineteenth-century renaissance of New England, where he located, not without some nagging contradictions, an arguable cycle of American literature. (In our later pages, we shall compare Robert Spiller's refinement of Wendell's cycle as a guiding principle of the cooperative *Literary History of the United States* in the 1940s, a specifically romantic thesis that he elaborated in *The Cycle of American Literature* in 1955.) Meanwhile, Wendell had many more writers to consider before, during, and after his favored episode in nineteenth-century New England. His admiration of Tyler notwithstanding, Wendell had small regard for seventeenth-century writers, when the typical American was but an Anglo-Saxon immigrant in colonial exile. He granted all of forty-two pages to that initial period and only seventy-seven to all of the eighteenth century. Thereafter, the nineteenth century received 379 pages (203 of them reserved for the New England renaissance). Unlike Richardson, Wendell avoided the living authors, since contemporary figures and their activities were "never quite ripe for history" (p. 10).

Wendell looked at colonial writing largely in relation to English tradition. This supposedly transcultural approach never provided him with real clues to literary continuity or distinctive national growth. But he did raise some fruitful questions about what may be uniquely "American" in thought, attitude, and character. Like Tyler and Richardson, Wendell underscored the Anglo-Saxon-Elizabethan racial temper of the early American puritan: "For all their mutual detestation, Puritans and playwrights alike possessed the spontaneity of temper, the enthusiasm of purpose, and the versatility of power which marked Elizabethan England" (p. 27). Virtually quoting Tyler, Wendell noted that, like their Elizabethan prototypes, both Virginians and New Englanders "were on the one hand men of action, and on the other, men of God" (p. 37). But Wendell had his own account of a diverging political and religious history in the two countries, and the differences influenced diverging national characteristics. The Revolution of 1688 brought to English government a freedom that in New England had already become a tradition. Because of this relatively untroubled continuity of colonial experience, "the native Yankees of 1700 were incalculably nearer their Elizabethan ancestors than were any of their contemporaries born in the mother country" (p. 33). In Elizabethan terms, that is, the Americans were relatively unchanged and, so to speak, more English than the English.

In the eighteenth century, disparities in experience and therefore national character continued to grow. In America, twin influences of religious and political ardor inherited from the King James Bible and English Common Law led, successively, from the popular enthusiasm of the Great Awakening to the revolutionary excitement of 1776 (p. 75). Wendell emphasized a further difference in political perception by 1776: While the English parliament was engaging in the technicalities of jurisprudence in regard to colonial government, "a century and a half of incessant theological discussion had made the native Yankee mind far more accessible to moral arguments than to legal" (p. 110). The same Yankee moralistic frame of mind welcomed the idealistic philosophy of radical human rights emanating from France (although this Rousseauistic tendency Wendell and the twentieth-century New Humanists would view as dangerous to individual discipline and merit). Pragmatic old England, on the other hand, was growing more conservative and middle class. While Americans retained "to an incalculable degree" the triple virtues of Elizabethan spontaneity, enthusiasm, and versatility—an indication of Yankee youthfulness as well as retardation—such was hardly the case with the native Englishmen who greeted the dawning nineteenth century with nary a trace of their Elizabethan forebears: "Whatever else John Bull may be, he is not spontaneous in his reactions to fresh impressions; he is not enthusiastic, except in irascibility; and he is about as far from versatile as any human being who ever trod the earth" (pp. 77, 64).

Wendell also focused on the American scene alone—perhaps with Taine's causal milieu in mind—to explain other character traits that had arisen, this time, from typically native conditions. Most salient was our national innocence, or what he had labeled in 1893 our inexperience (*Stelligeri*, p. 11). He now returned to this absence of American experience or "struggling complexity of social and political forces" to explain why the Elizabethan type had remained fairly constant in New England, in contrast to the English national character's being shaped under the duress and change of seventeenth-century civil war, restoration, and revolution. Our national inexperience continued in the eighteenth century and explained why Calvinism could not maintain a dominant hold on American minds: Human nature in the inexperienced new world was not exposed to the usual pressures and perversions of civilized society. Jonathan Edwards's premises and conclusions concerning human depravity appeared invalid to a people whose lives did not bear out the gloomy presuppositions of Calvin's world. Unfortunately for American letters, said Wendell in his closing sentence on the eighteenth century, one was reminded of "the commonplace that lack of experience does not favour literature or artistic expression" (p. 136).

Scarcely separable from this inexperience for Wendell was the rather static condition of what might be termed pastoral space and time in early America, a state of life relatively unaffected by social environment but conducive to the growth of individualism. He put it this way: "Such stagnation of social evolution as marks the seventeenth century in New England is humanly possible only under conditions where the pressure of external fact, social, political, and economic, is relaxed—under conditions, in short, where the individual type is for a while stronger than environment" (p. 33). With Tyler and Richardson, then, Wendell regarded the "geographical isolation" of a new-world frontier not to be an influencing environment; rather, it was free space, a sort of mythic prelapsarian virgin land whose American history Henry Nash Smith has studied so memorably. For Wendell, therefore, the result for American life in the seventeenth century was unprecedented in the history of nations—a time of "untrammelled national inexperience" (p. 34). Only once did he suggest for literature a salutary effect from this "relaxation" of the pressure that "a dense society brings upon human life"; it occurred in the unforced "enthusiastic spontaneity of Elizabethan English" present in Cotton Mather's *Magnalia* (p. 53). (And crucial to Wendell's cyclic theory of literature, the death of Mather in 1728 brought a shift in our literary history from New England domination to the rising prominence of the middle colonies, an interruption that would end a century later with the New England renaissance.)

Wendell ingeniously discovered a further ingredient in his new American that helped explain the tenacity of ardent colonial-Elizabethan traits through the centuries. Besides their "untrammelled inexperience" in the new world, these Anglo-Saxons possessed "the absorptive power of our native race to preserve the general type of character which America had displayed from its settlement" (p. 77). This "power of assimilating whatever came within its influence" marked both Puritan and "the less austere type of character which first planted itself on the James River" and remained undiminished in the eighteenth century, "as indeed it seems still to remain" (pp. 28, 70). Anglo-Saxon par-

tisans of the 1890s could hardly have asked for a better justification from an Ivy League intellectual. It was Wendell's version of
their dominant role in our melting-pot democracy, even though
they, like he, were currently less than hopeful that Anglo-Saxon
ideals did, in fact, leaven the democratic lump any longer.

Wendell had referred to American democracy privately five
years before as "little better than a caricature of government."
Idealistic individuals of "the better classes" were removing themselves and their "external graces and dignity" from the corrupt
center of leadership.[22] In a 1905 lecture at Lowell Institute, he
still saluted in commoners like Lincoln, at least (as earlier proper
Bostonians had), the character that popular democracy might attain; but in *The Privileged Classes* (1908), Wendell created a
slight furore with his supercilious observation that the newly
"privileged" laboring classes had no compunctions about be-
having discourteously even before their gentlemanly betters. In
short, the Anglo-Saxons, whose absorptive power had earlier
forged a national type in a purer America of untrammeled inexperience, were now either unable or unwilling to exert any racial
charisma in a decadent society.

Against this background of early national characteristics in a
colonial world of sparse and undeveloped intellectual and literary
life, Wendell moved to his preferred nineteenth century and the
emerging history of a now-definable American literature. Only
the chapters on prewar literature in New England warrant a close
rereading, and they are, indeed, the celebrated showpiece of his
literary history. Both in the weaknesses and strengths, they rank
as some of the most significant writing in all American literature
studies. Perhaps influenced by the entire drift of evolutionary,
and cyclical, thought in his lifetime—Hegel, Darwin, Taine,
Brunetiere, even Henry Adams and C. E. Norton—Wendell tried
to describe what to him was a complete cycle of a literary period
of florescence, maturity, and decline. How did New England rise
to this renaissance? He meant the term literally, a renewal of the
older but "untired blood" of the Puritan gentry invigorated by the
"fine flush of independence" in a New England society "in which
fixed traditions had prevailed" (p. 243). Blessed by these conditions, together with the unprecedented material prosperity of
new foreign commerce and domestic manufacturing, "the whole
region was suddenly flashed into unity" (p. 244). So far so good.
How then did these forces help bring about "the most remarkable
literary expression which has yet declared itself in America"?
Predictably, Wendell faltered: "To say that this resulted from
social and economic causes is too much; what can surely be

asserted is that the highest development of intellectual life in New England coincided with its greatest prosperity." The inevitable parallel with the Italian Renaissance occurred to him, but he did not see in his comparison the widely ranging causal possibilities—parallels or contrasts of wealth, power, cultural distinction, and provincial pride. All we are given is the description of the new intellectual spirit, "more like that which aroused old Italy to a fresh sense of civilised antiquity than like a spontaneous manifestation of native thought or feeling." The result of this rebirth was "the most mature school of pure letters which has yet appeared in this country" (pp. 244, 245).

Wendell devoted fifteen chapters to the New England period, with due attention to the Concord group and the antislavery movement, separate chapters on the chief figures (Emerson, Whittier, Longfellow, Lowell, Holmes, and Hawthorne), and a final essay, "Decline." He carefully delineated the youthful, rebellious imaginations that were being quickened in an atmosphere where older tradition lingered amid the vital new spirit of an age. Emerson's fondness for allusions reflected the "juvenile pedantry" of the newly awakened New England mind (p. 326); a juvenile Longfellow at Bowdoin was responding with similar "religious and philosophic buoyancy" (p. 379); George Ticknor was exciting the students at Harvard with the treasures of postclassical literatures; and Whittier, though less strident because of the long Quaker tradition of antislavery, had lent his individual talent and ardor to the company of more recently liberated Unitarian and transcendentalist converts. Of them all, however, Hawthorne was the quintessential "broadly American" romantic who expressed the flowering New England renaissance. He was also the boldly independent artist of Wendell's new literary cycle who possessed, as well, a general thirst for antiquity and a closeness to the peculiar New England heritage, "the darkly passionate idealism of the Puritans" with its "tendency toward conceptions, which when they reached artistic form must be romantic" (pp. 431, 432).

Why did this literary cycle in New England wind down? Internally, the centripetal individualism that gave rise to the renaissance bore the seeds of undisciplined excess, disintegration, and decline. The "three phases of one considerable movement"—Wendell was referring to Unitarianism, transcendentalism, and militant reform—"were based on the fundamental conception that human beings are inherently good" (p. 441). So long as New Englanders wedded "the discipline of tradition" to this buoyant and naïve individualism, "their vagaries were not so wild as to

seem socially disintegrating; but before long, excessive individualism began evidently to involve the neglect and decay of standards" (pp. 441, 442). Harvard men had shaped and anchored
these standards in the pages of the early *North American Review*
and the later *Atlantic Monthly*. But this continuity was severed
by the Civil War. In the postwar decades, material fortune had
now replaced New England's literary and cultural ideals in the
realm of American power and eminence (p. 441). (Material prosperity had earlier created a hospitable climate and audience for
Wendell's New England writer.)

After treating briefly the postwar ascendancy of New York, the
arrested postwar condition of the South, and the "swiftly changing" West (p. 513), Wendell pondered the oncoming demise of an
imperiled high culture in democratic America. Though he had
wearily concluded earlier that even New England's golden day
had left little of a lasting impact on a complex and bewildering
America at century's end (pp. 445–46), Wendell now returned to
the "gleams of counsel and help" to be found in the "simple,
hopeful literature of inexperienced, renascent New England." A
twilight nostalgia rather than gleaming hope, however, attends
his closing comment on that earlier time: "There, for a while, the
warring ideals of democracy and of excellence were once reconciled, dwelling confidently together in some earthly semblance of
peace" (p. 530). In this somber mood, he ended the *LHA*.[23]

Other literary and historical aspects of the *LHA* need not de-
tain us. On the historical evolution of American literary modes
and genres, Wendell traced briefly a tradition of native humor
and envisioned a strong future for the short story (as did Richardson) and a recently advancing American drama. (Wendell himself published two stories, left nine more among his manuscripts,
and wrote eight plays. He encouraged George Pierce Baker of
Harvard 47 Workshop fame and thus, indirectly, influenced
Eugene O'Neill.) After a perfunctory comment on Simms's native debts to Cooper and "perhaps" Brown, Wendell was silent on
the growth of long fiction in the century (p. 488) and necessarily
so on the living postwar novelists whom he had ruled out of his
bounds.[24] As an aesthetic commentator, Wendell belonged to the
same impressionistic school as Tyler and Richardson. Wendell
discovered a requisite moral scrupulosity, what he termed artistic conscience, in the American imagination of Bryant, Irving,
Cooper, Poe, Hawthorne, and Lowell. But not in Whitman. Wendell invited the reader to "feel" the "power," "vividness," "spontaneity," and "truth" in the separate literary works, and he excused
his unwillingness to explicate: "To dissect is too often to kill." He

also enjoined the reader to appreciate and judge our authors by reading them aloud. The suggestion was consistent with his practice in the Harvard classroom. A vivid and effective reader is how one class assistant remembered Wendell: "Generally he made no comment; he only read a passage aloud in such a manner as to impart to others the effect it had on him." [25]

Wendell's critical method did not disturb his equally impressionistic turn-of-the-century reviewers, and his history, for the most part, was cordially received (and Howells later apologized for his snippy comments in the *North American Review*). The unsigned review in the *Dial* praised Wendell in every aspect of the literary historian's duties, and even higher compliments were awarded by Wendell's colleague at Harvard, Lewis E. Gates. Several months before, Gates had written for the *Atlantic Monthly* his requirements for the ideal critic, one who wisely blends impressionism with historical understanding, technical explanation, and critical breadth. He was satisfied that Wendell had approached and executed his task in all these regards. The total work was "delightful reading: whimsical at times, challengingly paradoxical and wilful, here and there almost too debonair, and yet withal wise, judicious and fully appreciative of merit and genius" and destined to be our standard literary history. [26]

After Wendell, we must wait until Parrington to read a literary history as strongly unified by one man's rhetoric and singular point of view—Parrington's liberal outlook, of course, in many ways the diametric opposite of Wendell's New England biases in regard to social class, Anglo-Saxon tradition, and the legacy of Harvard. For all his limits as a critic and historian, Wendell in his time provoked a continuing debate over the shape of American literary history and the vitality of the New England tradition, as we shall see presently in the reactions of young Van Wyck Brooks, Waldo Frank, and others in quest of their "usable past." Beyond his generation, Wendell remains important for several pioneering theses: his notion of the renaissance in New England, accompanied by his speculations of the literary cycle; his suggested herding of most of his major writers in prewar America into the mode of romanticism; and his faithful pursuit of inexperience as the salient feature of American life and character. No doubt Wendell was strongly influenced in this last case by his friend Henry Adams's brilliant analysis in the *History of the United States* (which Wendell cited). But Wendell was more tenacious in tracking that potentially creative naïveté and can rightly be considered the chief forerunner of the spate of studies in the 1950s whose authors recognized (or believed they had discovered) the explanatory power of innocence in the various phases and subject areas of American history.

Finally, Wendell is important for the original reason he came into these pages, as a mind and conscience that inspired and goaded the editors of the *CHAL*. He was their final, and most visibly prominent, trailblazer. But he was not the last to appear. Surrounding him were many other aspiring literary historians in the years just before the *CHAL*, and they were not about to accept Wendell's as the standard literary history of America. His book, then, must be viewed among the steady flow of literary histories at the turn of the century. During this new surge of American literature scholarship, unleashed as it was by a renewed nationalism, sectional pride, and the quest for a usable past, William P. Trent himself, and many others, usually from the Eastern universities, added their own literary histories to Wendell's.

Publishers were still competing for a lively school and popular market, and they easily teamed with professors who were chasing their various life ambitions. It mattered little to many a publisher and author, apparently, if their literary history achieved originality or professional distinction, so that we suspect financial rather than scholarly motives were frequently ascendant. Still, without a brief glance at this publishing activity, our narrative would remain incomplete. In addition to Trent's history for Appleton (1903), a mercifully selective sampling of these authors and their sponsors to the eve of the *CHAL* includes Lorenzo Sears of Brown (Little, Brown, 1902); Thomas Wentworth Higginson, whose Lowell Institute lectures of 1903 were modified and supplemented by a younger Henry W. Boynton (Houghton Mifflin, 1903); George Woodberry of Columbia (Harper, 1903); Richard Burton of Minnesota (Scribner, 1904); Theodore Stanton and colleagues at Cornell (Putnam, 1909); William B. Cairns from Wisconsin (Oxford, 1912); William J. Long of Stamford, Connecticut (Ginn, 1913); and John C. Metcalf from Richmond College (Atlanta: B. F. Johnson, 1914).

None of these authors argued the foreign or native influences on the growth, fruition, continuity, and decline of literary periods, movements, modes, and genres. Following the lead of their predecessors, they equated literary with political periods—colonial, revolutionary, and national. There were quibbles about dating: Sears ended his colonial period at 1783, and then termed the rest of his history national. Cairns chose 1765. Stanton disdained any pretence of originality as a colonial historian and simply condensed Moses Coit Tyler. Less agreement occurred on the nineteenth century. Unable to trace national literary movements, most of the authors preferred a regional approach, usually including Philadelphia, New York, New England (with an occasional distinction between Cambridge and Concord), the South, and the West. Cairns separated his regional treatment into two periods, "Early" and "Central," casually dividing them at 1833 (the terminal year in his survey of early American journals, cited in Chapter 3 above). He saw by the 1880s a "noticeable weakening of the older sectional feeling" (p. 221). Long distinguished his periods as "First National" to 1840 and "Second National" to 1876, followed by "Recent Tendencies." In a seeming jibe at his fellow historians' dilemma over a national literature, Long commented flatly, without an argument of his own, that there were "no political and geographical divisions in the national consciousness" (p. v). Metcalf, who did follow the regional strategy, asked us to remember, too, the "larger union," the "national development" (p. 4). Burton gave most of his nineteenth-century chapters over to selected major authors. Stanton's friends contributed seven genre chapters.

Trent, too, showed very little originality in the historical conception of American literary history (nor would he gain any startling insights over the next decade for the structure of the *CHAL*). His four periods to the close of the Civil War were politically oriented. The colonial closed at 1764, the dividing event being the Stamp Act. The Revolutionary period continued to 1788, the formative to 1820 and Jackson, and the sectional to 1865 (with 1850 a crucial date regarding slavery). Even when he centered on literary genres within the major time divisions— "Writers of Fiction" (1809–29), "The Poets" (1830–50), and so on—the dating was important for political rather than literary reasons.

In the American aspects of American literary history—the foreign-versus-native mixture in national character, aesthetics, ideas, and language—these historians were, again, less distinguished for originality than Tyler, Richardson, and Wendell. Their discussion of national ideals in literature reminds us that most of them were writing textbooks tailored to edify the young American student in moral rectitude, love of country, and sufficient appreciation of our home-grown literature. Sears gave a Tainean emphasis in his definition of American literature as "the product of our race and of our soil" (p. 9). Like earlier historians, he viewed American humor as our distinctly native literary mode. Cairns defined American literature as the expression of American life, and the other writers commented on the general spirit of our life and literature. The unoriginal consensus was that the American spirit was deeply moral and our literature valuable to the end that it reflected and engendered that morality. To Long, the writers of our first centuries were especially valuable in encouraging a "deeper love and veneration for America" (p. vi). Metcalf and Burton agreed that American literature advanced patriotism and encouraged moral growth in the young reader. Stanton underscored the "general excellence of moral atmosphere" in American fiction and predicted that the future American novel would maintain a "sane and optimistic realism" (pp. 238, 240).

Woodberry tried the hardest to describe the precise mixture of native impulses in our literature—the Puritanism in Emerson, Longfellow, and Hawthorne; the American idea in Irving, Cooper, and Bryant; the transplanted, fragmented, and regional characteristics; and the national humor. Indigenous literary qualities of our writers, for Woodberry, included simplicity (p. 195), artistic conscientiousness, and purity (p. 204). And he anticipated Robert Spiller's embracing theory for the cooperative literary history of the 1940s in a conclusion on the romantic spirit of the country: "America was romantic from the first. . . . The spirit of life in America is an incited spirit" (p. 222). Woodberry sensed the power of this spirit in the recent novel and romance, which were casting out previous timidity and imitation and bringing "a closer welding of the literary spirit with the nation, a more perfect union of the people and their writers" (p. 247).

Trent, in his turn, had so little enthusiasm for colonial and Revolutionary writings as literature, despite his high esteem for Tyler and his treatment of these periods, that Trent did not praise them even as a possible source of moral and patriotic inspiration to later Americans. He recognized that the early writing could not be ignored when studying the evolution of our literary history (p. 1), but the concept of national literature and character in these formative years, so intriguing to Wendell and Tyler, held little excitement for Trent. Similarly, he and his *CHAL* editors did not impose on their corps of contributors a working formula of "American" national and aesthetic qualities in any literary period or movement or even encourage them to pursue the question. In his own history, Trent did inquire into some of the national intellectual currents that influenced nineteenth-century writers.

When American literature finally arrived at its latter-day flowering in the "sectional period," Trent acknowledged that transcendentalism was somehow the catalyst for "the greatest spiritual movement and the greatest body of literature" in our history (p. 285). Hawthorne, however, stood isolated within the movement as a solitary genius. (Erskine in the *CHAL*, on the other hand, would place Hawthorne firmly within the frame of transcendentalism.) Trent closed the history at 1865, not with a national literary event created by a distinctly native writer like Whitman (for whom he advocated a favorable verdict from history) but, instead, with Lincoln, and here Trent rose for a first time to fervent appreciation of Americanness. Lincoln epitomized American democratic virtues and American literature's utilitarian and moral function: "As we have seen, the most distinctive note of American literature is its applicability to the needs of a healthy-minded, sound-hearted people" (p. 578). By this criterion, Franklin, Cooper, Longfellow, and Whittier also represented the finest in Trent's American literary tradition to 1865.

Finally, Trent and his contemporaries addressed in variously limited fashion the questions of literature as art in an American literary history—the aesthetic definition of literature, periods, genres, and modes; the formal subtleties within the literary work; and establishing a canon and a literary pantheon. Higginson and Boynton stressed that theirs was a modestly historical sketch of "pure literature," but unlike Wendell, they pressed on to a definition of their term—the pure literary work (quoting Bacon) "'raises the mind and hurries it into sublimity,'" and also expresses ideas dynamically "in continuous and symmetrical form" (pp. 5, 6). Woodberry referred to pure or polite literature "in the narrower sense" but preferred to define literature in its highly serious moral power "to lift the thoughts of men, to educate the emotions, to shape character towards ideal ends, to exalt and to console, and always to minister to the spirit in its walk on earth" (pp. 31, 8–9). The great works of Burton's *Literary Leaders* possessed artistic quality, but, like Woodberry, he required, as well, "intellectual and moral significance" (p. v). Cairns valued American writing mainly as "an expression of American life" and excused himself from the bother of aesthetic scrutiny by announcing summarily: "There are few American writings that require careful analysis and merit intensive study as masterpieces" (p. v). Trent agreed that, up to the nineteenth century at any rate, American literature was hopelessly without "intrinsic aesthetic value" (p. 1), and he apologized for the inevitable space he must allow it. The other historians made no pass at an aesthetic definition of literature, and the entire group seemed unaware of the aesthetic distinctions that characterize literary movements, genres, and modes.

These literary historians were expectably as helpless as Tyler, Richardson, and Wendell in literary explication. Indeed, only

Cairns made any effort to consider literary style and method, but he was at a loss to explain how technique renders the aesthetic results. He referred to a stylistic "charm that cannot be analyzed," characters that "always seem essentially real," or Irving's intrinsic merit "of style rather than of content, though the two are inseparable" (pp. 319, 173). His approach to poetry was to remark on a literary trait and illustrate it, without explication, by quoting a passage. (Because Burton had more patently designed a combination history-with-selections, he quoted all of Whitman's "Pioneers" and "Lilacs" before he appended a typical comment about unspecified "definitely rhythmical approaches" [p. 293].) With fiction, Cairns paraphrased the plot and assigned the story an arbitrary epithet or two. In a single page on Melville, Cairns paraphrased *Moby-Dick* in two sentences and then concluded, "The conception of the story is a powerful one, but it is not adequately sustained." Moreover, the perceptive reader would detect in that work a change in Melville's art, a "deterioration of his style" (p. 369). Trent was an equally representative critic of the time, similarly struggling to argue aesthetic distinctions but with no clear criteria and method at his disposal. And so, like Wendell, Trent lapsed into impressionistic judgments of "imaginative power" here, "a true poetic note" there; or else he cited what some other critics had said or where certain authorities had agreed.

This impulse to literary judgment became most interesting when the historians nominated the figures who seemed in the first decade of our century the major authors of American literature. None of these historians was enthusiastic about the colonial writers, despite the obligatory praise of Tyler's volumes. For the nineteenth century, Sears was conventional in his nod to the eminence of the New England group but also surprisingly enthusiastic over the unconventional Whitman, who allowed us relief from "over-refinement, artificiality, and dilettantism in art or life" (p. 356) as we saw him steadily grow into a major poet. Higginson and Boynton admitted the difficulty of judging the present, or past, literary artist, but they did not hesitate to place Whitman at the bottom: "Of all our poets, he is really the least simple, the most meretricious" (p. 233). Freneau was their "first true American poet" (p. 36), Franklin "the first great writer in America" (p. 56), Brown the "first writer of imaginative prose" in America (p. 77), but Hawthorne the "greatest imaginative prose writer" (p. 185). Melville was not mentioned, but Emily Dickinson (whom Higginson had befriended) received a page of ambiguous praise.

Woodberry, in late pages, devised his pantheon of "great writers in pure literature" in America: Bryant, Irving, Cooper, Emerson, Hawthorne, Longfellow, Lowell, and Poe (p. 203). Pointedly inferior were the prewar Southerners and postwar Westerners. Burton's was a more limited gallery: Irving, Poe, Emerson, and Hawthorne. Collaborators in Stanton's *Manual* summarized the received opinions of excellence, though Stanton rather daringly concluded that "we have no supremely great novelists" and that "American poetry now seems moribund" (pp. 238, 321). Cairns's praise was even more sparse, as expected after the belittling comments in his preface. Among his negative judgments, he deemed Mark Twain, in particular, to be overrated: "Little of his ambitiously serious work appears to have the elements of permanency, and it is probable that with change of taste his purely funny writings will seem less and less interesting" (p. 452).

Trent, too, discussed reputations and critical debate, showing that he had completed his secondary-source homework assiduously but not dependently. And not least, he wrote with an occasional vigor that recalls Tyler and Wendell. Excepting Woodberry and Higginson, Trent was the least pedagogical of the historians discussed here, no doubt because he had not designed his literary history with the school trade in view. Trent's pages often were flavored with tart phrasing and an unwillingness to grant every authority a last word. (Tyler, for example, was plainly mistaken, said Trent, about the iambs in Freneau's poetry.) Because he wrote the history for Appleton when Tyler declined on grounds of ill health and it "was turned over to my less skilful hands," Trent may have aspired to meet the exacting standards of the man he replaced, even to the end of challenging some of Tyler's assumptions and conclusions.[27] Hardly a classic, Trent's American literary history is fully competent, and it reminds us that in those days when American literature was not a fully recognized field for the scholarly specialist, America had well-trained literary scholars who were taking time to read thoroughly in their native literature and trying to frame assessments to benefit students and scholars to come. Not a brilliant literary historian or critic, Trent was as well qualified as any member of the academy to direct the profession's first cooperative literary history. Though Carl Van Doren soon became the quarterback of the *CHAL* team, very likely it was Trent's hand that drafted the original preface to the first volume, for he was the one best acquainted with the work and times of Knapp, Griswold, the Duyckincks, Tyler, Richardson, and Wendell, the trailblazers in these six chapters of retrospective history who strongly contributed to the birth of a profession.

Chapter 9

The *CHAL* (Volume I) Appears

We return to Trent, Van Doren, Erskine, and Sherman in November 1917, almost four years after the *CHAL* was proposed. The public curtain was about to be raised on volume I. For this long delay, we can point to some of the disruptions of wartime, mentioned previously, though America did not declare war on Germany until 6 April 1917. More decisive were the unforeseen difficulties within the academy. After locating the ideal contributors, the editors, especially Van Doren, wrote time-consuming letters to professors who either accepted, declined, defected, or delayed. And when the huge manuscript had been assembled far beyond deadlines, the editorial team was left to harmonize the varied and uneven style and scholarship of these many chapters. Also unexpected was the protracted delay caused by the extensive bibliographies that the editors correctly sensed would supply the impetus for the true beginnings of mature scholarship in American literature. The literary historians in the 1890s and after had drawn on a wealth of materials supplied by American, and some English, publishers: editions, biographies, and critical monographs on the best-known authors. But bibliographies had been limited and inaccurate. For the first time, thanks to the *CHAL* contributors, who were aided in some instances by research assistants, twentieth-century scholars were now about to possess a full and reliable panorama of primary and secondary resources in their nation's literature.

Wendell's bibliography, valuable in 1900, was child's play compared to the hundreds of pages in the *CHAL*, which included a bibliography of bibliographies, anthologies, and literary histories, followed by the original and secondary resources for each chapter. The scholar was now apprised of manuscript holdings in America's special library collections, with manuscript dates included, as well as the availability of these materials in print. Listed for the first time in a single volume, too, were the writings of American authors in the periodicals of their day. And collected works were so conveniently recorded that Percy Boynton (Chicago), the first literary historian to profit from these bibliographies in his *A History of American Literature* (1919), easily noted in his bibliography that the 1843 four-volume edition of Edwards was reprinted nine times until 1881, and that Franklin's collected editions went through eleven printings—English, French, and German—from 1773 to 1905. Boynton merely tallied the data marshalled in this first volume of the *CHAL*.

The bibliographies also showed with special vividness the flurry of post–Civil War publishing of collected editions and monographs that followed the earlier ferment of literary creativity in America. Beyond the sizable editions of Edwards and Franklin, there were more than a thousand volumes. For Irving alone, we had the posthumous twenty-one-volume edition (1860–61), which had been preceded by a sixteen-volume edition (1849–51, 1855) and followed by twelve volumes (1880), twenty-seven volumes (1882), ten volumes (1884), twelve volumes (1887), forty volumes (1897, 1902–03), and twelve volumes (1910). Bryant's *Life and Works* had been assembled in six volumes during the 1880s by his son-in-law and biographer, Parke Godwin. The first collection of Cooper in 1854 ran to thirty-three volumes, and by the end of the century, nearly a dozen more editions had appeared, mostly of comparable size. Melville's sea fiction came out in two four-volume editions near the end of the century. Simms's border romances, first collected in 1859, enjoyed six more editions, usually in seventeen volumes. Emerson was duly served by James Eliot Cabot's Riverside Edition in twelve volumes (1884–93) and son Edward Waldo's Centenary Edition of the same size (1903–04), from which plates also appeared, respectively, for the Standard Library Edition and Autograph Centenary Edition, plus a Concord Edition. The uncollected writings appeared in 1912.

When volume II of the *CHAL* presently appeared, this impressive section on primary works of writers to the Civil War was completed in an additional 225 pages of bibliographies. Again, to cite only the collected editions of American authors now recognized to be the makers of American literature, Thoreau had his posthumous Riverside Edition of eleven volumes (1894) as well as two editions of twenty volumes (fourteen volumes being the journals) in 1906—the Manuscript and the Walden (without manuscript insertions) editions—and a Pocket Edition of eleven volumes in 1915. The Thoreau bibliography was supplied by Mark Van Doren, who wrote his master's thesis on Thoreau (1915) under Sherman at Illinois. (Houghton Mifflin published it in 1916.) Hawthorne's Illustrated Library Edition (1871–76) in twelve volumes was the first of some eighteen editions in the next thirty years, several of them over twenty volumes long.

Only the Longfellow bibliography, signed by H. W. L. Dana, was imprecise and erratic, so that we do not realize, for example, that the 1886 edition in eleven volumes was the Riverside Edition that became, with the addition of brother Samuel Longfellow's *Life*, the Standard Library Edition of *The Works* in fourteen volumes (1886–91). Neither was the illustrated Craigie Edition of 1904 listed. And there was more in the horn of plenty for literary scholars to come: The Standard Library Editions—formed from the Riverside Edition plates with an accompanying biography—served Whittier (nine volumes, with the *Life* by S. T. Pickard, 1894), Holmes (fifteen volumes, with the *Life* by J. T. Morse, 1896), and Lowell (thirteen volumes, with the *Life* by H. E. Scudder, 1902). Poe received the full treatment at last in the Stedman–Woodberry edition (ten volumes, 1894–95), the Virginia Edition of J. A. Harrison (seventeen volumes, 1902), and C. F. Richardson's ten-volume edition for Putnam (1902). And there were the huge recent editions of Stowe, Whitman, and others listed in the final installment of the *CHAL* in 1921.

Besides the standard biographies already cited, American scholarship in the decades between the wars had been graced by two monograph series of lasting value. Wendell's debts to the American Men of Letters series have been mentioned. The *CHAL* included, beyond 1900, additional titles: Woodberry's Hawthorne (1902), Higginson's Longfellow (1902), George R. Carpenter's Whittier (1903), Rollo Ogden's Prescott (1904), and Edwin Mims's Lanier (1905). The high quality of this series is still recognized today, and the volumes, in fact, were reissued in the 1980s by Chelsea publishers. The *CHAL* omissions included only studies of lesser interest, like O. B. Frothingham's George Ripley (1882), Henry Beers's N. P. Willis (1885), and Henry D. Sedgwick's Parkman (1904). In addition, the *CHAL* listed American authors in the English Men of Letters series, brought out after the turn of the century by the New York branch of Macmillan. (Henry James's classic *Hawthorne* in 1879 had also received New York publication in 1880.) The English Men of Letters series now included Higginson's Whittier (1902), Harry T. Peck's Prescott (1905), William A. Bradley's Bryant (1905), Woodberry's Emerson (1907), and Carpenter's Whitman (1909).

Reviewers of the *CHAL*, and scholars in the next two decades, agreed that the bibliographies earned a right to their extended space. What ballooned the *CHAL* less excusably was the editors' inability to define the limits of their history. This failure gave them a fair amount of unexpected labor, frustration, and delay. In the opening paragraph of their preface in 1917, prior to the sur-

vey of nineteenth-century precursors, the editors proudly announced their history to be "on a larger scale than any of its
predecessors which have carried the story from colonial times to
the present generation." This largeness was due to the editors'
concept of literary history as an expression of national life "rather
than a history of *belles-lettres* alone." The editors appeared sufficiently uneasy about this definition to return to it at the end of
the preface. Readers with "a taste and judgment unperverted by
the current finical and transitory definitions of literature" would
understand why Edwards, Franklin, *The Federalist*, travel writing, memoirs, and oratory all belonged in a generous literary
history of the American mind and the "national temper." Not addressed was the question of aesthetic worth, in or out of belles
lettres, nor the guiding principles of causation, continuity, and
recurrence in literary history.

In volume I, no "finical" subtlety could be charged to the editors in their definition of literary eras. As in so many of the previous literary histories we have looked at, these were political
periods: "Colonial and Revolutionary Literature" and then "Early
National Literature" (to be continued as "Early National," part II,
and followed by a "Later National Literature" of three parts in
the subsequent volumes). Nor was there a subtlety of literary–
historical development in the chapters within these periods. In
the first era, More's Edwards and Sherman's Franklin aside, these
were survey chapters with little effort given to evolution of separate forms and styles or the general development of an American
mind and sensibility. The chapters mainly read like isolated essays in a collection printed without benefit of transitions and
continuity, though an obvious editorial rationale was implied in
the progress from "The Puritan Divines, 1620–1720" by Parrington to the "Edwards" by More and thence to "Philosophers
and Divines, 1720–1789" by Riley. (For full names and academic
addresses of contributors previously mentioned, see Chapter 2
above.)

Among the contributors who offered a rudimentary literary
history of their subject, Tucker in "The Beginnings of Verse,
1610–1808" set out virtually alone to formulate a version of
genre development:

> The two centuries that cover the beginnings of American poetry
> may be divided into three periods. The first period is that of the early
> colonial verse which begins in 1610 with the publication of Rich's
> ballad on the settlement of Jamestown and ends with the seven-
> teenth century. With 1700 begins the second period, which is one of

transition in purpose, subject, and style. The third period, which is marked by the beginnings of nationalism, opens with the passage of the Stamp Act in 1765 and closes with the publication of Bryant's *Embargo* in 1808. (I, 150)

Suggestion of period contours or causal forces could hardly be more elementary. In the three submovements of early American poetry, Tucker discovered utilitarian and religious purposes, followed by a literary impulse from Waller and Pope, and finally the influences of political confrontation with England after 1765. Tucker then ventured into the next main period of the larger literary history, "Early National Literature," with a discussion of the Hartford group and Freneau, but not Bryant. But when Leonard continued that story five chapters into the second main period with "Bryant and the Minor Poets," no transitional linking occurred between Tucker's configurations and Leonard's new era of Bryant. It is not necessary to belabor the point with endless examples. Volume I was eighteen chapters of miscellaneous literary history that were everywhere in need of guiding principles of national literary evolution.

Several chapters can be read without condescension, however, for insights still valuable these many decades later. For example, after skimming the colonial travelers by Winship and the equally perfunctory chapter on colonial historians by Bassett, we arrive at Parrington's "The Puritan Divines," a stunning essay from his own literary history in progress. He was already writing with verve and confidence, aided by a clearly developed point of view on the intellectual and political importance of colonial literature. In twenty-five pages, he selected nine ministers for their political significance, sketched an old-world historical background, admired the intellectual vigor even of the Presbyterian conservative theocrats, and reserved his warmest praise for the divines who were stewards of a Congregational democracy in their religion and politics—John Wise, Roger Williams, and Thomas Hooker. Through it all, Parrington generated an urgency by means of his extraordinary style. The sentences, varied in length and syntactic design, were charged with lively and seemingly spontaneous imagery. Roger Williams was "an arch-rebel in a rebellious generation, the intellectual barometer of a world of stormy speculation and great endeavor" (I, 43). Arrogant and autocratic until he was at last "shorn of power," Increase Mather "sat down in old age to eat the bread of bitterness" (I, 49). The vanity of son Cotton "was daily fattened by the adulation of silly women and praise of foolish men," and while he censored the press to prevent "the pollution of the people," the credulous old zealot finally became the sorriest victim of the age when "the insularity of his thought and judgment grew into a disease" (I, 50, 51). (The aptness of Parrington's varied imagery will be our subject in an upcoming chapter.) The present-day student unable to respond to the colonial era can well begin with Parrington's succinct chapter in the *CHAL* and then move forward to his monumental *Main Currents in American Thought* ten years after—or backward to that other masterly stylist, Moses Coit Tyler. As a bonus, Parrington offered forty pages of primary and secondary bibliography on his nine church figures.

The case of Parrington strikingly poses the dilemma in a cooperative literary history: How do the editors avoid the effect of chapters bumping along with a diversity of style and outlook? Following Parrington's chapter, for example, came Paul Elmer More (on Edwards), the conservative friend of Irving Babbitt and the New Humanists and surely a strange academic bedfellow to continue the Puritan discussion after the liberal Parrington. More was predictably offended by the undisciplined side of Edwards's nature exhibited in the unrestrained "wave of superheated emotion" during the Great Awakening that Edwards considered valid religious inspiration. More underlined here the unpleasant "resemblance between the position of Edwards and the position of the apologists of the romantic movement in literature" (I, 62). (Parrington, by contrast, would regret in his *Main Currents* that Edwards could not fulfill his prophetic calling as "a transcendental emancipator.") More cared no more than Parrington for the Predestinarians but objected to this theological determinism not for its social and political restraints but on the private psychological ground that it undermined the freedom of human will and individual restraint. The gloves-off, rhetorical vigor of Parrington's style also contrasted with More's gracefully controlled polemic against Edwards on cause and necessity, will and evil.

More returned fourteen chapters later to write the chapter on Emerson, a fortunate editorial decision in the interest of interpretive continuity between the foremost spokesmen of two major epochs in New England. Unfortunately, just before More's Emerson came a chapter on "Transcendentalism" by Harold C. Goddard (Swarthmore), who was far more enthusiastic than More over the Emersonian liberation. (Goddard wrote his Columbia dissertation in 1908, "Studies in New England Transcendentalism," under Trent.) As he did with Edwards, More again adopted the unrelenting perspective of a latter-day anti-romantic humanist. He compared Edwards and Emerson as churchmen who abandoned their parishes over the question of the communion ceremony (though Emerson's departure was amicable and voluntary) and tried to achieve an "emotional realization" of dogma and ceremony. Emerson, however, became the evangelist of a new moral freedom that brought his New England followers "from theological dogmatism to romantic liberty" (I, 356, 357). More quoted approvingly from his mentor at Harvard, Charles Eliot Norton, who had listened in dismay on an ocean crossing in 1873 when his shipmate Emerson expounded a fatalistic optimism, with an "indifference to moral considerations, and to personal responsibilities" (I, 354). More traced part of this failing to the early influence of aunt Mary Moody Emerson, whose "pure but dislocated enthusiasms" pushed Emerson to "his weaker inclinations" when he should have summoned a strength of will to resist them (I, 350).

For More, the legacy of Emerson's time was a dubious compound of "rarity and beauty," with the man himself remaining a radiant messenger of hope and "assurance of present happiness"; it was also a legacy limited by his facile treatment of "the dualism of experience": "He accepts it a trifle too jauntily, is reconciled to its existence with no apparent pang" (II, 361, 362). More admired Emerson, of course, where he proposed checks and restraints on emotion and behavior. We are not to forget that Emerson anchored the freely floating symbolic truth of his *Nature* in the lesson of discipline (I, 352). Despite his romantic spontaneity, Emerson insisted on the moral imperatives of character, and he never confused "spiritual aspiration" with the "sicklier lusts of the flesh." He inherited the severe impulse of New England to discover her God, so that at its best, said More, "Emersonianism may be defined as romanticism rooted in Puritan divinity" (I, 358; this amalgam Barrett Wendell had also proposed). Similarly, Emerson was strongest as a poet in those moments when he imposed the discipline of the epigrammatic quatrain on his "spiritual ejaculations" (I, 358).

Though More made his chapter on Emerson coherent through a definable outlook and distinctive style, the effect became rather schizophrenic for the reader who had just completed Goddard's lead chapter treating transcendentalism as the American consummation of the great post-Renaissance "movement for the liberation of humanity." For Goddard, the ideals of Emerson's time envisioned, and partly achieved, the defeat of religious and political tyranny and the triumph of philosophical and literary imagination. Goddard made a temperate defense of Bronson Alcott, Brook Farm, and especially Margaret Fuller. On the intrinsic merit of her *Dial,* with its stimulating pieces on philosophy and art, he was less restrained: "We shall not be likely to overrate its significance in the history of American literature or the importance of the part it played in our literary emancipation" (I, 341). Reciting in a single paragraph the alleged weaknesses of transcendentalism—a rarefied idealism, paralyzing fatalism, the "atrophy of will"—Goddard countered with the strengths of this varied, complex, and fruitful movement. Unlike More, Goddard viewed transcendentalism to be free of sentiment and anarchy, owing to a "dash of Yankee practicality in the midst of the Oriental mysticism, a sturdy Puritan pugnacity and grasp of fact underneath its serenest and most Olympian detachments . . ." (I, 347). Thoreau, Parker, and Alcott were "no mere dreamers" but men of action impelled by a hereditary Puritan character, and their prophet Emerson voiced the enduring spirit of Edwards, "the innate idealism and individualism of the New England mind" (I, 347, 348). More then entered the *CHAL* with his less encouraging view of this merely "transient experiment in civilization" (I, 349). For all their disagreement, More and Goddard were equally provocative on the spiritual continuities between Edwards's and Emerson's America.

Greater harmony of historical approach and outlook wedded the two chapters on early nineteenth-century fiction, for both were written by Carl Van Doren, whose diligent homework we have previously traced. In "Fiction I: Brown, Cooper," he gave lucid and succinct accounts of the English backgrounds for the post–Revolutionary novel before Brown, and handled judiciously the inevitable comparison between Godwin and Brown and, after a barren interval of some two decades, between Scott and Cooper. Biographical summary and plot analyses characterized Van Doren's approach to both novelists, though when he advanced to "Fiction II: Contemporaries of Cooper," he proposed the genre distinction between the novel and romance, placing *Moby-Dick* in the latter category during a brief discussion of Melville that was superior to anything that had yet appeared in American scholarship. Even so, Simms received a fuller treatment, for Van Doren had subordinated Melville to the company of aspiring regional fictioneers of limited stature: Beverley Tucker, James Hall, Timothy Flint, Mrs. Child, and others. Van Doren concluded that Cooper was, at last, our "one novelist of first rank" in a period of fiction that he dated and defined as follows: "It is mere coincidence that Cooper was born in the year which produced *The Power of Sympathy* and that when he died *Uncle Tom's Cabin* was passing through its serial stage, and yet the limits of his life mark almost exactly the first great period of American fiction" (I, 324, 307). Such historical irrelevance recalls the more desperate pages of Barrett Wendell and leaves us with no conclusions regarding Cooper's national characteristics or the evolution of his thought and style.

Neither was it clear what literary values Van Doren had in mind that rendered Cooper our earliest novelist of "first rank." Near the end of their preface, Van Doren and his fellow editors stated that they intended to "enlarge the spirit of American literary criticism" beyond strictly aesthetic considerations, and they rather foolishly termed this larger spirit within and beyond belles lettres "more energetic and masculine" (I, x). While this vague statement of purpose indicated an editorial laxity that was amply reflected in Van Doren's chapters, some of the other contributors were surprisingly attentive to the requirement of literary art in chapters that fall well outside traditional belles lettres.

Cook discussed eighteenth-century newspapers and magazines with an eye alert not only to distinguished journalistic writing but also to literary advertising and fillers, poetic contributions, and echoes of English literary influence. MacDonald also attended to literary criteria in "American Political Writing, 1760–1789," though the discussion was less than expert. The opening sentence of "Travellers and Observers, 1763–1846" by Lane Cooper (Cornell) was a model of proper emphasis for a literary history: "The literature of travel, fresh, varied, and cosmopolitan, doubtless owes its principal charm to its effect upon the sense of wonder, and hence in the last analysis is to be understood in its bearing upon imagination and poetic art; but its relation to history and geography is not superficial" (I, 185). Major Putnam referred to Irving's imaginative force of characterization and narrative even in an historical work like *The Life of Washington*. And Goddard related the religious impulses and ideas of transcendentalism to their corresponding expression in the literary works of the major and lesser figures in the movement.

Among these contributors who insisted on literary criteria for selecting works in their chapters, the demand did not ensure that the discussion itself would then illuminate the literary form and style of the authors. The groping efforts at literary analysis that we have noticed in the previous literary histories reappeared in the *CHAL*. In regard to generic structures, MacDonald referred to the original and "attractive literary form" of John Dickinson's *Letters from a Farmer* and judged the form of the eighty-five *Federalist* essays "incomparably superior" to all the other political writings, but MacDonald never defined the form he presumably had in mind (I, 132, 148). Writers of the belles lettres chapters were somewhat more helpful. Quinn in "The Early Drama, 1756–1860" distinguished nine types of drama before the Civil War. On the American essay, Whicher saw in N. P. Willis a Romantic flourish and mixture that broke with the "smooth, dry, elegant" Addisonian essay (I, 242), while several numbers of the senior Dana's *The Idle Man* "illustrate the ease with which the periodical essay might merge with the then unrecognized short story" (I, 240). Van Doren wrestled with the distinctions of realism, romance, and novel, though with only limited success. Even More, concurring in Matthew Arnold's admiration for Emerson's pithy quatrains, ventured a generic clarification: "They have the cleanness and radiance of the couplets of Simonides. They may look easy, but as a matter of fact the ethical epigram is an extremely difficult *genre,* and to attain this union of gravity and simplicity requires the nicest art" (I, 359).

The contributors to volume I remind us of the limits of academic criticism, too, in their inability to elucidate their critical opinions with close textual analysis. Unlike the single-author histories in previous decades, the cooperative literary history, when written by a committee of independent scholars with no real consonance of critical method, can become a veritable nightmare of diverse and uncoordinated interpretations. The *CHAL* is our first example in America of this peril. Ironically, the very absence of critical precision among the contributors may have allowed the *CHAL* one of its few sources of unity. Most of the critical pronouncements were continuously impressionistic. At the extreme were peremptory judgments of an author's general artistic ability. Riley passed from Charles Chauncy and Jonathan Mayhew to the "far higher literary skill" of Connecticut's Samuel Johnson (I, 81), but the ingredients of Johnson's "sheer literary skill" (I, 84) were not explained.

Tucker dispatched our earliest rhymesters to oblivion without examining the evidence for his verdict. He announced that Michael Wigglesworth "had no real poetry in him; at no period and under no condition would he have been a poet" (I, 154). The Connecticut Wits, for all their vaunted independence, betrayed "in every line" their dependence on English models (I, 164). Anne Bradstreet, though interesting and pleasing, was no poet: "Perhaps in more fortunate times she might have written poetry" (I, 154). Lane Cooper, likewise, sensed that William Bartram was "not without poetical imagination" (I, 196), but Cooper was unable to explain its nature and expression. Throughout Irving, Putnam asserted, the author "always succeeds in coming into the closest sympathy with his environment. He has the *artist's touch* in the ability to reproduce the atmosphere in which the scenes of his stories are placed" (I, 254, italics added). Leonard judged Bryant "not one of the world's master-poets, because he was not pre-eminently endowed with intellectual intensity and imaginative concentration" (I, 275), to which we might assent had Leonard earlier demonstrated these shortcomings in some of the works. Van Doren's final assessment of Cooper's enormous vogue was equally vaporous, especially in the final two epithets: "Certainly it is difficult to explain why, with all his faults of clumsiness, prolixity, conventional characterization, and ill temper, he has been the most widely read American author, unless he is to be called one of the most impressive and original" (I, 306). Van Doren, however, had earlier commented on Cooper's literary manner with some clarity. He gave us, in fact, the nearest version of modern literary explication to appear in this first volume.

Comments on more specific aspects of literary tone and style, even when focused on individual selections, also recall the impressionistic vein of what was then passing in the academy for literary criticism. Various works carried an alleged power, charm, irony, levity, or sprightliness, but how this tone emanated from literary style was never revealed. John Smith's *True Relation* was "direct, vivid, and generally simple" (I, 16), William Bradford's *History* was written in a "direct and simple style" (I, 21), John Winthrop's style in his *History* was not "so interesting" as Bradford's (I, 22), and Samuel Smith's in *History of New Jersey* was "heavy" (I, 27). Edwards owned "a vividness of style uncommon at any age" (I, 57). John Adams was singularly "verbose and careless" (I, 147), but Jefferson, even in the "generally dry" *Notes on the State of Virginia,* was given to "occasional flights in a loftier style" (I, 201, where an illustrative passage was then supplied without comment).

Finally, William MacDonald made this elaborate, unargued claim for the literary preeminence of Revolutionary State Papers that flowed in the wake of the Stamp Act:

> Nowhere else in American literature does the peculiar gift of formal expression and logical exposition in politics show itself on so large a scale or in so great a cause, and in no country in the world has such expression moved so long and so consistently on a high plane, or voiced itself with so much dignity, condensed forcefulness, or formal beauty. (I, 130)

It is well to add that the historian-critics of a nation's entire literature are burdened with multiple obligations to their authors and works. How much close analysis can they allot in order to prove the generalized assessment? This question would remain un-answered even into the 1940s when we find that the profession, by then well beyond the innocence of the *CHAL,* was neverthe-less groping its critical way into a second cooperative literary history.

✷   ✷   ✷

When the first volume of the *CHAL* appeared in November 1917 (priced at $3.50), critical reception from the intellectual commu-nity was generally appreciative but not enthusiastic. (The uni-versities did not yet possess the journals to register an academic response to each arriving installment of the *CHAL.*) No doubt some critics were waiting to see the larger history to come. The earliest notice was probably that of the *Boston Evening Tran-script*. The reviewer created interest in the new history by para-phrasing a number of the chapters, though he offered no critical estimate. Several weeks later, however, he or she (or another critic) returned to the volume to comment mainly on Van Doren's two chapters on the early fiction. After quoting and paraphrasing from the paragraphs on Simms, the reviewer concluded: "This is one of many brief and acute studies of literary personalities and influences" to be found in this new assessment of our literature. The *New York Times* gave early and generous space to the first volume. After surveying the scope of the eighteen chapters, the critic specifically commended Parrington on the Puritan divines, Sherman's Franklin, and Goddard's transcendentalism, and re-garded the volume "a book of the utmost importance." George Putnam was upset, however, that the *Times* critic, and allegedly other readers, wondered why "The Star-Spangled Banner" and "My Country 'tis" were not mentioned in Tucker's chapter on early American verse. No doubt Putnam suspected that Trent was in part responsible for the rather sardonic references to early Americanism and patriotic zeal. "I should be glad to have a word from one of our editors," Putnam wrote Van Doren, "which would enable me to answer the inquiries concerning the ground for this omission, or rather these two omissions."[1]

The *Outlook* was not so convinced as the *Times* that this was a work of utmost importance and granted the book only a single, descriptive paragraph. Three other reviews, spaced several weeks apart and by no means thoroughgoing, are interesting to com-pare for their comments on editorial approach and for their judg-ment of distinguished chapters. The *Dial,* the *Literary Digest,* and the *American Review of Reviews* all noted the editors' dis-avowal of an aesthetic principle of selectivity, but none challenged it. The reviewers for the *Dial* and the *Review of Reviews* agreed that American literary history in the first two centuries should be written to reveal the necessary foundation or super- structure of intellectual history. Both anticipated in subsequent pages an emphasis on belles lettres, and the *Dial* "would wel- come a smaller measure of compilation and a larger manifes- tation of the critical and the appreciatory." For their favorite contributors, the *Dial* selected, as had the *Times*, Sherman and Goddard; the *Literary Digest* liked the four chapters on the Pu- ritans (by Winship, Bassett, Parrington, and More) but saved its laurels for George Putnam's "delightful" essay on Irving (a higher estimate, we recall, than Trent and Van Doren allowed Putnam). In the *Review of Reviews*, highest praise went to Sherman's Frank- lin and More's Emerson. Finally, the two hundred pages of bib- liography were exhaustive to the *Literary Digest* but merely laborious to the *Dial* (while the reviewer for the *Springfield Republican* wished the bibliographies had been even more comprehensive).[2]

The *Nation* reviewed volume I in February 1918, rather tardily in view of the critic's opening assertion that the appearance of a full-scale American literary history at last, after more than a dozen political histories, was an occasion truly "momentous." But this critic was only moderately happy with the result and hoped for the greater success of the next two volumes. Only one contributor (not specified) was an avowed specialist in Ameri- can literature; hence, one understood the omission of Morton's *New England Canaan* and the slighting of the literary effects in Nathaniel Ward, Madam Knight, and Judge Sewell. While he could not praise any chapter, the reviewer tartly criticized the two on early poetry. Tucker's "Beginnings of Verse" was "very dif- ficult to fathom," since his defensive praise of these early verses alternated with unsparing rebuke for their amateurish failure. The chapter was disappointing in its "carelessness as to fact and dogmatic certainty as to matters of opinion" (and the reviewer supplied examples). Leonard in "Bryant and Minor Poets," by contrast, had gone to the "extreme of laudation" with an enthu- siasm "indiscriminate and blurred." Finally, the bibliography, though of immense value, was at times disproportionate to chap- ter length (Parrington's was cited) and the index was both slender and poorly cross-referenced.

The *Nation*'s qualified conclusion: "It is ungracious work to carp and nibble at a noteworthy undertaking; but unevenness of execution, a lack of unity in method, and a certain disregard of proportion mar a book which for the most part is a distinguished

piece of writing and editing." One recipient of the *Nation*'s carp-
ing and nibbling found the review distinctly ungracious. Leonard
soon wrote a self-justifying letter to Van Doren. He had approached Bryant, he explained, through a method that would
allow critical evaluation. He was "much chagrined" for everyone—himself, the editors, even Bryant—after reading the *Nation*. The review "was as a whole, I thought, superficial, smart, &
schematic, and I suspect—with reference to me—personally
hostile. Who is the gentleman?"[3]

Finally came the review from the London *Times Literary Supplement,* its tardiness partly compensated for by generous length.
The estimate was somewhat more gracious than the *Nation*'s:
This history "would be difficult to better so far as judgment, moderation, balance, and a complete absence of 'Stars and Stripes
spread-eaglism' are concerned." The chauvinistic exception
noted (splendid irony, we suspect, for Trent and Van Doren) was
Major Putnam's "aggressively patriotic" treatment of Irving. Van
Doren's two chapters on the fiction were merely conscientious
and rather marred by too much praise for little-remembered
books—including *Moby-Dick* (!). More's chapter on Emerson
was the most striking. The reviewer agreed that Emerson was
"'the outstanding figure of American letters,'" though his was
the inspired voice of elevated morality rather than of a philoso-
pher or literary artist. The *Times Literary Supplement* critic welcomed the prospect of the next volume, hoping that figures like
Hawthorne and Poe might awaken the authors to some livelier
writing than in this initial volume, which he finally labeled a
"singularly moderate and non-provocative cyclopedia of American criticism."[4]

Chapter 10

And Then Volume II

The reviewers and readers who anticipated an imminent volume II were in for a frustrated delay of many months. In the previous August (1917), the editors were reading proofs of the last four chapters of the twenty-four that comprised the "Early National Literature" period. (Chapters 10–24 of that period began volume II, followed by the first seven chapters of "Later National Literature.") Van Doren had sent them to Trent, who, in turn, delivered them to Erskine, meanwhile writing to Van Doren a report invaluable for our knowledge of the editorial procedures. Trent had his fears that the "Newspapers, 1775–1860" by Frank W. Scott (Illinois), though "distinctly competent," was "too sectional— really too *New Yorky*" in his ignoring the Southern journalists. The "Divines and Moralists, 1783–1860" by Samuel Wolff (Columbia) "is one of the best we have had," said Trent, though he wished the pages on Timothy Dwight and Henry Ward Beecher had more precision. He also wondered if Wolff should not delete his implication that America's Protestants never "wrote anything worth while in divinity or ethics," however true this might be. Trent was also concerned that Wolff had left out Orestes Brownson. Was he present in another chapter? Trent asked Van Doren. "If he is not, we shall have the R.C.s [Roman Catholics] on our shoulders, and *entre nous*," Trent acidly reflected, "I guess he was worth as much as any of them, i.e. 0."

Among other pages in proof, Trent termed the chapter on Lowell by Ashley Thorndike (Columbia) "excellent" as it stood but was less cordial to the "Writers of Familiar Verse" by his colleague and war adversary, Brander Matthews. The treatment of Holmes seemed "thin but sufficiently readable and competent," though what was one to do about Matthews's having elevated H. C. Bunner's work above Eugene Fields's? "B. M.'s devotion to his friend must stand, but we can probably later get in something that will serve as a corrective," said Trent, mindful that Matthew's public reputation alone made him valuable to the *CHAL*. Finally, Trent looked ahead to filling a gap in the history— on "books and classes of books—e.g., church histories that got shoved aside in various chapters and fall, as it were, between them." His zeal for completeness, which partly caused the delays in publication, would be satisfied in subsequent chapters like "Later Theology" and "Popular Bibles."[1]

In response to Trent, Van Doren apparently convinced Wolff to revise and even pare his chapter. Erskine wrote Van Doren some two weeks later that he and Trent considered it "mighty fine" in its "shorn state." But they were concerned that he "ignores Roman Catholic and Episcopal names" (and Brownson never appeared), as well as Phillips Brooks and Bishop Coxe. Along with these comments, Erskine also sent Van Doren two packages of proofs.[2]

In the summer of 1917, the editors were also recruiting contributors whose chapters would not appear until the final volumes in the spring of 1921. In September, Trent argued for the nonacademic Montrose Moses over Arthur H. Quinn to write the "Drama, 1860–1918," even though Quinn, we would suppose, could bring some continuity of genre history from his earlier chapter on American drama to 1860. Conceptual integrity, however, continued to be of minor editorial concern, and Trent wrote to Van Doren regarding Moses and Quinn:

> On the score of securing the non-academic writer I prefer M., provided you are satisfied as to his competence. The only book of his I ever examined was an early one which was thin. Liberality as to race is also desirable, and as Q., I have been told, has recently poached on M.'s preserves, I incline all the more to M. But use your judgment.[3]

Volume II in subsequent reprintings carried an original publication date of January 1918, two months after volume I appeared. But the preface was dated 1 May 1918. By that time, the editors and publisher realized that a two-volume history was out of the question and as they expressed it in that preface, "the abundance of the material submitted and the importance of having the biography [bibliography] comprehensive and practically complete, made it necessary for the publishers to extend the work to four." They had also decided which living writers to include: "Certain contemporaries who before 1900 had written notable books and who have exerted important influence in our literary history" would appear in the later chapters (II, iii).

Volume II failed to appear in 1918, but the editorial correspondence does not reveal any impatience over the delay. Circumstances surrounding the Armistice may have caused Putnam to hold the volume from the market. In the summer of 1918, Van Doren and Trent were happily considering additional chapters for a fuller history, now that Putnam had granted them extra volumes. Trent suggested a "short chapter in American Bibliography . . . with incidental remarks on the growth of American libraries," another on American scientists, and he endorsed Van Doren's idea for an "Aborigines chapter." Of the three, only this last chapter, written by Mary Austin for volume IV, would be included. And so in the summer of 1918, with the entire history virtually mapped out and most of the participants committed, Trent exulted: "The *total contents* is very impressive, and, as we should not have dared branch out so with *two* volumes, I think we have reason to congratulate ourselves on the way things have turned out."[4]

Volume II continued the "Early National Literature" period after the previous nine chapters of the period had concluded volume I, the final chapter being More's essay on Emerson. The fifteen additional chapters were designated "Early National Literature: Part II," but with no intention of arguing a separate literary movement. The opening chapter on Thoreau by MacMechan suggested no transition from More's previous chapter on Emerson. Nor did the editors provide any literary–historical continuity from volume I, let alone among the fifteen individual chapters here. Five single-author chapters on Thoreau, Hawthorne (Erskine), Longfellow (Trent), Whittier (William M. Payne, our earlier friend from the Chicago *Dial*), and Poe (Campbell) were separate beads on a string, followed by four chapters perhaps implicitly related by prewar political and historical interest: "Publicists and Orators, 1800–1850" (A. C. McLaughlin) and "Writers on American History, 1783–1850" (Bassett) were followed respectively by "Webster" (Sen. Henry C. Lodge) and "Prescott and Motley" (Ruth Putnam). Then appeared four chapters in random order: "Early Humorists" (Howe), "Magazines, Annuals, and Gift-Books, 1783–1850" (W. B. Cairns, Wisconsin), "Newspapers, 1775–1860" (Scott), and "Divines and Moralists, 1783–1860" (Wolff). Finally were two chapters, related but curiously placed at the end, "Writers of Familiar Verse" (Matthews) and "Lowell" (Thorndike).

Volume II, as we previously realized, also picked up the initial seven chapters once intended for volume III. They introduced the second post-Revolutionary period of our literature, designated by the editors "Later National Literature: Part II," which they began with Whitman and followed with Civil War poets, presumably adopting that war as a historical watershed of sorts in our national literature. This "Later National" period would complete the *CHAL*, being subtitled Part II and Part III in volumes III and IV, respectively. These parts again had no real significance as literary history, though rather casually they did reflect chronology.

As in the first volume, we learn of the historical evolution of forms and modes, and of the American mind, spirit, and sensibility, chiefly by extracting and patching together for ourselves the scattered comments within and among the quite isolated chapters. MacMechan, relying on Lowell's famous condemnation, cited the adverse influence of Emerson on Thoreau's oracular sentences and, in the poetry, on what Lowell punned as "'worsification'" (I, 4, 5). Trent remarked on Longfellow's shaping of legend and history from colonial and Revolutionary times; Cairns stressed that magazines, gift books, and annuals helped literary forms evolve by giving authors a generous hearing; Wolff suggested a continuity of literary Calvinism transmitted from Edwards to Mark Hopkins to Harriet B. Stowe; and Matthews perceived "the fortunate influence of Hawthorne in the treatment of the abnormal heroine" in Holmes's *Elsie Venner* (I, 232).

More extended were the valuable comments by Fred L. Pattee on the evolving short story, and he was aided by more than a dozen studies since 1900, which he dutifully listed in the bibliography. He traced the American short story through various stages: the eighteenth-century moralistic tale found in Carey's *Columbian Magazine;* the professional advances made by Irving, Hawthorne, and Poe; the transitional 1850s and 1860s, when a new localized actuality appeared in works by Rose Terry Cooke, Fitz-James O'Brien, and Edward E. Hale; the new scientific method of James (1865–75); the culmination of the genre from 1875 to 1895, as sentimentality and an exaggerated localism challenged the "realistic" school of James and Howells; and since the later 1890s, the popular sensationalism of Jack London, Richard Harding Davis, and O. Henry. Pattee also traced the shifts in content and taste in a concise and judicious essay that stands up well in the company of later studies in short fiction. Typically independent and assertive, he labeled the period between the civil and world wars "The Era of the Short Story" (II, 367) and termed the phenomenon a dubious compliment to the American reader's attention span.

Will D. Howe sketched the growth of native American humor with equal care and even greater concision (eleven pages). Briefly surveying American humor from Nathaniel Ward to the era of Jackson, Howe then described two main streams of indigenous humor: homespun political wisdom and social satire from Seba

Smith's Jack Downing to Dunne's Mr. Dooley; and the varieties of outlandish frontier humor in the forerunners of Mark Twain. But this fine chapter, it seems, was secretly coauthored. Carl Van Doren noted in the margin of a letter from Trent, 30 August 1920, that brother Mark "had completely re-written the chapter on Early Humorists, though it was credited to Will D. Howe, 'the ostensible author.'"

Foreign aspects of "Early National Literature" emerged, likewise, here and there among the chapters, but the reader received no clear sense of the intense debate over the foreign heritage of our national literature in the period, as we have considered it earlier in this study. Among the foreign literary influences noted were English (on Thoreau, Whittier, Holmes, Poe, Harte, and Lowell), French (Henry James), German (Poe and Longfellow), Scandinavian (Longfellow and Whitter), and classical (on Thoreau and Webster). Reciprocal national influence belonged to Poe, whose posthumous fame brought imitators of his poetry and tales, chiefly in England and France; and to Whitman, who enjoyed in his later lifetime a celebrity as poet and sage and became the object of correspondence and pilgrimages of European admirers.

Equally diffuse were the separate insights and partial discussions of an evolving Americanness of mind, spirit, or sensibility in this period of decisive nationalism. After the relative absence of inquiry into the making of an American spirit in volume I, however, we can at least appreciate what now emerged. MacMechan and Erskine treated the tensions of Puritanism in Thoreau and Hawthorne, but the subject did not appear again until ten chapters later, and Wolff did not refer to the earlier discussions. American transcendentalism was properly reemphasized, though ironically, it first reappeared not in Thoreau but in Erskine's subsequent Hawthorne. Erskine argued that Hawthorne was attracted to transcendentalism not for the mysticism but for "its free inquiry, its radicalism, its contact with actual life." Erskine demonstrated that Emersonian themes of self-reliance, compensation, and cosmic optimism provided the central moral problems of Hawthorne's long romances (II, 26). Not again until F. O. Matthiessen's *American Renaissance* (1941) did the goading influence of Emerson on Hawthorne receive this enlightened attention (and Matthiessen, as we have said, did not acknowledge Erskine).

Sprinkled within other chapters were tantalizing suggestions of the American character. In "Publicists and Orators," McLaughlin challenged the claim that Americans had an "incapacity for sustained theorizing, or for prolonged logical discussion" by pointing to the mixture of philosophical idealism and practical legalism in the developing American mind: "Even the unlearned could not speak and think of democracy and its hopes without indulging in visions; they could not discuss the presence of slavery without touching the border of the deepest problems of social order; they could not speak of union or states' rights without entering at least the outer portal of philosophic argument" (II, 70).

Cairns suggested a further American trait, the appetite for the sentimental, which the annuals and gift books of the 1830s both served and whetted. Newspaper editors like James Gordon Bennett of the New York *Herald,* said Frank W. Scott, were cynical of democratic tastes, though C. Alphonso Smith believed that dialect writers after the war gained a popular American audience because the average reader had an informed and genuine sympathy for "how the other half lived" (II, 360). In another vein, Thorndike, writing on Lowell's passion for moral reform, wryly observed, "The American reader should indeed have a special sympathy for this avowal of high purpose, for is not this gospel of reform the better genius of our nation?" Thorndike attributed to Lowell an American temper derived from a native pioneering cockiness, our certainty that we can conquer, rebuild, move on, and forever improve our lot. Morally, we discover new causes to promote, all the while unreflectively imposing our wishes and virtues on others. On Lowell's vaunted expression of an elusive American idea, Thorndike concluded, "If we ever determine what the American idea is, we shall evangelize the world" (II, 250). Finally, in the last chapter of volume II, Algernon Tassin (Columbia) wrote on "Books for Children," partly to show how the characters and actions in these books inculcated in the young reader our national ideals—patriotism, self-reliance, resourcefulness, and moral probity. Also implicit in such publishing activity was adult America's conviction that well-read and well-instructed children are important to the future of a democracy.

In volume II, the editors remained faithful to their broader definition of literature despite the abundance, now, of belles lettres. Some authors of the marginally literary chapters occasionally honored the aesthetic justification of their subject. McLaughlin admitted that the orators, eager for popular approval, addressed a multitude "uncritical in its attitude toward literary form"; but he insisted that literary art triumphed over demagoguery in the best speeches of our age of oratory (II, 71). Lodge treated Webster first and last as a literary figure. Scott did not clearly distinguish literary values from the journalistic, but he argued for a general literary consciousness among the earlier nineteenth-century editors, whose "newspapers owed their character to men of literary tastes and pursuits" (II, 185).

Cairns, however, saw no profit in making close literary distinctions in the early journalism, of drawing "any sharp line between 'literary' magazines and those that were largely religious or scientific" or of evaluating the annuals of the early national period: All had their "especial admirers, and the critic of today hardly need attempt the task of deciding on their respective merits" (II, 160n, 175). Nor did Bassett worry about literary niceties. When he reported that Jared Sparks retired as president of Harvard in 1853 "to do literary work," that is, to work at history, literature became a synonym for writing of any type and worth (II, 117). Erskine adopted a biographical approach to literature, but it reaped aesthetic benefits, for he astutely centered his attention on the instances in Hawthorne's life where "biography aid[s] directly in the understanding of his works" (II, 19). The same virtue could not be claimed for the excessive and unimaginative biography in Campbell's chapter on Poe and Holloway's on Whitman.

Diverse criteria and philosophies of literature, the ever-present danger of the cooperative literary history, emerged in other guises as well in volume II. Should the literary history of a democracy consider authors and works to be important on the basis of their wide popularity, aesthetic thinness notwithstanding? The editors implicitly answered the question by including chapters on oratory, children's stories, and other examples of popular taste. Trent seemed aware of the editorial dilemma in his dual focus on Longfellow. First was the popular "lyric interpreter of the simple thoughts and feelings of an unsophisticated people" and equally popular transmitter of Old and New World legends. The other Longfellow was the serious artist who must face the sterner critical verdict of history. Trent's admirably reserved literary and historical opinion of our people's poet came at the end of a concise ten-page chapter:

> His place is not with the few eminent poets of the world, or even of his century, as the admiration of the mass of his countrymen and the critical lucubrations of some of them might be held to imply; but it is, legitimately and permanently, in the forefront of the small band of important writers in verse and in prose who during the first century of the republic's existence laid firmly and upon more or less democratic lines the foundations of a native literature. (II, 32, 41)

Payne faced similar difficulties with the other popular New England poet, Whittier, but failed to achieve Trent's objective distance. Payne finally argued that while Whittier was probably "third rank" with his careless rhymes, diffuse stanzas, and uncertain voice, such aesthetic criteria must be suspended in assessing the native importance of Whittier's poetry in the passionate years of abolitionism: "It cannot be coldly and critically considered by any one who has had a vital sense of the agonies and exaltations of that critical time" (II, 53).

Payne's claim for Whittier suggested the criterion in volume I that an author be partly judged on the basis of moral engagement with the life of his time. The moralistic approach reappeared in several ways. Wolff concluded his "Divines and Moralists, 1783–1860" with enthusiastic approval of Mark Hopkins's prescient reaction against romantic naturalism and his favoring the truer moral inferences of "a controlling humanism" (II, 223). For a moment, we encounter a rare continuity with More's pages in volume I. Howe gave a different shading to the moral criterion when he praised Northern poets of the Civil War as "workers in the real material of human experience . . . who, though surrounded by much that was crude and raw, petty and vulgar, still had visions and felt pulses throbbing beneath the rude exterior of American life." These morally engaged singers—Lowell, Whittier, Whitman, and lesser poets—contrasted with Longfellow, Bayard Taylor, and the early R. H. Stoddard, who, in their dreams of the past or yearnings for the "land of the Lotos Eaters," were merely aesthetic "practitioners of the poetic art" (II, 276).

The most forceful and individualistic proponent of a nonaesthetic approach to literature in volume II was Fred L. Pattee in "The Short Story." His pioneering classroom work at Penn State in 1895 has been mentioned. Pattee then committed his class notes and lectures to the printed page. In 1896, he entered the thriving market for literary history textbooks with his own *A History of American Literature: With a View to the Fundamental Principles Underlying Its Development, A Text-Book for Schools and Colleges*. At Penn State, he worked under the familiar handicap of limited library resources and achieved much of his research through interlibrary loans from the Library of Congress. As a literary historian, Pattee's fundamental principles included a Tainean national explanation of American mind and spirit (race, milieu, and epoch). To account for the diversity of literary voices within a nation, he added the causal force of personality. Pattee's book was recommended by Tyler and Richardson, well reviewed in the *Nation* (jointly with Brander Matthews's *Introduction to the Study of American Literature*), and soon adopted at more than thirty universities. Four printings were issued in the first year, with a sale of 12,426 copies by July 1903. Pattee reported an eventual market of one-quarter million.[5] In the book, Pattee had discussed later nineteenth-century literary trends and America's preeminence in the short story. In his class preparations, he was venturing, in fact, into the early years of the new century. He realized the need for a literary history of the modern period and was not afraid to judge the living writer.

To that end, Pattee undertook *A History of American Literature Since 1870* (1915). Previously, we have seen that living writers had been mainly off limits in American literature scholarship. "There were no biographies of contemporary writers and few reliable biographical sketches," Pattee wrote years later. Much of the information came to him, then, from time-consuming interviews or correspondence with every prominent living writer.[6] For the modern period, he again relied on Taine to highlight the relation of American life to literature; and Pattee valued artistic personality (or passion, heart, or soul) over the calculations of aesthetic craft. He now insisted, too, that the national period in American literature began in 1870, the prewar literature of the Knickerbocker and New England writers being regional and derivative. Of Pattee's eighteen chapters on genres and regionalists, and an emerging national literature (individual chapters on Whitman, Twain, Harte, and Joaquin Miller), the sixteenth, on "The Triumph of the Short Story," agreed with his approach and conclusions in the chapter for the *CHAL*.

In this chapter, Pattee interpreted the stages in the historical evolution of short fiction in America by persistently referring to moralistic criteria similar to those of Wendell, Woodberry, and others. Pattee's doctrine of moral personality worked in favor of Hawthorne, who added "soul" to Irving's essayistic form, but against Poe, who was "an artist and only an artist" without Hawthorne's "deeps of the human heart" (II, 369, 370). In the two ensuing, transitional decades, Pattee emphasized the effects of environment and epoch in a "dawning of definiteness, of localized reality, of a feeling left on the reader of actuality and truth to human life' (II, 372). Then came the fastidious James, who worked "in the clay of actual life," to be sure, but in his mastery of French form, he neglected the spiritual, the heart, rendering his short fiction "an art form simply, cold and brilliant" that reduced him to "second place as an interpreter of human life" (II, 376).

From 1875 to 1895, Pattee again esteemed moral personality more highly than literary craft. Bret Harte suffered from "his lack of sincerity and of moral background." Ambrose Bierce lacked "sincerity" as well as "truth." Like Poe, "he was a man of the intellect only, a craftsman of exquisite subtlety, an artist merely for the sake of his art" (II, 380, 387). H. C. Bunner, however, was not only an exquisite artist, but more American than James, and his stories conveyed "more depth of soul" than Aldrich's and Stockton's (II, 386). Among the very recent writers, London was deficient both in "moral background and beauty of style" (II, 392); Richard Harding Davis was "a craftsman rather than a critic of human life" (II, 393); and O. Henry, though an artist, must be condemned with Bret Harte for having "lowered the standards of American literature, since both worked in the surface of life with theatric intent and always without moral background" (II, 394).

Volume II rates only average marks in defining the emerging forms and modes of American literature. MacMechan complained of a "tendency to formlessness" in Thoreau's *Week,* a generic failure resulting in "neither a record of a week's excursion nor a book of essays, but a jumble of the two." *Walden,* however, was the "most closely jointed of his books," though we were not told what closely jointed structure Thoreau successfully imposed on those subsequent adventures and musings (II, 9, 12). Bassett referred altogether vaguely to literary form in Sparks's historical writing, but Ruth Putnam was slightly more adept when she explained Prescott's narrative and thematic approach to structure in *Ferdinand and Isabella:* "He would think out a chapter on the same structural plan as for a romance or a drama, letting the events develop towards some obvious point or conclusion" (II, 127). The reader missed the illustrative example here but received it in *The Conquest of Mexico,* an historical narrative shaped and focused by the progress of the central actor, Cortes. Brander Matthews provided a concise definition of familiar verse as "the metrical equivalent of the essay in its charm, in its grace and in its colloquial liberty," but even more precisely, it was "the lyric commingled of humour and pathos, brief and brilliant and buoyant, seemingly unaffected and unpremeditated, and yet—if we may judge by the infrequency of supreme success—undeniably difficult, despite its apparent ease" (II, 239). But Matthews did not then illuminate a Holmes poem with this workable genre definition. Emory Holloway labored profitably to describe Whitman's "flexible prose-poetic form" and speculated on the literary origins aside from "the unquestioned originality of his own genius" (II, 266).

In American fiction, Erskine explored the transcendental argument in Hawthorne's long romances without explaining how the romance was an aesthetic form in various ways congenial to Hawthorne's mind and literary genius. Neither did Erskine inquire into the special form of the Hawthorne tale, except to observe that it more elaborately contained the ironic contrasts that were implicit in the "possibilities, hints, causes, and coincidences" of the nondramatized essay sketches (II, 23). Killis Campbell adopted a version of Poe's own famous generic definition by contrasting his tales with Hawthorne's: "Although the New Englander is infinitely Poe's superior in some respects—as in the creation of character and in wholesomeness and sanity—he must yield place to him in the creation of incident, in the construction of plot, and in the depicting of an intensely vivid situation" (II, 67). Finally, Pattee surveyed the development of short fiction in America, clarified the trends in moral purpose (or its absence), and marked the degree to which American life became a "localized reality" in the three "phases" of local-color writing. But his few comments on the American tale as an art form were not very helpful.

Lastly, Will D. Howe (and secretly, Mark Van Doren) bravely anatomized the pre–Civil War mode of humor in America. Howe mentioned a classical tradition, with English models from Addison to Dickens, to which Franklin, Irving, and Holmes, belonged. But he analyzed a group "more essentially native, at least in form and tone" (II, 148): From Nathaniel Ward to William Byrd and Madam Knight to Artemus Ward, America had experienced an historical fondness for poker-faced exaggeration that "long drew its principal inspiration from the differences between that frontier and the more settled and compact regions of the country" (II, 158–59). To the credit of Howe and Van Doren, this analysis, which seems hardly surprising, was not so easy to phrase in their time, coming before the fruitful twentieth-century studies in American humor that we now enjoy.

The impressionism of volume I reappeared even more extensively amid the ampler belles lettres of volume II and provided, again, an inadvertent unity to many of the chapters, whether in pronouncements on style, form, substance, or a total career. Trent wrote that Longfellow, early and late, never showed himself to be "a consummate metrical and verbal artist of the highest order or a poet of sustained imaginative flight" (II, 37), but Trent remarkably avoided quoting even once from Longfellow's work in the entire chapter. Payne reserved a higher opinion of Whittier but fell back helplessly on the impressionist's aesthetic and moral vocabulary reminiscent of Barrett Wendell ("truth," "force," "sincerity," "power") to deliver his uninspected judgments. Campbell never quoted from Poe's creative work (he gave two pages to the poems, two to the tales) but was convinced that "the best of his verse exhibits a spontaneity and finish and perfection of phrase, as well as, at times, a vividness of imagery, that is difficult to match elsewhere in American poetry" (II, 65).

Perhaps the harmony (or common haziness) of impressionistic method and diction in volume II becomes more apparent when individual contributors are not named and we discover how their opinions might have been written by a single critic. Thoreau's simple style in Walden, for example, could best be explained in a comparison to the Pond, "clear, colourless and wholesome." Moreover, "Thoreau is a careful writer, with an instinct for the right word which was developed and strengthened by a lifelong devotion to the best books" (II, 14). A passage quoted from John Marshall gives us "some idea of the simplicity of the style, the evidence of power and confidence, the eloquence which can raise a judicial opinion into the realm of literature" (II, 75). Among historians, Wirt had "a polished style" and Bancroft "a lofty and sonorous sense of detachment in his sentences" (II, 105, 111). Frank Stockton had a "wise humorous style" and Hawthorne's was, in a word, superb (II, 407, 19). George Boker's verses were not so successful as Henry C. Brownell's, for they lacked "the passionate truthfulness of Brownell's" (II, 278). Henry Timrod was author of three effectively "passionate" poems and James R. Randall of "a splendid impassioned utterance" in "My Maryland" (II, 294, 295).

At other times, the common impressionism was heard in the familiar demand that readers allow their power of feeling to respond to the author's touch or taste or style or capacity of feeling. One enjoys *Walden* "with a zest he can hardly explain to himself" (II, 12). After reading a full-page quotation from Webster, "We feel all through it the literary value and quality which make it imperishable," an emerging "literary touch," and "as the sureness of the literary touch increased, so did the taste become refined until it was finally almost unerring" (II, 98). Much of Andrews Norton's Unitarian writing "is ascetically pure in taste as in style. It can still be read with pleasure, indeed with a certain intellectual thrill" (II, 211). Nor should the reader fail to notice that in Lowell's postwar poems, "there is a greater depth of thought and a maturity of feeling" (II, 252), though Holmes's serious poetry at its best appears "the result of his intelligence rather than of his imagination. It lacks depth of feeling and largeness of vision" and is somehow French in adroitness and "inadequacy of emotion" (II, 237). Hayne's best poems, on the other hand, "are characterized by delicacy of feeling, conscientious workmanship, and a certain assimilation of the best qualities of other poets" (II, 311), and "the deep and sincere religious feeling of the *Centennial Hymn* is characteristic of the entire body of Whittier's verse" (II, 51).

The chapter that best illustrated how language does in fact operate in literary expression came not from a member of the academy, ironically or perhaps understandably, but from the U.S. senator from Massachusetts, Henry Cabot Lodge. Though in many of his pages, Lodge was as intolerably impressionistic as his professorial coauthors, once or twice he showed a critic's best instinct to invite his readers into the making of his judgments. After one of his quotations from Webster came this comment:

> Rhetorically this passage is all that could be desired. The sentences are short, effective, possessing both balance and precision. But when we come to the last we find the literary touch. It is only one word, "mildew," but that single word is imaginative and strikes us at once.[1]
> (II, 101)

Even though Lodge stopped well short of a satisfying explanation, he convinces us that his eye here is closely fixed on the literary medium. Unfortunately, he lapsed on the next page into a disjunction of thought and style: "It is not the thought which has carried these words so far through time and space. It is the beauty of the imagery and the magic of the style." And in praise of another passage: "Here the thought is nothing, the style everything" (II, 102). Assigning praise and blame to Lodge is complicated here, however, by Carl Van Doren's later marginal note on a letter from Trent (18 June 1921). "I made enormous cuts and changes in the chapter as Lodge sent it," Van Doren wrote, but "we could not do too much to a senator who had been asked—by G. H. Putnam without the knowledge of any of the editors—to be a contributor." Van Doren and Trent's shared verdict that Lodge's was the worst chapter in the entire history may be too harsh.

When volume II appeared in early 1919, tardy by a full year, the reception was markedly wider than for the first volume. Although early reviews in the two separate issues of the *Boston Evening Transcript* (12 and 15 February) were, as before, rather flatly descriptive, other critics now sensed that the *CHAL* might well be a landmark effort in American literature scholarship. The *Literary Digest* termed the contents a "well-varied menu," and liked the breadth afforded by the various chapters marginal to literature. The critic did remark on the uneven style among contributors, with MacMechan's writing on Thoreau being superior to Payne's Whittier or Thorndike's Lowell. The extensive bibliographies again won the approval of this journal, and the first two volumes were seen to be the beginning of a successful and worthy series. *The Outlook* was again stingy with space but not, this time, with enthusiasm. "There is not a dull page in this entertaining and instructive volume," the reviewer exclaimed, rather curiously citing as favorite chapters the two essays on Civil War poets. He firmly approved the scope of the literary history: "The stretch given to the rigorist definition of literature . . . [allows] an inclusiveness not reprehensible in a complete account of American life and letters." [7]

The *Dial* complained again about the unnecessary bulk of the bibliographies and blamed them for the delay that was sending the work into even more volumes. But the reviewer had no complaint about the text, singling out for favorable mention the chapter on Lowell by Thorndike, on Bancroft by Bassett, and on Whittier by Payne (the *Dial*'s own). The critic predicted that a current postwar interest would be directed on the chapters on our earlier poets of the Civil War. And he liked, in particular, Tassin's entertaining chapter on children's books. [8]

Walter C. Bronson, professor of English at Brown, whose undistinguished *A Short History of American Literature* (1900) was discussed earlier, raised crucial issues of editorial conception in a review that proved him a better critic than writer of literary history. He conceded that an absence of "unity in method and point of view" could be expected in a composite work, but he felt that the editors had allowed the history to get out of hand as it ranged from the diverse treatments of Hawthorne to Webster to Whitman. Though Bronson rated Erskine's essay on Hawthorne one of the best, he questioned the historical emphasis on transcendentalism that rendered the chapter "inadequate as an interpretation of the art of our greatest romancer." Pattee did little for either "the form or the substance" of the short story, Holloway's Whitman chapter was "little more than a biography," and the varying lengths of various chapters seemed capricious. Even so, Bronson regarded this volume to be in material richer and in contributors superior to the first, and he applauded it for scope, accuracy, the balance of major and minor figures, and the fine bibliography (especially the periodical items). With T. S. Eliot's now-classic review, which we shall notice in a moment, Bronson's was the most perceptive commentary on the *CHAL* at its halfway mark. [9]

The review in *Nation* appeared unaccountably late, at the end of August 1919, perhaps reflecting a slowly developing reaction against this new appropriation of American literature by "the professors," our subject in the chapter to follow. (The review was titled "American University Criticism.") The *Nation* considered the volume generally deficient in literary criticism (as it also had the first volume), pointing to Campbell's Poe and Holloway's Whitman as especially weak, along with Lodge's "invertebrate and unfortunate article on Webster." (Some political animus may have colored this judgment.) The reviewer also regretted that contributors had failed to interpret, rather than merely indicate, the symptoms of national taste: "The question, all-important for the literary historian, 'Why did (or does) such-and-such a work please?' is not frequently answered in the work." Presumably, this might be construed as a shortcoming in editorial prescription and guidance, but the reviewer did not see it that way and even went on to praise the editing, not least for "the exhaustive and admirably arranged bibliographies."[10]

Unlike the first volume, the second received ample and judicious attention in England, and this reception seems especially historic, for it marks almost exactly the centennial of Sydney Smith's jibe about the poverty of American literature. Early reviews in the *Spectator* and *New Statesman* appeared on the same day, with agreement that the volume was weak as literary criticism. The *Spectator* termed the chief defect an "absence of illuminating quotations," even in the chapters treating Poe and Whitman, and cited Lodge's chapter on Webster as a fortunate exception. The *New Statesman*'s reviewer, even more negative, noticed this "dread of tangible example" also in Trent's Longfellow and Payne's Whittier, and while he hesitated to be numbered among England's sneering band of anti-American critics, "this production of the associated professors of America," he promised, would surely add grist to the critical mills of England. The reviewer for the *Spectator* was more generous. He found something to like even in some of the chapters he criticized: MacMechan's Thoreau was "brilliantly written," Campbell's Poe "eminently judicial," Holloway's Whitman "sympathetic and moderate," Smith's survey of dialect writers "admirable," and Pattee's discussion of the short-story writers "remarkable" in scope and assessment. He also admired the spirit of American self-criticism—"patriotic bias is in the main rigorously excluded."[11]

Among the other English reviews, T. S. Eliot's in the *Athenaeum* was the most revealing and remains the most famous contemporary response that the *CHAL* would receive. He was dutifully specific on selected chapters—Lodge did not explicate Webster's style, Miss Putnam discussed the influence of Prescott's wife rather than of other historians, and MacMechan was good on Thoreau though he had no "fresh or surprising point of view." And Eliot liked the "important and encyclopaedic bibliography." Permeating the rest of his review was the important underlying issue of his critical ruminations at this time, namely tradition versus originality. Eliot began by detecting in this second volume an absence of common aim and method; it was not a history but a collection of essays on "various fragments of American letters." Perhaps, though, the miscellany of chapters properly reflected the "lack of cohesion" in American literature, the peculiar isolation of our greatest writers that led to their originality. The big three he had in mind were Poe, Whitman, and Hawthorne. Eliot first considered their treatment in the present history and then submitted the Eliot critique that his subsequent cult worshippers would learn by heart.

Eliot approved Campbell's treatment of Poe as a critic but was disappointed that nothing was ventured on Poe's "peculiar originality" as a poet and his ambiguous presence as "both the *reductio ad absurdum* and the artistic perfection" of the great romantic movement. Holloway told the reader everything about Whitman *except* the poetry. Erskine's Hawthorne, however, was "surely the most serious and most intelligent essay in the volume." Eliot missed a background sketch of the New England society that impinged on Hawthorne's imagination—we must go to Barrett Wendell for that—but admired Erskine's insight on Hawthorne's philosophical detachment and Hawthorne the moralist.

At this point, Eliot launched his own essay in American literary history on these writers and their times. Hawthorne rather than Emerson and his circle, said Eliot, was the clear-eyed "realist" and perceptive "observer of the moral life" of the age, while the personalized essays of Emerson were "already an encumbrance." Hawthorne's work, with its "hard coldness of the genuine artist," was "truly a criticism" of the Puritan, transcendental, and other strains of American morality, and Eliot ranked him as a moral historian the equal of Henry James, Flaubert, and Turgenev. Like Poe and Whitman, however, Hawthorne was a "pathetic" case. Living in a "starved environment" amid the "lack of intelligent literary society," he was left to survive on his "*originality.*" All three suffered, we could now see, because American civilization was "thin; it was not corrupt enough. Worst of all it was secondhand." Poe and Whitman filled and then drained their solitary selves like a suction bulb in a bottle, while Hawthorne "sucked every actual germ of nourishment out of his granite soil." [12]

Eliot's disaffection from (but intimacy with) American culture, together with his insinuation that the American university professors of the *CHAL* had offered little in the way of a vital interpretation of our premier writers of the past, leads us to the larger cultural debate of the second decade of this century. The interval before volumes III and IV of the *CHAL* see the light of 1921 will be an opportune moment to consider how the academy had been coming under attack from the outside by insurgent young men of the time, some of them about to become the most vigorous and resourceful critics of our literary past and present.

Chapter 11

Interim: Some Insurgent Critics versus "the Professors"

Eliot's review of the *CHAL* was part of the postwar reassessment that brought a new spirit to American literature and introduced a new cultural debate in criticism and scholarship. From another viewpoint, his oracular pronouncements came at the end of a dozen years of cultural assessment wherein the academic figures, both in and out of the *CHAL*, had seemed the reincarnation of Alexander Pope's Dunciad to insurgent critics like Van Wyck Brooks, John Macy, Randolph Bourne, H. L. Mencken, and Waldo Frank. The irony here is that many of these scholars, we have seen, were themselves an embattled group facing an entrenched opposition within the academy that was inhospitable to American literature as a worthy subject of historical and philological inquiry. To the younger generation unaware that this struggle had been occurring, the professors of literature were united in antiquarian pursuits, a monolithic army smugly on parade in doctoral hoods and gowns and square black caps. The American "usable past" these rebellious young were agitating for in literature would easily have included the moment of Freneau's sarcastic warning to authors at the beginning of our national period:

> Be particularly careful to avoid all connexion with . . . masters of arts, professors of colleges, and in general all those that wear square black caps. A mere scholar and an original author are two animals as different from each other as a fresh and salt water sailor. There has been an old rooted enmity between them from the earliest ages, and which it is likely will forever continue. ("Advice to Authors: By the Late Mr. Robert Slender," 1788)

Norman Foerster (North Carolina), whose chapter on "Later Poets" soon appeared in the third volume of the *CHAL*, recalled in 1930 this climate of rebellion:

> Particularly after the year 1910, large numbers of young men keenly interested in life and in letters refused to follow the lead of the pedants, historians, and scientists of literature who seemed to have

the *belles lettres* in their keeping, . . . who wrote books and articles and read papers before the Modern Language Association in a factual and mechanical language that gave scant promise of really illuminating the language of the poets and dramatists, who in their addiction to dates, texts, emendations, influences, evidence external and internal, appeared to have lost the power of enjoying life or literature in terms of feeling, imagination, and reason in its freer activities.

Foerster did not distinguish between the study (and instruction) of American literature and the older literatures, though most of the professors teaching American literature in 1910 had been trained, of course, in English literature scholarship and philology; and they were teaching largely in that area. Yet many of these professors resented the current pedantry of MLA meetings nearly as much as the rebel critics and, by 1921, would form their own American Literature Group within the association. Foerster also ignored a distinction between the professors and the young men when he remarked, further along, on the "rise and triumph of impressionism" in American criticism. This romantic movement he ascribed to Mencken and others who "remade old organs of opinion and established new ones" until "at length they carried their impressionistic programme to triumph in the years just following the World War." To be sure, these younger critics followed, here and there, the aesthetic doctrines of Coleridge, Sainte-Beuve, Pater, Wilde, Symons, Anatole France, Croce, and even America's Crocean disciple at Columbia, Joel Spingarn. But a number of professors who wrote our first American literary histories were in the actual vanguard of an impressionistic criticism that was now bringing an aesthetic appreciation of American authors, however inarticulately, into a reluctant academy and beyond.[1]

That campaign for American literature study, as it advanced now from the turn of the century to 1920, formed the essential background to the controversy between professors and the twentieth-century version of our earlier Young Americans of the 1840s. The period has been partly characterized and summed up by Fred L. Pattee, John S. Lewis, and John Hite. Their conclusions vary. To Pattee, who participated in the movement, the European war indirectly played a vital part in encouraging more work in American literature scholarship in these years "by cutting off research visits to England and the universities of the continent and by its stimulation of national consciousness."[2]

From the later perspective of the 1940s, John Lewis and John

Hite were not so impressed, however, by the impact of the first World War. Lewis tallied the setbacks along with the advances in the academy and warned that statistics should be studied comparatively. By the end of the war, exclusively American literature courses had nearly doubled since 1900—from fifty-seven to ninety-eight—in the colleges he was surveying. But English literature offerings were also expanding in these years, so that advocates of native authors were still a pronounced minority in the literature department. Lewis recognized, with Pattee, the surge of nationalism brought on by the war, rather like the fervor attending the Spanish-American War, and no doubt it encouraged serious study in the past and present achievements of the proud young nation now become a new world power. In the third survey of American literature instruction, John Hite informed the American Literature Group of the MLA in the mid-1940s that of the one hundred institutions that responded to his questions, thirty-nine had first offered American literature before 1900, and a mere twenty-eight more joined the group by war's end. Hite concluded that the popularity of American literature did not really swell in the first two decades of this century.[3]

More clearly, there was progress of another kind in these years. A growing number of literature professors of scholarly reputation in universities of high prestige were now teaching American authors and writing on them. At Harvard, Barrett Wendell was joined by Chester N. Greenough and then Bliss Perry, who offered a graduate course on Emerson in 1911.[4] Brown had Walter Bronson and until 1906, Lorenzo Sears. C. F. Richardson taught his American literature course at Dartmouth until retirement in 1911. At Yale were Henry Beers (until retirement in 1916) and William Lyon Phelps. American literature at Columbia was in the capable hands of *CHAL* editors Trent (he offered a first graduate seminar in 1903) and in the second decade, his protégé Van Doren. But Erskine never strayed from his classrooms in English literature—except for a wartime assignment in France from 1917 to 1919. Also at Columbia in this period, as Alfred Knopf (class of 1912) recalled a half-century later, Brander Matthews was teaching a very popular course on American writers, which Knopf, however, did not take: "I had a priggish notion, based on complete ignorance, that there was no such thing as American literature." Among Columbia's graduate students in the second decade was Jay B. Hubbell, defector from Harvard (M.A., 1908) where, he later complained, no graduate course in American literature was offered during his two years from 1906 to 1908 (though four Chaucerians were busily employed in the

English department). Hubbell studied for the doctorate in 1914 and 1915, and, after the war, completed his dissertation on "Virginia Life in Fiction."[5]

Elsewhere in the East, Pennsylvania offered an undergraduate course in 1903, "English Literature in the United States." Two years later, Arthur H. Quinn gave a graduate course, "Forms and Movements in American Literature"—perhaps the first American literature offering ever at the advanced level. In 1913, he was teaching the basic course in American literature for two terms, as well as a class on Emerson and Poe. In 1917, Quinn introduced the first native drama course in the American university. At Penn State, Pattee in 1907 was alternating between his 210 composition papers a week and the "'mere relaxation'" of teaching American authors. Several years later, he expanded the curriculum of his English and American Literature department (so titled in 1914) to include a survey and two period courses in American literature. The contemporary poetry course in the year 1909–10 included American authors, as did the novel and contemporary drama courses in 1911 and 1913, respectively. In 1920, Pattee was awarded the title Professor of American Literature. At Pittsburgh, an American literature course was being taught by E. B. Burgum. No American literature classes appear to have been offered at Yale, Princeton, or Johns Hopkins in these two decades.[6]

To the south, C. Alphonso Smith arrived as Poe Professor of English Literature at Virginia in 1909 and immediately introduced three American courses for seniors. Smith left Virginia in 1917 to head the English department at the U.S. Naval Academy; his new academic address is given in his *CHAL* chapter on "Dialect Writers." Teaching American writers at West Virginia in this period was R. A. Armstrong. North Carolina gave the first M.A. in American literature as early as 1896 and by 1920 had the semblance of a graduate program. Young Jay B. Hubbell taught his first course in American literature at Wake Forest College in the year 1913–14, before departing for doctoral study at Columbia. At Texas, Killis Campbell was offering "Literature of the South" in 1900. In 1902, Texas awarded an M.A. in American literature. Finally in the South, LSU resumed, in 1909, an American literature course after an eleven-year hiatus.[7]

Professors in the Middle West did not have the luminous reputation of their Eastern counterparts, but their commitment to American literature might have been stronger. At Michigan, Isaac Demmon was continuing the work begun in the 1870s by Tyler, and Wisconsin's program was prospering with W. B. Cairns (his dissertation in 1897 from Wisconsin, mentioned earlier, was in American literature). He carried the title Assistant Professor of American Literature. His colleague, F. W. Roe, offered a course on Emerson and Arnold from 1915 to 1918 in an American program that included also a survey, an individual-author course, and a graduate seminar. The University of Chicago had Percy Boynton and George Sherburn, who were giving three full-quarter courses in 1913 and an additional one by 1917. Joseph Warren Beach was teaching American literature at Minnesota by 1907, and his colleague Hardin Craig taught a survey in 1911. Vernon Parrington was in his seventh of ten years at Oklahoma in 1905 when an American literature course was offered for one year. But his colleague Wilbur Humphreys, not Parrington, taught the course. Not until Randall Stewart arrived in 1917 was the cause of American literature revived at that institution. Meanwhile, at Nebraska Louise Pound had been teaching the American course since 1904 (listed in the catalog since 1883) and continued it over the next forty years. Bernard DeVoto entered Utah in fall of 1914 and was delighted that two courses were given in American literature. (Transferring to Harvard the next fall, he discovered only one course—Bliss Perry's American poetry up to Emerson, with literary–historical backgrounds courtesy of Barrett Wendell.)[8]

On the Pacific Coast, the state universities, once again, were more committed to American literature than were the private institutions. The University of Washington welcomed Parrington after he was fired from Oklahoma, and in 1909, he began a program in American literature. He was joined by L. D. Milliman the following year. The curriculum expanded, and in the catalog for 1915–16, six undergraduate and two graduate courses were listed. This was perhaps the most impressive array in American literature anywhere in the nation up to that time. The University of Oregon was not far behind. In 1909, it introduced a major in "Rhetoric and American Literature," and, by 1917, listed ten undergraduate courses in American literature, ranging from genres—including the short story—to single authors such as Poe and Whitman. As in other catalog listings, we would like to know how many of the courses were actually being taught in a given year. Belletristic rather than, like Washington, biographical–historical in design, Oregon's program did not include graduate work and boasted no faculty luminaries. At the University of California, William D. Armes was campaigning for American literature during the nineteen years before his death in 1918. In 1908, the catalog from Berkeley listed "California Literature." Armes may have taught the course. Remembered as the

professor whom Frank Norris despised, Armes was described in
Who's Who in America (1914–15) as Associate Professor of
American Literature, though it is not clear how he received this
title.[9]

This summary of the data supplied by Pattee, Lewis, Hite, and
other sources hardly fulfills the historian's ideal of clear and sufficient documentation. Omitted are an indefinite number of institutions that could hardly have been without some version of a
class in American literature. And in many of the colleges included in these surveys, as we have seen, we cannot be certain
which courses mentioned in the catalogs were, in fact, being
taught at the time. Perhaps the evidence does point to the wider
stirrings of an academic recognition of our literary history. Yet
Lewis discovered that even as fourteen of his colleges began to
list an American literature course in the years from 1910 to 1918,
this apparent gain, a distinctly modest one, was then undercut by
the defection of eleven others. We can read these and other figures and quite easily reject any conclusion that American literature study had finally arrived. For all the breakthroughs in New
England or the South or Far West, it turns out that no more than
10 to 15 percent of the "English" curriculum in the American
academy was apparently reserved for American literature.

Also to be cautiously interpreted are the growing number of
Ph.D. dissertations written in English departments between 1900
and 1920, for these figures usually do not reflect a thriving
graduate program in American literature itself. As in the nineties, they were studies written in universities usually providing
little or no graduate work in American literature. Even at Columbia, for all the popularity of the undergraduate program, American literature dissertations completed in these two decades—an
average of nearly one a year—were not the result of a rich graduate curriculum in the subject. Still, the dissertations indicate the
new academic spirit being encouraged by Trent and then Van
Doren. The dissertations by *CHAL* contributors were William E.
Leonard's "Byron and Byronism in America" (1905), H. C. Goddard's "Studies in New England Transcendentalism" (1908), Earl
Bradsher's "Mathew Carey: Editor, Author, and Publisher . . ."
(1912), and Elizabeth Cook's "Literary Influences in Colonial
Newspapers, 1704–1750" (1912). Other English departments
hospitable to the occasional doctoral dissertation in American
literature in these two decades, but with little if any seminar
work in the American area, included Harvard, with eleven theses, followed by Virginia (ten), New York University (eight),

Pennsylvania (six), Illinois (four), and Yale (three). The most popular single-author subjects were Emerson (four theses), Whitman (two), and Poe (two). One dissertation each went to Lowell, Howells, Mark Twain, Longfellow, Dunlap, Bird, and J. C. Harris.[10]

Although there is not space in this book to pursue the study of American literature at the precollege level, a revealing article in 1903 indicates that the high schools were still, as in previous decades, more realistically attuned to our national literature than were the hidebound arbiters of college curricula. In Iowa during that year, 113 high schools reported that American classics were receiving abundant time in the classroom, an attention almost equal to British authors. Yet in the college entrance examination for 1903, the four books to be read carefully and ten cursorily were in "English literature." One of these books, be it noted, was Lowell's *Vision of Sir Launfal,* presumably admissible because it was "'English rather than American in narrative and atmosphere.'"[11]

American literature in the high schools and colleges was intimately linked, also, by the textbook anthologies produced increasingly by professors, some of whom were also the authors of literary-history texts—notably W. B. Cairns, Walter Bronson, Percy Boynton, and Fred Pattee. The course most frequently listed in college catalogs was the survey, with emphasis on backgrounds and occasionally aesthetic values, though it is hard to grasp just how the two varieties of textbook were used in the approach and conduct of these survey courses. Cairns explained in the preface of his *Selections from Early American Writers, 1607–1800* (1909) that his book not only would aid classroom study but was needed also on the shelves of college and secondary-school libraries, for they were sadly deficient in our early writers. Because these books were not designed exclusively for college students, we cannot estimate the degree to which their considerable sales were an index of the activity and learning in American higher education.

Bronson's *American Poems* (1912) handsomely rewarded its academic publisher, the University of Chicago Press, with seven impressions by 1918 and thirteen by 1927. Bronson's *American Prose* (1916) by the same press turned out sufficiently profitable, too, going to a seventh impression after twelve years. In 1916. also, Norman Foerster edited *The Chief American Prose Masters* (Boston: Houghton Mifflin); its sales were steady enough to warrant an enlarged edition fifteen years after. Boynton's *American Poetry* (Scribner, 1918), edited with the assistance of Howard

Mumford Jones, George Sherburn, and Frank Webster, received three additional printings in the next six years. Even more widely used was Pattee's *Century Readings for a Course in American Literature* (Century, 1919), which he introduced by echoing his wartime thesis that a true appreciation of Americanism was on the rise in our schools and colleges and in public discourse at home and abroad. His *Century Readings,* of course, would be the ideal literary source of such knowledge. The argument, together with Pattee's skills as an anthologist, helped *Century Readings* to a flourishing life in the twenties, with two enlarged editions and a total of five reprintings. A last notable anthology from Century brought a collection of American drama to the schools and colleges, Arthur H. Quinn's *Representative American Plays* (1917).

One last merging of literary concerns in the high schools and colleges also carries us into the specific critical controversy we are moving toward in this chapter. Instructors at both levels were listening and contributing to the growing debate over the apparent mediocrity that had seemingly descended on American literature since the turn of the century. John W. Berdan of the Toledo schools wrote in 1903 for the *Arena* his suspicion that democratic education and growing literacy had not nurtured good taste and a demand for "fine literature" from our authors. The populace (or that portion not totally consumed by materialistic ends) preferred the "light novel," and their craving for such cheap fare had determined the quality of our literature. Berdan's solution: "The future of American literature rests in the hands of the English teachers of the high school." Other explanations for the poor state of our fiction included the popular resurgence of an uncritical Americanism, harmful to both our political and literary intelligence. But another article in the *Arena* seconded the analysis of Berdan. Francis L. Pierce rephrased Sydney Smith's century-old question to read, "'Who cares to read a contemporary American book?'" Except for Jack London's *The Sea-Wolf* (1904) and Upton Sinclair's *The Jungle* (1906), American literature was currently enfeebled by "barrenness, timidity, [and] frivolity"; the business novels by a "bald, prosy, slipshod style"; and the poetry by a spirit (quoting Ludwig Lewisohn) "'mild, bourgeois, and proper.'" Like Howells in his "Editor's Easy Chair" columns for *Harper's Monthly,* Pierce also assailed the craze for utterly forgettable new romances. Why was American literature so "trashy"? Partly because modern authors were shallowly engaged in life and art, but also because "so many of the American people like trashy things." [12]

By 1914, a new American poetry was being defended by Louis

Untermeyer, who saw in it the healthy signs of breaking away from stodgy Victorianism. But the scholarly and critical journals continued to assume that our literature was in the doldrums, and they looked for causes and, if any were possible, for remedies. In the *South Atlantic Quarterly,* H. St. George Tucker repeated a current list of presumed culprits—commercially minded magazine editors, writers, theater managers, actors, and even critics—but he chiefly ascribed our literary mediocrity to the writers' narrow vision of the American "soul" as being conditioned and shrunken in a regional environment. In the same journal, H. Houston Peckman traced the main ailment of modern fiction not to neoromantic "rubbish" or the tyranny of democratic taste (our nineteenth-century novelists, after all, thrived amid the popular bestseller); rather, the sane realism of Howells had been superseded by a "lopsided realism" glorying in the bizarre and exceptional. Edwin Björkman, in the *Century,* took a different route. In an open letter to President Wilson, he urged federal support and encouragement of American writers.[13]

Charles Wager offered *Atlantic Monthly* readers no proposal for raising the standard of American writing and, in fact, considered it very unlikely that any future literary genius would emerge out of a democracy that had no perspective on the past and could neither encourge nor judge literary excellence in the present. But in the same issue of the *Atlantic,* Katherine Gerould did have a solution of sorts. After acknowledging the decline of culture in our society of democratic levelers, inferior immigrants, and idolators of science and money, she rebuked the colleges for the state of the arts, and implicitly, at least, she enjoined them to return to their former high office of "custodians of culture." She observed that the state universities were teaching "hat-trimming" while the humanities were lying neglected, as they were also in the high schools. Percy Boynton, in the *Nation,* attributed this sorry condition, especially in the case of American literature, to our native works being taught in the high schools by teachers with no background in American literature, while in higher education, "not one eminent university man in this country today has devoted his whole career to studying or teaching the literary history of America."[14]

The most celebrated critique of American culture and literature, phrased in the conservative vein, came in these years from Irving Babbitt and the New Humanists (about whom we shall hear more when their following increases at the close of the 1920s). Along with Paul Elmer More, Stuart Sherman, Frank Jewett Mather, and others of less prominence, Babbitt became for the young liberal critics the very image of the puritan, Anglo-Saxon, anti-modernist professor. He fired his first book-length volley in 1908 with *Literature and the American College: Essays in Defense of the Humanities,* at a time when the modern function of the university was being revaluated not only here but in England, with special concern for the place of modern literature in the course of study. We are astonished to remember that English literature was not firmly certified as a college subject at Oxford until 1894, when the faculty was assured that its romantic-minded colleagues would tie the literature to responsible philological instruction and examination. (Cambridge did not fully admit post-Renaissance British authors into the curriculum until 1917.) In America, concerned histories of education just before Babbitt's first book were being written by Edwin G. Dexter and Charles F. Thwing; Professor Albert S. Cook of Yale published his essays on teaching English in the university; and the elective system instituted at Harvard just after the Civil War by President Eliot was one of several issues undergoing a stern scrutiny.[15]

Into this arena of educational reassessment and argument, Babbitt came well armed and eager for combat. Anything but the cloistered humanist, he had been attacking the excesses of modernism in articles for the *Nation,* the *Atlantic,* and elsewhere. Like his counterparts at Oxford, he abhorred romantic unrestraint; but he distanced himself from their scientific spirit of philology. In his book, he cut a broad swath, ridiculing the smorgasbord education implied by the elective system; urging that study of modern literature be tempered with the classics; and arguing for the recovery of permanent values in literature rather than the comparative and relative findings of literary history, the nationalism and self-expression derived from Rousseau and Herder, and the hazy readings of dilettante impressionists.

Babbitt's humanistic assault was strengthened in these early years of the movement by his prolific disciple, Paul Elmer More, whose analysis of Edwards and Emerson in the *CHAL* must have cheered his mentor at Harvard. More first gathered his philosophical and literary meditations and articles into the Shelburne Essays, First Series, in 1904 (there would be eleven volumes by 1921). Not so exasperating to liberal opponents as Babbitt—More's verdict on Whitman in the Fourth Series of the essays was surprisingly favorable—he still adhered to the higher law of restraint that gives control and significance to behavior and humanistic art. His social outlook was equally tiresome to young Americans like Randolph Bourne. Reviewing in 1916 the Ninth Series of Shelburne Essays, *Aristocracy and Justice* (1915),

Bourne recognized More as the "ablest spokesman of our intellectual plutocracy," a dubious compliment, for this was a man unaware that the institutions he was defending (church, university, industrial plutocracy), said Bourne, were forces not of social control and stability but, in fact, the underlying causes of our dehumanizing and chaotic present. Confronted by the more generous and creative social purpose of our exhilarating democracy, More shrank into the "tight little categories" of his Greek classics. But More's and Babbitt's humanism was not without eloquent support, chiefly from Stuart Sherman, whose spirited jousting with H. L. Mencken we shall turn to in a moment. Frank Jewett Mather was another ally. By 1906, he had attained a perspective on the philological program at Johns Hopkins that had left him a dessicated student, but one well-schooled in the anti-humanistic effects of what he now termed, in a *Nation* article, the "false ideals of research inherited from Germany."[16]

Another critic somewhat in Babbitt's camp, at least in the common quest for critical standards and genre definitions (à la the French critic Brunetière), was William C. Brownell. His *American Prose Masters* (1909) was the only distinguished volume in a parade of genre or period studies that, today, has scholarly as well as historical significance. Jessie B. Rittenhouse's *The Younger American Poets* (1904) reminds us how forgettable was most of American poetry since the Civil War; and Annie R. Marble, *Heralds of American Literature* (1907), included the figures Moses Coit Tyler would have next discussed had he lived—Dunlap, Brown, and others. *American Literary Masters* (1906) by Leon Vincent, the best scholar of the three, comprehended nineteen authors from Irving to Whitman (typically, he excluded Melville) in an effort to define a canon of earlier nineteenth-century literature. John Erskine worked to the same purpose in *Leading American Novelists* (1910), discussed in an earlier chapter.

But Brownell possessed the most urbane and enduring critical intelligence of the group. The long-time literary adviser to the house of Scribner, he had an editor's firm set of literary guidelines for excellence in substance and style. Like Babbitt, Brownell viewed literature as a force in the humanization of mankind, and he mainly ignored the historical issues of his literary period. In his focus on the individual author and work, Brownell was less like Babbitt, despite their common emphasis on rational judgment and control, and closer to Columbia's Joel Spingarn, whose lecture on "The New Criticism" rattled a few academic windows the following year. But in that focus, Spingarn also assumed his tight Crocean stance of "criticism as the study of expression" in the separate, organic work of art. We have had enough study, said Spingarn, of conventions, genres, modes, rhetorical theory, terminology, and literary origin and evolution. He had little patience with droning moralists, rules-bound pedants, and cultural critics with their Tainean diagnoses. The time had come for criticism to merge "genius" and "taste," to realize that "fundamentally the creative and the critical instincts are one and the same." [17]

Although he disparaged their scholarly enterprise, Spingarn may have given some comfort to the literary historians in their aesthetic moments of "feeling," when they turned from history, nationalism, and life to flounder in a critical impressionism of the literary work. For culture-oriented literary critics, radicals and conservatives alike, Spingarn was of little use and became, in fact, a thorn in Babbitt's side three years later after a slashing review of *The Masters of Modern French Criticism.* Babbitt, said Springarn, was bereft of aesthetic theory and oddly ignored the literary criticism of his French literary critics. Moreover, Babbitt had no central idea, so that he expressed a personal bias against comparative, historical, and scientific values while himself a follower of Brunetière's scientific investigation of tradition and genre.

In his reply to Spingarn several months later in the same journal, Babbitt charged that it was today's aesthetes who were lost without a central idea in an impressionistic fog. Philosophically, they were in love with the relativity of William James and Henri Bergson. Babbitt bade them return to the classical tradition, especially in its dualistic view of man, and rediscover the permanent standards of value that govern taste. Philosophy, in short, should precede aesthetics, especially when Crocean enthusiasts adopted the instinctual formula of expression to destroy the boundary between creation and criticism. Babbitt wickedly reversed the terms of the debate and suggested that the Bergsonian instinct of an *elan vital* be replaced by humanity's older dualistic instinct of a *frein vital,* the anti-romantic discipline of the "inner check." In another shrewd reversal, he placed Spingarn and the aesthetes in an ivory tower, for they (unlike tradition-oriented New Humanists) separated literature from experience and ignored, in particular, the life-tested standards of a classical morality. [18]

Spingarn and other critics of equally irritating and benighted persuasions effectively goaded the "Warring Buddha of Harvard" to carry the program of the New Humanists through and beyond the years of World War I. The crowning expression of Babbitt's argument against aesthetes, social radicals, and romantic and scientific naturalists appeared in 1919, *Rousseau and Romanticism*. The book was also an affirmation of "moderate and sensible and decent" individualism, an Aristotelian "positive and critical" humanism. But Babbitt's inner check did not totally govern his immoderate irritation with his current antagonists. By the close of the decade, he had grown particularly irked by "the ineffable smartness of our young radicals" who were puffed up with "the conviction that . . . they are the very pink of modernity" (pp. xxi, x, xi).

First on Babbitt's mind among these smart young radicals may have been Harvard alumnus, Van Wyck Brooks. The year before, Brooks had published in the *Dial* his astringent views on literature and the academy, with particular antipathy directed toward professors who had diluted or distorted our literary past. In this now-classic essay, "On Creating a Usable Past," Brooks did not mention the *CHAL*, whose editors were agonizing in that same year over the difficult inclusion of certain living writers in the later chapters. But it seems inconceivable that Brooks should not have that literary history and its makers at least partly on his mind. (Volume I had appeared only months before and been rather critically reviewed in the *Dial*.) The professors, according to Brooks, had fashioned an American literary tradition that was stagnant with moralistic and commercial motives, a "literature of exploitation" that failed to reflect the "creative impulse in American history." If America were to achieve a vital literary culture, the first step, said Brooks, was obviously to ignore the professors' version of American tradition and create a truly usable past. He did not ask for a more sophisticated aesthetic approach to the creative impulse in that past: "The real task for the American literary historian, then, is not to seek for masterpieces—the few masterpieces are all too obvious—but for tendencies." The vital questions were such as these: Why did Bierce fail? Or why had Stephen Crane's legacy borne no fruit? Would not this creative search for underlying tendencies in our literary past provide an inspiriting common ground for writers of the present, "that sense of brotherhood in effort and in aspiration which is the historical promise of a national culture?"[19]

Brooks was admirably equipped to speak for young Americans who were waging combat, as their spiritual predecessors in the 1840s had, against anglophilia and an American cultural inferiority complex, as well as a spiritual toryism traceable to the New Humanists and the environs of Harvard Yard. Brooks at-

tended Harvard from 1904 to 1907, at the same time that young
Stuart Sherman was chafing there under the Germanic stuffi-
ness of Harvard literary study. In his autobiography half a century later, Brooks remembered that the academic mood of the
period was to equate Americanism with philistinism, following
Matthew Arnold's view that American life and culture were,
frankly and simply, not interesting. The presence of Barrett
Wendell did little for American literature, Brooks wrote, for he regarded our writers "of little lasting potence," including even, as
we have noticed in an earlier chapter, the authors of his New England renaissance. Babbitt, meanwhile, was railing against the
romanticism of the recent century and Charles Eliot Norton
against a generally decadent or at least degenerating age. In his
retreat to high culture, Norton was holding his Sunday "Dante
evenings"—Brooks attended twice—while others looked to Italian art with Bernard Berenson and Mrs. Jack Gardner, or to
Shakespeare or Flaubert or the French symbolists or Sanscrit.
(T. S. Eliot, be it recalled, was a Harvard student with Brooks.)
When Henry James came through in 1905, he lectured not on
American writers but on Balzac.

The effect of this estrangement from our native culture was to
create "a special frame of mind that made 'the Harvard graduate,'
as Henry Adams put it, 'neither American nor European'";
and Adams, who bore in his consciousness nary a line of Emily
Dickinson or Stephen Crane, was a fit spokesman for this academic state of mind. Brooks's selective evidence here shows that
the seeds of his *The Pilgrimage of Henry James* (1925) clearly
were planted in the student years at Harvard. Above all, Harvard
was suffocating from the traditional American deference to English culture. In and out of the classroom,

> English authors were always cited in preference to Americans. . . .
> Invariably one heard of Thackeray, rarely of Hawthorne—Carlyle,
> not Emerson—Charles Lamb rather than Thoreau; and merely to
> have mentioned this would have been thought chauvinistic, a word
> that was applied to me when later I did so.

One faculty member, Charles Copeland, the legendary "Copey,"
who was also a newspaperman and Boston theatre critic, did
manage to spirit into his classes now and again a reference to
American writers, but not Emerson or Howells. His examples
came from his favorite journalists—a Richard Harding Davis or
O. Henry. When Brooks, in 1909, visited Howells a second time
(the first was in 1907), he was chagrined by his own continuing

ignorance of Howells' novels: "I doubt if I had read more than one."[20]

Such was Brooks's meager preparation in American literature at Harvard before he departed for the West in 1911. During his brief tenure at Stanford, he married and settled in to become not a professor but a writer. Indeed, he was already pointed toward a career in American literature study with various publications, most importantly *The Wine of the Puritans: A Study of Present-Day America* (1908). Now within two years, Brooks finished the parts of three different books, on French pensée writers (which became *The Malady of the Ideal,* 1913) plus John Addington Symonds (1914), and H. G. Wells (1915). Brooks was fully primed to write *America's Coming-of-Age* in 1915, wherein he distilled the mood of his time and, more crucially, diagnosed the historic ailments of American life and pointed to a remedy. This classic work became a new *Democratic Vistas,* and Brooks even reaffirmed some of the critical and meliorating vision of Whitman's essay.

In his initial chapter, Brooks described (and lamented) the division in American culture between highbrow and lowbrow, by far the most memorable pages in the book. The highbrow in Brooks's cultural dialectic was the professor, an embodiment of the American mentality that worshipped old gods, writers safely dead, the heritage of Jonathan Edwards, and even more devotedly, the literary tradition of England. The highbrows isolated themselves from the writings of living authors, and this "habitual remoteness from the creative mood has made American professors quite peculiarly academic." Moreover, the professors communicated to college students the fatal charm of this remoteness. The college years then became, in memory, a lovely ivory-tower period presided over by idealistic mentors, a time of insulation from the harsher realities of a practical business America that awaited the student after graduation—the lowbrow, nonpoetic world of Franklin and his American disciples. Brooks regretted that this chasm had opened between the competing cults of Edwards and Franklin, or the professor and the businessman, and proposed a middle way, the life goals of which would be the American ideal of self-fulfillment over against self-assertion. For the moment in his argument, he announced that "on the economic plane, that implies socialism."[21]

In his second chapter, Brooks wrote a truncated literary history of "'Our Poets'" of the nineteenth century, the leading spirits who tried to forge significant literary expression in an America unresponsive to the creative life. Only Whitman explored the

contradictions of his society with a memorable art that also liberated his own personality and genius. Brooks then devoted his
third chapter to a separate consideration of Whitman ("The Precipitant"). Significantly, two chapters remained thereafter, so
that Whitman was not destined to be Brooks's climactic, grand
redeemer. In the modern era when American poets had retreated
from the rugged stuff of life to court an "unworldly refinement," a
sublimated and rarefied idealism, we would, however, need to return to Whitman for the beginning of a solution. His voice suggested the possibility of a middle tradition that might wed the
ideal and the earthy, "the sense of something organic in American life," a fusing of "hitherto incompatible extremes of the
American temperament" (pp. 110, 112). But Whitman alone did
not crystallize the twentieth-century answer America needed.
His instincts were sound, but on the plane of ideas, he embraced
all concepts too uncritically and thereby failed to mold the contradictory impulses of a chaotic America. He remained, in short,
only "the precipitant."

So Brooks moved on from Whitman rather than conclude here
the diagnosis and cure for a schizoid America come of age. In
chapter 4, "Apotheosis of the 'Lowbrow,'" he recognized, in fact,
the deleterious effect Whitman had brought to misguided followers like author Gerald Stanley Lee, who imagined his mediating
Whitman figure, his ideal materialist, in the "inspired millionaire" capitalist—to Brooks, "a sort of Marshall Field with a halo"
(pp. 133, 134). The fallacy here was that in a land where mil-
lionaires had usually not inherited their wealth, they were unable, according to Brooks, to play both disinterested highbrows,
who cultivate and harvest ideas, and capitalists who pursue the
margin of profit. Whitman, then, could become an unreliable
precipitant by encouraging capitalistic solutions for our culture
when a very cause of America's chaotic civilization lay in the
lowbrow acquisitiveness spawned by capitalism itself. But at the
end, Brooks could only face the other direction and hope that
within a transformed and redeeming highbrow America, we
could forge a middle way. In the Sargasso Sea of modern America,
he exhorted a resisting and engaged literary class and intelligentsia to promote the mediating answer, an aesthetic, intellectual, and moral vision leading to a humane socialism for America.

The following year, 1916, Brooks elaborated his program for a
revitalized America guided by accessible and well-informed critical opinion. First, he helped establish the *Seven Arts* and, with
Waldo Frank, kept it alive as a critical and pacifist journal until
October 1917. Randolph Bourne and H. L. Mencken were

among the contributors, who also included Theodore Dreiser, Sherwood Anderson, and young John Dos Passos. Seven of his own essays in the journal Brooks collected for his next book, *Letters and Leadership* (1918). Of particular interest was "Our Critics," which had appeared in the May 1917 issue of the *Seven Arts*. Here Brooks touched, again, on the failure of our classic authors to create their literature out of the web of American life or even the "congruous world of human life in general" that could bind the writer to his audience. But Brooks was more deeply concerned that this historic separation of American consciousness from the tap roots of our everyday life was being perpetuated by academic critics of the present. Babbitt's and Brownell's assiduous study of French critical traditions and Spingarn's cultivation of Croce could not contribute to the primary business of American criticism. Theirs were European critics who had understood how their own national literature was organically related to their civilization. But how could they suggest "any principles of order adapted to a spiritually unorganized society" such as ours (p. 116)?

✴   ✴   ✴

Brooks's cultural diagnosis of America and his assault on the unresponsive academy were in some ways sharply amplified by our next torch-bearing insurgent, John Macy (1877–1932). His *The Spirit of American Literature* (1913) preceded by two years Brooks's *America's Coming-of-Age*. Why Brooks's work, not Macy's, ended up igniting the imagination of the discontented in the period of progressivist agitation needs to be answered. In his essays on sixteen separate literary figures (including William James), Macy derived his literary judgments from a variety of social and aesthetic propositions that closely paralleled the shaping principles in Brooks's program for a reinvigorated American literature and society. In Macy's book, these ideas came together in two predominant themes. First, the best American literature survived through its relation to life, including especially the American life closest to the heartland and common concerns of the people. Second, this life-enhancing literature was threatened by an institutional conservatism bearing the three monster heads of the professor, the puritan, and the capitalist, who frequently voiced their reactionary opinions in compulsive unison. This was virtually the American mentality Brooks soon dubbed highbrow.

Macy was not blind to the distinctly aesthetic rewards in Irving, Cooper, Hawthorne, Poe, and others, and he discussed their works in a style delightful for its crispness and lucidity. But for his ultimate judgment of their legacy, Macy returned always to the touchstone of life and actuality, both American and universal. More central to our purpose is the manner in which Macy's animus toward the American academy flowed through virtually every chapter—an antipathy he appears to have cultivated as a student in the Harvard class of 1899 (Brooks entered in 1904). Born in Detroit, Macy had gravitated back to the land of his seventeenth-century Puritan forbears less than happily, as it turned out. A Phi Beta Kappa student, editor of both the *Advocate* and the *Lampoon,* and class poet, he was hired at graduation as an assistant in English. Despite his success, Macy recalled (in the chapter on William James) that the Harvard experience was quite deadly. Only James and some few others "redeemed the 'humanistic' departments of Harvard University from the sterility and impotence into which they had fallen during the past twenty-five years" (p. 298). To Macy, one of these redemptive figures was Charles Eliot Norton, an admirable "survival of a generation that read literature and knew not Ph.D's" (p. 298), unlike Brooks's Norton, a defector into the sublime regions of Dante and the past. Macy left Harvard in 1901 to become associate editor of the *Youth's Companion* until 1909, the year he officially became a socialist. In 1912, he served as secretary to the Socialist mayor of Schenectady and in 1916 published *Socialism in America,* a book for which he was subsequently denied membership in the Harvard Club.

From his Harvard years on forward, then, Macy viewed the conservative American (and distinctly New England) mentality to have been shaped by the unholy marriage of professor, puritan, and capitalist. To the degree that our values were dominated by this triumvirate, American life was poisoned. Our literature was vital only as authors affirmed the true spirit of our democracy subverted by this enemy. Macy's strategy in *The Spirit of American Literature,* then, was not only to uncover this democratic spirit in the vital writers, but also to identify and vanquish the enemy in his strongholds of school, church, and state. His argument was symptomatic of the pre-1920s rebellion and spirit of reform, too familiar to recount much further were it not for the power and exhuberant disdain with which he so delightfully made, and reiterated, his case. The university as an enemy of American literature has seldom taken a more severe shellacking than the one Macy administered. To Professor T. R. Lounsbury's claim that leaving Yale in the third year might explain the defects in Cooper's writing, Macy replied scornfully, "as if good old Yale or any other American college ever helped a man of genius to write!" Indeed, the "preliminary intellectual drill" that a writer could profit from "is not the sort which our beloved universities have shown themselves competent to adminster" (p. 40).

Dulled by his textbook approach to dead writers, the conventional professor of the past, Macy wrote, could not be expected to respond, say, to the "new genius" of Whitman in 1855, and even in the present, "the essay by Professor George Santayana in 'Poetry and Religion' is a perfect justification of Whitman's dislike of aesthetics" (pp. 235, 247). Professors were unresponsive to life in literature because they were themselves severed from life. Among lonely exceptions to ivory towerism, Longfellow at Harvard tried to reach the popular ear even though he was "in an institution monastically remote from the life of the toiling many," the American academy wherein "as a rule professors write books which are useful only to other professors and to students obedient to academic prescription" (p. 99). Longfellow, and then Lowell and Norton after him, "bore a torch of living culture among rusty grammarians and the hebraical sons of a decadent but still stupid Puritanism" (p. 99). Late in the century came a time "when the teaching of modern literature in American universities, at Harvard certainly, was divided between the philologists on the one hand, men with no literary sense, who reduce Shakespeare and Milton to archeological specimens, and, on the other hand, amiable dilettanti" (p. 100). Thoreau's *Civil Disobedience* once sent shivers through official Harvard, and this liberating anarchy, still alive, still terrified the timid leaders of his alma mater. Macy quoted the recent Harvard ruling that "'the halls of the university shall not be open for persistent or systematic propaganda on contentious questions of contemporaneous social, economic, political or religious interests.'" Macy paraphrased this ultimatum to read, "let the university offer fifty courses in philosophy, history, and literature which is dead enough not to be dangerous to vested authority, but let it not take any part in philosophy, history, or literature which is in the making!" (p. 173).

Therein lay Macy's final castigation of the American university, which had defined its ultimate role to be custodian of vested puritan–capitalist interests in our society. He did not assault the aesthetic, moral, and material blight of puritanism with the sustained vehemence of Brooks in *The Wine of the Puritans* (1908). But Macy's periodic thrusts were nevertheless deadly when he portrayed Hawthorne or Holmes or Howells in confrontation with the New England guardians of this sickly and dated morality. Indeed, the historic assignment for American writers had been to recognize and expose this conservative puritan ethic of our commercial civilization, and they had received almost no support from the professors. What had been "inculcated by most of the 'savants' in obedience to the economic powers that endow and dominate the universities" were not the democratic ideals of a Whitman, but the bourgeois values of the "capitalistic oligarchy" (pp. 212, 214). Macy went on to adopt the touchstone of socialism in his most memorable chapters, where he analyzed and evaluated the American spirit of the authors. But for all the lively substance, range, and style of his socially—and socialistically—oriented, but by no means aesthetically undiscriminating, literary history, why did Macy not become a sharper rallying voice for a new generation than Brooks in *America's Coming-of-Age* two years later? No single cause can be isolated. Macy's *Spirit* was packaged in a commercial series, the Modern Library of the World's Best Books, and he hoped, in his preface, that it would be an appropriate introduction for the student (p. v). To that end, he included the obligatory biographical note, with a modest bibliography, at the close of each chapter. And while he complained of academic critics "who write with such modified judgments and well-tempered compensations that they elaborately kill their discourses" (p. 205), this rather anti-intellectual strain in Macy may have prevented him from necessary rigor of method and definition. He freely owned that his book was "a little nearer to a collection of appreciative essays than to a formal history or bibliographic manual" (p. v). It did achieve a semblance of thematic unity, though the selective analysis here may have exaggerated any cohesive structure.

Perhaps most damaging was the vagueness of Macy's terminology. In the introductory chapter on "General Characteristics," he discussed, but did not clarify, the terms in his title. What is literature? What is American literature? What is the American spirit in or out of our literature? Macy stated that literature "springs from life ultimately but not immediately" and the history or tradition of literature is somehow "a succession of books from books." On American literary nationalism, he repeated the argument as old as one hundred years or as recent as Brander Matthews: Ours was a "branch of English literature" and (implicitly) Tainean analyses were inadmissible due to the primacy of our shared English language; for "in literature nationality is determined by language rather than by blood or geography." No critic, Macy wrote, had satisfactorily defined American characteristics, so that a poet like Whittier might seem "pugnaciously American, but his sympathies are universal, his vision is cosmic." At one point, Macy flatly stated (his title notwithstanding) that "the American spirit in literature is a myth." Later, he asserted, however, that

"American literature is on the whole idealistic, sweet, delicate, nicely finished," and he would have our writers more local, or "provincial," for our literature was "too globe-trotting, it has too little savour of the soil." We needed more Ethan Fromes and Jennie Gerhardts (pp. 3–17). After moving through Macy's subsequent chapters, from Irving to Henry James, the reader might be invigorated by the opinionated liberalism but was left asking precisely what the American spirit in literature was or is, might be or ought to be.

In his varied career after the war, Macy never courted academia, nor did he abandon his fighting credo of 1913. Always a tart literary critic, he also served as adviser to William Morrow (after 1926). Macy died of a heart attack in 1932, characteristically in the middle of a series of lectures on the rebellious aspects of American literature, being delivered not to a university audience but to trade union workers at Unity House, Stroudsburg, Pennsylvania.[22]

★   ★   ★

Randolph Bourne (1886–1918) was more influential than Macy in the short run, though his literary and cultural criticism were even less sustained. Brilliant, deformed, and pampered, Bourne grew up in Bloomfield, New Jersey, suffocating from the middle-class puritanism of small-town America. He recounted these years in his first book, *Youth and Life* (1913). His mother proper and compliant, his father an irresponsible businessman who disappeared in Bourne's late teens, Bourne came to view his early alienation as the representative experience of American youth in the early twentieth century. At age twenty-three, he was belatedly awarded a scholarship to Columbia. There he attended classes of Erskine but apparently none taught by Trent. Van Doren, recently arrived as a graduate student, recalled in his autobiography that Bourne made a considerable stir around campus in these years with his opinions on behalf of the younger generation, some appearing early in the *Atlantic Monthly*. Bourne anticipated our later youth culture of the 1960s ("don't trust anyone over thirty") by advancing a slogan that nobody over twenty-five ever absorbed a new idea. His professors reminded the young radical that he was twenty-five (it was 1911). His posthumous *The History of a Literary Radical*, said Van Doren, became the "whole history of the thoughtful young men of his decade."[23] Bourne there described his literary education in the American academy.

He arrived at Columbia with a prep-school background in the

classics. His interest soon turned to English literature, not in the lackluster courses at Columbia but during a pivotal moment on holiday when he heard Yale's William Lyon Phelps lecture on the modern novel in England and Russia. Bourne later realized that Phelps was a rather "pale and timid Gideon" after all. But Bourne's revolt and emancipation were under way, and he fashioned his own literary educaton, seeking out writers of social purpose—Tolstoy, Wells, and Chesterton. At Columbia, Bourne forswore literary classes after experiencing them as "dead rituals in which academic priests mumbled their trite commentary." One of these academic high priests was Erskine, whose popular (English) literature classes gave Bourne little help "through the current literary maze," for Erskine avoided the young living writers. He allowed discussion of socialism in the classroom and in after-school student gatherings and even offered his own asides, but he was "inclined to deprecate the fanaticism of college men who lose their sense of proportion on social questions," and he cautiously prevented the shock of radical issues from fracturing "the sacred chalice of the past."[24]

During his postgraduate year in Europe (1913–14) on a Gilder Fellowship from Columbia, Bourne made two discoveries almost simultaneously that helped to complete the education of a young American literary radical. First, he conceived an overpowering distaste for the anglophile American. (Earlier at Columbia, he had thought of becoming a professor of English literature.) And second, he realized that, consequently, he must turn, as Brooks had done, to "inventing a 'usable past'" for his generation, to cull somehow a legacy derived from the "terrible patronage of bourgeois society." Bourne read *The Adventures of Huckleberry Finn* and *Tom Sawyer* for the first time and, along with the works of Thoreau and Whitman, hoped "to tap through them a certain eternal human tradition of abounding vitality and moral freedom, and so build out the future" (p. 42).

On his return from Europe in 1914, Bourne published in the *Atlantic* his impressions of American literary opinion and tradition as he had gathered them from a transoceanic perspective. Most galling to him were Americans' admiration of virtually any national culture but their own and especially their worship of England's literature. He had noticed that even the English were amused by "the bated breath of the American, when he speaks of Shakespeare or Tennyson or Browning." Bourne could have been staging a modern-day dialogue with his alma mater's Brander Matthews on this century-old debate over American literary nationalism. Matthews, for example, had written a celebrated piece urging a proper humility on teachers of American literature. Really by then a litany of anglophile platitudes, Matthews's article had stressed that "American literature is only a branch" of English literature, that the American student's "roots in the past" should therefore be nourished by a literary pride in his Shakespearean heritage, and that we should beware an "excess of patriotic bias," for we had not even a second-rank American poet. No doubt Emerson, Hawthorne, and Poe had unique gifts, but the English Victorians were clearly superior and we should modestly inquire into reasons for our literary shortcomings.[25]

Bourne in 1914 countered this perennial cultural humility by arguing, instead, that we needed to cultivate "a new American nationalism" similar to the "cultural chauvinism" of the French, to judge authors past and present with a modern response and creative pride. ("When shall we learn to be proud? For only pride is creative.") In Europe today, or even over the past half-century, "one will go far to find greater poets than our Walt Whitman, philosophers than William James, essayists than Emerson and Thoreau, composers than MacDowell, sculptors than Saint-Gaudens." These artists who expressed the American spirit, rather than the foreign writers who expressed *their* national spirit, were to Bourne "immensely more stimulating, because of the very body and soul of to-day's interests and aspirations."[26]

Two years later, again in the *Atlantic*, Bourne completed his diatribe against the American anglophile, this time attacking our mainstream Anglo-Saxon culture. "English snobberies, English religion, English literary styles, English literary reverences and canons, English ethics, English superiorities," he wrote, "have been the cultural food that we have drunk from our mother's breasts." By then, he was also firmly opposed to American intervention on the side of the English in the current war. A pacifist on idealistic grounds, to be sure, he must have been gaining from this cultural animus at least subliminal argument for his antiwar position. Moreover, he remarked on the hue and cry by our nation's official publicists whenever they detected any "evidence of vigorous nationalistic and cultural movements in this country among Germans, Scandinavians, Bohemians, and Poles, while in the same breath they insist that the alien shall be forcibly assimilated to that Anglo-Saxon tradition which they unquestionably label 'American.'" Bourne heralded the "indigenous genius" of our immigrant democracy, "the distinctively American spirit—pioneer, as distinguished from the reminiscently English—that appears in Whitman and Emerson and James."[27]

Bourne died in 1918 before he could fully explore this usable past in our literature. That his legacy as an author seems so much larger than it actually is can serve as testimony of his charismatic flair as a hero of the radical youth culture of the time. Even today, many believe that he died somehow as a martyr cut down by the entrenched forces of Anglo-Saxon militarism, capitalism, journalism, puritanism, academicism, and so on. In fact, he fell victim to the influenza epidemic of 1918.

✸   ✸   ✸

More intemperate than Bourne's attack on traditional American values and institutions, including the academy and its literary professors, was the longer lasting campaign of H. L. Mencken (1880–1956). Though he sprayed his fire at countless enemies in the bastions of American puritanism, gentility, plutocracy, and democratic stupidity, the happy warrior and coeditor (with George Jean Nathan) of the *Smart Set* (1914–23) was never more gleeful than in moments when his barbs and shafts struck a "Professor Doctor," Mencken's mock-Germanic title for adversaries in the "groves of sapience." Son of a prosperous tobacco merchant, Mencken did not share the eager socialism of Brooks, Bourne, Macy, and the rest, but he fully sympathized with their revolt against the mentality of the university pedagogues who consistently denied a seat on Parnassus to America's provocative new authors. Even here, Mencken sometimes promoted fiercely independent opinions that his allies in rebellion were not able to endorse. He was also vulnerable to a charge of academic sour grapes in his unrelenting war on the professors because, as Sherman noted in reviewing the early *A Book of Prefaces,* Mencken had never attended a university. (His final schooling was at Baltimore Polytechnic.) Even his most dogged admirers agree that while Mencken's critical instincts were brilliantly journalistic, he was often careless and inaccurate as a scholar.

In *A Book of Prefaces* (1917), his first important critical volume, Mencken propped up most of his favorite targets and established the Mencken style of attack. Of the four chapters, three were on Mencken heroes—Conrad, Dreiser, and Huneker. Here the method was to extol the object of Mencken's praise and at the same time expose the ignorance of his antagonists, usually the professors. In chapter 4, "Puritanism as a Literary Force," his literary heroes, from Poe and Whitman to Dreiser and George Ade, popped in and out as victims during the course of Mencken's tirade against the prevailing culture in America with its puritan-sponsored "campaign of repression and punishment" and the philistine "distrust of beauty, and of the joy that is its object" (pp. 210, 240).

While praising Conrad, Mencken took his swipes along the way at the moralistic Anglo-Saxon, old-maidish American literary tradition. He arrived at Dreiser in full stride. After some sixty pages explaining the phenomenon of Dreiser's American career, Mencken assessed the country's academic critics, beginning with "an ass named Professor Richardson" in whose literary history for colleges Mark Twain was barely noticed, was ranked below Irving, Holmes, and Lowell, and "dismissed by this Professor Balderdash as a hollow buffoon" (p. 132). William Lyon Phelps admirably deplored this lapse in Richardson and others, but "college professors, alas, never learn anything," for Phelps then left out Dreiser in *The Advance of the English Novel* while hailing the genius of O. Henry and Henry Sydnor Harrison (p. 133).[28] Other tone-deaf members of "the new Dunciad" included those whom Brooks had recently identified in *The Seven Arts,* "most of the acknowledged heavyweights of the craft— the Babbitts, Mores, Brownells, and so on" (p. 134). The attack against them and other worshippers of "fossil literature" was enlarged in the next chapter on James Gibbons Huneker, where Mencken not only blamed the professors for the literary ignorance of students who become our critics, but also regretted that they published their Victorian-style opinions in journals like the *Nation,* their pretentious learning "precisely the sterile, foppish sort one looks for in second-rate professors" (p. 158). Exempted from Mencken's roll call of incompetent literary critics were Ludwig Lewisohn, Joel Spingarn, and John Macy ("I recently found his 'The Spirit of American Literature,' by long odds the soundest, wisest book on its subject, selling for fifty cents on a Fifth Avenue remainder counter" [p. 157]), and most prominently, his cherished Huneker.

After the chapters on Dreiser and Huneker, Mencken presumably established his credentials as a worthy foe of the professor-critics, so that he could write his own essay in American literary history, "Puritanism as a Literary Force," which completed the volume. The reader looking for scholar acumen or even fair play in this culminating essay will not find either amid Mencken's casual homework and sophomoric rascality. Measured against the solidity and eloquence of a scholarly professor like Moses Coit Tyler, Mencken is little more than a peevish amateur in his analysis of the Puritan spirit in American literary history. So familar now is the Mencken line that it can be easily capsulized. The colonial Puritan established a "commonwealth of peasants and small traders, a paradise of the third-rate" that was guided by a national philosophy almost wholly unchecked by the more sophisticated and civilizing ideas of an aristocracy." Mencken's social and intellectual propositions were almost frivolously uninformed, but the polemicist in him was undaunted. When he advanced the historical sketch into the early nineteenth century, he remarked on the supplanting of the old theocracy by its puritan twin brother, philistinism.

This enemy of beauty and joy now handed over "the cultivation of belles lettres, and of all the other arts no less, to women and admittedly second-rate men." The philistines defeated Poe and Whitman, but writers like Mark Twain, Howells, and James waged a campaign to bring life back to literature. Sad to say, all three soon exhibited a "timorousness and reticence," and the puritans renewed their authority, beginning with the Comstock Postal Act of 1873. Since then, the "new will to power" of the American puritan had "developed an art of militant morality as complex in technique and as rich in professors as the elder art of iniquity." Mencken closed with an obligatory gesture of hope in a new day, "at least the beginnings of a revolt, or, at all events, of a protest" (pp. 210–82).

Of the reviews that greeted *A Book of Prefaces,* the one that commands the keenest historical interest was by the *CHAL's* Stuart Sherman in the *Nation.* Sherman had appeared in Mencken's Dreiser chapter as the beneficiary of a left-handed compliment: With W. H. Boynton, he stood at the head of "the other group" in Mencken's new Dunciad, in "a more courageous and more honest" gathering that at least recognized the presence of Dreiser, unlike the "lady critics of the newspapers" in their genteel ranks. Sherman alone was capable of "any intelligible reasoning," but Mencken promptly ridiculed Sherman's case against *The "Genius"* (1915) in which he had typed Dreiser a French naturalist propagating a theory of animal behavior. So much for "the folly of college professors" and their "pigeon-holing pedagogue" Sherman, who "may well stand as archetype of the booming, indignant corrupter of criteria, the moralist turned critic," the embodiment of Christian–Comstockian Americanism (pp. 134–39).

Sherman replied in a scathing review, "Beautifying American Literature" (*Nation,* 29 November 1917). Throughout the years of their combat, Mencken usually admired Sherman's clever attacks in kind, but this one carried the wartime implication that Mencken was a partisan of all things German, a gutter-level tactic impugning his patriotism, Mencken believed, and he never forgave Sherman for it.[29] At the time of his review of Mencken in 1917, Sherman had been readying his own first volume of American criticism, *On Contemporary Literature* (1917), where he reprinted various earlier essays, most prominently "The Naturalism of Mr. Dreiser," the review in *Nation* (1915) that Mencken was angrily refuting in the book under review. Mencken soon discovered that Sherman had sardonically retitled the essay "The Barbaric Naturalism of Theodore Dreiser" in the forthcoming book. Sherman, then, was emotionally primed to duel with Mencken in late 1917. And Sherman was superbly prepared intellectually, as we can appreciate in the pages of *On Contemporary Literature,* one of the most eloquent and readable treatises ever to appear under the unofficial aegis of the New Humanism (it was dedicated to Paul Elmer More who, it will be recalled, had brought young Sherman onto the *Nation* with a recommendation from Irving Babbitt, Sherman's favorite professor at Harvard).

The larger setting for Sherman's review of Mencken's *Book of Prefaces* takes us back through his ten years since Harvard, during which he had been using literature as a weapon of moral combat, with all the energy of Mencken, Brooks, or Bourne. As Mencken generously conceded, Sherman in these years courageously and directly entertained the issues of modern literature rather than discount current writers with the professor's usual oblique, antiquarian disdain. For *On Contemporary Literature,* Sherman was assembling, in 1917, some of his most incisive pieces and updating them here and there in the recent months since American entry into the war. For example, in the original review of Brooks's *The World of H. G. Wells* (1915), Sherman had needled Brooks and the immature followers of Wells and his naturalism. For the book, Sherman was bringing the review up to date and wondering if the younger generation might feel lately betrayed by Wells's wartime conversion to human over biological purpose, of ideals over instincts, "such ideas as right, liberty, happiness, duty, and beauty, in behalf of which, indeed, they are now shedding their blood."[30] But the liberated young would inevitably search out the naturalist in Wells. Just as surely, they would ignore Arnold Bennett's conventions that enlarge life by curbing wayward desires, for "the young, as Mr. Randolph Bourne tells us, the young are in love with life; and to accept conventions is to refuse life" (p. 119). Turning to American writers Mark Twain and Dreiser (whom Mencken had complained that most American professors shun), Sherman forcefully argued his case against any naturalism in Twain, deplored it in Dreiser, and

also injected into his pages on Dreiser the anti-Teutonic argument that especially irritated Mencken.

Having prepared for republication these earlier arguments,
some of them newly sharpened from the unified perspective of
the New Humanism, Sherman may well have reviewed *A Book
of Prefaces* in late 1917 virtually at a sitting, so ready was he to
impede Mencken's offensive and repudiate his central themes.
Sherman now bracketed Mencken and Dreiser as Germanophiles
and then summarized the entire spectrum of Mencken's un-
American credo: in "Kultur" Germanic; in politics, a spokesman
for an anti-democratic federalism; in social thought, antifeminist
and in favor of a "somewhat severe male aristocracy"; in education, against universities and professors; in religion, against
Christianity and for *Herrenmoral;* in nationalism and race,
against the Anglo-Saxon and for a "Teutonic-Oriental pessimism
and nihilism." [31] Sherman then gave to Mencken's "learned style"
a searingly ironic analysis (a treatment that Mencken would use
one day soon, in turn, on "Prof. Dr. Thorstein Veblen"). Sherman
observed that "a brave little band of sophomores in criticism"
were defecting to this "quiet drummer of beauty" who urged us
to abandon the "ruck and muck of American 'culture'" in ex-
change for his foreign values. [32]

Mencken, meanwhile, was stimulated into even more vocif-
erous combat in *The Smart Set,* pages that he reworked for the
first of six volumes of *Prejudices.* The first series appeared in
September 1919 and went through eight printings in the next
five years. True to the title, it was a grab bag of enthusiasms and
antipathies, most of them already spotted and labeled by Sherman
in the review of *A Book of Prefaces.* Of Mencken's twenty-one
chapters, only two were sustained essays, and their common subject was the professor. The occasion for "Criticism of Criticism of
Criticism" was Henry Holt's reissuing in 1917 of Joel Spingarn's
Creative Criticism (1911). Mencken imagined the effect wrought
by the Columbia professor when his radical dogma of aestheticism
reached the stodgy critics in academe and specifically the reactions of indignation and horror from Yale's moralistic Prof. Dr.
William Lyon Phelps; of the "Amherst Aristotle" with his iron-
clad standards, Prof. Dr. W. C. Brownell; and above all, of "the
gifted Prof. Dr. Stuart P. Sherman, of Iowa," he of the "loud patriotic alarm" and the quaint "maxim that Puritanism is the official philosophy of America, and that all who dispute it are enemy
aliens and should be deported" (p. 11). [33] Though Mencken welcomed the further havoc that Spingarn would spread among the

critics in academia, Mencken pointed out instructively that
Spingarn, "the ingenious ex-professor, professor-like" claimed
too much (p. 17). Beauty cannot be considered in a vacuum. It
has "its social, its political, even its moral implications" (p. 18).
Not to denounce all categories and approaches but to use them
eclectically and wisely was the program of the free-spirited
Huneker, a critic superior to "all the prating pedagogues since
Rufus Griswold" (p. 19).

The chapter "Professor Veblen" embraced the parallel concerns of new rebels like Macy, Brooks, and Bourne, who hoped to
reform American society through socialism so that a national
literature might realize and express our traditional democratic
faith. Mencken described himself as an early dabbler in socialism
and the writings of Veblen until about 1909, when he lost all of
his "superior interest in Socialism, even as an amateur psychia-
trist, and thus lost track of its Great Thinkers" (p. 60). He then
graduated to other putative great thinkers of the American campus, Prof. Dr. William James and Prof. Dr. John Dewey. (Macy, we
have seen, admired James, and Bourne idolized Dewey before the
pragmatist rationalized American intervention in the war.) Since
1914, Dewey had been dethroned by the "intellectual soviets"
and Veblen was back. Returning to *The Theory of the Leisure
Class* (1899), Mencken pronounced it "simply Socialism and
water" written in "the most cacophonous English that even a professor ever wrote." He then implicitly recast Brooks's highbrow–
lowbrow America into the plutocracy and the populace and
termed both groups ignorant in a society that sorely required a
saving, a mediating "intellectual aristocracy." What America
owned, instead, was "an indistinct herd of intellectual eunuchs,
chiefly professors—often quite as stupid as the plutocracy and always in great fear of it. When it produces a stray rebel he goes
over to the mob; there is no place for him within his own order."
Thus the American professor was the indecisive and craven
man-between who "gets no respect and is deficient in self-respect"
(pp. 60–81).

*   *   *

Joining Mencken's chorus in 1919 were still other voices reassess-
ing American life, literary history, and contemporary values. The
two most important were Louis Untermeyer, *The New Era in
American Poetry,* and Waldo Frank in *Our America.* Untermeyer
(1885–1977), like Mencken, had no college training in literature
and criticism. He recalled in his autobiography, *From Another*

World (1939), that he worked during these years in the family jewelry business by day and, after hours, nurtured the ambition to be a composer, a pianist, and finally a poet. In the process, he became, instead, a gifted anthologer and a slightly above-average critic at a time when the new poets could dearly use his services. His best work as a critic appeared in the *New Republic,* the *Seven Arts,* and the early *Masses.* For the *New Era in American Poetry,* he presented some of this criticism, written in the second decade of the century, that bore the new temper of rebellion. In his "Introduction: The New Spirit," he quoted Brooks and inveighed against America's Europeanized graybeards who could not appreciate Whitman's "keen and racy originality." The Mencken doctrine, too, was lively in his mind as Untermeyer identified in America's poetic expression a peculiar hypocrisy that was "rooted in its old puritanism." But that was largely in the past, and he was heartened by the new poetry, far more than was Mencken. The distance it had come in the two decades since Stedman's *American Anthology* could be measured in qualities of the "human, racy and vigorous; it is not only closer to the soil but nearer to the soul." Within this new democracy of spirit and of speech, America's new poets were engaged in a restless searching for new values, for a new awareness of the self (pp. 5–14).

Waldo Frank (1889–1967) was born in New Jersey, like Brooks and Bourne, but grew up in New York City a precocious and advantaged child. He fills out our academic survey by representing Yale, where he took courses (though not American literature) with Henry Beers and William Lyon Phelps. To Frank, Phelps was something less than the emancipating lecturer who inspired Bourne. Years later, Frank profiled Phelps in the *New Yorker* and recalled his old professor as a kindly sentimental purveyor of beauty and culture, as well as a courageous pacifist who predictably saw the light and decided to go with the popular war-majority (becoming the same "pale and timid Gideon" Bourne later recognized).[34] After graduating with honors from Yale, Frank traveled, then tried to establish a literary and journalistic career commensurate with his egocentric and mystic sense of his vast personal gifts and ended up contributing to Mencken and Nathan's *Smart Set.* From November 1916 to October 1917, Frank joined Brooks and others as associate editor and contributor to the *Seven Arts.* Frank also wrote a first novel, *The Unwelcome Man* (1917). Avowedly a pacifist like Bourne, Frank ventured west in the last year of the war to understand not only the nation's heartland and the Chicago literary scene, but also to experience the final result of pioneering in the reaches beyond traditional Anglo-Saxon America on the Pacific slope and the Southwest. Out of this journey came *Our America* (1919), Frank's personal odyssey toward recognitions occasionally novel and deeply independent in spite of his spiritual allegiance to the main party line of young America.[35]

Frank established his point of view in the foreword and introductory remarks and took aim at the traditional enemies of his generation with a critical certainty that belied the frequently rambling progress of his nine chapters. At the outset, he presumed to be the unofficial voice in 1919 on behalf of his peers, "the first generation of Americans consciously engaged in spiritual engineering." He named three familiar villains who were captives of a dying order in twentieth-century cultural America: the professor, the anglophile, and the industrialist. (Macy's highbrow triumvirate were the professor, the puritan, and the capitalist.) They typified and expressed the opposing values that had fired the revolt of Frank's idealistic and hopeful younger generation (pp. ix–xi, 3–9).

Before he embarked on a new exploration of America, Frank devoted three chapters to the fateful materialistic effects of three centuries of the pioneering experience in America. He then explored the regional life in the Far West before back-tracking to Chicago, New England, and New York. (Characteristically, the South was ignored.) The book comes alive as literary history impinging on the academy when Frank returns eastward to New England. (He had nothing to say about writers or academic figures on the West Coast, nor had he any interest in the Chicago critics, though his comments on despair and hope in the Midwestern writers were frequently incisive.) In "The Puritan Says 'Yea,'" Frank discovered an authentic hero for "revolting America—young America" in Thoreau "who faced reality," revered the Indian's America, and embraced Rousseau's doctrines of nature and self. Frank's middle name, David, came from Thoreau. But his first name, after Emerson, did not tie him spiritually to the sage of Concord. To a postwar America, Emerson's words had become "vague and impalpable and abstract"—or as T. S. Eliot commented in his review of the *CHAL* this same year, though with other reasons, Emerson was now an "encumbrance."

Frank's modern yea sayers in the land of the Puritans included Robert Frost, tortured and ambivalent to be sure, but still creator of lyrically beautiful poems.[36] In the example of Amy Lowell, Frank adopted the Mencken ploy of linking this descendant of

official Puritan New England to the stifling academy. But Frank
anticipated a happy outcome. She had triumphed over her Anglo-
Saxon origins and upbringing. In this latter-day Lowell, "the
American cultural tradition at last strikes free from its ancient
bondage whose arsenals-in-chief have been the Eastern univer-
sities." Like Untermeyer, Frank detected in her a champion of
European literature and modern American poets rather than of
English authors, a liberating rebel who had defected from her
"puritan clan" that "kept the Colonial American, the unconscious
Anglophile, on top." But their mastery was still formidable in
politics, the academy, and the press: "They speak in the United
States Senate through such men as Henry Cabot Lodge; they
preach in the schools through W. C. Brownell, Barrett Wendell,
William Lyon Phelps; they set the journalistic standards in the
leadership of the *Atlantic Monthly,* the *Boston Transcript,* the
New York *Evening Post*" (p. 163). And, Frank might have added,
their G. R. Elliott had recently repudiated the anti-Victorian
battle cry sounded by Miss Lowell in her *Tendencies in Modern
American Poetry* (1917). Elliott disavowed the kindly mystical
individualism of the modern poets' Whitman as having any force
amid the selfish materialism and blazing romanticism of "our
present national temper."[37]

But for Frank, back once more in New York, Whitman helped
to climax this modern religious quest for new gods. *Our America*
closed in an upbeat fashion as Frank envisioned how our de-
pleted puritan pioneering energies could be replaced by the emotional and religious spirit of a Whitmanesque "love of life, love of
being." But first, he felt impelled to hurl one last grenade in the
direction of the American universities. Those "incubators of reaction," founded largely by puritans and pioneers, were now "endowed by the successors of these: the industrial masters." And
lately, they had become the wartime persecutors of all deviant
professors courageous enough to challenge with alternative views
of society and art what Frank rather ominously termed the "academic powers of America" (pp. 230, 209).[38]

✱   ✱   ✱

In that academy, meanwhile, the editors of the foremost cooperative effort in American literary history were preparing the final
two volumes of the *CHAL*. While these third and fourth shoes
were still to drop, H. L. Mencken, ever wide-awake and opinionated, was preparing his special reception for the event. In the
Smart Set of February 1918 (pp. 138–40), he had already no-

ticed volume I and even ventured a few words of backhanded praise. The "professor doctors" had turned out a "diligent and comprehensive work" nicely suited to their talents, since "it demanded, not any capacity to make the thing charming, nor even any capacity to work out accurate valuations, but merely an encyclopediac [sic] knowledge of the indubitable, and a sure skill at cataloguing." Especially meeting these purposes of "embalming and laying out" were the praiseworthy chapters by More, Parrington, and even Sherman, together with the admirable bibliographies (in which the one prominent omission was the work of John Macy). Where the *CHAL* had failed, however, was painfully clear: "The college professor, as I have often argued in this place, is almost devoid of any true critical sense." The stage was set, then, for an "intelligent critical history" of American literature, and Mencken now framed his own version of that history in *Prejudices: Second Series* (1920). The eleven-part essay, "The National Letters," ran to one hundred pages, or 40 percent of the volume. Drawing partly from his columns in the *Smart Set,* he did not, however, repeat his earlier praise of the "necessary and long-awaited" *CHAL.*[39]

The underlying theme of Mencken's essay proper was that the official canon of American literature had attained only a "respectable mediocrity," a "timorous flaccidity, an amiable hollowness" and the best living writers created under duress because our experiment in democracy had been an enormously depressing cultural flop. One of the chief causes for this American "disease" was the presence of "a forlorn *intelligentsia* gasping out a precarious life," and it was on the failure of these campus critics and pedagogues that Mencken vented his spleen anew. They had failed to lead us toward a sanity of national ideals or a pride in our most vital and courageous authors of the past, and they offered neither creative direction nor encouragement to our living writers. Aware that they were barely tolerated by American society and threatened with expulsion for any deviant ideas or actions, professors knew "they are safe so long as they are good, which is to say, so long as they neither aggrieve the plutocracy nor startle the proletariat" (p. 79). When professors eagerly became relevant and went public as intellectual framers of national sentiment, they were "almost as timid and flatulent" as the press (p. 82). And just as dangerous, Mencken had discovered during the recent war (no doubt Sherman, among others, was on his mind): "They constituted themselves, not a restraining influence upon the mob run wild, but the loudest spokesmen of its worst imbecilities. They fed it with bogus history, bogus philosophy, bogus idealism, bogus heroics" (p. 83).

Once more, Mencken had accomplished only cursory homework. He noted that the historians of our literature in the last century had produced a sorry intellectual record that stretched from the naïve and extravagant nationalism of Samuel Knapp, the elder Channing, and Noah Webster to Barrett Wendell's end-of-the-century "sour threnody upon the New England *Aufklarung*" (p. 13). (In *Prejudices: Fifth Series,* 1926, Mencken would term Wendell's *Literary History of America* "arbitrary and ignorant but highly amusing" and then pay his respects to this fellow aristocrat whose verve, at least, showed other professors how they might descend from their ivory towers and breathe the living air at sea level.) Since Wendell, we had "the solemn, highly judicial, coroner's inquest criticism of More, Brownell, Babbitt and their imitators," including W. L. Phelps, Percy Boynton, and Bliss Perry (whose *American Spirit in Literature,* 1918, blandly all things to all readers and published by Yale, would inevitably have angered Mencken).

Chief among the New Humanist tag-alongs, of course, was the moralistic Sherman, who had given the younger generation strict warning "that Puritanism is the lawful philosophy of the country, and that any dissent from it is treason" (pp. 19, 27). In the hands of these professors, literature was "an academic exercise for talented grammarians," as well as "a genteel recreation for ladies and gentlemen of fashion" (p. 19). Our living writers, agonizingly at work to portray and criticize American contemporary life, needed an "intelligent sympathy . . . its roots in the intellectual curiosity of an aristocracy of taste" (p. 89). The modern writer received, instead, the professors' corrective rebuke: "His representation is indecorous, unlovely, too harsh to be borne. His criticism is in contumacy to the ideals upon which the whole structure rests" (p. 88). Mencken recalled that when he looked to the academic intelligentsia for support of Dreiser's The *"Genius,"* he realized that the professor arrayed himself with the Comstocks: "No instinctive urge of class, no prompting of a great tradition, moved him to speak out for artistic freedom" (p. 91).

At the close, Mencken admitted that perhaps "insurmountable natural obstacles stand in the way of a distinctively American culture, grounded upon a truly egoistic nationalism and supported by a native aristocracy" (p. 99). Still, he had culled some hope along the way: in the "natural revolt of youth against the pedagogical Prussianism of the professors" (p. 26); in the "operatic rebellions" of Greenwich Village from which had emerged the dramas of Eugene O'Neill, "many cuts above the well-professored mechanicians who pour out of Prof. Dr. Baker's *Ibsenfabrik* at Cambridge" (pp. 100, 30); and in the wisely skeptical critical spirit expressed in "the iconoclastic political realism of Harold Stearns, Waldo Frank and company" and in Van Wyck Brooks, "a young man far more intelligent, penetrating and hospitable to fact than any of the reigning professors" (pp. 100, 12).

Chapter 12

The *CHAL* Completed

In the meantime, during summer of 1919, Mencken's reigning professors were either completing assignments for the last two volumes of the *CHAL* or awaiting publication of their chapters already completed or, in the case of the four editors, either soliciting a few last contributors or awaiting manuscripts in progress while reading proofs of others. In June, at his summer retreat in Westport, Connecticut, Trent returned to Van Doren the proofs of "Later Philosophy" by Morris Cohen (CCNY), earlier misplaced and presumably lost until Mrs. Trent had located them in a bureau drawer of their hotel in Northampton. "The chapter seems to me excellent," Trent wrote, "but needs special consideration on one point—i.e., the conspicuous amount of space devoted to contemporaries, who are perhaps essentially of no greater importance than any men in other lines who are omitted or briefly mentioned," though he did not see how the space for Dewey and Santayana could be reduced.[1] Here is the basis for the complaint we have just heard from young critics of the orthodox literary historians, the reluctance of the academy to welcome American writers of the present.

The final chapters of the *CHAL* were moving ever closer to the contemporary scene, but the end was not in sight, and the year passed into still another summer. In July 1920, Trent was commuting from Norwalk, Connecticut, to teach in the Columbia summer session and returned still more proof sheets, corrected with his usual thoroughness. He wearily asked Van Doren, "How many chapters remain to be set up?" Causing their chief exasperation was Columbia colleague Samuel Wolff and his late chapter, "Scholars." On 24 July, Trent returned Wolff's proofs to Van Doren with the comment, "Your cutting must have been a job!" The chapter now was, at least, useful. But when the proofs came to Wolff's hands, more than a month's delay followed, and Van Doren was to recall years later that "at the last I was a good deal irritated, and spoke roughly to him over the telephone. Afterwards I was ashamed of this."[2]

The last proofs were finally returned by summer's end, and the editors penned their final preface, at last ready to enjoy the consummation of a labor that had extended to more than six years. In the winter of early 1921, the final two volumes were printed, and Trent soon mailed each editor a check for $187.50, with an extra $50 to Van Doren for clerical expenses. (Van Doren noted on Trent's letter that his wife Irita worked especially on the index.) Somewhat plaintively (or was it a grumble?), Trent requested of Van Doren on 16 March, "If you can suggest to G. H. P. that the oldest editor would like to see the volumes, I should be obliged." The closing weeks were also the occasion for a tribute to Van Doren from the other editors for his disproportionate share of the work. Some time before, Trent had proposed to Sherman the idea of an appropriate gift, and Sherman selected a handsome volume of Charles Lanman's *Letters from the Allegheny Mountains* (1849). The three editors inscribed their gratitude to Van Doren "in recognition of the part his Atlantean shoulders have borne in carrying through the Cambridge History of American Literature."[3] Unfortunately, it was premature even for so reserved a celebration. One last painful episode began within days after publication. On the front page of the *New York Times* of 19 April 1921, Albert F. Gilmore, a prominent New York Christian Scientist, took exception to the irreverent remarks about Mrs. Eddy and *Science and Health* in the chapter "Popular Bibles" by Woodbridge Riley. Putnam immediately gave in to the pressure and tried to recall volume IV, though *Nation* and some few others had already reviewed it, and other journals had the original volume as review copy. Van Doren objected to a substitute chapter, but Trent went along with the publisher and persuaded Van Doren to do the same. On 22 April, Putnam announced on an inside page of the *Times* that theologian Lyman P. Powell was writing the new chapter.

It is easy today to argue that the editors should have been thankful for such gratuitous publicity in the *Times*. It turned out to be the most lively public notice the *CHAL* was ever to receive. But for Trent in particular, handling one last manuscript was a dismal return to battle after a false armistice. As he told Van Doren, Putnam had laid the burden on him "as they have done throughout when anything was not to their liking. You know, of course, how genial my feelings have been toward them ever since I wanted to throw up the job on account of I.[rving] P.[utnam]'s letter about my [antiwar] verses." Powell, mercifully, wrote the new chapter with dispatch. Trent then suggested revisions, and Powell speedily complied. Trent was unable to send Van Doren the revised manuscript because Erskine sat on it too long, but

Trent assured Van Doren of veto privileges when the proofs arrived. Exhausted from it all, Trent hoped that Van Doren would see his way to letting the chapter go through without alteration. "My nerves are pretty well knocked out," said Trent, "and I can do but little work." He had resisted a Putnam effort to grant censoring privileges of the new chapter to the Publication Committee of Christian Science and was anxious to get volume IV "out of 'hock.'"[4] Late reviewers like William Lyon Phelps were sent the original volume IV with Powell's new chapter as an accompanying leaflet. Meanwhile, Putnam reissued the volume officially with Powell's substitute chapter within the new bindings, and Riley's censored version of Mrs. Eddy went the route of a collector's item.

In their brief preface to the joint volumes, dated 10 September 1920, the editors hoped that the completed *CHAL* would establish "a new and important basis for the understanding of American life and culture," and attributed their delay to the recent war ("the unsettled conditions of the time") as well as to the many unforeseen "pioneer tasks" in American literature study. Much of the delay, of course, had come from the editors' genial vagueness in defining historical and aesthetic guidelines for the chapters. They had also failed to discipline the more verbose of the contributors. Wolff's "Scholars," despite Van Doren's assiduous pruning, still ran to forty-seven pages. Frederick Dellenbaugh's "Travellers and Explorers, 1846–1900" was forty pages (with forty-seven pages of bibliography), the same intolerable length as Cohen's "Later Philosophy" and the "Education" by Paul Monroe (Columbia). "Political Writing Since 1850" by William Boyd (Trinity College, Durham, North Carolina) and "Later Historians" by Bassett occupied thirty pages each. Yet the main poetry and fiction since the Civil War, including the attention to Mark Twain (twenty pages by Sherman), James (thirteen pages by Beach), and Howells (nine pages by Van Doren), received fewer than one hundred pages, and in this total, Crane, Norris, and London shared just under two pages.

The final two-volume installment opened auspiciously with the chapter on Mark Twain by Sherman, the most celebrated professor in Mencken's enemy camp. Sherman surveyed the life and discussed the travel books and fiction in a succinct twenty pages. He also touched on essential questions of American literary history more than most of the previous (or subsequent) contributors, though he often lacked precision in basic principles and terms. He tried to account for Mark Twain historically with regard to both literary tradition and American traits and then evaluated the literary performance and legacy. Sherman admitted the commonplace that Mark Twain was independent of most of his literary contemporaries and strongly indebted to the American oral tradition. Twain had affected America's general literary current at one extreme with his "'free-born American'" hero and at the other, with his pessimistic view of unheroic man. Sherman considered national traits that entered into, and evolved through, his writer. Mark Twain belonged in the company of Whitman and Lincoln as "an unmistakably native son of an eager, westward-moving people—unconventional, self-reliant, mirthful, profane, realistic, cynical, boisterous, popular, tender-hearted, touched with chivalry [in *Joan of Arc,* not *The Connecticut Yankee,* Sherman clarified later], and permeated to the marrow of his bones with the sentiment of democratic society and with loyalty to American institutions" (III, 1–2). *Innocents Abroad* was guided by the "thoroughly honest Western-American eye" (III, 9) and *Life on the Mississippi* by a renewed Emersonian spirit of place, a "new national pride declaring the spiritual independence of America" (III, 12). But Twain's late naturalistic pessimism introduced a strain "of which American literature before Mark Twain showed hardly a trace" and may have had an influence "unfortunately, not always in connection with the fine bravado of his American faith, which occasionally required an antidote to its natural insolence" (III, 20). Only in this final sentence of the chapter did Sherman expose the anti-naturalistic bias of the New Humanist that so irritated Mencken.

Sherman also addressed the third large question of the literary historian, "What is literature?" And refreshingly, it became a nonmoralistic and largely aesthetic issue. At the outset, he asked, in effect, if the author who achieves "a tremendous popular vote" belongs in the nation's literary history, and the implicit reply was yes, if the author has exhibited aesthetic excellence "in the opinion of severe critics." So Mark Twain's work possessed not only "a large illustrative value" but also a necessary "strictly literary significance" (III, 1). Sherman defined Mark Twain's humor as the abrupt Byronic transition from "the sublime to the ridiculous or *vice versa*" (III, 9). (Barrett Wendell traced this mode in much the same terms but as an American tradition, stretching from Franklin and Irving through Twain to Dunne.) Sherman also tried to describe Mark Twain's lifelong struggle with literary form, first in the "joyous miscellany" of the travel books (III, 8) and then in the fiction. For all Twain's fine instinct for plot and character, he usually lacked unity of tone and form, since he liked to begin "on the key of impressive realism, shift to commonplace melodrama, and end with roaring farce" (III, 13). Sherman

then moved on to each of the major fictions, though he never defined realism, let alone "impressive realism," or distinguished it
from melodrama, be it commonplace or otherwise. But he managed to discuss seven novels in as many pages, with discriminating judgments derived from explication of precise details of
character and incident within the works. His Eastern coeditors
might profitably have distributed this chapter to all the contributors. It was the high-water mark of the final installment of the
CHAL. The two dozen chapters that came after Sherman too frequently illustrated the dissonance of principles, definitions, and
methods in American literary history that characterized the two
previous volumes.

As an inquiry into historical evolution in our literature, volumes III and IV offered little more than haphazard chapter organization and uncoordinated discussions. The period "Later
National Literature: Part I," begun at the close of volume II with
the Civil War (or, when more convenient, 1850), continued in
volume III as "Later National Literature: Part II" and became, in
volume IV, "Later National Literature: Part III." Serious belles
lettres occupied just over one-fourth of the chapters, and only
the chapter on Howells's circle by Van Doren and on James by
Beach give us a sense of genre development. Van Doren traced
the various roots of Cooper romance as it survived among the
"fertile hacks" of the dime novel and idealized antebellum South
of John Esten Cooke and then virtually exploded in the native
and foreign subjects of historical romance in the 1880s and
1890s. Contributing also to this last outburst was a reaction to
realism, a mode that Van Doren designated (but never defined) as
"the dominant creed of the eighties" (III, 89). The reaction to realism, in turn, came from the bolder naturalists. Mainly, Van
Doren was inclined to simplify the evolution of native fiction as a
story of "tendencies" conveniently pocketed within decades rather
than as a development in which elements of the genre continued
or changed or were transformed into difficult mixtures. He left
the reader with the facile assertion that "no tendency quite so
clearly prevails as romance in the thirties, sentimentalism in the
fifties, realism in the eighties, or naturalism at the turn of the
century" (III, 95). (Elsewhere, he had nominated the seventies
as the decade of local-color short fiction.)

Beach's chapter on James was notable as a condensed version
of his recent *The Method of Henry James* (1918), the first distinguished study of James by an American. To explain the literary
technique, though not the themes, of James, Beach discounted
any important influence in American fiction, even Hawthorne,

and attributed the form and style of the long and short fiction to George Eliot, Flaubert, Turgenev, Pater, Swinburne, and Wilde. James became international rather than native in his adherence to "the cult of impressions," his attenuation of dramatic scenes, the minute concern with psychological states, and the "'initiation' into some social or artistic or spiritual value not obvious to the vulgar" (III, 107, 105).

Elsewhere and beyond fiction, the history of genres fared less well in these final chapters of the *CHAL*. Norman Foerster (moved from Wisconsin to North Carolina) separated the postwar versifiers (all were minor in his opinion) into regional schools—New England, New York, Midwestern, Western dialect—with none of them continuing the poetical note of earlier writers or even echoing strongly any single voice of the prewar era. He approached the new poetry through William Vaughn Moody (d. 1910) and discovered the tenuous beginnings of an American tradition for twentieth-century poets in the legacy of Whitman, at which point Foerster identified himself as a budding New Humanist: "To him, and of course to others, they owe their usual form, free verse, and their point of view, that of an exaggerated individualism" (III, 65). Montrose J. Moses also failed to discover any strong literary movement or school in American drama since the Civil War until recently. Playwrights serving the Washington Square Players, the Provincetown Players, and the Wisconsin Players were creating lively community theater and awakening an "art consciousness" in America (III, 298).

Other historical observations on genres and modes appeared briefly in various chapters. The essays of Donald G. Mitchell ("Ik Marvel") and George W. Curtis, said George Hellman, continued the tradition of Irving's "tender sentiment and gentle satire" (III, 110), and the travel essays of Charles D. Warner likewise recalled Irving. The postwar literary critics continued the tradition of criticism in America that Hellman identified as a "courtesy of spirit and courtesy of phrase" unlike the raspier voices of eighteenth- and nineteenth century English critics who otherwise influenced them (III, 129). George Whicher (Amherst) felt postwar humor to be less racy, crude, and eccentric than before, but there had also been a loss in "native flavour and homely philosophy," as well as instructive social satire (III, 21). Louise Pound (Nebraska) argued, oddly, that our oral literature tradition seldom possessed any serious artistic interest. But Mary Austin, in a welcome discussion of aboriginal American literature that fittingly completed the *CHAL*, maintained that "both the mood and the method of Amerind folk-tales are as distinctively American" as the work of Mark Twain or Edgar Lee Masters and as excellent. They directly influenced the Br'er Rabbit stories, which were "original Cherokee inventions" that passed from Indian to Negro slave to Joel Chandler Harris (IV, 615).

American ideas and character traits that had evolved in our life and literature since the Civil War received some comment from Whicher ("Minor Humorists"), who distinguished in this later American humor a national flavor less acerbic than the comedy of the Old World, our preference leaning to "unreflective merriment" or an exposure of the weaknesses of human nature "by the lenitives and tonics of mirth instead of by the scalpel of criticism" (III, 23). To Foerster, postwar poetry achieved no strong "national accent" but only a scattering of provincial voices, although the dominant New England spirit of Emerson continued in Emily Dickinson. And in Aldrich, "Puritan morality, after passing through Hawthorne, half artist and half moralist, becomes wholly artistic" (III, 31, 35). Beach credited both Emerson and Hawthorne for the Americanism of James's characters abroad: "There is something in James's estimate of spiritual values so fine, so immaterial, so indifferent to success or happiness or whatever merely practical issues, as to suggest nothing so much as the transcendentalism of Emerson, the otherworldliness of Hawthorne" (III, 99). Intensely American, too, was the "passion for Europe" in these characters and James himself (III, 98). The same passion, said Cohen, had also dominated our philosophical indebtedness to England and Scotland, though French and German influences were right behind. Wolff argued that our scholarly tradition had developed, more precisely, out of three foreign modes—British individual inquiry, French coteries and learned societies, and by the second quarter of the nineteenth century, the German universities, which "supervened upon the other two modes, and were added to them, as stimulus and audience, outlet and patron" (IV, 444).

Harry M. Ayres (Columbia) in "The English Language in America," returned to indigenous influences, including slang, regional variants, and dialectal growths, though he doubted that Whitman's dream of an expansive new word hoard of Americanisms was likely ever to be realized. Echoing Moses Coit Tyler, Ayres attributed also to Americans "an Elizabethan love of exuberant language" (IV, 570). This Anglo-Saxon observation was followed by two final chapters on "Non-English Writings" in America—German, French, Yiddish, and aboriginal—and the editors' unusually foreward-looking implication seemed to be that the quest for what is American in our literary history must account for a complex phenomenon, the preserving, dissolving, and transforming of various cultural elements and traditions, foreign and indigenous, in America.

Lastly came the question of the literature proper to a literary history of America in the final half-century of the *CHAL* survey. Again, the reader was offered a bewildering array of criteria, terminology, and definitions (or failures to define) from twenty-seven contributors. The worst offenders were the authors of the non–belles lettres chapters who termed their writings literature and then failed to show how this writing either possessed or contributed to aesthetic expression. In various chapters, artistic qualities of literature were acknowledged while not deemed utterly essential for an author or work to receive due attention in a literary history. Van Doren conceded that *Uncle Tom's Cabin* "stands higher in the history of reform than in the history of the art of fiction" (III, 70). Hellman stamped N. P. Willis "the prototype of later semi-literary American journalists" (III, 109). In "Book Publishers and Publishing," Earl Bradsher (Texas) unequivocally gave literature a qualitative label, and his subject was, therefore, "the publication of notable literature" (IV, 552). But Louise Pound ("Oral Literature") asserted that in "genuine folk-literature," issues of style, technique, or quality were secondary to popularity, so that the main criterion for noticing these works was that "the people have liked them and preserved them" (IV, 503).

Pound's comments on oral literature posed a basic question for printed works as well. Should contemporary, or even long-lasting, popularity of a work ensure it a significant place in the history of a democratic culture, of American life and literature? Carl Van Doren mentioned Lew Wallace's immensely popular *Ben-Hur* as "a true folk possession" comparable to *Uncle Tom's Cabin*, works that belonged "not only to literature but to folklore" (III, 74, 70). (Either Van Doren ignored or overlooked Pound's treatment of the two terms.) Foerster judged Bayard Taylor's popularity harshly—"In most of his work he was acceptable to his age; in very little is he acceptable to a later time" (III, 42)—but that contemporary vogue still rated Taylor five pages of discussion. Another minor poet, James Whitcomb Riley, lacking profundity in either emotion or thought, earned more than two pages, for "it is undeniable that he appeals urgently to the normal thoughts and feelings of the divine average" (III, 61, 62). Ik Marvel's *Reveries of a Bachelor* and *Dream Life,* "despite that naïve sentimentality frequently displayed by American literature in the period just preceding the Civil War," were deemed by

George Hellman important to literary history because of "their hold on the affections of later generations" (III, 100).

Montrose Moses recognized in the later drama the confusing claims of "popularity and permanence" (III, 290), and he held that the frequent tyranny of popular taste had been a hindrance to creative experimentation. Cairns ("Later Magazines") was more optimistic about the literary quality he found in the popular magazines, but Percy Boynton dismissed "Patriotic Songs and Hymns" in fewer than ten pages, for he regarded Americans as "a relatively untuneful people" and their songs important mainly as "expressions of popular feeling." We had enjoyed relatively few public occasions of historical interest, said Boynton, and in fact, there were none at all since the Civil War, unless we included 1917, with its native moment memorialized in "Over There," an item that "belongs to the same public that delights in O. Henry, Walt Mason, Irvin S. Cobb, and Wallace Irwin, all in the main sane, wholesome, obvious people" (IV, 492, 498).[5] Mary Austin, however, held in high regard the "democracy" of style and content of aboriginal expression, wherein "the language of literature was the common vehicle of daily life," and she hoped to see a day in America when "all the literature will be the possession of all the people, and the distinction between 'popular' and real literature will cease to exist" (IV, 611).

The final two-volume installment was expectably disappointing in the critical and interpretive explication of the authors and works since the Civil War, despite the analyses in Sherman's Mark Twain and Beach's James. Van Doren included too many third-rank novelists and neoromancers in his survey chapter, omitted by design the living writers, and slighted those who were recently deceased (Crane and Norris received one page together). Van Doren's nine pages on Howells's career, however, were a more judicious estimate than readers would meet again for many years. Foerster placed Emily Dickinson at the head of the poets, all "minor," since the Civil War and devoted three pages to this gifted woman who "despite her defective sense of form" (Foerster did not explicate so much as one line) possessed "extraordinary insight into the life of the mind and the soul." He cautiously predicted for her an "inconspicuous but secure" place in literary history (III, 32). It soon grew obvious, though, that he had placed her first in the chapter by virtue of chronology. Aldrich also rated three pages while Bayard Taylor received five. Foerster, like Sherman, indulged himself in one parting shot as a moralistic or Arnoldian New Humanist. While modern verse seemed "not always sincere," the best poets "have for the most part honestly sought to see life more truly than it has been envisaged by the poets of the past" (III, 65).

And so the *CHAL* was again, somewhat negatively, significant as literary criticism in that it reflected the spirit and method of artistic judgment and limited explication characteristic of American professors sixty and seventy years ago. Few critics today would have Foerster's audacity to complain of Joaquin Miller's "lack of proportion, his crudity in music and in taste" (III, 56) and yet fail to supply a single example from the poetry. Equally audacious, or just uncontrollably glib, were the other critics who merely submitted without a trace of textual evidence that Moncure Conway lacked "the authentic fire of genius" (III, 120); that historians Parkman, Fiske, and Eggleston were "artists in expression" (III, 188); and that some of the political writing of the Populists had "real artistic merit" (III, 357).

Stylistic power and grace were again demanded by the impressionistic critic, but only a few asked that style be considered in vital relation to the writer's subject. Beach presented James's fiction as the melding of frequently American themes with largely European aesthetic form, and Foerster noted that Aldrich's best poems "have substance enough to deserve the embalming power of fine form" and that the best living poets had begun "to reveal their findings . . . by means of a form entirely dictated by the substance—the very substance externalized" (III, 37, 65). Nathaniel Stephenson (College of Charleston) said of Lincoln that "when his vision deserted him, his style deserted him," that his style was "but the flexibility with which his expression follows the movements of a peculiar mind" and even quoted (though without explication) several illustrative passages of Lincoln's "applied art. . . . Never for an instant does it incrust the business—as the rhetorician would do—nor ever overlay it with decoration" (III, 381, 368, 383).

At the close of the history came the bibliographies for volumes III and IV, equal to one-quarter of the completed text. Though they have long since been superseded, these listings would be priceless to scholars of American literature in 1921 and in the two decades to follow. Beach's, to cite just one example, provided for a first time the data on serial publication of James's novels and also recorded the scholarship up to 1920, even to the recent *Letters* edited by Percy Lubbock. Indeed, most of the contributors listed primary or secondary matter as late as 1919, suggesting that the editors postponed these final pages long after the text of some of the chapters were submitted, perhaps urging the authors to make their bibliographies as valuable and recent as possible. The four volumes of the *CHAL* contained 623 pages of bibliography on original sources (including manuscript holdings) and the historical, critical, and biographical works of a dawning scholarship. American scholars were now in convenient possession of the indispensable basis for advanced study of their nation's literature.

The bibliographies were also to become, as before, the object of special praise from the reviewers. Walter Bronson of Brown, writing on the history once again in the *American Historical Review,* called them "very full and valuable," and William Lyon Phelps of Yale, in the *New York Times Book Review,* anticipated from them a new wave of studies that scholars would soon "'work up'" from merely this feature of the *CHAL*. Samuel Chew (Bryn Mawr), writing in the *Nation,* praised the bibliographies, but he also concluded that the entire history would "provide a foundation for literary study and research," thanks to the generous, if somewhat confused, range of the literature, preliterature, and subliterature. Bronson also liked the many chapters that went beyond "literature in the narrower sense of the word" and etched in the larger "record of American culture." Contributor Norman Foerster had no compunction about reviewing the volumes, though he avoided all-out praise and challenged the editors' attempted catholicity that, for all the inclusiveness, had left out a chapter on literary criticism and a "scientific treatment" of literary evolution within the national culture. Phelps suggested as a more accurate title, the "Cambridge History of American Thought," but allowed that the history was a "treasure-trove" in its extraliterary range. Henry Canby, also of Yale, considered the last two volumes deficient as literary criticism, but he rather ambivalently noted that "as an annotated bibliography rising in many instances into admirable historical criticism it succeeds." John Macy, in a predictably tart review for *New Republic,* ranked the belles-lettres chapters the least stimulating, steeped as they were in a "dreariness" possible only from a team of university professors of literature "who have inevitably chosen as fellow contributors their own unimaginative kind." Macy's estimate closely matched Mencken's in the *Smart Set*. Together, they can probably be taken as the official response of the rebel critics on the literary scene in 1921.

Macy also criticized the editorial vision, or rather its absence, especially in the confusing organization of the chapters in these final volumes. And Chew, like reviewers of the earlier installments, cited the difficulties of multiple authorship—the diversity of method and manner, the uneven quality among the chapters. On the treatment of the glamorous figures, Macy considered

Beach's James the weakest for American literary history. Canby remarked on the lack of "unity of subject and treatment," but enjoyed the "brilliance" of Sherman's Mark Twain. Phelps pointedly applauded Beach and Sherman, and also Van Doren, but Foerster praised just Beach and Sherman.

On the value of other chapters, Bronson liked the Amerind chapter, while Chew dismissed it: "Miss Austin offers a not altogether convincing plea for the Amerind myths as a proper subject for modern imaginative treatment." Bronson praised Ayres's chapter on American English, but Phelps berated it as "polemical rather than descriptive." Phelps complained that Foerster had done little with the new poetry, unlike Moses who recounted very fully the gains in modern drama over the recent twenty years. Phelps was also pleased that Wolff gave philologists James Hadley and William D. Whitney, Phelps's predecessors at Yale, their deserved notice. Canby also praised Wolff's chapter, calling it a difficult but useful essay on American scholars. He also liked the "penetrative insight" into the theologians by Ambrose Vernon (Carleton College) and the sense of literary–historical movement in Foerster and Von Doren.

Phelps considered the *CHAL* in its final, completed appearance a scholarly triumph, and Chew called it admirable in scope, variety, and authority. Foerster looked back to volume I as an inadequate substitute for Tyler's histories and to volume II as a rather pedestrian survey of familiar writers. But Foerster believed volumes III and IV to be valuable new history of unfamiliar and sometimes radical new voices of a finally achieved literary independence in America. Macy, however, reiterated that the "flatness of the material" from this academic team had rendered American literary history a prolonged episode in "dreariness" and "dullness." Canby was only slightly more generous, seeing the *CHAL* as a prime illustration of both "the merits and defects of American scholars to-day." Along with "clear and penetrating interpretation," and a Germanic thoroughness of research and documentation that made it indispensable, there was a fair amount of undigested scholarship. He would like to have seen a unified single volume written by a smaller team—say, Sherman, Van Doren, Erskine, Cohen, Bassett, and Harvard's John Livingston Lowes. Canby predicted that one day a single historian would mold these raw materials into a proper literary history. (Six years later, he was gratified that Parrington's *Main Currents in American Thought* had become that history.)

Perhaps as an escape to something livelier for his taste, Macy devoted more than half of his review to a tirade against the Christian Scientists' objection to Riley's original essay on Mrs. Eddy, with his sportive reference to her as a "thrice-married female Trismegistus." Macy pronounced Putnam "guilty of pusillanimous conduct, of treachery to an honest critic, of violation of the right of free discussion." He understood (in early June 1921) that volume IV might be reissued without Riley's chapter. Canby, writing in late July, also deplored the rumored suppression of Riley's chapter. By September, Phelps had received in his review copy the inserted leaflet of Powell's substitute chapter and was puzzled that the new treatment was less than reverent as well. Perhaps the *Christian Science Monitor* might have supplied a qualified believer to rewrite the chapter?[6]

Readers today may wish to learn a bit more about this interesting episode in the censorship of an American scholar that strangely climaxed the story of the *CHAL*. It all began in 1918 when Riley was working diligently to produce a responsible essay on the *Book of Mormon* and *Science and Health* and writing periodically to Van Doren on the progress and sticking points. The first serious trouble appeared in early 1920 when a Putnam editor, a Miss Lovendhal, asked for revisions of sentences carrying questionable facts and interpretation regarding not the Christian Scientists but the Mormons. These problems concerned the inevitable matter of plagiarism in the *Book of Mormon* and, despite the Woodruff Manifesto, the continuing practice of plural marriages. (Riley told Van Doren that private observation, plus assurance from friends, verified for him that polygamy still was "practiced on the sly.") In March 1920, Riley sent a number of corrections from the Sorbonne, where he was lecturing, and as late as November was adding to his bibliography. By the end of the year, the chapter "Popular Bibles" seemed to be thorough and finished at last.[7]

But when volumes III and IV appeared several months later, Riley became the center of the controversy that broke on the front page of the *New York Times* of 19 April 1921. He was now attacked not for his assessment of *The Book of Mormon*, but for the treatment of the Christian Scientists and their own popular bible. The objection had been lodged by Albert F. Gilmore of the Christian Science Committee on Publications for the State of New York. Putnam had stopped the sale of volume IV, discontinued the printing, and tried to recall the fifteen hundred to two thousand copies still out. The news item mentioned that Putnam had already arranged for substitute pages on Christian Science by Lyman P. Powell, former president of Hobart College, and quoted Irving Putnam who had termed the chapter outrageous in its "'tone of contempt and ridicule,'" its "'light and flippant'" attitude toward a religion with several million believers. The responsibility, said Irving, rested with Professor Trent (!) and his colleagues, for Putnam granted its authors freedom to express their views. The publisher expected, naturally, that they would do so in "'decent parliamentary language and with due respect to the subject.'" In the article, Riley was allowed the space to defend his scholarly diligence. He commented on spending much time and travel expense to ensure that his chapter would be accurate and responsible.[8] Two days before (Sunday), Riley had received a special delivery letter from Van Doren that there was belated trouble from Putnam. Riley's telegram in reply to Van Doren on 17 April read, "YOUR LETTER RECD KINDLY ARRANGE INTERVIEW FOR ME WITH MAJOR PUTNAM MONDAY MORNING BETWEEN ELEVEN AND ONE[.]" Trent and Van Doren, emotionally emptied by the affair, had acquiesced to the substitute chapter by Powell.

The next week, the Mormons were alerted to Riley's treatment of them after reading a newspaper excerpt from the chapter. Their President Macune now wrote to Putnam. Shortly after, the Mormon's *Salt Lake City News* printed Irving Putnam's answer: "I thoroughly agree with you that the effusion quoted from Riley in the *New York World* on April 25 renders any further comment by intelligent people unnecessary." Riley discovered the insult and wrote to Van Doren, "I apparently no longer belong to the intelligentsia." Van Doren sympathized and regretted as well that editors were apparently shying away from reviewing the final volumes until the Powell chapter came out in the new volume IV.[9]

Lyman Powell, meanwhile, was working hastily to supply the new pages so that he could escape on a summer vacation. The Putnams, quite predictably, had gone around Van Doren during this flap and resumed direct correspondence with their old wartime antagonist, Trent. Powell's manuscript, therefore, went directly to Trent. He persuaded Powell to make changes that would not leave the new impression of a pro-Christian-Scientist bias. He also resisted the publisher's effort to allow a representative of the Christian Science Publication Committee to approve the chapter, now bearing the more respectful title, "Two New Religions." Erskine read the revised manuscript none too hastily, so Trent then bypassed Van Doren and sent it at once to the printer. Since the proofs would soon be in Van Doren's hands and he could have his editorial say, Trent pleaded, "Confine your remarks to sighs and groans," for Powell's chapter probably was even worse than the earlier Webster by G. H. Putnam's selected contributor, Senator Lodge. Trent wickedly imagined the two men in competition for the booby-prize chapter: "I understand that H. C. Lodge is preparing to bring suit against Powell for ousting him, Lodge, from a proud, unspecified position he has occupied since the very inception of the work!"[10]

The final skirmish was fought in the pages of the *New Republic*. Two weeks after Macy's review in the 8 June issue, the Christian Scientists' Gilmore reentered the fray with correspondence on the review and a return to the fracas in April that ended up in the *Times*. He had not urged Putnam to expunge the chapter by Riley, he explained; he had merely lodged a courteous protest with the publisher. Irving Putnam had then joined brother George in a reading of Riley's essay, and they "were both shocked not only at the offensive personal allusions [to Mrs. Eddy] but at the outrageous tone of ridicule and worse that permeated the article." Thereon, they wrote to Trent and told him to locate a fair-minded scholar with a decent respect for Christian Science.[11]

In the next number of the *New Republic*, Gilmore and the Putnams were supported by an Elizabeth Grabo of Chicago. The issue, she wrote, was that the Christian Scientists deserved an "adequate statement" of their creed, without sardonic asides, "in what purports to be an authoritative history of American literature." About Macy's criticism of Putnam for gaining "'some advertising without expense except the trivial price of a little honor,'" Ms. Grabo observed that to recall a volume and replace it amounted to no small expense. In July, Morris Cohen wrote an ostensibly objective letter to the *New Republic* on Macy's review. While he disagreed with Macy's belletristic approach to literature, Cohen was able to concur with Macy in his "indignation at the suppression of Professor Riley's scholarly article on Christian Science."[12]

Riley, in the meantime, was preparing his own defense. He wrote to Van Doren at the end of July of plans to coauthor a volume on Christian Science from three points of view. The first would be psychological, drawing from his own earlier piece in the *Psychological Review* (1903); the next legal, to be written by Frederick Peabody of Boston, who twice served as counsel against Mrs. Eddy in her sanity trials; and finally, a medical opinion, the author to be determined (with Van Doren's suggestions welcomed). Riley planned to mention the Christian Scientists' opposition to serums for the American Expeditionary Force, to vaccinations in Chicago, and medical examinations for school children of Washington State in an upcoming referendum. Riley then sent a reply to the *New Republic* in response to Gilmore's letter in the June issue. Rather than attack Gilmore, Riley quoted from Irving Putnam's letter to Gilmore, noting the pious and "meaningless quotations from scripture," and accused Putnam of straying from the issue, which was the scholarship appropriate to an "article on *popular* bibles in a *literary* history." Besides, if the Putnams were so sensitive to religious feelings, why had they recently published the anti-Semitic *The Cause of the World's Unrest?* On the ignorance attending religious censorship, Riley permitted George H. Putnam to speak on the matter through a quotation from his own two-volume *The Censorship of the Church of Rome and Its Influence upon the Production and Distribution of Literature* (1906–7): "'There is something almost pathetic in the long series of attempts made by poets, councils, bishops, congregations, and inquisitors to protect the souls of the faithful against the baneful influence of the ever-increasing tide of literature that was pouring forth from the various publishing centres.'"[13]

And with that coup de grace, if such it were, the long story of the making and reception of the *CHAL* ground to a halt after seven historic, troubled, frustrating years of exhausting editorial work, especially for Van Doren and Trent, in the midst of literary and scholarly controversy and the personal and national agonies of a global war. But the rewards had also been there, and they multiplied for others in the years to come. American literature now possessed a respectable foothold within the academy, and spiritually, at least, an academic profession was born. Over the next two decades, American literary scholars would build on the foundations of the *CHAL* until the profession, in the 1940s, crowned that growing achievement with a new cooperative literary history.

Moses Coit Tyler (1835–1900)
(*Michigan Historical Collections, Bentley Historical Library, University of Michigan*)

Charles F. Richardson (1851–1913)
(*Dartmouth College Library*)

Lorenzo Sears (1838–1916)
(*Brown University Archives*)

Barrett Wendell (1855–1921)
(*Harvard University Archives*)

Brander Matthews (1852–1929)
(*Columbiana Library, Rare Book and Manuscript Library, Columbia University*)

George Woodberry (1855–1930)
(*Columbiana Library, Rare Book and Manuscript Library, Columbia University*)

William P. Trent (1862–1939)
(*Columbiana Library, Rare Book and Manuscript Library, Columbia University*)

John Erskine (1879–1951)
(*Columbiana Library, Rare Book and Manuscript Library, Columbia University*)

Stuart P. Sherman (1881–1926)
(Photographic Subject File (39/2/20), University Archives, University of Illinois, Urbana-Champaign)

Carl Van Doren (1885–1950)
(Columbiana Library, Rare Book and Manuscript Library, Columbia University)

Fred L. Pattee (1853-1950)
(Penn State Room, Pennsylvania State University Libraries)

Percy Boynton (1875–1946)
(University of Chicago Archives)

William B. Cairns (1867–1932)
(*State Historical Society of Wisconsin*)

Book Two Growth

Professional Scholarship and
Politics (1921–1939)

Chapter 13

A New Era: The Profession Establishes a Political Voice

Fred L. Pattee prefaced his postwar *Century Readings for a Course in American Literature* (1919) by explaining the salutary effects of the recent global conflict:

> The recent manifestation of American patriotism, the new description of Europe of the soul of America, the new insistence upon the teaching of Americanism in our schools and colleges, especially in those that for a time were under government control, has brought the study of American literature into the foreground as never before.

In April 1919, Pattee repeated Whitman's urging of a new vision for America, for now "a new future opens" up for the nation after the war. In particular, Pattee looked forward to a revolution in study of our national culture: "I call first of all for a chair of American literature, side by side with the chair of American history, in every college and university . . . [filled by] a man of vision, an American who thrills with the past of America and the lofty promise of the years to be." [1] The next year, Penn State went a good part of the way and awarded Pattee himself the title Professor of American Literature.

A similar feeling of postwar exhilaration and renewal of purpose emanated from the intellectual community of liberal critics. Ludwig Lewisohn agreed that "the spirit of Whitman is not dead" in America, but to him it was newly endangered by Volstead repression, racist Americanism, and the academy itself. In his edition of *A Modern Book of Criticism* (1919), Lewisohn ranged his intelligently responsive critics—Huneker, Spingarn, Mencken, Brooks, and others—against the authoritarian and anachronistic Babbitt, Sherman, and More. And Lewisohn elaborated on this modern battle of the books in the *Nation,* newly liberalized under the guidance of Oswald Garrison Villard. Lewisohn argued that the tradition-bound humanist who "loves the ivied wall, the studious cloister, the cadence of great verses heard in youth" was also the American nationalist who invoked puritan restraints and ignored the freedom of the individual soul heard in other, more truly American, writings by Whitman, Emerson, and Mark Twain. Lewisohn concluded that "the American spirit must be liberated for a new contact with reality" through a new anti-puritan literature and criticism ventilated also by contemporary movements in France, Germany, England, and Ireland.[2]

Other voices, too, were proclaiming a new era in one symposium after another. Harold E. Stearns edited *Civilization in the United States* (1922), with the hope of "making a real civilization possible" in the face of "dull standardization" and a "pioneer point of view" that resisted serious and refined thought (pp. iii, 150, 136). "The most hopeful thing of intellectual promise in America to-day," Stearns wrote, "is the contempt of the younger people for their elders; they are restless, uneasy, disaffected" (p. 149). Harmonious with Stearns's views of our emotional repression, schizoid separation between theory and practice, and a potentially vital culture more heterogeneous than merely Anglo-Saxon, were essays by Lewis Mumford ("The City"), H. L. Mencken ("Politics"), Conrad Aiken ("Poetry"), and Van Wyck Brooks ("The Literary Life").

Ernest Gruening corralled more criticism of American values in the two-volume *These United States: A Symposium* (1923–24). Essays on the various states came from critics Mencken (Maryland), Edmund Wilson (New Jersey), Lewisohn (South Carolina), Macy (Massachusetts), as well as novelists Sherwood Anderson (Ohio), Dreiser (Indiana), Sinclair Lewis (Minnesota), and Cather (Nebraska). Many of these critiques first appeared in *Nation*, as did Freda Kirchwey's selections in *Our Changing Morality: A Symposium* (1924), written by Lewisohn ("Love and Marriage"), Floyd Dell ("Can Men and Women be Friends?"), Joseph W. Krutch ("Modern Love and Modern Fiction"), and others. Another collection, Joel Spingarn's *Criticism in America: Its Function and Status* (1924), was a chronological assembling of seminal essays since 1910, immodestly beginning with his "The New Criticism" and continuing forward with a representative sampling of the debate previously chronicled two chapters ago: figures included Brownell, Woodberry, Babbitt, Eliot, and Sherman, together with Brooks, Mencken, and more recently, Ernest Boyd.

At about 1921, then, we can reasonably date the transition into a new age and validate the period with a variety of occurrences. Van Wyck Brooks in February invoked the spirit of Randolph Bourne and scolded Americans for their cultural humility in welcoming the postwar hordes of British poets and novelists on American lecture tours.[3] Within the week, Barrett Wendell was dead. His funeral seems almost to have signaled the passing of the old order. Shortly after, the last installment of the *CHAL* appeared, "a pre-war history of pre-war literature," Van Doren later modestly and accurately termed it.[4] Planning their strategy at the MLA convention that year, the American literature devotees conceived a campaign to achieve a larger professional role within the national society.

Meanwhile, each of the *CHAL* editors began to behave as though the completion of their seven-year scholarly enterprise called for the beginning of a new professional career. Senior editor Trent in 1921 survived the terminal nuisance with Putnam over the Christian Science flap, but Trent never recovered from an accompanying setback, the death of his wife in the same year. He remained at Columbia the imposing patriarchal figure estranged from the 1920s generation but, in 1924, was reconciled with Brander Matthews when his old war adversary retired. Trent was never again a living force in American literary scholarship, though his legacy before the 1920s would not be forgotten by former students like Lewisohn, who credited Trent with having "aroused my interest in American literature" at Columbia. Lewisohn avowed that *Expression in America* (1932) "would never have been written had he not been both my teacher and my friend." In 1927, Trent suffered a stroke that periodically impaired his mind and also left him emotionally a child. In 1938, the cooperative Columbia edition of Milton, which Trent had envisioned at the school's Milton Tercentenary in 1908, was completed. Not American literature but Milton had actually been Trent's great love all along, both as a scholar and teacher. He died of a heart attack on 7 December 1939.[5]

Far less committed to the *CHAL* than Trent, and to the academic world at large, was John Erskine. In the 1920s, he withdrew from American literature scholarship even more decisively. After America's late entry in the war, he had served as chairman of the Army Education Commission of the American Expeditionary Force in France and, after the armistice, as educational director of the American Expeditionary Force at the University at Beaune. He returned to Columbia in 1920 but was untouched by the new ferment in American literature. Alternating with his English literature classes were equally strong inclinations toward (non-American) historical romance and classical piano. He gained his greatest literary celebrity in 1925 with the success of his novel *The Private Life of Helen of Troy*. Erskine dabbled in more fiction, gave piano recitals, and enjoyed being interviewed for his opinions on bootlegging (he was a wet), sexual fads, and other trends and goings-on of the postwar decade. He popularized a "Great Books" course in these postwar years and thereby helped his student Mortimer Adler discover a profitable vocation in the 1930s and after. The new American literature Erskine dismissed to one interviewer as "sexual bookkeeping." Another writer described him as unfortunately one who "loves the old world much more than he does the new: he has too much, indeed, of the typical condescension for things American." Beginning in 1928, Erskine served as president of the Juilliard School of Music, received several honorary degrees, and after 1937, became professor emeritus at Columbia and a trustee of Juilliard. He continued to write a bewildering variety of books, from fiction to the fine arts. In the late 1940s, he composed his memoirs. Death came in 1951.[6]

Sherman at Illinois also changed with the times, but rather than defecting from American literature study, he shifted in the 1920s toward a new involvement. He relaxed his stiff, antiromantic humanism, thanks to a war-inspired, more favorable attitude toward the younger generation. Their sacrifice and idealism had led him, he claimed, to a "fresh interest in American life and letters." He now rebuked his old mentor, Paul Elmer More, for his puritanic view of human nature and unwillingness to discuss contemporary American literature or to write at the level of the American democratic reader. This new stance by Sherman, plus a not unkindly review of Mencken's continuing *Prejudices* ("He is alive. . . . He has a rough prodding wit . . . [and] he will scoff at a sham"), appeared in the collected essays *Americans* in 1922 (pp. 318–35, 7). In response, Mencken, while castigating More in the next series of *Prejudices* (1922), rather disappointedly noted that his old antagonist Sherman was "showing signs of late of a despairing heart: he tries to be ingratiating, and begins to hug in the clinches" (p. 178).

Some later critics have demeaned the new critical intelligence of Sherman by reading him selectively in these years and concluding that he made a volte-face, perhaps because he had felt isolated at Illinois and craved the Eastern limelight. More likely Sherman was experiencing a transition after the war into his forties, a new season, as we now say, in his life and career. Too, he was demonstrating in his own person a bridging of the distance between society and the academy. His modified humanism was expressed again in the collection of 1923, *The Genius of America,* subtitled *Studies in Behalf of the Younger Generation.* He instructed his younger contemporaries that their revolt against puritanism was itself an act of mindless conformity, for they were closing their eyes to certain spiritual resources that have sustained the national genius. The puritan spirit, after all, had always been vital, individualistic, iconoclastic, idealistic, formative, and creative. (These were the same components of an American tradition that the anti-puritan Mencken, too, had been loudly proclaiming.)[7] Sherman blended this plea for a discriminating tradition of historic Americanism with a newly found hospitality to the pessimism of modern American literature, including what Carl Van Doren had recently labeled the revolt from the village in the American novel. Sherman viewed this pessimism to be a critical inspection of humdrum America, a movement Matthew Arnold would have approved and perhaps the basis for a rebirth of national will and a "genuinely democratic humanism" for all the people.[8]

In April 1924, Sherman became editor of the literary supplement of the New York *Herald Tribune* and plunged into his assignment with professorial thoroughness of preparation and a fierce expense of energy that probably contributed to his death just two years later. He read prodigiously into the night to review not merely a recent book from an American, English, or continental author, but also to catch up on the writer's previous work. The results appeared in reviews of informed appreciation but with little of the tough-minded point of view that spiced his earlier criticism. In the first collection of these essay reviews, he declared that the duty of the literary commentator was "not to exploit his own predilections; it is rather to understand the entire 'conspiracy' of forces involved in the taste of his day." He denied that this approach amounted to a Spingarnian "expression for expression's sake," Sherman was merely seeking "'the good life'" accessible in the enjoyment of literature. In his review of Anderson's *Dark Laughter* (1925), he announced his sympathy with the contemporary movement in American Literature "however impatiently I may have contemplated some of its bungling preliminary operations." Mencken spared Sherman from the roll call of stuffy pedagogues in the fourth series of *Prejudices* (1924; though Mencken never forgave Sherman for the wartime slurs against his and Dreiser's Americanism, and they never became friends). Sherman, in turn, praised parts of this new volume and repeated his admiration of Mencken's "rare gift at stirring people up and making them strike an attitude, and at least start on the long process of becoming intelligent beings."[9]

One last collection, issued posthumously, included more of Sherman's mellowings. He now was pleased to mark Dreiser's progress in "tragic realism" since those years when Sherman had sounded his disapproval of *The "Genius."* Reading his review of *An American Tragedy,* the reader might believe the piece to have been ghostwritten by Mencken, especially in the praise of Dreiser's "comprehensive veracity," "unexceptionable moral effect," and "massively impressive" structure.[10] Sherman drowned in Lake Michigan near his summer home in August 1926 during a heart attack possibly caused by exhaustion from his arduous work schedule. He was forty-five.

Carl Van Doren's career after the *CHAL* resembled that of Sherman in pursuing a wider role for the literary humanist in the intellectual community outside the academy. In 1919, Van Doren had undertaken a three-year term at the literary editor's desk of Villard's *Nation.* A new season was at hand, Van Doren sensed, and with his customary instinct for the main chance, he adjusted to the shifting tides of literary and critical mood and taste. He recalled in his memoirs of the mid-1930s that the younger-generation heirs of Randolph Bourne had broken with the traditional wisdom and leadership that had culminated in global war: "Down with authority. Up with instinct. Youth was as likely to be right as age. Youth, the Younger Generation held, was always right." The expression of this new spirit "flowed in a stream of new books across my desk at the Nation." And Van Doren found himself hospitable to this "fresh literature in a fresh language." (Symptomatically, he noted, the *Nation* was turning away from Sherman and bringing Mencken in as a contributing editor.)[11]

Van Doren next became literary editor of the *Century* (1922–25) where he earned more money for less work and was able "to publish what I liked as well as to talk about it."[12] Thereafter, he advised on various commercial publishing ventures, served on the committee on management of the new *Dictionary of American Biography* (1926–36), became chairman of the Readers Club (1941–44), and then editor of the Living Library (after 1946). Van Doren also edited a number of profitable anthologies and published a biography of Franklin that sold 270,000 copies and won the Pulitzer Prize in 1939. In that same year, Professor Robert Spiller wrote to Van Doren asking him to serve on the American Literature Group of the MLA Committee for a Literary History, with the hope that Van Doren would transmit some of his editorial experiences from the *CHAL.* But Van Doren, his secretary informed Spiller, was on a lecture tour. Though Van Doren never joined the editorial team of Spiller's *Literary History of the United States,* he did write the chapter on Franklin. He died in 1950, two years after that three-volume cooperative literary history appeared. There is no record that he ever undertook to read this ostensible successor to the *CHAL*.[13]

Van Doren's career after the *CHAL* still included scholarly services to the study of American literature in the academy. Even as he was working on the staff of the *Nation* in 1919, he dropped in at Columbia to teach on Friday afternoons a popular graduate class in American literature, his title being Associate in English. He remained on the faculty part time until 1930. In his memoirs, he was justly proud of his many graduate students who went forth to teach whatever American literature courses their English departments elected to offer. And Van Doren accurately assessed his own strengths as a scholarly editor who sifted into anthologies the selections of enduring vitality from Edwards, Franklin, Paine, Irving, and Hawthorne. Van Doren helped to bring compositional order out of *Leaves of Grass* and rightly claimed a role in the recovery of Melville: "Having done, for the Cambridge history, the first detailed study and the first bibliography of his work, I set Raymond Weaver at Columbia to writing the first life of Melville."[14] In fact, Van Doren was one of our first critics to appreciate *Moby-Dick*.

Serious literary scholars today who respect Van Doren point to his *The American Novel* (1921), our first thoroughgoing history of that genre. The book was completed during the final delay of *CHAL* volumes III and IV, while Van Doren was also abridging the parent history as the *Short History of American Literature* (1922). The history of the novel, in lesser degree, was a spinoff from these same pages, "considerably indebted," he admitted, to his chapters on American fiction in the *CHAL* (p. ix); and he also relied considerably on the bibliographical listings of the *CHAL*. Van Doren went well beyond his studies in the *CHAL,* however, and markedly expanded his earlier appreciation of Melville. Now, too, he wrote his own chapters on Hawthorne, Twain, and James. The survey can be recommended sixty years later for the concision, clarity, and grace with which Van Doren summarized the fictional influences and trends in the nineteenth century and effortlessly laced together historical background, thumbnail biographies, and interpretive paraphrases of the works of major and lesser novelists. The single-author chapters are still reliable. Much of the criticism of Hawthorne, Howells, Twain, and James up to our present day is an exploration and refinement of the early opinions Van Doren submitted here (though never asserted with great boldness). He overstated, as he did in the *CHAL* chapter, the quiet sanity of Howells, but he rightly pointed to a lack of gritty texture in Howells's fictional worlds of Boston and New York.

On Mark Twain, he repeated (and acknowledged) Brooks's recent allegation in *The Ordeal of Mark Twain* that Twain's genius was cramped by the genteel censorings of wife Livy and friend Howells; but Van Doren also reserved some skepticism about Brooks's theme. Van Doren was weakest in failing to discover the serious aspects of *Huckleberry Finn*. In the chapter on James, he appreciated the artistry, though he did not reveal the Jamesian subtleties. And he mistakenly predicted that James's fiction was too rarefied to command a lasting place in our literary history. Generally in his interpretations of the novel, Van Doren perceptively judged the validity of the fictional characterizations but was not sensitive to the fusion of meaning that arises from setting, plot, dialogue, angles of vision, and the like. He viewed as an advantage his nonpartisan, historical approach to American fiction and "to this lack of partizanship may be ascribed a disinclination to define the term 'novel' too exactly." Not only did Van Doren not build on (after citing) Hawthorne's distinction between the romance and the novel, but he indiscriminately gave more space to the fiction of F. Marion Crawford than to the combined output of Stephen Crane and Frank Norris. Failing to define the techniques and attitudes of realism, Van Doren then compounded the vagueness by treating naturalism as primarily more frank and pessimistic realism.

The next year, Van Doren drew on pieces written for the *Nation* to assemble *Contemporary American Novelists: 1900–1920* (1922). He discussed here a full score of authors, achieving a near brilliance in compression, though penetration and focus were missing in both literary history and criticism. Such was the troubled wedding of scholarship and journalism. He assembled the authors vaguely according to their relation to "the drift of naturalism," which in turn Van Doren defined, once again, so vaguely that it became an umbrella to cover anyone from Dreiser to Booth Tarkington. The final section, organized under "The Revolt from the Village," would become the most familiar criticism in all of Van Doren, though later students picked up the coinage without returning to appreciate Van Doren's subtle shadings in the revolt. He detected in Howe, Masters, and Anderson not only a repudiation of the sentimental myth of small-town America but also an embracement of the sustaining human ideals in the village. Only in Lewis's *Main Street* did Van Doren rashly overstate the author's vengeful assault on the "village virus" of complacency and dullness.

Over the next ten years, Van Doren's contributions to American literature study amounted to routine monographs on Cabell (1925, revised in 1932) and Lewis (1933), plus the intellectually lazy *American Literature: An Introduction* (1933, retitled in 1935 *What is American Literature?*). Then, rather miraculously, he surged into serious scholarship once more to write the prize-winning *Benjamin Franklin* (1938), possibly aided by the therapeutic lift of his autobiography, *Three Worlds,* in 1936. But after Franklin came more symptoms of intellectual fatigue. In *The American Novel: 1789–1939* (1940), Van Doren borrowed largely verbatim from his previous genre histories of 1921 and 1922. He did expand into a separate chapter the treatment of Melville in the light of scholarship in the twenties, much of it work he had no need to search out, for he had encouraged and guided it at Columbia. He traced the later careers of the novelists from 1900 to 1920 who appeared in his second volume (1922). Van Doren also compiled a valuable bibliography on monographs and genre studies since 1920, yet he did not recast his earlier books in the light of the vast scholarly discoveries in the new era. And he amiably included dozens of practicing or occasional novelists, including brother Mark and *CHAL* colleague Erskine. The volume stands as a pleasant reader's companion, granting bits of biography and literary background, along with various trends slightly illustrated and defined loosely, if at all, together with a series of plot summaries and sensible appreciations: an ideal selection for a popular book club. (Macmillan's advertisements after publication did not mention any adoptions, however.)

This final work perfectly mirrored Van Doren the assiduous historian and gentlemanly writer in both his shortcomings and strengths. In his puzzlements over literary tradition and the individual talent, he decided as an historian to come down on the side of literary discontinuity; and as a practicing critic, he tried to remain the hospitable skeptic with a mind open to the random uniqueness of any distinguished literary talent. While Van Doren realized that he was thereby rendered an ineffective critic, he claimed in *Three Worlds* (1936) not to have envied those who cultivated a more certain evaluative stance: "More and Babbitt, Sherman and Mencken, Lewisohn and Van Wyck Brooks, all demanded that literature take more certain courses toward more certain ends than I felt any need for" (p. 195). Large in person and spirit, Van Doren deserves ample room in our memory and affections as the tireless managing editor of the *CHAL* and then the generous host of American letters in the period between the wars when he opened doors to the publication of countless poets, writers, and critics. In this latter role, he also educated the reading public to appreciate modern American authors. As a professor at Columbia until 1930, Van Doren inspired many a graduate student to pursue the serious study of American authors. Finally, he created a modest sheaf of chapters on the American novel for scholars and critics of the twenties (and after) to profit from before indulging an American spirit of reinterpretation, repudiation, and casual ingratitude.

* * *

Van Doren and his fellow editors can be credited in large measure with the gestation of a new professional guild. But they stepped aside after the *CHAL,* as if to say to their professorial readers, we have defined the historical scope and particulars of your subject. Now build a profession on them. And so to other postwar members of the academy was left the political task of organizing the teachers of American literature. The logical strategy was to bore from within the Modern Language Association and capitalize on the changing temper of a new era. Fortunately, the MLA membership was responding to the postwar spirit of fresh beginnings. In 1920, with that membership swelled to more than 1,500, president John M. Manly of Chicago reviewed the association's thirty-seven-year history with satisfaction but sensed that the new decade required enlarged aims and procedures. The most radical change he proposed was to include within the three Sections (English, German, and Romance) groups that would stimulate discussion and encourage specialized research. "New Bottles" was the title of his address. But American literature was left out. Afterward, the *CHAL*'s Killis Campbell assured Manly that a fairly sizable body of professors interested in American literature had been slighted, and Manly agreed. In 1921 and 1922, the American group was English XI. Through the rest of the twenties, it became English XII. It is at least amusing that Manly, in 1922, proceeded to publish with fellow Chaucerian Edith Rickert, *Contemporary American Literature: Bibliographies and Study Outlines* for Harcourt Brace.[15]

Thus the American Literature Group (ALG), as the members presently dubbed themselves, attained a rather belated welcome to the MLA. Campbell became the first chairman in 1921. The initial program that year in Baltimore was given over to Arthur H. Quinn's paper, "The Graduate Teaching of American Literature," and Walter Bronson's "The Place of American Literature in the College Curriculum."[16] Quinn, whose published paper will be discussed in the following chapter, was elected chairman for the next year's meeting in Philadelphia. The program in 1922 included two papers. Percy Boynton read "A Proper Critical Attitude to American Literature," a paper on the growth of national consciousness and the decline of literary self-consciousness, as secretary Francis A. Litz (Johns Hopkins) phrased it. Henry Canby discussed "Some Standards of Criticism," advocating "more rigorous and scholarly" criticism of American writers. Boynton was elected chairman of the group for 1923.[17]

Jay B. Hubbell, by then at Southern Methodist, recalled that he attended his first ALG meeting in Ann Arbor in 1923, which Quinn chaired in Boynton's absence. One paper was read— Pattee's historical survey of "American Literature as a College Course"—followed by a discussion among the twenty-five or so members present. (Total MLA attendance at this meeting was 467.) A youthful Robert Spiller, acting secretary at the meeting, summed up the group response to Pattee's comments: "The discussion that followed favored presenting American Literature as expression of national (historical) consciousness and not as aesthetic offshoot of English Literature."

In accord with this spirit of autonomy and a fresh, historically oriented approach to our literature from an American, not English, perspective, Ernest Leisy (Illinois Wesleyan) then cited scholarly articles appearing in the journals, doctoral theses in progress, and American subjects that awaited investigation. Thomas O. Mabbott (Columbia) added that bibliographical and biographical studies of local authors had been neglected, and Pattee argued that existing biographies of the major figures were biased and should be written anew. Hubbell, speaking in the light of Pattee's conference paper, suggested how these literary backgrounds should be adapted to the college classroom. Members agreed that the profession acutely needed finding lists of manuscript materials and a bibliography of American literature scholarship in progress. A committee of Hubbell, Mabbott, and Leisy (chairman) were enjoined to compile a list of theses completed and in progress, together with a report on special research collections in American libraries. (The completed report, later published in *Studies in Philology* of January 1926 also included a bibliography of articles on American literature.) Pattee was elected chairman of the group for the meeting in 1924 at Columbia.[18]

In only three years, then, the ALG had achieved both identity and purpose. A nucleus of the most prominent members were assuming their position as the political elite of the new profession to lead a constituency soon to number in the hundreds.

The professional awareness of the membership continued to grow each year thereafter. During the meeting at Columbia in 1924, with the venerable Pattee as chairman, and the next two years under Hubbell's leadership, they advanced toward two notable achievements—the scholarship for *The Reinterpretation of American Literature* (1928) and preliminary discussions leading to the ALG's own professional journal, *American Literature*, in 1929. The 1926 meeting at Cambridge was, in Robert Spiller's words, particularly "epochal. . . . We carved out a viewpoint as the foundation of scholarship in our field."[19] An advisory committee at this meeting recommended that three sections be formed, with the purpose of focusing study and discussion on (1) the Puritan tradition (and other colonial areas), (2) romanticism in American literature, and (3) the frontier spirit.

In a mailing of early 1927, Ernest Leisy, the group's secretary, asked members to indicate which session they wished to attend and their choice of a section leader. He also solicited their suggestion for papers, perhaps to include one in each group that would treat scholarship both existing and needed. He also asked for names (and addresses) of prospective members for the ALG, either currently in MLA or out. In addition, members were asked to send $1.00 if they wished to receive from Leisy titles of doctoral dissertations and current research, plus $.50 for titles of masters' theses. Leisy's tally of responses showed six replies to attend the Puritan section, thirteen for romanticism, and eight for the frontier.[20] More than fifty years later, these numbers seem insignificant, until we realize who the respondents were. They included Henry S. Canby (Yale), Ernest Bernbaum (Illinois), Stanley T. Williams (Yale), Harry Warfel (Bucknell), Clarence Gohdes (Southern Methodist), Kenneth Murdock (Harvard, who volunteered to do a paper surveying the Puritan field), Gregory Paine (North Carolina), John H. Nelson (Kansas), Thomas O. Mabbott (at Northwestern until 1928), Robert E. Spiller (Swarthmore, who suggested the three subdivisions might rather be established on philosophical, aesthetic, and critical bases, with each annual meeting centered on one), and Wisconsin's W. B. Cairns (who also felt that the three sections were a restrictive grouping).

A dissenting voice arose from this new movement toward scholarship and specialization. Franklyn B. Snyder (Northwestern) suggested to Hubbell that the success of the ALG depended on their making the annual program more appealing to the rank-and-file teacher of American literature, and this group, to Snyder, was too unsophisticated to appreciate the ALG's new emphasis on specialized areas of American literature scholarship. Snyder was echoing a continuing debate during the decade within the Association of American Universities (established in 1900) whether the academy should not institute a doctorate in teaching as well as research. Each time the question had come up, the degree in teaching had been defeated as "too 'educationist.'"[21] Snyder's proposed hospitality to the unscholarly professor might have been further prompted by the fact that he was currently preparing a classroom text for Macmillan. But he was opposed in the ALG by, among others, Ernest Leisy, who felt that the foremost need was to approach American literature as a legitimate field of scholarly inquiry. Anything less would suggest that American writers were "for the dilettante."[22]

The ALG meeting at the University of Louisville in 1927 was also decisive for the progress of the profession. The group now undertook serious plans to create its own journal—to be fully recounted in an upcoming chapter—and chairman Murdock appointed a Committee on Publications. The meeting in the following year at Toronto was also productive, for now the political organization of the ALG was strengthened and defined. Murdock presided at a meeting of the Executive Committee and Advisory Council on 27 December 1928, where a committee of nine was appointed to regularize the organization and elections of the group. Quinn also suggested at this preliminary meeting at the Toronto convention that the ALG become the fourth Section within the MLA "to allow more time for the expanding and diversifying interests of American literature." It was agreed that Quinn's suggestion be put to ALG members. Two days later, forty-eight people gathered to give their "thorough approbation." Officers would therefore try to secure permission from the MLA Executive Committee to bring the American Literature Section into being.[23]

Although Quinn's suggestion came to naught within the parent organization (an American Literature Section was finally approved in 1966), the committee of nine conducted their particular work efficiently, and at the Cleveland meeting in 1929, the ALG finally enjoyed a tentative modus operandi:

Membership: MLA members
Officers: Chairman, Secretary-Treasurer, and Bibliographer (by annual elections)
Advisory Council: Chairman, Secretary-Treasurer, Editor of *American Literature* [newly created: see Chapter 16 below]. Ex Officio: Bibliographer. Plus six members to be elected to one-, two-, and

three-year terms. Duties will include the nominating of successive editorial board members of *American Literature*, these choices to be ratified by the Group.

Executive Committee: Chairman of ALG, Secretary-Treasurer, plus one member of the Chairman's choice. Duties will include preparation of programs, yearly plans, and emergencies.

Nominations and Elections: The Chairman will appoint a nominating committee of three, with no more than two to be from the Advisory Council. Elections will be held from the floor.[24]

So ended the first decade of the ALG. At last having attained a cohesive organization with a quickened sense of scholarly and pedagogical mission, together with a stronger political identity than any other "group" within the MLA, American literature professors now pointed to the 1930 meeting in the nation's capital, led by chairman Spiller, secretary Sculley Bradley (Pennsylvania), and an Advisory Council of Quinn and Paine elected for three years, Murdock and Cairns for two, and Williams and H. Milton Ellis (Maine) for one.[25] But this is only the sparse outline, the outer contours, of the progress achieved in the community of American literature professors during this crowded postwar decade. Another four chapters will help complete this narrative of scholarly life in the American academy during the 1920s.

Chapter 14

American Literature in the University: Study and Debate in the 1920s

The professional self-consciousness of the American Literature Group of the MLA was both a response to postwar study of American literature in higher education and a state of mind that stimulated further growth, as well as intramural professional politics. Very few of America's leading universities were totally neglecting American literature at the outset of this decisive period—only Duke, Notre Dame, University of the South, and some seven others.[1] Regarding the scene at Duke, Jay B. Hubbell recalled that when he came there from Southern Methodist in 1927, hoping to arouse an interest in American literature, the library did not have so much as a copy of such standards as *The Scarlet Letter.* He and Clarence Gohdes, who arrived at Duke in 1930, had to build an American literature library virtually from scratch.[2] Remarkably, within two years of his arrival, Hubbell became the founding editor of the profession's journal, *American Literature,* and the Duke campus was a beacon to which the foremost scholarly articles on American literature were directed.

Where American literature was being taught at the more adventurous universities in the 1920s, the survey course was the staple, with a new stress, in many instances, on American life and thought. (References to social, political, and economic forces markedly increased at the end of the decade after publication of Parrington's *Main Currents in American Thought.* Parrington's own teaching in the 1920s at the University of Washington is treated in Chapter 17.) Publishers of textbook anthologies willingly accommodated these survey courses. Scribner's *American Poetry* (1918), edited by Boynton, Jones, Sherburn, and Webster, continued to be popular in the twenties, with a fifth printing by 1925. Pattee's *Century Readings* (1919) was in a third enlarged edition by 1926, accompanied the next year by Irving Garwood's *Questions and Problems in American Literature: Based upon the Text of Pattee's Century Readings in American Literature* (205 pages).

Four other leading anthologies appeared in the decade, also edited by professors rather than men of letters outside the academy, as in the days of E. C. Stedman. Houghton Mifflin brought out Norman Foerster's *American Poetry and Prose: A Book of Readings, 1607–1916* (1925), valuable for the early periodizing of an American Romanticism and the suggested grouping of authors under the "Advance of Realism" (1870–90) and the "Triumph of Realism" (1890–1916). By the third edition (1947), Foerster refined this "Triumph" segment in the light of a more sophisticated scholarship since the twenties, to include naturalism and eliminate the period dates. By the fourth edition in 1957, the era after "Realism" became even more cautiously "New Directions." In 1926, Doubleday and Page published *American Literature,* edited by Robert Shafer (University of Cincinnati), an ample two volumes in one, with the Civil War already the convenient watershed of the large anthology. A second printing appeared in 1927 and, in 1933, a separated two-volume edition. In 1927, also, Franklyn B. Snyder, with Edward D. Snyder, collected *A Book of American Literature* for Macmillan. Finally, in 1929, Arthur H. Quinn, with Pennsylvania colleague Albert C. Baugh and Indiana's Will D. Howe, made Scribner competitive in the survey–anthology race with a two-volume *The Literature of America: An Anthology of Prose and Verse.*

Beginning to complement the literary survey in the postwar decade were genre courses in the novel and short story. Spotty in the second decade, they were fairly well established by the mid-1920s, an impetus due in part, perhaps, to Van Doren's study of the novel and Pattee's *The Development of the American Short Story* (1923), as well as to the growing popularity of the survey course itself. Facilitating a wider curriculum in separate genres, too, was the new publication of works by American authors in rather inexpensive format. American poetry courses were mentioned less frequently than fiction, while the genre course in American drama appeared in a number of college catalogs during the later twenties. Quinn had been teaching such a course since 1917 at Pennsylvania, the year of his *Representative American Plays* (Century), which was in a fourth revised and enlarged edition by 1928. He supplemented that collection in 1923 not only with his *Contemporary American Plays* (Scribner) but also the *History of American Drama from the Beginnings to the Civil War* (Harper), which he brought forward to the present in the two-volume sequel in 1927. No area of American literature study was more dominated by one professor than drama under Quinn in the 1920s.

The decade also enjoyed a modest variety of individual-author courses. Emerson appeared in eleven catalogs (Bliss Perry was teaching it at Harvard in the previous decade), followed by Poe (seven), Whitman (six), Hawthorne (three), Thoreau (two), and even a course on Abraham Lincoln, predictably at Illinois. The twenties also marked a beginning of sporadic offerings in regional and state literatures, including folklore, as well as pioneering courses in ethnic writers, from Negro (Howard) to Slavic (Dartmouth). In 1921, Ralph Rusk offered "Literature of the Midwest" at Indiana University; and in 1929, at the University of Texas, J. Frank Dobie was teaching "Life and Literature of the Southwest."[3]

New York University rose to apparent leadership in American literature offerings in the postwar period. Led by Arthur H. Nason, who had fashioned a separate American course as early as 1906, the department was now giving one graduate and three undergraduate courses by the midtwenties. In 1929, the faculty included Nason, Oscar Cargill, Nelson F. Adkins and, in summer, Arthur H. Quinn, who had come from Pennsylvania to teach a course in American drama. Quinn, meanwhile, was still hoping to develop an integrated program at Pennsylvania. In 1923, he was also spreading his gospel to the West as a visiting professor in drama at the University of Chicago, where Napier Wilt had just completed his dissertation on the Chicago theater (1847–57). The mainstay, of course, was Percy Boynton, who joined the Chicago faculty in 1905 after his own graduate study there (though not with a thesis in American literature). After the war, he opened the way for American literature to become a requirement for English majors. In 1923, the department was offering four undergraduate and four graduate courses. Quinn's neighbor, Penn State, was still a leader in American literature under the postwar guidance of Professor of American literature Fred Pattee. By 1923, the curriculum in native authors included five undergraduate and three graduate courses, plus two graduate seminars. To the north, Wilfred E. Davison in the same year established a Department of American Literature at Middlebury, perpetuated after his death in 1929 by Reginald L. Cook. American literature study continued in the leading universities of the West on approximately the same road of gradual expansion traced in the second decade, but with nothing so dramatic as Middlebury's commitment.[4]

In the graduate programs during the twenties, we assume there would be a correlation with the vitality of the undergraduate curriculum, as well as a connection between the number of doctoral dissertations completed and the abundance of graduate offerings. Such correlations, however, are difficult to establish, though we may be tempted to conclude that Harvard's rather indifferent and intermittent course of study in American literature explains why Charles Grandgent, in surveying the history of graduate work at that institution to the year 1926, discovered only four doctoral theses in American literature.[5] Grandgent's tally was confirmed and given wider perspective in the same year when Ernest Leisy (Illinois Wesleyan) published in *Studies in Philology* the report authorized by the American Literature Group in 1923, "Materials for Investigations in American Literature." Leisy's findings included the first national survey of doctoral dissertations in American literature. The value of this landmark bibliographical article is incalculable, for it not only alerted the academic community in 1926 that American literature study on the graduate level could no longer be given a merely patronizing nod, but it also began a tradition of orderly reporting of graduate-level research in the decades to follow. Leisy printed addenda and errata in 1927, brought the list up to date in *The Reinterpretation of American Literature* (1928), and the next year the profession's journal, *American Literature,* began regularly listing theses in progress or completed. In that journal in 1933, Leisy and Hubbell compiled a new cumulative list of 406 dissertations through 1932; and the addendum in 1948 by Lewis Leary (Duke) increased the sum by 1,142 titles when he gleaned the continuous records in *American Literature* compiled by Leisy (to 1938), Gregory Paine (1938–40), and Raymond Adams (1940–47). In 1957, James Woodress (San Fernando Valley State) published more than 2,500 titles, accumulated since 1891 and in a second edition (1962) added 809 new dissertations.[6]

Leisy's dissertation count in 1926 and the supplementary titles through 1929 showed Columbia, with seventeen doctoral theses, leading all English departments in the 1920s, followed by Chicago (fourteen), Virginia (seven), North Carolina (six), Pennsylvania (five), and Cornell (five). These totals did not necessarily reflect, as we have seen, the interest and activity in American literature within the various graduate and undergraduate programs during the decade. Harvard graduated five American literature candidates by the end of the 1920s, but their program in the subject remained quite minimal. New York University, with a department more active at both graduate and undergraduate levels, produced only four dissertations, as did Wisconsin, while Penn State, for all its curricular strength and variety, showed only one successful candidate for the doctorate. In the Far West, the University of Washington, during Vernon Parrington's era, boasted only three Ph.D.'s in American Literature.

Leisy's listings were valuable in their evidence that general topics rather than single authors usually comprised the earliest dissertations. Of the latter, Poe was the subject of five theses. Henry James, Cooper, Franklin, Emerson, and Whitman received three dissertations each. Significant, too, were the number of future professors of American literature who were now writing their dissertations in American, not English, literature. Those who would become leaders in the profession, or in some cases whose theses at least would become a valuable contribution to scholarship, were emerging from the various graduate schools of the twenties from year to year (theses later published as books are marked with an asterisk):

1922

Jay B. Hubbell, "Virginia Life in Fiction"* (Columbia)

1923

Ernest E. Leisy, "The American Historical Novel before 1860"* (Illinois)

Thomas O. Mabbott, "An Editon of Poe's *Politian*"* (Columbia)

Kenneth B. Murdock, "Increase Mather: Foremost American Puritan"* (Harvard)

Napier Wilt, "History of the Chicago Theatre from 1847 to 1857" (Chicago)

1924

Dorothy A. Dondore, "The Prairie and the Making of Middle America"* (Columbia)

Gregory L. Paine, "James Fenimore Cooper as an Interpreter and Critic of America" (Chicago)

Ralph L. Rusk, "The Literature of the Middle Western Frontier"* (Columbia)

Robert E. Spiller, "The American in England during the First Half Century of Independence"* (Pennsylvania)

1925

E. Sculley Bradley, "George Henry Boker: Poet and Patriot"* (Pennsylvania)

Lucy L. Hazard, "The Frontier in American Literature"* (California)

1926

Nelson F. Adkins, "Fitz-Greene Halleck: An Early Knickerbocker Wit and Poet"* (Yale)

G. Harrison Orians, "The Influence of Walter Scott upon America and American Literature before 1860" (Illinois)

1927

Tremaine McDowell, "William Cullen Bryant" (Yale)

1928

Raymond W. Adams, "Henry Thoreau's Literary Theory and Criticism" (North Carolina)

Frank L. Mott, "American Magazines, 1865–1880"* (Columbia)

Henry A. Pochmann, "The Influence of the German Tale on the Short Stories of Irving, Hawthorne, and Poe" (North Carolina)

1929

Harold Blodgett, "Walt Whitman in England"* (Cornell)

Frederic I. Carpenter, "Emerson's Use of Translations from the Oriental"* (Chicago)

Leon Howard, "Whitman's Evangel of Democracy" (Johns Hopkins)

In previous decades, universities expected the thesis to be published—if necessary, at the author's expense. (Fourteen of the foremost universities had begun their own presses before 1920, and seven others followed in the twenties.) But as the program for the Ph.D. was lengthened and the scope of the dissertation expanded—to prove that American requirements were every bit as demanding as the European—one result, as John Higham remarks, was that "ironically, the swollen size of theses" coincided with inflated printing costs and "gradually forced universities to suspend the traditional rule that theses must be published, thereby permitting a further sacrifice of quality."[7] All of this intensive Europeanizing of the American doctorate, President Lowell of Harvard believed as early as 1909, was creating an "industrious mediocrity" of future professors, and Dean West of Princeton complained that graduate students were generally motivated to earn the degree not out of the love of learning but to acquire "a union card."[8] Be that as it may, by the later 1920s, the author of the American literature dissertation began to have bright chances of employment, said Cairns in a letter to Hubbell in late 1927: "Three or four big state universities are now looking for men in American literature, willing to give any reasonable salary and rank for the right man."[9]

Cairns, Hubbell, and younger professors who were shaping the graduate programs in American literature in the twenties were also leading the American Literature Group, and when the MLA met at Harvard in 1926, they addressed their shared concerns and difficulties in pedagogy and scholarship. The Advisory Council unanimously passed a report on "Recommendations for the Doctorate in American Literature," obviously an outgrowth of the new theories of American literary history that were forming and soon to receive expression in the *Reinterpretation of American Literature*. The report was the work of Cairns, Hubbell, Howard M. Jones (North Carolina), Ernest Leisy, T. O. Mabbott, Kenneth Murdock, Stanley T. Williams, and chairman Norman Foerster. They intended to remedy the vagueness of doctoral requirements by addressing such basic questions as whether graduate students preparing for a professorship in American literature should receive the bulk of their courses in the national literature; or equally in English literature, with American literature viewed as a by-product of English rather than as a national literature; or in all of English literature, with some fraction of American literature.

The council agreed that American literature, so-called, was not purely national but yet was more than a reflection of English literature. Properly it should be understood as *comparative*. Questions guiding the curriculum, then, should be the following: (1) How is American literature distinctly American? (2) How is it like English and other literatures? and (3) How has it been influenced by American life and thought? To answer these questions, the council agreed that five areas of study would be essential to the American literature doctoral candidate: (1) American history—specifically, political, social, and economic; (2) modern European history, especially since the death of Elizabeth in England and the Napoleanic revolution in France; (3) history of modern philosophy and religion; (4) English literature from the Renaissance to 1800, with emphasis on the [early?] romantic movement; and (5) American literature—the primary texts and history—from 1607 to 1890. For the language study that best supported an emphasis in American literature, the following were deemed "neither relevant nor practicable": Old French, Gothic, Anglo-Saxon, and Middle English. German and French should be studied if they were related to the area of a dissertation. And if faculty colleagues urged that linguistic study were a worthy discipline for every student, American literature candidates might study Latin and Greek, since these were languages known to the older American writers. The council agreed, too, that a one-year M.A. in American literature was too slight a degree. The doctoral candidate would more profitably earn a master's in English literature; otherwise, he or she could skip the intermediate degree altogether.[10]

In view of this enlightened activity in 1926, professors in American literature some decades later may ask why graduate study should have continued to include such requirements as

Anglo-Saxon or have maintained the familiar five-to-one imbalance of English literature over American in the doctoral examinations. The radical innovations discussed in 1926 were not,
in fact, pursued even then. As Murdock acknowledged after the
meeting a year later, had the ALG vigorously argued these new
requirements, they would only have alienated the majority of
their tradition-oriented departmental colleagues. At the Toronto
meeting of 1928, in a joint session of the ALG's Executive Committee and Advisory Council, members agreed to "table as premature the efforts of the last year to stabilize Ph.D. requirements."
Intramural political realities had to be faced.[11]

Beyond the confines of their professional meetings, ALG professors further advanced the rationale for the serious study of
American writers. Leaders in the academy now brought the
issues into public print with far greater energy and confidence
than in the previous two decades. In his memoirs, Van Wyck
Brooks recalled, with some exaggeration, the low state of the profession at the advent of the twenties:

> American writing itself had come to seem important, although it
> was still ignored in academic circles, where Thackeray and Ten-
> nyson were treated as twin kings of our literature and all the
> American writers as poor relations. It was regarded as "a pale and
> obedient provincial cousin about which the less said the better," in
> the phrase of Ernest Boyd, and Christian Gauss at Princeton, as
> Edmund Wilson soon pointed out, chimed in with Woodberry at Co-
> lumbia and Wendell at Harvard. He [Wilson] too looked down his
> nose at American studies.[12]

That portion of the American reading public concerned with life
inside the universities now increasingly learned of the stubborn
opposition to academic study of American literature. Within
months after the Armistice, an article titled "American Literature in the Colleges" appeared in the *North American Review*.
Writing under a pseudonym of T. J. Baker, the author called public attention to the neglect suffered by American literature within
the most prominent universities in the country, while literatures
from across the seas were honored in the curriculum. A large
New England university that he did not name was offering but
one two-hour survey course, from Benjamin Franklin to the
present ("'omitted in 1917–1918'"). In all the large Eastern-
college catalogs, he could not find a single course in American
literature specializing in a genre (he had obviously missed Quinn's
drama course at Pennsylvania in 1917–18). At Harvard, Bliss

Perry had devoted a half-term to Emerson. Baker emphasized that American literature was not an appendage to English literature but reflected our American life and American spirit.[13]

More systematically, Arthur H. Quinn repeated and elaborated these data and opinions in his paper, "American Literature as a Subject for Graduate Study," for the 1921 MLA meeting in Baltimore, the convention where the ALG was born. His remarks received wider currency in the pages of the *Educational Review* some months later and helped form the ALG's subsequent inquiry into Ph.D. requirements. Quinn, too, had gone to college catalogs for his data, but he had also written to seventeen universities across the country. Three reported an annual graduate course in American literature (Columbia, Michigan, and Pennsylvania), and four gave one every other year (Illinois, Stanford, Virginia, and Wisconsin). A mixed graduate–undergraduate course was given at Chicago, Cornell, North Carolina, Texas, and Virginia each year, and at Harvard and Yale every other year. Brown, Princeton, and Johns Hopkins did not have any sort of graduate course in American writers. Where courses were offered, they ranged from periods and regions to genres (four in the novel, two in drama) and single authors—Emerson, Poe, Hawthorne, Lowell, and Whitman. Proposed dissertations on a single writer predominated, followed by regional phases, drama, and the novel.

Quinn's article remains significant historically not so much for the data—they give a rather limited picture of graduate-school activity in 1921—as for his professional and public effort to awaken the nation's English departments to a new spirit of letters in postwar America. He recommended changes in both policy and attitude: that American literature be recognized as a subject of ample substance for serious scholarship and not as a by-product of British literature; that the graduate student pursuing a Ph.D. in American literature be asked to read, secondarily, only the British literature clearly related to his or her subject; that the historical survey of American literature be relegated to the undergraduate curriculum; that pure graduate-level courses predominate over offerings on the mixed graduate–undergraduate levels; and that the work of modern and contemporary authors—a Frost or Robinson—be granted equal status with older authors as deserving of graduate study when subjected to the most rigid standards of scholarship.[14]

When the ALG framed Quinn's and other recommendations in the report at the Harvard meeting of 1926, as we saw, it was soon realized that the time, even by the late 1920s, was not ripe for any seriously altered temper and structure in the parent English department. But American literature professors, like other human beings, do not see far into the future. And so in the year after Quinn's article, Stuart Sherman, still a teacher at Illinois, hurled his own considerable energies and bright hopes into the same campaign "For the Higher Study of American Literature." His remarks appeared in the *Yale Review* of 1923, and he promptly gave them more prominence in his collection *Points of View* the following year. Sherman reminded readers that as children they grew up with American literature favorites, but these authors and books were not deemed fit subjects for disciplined study by the time American youth entered college. Those who progressed to graduate study and became professors of literature were ill equipped to turn the tide: "At the present time it is a conservative estimate to say that nine-tenths of our university teachers are more competent to discuss the literature of England than the literature of America." Sherman did not belittle the study of English literary tradition, of which American literature was no doubt an inevitable part. But somewhat like Quinn, he reversed the prevailing emphasis or priority: "The older literature must forever be *a part of American literature.*" Though American literature was still inferior artistically, and currently needed evaluative criticism and responsible guidance, Sherman echoed the case Baker had previously argued in the *North American Review:* To understand American life and society we must appreciate our own literature.[15]

During these months, Fred Pattee, too, surveyed American literature study in the academy, reaching back to the beginnings in the previous century, and thereby provided historical perspective and depth to the articles by Baker, Quinn, and Sherman. The results were presented to ALG members at the meeting in Ann Arbor, December 1923 (see Chapter 13). Published in 1924, the essay concluded with a variation on Sherman's left-handed compliment to our literature—the important social values in American writings deserved serious study, even if our authors were aesthetically deficient. Pattee quoted approvingly from a recent letter from C. Alphonso Smith (U.S. Naval Academy), his colleague on the *CHAL* team:

> "I am inclined to think that the colleges are coming gradually to the idea that while in purely artistic excellence English literature is superior to our own, our own is far superior to the literature of England as an expression of the vast implications of democratic citizenship. The moment one begins to think of citizenshp as a worthy objective, our literature begins to be seen in its true proportions."[16]

In May 1925, Ernest Leisy, secretary of the ALG, mailed a questionnaire to three hundred colleges, a sizable cross-section of regional institutions large and small, and solicited data on courses, prerequisites, texts, and instructor's expertise in American literature. He summarized the 148 replies at the ALG meeting in December in Chicago. Consistent with the missionary efforts of ALG leaders, Leisy published the findings in *School and Society* two months later. His paper to ALG members, "The Status of American Literature in the Colleges" (with Pattee a respondent), variously supported Quinn, Sherman, and Pattee, though with occasional qualifications obtained from a more extensive and updated inquiry. Among the important revelations, he reported that Pattee's collection of *Century Readings,* often in combination with Percy Boynton's *History of American Literature* (1919), enjoyed the most popularity in the college textbook market at mid-decade. Regarding pedagogical approach and expertise, Leisy learned that historical considerations were stronger than the aesthetic, and the national spirit in our literature more important than the regional. Among the questionnaires returned, he tallied thirteen professors who had written doctoral theses in American literature, while thirty-eight had received some graduate work in the subject.[17] Also in 1926, Leisy completed the bibliography, previously mentioned, that brought together a wider range of findings on dissertations and scholarly activity, and again, the results were promptly published, this time in *Studies in Philology* (Norman Foerster and Howard M. Jones were advisory editors).

At the ALG program in December 1926 at Harvard, after the Advisory Council passed its short-lived recommendations for the doctorate in American literature, more interest and debate stirred not only within the convention rooms but also in the larger intellectual community. Franklyn B. Snyder of Northwestern read a paper, "What is American 'Literature'?" It presently appeared in the *Sewanee Review.* Snyder answered the question in his title by echoing Sherman and Pattee: Ours is a literature distinguished not as belles lettres of a high order, but as a window to the national and regional issues of American social and political history. The survey of native literature in the English department should become primarily a course in "American civilization, reflected in American literature." Snyder argued for subliterary documents that illuminate our wars and historical watersheds, but figures of literary merit like Emerson and Whitman, or Hawthorne and Mark Twain should, of course, be included for the insights they also provide for the historical era. The Alfred Kreymborgs and Vachel Lindsays, however, could easily be eliminated.[18]

Within days after Snyder had read his paper, Henry S. Canby editorialized in the *Saturday Review of Literature* on "Teaching Our Literature." He regretted that when our literature received a hearing, along with the English writers, in the classroom, America was represented by inferior moralists or mediocre regionalists. It was equally wrong to regard our great authors only as they reflected American culture. Canby proposed a blending of history and belles lettres, so that the works of Hawthorne, Whitman, Poe, Melville, Thoreau, Emerson, Cooper, or Twain could be understood as "art conditioned by the American environment." In short, Canby concluded, "read the great Americans as they wrote, not to illustrate America (except for Cooper in his decadence), but because they had something to say, and could say it finely, and not without reference to the America that bred them." Jay B. Hubbell, and no doubt others in the ALG, soon suspected that Canby knew about Snyder's remarks at the recent convention and was directly responding to that narrowly historical approach to American literature.[19]

In 1928, H. L. Mencken considered this advocacy of American literature lively enough to merit some pages of his *American Mercury*. The article, "Teaching American Literature in American Colleges," was written by Ferner Nuhn, once more a pseudonym—this author was Ruth Suckow. Nuhn claimed to have consulted college catalogs for her findings. They merely documented, with some vivid new data here and there, the state of American literature in the college offerings already described by Leisy, Pattee, and others; but now the message was being sent even to the smart-set readers of the *American Mercury*. First, Nuhn contrasted the neglect American writers suffered by comparison to the English. On average, one of eleven English department undergraduate courses were in American literature. On the graduate level, the ratio was one to thirteen, with courses in Chaucer equaling the sum of all American literature offerings. Seven of eight theses were in English literature. At Harvard in 1927, however, all thirteen literature theses were on English topics, and all thirteen sounded singularly dull but indubitably were prosecuted with a requisite scholarship.

Nuhn also contrasted the neglect of American literature with the now-thriving study of American history. American history courses outnumbered English history in the colleges two to one. In the world history curriculum, one of every three courses was American, as opposed to the literature curriculum of one American course in every twenty-five. Nuhn offered graphic examples: "Contemporary Drama" at Ohio State did not list even Eugene

O'Neill; no American writer appeared in "Comparative Literature" at Illinois; and at Pennsylvania, "A Study of Nineteenth-
Century Prose" meant the prose of England. Pattee's program at
Penn State drew her highest acclaim, with six of twenty-seven
undergraduate and five of eleven graduate literature courses belonging to the American field. This article, written more than
fifty years ago, recommended the separate American literature
department with a logic that has not penetrated academic committee rooms to the present day: "It seems little enough to ask:
that the national literature be granted a status equal to that now
generally accorded such subjects as journalism, the Spanish language and literature, band instruments, horticulture, animal
husbandry, and military science and tactics."[20]

Chapter 15

The Reinterpretation of American Literature (1928): Professional Scholarship after the *CHAL*

Revaluation and reinterpretation of America's literature during the 1920s were an inevitable outcome of the many-sided upheavals and questionings provoked by the nation's engagement in a first global conflict. Add to the pervasive effects of World War I the completion of a first cooperative literary history, and the stage was prepared for a skeptical, postwar generation of young intellectuals to scrutinize the achievements and failures of their academic elders. In literary scholarship, Norman Foerster registered an early note of dissatisfaction in his review of the completed *CHAL* in 1921. Though himself a young contributor to the history, he was disappointed that no account of American literary criticism had appeared in these pages and that the work offered no clear sense of how American literature had evolved. Foerster eventually tried to remove the first deficiency with his *American Criticism* in 1928. A remedy of the other appeared the same year in *The Reinterpretation of American Literature,* the result of a movement inside the young profession to reassess American literary history more adequately than had the previous generation represented in the *CHAL* (and, it should be added, to do so with a professional disregard of postwar British views on American literature). In this volume, Foerster again played a major role.

Preceding these two works, Foerster served the infant profession in still another capacity, as the first compiler in *PMLA* of the annual scholarship in American literature. In his initial "American Bibliography for 1922," he discussed the articles and books treating the two previous centuries of American writing, together with essays proliferating at a "furious rate" on contemporary authors. He observed that the "rapidly growing interest in American letters . . . is more popular than scholarly," and his conclusion foreshadowed the major reinterpretation of modes and movements in which he would soon be engaged: "Substantial studies of American subjects are still rare" (p. 25). He continued to list the annual studies in the same format over the next three years and repeated, in the bibliography for 1925, that while the scholarship was marked by accelerating quantity and diversity, the profession needed direction and definition, a "more concerted effort." He noted, in fact, that in his own *American Poetry Prose* of that year "a partly new conception of American literary history determines the arrangement, text, and notes."[1] Thereafter, Foerster abandoned the essay form in favor of the format that would be adopted when *American Literature,* in its third issue (November 1929), began to list current articles: a bibliography (frequently annotated) of general subjects, followed by sections on authors chronologically arranged. (Gregory Paine substituted for Foerster in the *PMLA* listings for 1927 and 1929.)

We can reenact through still other sources the motions of the scholar in the 1920s who was trying to keep current in studies of American literature. In addition to Foerster and Paine in *PMLA,* we have noticed the valuable bibliographical labors of Ernest Leisy for the ALG in the issues of *Studies in Philology* during 1926 and 1927, where scholars now learned, in particular, about doctoral dissertations under way or completed. Scholarly monographs in the twenties, too, were consistently helpful in reminding the student not only of recent work in the field, but also of the bibliographies in the *CHAL.* Vernon L. Parrington prefaced the bibliography of both volumes of *Main Currents in American Thought* (1927) by sending his reader, above all, to the *CHAL.* His full bibliographies also gave an excellent portrait of a superb scholarly mind prepared to comprehend our literary history with the aid of the most up-to-date sources.

Somewhat more modestly, Henry S. Canby's bibliography in *Classic Americans* (1931), prepared with an assist from Randall Stewart (Yale), did the same and also reminded us of the impressive flow of new scholarly editions and monographs that arrived just after Parrington. These included Stanley T. Williams's four volumes of Irving, Robert Spiller's two volumes of Cooper's *Gleanings,* and the editions of Thoreau's and Hawthorne's journals by Odell Shepard and Newton Arvin, respectively. Parrington must have felt a bit overwhelmed in 1926 as he witnessed the outpouring of monographs appearing too late to be comprehended in his first two volumes. Perhaps he also felt relieved. In that single year came Ernest Leisy's study of Cooper; John Freeman's Melville; studies of Poe by Hervey Allen and Mary E. Phillips, both in two volumes, plus Joseph W. Krutch's monograph; and volumes on Whitman by John Bailey, Havelock Ellis, and Emory Holloway. These works were followed in 1927 by Brooks Atkinson's

Thoreau and the monographs on Hawthorne by Herbert Gorman and Lloyd Morris. Two years later came two studies that stimulated far-reaching scholarly interest and discussion—Newton Arvin's Hawthorne and Lewis Mumford's Melville.

Foerster's dissatisfaction with American literary scholarship in the twenties resulted not from a paucity of work on individual authors. He lamented, instead, the absence of the larger vision that could shape a more accurate literary history. Some limited efforts to that end appeared, of course, in several genre studies. Louis Untermeyer, in *American Poetry Since 1900* (1923), recast and updated his *New Era* (1919), organizing our twentieth-century poets into their various *isms:* Lyricists, Rhapsodists, Traditionalists, Cerebralists, Imagists, and so on. Bruce Weirick (Illinois) cut a wider swath the next year in *From Whitman to Sandburg in American Poetry* (1924), bravely fashioning a version of literary history with Whitman the supreme influence on modern poetry and his disciple Sandburg the chief living poet who had risen above a time of bizarre and incoherent expression. T. S. Eliot received no mention.

In American prose, after Van Doren's studies of the novel and Pattee's on the short story, we had two works in the midtwenties, Joseph W. Beach's *The Outlook for American Prose* (1926) and Percy Boynton's *More Contemporary Americans* (1927), both published by the University of Chicago and both evincing the lack of a sustained historical sense—they were collections of the authors' published articles. Nor was a sense of literary past and present gained in Stanley T. Williams's *The American Spirit in Letters* (1926). Designing it as volume 11 in Ralph Gabriel's fifteen-volume Pageant of America series, Williams wrote an urbane commentary (without footnotes) that served largely to caption the illustrations that accompanied his 326 pages of text. Also written for profit as well as edification in 1926 were two distinguished period histories. Lewis Mumford's *The Golden Day* ranged impressively into, before, and after his golden period of "disintegration and fulfillment" from 1830 to 1860. And Thomas Beer added a graceful and witty five chapters to Mumford's later pages with *The Mauve Decade: American Life at the End of the Nineteenth Century,* useful for the cultural backgrounds to the American literary history that Foerster and his colleagues were now agitating to reassess and recast.

The origins of their pivotal study can be traced to the middle 1920s. For the American Literature Group meeting in Chicago in 1925, Foerster read a paper, "New Viewpoints in American Literature." The content was derived from his preface to the first edition of his anthology, *American Poetry and Prose,* which appeared earlier in the year. After a fair amount of rewriting, Foerster published the paper as "American Literature" in the *Saturday Review of Literature.* Houghton Mifflin then issued the article in pamphlet form. In this formative essay, Foerster subsumed all of American literary history under European culture and American environment and then isolated four "factors": "(1) the puritan tradition, (2) the pioneer spirit [nature, frontier, physical America], (3) romanticism, and (4) realism . . . the application of the scientific spirit to art." Recognizing these forces would help to arouse fresh interpretations, perhaps in four separate books, to allay "the danger that confronts the higher study of American literature," namely "an aimless accumulation of small facts."[2]

Though Foerster's four shaping factors in American literature will seem even to an undergraduate today both obvious and incomplete, the effect of his paper in 1925 became well-nigh electric within the ALG. Hubbell wrote to him shortly after the Christmas meeting to debate the viewpoints and suggest that all but the frontier were really foreign influences, unless we regard puritanism as a native phenomenon. But even here, Hubbell asked, was not the New England environment more crucial than the religious import of Puritanism? He suggested that American literature might more correctly be shaped under the headings of (1) race, (2) environment (geographical, social, and economic), and (3) literary influences from the outside—including romanticism and realism. Foerster allowed that his four divisions did not cover the field, were only "leading" indicators, and no doubt Hubbell's three headings were more inclusive. Even so, Foerster did not modify his thesis.[3]

The next ALG program was arranged by Foerster and Chairman Hubbell almost at once. They wanted to consider "Factors in American Literary History," with papers centering on Foerster's four points. Foerster recommended for participants Hubbell himself (or Howard M. Jones), Canby of the *Saturday Review* (or Van Wyck Brooks or Stuart P. Sherman, who died, however, in the summer of 1926), and John Erskine (or Carl Van Doren or Foerster himself). To consider three of the four editors from the recent *CHAL*—Sherman, Erskine, and Van Doren—probably revealed Foerster's search for continuity rather than radical departure. Or perhaps he wanted strong confrontation and debate. Among the other names, Canby was primed, as he told Foerster, with a concept for a book on the subject of the program. (In *Classic Americans,* 1931, Canby explained that he had been envisioning a more elaborate history of American literature but had forsaken it in favor of these single-author chapters.) For his part, Jones was contemplating an article on his conception of American literature.[4]

In the summer of 1926, Hubbell met with Foerster at Chapel Hill and suggested that what they now had was the basis for a book reinterpreting American literary history. Foerster's essay, along with Hubbell's paper on the frontier at the 1924 meeting of the ALG, were already known quantities. And Ernest Leisy, who had just published his American literature bibliography in *Studies in Philology,* could easily contribute. As the ALG program in December 1926 drew nearer—the meeting Robert Spiller was to call epochal—Hubbell courted Jones for a paper that could also become a contribution to the book. Canby, said Hubbell, seemed prepared, and with "one or two other things," the book would virtually have taken shape, perhaps bearing the title of Foerster's seminal paper of the year before, "New Viewpoints in American Literature."[5] Then came the 1926 MLA convention in Cambridge, one of the meetings that, in retrospect, would have a crucial bearing on American literature scholarship for years to come.

The issues in the projected volume of essays not only received further airing and debate, but the authors also found a likely publisher. Houghton Mifflin seemed "generally disposed," Foerster wrote to Hubbell after the convention. "Their chief argument for publishing is that they don't want anybody else to publish the book!" (Houghton Mifflin had been Foerster's publisher not only for the recent pamphlet but also his anthology *American Poetry and Prose* in 1925 and his composition handbook *Sentences and Thinking* in 1923.) Foerster wondered if the ALG might help sponsor the book by assuring Houghton Mifflin of certain funds. For editor, Hubbell nominated Foerster, but Foerster suggested they wait with that decision.[6]

Several months later, Foerster wrote Hubbell that Houghton Mifflin had turned down the proposed book. Foerster was now offering it to Harvard (who also declined in very short order, unwilling to assume the financial risk).[7] Foerster described to Hubbell the contents he was currently proposing to publishers under the title *The Study of American Literature.* They included the eventual chapters by Pattee, Foerster, Hubbell, and Murdock. Foerster's letter made no mention of Parrington's chapter on realism nor "American History and American Literary History" by A. M. Schlesinger (Harvard); presumably they were not yet envisioned. And Foerster eventually turned his "Romantic Movement" chapter over to Paul Kaufman (American University). Either Arthur H. Quinn or Stanley T. Williams, Foerster hoped, would write on "American Literature and the Graduate School."

Of the three appendices that Foerster described, two appeared in the published volume, prepared by Gregory Paine and Ernest Leisy, respectively: a bibliography for students of American literature, and a list of materials for investigation (the data updated from Leisy's two recent articles in *Studies in Philology*). The third appendix was to have been labeled "A. Recommendations for M.A. and Ph.D. Degrees." Hubbell passed Foerster's contents along to Leisy with a postscript: "Leisy: How about a chapter on the nature of research problems in Am. Literature, etc., leading up to Appendices A and C, written by Cairns or Parrington? Do we need Jones's ["Middle Class Spirit"] chapter? J. B. H." Leisy agreed that Jones's chapter, the subject of his paper at the 1926 meeting, should go; Jones then lent his more formidable knowledge to the chapter, "The European Background." Parrington, said Leisy, should write the chapter on research problems. But Appendix A, on recommendations for advanced degrees, was then abandoned along with the research chapter, and Parrington contributed, instead, the chapter on realism.[8]

As the book approached completed form, Carleton Brown, secretary of MLA, wrote to Foerster that he was pleased with Foerster's notion that the book be issued under MLA auspices. And to Foerster's amazement, Harcourt Brace not only agreed to bring out the book, but did not seek financial aid in the publication. Indeed, Foerster secured royalties for the contributors. His own reward later amounted to $104.17 in the next five years from a sale of 2,135 copies. That good fortune was only slightly dimmed by the awkward defection of Canby ("The Backgrounds of American Literature") as the venture approached the manuscript deadline. But Harry Hayden Clark (Wisconsin) was rapidly delegated to write on "American Literary History and American Literature."[9]

The Reinterpretation of American Literature is indispensable reading today for every person who would understand the rise of twentieth-century studies in American literature. A decade after publication of the initial volumes of the *CHAL*, the authors reflected here and there an awareness that scholarship since then had inevitably developed under the long shadow cast by that massive literary history. In his introduction, Foerster recalled the ferment of the war years that stimulated the drive to American self-knowledge and encouraged a strong link between literary scholarship and cultural history. Still, the *CHAL* suffered from the paucity of earlier studies, resulting in an inadequacy of facts to support generalizations about our literary history. And, said Foerster, our national literature even yet had not been studied thoroughly because (here echoing the litany of complaints we have earlier recorded) American literature was regularly viewed either as merely one more field of English literature or, even worse, as "a hobby that may be tolerated."[10]

Faced with this perennially condescending attitude and its debilitating effect on American literature study, Foerster and his colleagues intended to present not "striking discoveries and novel conclusions" but rather a suggestive "spirit and manner in which a fresh interpretation should be undertaken" (p. vii). The suggestions would point to the external, but also the internal, approaches to an understanding of our literary works, to the claims both of history and of criticism. Historically, three questions of literary history—how our literature was peculiarly American, in what ways like European literature, and how local conditions of life and thought had made a difference—must now be addressed by giving attention to Foerster's four causal forces: the puritan tradition, the frontier spirit, romanticism, and realism. (By leading us toward Western European origins of romanticism and realism, Foerster was helping cut the umbilical cord to England without relying wholly on native cultural influences—a momentous step in redefining the tradition of American literature.) Finally, said Foerster, the internal demands of interpretive explication and criticism, of aesthetic revaluation, were crucial for the current professor and literary historian in the American field. The historical approach alone would not do (and though unnamed, the aesthetically indiscriminate *CHAL* had to be on Foerster's mind). The professor who required the historical mastery of texts, background, and genesis, but also proceeded to questions of aesthetic interpretation and criticism, would send forth young humanistic teachers of American literature who realized that "the life of scholarship is not a mechanism to be manipulated but indeed a life to be lived" (p. xv).

Fred L. Pattee led off the volume with "A Call for a Literary Historian," his submission to Mencken's *American Mercury* in June 1924. That date points significantly in two directions. In less than three years after the completed *CHAL*, Pattee was already clamoring for a comprehensive new history; and his reprinting the article in 1928 suggests that the need had been continually felt in the intervening four years. Pattee issued "the fundamental ten commandments" for making a totally American literary history. His injunctions were that the new history must be (1) a living and original history with no aim to being a classroom textbook; (2) impartial and unprovincial; (3) a revaluation of older writers from "the new perspective"; (4) based on newly discovered facts and emptied of myths about the "major writers"; (5) a unified blending of nineteenth-century historical backgrounds, including Eastern cultural centers, European influences, the ferment of the 1830s and 1840s, and the pre- and postwar West; (6) a democratic story that embraces the popular and subliterary as well as belles lettres; (7) a reassessment of periods; (8) unrelenting criticism (for example, of the venerated Cambridge poets); (9) aware of the important role of the magazine, especially in the development of American humor, the short story, and the essay; and (10) written with an encompassing "force and beauty, with a style simple and clear."

The second chapter, Foerster's "Factors in American Literary History," established the four bases for the following chapters 3–7: (1) the puritan tradition, to be considered in the chapters by Jones and Murdock; (2) the frontier, Hubbell's chapter; (3) romanticism (Kaufman); and (4) realism (Parrington). Foerster pointedly rejected the political and geographical periods of earlier literary histories (quoting, without naming his source, the period titles in the *CHAL*), for they had missed the "organic relationship of American and European literature" (p. 24).

Hubbell began the discussion with his chapter on factor number two, the frontier. Perhaps the editorial reasoning for violating the order of Foerster's list was to consider this indigenous influence before returning to the three forces that had affected our literature from abroad. In fact, however, Hubbell commented almost at once that American frontier literature was not overly American, for it was directly indebted to European literature in matters of "form or technique" (p. 43); and we must understand European social and industrial influences to comprehend the frontier (as Mrs. Hazard's recent book did not). Still, the frontier had been a regenerative and original force, giving to American authors—whose backgrounds had usually been quite separate from the frontier—both new native materials and a new point of view and spirit, or at least a rekindling of the older spirit of American independence. This renewal continued even into the 1920s, Hubbell argued, for the Midwest, and especially Chicago, was creatively the "most productive center of American literature" (p. 55). He concluded that literary scholars must define "frontier" more carefully than historian Frederick Jackson Turner

(1893) and Frederic L. Paxson (1924) had done. We might have expected Hubbell to illustrate how "frontier" had been employed within the three books of the midtwenties: Ralph Rusk's *The Literature of the Middle Western Frontier* (1925, two volumes), Dorothy Dondore's *The Prairie and the Making of America* (1926), and Lucy Hazard's *The Frontier in American Literature* (1927). Hazard and Rusk were cited vaguely and Dondore not at all.

In his "The European Background," Jones deplored the naïve references to European writers made by our literary historians, as well as holistic theories of American literature that had failed to account for the international backgrounds of seventeenth-century Calvinism, eighteenth-century Jeffersonian liberalism, and nineteenth-century moral and aesthetic revival and revolution. He, too, scored the *CHAL* for its deficiencies, such as devoting ten times the space and emphasis to political over religious thought in America when the latter was more vital to our literature (and demanded that the literary scholar be firmly grounded in European influences). Where a lesser scholar would have paraded the learning of his recent book—Jones had just published *America and French Culture* (1927)—Jones easily ranged among the diverse national influences of Europe. In the process, like Foerster, he thus directed us away from merely British antecedents in our literature. The chapter heralded the appearance of one of the most far-ranging and synthesizing minds American literature scholars would come to know in the decades ahead.

While Jones touched on puritanism, Foerster's initial factor, Kenneth Murdock, whose Harvard thesis (1923) on Increase Mather had recently been published by his alma mater, focused directly on the concept in "The Puritan Tradition in American Literature" (originally a 1927 lecture to the Bread Loaf School of English, Bread Loaf, Vermont). He anticipated a more exacting Puritan scholarship after the strident 1920s, when "puritan" had been employed loosely by ancestor worshippers and with similar vagueness as a pejorative catchword in the criticism of Mencken, Brooks, Lewisohn, and James T. Adams. New literary studies must deal with the theological, political, social, and economic aspects of the Puritan tradition and also examine the aesthetic of holiness, the practical idealism, the operation of the plain style, and the generally rewarding complexity in Puritan writing. Finally indispensable to such study would be accurate reprints of colonial texts (pp. 100, 105, 111).

In "The Romantic Movement," Paul Kaufman admitted that he was not presenting an original theory but rather—and this was often true of the companion chapters as well—assembling the data "which are familiar enough, but which hitherto have not been isolated and rearranged in the present pattern" (p. 136). In 1923, Kaufman had delivered a paper on romanticism at the MLA meeting in Ann Arbor. Before Kaufman could bring out his "Defining Romanticism: A Survey and a Program," Arthur O. Lovejoy had published his now-classic "Discrimination of Romanticisms."[11] Kaufman, characteristically self-effacing and generous, hailed Lovejoy's "brilliant and comprehensive" essay. Now in *Reinterpretation,* he also acknowledged in an introductory footnote the recently valuable interpretations of American romanticism formulated in Foerster's *American Poetry and Prose* (1925) and Parrington's volume 2 of *Main Currents in American Thought* (1927). The critic in Kaufman, however, could not resist pointing to the conceptual weakness of the *CHAL* (unnamed), as he quoted its nonliterary title, "Early National," for the period. On the other hand, he generously cited Van Doren's and Quinn's contributions to the *CHAL* for their attention to romantic elements in American fiction and drama. Kaufman argued for research that would go beyond geographical divisions (the New England school or the New York group) and discover a coherent romantic character in American literature of the post-Revolutionary decades from Crevecoeur and Freneau to Whitman, along the way taking account of the variations in the romantic mode, whether derivative in Brown, Cooper, and Irving or more distinctly American in the creations of Poe, Melville, and their New England contemporaries. Causal explanations must include the spirit of freedom that had fired the energies of our writers during the American Revolution, in the period of Abolitionism, and over the many decades on the frontier.

In the remaining three chapters, Parrington discussed Foerster's fourth, and last, factor in "The Development of Realism," while A. M. Schlesinger, Sr., and Harry Clark wrote summing-up essays on various matters historical and literary that would affect writing a new American literary history. Parrington condensed the materials that awaited the third (posthumous) volume of *Main Currents.* Displaying his genius for the literary-historical synthesis, he viewed the six decades since the Civil War as largely realistic in literary expression, caused by a middle-class society and economy, including a critical reaction to reigning bourgeois values. Anti-capitalist discontent and "changing social ideals" at home had been complemented by a scientific and philosophical pessimism imported from Europe. Parrington detected a simmering of social discontent within four marked stages of realism: the commonplace in the literature of the early 1870s, culminating in the work of Howells during the mid-1880s; social protest from the early Garland to the flowering of this critical spirit, 1903 to 1917; Zolaesque naturalism from Crane and Norris to Dreiser; and impressionism—and perhaps expressionism—in *The Red Badge of Courage,* renewed by writers since World War I. For Parrington, realism was a pronounced *movement* rising out of the "ashes of romantic faith" (p. 140); it was a method devoted to "simple objectivity" or "a crisp objective impressionism" (p. 158); it was a salutary attitude critical of the status quo and liberated from "Victorian reticence" (p. 159). And it was a Zolaesque *philosophy* most recently expressed by Sherwood Anderson and his contemporaries, in which "the animal called man stands before us naked and unashamed." Parrington welcomed this evidence that America, grown more candid, introspective, and rational, was now "coming of age" (p. 159). For readers in the late twenties, he thus presented many valuable dimensions to the concept of realism—far too many, we now realize. It is also easy to fault him today, in particular, for the extravagant overlapping of his modal categories. To his suggestive insights and often transparent contradictions in the larger treatment of realism within *Main Currents in American Thought* we shall return in Chapter 17, devoted exclusively to Parrington.

Historian Schlesinger, whose *New Viewpoints in American History* (1922) had revealed the advances in "the New History," urged literary historians to understand the entire cultural matrix of a period, including activity in the fine arts, education, and the publishing industry. But Schlesinger argued his case with a vehemence that strangely implied a long-term neglect of the historical approach to literature. He found fault even with "the admirable and encyclopedic *Cambridge History of American Literature*" for slighting "the vital relation between the new education and literary production" before the Civil War (p. 171).

Clark concurred only to a degree on the importance of cultural backgrounds and their organic relation to literary creativity in his summary final chapter, "American Literary History and American Literature." He then insisted that for the literary historian, "literature itself remains the true subject, and the proper focal center is finally the acknowledged masterpieces" (p. 193). Furthermore, the literary work belongs at once in the foreground, and the social and economic forces should be viewed through the "windows" provided in the primary aesthetic interpretation of the work. Clark tried to demonstrate this dual approach with examples from Freneau's poetry and Melville's *Moby-Dick*. But he provided very little in the way of an aesthetic window for either writer. He merely quoted Freneau. For *Moby-Dick,* Clark acclaimed the "framework" and the "power as a work of art" and collapsed the contents into three sentences. Then he showed, with far greater success, the way to explore contemporary backgrounds that illuminate the texts. In short, Clark, with his contemporaries, insisted that the reinterpretation of American literature called for an aesthetic approach, the "careful and intelligent reading of the literature itself" (p. 213), but they had not yet discovered the techniques and principles for such explication and insight.

The *Reinterpretation* contained two appendices of concise bibliography that rivaled in importance the chapters that came before. Updating parts of the *CHAL* bibliographies, these listings remind us that American literature studies were fast approaching an era in which the mere tallying of a burgeoning scholarship was becoming a major industry in itself. In Appendix A, Gregory Paine listed in fourteen divisions, with occasional annotation, twenty pages of historical and literary works, reaching back to Griswold and Duyckinck and forward to Parrington. The student of 1928 could not have asked for a more judicious selection, ample and helpful and yet spare and unintimidating. Appendix B by Ernst Leisy (now at SMU), titled a "List of Dissertations and Articles, and of Americana in Libraries" was more valuable even than Paine's listings because more original. Leisy updated the dissertations and studies compiled recently for *Studies in Philology,* and also provided a second listing, of dissertations in progress on American topics, though it was unaccountably separated (as in the earlier listing) by the section "Articles on American Literature in American Scholarly Journals." Here, he had reproduced the 3½ pages of items from his *Studies in Philology* article of 1926, those studies published up to 1921, the year when *PMLA*'s annual bibliography succeeded *The American Year Book.* (Its publication had ended in 1920.) Graphically significant in Paine's listing were the limited outlets for scholarly articles in American literature during those earlier decades— *PMLA* (founded 1884–85), *Modern Language Notes* (1886), *Journal of English and German Philology* (1897), *Modern Philology* (1903), together with *Sewanee Review* (1892) and the occasional nonscholarly magazine. Finally, Leisy gave the American scholar a convenient package of twenty pages describing historical and literary materials of Americana in collections of twenty-four states and at the Library of Congress. In short, the appendices of *The Reinterpretation* not only reflected current American literature study but also offered a model for the bibliographer of American literary scholarship whose labors would vastly increase in the years to come.

Although Canby had defaulted from his chapter for the book, his absence from these pages created a large dividend in the end. Hubbell persuaded him to review *Reinterpretation* simultaneously in Canby's own *Saturday Review of Literature* (2 March 1929) and in the initial issue of *American Literature*, also in March 1929. Canby termed the publishing event "of the greatest importance" for scholars, critics, and teachers at a time when all of the major writers in our history "need orientation, explanation, appreciation on the sound bases of exact knowledge, and by the fine intuitions of trained taste" customarily devoted to older literatures. The importance of exact knowledge of backgrounds was admirably advanced in the book, and perhaps even overstated by Schlesinger, so that Canby repeated the warning by Clark that "'the background . . . must not be allowed to obliterate the foreground, the literature itself.'" Canby concluded that the *Reinterpretation* had served an invaluable purpose, "provided that purpose is understood to be preliminary to a more difficult task," which was the writing of a "much more radical volume . . . [that] engages the problems of intuitive appreciation." But he remained as helpless as the authors in knowing how to proceed: "If this means that we must risk the vagaries of impressionistic criticism—well, we must risk them, and go on." Canby's notice in the *Saturday Review*—perceptive, appreciative, and forward looking—was honored by Hubbell when he moved it from those pages to the position of lead review in the first issue of the profession's new journal. Thus were two youthful forces of American literature criticism and scholarship, in and out of the academy, consolidated in a strategic moment at the end of the twenties.

Chapter 16

American Literature (1929):
The Profession Has a Journal

Amid the growing professional awareness of American literature scholars in the 1920s, and the intellectual ferment that inspired *The Reinterpretation of American Literature,* an official journal for the movement became as inevitable as it was necessary. The story of *American Literature* can properly begin in December 1924, when Norman Foerster, an advisory editor of *Studies in Philology* (*SP*) at Chapel Hill, was planning to give the journal an increasingly American emphasis. He asked Jay B. Hubbell for a list of American Literature Group members who might be told about the new hospitality of *SP*. "Our pages are open," he wrote Hubbell.[1] With his usual instinct for projects to advance the profession, Hubbell as chairman of the ALG in 1925 went Foerster one better; he solicited the membership for their opinions on the idea of a new quarterly exclusively for American literature. A proposal then arrived from Louise Pound at Nebraska: The ALG might consider adopting *American Speech* as an official outlet for the profession. That journal had just published its first issue (October 1925) under the editorship of Pound, Kemp Malone (Johns Hopkins), and Arthur Kennedy (Stanford). Literary interpretation would nicely complement the linguistics articles, and she could make generous space available. Besides, so many journals were already in business for MLA members to buy that a new one seemed ill-advised. Hubbell promised to bring her offer before the ALG at the 1925 meeting in Chicago. But when Foerster heard of this offer, he promptly opposed an ALG endorsement of *American Speech* because of its "popular slant." He favored, instead, a closer arrangement with *PMLA* or *Modern Language Notes* (and, presumably, his own *SP*). "The fact that we Am. lit. folk are more or less on trial," he wrote Hubbell, "must make us sensitive to criticism."[2]

In 1926, Hubbell pushed on to other fronts—the program on reinterpretation, for one—but he kept alive the notion of a quarterly solely for American literature. Pound now favored such a journal, to be sanctioned by the ALG and, as she suggested, to be located at the University of Nebraska. Her university might willingly sponsor it in light of the increasing national interest in American literature. At the annual meeting in 1926 at Harvard, the question of a journal was secondary to the reexamination of Foerster's four-factors paper of the year before. But Hubbell kept the issue before ALG members in his correspondence during 1927. Among the respondents, Killis Campbell felt that the journal should be launched only if success could be guaranteed. In any event, he opposed Nebraska (though he admired Louise Pound): "I should wish it, in a word, to be published from some more central place."[3]

Later in the year, Campbell wrote to question the timing of a new journal. Were not *SP, PMLA, Modern Language Notes,* and *Modern Philology* sufficient outlets for scholarship in American literature at present? More encouraging was Percy Boynton, who assured Hubbell not only that existing scholarship was adequate for a separate journal, but also that new doctoral candidates of high ability (Boynton knew twelve at Chicago) were "doing very definite and valuable research." Pattee pointed to the encouraging expansion of American literature in the college curriculum. W. B. Cairns echoed Boynton and Pattee, seeing an impending boom for American literary study that would be felt in both publishable research and the professional job market. (Other professors were not so encouraged, however, by the progress of American literature study in the universities, and their dissatisfaction would be echoed well into the 1930s.) Kenneth Murdock, soon to launch the *New England Quarterly,* wondered, on his part, where money would come for subscriptions: Membership in ALG totaled roughly one hundred persons. Any university press would need to foot a considerable bill over the first several years. Nor was he confident that scholarship of an adequate level could yet fill the initial issues of a specialized journal. Aside from fears that it might be slightly premature, however, Murdock favored a journal for American literature. Stanley Williams, on the other hand, openly opposed those who warned that "'the time is not ripe,' etc. I shall be glad to do anything, edit, solicit, etc."[4]

Before he moved to Duke in the summer of 1927, Hubbell argued unsuccessfully with his graduate dean at Southern Methodist that an American literature journal would enhance the reputation of their university (Hubbell had been editing its *Southwest Review*). And so he carried to Duke his ambitions for the journal and hoped it might be stationed at his new campus. In the summer of 1927, Williams wrote again, this time with a more qualified assessment of the new enterprise. The study of American literature, he feared, was still besieged by hostile critics who charged that it dealt in huge vaguenesses and lacked, as yet, sufficiently academic discipline. Such critics would probably sniff at an American literature journal if it were located, as he knew that Hubbell planned, at a somewhat raw new university like Duke (Trinity College until 1924), with an editor allegedly a student primarily of the frontier. These critics, actual and potential, could be held off, though, if the journal demanded patient, focused scholarship judged by a board of editors of unquestioned achievement from our strongest universities. Pattee noted that the American literature movement was "growing with marvellous rapidity" and sent his support both of Hubbell and Duke. Robert Spiller was similarly excited and gave his unequivocal endorsement. The timing was splendid, he felt, coming on the heels of the remarkable meeting of 1926 on the reassessment of our national literature. Bibliographer Ernest Leisy echoed Spiller and pointed to a mere five years past when he counted only forty-one articles on American literature in all of our learned journals. But the *PMLA* bibliographical listing of 1926 (compiled by Foerster) showed that figure to have doubled. Clearly American literature needed the space afforded by the profession's own journal. And clearly, Hubbell was the experienced editor to be placed at the helm.[5]

The stage was now set for the 1927 meeting in Louisville. Shortly before, Williams wrote to Hubbell about a rumor that Brown University was planning to make a bid for the new journal.[6] At the Louisville meeting, Hubbell presented the case for Duke, but Chairman Murdock ensured an orderly presentation and review of all interested sponsors by appointing an ad hoc Committee on Publications of the group, with ALG secretary Spiller as chairman, along with Cairns, Ralph Rusk (from Indiana to Columbia since 1925), Hubbell, and Murdock (exofficio). Negotiations for a publisher would also be channelled through Spiller's committee. After the Louisville meeting, Leisy reported to Hubbell on 15 January 1928 some of the sotto voce sentiments at the recent convention. Members were heard to fear that if the journal went to Duke, Hubbell would have on his hands a Rasputin as assistant next door at North Carolina, namely, Foerster. To combat this apprehension, said Leisy, Duke should clarify its planned arrangement for the advisers to the editor. And he suggested quite delicately that the journal should espouse a more scholarly intensity than Hubbell's previous *Southwest Review*. Meanwhile, with the efficiency and acumen that would characterize his administrative labors throughout the next three decades, Spiller quickly organized his committee. By January 1928, he had sent his members (1) excerpts from letters solicited from editors of other journals regarding matters of ownership and editorship and (2) statements regarding possible location of the new journal—including proposals from Duke and Brown. Pennsylvania also had an offer pending. Spiller was moving cautiously because, as he wrote to an understandably impatient Hubbell, he did not wish to anger, by undue haste, some who might be planning to make late offers.[7]

On 4 February 1928, Spiller mailed to his committee a six-page "Preliminary Report of the Committee on Publications" and also advised them of a proposed luncheon in New York on the eighteenth to be hosted by member Ralph Rusk at Columbia University Men's Faculty Club. In addition to committee members, invitations were going out to Lindsay Todd Damon (and one other representative from Brown), Stanley Williams, and Arthur Quinn. The following day, Spiller wrote to Hubbell suggesting that it would be in Duke's interest to make its offer quite specific. On 10 February, Phelps Soule, recently arrived as editor and manager of the University of Pennsylvania Press, informed Spiller that Pennsylvania did not have the required financing and was withdrawing from the competition. And so Brown emerged as chief rival to Duke, though its plan to include three or four Brown professors on the editorial board alarmed men like Rusk. He asked Murdock, what would then become of ALG control of the journal?[8] These and other problems fully surfaced when the proposals of Brown and Duke were presented to the ALG representatives at the New York luncheon.

In his memoirs thirty-seven years later, Hubbell tried to reproduce the particulars and dramatic tensions of that occasion. He recalled that Murdock was unable to attend; nor did he mention Quinn. Williams arrived with the presumed intention of supporting Brown, and "this he did but with little enthusiasm after the discussion got well under way," as Hubbell sensed it. From Brown came Damon and a pair of younger colleagues—none of the three with any record in American literature scholarship. As Hubbell remembered it, their plan included at least seven editors, all to be appointed by Brown: three to be professors at Brown, with one representative each from Harvard, Yale, and Columbia. The delegation then withdrew while the committee deliberated, in particular, the apparent lack of any editorial control by the ALG in the Brown proposal. In a session later in the day, or into the night, Brown questioned how Duke, with its presently limited capacity for research, could properly screen scholarly manuscripts. And while Brown deemed a sixteen-page quarterly adequate to publish or review current research, Hubbell was proposing a journal closer to one hundred pages.[9]

Following Spiller's previous advice, Hubbell presented a firm and detailed offer from Duke in a formal communication from Duke treasurer, R. L. Flowers (written in advance of the meeting, with explicit prompting from Hubbell) to Chairman Spiller. Duke guaranteed two thousand dollars annually for five years to establish a journal of American Literature that would be the property of Duke. That university would appoint one of its own as editor-in-chief and further agreed that the journal would be the official organ of the ALG. Other details could be left to the committee. Brown was then allowed necessary time to return home and revise the original plans in the light of Duke's offer and the committee's misgivings. Spiller so advised Flowers of Duke. But this delay and concession to Brown, Hubbell wrote Spiller, was irritating and unfair to Duke. And he continued in a fuller vein to Rusk that allowing Brown to modify Duke's offer was inviting it, in effect, to equal or outbid Duke. He repeated to Rusk a warning he had given to Spiller: Unless Brown were prodded along, Duke might withdraw its offer, and he doubted that Brown could match the longevity and editorial expertise Duke could bring to such a journal. Three days later, Spiller sent a telegram and Rusk a letter to Hubbell, both reporting the climactic news: Damon of Brown had asked Murdock's advice about Brown's continuing in the competition with Duke, and Murdock had suggested that Duke's resources as publishers were superior. He had advised Damon that Brown might best withdraw, and Damon apparently had assented.[10]

Slightly more than a week later, Spiller's Committee on Publications met to complete its assignment on the *Studies in American Literature* (its preferred title for the journal) and then to disband. In his final report to the ALG, Spiller described and then recommended Duke's plan, which allowed the ALG to control the election and geographical distribution of an editorial board. Spiller also underscored the state of scholarly publishing in American literature that the new journal would markedly improve: "Scholarly manuscripts in this subject are now scattered and often appear in obscure journals, lie in manuscript or type for two years or more after acceptance, or fail of publication entirely."[11] Finally, seven weeks later, on 23 May 1928, Hubbell sent to Spiller Duke's formal approval of the ALG negotiations but with two reservations: (1) Duke preferred that the annual issues begin in November and January, not October and December and

(2) Duke would bear the expenses of editorial board meetings only if business could not be fully conducted at the annual MLA convention. Spiller forwarded these emendations to Chairman Murdock for approval by the Executive Committee of the ALG.[12]

With the new journal in Duke's lap, Hubbell wasted no time putting the wheels in motion to turn out the first issue. Indeed, he had anticipated Duke's successful bid. Well before the end of 1928—in retrospect, a truly momentous year for American literary scholarship—he had already advanced beyond the initial stages of creating a journal. In March 1929, Hubbell's efficient labors of many months culminated in the first number of *American Literature*. An editoral board had been selected, a title agreed on, and the editors had established—through the initial articles and reviews—a standard that would characterize the journal in the decades to follow. A close look at the making of this first issue illustrates how the ALG had attained, by the late 1920s, a scholarly identity and professional organization that made possible this rapid shaping of its own house organ.

Of first importance in launching the journal was naming a board of editors to determine the contents of the first issues. Hubbell had earlier wanted Foerster, from nearby North Carolina, as coeditor. But as already mentioned, Hubbell soon realized that some members of the ALG were opposed to Foerster. In February 1928, Hubbell wrote to Spiller before his ad hoc Committee on Publications had been dissolved and suggested that Spiller or Rusk serve on the editorial board. Spiller declined because he felt that Swarthmore, which carried only an undergraduate survey course in American literature (Spiller's), did not own the prestige to justify a representative on the editorial board. Hubbell also corresponded with Murdock, who suggested several names: Percy Boynton, Louise Pound, T. O. Mabbott, Arthur Quinn, and Ralph Rusk. But Murdock thought it desirable also to consider people from the Southwest or Southern Midwest. The next month, Rusk (a member of the ALG Advisory Council) informed Hubbell that ALG members themselves expected to determine the membership of the editorial board.[13]

To form the initial editorial board, however, it was necessary for the ad hoc Committee on Publications to improvise a procedure. They nominated Murdock for five years and Cairns for two. With editor-in-chief Hubbell, these three nominated Rusk to four years. Then at the ALG meeting in Toronto in 1928, the group named Pattee (retired from Penn State and presently at Rollins College), the final member, to a three-year term. As advised by the Committee on Publications, the chief editors then selected an advisory board "to be chosen for their accomplishment and for their special qualifications in the field of American literature and related subjects." The chief editors chose fifteen members—seven for one year and eight for two years. The names gave the journal both regional balance and national distinction: Percy Boynton (Chicago), Killis Campbell (Texas), Norman Foerster (North Carolina), George Krapp (Columbia), Ernest Leisy (Southern Methodist), Thomas Mabbott (Brown), John Moore (Michigan), Vernon Parrington (Washington), Bliss Perry (Harvard), Louise Pound (Nebraska), Arthur Quinn (Pennsylvania), Robert Spiller (Swarthmore), Frederick J. Turner (Huntington Library), Stanley Williams (Yale), and Lawrence Wroth (John Carter Brown Library).[14]

Earlier in 1928, Hubbell had been soliciting various titles for the journal. In June, he sent a list of seven to ALG Chairman Murdock:

1. The American Literature Journal
2. The Journal of American Literature
3. The American Literature Quarterly
4. American Literature
5. The American Literature Review
6. Studies in American Literature: A Quarterly Journal of American Literary History, Criticism, and Bibliography
7. Journal of Studies in American Literature

Murdock listed his preferences, in order, as 4, 2, and 3. Among other correspondents, Cairns replied with a preference for 2. Tremaine McDowell (Minnesota) wrote, "May we not be conservative and have a *Journal,* a *Review,* or the like?" Hubbell and Pattee favored 4, with a near duplicate of 6 as subtitle, and the rest of the board later concurred to this official title, *American Literature: A Journal of Literary History, Criticism, and Bibliography.*[15]

Although a glance at the initial issue of March 1929 leads us easily to assume that the contents had been arbitrarily solicited by Hubbell—Spiller, McDowell, Gohdes, Leisy, and Murdock wrote five of the articles and notes—it happened that by December 1928, Hubbell had been screening, with his editors, more than twenty articles. Six were accepted, five rejected, and another dozen were circulating. McDowell's "Bryant and *The North American Review*" was returned with editorial suggestions for revision that seemed to him admirable for their concern with quality, though he ultimately did not agree to most of them. McDowell also suggested that *American Literature* should encourage graduate students to submit articles, and Leisy added that thesis directors might be asked to send a brilliant chapter by their students. He also wondered if Hubbell should not try to have an article from a major scholar in every issue. Policy formulated at the 1928 ALG meeting in Toronto ruled out articles on pedagogy or living authors; required an American literature emphasis in all essays on folklore, linguistics, and comparative literature; and welcomed bibliographical essays carrying fresh discoveries. Hubbell expressed a concern to the assembled group (perhaps recalling Leisy's suggestion to include a major scholar in every issue) that the established members in the field were, as yet, failing to send him their work for the initial numbers.[16]

Together with their demand for scholarly articles of high quality, the editors intended the journal to be the most authoritative review of recent publications. Today, some will even argue that, in the long run, the reviews have been the more valuable feature of *American Literature*. As early as January 1928, Leisy wrote to Hubbell that Rusk considered a quarterly review of books to be of the first importance, with authors easing the labor somewhat by supplying an outline with their book. Leisy added that the journal might also want to give a similar review of dissertations. To shoulder the burden for all this work, Spiller, who had modestly declined to serve on the editorial board, volunteered to be the book review editor. Pattee, however, suggested a regular book review staff of editors.[17] It turns out that Hubbell was left with the brunt of such chores, selecting and corresponding with reviewers, writing the bulk of the "Brief Mention" reviews himself, but receiving aid in selecting books suitable for reviewing. In the first issue, we have already seen, he elected Canby to review *The Reinterpretation of American Literature* and gave it first place among the reviews.

The "Research in Progress" conducted by Ernest Leisy—in the first issue it was titled, "A List of Research in Progress Supplementary to that Given in *The Reinterpretation of American Literature*"—was a section that met a need that Leisy had previously expressed to Hubbell in a long letter of late 1927. At Southern Methodist, as elsewhere in the country, doctoral candidates were pursuing research on a dissertation while having no inkling if the same subject were a thesis topic elsewhere. Pattee also advised Hubbell of the obvious value of dissertation lists.[18] Leisy sent out a call to various universities and reported the current research in the first issue: Five dissertations were under way on individual authors and four on topics of a general nature, as well as postdoctoral work in progress by Harry Clark, Hubbell, Howard M. Jones, McDowell, Rusk, and some few others.

Finally came the listings of recent articles on American literature. Earlier, Pattee had written to Hubbell that the journal should have frequent bibliographies and these might later be bound for the convenience of scholars. Murdock later questioned the usefulness of such a printing, however, since *PMLA*'s bibliography should be adequate. A third suggestion came forth at the December 1928 meeting in Toronto when ALG members recommended that the annual bibliography Leisy previously circulated among the group might well become the model for a "yearly appendix to 'American Literature.'"[19] The current bibliography of articles on American literature, designed to appear in each issue, was inaugurated in the third number (November 1929). Over the summer of 1929, Hubbell worked with the editors to determine a list of appropriate journals (and to include relevant articles on European literature and American history), to arrange the magazine assignments for various professors, and to establish deadlines. The November 1929 issue comprehended 145 journals, the listings prepared by a work force of eighteen professors. The periodicals cited would become increasingly specialized and native, though Hubbell asked Cairns, in London early in 1930, to try to find an Englishman who might provide a bibliography on British articles in American literature.[20] The initial bibliography appeared essentially in the style and organization of the *PMLA* listings, with similarly random annotations, a format that would continue relatively unchanged through the next half-century.

And so *American Literature* sprang rapidly into existence with a character almost fully formed. Members of the ALG awaited the inaugural issue with faithful support—at the Toronto meeting of 1928, Hubbell reported that 250 readers had already subscribed. Something of the professional excitement that surrounded the imminent first issue could be detected in Pattee's letter to Hubbell: "It is a tremendous moment in the history of literature on this planet," he exclaimed. "Think of a magazine devoted to *American* Literature!" Hardened by his many years devoted to the struggle, and aware that academic custom and form still hindered the study of our home-grown literature, Pattee slightly tempered his optimism. "We have a great inertia to overcome," he realized, and he recounted the embarrassment visited on a recent youth who was laughed at when he presented himself as a serious student of American literature. "They said American literature is a very minor subject taught only incidentally in the schools. No one specializes in it, etc." Pattee then sent up his battle cry: "It is up to us to change all that." Much the same spirit could be heard in Rusk's letter to the new editor: "I think if we continue as we have begun we shall succeed in giving the field of American literature a place in the sun and help put an end to the snobbish disdain that some narrow-minded scholars . . . still exhibit when the subject is mentioned."[21]

As the histories of maiden issues of scholarly journals go, that of *American Literature,* then, was a remarkable instance of efficient planning by a corps of intelligent scholars and experienced editors. In his "Foreword," Hubbell may have exaggerated slightly the historical neglect of our literary history in his excitement over the recent activity within the ALG that now peaked with this inaugural number. "Until recent years our scholars were slow to study the national letters or their relation to European literatures and to American life and thought," he observed, but now the academy was finally alive to this rich vein of new learning. "Within the last few years American scholars have awakened to the fact that our literary history supplies a rich and comparatively unworked field." Journals were at hand to publish criticism of living authors, "but *American Literature* is the only scholarly journal devoted solely to research in the field as a whole" (1, 2). Farther along, the editors printed a "Note to Contributors," in which the purpose of the journal—not pedagogical, not contemporary, not popular, but *scholarly*—was clarified:

> Articles of particular value, we think, are those that bring to light new materials or new facts which might assist in the critical interpretation of an author or in a fuller understanding of some aspect of our cultural history. Only less important are articles which, though based on old facts, present a new interpretation of some work or movement, made convincing by sound reasoning and the citations of adequate evidence. (1, 75)

The articles in the first issue fulfilled this stated intention of the journal. The first was an inspired choice, Robert Spiller's "The Verdict of Sydney Smith." The English critic who belittled the enterprise of American bookmaking in 1818 was not relegated to eating crow a century later, however, for Spiller assembled old facts with new to create a balanced portrait of our early "often-misguided but frequently penetrating critic and friend" (1, 73). Not least, Spiller was a bona fide student of American literature, with a dissertation from Pennsylvania in 1924 in the area of his article. The next two essays were also on the early years,

Tremaine McDowell on Bryant and Clarence Gohdes on Emerson, and were similarly derived from doctoral dissertations. Then came three varieties of contribution: unpublished correspondence of Lanier to Hayne by Aubrey H. Starke (Northwestern); a study of the influence of Arbuthnot's *The History of John Bull* in America, by George E. Hastings (Arkansas, his Harvard dissertation on Francis Hopkinson coming in 1918); and a bibliographical inquiry by J. R. Bowman (Cambridge, Mass.). Two notes called attention to scholarly errors: Kenneth Murdock corrected an unwarranted inference in Higginson's American Men of Letters volume on Longfellow, and George R. Stewart, Jr. (California) cited Thomas Pemberton's inaccurate date of Bret Harte's birth (Stewart's own biography of Harte was under way).

Just as authoritative were the scholarly reviewers in this first issue. Besides Canby's on the recent *The Reinterpretation of American Literature*, others were written by the luminaries of the profession on subjects they were eminently fit to address: Cairns on the historic first volume of the *Dictionary of American Biography*, Quinn on George Odell's *Annals of the New York Stage*, Murdock on the Boases' *Cotton Mather*, Parrington on Albert Beveridge's *Lincoln*, Killis Campbell on Mabbott's selections from Poe, Mabbott on William M. Forrest's *Biblical Allusions in Poe* (Mabbott had explored this particular territory), Howard M. Jones on a selected volume of Thomas Paine, and John H. Cox (West Virginia, with a Harvard dissertation in 1924 on "Folk-Songs on the South") on *American Negro Folk-Songs* by Newman I. White. Finally, under "Brief Mention," largely by Hubbell, a variety of current works—on balladry, linguistics, theory of the novel, and so forth—were called to scholars' attention.

The book reviews, expectably, became a sensitive area of academic politics from the initial issue and on. At the outset, Hubbell asked Foerster to suggest a reviewer of Foerster's own *American Criticism*, an instance of the old-boy network that Hubbell, perhaps unavoidably, worked in one guise or another throughout his twenty-five-year editorial tenure. Foerster's choice was Harry Clark, who then wrote an appropriately critical review but ended with a paragraph rather excessive in admiration and flattery. Cairns and Hubbell asked Clark to remove the final paragraph, since it might raise some eyebrows among the ALG members. Foerster, for example, had helped Clark, at Middlebury from 1925 to 1928, to receive a summer job and subsequent appointment at Wisconsin. Also, Hubbell informed Clark that "the Group objected to my original proposal that Foerster and I should edit *American Literature*."

Foerster, to whom Clark had sent a draft of the review, soon knew, probably from Clark, about the requested deletion and wrote to Hubbell, citing the matter of editorial ethics when a signed review is censored by an editor. As an afterthought and clarification four days later, Foerster wrote again to say that he was not personally impressed with the paragraph in question or strongly concerned with its deletion, except that the issue of censorship remained important to him. The next week, Murdock wrote Hubbell, with regard to the matter of editorial ethics, that editors have their own rights and obligations where questions of content are at issue. He also advised Hubbell that it was unwise for an editor to ask an author to suggest his own reviewer. Pattee submitted a literary rather than editorial criticism of the review: Clark had erred in his judgment that Foerster's anthology was the best of its kind. Pattee claimed that his own *Century Readings* had given Foerster his model and Foerster had admitted as much. "I have never seen much in Foerster's work," Pattee added tartly, "that deserves superlatives." Because of the suggested excision, Foerster's objection to it, and the protracted editorial debate that had followed, Clark's review never made it into the opening issue of *American Literature*. It appeared in the second issue, May 1929, pages 206–12. No mention was made of Foerster's *American Poetry and Prose* anthology but otherwise any rewriting was impossible to detect. The final paragraph, in fact, included over-weening praise of this "gifted spokesman of the soundest, sanest, and most purposeful tradition in modern American scholarship" (p. 212). (*American Criticism* and Foerster's other work in the company of the resurgent New Humanists are discussed in Chapter 19.)[22]

Perhaps because of the Foerster–Clark incident, Cairns raised to Hubbell a further question of selecting appropriate reviewers: "In general, I think the reviewing should be done largely by people off the board, except where there is special fitness." (Clark, however, was neither on the board nor among the advisory editors.) Hubbell could, of course, have responded that his editors, above all, represented the scholarly authority and "special fitness" to judge the profession's scholarship. But Cairns rightly sensed that the dangers of editorial favoritism were inevitably there. And they continued to taint the journal in succeeding volumes. Professional careers and reputations were accordingly influenced. When Oscar Cargill (NYU), in 1937, wrote to Hubbell that the established senior people in the academy received kinder reviews in *American Literature* than the nonestablished, Cargill's view of the matter was not only on the mark but also amply verified in the editorial correspondence of the journal in previous years, wherein rank and seniority assuredly enjoyed their privileges.[23]

The insiders, first of all, were assured that their own work would be selected for review. Inevitably (and for the most part justifiably), they were also asked to review the works of others, including their fellow seniors. Many a time, insiders merely had to request a certain book to review and Hubbell obliged them. In the process, the sensibilities of a colleague under review were thoughtfully protected. When Gregory Paine had bad moments trying to review Ernest Leisy's survey history, *American Literature*, which Paine unhappily discovered to be "very superficial," he wrote to Hubbell that, even so, "I do not wish to say so in a review." So he managed, after a polite critique, to praise Leisy as a "wise, well-informed critic" and a good bibliographer, though Paine closed by subtly recommending the book for "college students who are beginning their studies."[24] Though Cairns privately was "not much in sympathy with Foerster's ideas" or convinced that they were receiving eloquent expression in a current pair of books, he, too, treated his established colleague politely; and his comments on Foerster's *Toward Standards* and *American Critical Essays, XIXth and XXth Centuries* became the lead review.[25]

When Pattee, however, was given an unexpectedly severe review from Assistant Professor Fred B. Millett (Chicago), Pattee was accorded at once Hubbell's commiseration and the expressed hope that the commentary "doesn't irritate you unduly." (But it did.)[26] Usually, such irritation was averted for scholars of favored status, especially when they reviewed each other's work. In 1934, Henry Pochmann (Mississippi State College) wrote to Hubbell that Stanley Williams wanted to review Pochmann's new book (*Washington Irving: Representative Selections*) when it appeared. For whatever reason, the book was never reviewed in *American Literature*. The next year, however, Pochmann reviewed, with due respect, Williams's *Washington Irving: Journal, 1803*, and the year after, his *The Life of Washington Irving*.[27] In 1937, Howard M. Jones apologized for his blandly uncritical review of Percy Boynton's *Literature and American Life*. Boynton was, after all, Jones's one-time teacher (at Chicago); and this might well be Boynton's final book.[28]

Prominent and hyperactive in the early annals of *American Literature* reviewing was the figure of Harry Clark. He suggested to Hubbell the reviewers for the first four volumes of his American Writers Series (American Book Co.). (Pochmann's *Irving* may have been pointedly ignored by Hubbell out of pique over Clark's—and Pochmann's—behavior.) Later, Clark hoped that Hubbell would see that Clark's anthology of *Major American Poets* went to a friendly reviewer, because Clark, after all, had worked on the book during the past four years. The book, instead, was not reviewed at all. Undaunted, Clark petitioned over the years, also, to review one book or another. On one occasion at midcentury, Clarence Gohdes had to remind him that he was tardy in delivering on *four* books he had asked to review.[29]

This risk of academic climbing and politicking through manipulation of the ALG's own journal was not lost on the original board of editors, including, as we have just inferred, the editor-in-chief. Firmly established in the field, they were inescapably open to the charge of privileged seniority and an establishment mentality in a profession that viewed itself as youthful, embattled, and vigorous. To his credit, Cairns posed the problem early on. The editorial board, he felt, should be members of Hubbell's generation (b. 1885) and younger. Cairns noted that Pattee (b. 1862) and himself (b. 1867) were at least one oldster too many. The issue of representative democracy also extended to geographical distribution of board members. As Pattee's three-year term was ending, Hubbell wrote to Cairns, asking for suggestions for a successor. Hubbell did not feel that the journal, editorially, was bound to be specifically represented by the profession across the land. In fact, the Pacific Coast men, he added, "are pretty far away to attend meetings or to return MSS promptly." Realistic as this observation may have been, it smacked of an Eastern proprietary view of the profession that, on occasion, rankled even an elderly insider like Cairns. He was especially irritated that Eastern members were apparently planning to skip the MLA meeting in 1931 on Cairns's campus because Madison was too far away to the west. But Midwesterners, naturally, were expected to attend the meetings in the East. Hubbell did appear to act on Cairns's suggestion to try to go with a younger board of editors, and Pattee assured Hubbell that he, too, sympathized with the suggestion that his own place be filled by a younger man. Robert Spiller replaced him in 1932. Yet when Cairns died in that same year, he was replaced on the board by the sixty-year-old Killis Campbell.[30]

One additional problem of editorial democracy was the role of the twenty advisory editors. No doubt this generous representation gave at least an illusion that many universities were making their influence felt in the profession's journal. In practice, this was not the case. Many editors, apparently, were not consulted at all. Murdock advised Hubbell in 1933 that the advisory group might as well be reduced to five or six members.

Even by 1939, when the advisory editors did number only six, Howard M. Jones, recently one of them, wrote Hubbell that he had been miffed for some time because he was not being consulted. Had he been, he would never have approved the articles that were then appearing in the recent (January 1939) issue.[31]

Chapter 17

Parrington's *Main Currents in American Thought* (1927–1930)

One of the Pacific Coast men whom editor Jay B. Hubbell deemed pretty far away to attend meetings or to return manuscripts promptly in the service of *American Literature* was, no doubt, Vernon Louis Parrington from the University of Washington. Like his admired Whitman, Parrington was both in and out of the game. As a cooperating participant in the profession, he contributed the chapter on realism to the ALG's *The Reinterpretation of American Literature* and agreed to serve as an advisory editor of *American Literature*. But over the years, he was also an individualistic loner. He felt little interest in the goings-on of the ALG or in the annual conventions of the MLA; and he died in England while engaged in his solitary research shortly after *American Literature* was born.

The strategic maneuvering and infighting that accompanied a fair part of the professional scene in the 1920s were activities from which Parrington, in faraway Seattle, was blessedly removed as he completed, near the close of the decade, a monumental, one-man American literary and intellectual history, the product of virtually his entire career in American literature scholarship. His initial volume of *Main Currents in American Thought* had first been sketched for a publisher in 1914, when the *CHAL* itself was little more than a sketchy proposal. When Parrington's study of American literature to the Civil War appeared in 1927, the event was hailed as a climax of American literature scholarship since the *CHAL*. (Ernest Leisy stated, in 1929, that his own *American Literature: An Interpretative Survey* was "perhaps the first connected account of our literature to be written since the newer stock-taking" [p. vi], a surprising claim for a small, undistinguished history that was lost somewhere in the immense shadow of Parrington's volumes.) As it turned out, Parrington's career and life closed shortly after volumes I and II of *Main Currents* dazzled a grateful, admiring profession. But he lived long enough to enjoy the reception of the old and new community of scholars, from Pattee, Foerster, and Van Doren to Hubbell, Spiller, and many others. Lionel Trilling, writing as late as 1940, assessed *Main Currents* to have had "an influence on our conception of American culture which is not equaled by that of any other writer of the last two decades."[1]

Before he became a historian of American literature, Parrington was a Midwestern professor of (what else?) English literature, in a career that began in 1893 at Emporia College in Kansas after his final two student years at Harvard. He departed from the Ivy League with strongly mixed feelings, so that the trip westward was, for the most part, a welcome return to his home turf.[2] The family had migrated from Aurora, Illinois, to farm land near Americus, Kansas, in 1877, when Parrington was six. He attended country school in winters until 1885, when his father was elected probate judge in Emporia. There Parrington went to prep school and, from 1888 to 1891, attended the College of Emporia. The college had no English department, but the town library offered him ample fare in his favorite reading, the Victorian (not American) novel. During summers, he worked on the farm. In 1891, with the help of a tuition scholarship ($150), the family was able to send him to Harvard for two years.[3]

At Harvard, Parrington received a *B* in composition from Barrett Wendell. He studied modern languages but no American literature or history. (Wendell did not present English 20, "Research in the Literary History of America," until 1897). Parrington took eighteenth-century English literature from Lewis Gates, earning the grade of *A*−. He remembered Wendell and Gates as "fair second rate teachers," although he added that they passed on to him an indispensable "method of teaching English composition and literature." Parrington's study of American literature while at Harvard was informal and desultory. He recorded in an 1892 diary that he had read some Howells and did not like his "bald, crude realism"; after *The House of Seven Gables,* "I fairly love Hawthorne"; and he read for the first time, and liked, "Hiawatha." At year's end, Parrington wrote: "From a literary standpoint the year has brought noticeable development. I am beginning to get an idea of the spirit and meaning of our literature."[4]

After graduating in the Harvard class of 1893, then, Parrington began his teaching career at his other alma mater, Emporia College (they awarded him a B.A. in absentia in 1892). For a salary of five hundred dollars, he was hired to teach English and French and recalled that he merely drifted into teaching for lack of opportunity in some other field. But he remembered, too, that the four years at Emporia were vital and decisive. He created an English department and organized its curriculum (apparently with no American literature), read further in English literature as he wrote out complete lectures, composed some poetry, received the master's degree (in 1895), and even coached football.

Parrington's now-famous tenure at Oklahoma, ending when he was abruptly fired in 1908, began in 1897 when Emporia could not afford to raise his salary. Beset with personal expenses, as well as family debts on the farm for which he felt responsible, Parrington accepted the offer of one thousand dollars at Oklahoma to teach English and modern languages and organize an English department. He was chairman of a department of one until 1903, when Wilbur Humphreys, a recent Harvard M.A., was brought in to handle composition and Old English. Parrington taught the gamut of English literature courses from Chaucer to Tennyson, and in his last two years, a special course in Morris and Ruskin. Apparently he never gave a class in American literature at Oklahoma, although the university bulletin announced that Humphreys would offer, in the year 1905–6, English XVIII, a survey from the colonial times to the present, with special emphasis on Irving and Cooper, the New England and Southern writers, and recent authors.[5]

Parrington never developed an American literature curriculum at Oklahoma before he was dismissed, with others, in the notorious political and pietistic house cleaning of 1908. He was viewed as a morally permissive instructor who smoked, condoned dancing, and had been educated in the East (fellow Harvard man Humphreys was likewise tainted, and so terminated). Parrington moved to the University of Washington in 1908, where it has been usually assumed that he first caught fire in the field of American literature. Unpublished materials, however, reveal that he was already immersing himself in this study while at Oklahoma. Found among his papers are an uncompleted syllabus for the English XVIII survey course already mentioned, including assigned readings in literary history from the colonial sections of Wendell (pp. 1–55) and Trent (pp. 1–78) plus reading notes on authors he had been studying, from Cotton Mather to Whitman. Most important is the evidence that an early version of *Main Currents* was forming in his mind during the Oklahoma years. The subtle shifts within his new leanings toward American literary and intellectual history, possibly influenced by a fourteen-month trip to England and France, from which he returned to Oklahoma in 1904 with a new awareness of our native traits, strengths, and weaknesses—these await an accounting from Parrington's intellectual biographer steeped in the as-yet-unpublished papers.[6]

After 1908, Parrington lived his final two decades at the University of Washington. This climactic period constitutes, at least for his admirers, a saga with mythic overtones in which the indomitable scholar, routed from a distinguished position at Oklahoma, came to his rather solitary flowering in the Northwest, where he won the Pulitzer Prize for history by writing a work that Easterners could have achieved only through a team effort. Surely he arrived in Seattle inauspiciously, as he noted in his autobiographical sketch of 1918. He suffered a reduction in rank from full to assistant professor, and in salary from eighteen hundred to fifteen hundred dollars. His assignment the first year was in the Rhetoric and Oratory rather than the English department. In 1909, he entered the English Language and Literature department, an exclusively British literature group of four members, including Frederick Morgan Padelford, Yale man and Elizabethan specialist. Though assigned to teach English literature, Parrington also offered Washington's first course on American authors, a two-semester survey. With this course in 1909–10, the Parrington era at Washington officially began. Moreover, he was prepared to work in earnest on the literary history that, after various titles, was to become, in 1927, his *Main Currents*.

His classroom and scholarly work now happily converging, Parrington proceeded to create at Washington one of the country's most flourishing curricula in American literature. In 1911–12, the American course was described as "a study of literary production of America before the year 1820, with special attention to social forces and ideals. The greater part of the time will be given to the investigation of puritanism and the beginnings of democracy."[7] The department was thriving, its faculty having more than doubled in the three years since Parrington's arrival.

Joined by Loren Milliman, who offered a two-semester course in selected American figures, Parrington in the next year (1912–13) enlarged the American curriculum with the first graduate seminar, surprisingly beginning with works published since 1890, a focus that continued over the next dozen years. In this same year, now owning the rank of full professor, he also offered for the first time a full-year sequence in "American Literature Since 1870." (Pattee's literary history bearing this title did not appear until 1915.) The catalog described the emphasis in both this sequence and its earlier companion course to be on ideals, with the earlier writers representing national ideals reflected by "theological, political, and social movements in literature," while the later figures were to be studied in the light of "current *literary* movements and ideals in America" (my italics). Apparently for the later survey Parrington adopted more the belles lettres approach.

The 1916–17 catalog announcements (for the year following) showed Parrington's heavy teaching duties for the year to include English 135 and 136, "Main Tendencies in English Literature from 1590 to 1900" (three credits each); English 161, "Early 19th Century Literature in America" (three credits, first semester); English 162, "Middle 19th Century Literature in America" (three credits, second semester); English 163, "American Literature from 1870 to 1890" (two credits, first semester); English 164, "American Literature from 1890 to 1917" (two credits, second semester); and a graduate seminar in American authors, English 211–212, carrying the annotation: "The field of this work is determined by the wishes of the class. During the past two years the period from 1890–1914 has been studied." For the same year, Milliman was slated to teach English 163 and 164, as well as his "Great American Writers" courses 165 (Emerson, Whitman, Hawthorne, and Poe) and 166 (Longfellow and Lowell). Almost one-fourth of the undergraduate offerings in English, then, were American literature classes taught by Parrington and Milliman, a notable percentage when the nationwide average, as we noted in an earlier chapter, was closer to 15 percent. In graduate study, however, Parrington's single course was outnumbered, seven or eight to one, by British literature and British-related European literature courses.

In the 1920 catalog, the same American literature courses were listed but now divided and renumbered to accommodate the new quarter system (since 1918). Some minor changes show that the scope of early nineteenth-century courses had been expanded to cover in three quarters "American Literature from the Beginnings to the Year 1870," and the "Great American Writers" courses had been renumbered and appear to have been strictly lower-division offerings. A new course, added the previous year by Parrington, though not offered in 1921–22, was "Present Day Tendencies in American Literature," a continuation of the year-long sequence from 1870 to 1914. For 1921–22, Parrington was listed to teach a graduate course, "Modern English Literature," beginning at the midnineteenth century and including American authors, but his American literature seminar was not offered. Possibly the new course resulted from a petition by graduate students, since the content of Parrington's seminars, we have seen, was characteristically "determined by the wishes of the class." Of interest in the undergraduate status of American literature was the requirement that English majors were now to take "a course of individual reading in English and American literature under departmental tutors, extending throughout the senior year." But the senior examination covered only "the history of English literature."

Sampling the Washington catalogs through the twenties, we find an occasional new note in Parrington's teaching. In 1923, his survey to 1870 was retitled "American Culture" and in 1925, "The History of American Culture," symptoms of his concentration now on the broader substance of the soon-to-be-consummated *Main Currents*. Likewise, the graduate seminar had shifted to "intensive studies in early American literature," no doubt to center his teaching, as in the early survey course, on the larger questions of American culture. While the American literature program in the department, compared to English literature classes, remained proportionally what it had been over the previous eight or ten years, the senior examination, by the midtwenties, now required majors to answer questions in American, as well as British, literature.

Beyond these clues and inferences regarding his teaching, culled from the university catalogs, we have the written evidence of Parrington's syllabi and lecture notes, edited by Harold Eby in the posthumous volume III of *Main Currents* (1930). (More material is deposited among the Parrington family papers and in the Eby Papers in the archives of the University of Washington libraries.) The syllabi reveal what we expect from their author— a remarkably well-ordered, topical approach to the period and authors, with emphasis on humane elements in the literature. But Parrington can surprise the later reader with various judgments of this literature as art. (Presumably, this aesthetic side of Parrington was no surprise, however, to his students, one of them being Eby himself, and we shall presently consider the aesthetic aspect in Parrington more closely.)

The lecture notes Eby printed posthumously open vistas also onto the intellectual Parrington. They should not, however, deceive us into imagining Parrington a classroom spellbinder, the elderly version of his youthful self when he was an aspiring debater with a pulpitlike demeanor. Eby clearly warned against this false impression of an oratorical pedagogue. Parrington's classes in the 1920s were filled instead, Eby remembered, with the atmosphere of student debate, heightened by strategic provocations from Parrington. In Eby's prefatory essay to volume III of *Main Currents*, he recalled this technique of Socratic cross-examination that "made the student discover his intellectual deficiencies; while the class, to its astonishment and delight, found the quest for truth both elusive and exciting" (III, vi). Another of these students was Russell Blankenship, whose office in the late 1950s was next to this author's in Parrington Hall (the turn-of-century science building deemed appallingly ugly by Parrington, but renamed for him in 1931). Blankenship remembered, like Eby, the excitement Parrington created in the classroom, where seemingly random and spontaneous group discussions were, in fact, the product of the professor's highly organized mastery of the subject.[8]

No doubt Parrington continued to be this same Socratic instructor when he left his Northwest campus to teach as a guest professor elsewhere—at Berkeley (summer of 1922) and Columbia (summer of 1923). The invitations show Parrington's reputation as an eminence beyond the Washington campus to have been growing at a time when his published work was still meager. When publication of *Main Currents* by Harcourt, Brace was imminent, Wisconsin tried to lure him away from the Northwest in 1926 with an offer of $6,000. Parrington hoped that Washington would respond with a raise, and in a rather parsimonious fashion, his university did so, voting him a salary of $4,650. Meanwhile, he taught at the University of Michigan in the summer of 1927, and that institution then offered the recent author of *Main Currents* a professorship at $7,500. Washington responded with an offer to raise his salary to $5,000. Going 12 percent of the way did not quite illustrate a generous spirit of negotiation and bargaining. But Parrington elected to stay at Washington. He was somewhat flattered, at least, to learn that he was now their highest paid professor.[9] In early 1928, Parrington justified his university's faith and favor, such as they were, by winning the Pulitzer Prize.

Parrington remained at Washington for a variety of reasons, personal and professional. In love with gardening in Seattle and popular with the students despite (or, in those earlier days, perhaps because of) his courtly manners, he had, by the late 1920s, adopted the Northwest as the region where he meant to live out his increasingly celebrated professional life. Perhaps the decision was also inspired by his lingering dislike of the Eastern intelligentsia. He continued to avoid the MLA and was unenthusiastic over its influence on literary scholarship. His famous comment in *Main Currents* on Henry James—"Like modern scholarship, he came to deal more and more with less and less"—can only have been a double-edged gibe directed at his contemporaries in the MLA. But the Northwest was not without its disadvantages for the literary scholar-professor of the 1920s. The library resources at Washington were almost as inadequate as Tyler's earlier had been at Michigan. Still, Parrington found the Northwest's academic and political climate a congenial atmosphere for his American literature studies almost from the moment of his arrival. The earliest version of *Main Currents*, we have seen, was under way in 1910. By 1914, he had brought his work in progress at least to a stage where he could approach Macmillan—and be rejected.[10] He claimed (in the 1918 "Sketch") to have completed the literary history to 1870 sometime in 1916. Houghton Mifflin then rejected it, as did Putnam in 1917 (already committed to the *CHAL*) and Holt in 1918.

To track Parrington's scholarly growth in these years and through his last decade, we are left, at present, with the evidence in his classroom work already discussed, together with the bibliographical references in *Main Currents*, and his modest corpus of essays and reviews published over some dozen years.[11] The *Main Currents* bibliographies for volumes I and II reveal that Parrington was not peddling a dated eight-years-old literary history when, in 1924, he signed the contract with Harcourt, Brace (and he continued to update his sources as late as 1926). The reader for Harcourt, Brace who confirmed Parrington's responsible and current scholarship was Van Wyck Brooks. The year before, Brooks had read and recommended the manuscript for New York University Press. The title was *The Democratic Spirit in Early American Letters, 1620–1800*, which indicated that Parrington had decided to present his total history in more than a single volume. The manuscript was accepted by NYU, but Parrington was asked to contribute five hundred dollars toward publication expenses. He declined, and the manuscript went to B. W. Huebsch, again recommended by Brooks. But after agreeing to publish the work, Huebsch was reeling from the failure of its journal, the *Freeman*. So Brooks, literary adviser to the new house of Harcourt, Brace (founded 1919), steered the volume to its last destination. Parrington now sent his publisher the outline of volume II, titled *Democracy and Individualism, 1800–1870*, which was to be published with volume I. A third volume, presented in outline, was expected to come out somewhat later.[12]

When volumes I and II of *Main Currents* appeared in 1927, Parrington demonstrated in the bibliographies that his scholarship was indeed largely up to date. Though he had written privately in 1924, "Pretty much everything is yet to be done in the field of [the] History of American Literature," he had consulted the biographical and critical studies available in the unsatisfactory holdings at the University of Washington, supplemented by

his own purchases.[13] The milestone literary studies since the
CHAL were listed: Van Doren's *The American Novel* (1921),
Arthur H. Quinn's *A History of the American Theatre* (1923),
Raymond Weaver's (1921) and John Freeman's (1926) pioneering
works on Melville, George Hellman's *Washington Irving* (1925),
and the frontier literature studies by John D. Wade (1924) and
Ralph Rusk (1925). For the posthumous volume III, editor Harold
Eby inferred a bibliography from Parrington's personal books,
plus his recorded borrowings from the University of Washington
library. These included the sources that have appeared in the
present chronicle: standard or memorial editions of the major authors, several literary histories, and critical studies both in and
out of established series.

Beyond the scholarship of *Main Currents,* Parrington's primary contributions to American literature study scarcely exist as
separate entities. But he must have been gratified that his scholarly work had been largely concentrated into the single matrix of
that expansive undertaking. Had he lived into the 1930s, he
would doubtless have multiplied his minor publications many
times over, since the outlets for American literature studies had
steadily increased and he would have been any editor's prized
contributor. As it was, in his lifetime, he published just one article for a journal, "The Incomparable Mr. Cabell" in *Pacific Review* (1921). The Washington Bookstore issued his pamphlet,
Sinclair Lewis: Our Own Diogenes (1927). He edited *The Connecticut Wits,* with an introduction (1926), and introduced an
edition of Rolvaag's *Giants in the Earth* (1929). He contributed
the chapter on Puritanism in *CHAL* and on realism in *Reinterpretation.* And he wrote two entries ("American Literature"
and "Hawthorne") for *The Britannica,* fourteenth edition. Finally, he reviewed some three dozen books, all in his final ten
years, with roughly one-half appearing in the *Nation* and the majority solicited after the publication of *Main Currents* in 1927.
Together with the Pulitzer Prize in 1928, most of the honors for
his life's work multiplied just barely in time for him to savor before his death in 1929.

✷　✷　✷

From the early reviews of *Main Currents* in 1927, through the
succeeding two decades when those two volumes, with posthumous volume III, became for American intellectual (and some
literary) historians one of the formative "books that changed our
minds," and in fact to the present day, the main interest and admiration in Parrington's scholarship have been directed on his

vigorous ideological approach to American literature. Indeed, for many a scholar, Parrington is valuable only as an American historian of ideas. It is now time to consider more fully the literary–historical aspects of *Main Currents* that early reviewers and later critics minimized or misread. Typical is the judgment of Howard Mumford Jones who, in 1948, said of *Main Currents:* "That the book is blind to aesthetic charm and callous toward what I may call the total literary problem . . . all this is true enough." Jones, however, then repeated what so many others before him had marvelled at, Parrington's own "brilliant individual characterizations," his masterly structure, historical drama, and the "driving power" of his style. Jones relived the excitement he felt two decades before: "Who can forget the tingling sense of discovery with which we first read these lucid pages . . . !" But he did not then alter his view that Parrington was scarcely a literary historian and was unmistakably "blind to the aesthetic charm" of American writers.[14]

We can begin by appreciating that there was a strong artistic and literary side of Parrington himself. The Kansas farmboy nursed ambitions to become a painter. At Harvard, he enrolled in a fine arts class, and he was chiefly in love with literature for its own sake. And while his early aesthetic delight in Ruskin and Morris merged, after the 1896 election, with his new interest in their social and political doctrines, Parrington at Emporia College and at Oklahoma was the professor of literature whose first pleasure was his own creating of literature and most of all poetry, though he also ventured into novel writing—the uncompleted "Stuart Forbes: Stoic." Given this background, we should expect a degree of pure literary impulse in the University of Washington professor who turned from his own poetry and fiction and began to write the first version of *Main Currents* in 1910. Not even his later critics could have stated better than Parrington in 1917 the aesthetic value literature held even for the intellectual historian:

> If literature be the product of estheticism and not of protest and propaganda; if it has had its birth out of that persistent love of beauty which is the mainspring of creative art, it is a thing spiritual or esthetic rather than economic.[15]

By applying to *Main Currents* the criteria of literary historiography, we quickly find that Parrington addressed quite fully the central questions of *literary* history in America, despite his writing, as well, an *intellectual* history that required its own methodology. For the literary historian, as we have noted before,

there are three fundamental issues: What are the historical–
evolutionary, the American cultural, and the aesthetically literary aspects of American literary history? While we shall attend
most fully to the third, the neglected aesthetic, consideration of
Main Currents, Parrington's approach to historical and nationalistic questions of American literary evolution must also be more
appreciated, for it helped frame the aesthetic issues. As he stated
at the outset, his organization of the history had "been fixed
by forces that are anterior to literary schools and movements,
creating the body of ideas from which literary culture eventually springs."[16] This comment appeared to confirm Parrington's
greater allegiance to intellectual history. Yet he may have been, in
fact, affirming that our literary culture, with its schools and
movements, was to be viewed as the climactic outcome of previous intellectual backgrounds. And throughout volumes I and II,
the more nearly "pure literary" figures did arrive in his discussion near the climax of the historical phase. They gave final
aesthetic expression to the main tendencies in a period of intellectual history.

Regarding these schools and movements, Parrington made no
effort in volume I (*The Colonial Mind*) to define any evolution of
a literary period in the first two centuries. But in the two volumes
that followed, he is our first literary historian to assign to the
American nineteenth century two dominant periods with their
attendant literary characteristics. He designated these periods in
the titles of the volumes: *The Romantic Revolution in America*
and *The Beginnings of Critical Realism in America.* In tracing
romanticism in America, Parrington ranged outside the common
literary–historical treatment of New England by describing and
documenting the less familiar aspects of the movement in the
Middle and Southern states, pages in *Main Currents* whose
freshness has never been fully appraised.

For his third volume, Parrington charted an emerging realism
in which a lingering native spirit of pre–Civil War optimism continued to be expressed by writers as yet unaffected by the harsh
new winds of scientific speculation from Europe and the impact
of industrialism on American life. The transitional figure in the
later 1880s was W. D. Howells. In his columns for *Harpers,*
Howells was "summing up the achievements of American realism and somewhat overconfidently forecasting its future temper," unaware that "he was in fact writing the history of a past
phase" (III, 216). A new literary mode, naturalism (a "more
adequate realism"; III, 238), held sway through the 1890s, but
presently (1903–17) it became "well-nigh submerged under a

wave of social speculation and inquiry" as the muckraking and problem novel created a "diversion from naturalism" (III, 346). Parrington completed his broad divisions of our literary evolution with a "new literary period" discernible after World War I in "three major movements"—(1) a new naturalism characterized by psychological rather than economic interests, (2) a new romanticism tinged with irony, and (3) a new school of anti-Howellsian satirical realism (III, 360, 373).

Parrington understood historical evolution in nineteenth-century American literature, then, to be primarily a growth, flowering, and decline of the two literary modes that reflected the reigning spirit, respectively, of each period. Just as he tried to define both foreign and native influences in American romanticism, Parrington traced both the foreign sources and the "native growth" in realism's chief architect Howells (III, 247–48). But as Parrington wrote more broadly on this new postwar mode, he emphasized its largely native evolution:

> The new realism was a native growth, sprung from the soil, unconcerned with European technique. In its earlier expression it inclined to a romantic or idyllic coloring, but as it developed it came to rely more and more on the beauty of truth. This primitive realism issued chiefly from the local color school of the short story, but it was supplemented by the sociological school. (III, 238)

Parrington identified naturalism as an offshoot of realism, and he accounted for important European as well as native influences here, as he had in the consideration of the previous literary periods. For one other literary mode in the century, humor, he located no foreign influence, however, nor any historically related mode. He did emphasize, though, that a "pronounced romantic" like Bird "put all his romanticisms aside" when he contributed to the mode of humor in *Nick of the Woods* (II, 192). Parrington defined the humorous *Narrative . . . of David Crockett,* however, as "romantic in spirit" if "realistic in method," a forecast that *Main Currents* would be an excursion, at times, through a rather slippery mixture and overlapping of literary terms. On the origins and evolution of American humor in the 1830s, he considered *Georgia Scenes* the fountainhead and its author Longstreet an original who "set the style that was followed in a long series of frontier sketches, and established the tradition of frontier humor that flowered at last in Mark Twain" (II, 172).

Parrington gave a literary historian's attention, also, to the evolution of literary genres, though his most faithful supporters would have to admit the treatment to be quite cursory. Of foreign influences on poetry and the novel, he was best aware of the English (he had taught English literature for a decade at the University of Oklahoma), though he suggested that, in the main, our fiction, in contrast to the poetry, had flourished as a largely native product. The passages are too scattered to suggest a formulated theory. But he stressed Cooper's aversion rather than extended obligations to Scott. Paulding harbored a strong distaste for the sensationalism of English "blood-pudding" romance (II, 216). The chief influence on Kennedy, early and late, was not the English romancers but the American Irving. Niceties of evolving literary form in the romance and the novel were beyond Parrington, but in his late lecture notes, he sketched the undermining of the turn-of-century romance and the naturalistic novel by the more distinctly American ferment of a progressive spirit that helped shape the new political and economic novels in the twentieth century.

Why Parrington should stress an evolution of mode and genre separable especially from their English sources or counterparts becomes clearer when we recognize the pervasive liberalism of his social and political sympathies. They lead us directly to an anglophobic bias. In the growth of authentic American ideas that he viewed as having gained the most vital currency in our national life and most vigorous expression in our literature, the role of conservative England from the beginning had usually been, at best, a catalytic goad and irritant, incompatible with the colonial American spirit. By 1800, it was the "European liberalisms" that Jefferson knew and breathed, apart from English colonialism and religious dogma, "that provided the mold into which ran the fluid experience of America to assume substantial form," even into backwoods and agrarian America (I, 397). With an eye on literary history, Parrington singled out authors like Freneau and Barlow who gained a salutary initiation into these European liberalisms, especially French democracy. Moving into volume II, Parrington admitted that the English did contribute a liberalizing influence in their romantic individualism, though he pointed out that "the first stage in the romantization of American thought resulted from the naturalization of French revolutionary theory" (II, vi). And running counter to this primary American import from France were the English middle-class, business-oriented laissez faire doctrines of Adam Smith. (In the South, the chief foreign influence appeared in a strained reenactment of anachronistic Greek democracy.)

After recording the familiar European (and English) influences on Emerson, Thoreau, and Longfellow, Parrington in volume III traced Whitman to German sources for the "monistic idealism" that he tried to wed with Spencerian science (III, 74). Whitman thereby played a transitional role for Parrington's final volume, *The Beginnings of Critical Realism in America*. In this postwar climate of evolutionary science, Parrington now regarded as unfortunate the influx of European ideas, though some of the literary offshoots were valuable to the critical realism of Howells and Garland and to the turn-of-the-century naturalism of Norris and London.

While his treatment of European ideas in American literature was neither original nor enthusiastic, Parrington brought genuine commitment to the companion issue of home-grown alterations of imported social and intellectual thought in America's three centuries of post-Renaissance history. In the preface to volume I, he announced his view of the nature and role of ideas in America's past. The "political, economic and social development of the country" comprised that determining milieu in which our most vital ideas had been shaped. In other words, Parrington offered an environmental explanation of the formation of these ideas. And in the preface to the second volume, he summarized the importing and domesticating of American thought as "the incoming into America of certain old-world ideals and institutions, and the subjection of those ideals and institutions to the *pressure of a new environment,* from which resulted the overthrow of the principles of monarchy and aristocracy, and the setting up of the principle of republicanism" (II, iii, italics added). But he was not consistent in the way he described the conditioning of ideas. Occasionally, Parrington characterized them as developing independently of any American social and economic environment. His reformist sympathies appear to have determined whether or not he placed emphasis on environmental forces. The liberal–Jeffersonian ideas for which Parrington had sympathy (in Roger Williams, Franklin, Paine, Bryant, Emerson, Channing, and above all, Whitman) he usually depicted with no reference to environment. But the conservative–Hamiltonian aspects of a Samuel Sewall and Increase Mather, or Webster and Clay, Parrington related to, or explained by, the unfortunate environment from which they were presumably shaped. Despite this philosophical inconsistency, Parrington was able to distinguish some salient contrasts and similarities among the emerging American mind in New England, New York, the middle Atlantic states, and the South.

But it was in the socially uncomplicated West that Parrington drew strongest support for his liberal theory of American mind and character. From the early nineteenth-century pioneer ambitions in the unsettled Mississippi Valley issued "the most romantic dream that ever visited the native mind of America" (II, vi). The passage reminds us that for Parrington, environmental pressures were inimical to the expansive idea of individual fulfillment, the American dream. In volume III, it followed that the Mississippi Valley's own Mark Twain, for all the inhibitions to his native frontier genius (Parrington obviously agreed with Van Wyck Brooks's explanation of Twain's career), became the quintessential American:

> Here at last was an authentic American—a native writer thinking his own thoughts, using his own eyes, speaking his own dialect— everything European fallen away, the last shred of feudal culture gone, local and western yet continental . . . indubitably an embodiment of three centuries of American experience—frontier centuries, decentralized, leveling, individualistic. (III, 86–87)

Unhappily, into this fulfilled embodiment of the complete American came also the new spirit of naturalism, an unfortunate intrusion of European thought that Twain and other Americans should have resisted. It quickened a dormant Calvinistic pessimism, which Parrington viewed as a sadly enduring characteristic of "the traditional American temper," though essentially an alien and old-world dogma that Emersonian liberalism was not quite able to rout from our being. Parrington gloomily continued: "Since Emerson's time a new world has been emerging. The old shadow is falling across the American mind. Determinism is in the air" (III, 326–27). And like Sinclair Lewis, Parrington detected a second blight after the Great War—a pervasive philistinism that was reaching into the American character at every social stratum, from the common "herd" to the banker, merchant, and realtor. In Lewis's George Babbitt, Parrington read the "symbol of our common emptiness. Historically he marks the final passing in America of the civilization that came from the fruitful loins of the eighteenth century" (III, 362, 369). Out of his late disillusion and despair, which was not unmixed with residual liberal hopes, Parrington then wrote a beautifully elegiac finale to *Main Currents*.[17]

✱ ✱ ✱

After these excursions into Parrington's sense of national character and thought in American literature, we can enter our third main question of literary historiography: Did Parrington, in fact, almost totally ignore the *artistic* expression of ideas in our literature, including the way American and historical content relates to literary form? To what degree did he deliver aesthetically on the promise of his subtitle, *An Interpretation of American Literature from the Beginnings to 1920*? Literary historiographers look to aesthetic definitions of literature in general, as well as of literary periods, modes, and genres. They also inquire into the literary–critical demonstration of organic excellence in the literary form—the functional relation of art and substance. And they notice the larger aesthetic judgments with which the critic establishes, or reaffirms, a canon of the major works in our literature.

Making a new case for Parrington as a literary historian and critic who appreciated the aesthetic criteria essential to the questions just posed, we must be initially frustrated by Parrington's well-known and rather self-defeating attacks on belles-lettres criticism in the preface of volume I. And it is true that in his vigorous treatment of colonial literature, he did rivet his interest on the nonaesthetic side of his liberal-versus-conservative debate. The final paragraph of the volume sounded not a literary, but a political, note—Jefferson's election in 1800 and the uncertain future of democratic liberalism. Moreover, Parrington had observed in the penultimate paragraph that the literature at the close of the eighteenth century that did carry aesthetic pretentions was also derivative, irrelevant, and anachronistic: "Polite letters were still content with the old wit ideal, still enamored of the couplet, still in love with caustic satire, still transfixing democracy with its sharp quills" (I, 397).

Parrington reiterated in volume II that he would not devote his study of literature to "the narrow field of *belles lettres* alone." He chided "our belletristic historians" for neglecting the great liberal journalist in the poet Bryant, and he willingly gave Poe over to "the belletrist to evaluate his theory and practice of art" (though Parrington then tallied the items for such an evaluation and paid a left-handed compliment to this romantic rebel). Various subtitles pointed, as well, to Parrington's nonaesthetic interests. Emerson was the "Transcendental Critic," Thoreau the "Transcendental Economist," Theodore Parker the "Transcendental Minister," and Margaret Fuller the feminist "Rebel." (See II, ix, 58, 239, 386, 400, 414, and 426.)

In the foreword of volume III, Parrington reported that the preceding two volumes had been visited with "many gentle reproofs" from critics, due to his failure to write "a history of American literature" that accounted for individual artistry within his allegedly "rigid scheme of economic determinism." He repeated his earlier purpose to study "the total pattern of American thought"; he denied a rigid pattern of economic determinism; and he asserted that writing a literary history of America remained a "rather difficult task for which no scholar is yet equipped" (III, xx). Nevertheless, he seemed increasingly sensitive in this third volume to aesthetic criteria, perhaps in response to the criticism of the earlier installments. In addition, of course, belles lettres had now come of age in later nineteenth-century America. As Parrington remarked, literature in this postwar era became the product not of politics, theology, and philosophy, but was now being fashioned by professional "men of letters—poets and essayists and novelists and dramatists" (III, xxvii). But he still intended to include inferior authors who undertook serious cultural criticism. When he later discussed the sociological novelists of the 1890s, he rather testily interjected, "Their work might be bad art—as the critics love to reiterate—but it was the honest voice of a generation bewildered and adrift" (III, 181). Near the end of volume III, however, Parrington was swinging, rather perplexingly, to the opposite imperative of literary aesthetics in the sympathetic appraisal of Cabell's romances and that author's insistence that "the function of art in society . . . is to comfort and inspire man with its divine beauty" (III, 340).

Parrington's regard for the peculiarly romantic, including aesthetic, qualities of Cabell need not seem all that perplexing, however. Nor was it an utterly belated and exceptional focus in *Main Currents*. We can now return to the earlier pages to discover his frequent attention—often uncertain and ambivalent, to be sure—to literary definitions, values, and authorial performances. Indeed, romanticism and realism for Parrington were key literary modes, for they not only pertained to literary genres, but also dominated the literary periods, respectively, before and after the Civil War. Unfortunately, he sacrificed a good deal of clarity in his literary interpretation because of the generous scope of his other sympathies, so that romantic and realistic also incorporated attitudes in politics, economics, psychology, and the judiciary. The historian of literary modes and periods was not always in harmony with the method and terminology of the intellectual historian.

To account logically for the way Parrington was employing romanticism and realism in a given area of American life or thought or literature at a particular moment, the reader can often merely ask, How did Jeffersonian liberalism, in Parrington's view, fare in this instance? Writers whom Parrington esteemed in American thought or belles lettres could be admirably romantic if they envisioned a humanely egalitarian society, and others could be admirably realistic in their critical awareness that complex forces operate in history and human nature to frustrate liberal–democratic hopes. Writers not permitted entry into Parrington's liberal pantheon could, in turn, be unfortunately romantic or unfortunately realistic. Put another way, he had romantic and realistic liberals; but he had, also, his romantic and realistic conservatives.

In his first volume, Parrington drew the economic, political, and social lines between the realism of England (generally, but not quite always, bad) and the romanticism of France (singularly good). Whereas "French romanticism popularized the doctrine of social equalitarianism" and its proponents were economic liberals leaning to humanitarian ideals, the English were political realists honoring property rule and middle-class, puritan-oriented ideals of work, commercial acquisition, and the "economic basis of politics" (I, 267). While Parrington did not inquire into aesthetic areas of literary romanticism in the later eighteenth century, he did recognize psychological aspects that were basic to literary outlook and imagination. Freneau was "endowed with a romantic imagination and love of natural beauty, a generation before the romantic revival," and his social sympathies were properly French and romantic—liberal and idealistic—rather than English and realistic (I, 368, 370). Barlow's years abroad (1788–1805) transformed him into a French romantic socially and politically; and like Freneau, he was similarly idealistic in his view of the human psyche, "accepting the romantic doctrine that human nature is excellent in its plastic state, and capable of infinite development" (I, 382, 385–86).

In the other camp were conservative "realists" like John Adams, who abhorred the "romantic idealisms" of Jefferson and Paine and adhered to the Calvinistic psychology of man, convinced that "the malady of human nature is a disease beyond the reach of romantic plasters" (I, 307, 312). Interestingly, Parrington somewhat dissolved his dichotomy in the portraits of Jefferson and Paine, discovering instead a welcome amalgam of the romantic French and the realistic English in the liberalism of both men. Parrington stressed that Paine, for example, though "Gallic in his psychology of human nature and his passionate humanitarianism," was also "English in his practical political sense and insistence on the economic sources of political action" (I, 341, 344).

The comment foreshadowed Parrington's more complex interpretations in the two volumes to come.

In volume II, *The Romantic Revolution in America*, Parrington painted so many aspects of American life and literature with a romantic brush that Arthur Lovejoy must have been relieved that his recent tally, "On the Discrimination of Romanticisms" (in *PMLA*, 1924), was already completed. Besides noting the political and economic doctrines of egalitarian liberalism transplanted in America, Parrington entertained further "ebullient romanticisms" in nineteenth-century psychology, theology, and now literature. "The days of realism were past," he wrote of the anglified wig and smallclothes mentality of the previous century (II, iii–v). Yet the still-powerful and realistic middle-class "economic man" of Adam Smith was among us, together with the proslavery "appeal to realism" in the South. At the same time, the South had inherited a paradoxically anachronistic and *un*realistic Greek master–slave "democracy," "the most romantic ideal brought forth by our golden age of romance" (I, vii–ix), so that Parrington later would admire Simms for a "strong bias toward realism" (II, 133). In volume II, Parrington fashioned from his all-embracing romanticism a net so vast that he gathered the multiplicity of sectional aspirations and literary contrasts—South and West, middle states and New England—into one romantic revolution. Adventurous and challenging, this was also critical overreaching. But if Parrington did not quite succeed in defining a coherent literary romanticism intersecting our regional similarities and contrasts, neither, for that matter, did F. O. Matthiessen fourteen years later.

In New England's romantic period, Parrington expectably endorsed the liberal aspects of Emerson—"a child of the romantic eighteenth century who by his own transcendental path had come upon the Utopia that an earlier generation had dreamed of"—and of his Concord neighbor Thoreau, whose romantic errand at Walden was "to seek Pan in a tired world and recover joys that have long been forgotten" (II, 397, 403). But elsewhere in the region, the romancers were a motley and less worthy tribe. Harriet Beecher Stowe: "Theocratic New England lay enveloped for her in a haze of romance" (II, 371). The Europeanized Longfellow: "In his work the romantic, the sentimental, and the moralistic" blended to make a literary reputation the twentieth century can scarcely understand (II, 439). Here Parrington made the sentimental and moralistic, by strict definition, separate from, rather than aspects of, the romantic. In still another vein, he referred to the "romance of ethics" in Hawthorne: "With the romance of love and adventure he was never concerned; what interested him was the romance of ethnics—the distortions of the soul under the tyranny of a diseased imagination." Then on the next page, Parrington separated romance from ethics: "Hawthorne was concerned with ethical rather than romantic values . . . in the problem of evil than in the trappings of romance." And yet on the following page, we are told that Hawthorne, in fact, created "romance out of the problem of evil" (II, 444–46). Parrington located further species of the romantic in Holmes, with his "half-hearted ventures in romanticism . . . patched with Victorian sentiment," and in the representative "romanticism of Brahmin culture" in the anglophile, Lowell (II, 453, 436, 472). For all these multiple denotations in Parrington's use of literary romanticism, the connotations were, on the other hand, quite easily known. The reader must ask if the literary case at hand coincided with the central articles of faith in Jeffersonian democracy or if it conspired to defeat them. And indeed, in the twilight mood with which Parrington closed volume II, the enthusiasms and vitality of that "romantic liberalism" had pretty much been played out and defeated. A postwar era was about to herald the new "spirit of realistic criticism" (II, 474).

✱   ✱   ✱

Between volumes II and III, Parrington had written his conceptual essay, "The Development of Realism," for *The Reinterpretation of American Literature* (1928). In an obvious effort to clarify the term realism, he had there widened its application to denote, all at once, a movement, a method, a spirit, and a naturalistic philosophy. In the introduction to volume III, he seemed, in fact, rather unconcerned with his problem of defining the crucial term and, instead, fervently expressed his personal discouragement over the decline of liberal idealism in American life since the Civil War. He concluded with an ambiguous plea for a romantic liberalism wisely monitored and guided by an alert critical realism. First would be the struggle to think realistically, to believe that in "wedding the new psychology to the older economic determinism, we may hope in a spirit of sober realism to make some progress in our thinking." Second was a plaintive request that our earlier romantic hopes in Jeffersonian democracy, including the benefits of a humane and individualizing education, be not abandoned too hastily (III, xxviii).

Parrington organized volume III as a literary history of realism, and the uncompleted study was inevitably spotty and truncated. His preferred romantics once voiced the agrarian and egalitarian spirit of the Jeffersonian adventure; his preferred realists now viewed, through corrective and unflinching critical lenses, the betrayals of the Jeffersonian dream. Parrington welcomed the postwar fiction of New England, especially among the women writers—Phelps, Stowe, Cooke, Spofford, and Freeman—for the successive shifts "from the moralistic to the sentimental, then to the idyllic, then to the realistic." Regrettably, though, "even the starkest New England realism was not very critical of the industrialism that was destroying the traditional New England" (III, 60, 63, 68). His traditional New England this time referred, of course, to the legacy of her liberal idealists. He placed the postwar Whitman in the realists' camp, despite residual flashes of the "romantic splendor" of the French Enlightenment in the later editions of *Leaves of Grass,* since Whitman was mindful of the new "lessons of science" and knew himself to be a "realist who honored the physical as the repository of the spiritual" (III, 69, 70). Parrington approved "the impress of authenticity" in Mark Twain's "honest realism," from the early humor to the later "rebellion against sham . . . [and] the aristocratic romanticism" of Scott evident in *A Connecticut Yankee*. Twain was therefore both realist and "incorrigible idealist" (III, 92, 95, 96). Bret Harte, however, lacked a realist's critical vision of the West as it had become; he was "not realist enough, nor honest enough, to portray the West in its stark, grotesque reality" (III, 93).

In another chapter, Parrington located a further variation of his literary mode in the "Victorian realism" of Howells and James, an interpretation of life "amid the middle and upper classes." The pages on Howells, nevertheless, constituted Parrington's surest handling of realism as a literary mode, technique, and a definable movement, thanks in part, no doubt, to Howells's own critical articulation in *Harpers* of his mission as a practicing realist in the 1880s. Thereafter, Parrington strained for definition of the literary modes and genres that had followed the reign of Howells, and he now embarked on a confusing venture into descriptive criticism. He uncovered a "mordantly realistic vein" in Garland, Frederic, and Kirkland; Rousseauistic traces in Lewis's updated realism; the "growth of a maturer realism" in Rolvaag; and in Cabell, the unexampled compound of romantic and realist, idealist and pessimist, that somehow reached into a deeper "reality" (III, 288, 338, 387).

As if he were not sufficiently pestered by an elusive romanticism and realism, Parrington also wrestled with the perplexities of a third literary mode, turn-of-the-century "naturalism."

Earlier, he had contrasted prewar agrarian optimism with post-war naturalism shaped by industrialism and scientific pessimism (III, 238–39). In literature, "oddly enough it was in the West that the new spirit first expressed itself most adequately," said Parrington in a manuscript fragment, citing Norris (California), Dreiser (Indiana), Anderson (Ohio), and Illinois poets Masters, Sandburg, and Lindsay as authors conscious of a dwindling American individualism (III, 319). Perhaps in a completed essay, Parrington might have elaborated his literary history of Western naturalism by tracing an evolution reaching back to earlier pre-war and even eighteenth-century frontier writing. In 1922, he lectured on the tenets of naturalism at the University of California, and he returned variously to this formulation in his practical criticism for volume III of *Main Currents*, his six criteria being (1) scientific objectivity; (2) anti-Victorian frankness, especially regarding fear, hunger, and sex; (3) an amoral and literal-presentational approach; (4) a philosophical determinism "setting it off from realism"; (5) an anti-romantic pessimism regarding "purposive will"; and (6) character types influenced by inner or outer forces that can lead the writer, respectively, toward grotesque distortion or to partisan reformism (III, 323–35). Unfortunately, when Parrington tried to apply these criteria to the postwar writers, he often tripped over his uncertain and shifting assumptions of realism and romanticism within the definition of naturalism.

There are moments in volume III, however, when Parrington directed his eye on naturalism as a philosophically based *aesthetic*, and he then became a credible literary critic. Norris's *McTeague* ("the first considerable contribution to naturalism by an American writer") he judged in nonsociological terms, admired the naturalistic psychology, and objected to Norris's marring this "severe study" by yielding to his "romantic tendencies," by which Parrington meant aesthetic tendencies rather than any misguided conservative-romantic social or political views. Norris's aesthetic devices unsuitable to naturalism included the romanticist's symbolism, grotesque characterization, use of foils, the "revenge motive," and the obtrusive moral judgment of sex and environment (III, 330–32). But in the work of Lewis and Dreiser, Parrington returned to his confusions of romanticism and naturalism that the reader can resolve only by recalling the social liberalism usually lurking within Parrington's formulations of his literary modes. With sad whimsy, he sided with Lewis, who implicitly bemoaned the passing of "the old romantic creed," in other words, an American "faith in justice, progress, the potentialities of human nature, the excellence of democracy." Lewis portrayed the impercipient Babbitt or the knowing Arrowsmith at grips with an America sustained not by Enlightenment or romantic dreams but by an "encompassing materialism" and the creed of a new science whose "psychology and physics is fast reducing man to a complex bundle of glands, at the mercy of a mechanistic universe" (III, 369). Here the romantic in Lewis was admirably contending with an alien, nonliberalizing naturalism.

We then expect Parrington to judge severely the naturalistic novels of Dreiser, with his creed of science and the glands. Perhaps Parrington would here side with Stuart Sherman's humanistic critique of the predatory world of Frank Cowperwood. But Parrington viewed Dreiser as a compassionate, Whitmanesque ally confronting both genteel and bourgeois timidities and hypocrisies that had stifled a truthful portrayal of American life. To resolve Parrington's praise of both Dreiser's naturalism and Lewis's anti-naturalistic romanticism, we ask again, How does Jeffersonian liberalism fare in this instance? For Parrington, both Lewis and Dreiser were aiding some part of that cause, each in his way. Parrington went on to call intelligent the earlier favorable estimates of Dreiser offered by Bourne, Mencken, and Van Doren; and, Parrington added, "All other commentators are stupid." To Sherman's simile that *The Financier* and *The Titan* were "'like a club sandwich composed of slices of business, alternating with erotic episodes,'" Parrington replied in notes for a classroom lecture, "What would Sherman have? Shall these impulses be eliminated from literature, or from human nature itself?" Parrington also moved the argument to the level of Dreiser's aesthetic performance: If the Cowperwood novels separated into layers of a business-and-sex club sandwich, "the failure is one of art that does not merge them" (III, 359).

Parrington did not doggedly pursue the aesthetic question of Dreiser's literary art, however, and we have come to accept the verdict that *Main Currents* is a book of its time, the literary historian and critic still inept at demonstrating how literary technique effectively serves the author's ideas. Still, Parrington has moments of aesthetic demonstration that hint at a further range that he might have achieved as a literary historian were it not for the demands of his intellectual history. We need only recall the vapid impressionism—or no aesthetic commentary at all—by our earlier literary historians to appreciate what Parrington does accomplish in literary explication.

Several instances of his aesthetic approach lead us to regret that Parrington did not supply us with more of the same. Of

Simms, he wrote, "If he had served his art more jealously, if he had learned from Poe to refuse the demands of inconsequential things, he would have viewed his beloved Charleston with keener eyes and portrayed it more adequately." Parrington then attended to Simms's art, first with a general analysis, easily graced with literary analogies and sprinkled with Parrington's gift of colorful metaphor, followed by Simms's artistic similarities to Dickens, Fielding, Smollett, Shakespeare and other Elizabethans, and on forward to Melville, Baldwin, Bird, and Cooper. In a stroke, Parrington highlighted the contrast between Simms's plotting and Cooper's: "In simplifying his plots to the uncomplicated problem of flight and pursuit, the latter gains in dramatic swiftness of movement, but he loses in abundance of accompanying action—the sense of cross purposes and many-sided activities, which *The Yemassee* so richly suggests" (II, 127–35). Though less incisive as a critic of poetry, Parrington delineated the exacting poetic art that achieves organic power—or fails to, as in the example of the derivative Robert Treat Paine:

> Little of his wit, unfortunately, found its way into his verse, which, modeled ostensibly on Dryden and Pope, lacks their vigorous common sense, and laboring to be sublime succeeds in being heavy. His couplets swell sonorously, but his thought does not keep pace with his rhetoric. He follows his recipe carefully; adjectives duly support the nouns; the caesuras are justly spaced and the balance of the parts is as nice as if weighted in an apothecary's scales. He seasons the whole with the staples of personification and poetic diction; everything has been provided for, and yet the cake is fallen that he takes from the oven. (II, 289)

Elsewhere, Parrington alternated between the two approaches we noticed to have been increasingly traditional in American literary criticism. One was to render an aesthetic judgment and supply an example or an extended quotation but without an explication of appropriate technique. The other was to send down an aesthetic judgment thumpingly, without so much as an illustrative example or quotation. But Parrington's enthusiasm for artistic performance was clearly present in *Main Currents*. More important, he was able to set aside his ideological bias in favor of liberal writers when he established through his many judgments of aesthetic excellence a canon of sorts for American literature and a miniature pantheon of authors chosen solely on artistic grounds. And some of his liberal writers, in the process, did not fare too well this time around. He valued Longstreet as a Jeffersonian agrarian and a literary forerunner of Mark Twain.

Still, "there could be no more telling commentary on the literary poverty of *ante-bellum* Georgia than the extraordinary popularity of Longstreet's sketches. . . . Longstreet was as uncritical as his readers and his frequent failures are glaring in their badness." Parrington named the "worst of the sketches" in *Georgia Scenes* and labeled their artistic failures (II, 171–72). He honored Mrs. Stowe for her humanitarian passions, but he closed with this verdict: "She never trained herself in craftsmanship . . . her work has suffered the fate that pursues those who forget that beauty alone survives after emotion subsides" (II, 378). And Whittier, who shared her emotions, remained neither "a great, [nor] even noteworthy poet" (II, 366). Though admirably liberal, Bryant was "narrow in range and barren in suggestion" (II, 246).

We need to be reminded of still other adverse estimates that Parrington arrived at from a strictly aesthetic basis. There was Paulding "who never took the trouble to master his technic. There was excellent stuff in him, solider perhaps than in Irving, but his failure suggests the difference between the journeyman and the artist" (II, 221). Cooper, for all his critical acumen, "said many wise things so blunderingly as to make truth doubly offensive, and he hewed his art so awkwardly as well-nigh to destroy the beauty of his romance" (II, 237). Holmes was too much the bon vivant "to take the trouble to become an artist" (II, 459). We are disposed to remember Parrington's notoriously brief aesthetic treatment and dismissal of Poe and James and to conclude that his liberal political bias had produced an aesthetic myopia nearly uncorrectable. Yet many another writer who should then have received Parrington's plaudits did not. He noticed the "art submerged by propaganda" in Upton Sinclair as well as in Herrick (III, 349, 353). Dreiser was the spiritual heir of the great Whitman, but in the novels "the artist suffers at the hands of the disputant" (II, 354). Parrington praised Norris as "the most stimulating and militant of our early naturalists" but discovered artistic flaws in the fiction: In *McTeague,* Norris "yielded to his romantic tendencies"; *Vandover* was "insufficiently motivated"; and *The Octopus* was marred by touches of melodrama (III, 329, 331, 332).

For too long, we have obviously taken Parrington at his word when he announced in the foreword to the second volume, "With aesthetic judgments I have not been greatly concerned. I have not wished to evaluate reputations or weigh literary merits, but rather to understand what our fathers thought and why they wrote as they did" (II, i). He evaluated reputations and weighed literary merits within all three volumes. He ranked Jonathan Odell the foremost Tory poet, placed the "French Group"—Freneau,

Barlow and Breckenridge—over Barlow's fellow Connecticut Wits (this despite Parrington's having edited the Wits in 1926), urged a permanent place on our bookshelves for Breckenridge's *Modern Chivalry* and Caruthers's *Kentuckian in New York* and Kennedy's *Quodlibet*. He ranked the *Knickerbocker History* Irving's best and demoted Simms's *The Yemassee* in favor of the "realistic" *The Partisan, The Forayers,* and *Woodcraft*. (Simms scholars in the 1980s have continued to launch interpretations of the fiction by quoting Parrington's provocative literary judgments). In addition to *Leaves of Grass* and *A Hazard of New Fortunes,* he argued the permanence of such landmark works as Kirkland's *Zury,* Garland's Middle-Border fiction, and Twain's *Connecticut Yankee*. More recently, there had been the excellent craft of Wharton's *The Age of Innocence,* and her earlier *Ethan Frome* was even better. Finally, Parrington virtually exhausted his vocabulary of superlatives to extol the literary art of Sinclair Lewis and, even more, of the "incomparable" Cabell.

✷   ✷   ✷

Another part of Parrington's vocabulary, however, may be viewed as inexhaustibly creative. Not since Moses Coit Tyler had fashioned his brilliant portraits and historical drama a half century before had students of American literature met with a literary history written with such verve and stylistic power. Nor have we seen Parrington's equal since. *Main Currents* itself is a distinguished work of literary art. In his "Call for a Literary Historian" in 1924, Fred L. Pattee ruled, in his final requirement, that the new candidate "be himself a writer of force and beauty." Parrington more than answered the call. Among the most prominent aspects of this literary art were the dynamic Jeffersonian angle of vision, together with a novelist's sense of structure, drama, character conflict, and the poetically explanatory uses of functional metaphor and imagery. His occasional grandiloquence, reminiscent of Tyler's exuberance, may not, however, have been precisely what Pattee had in mind for "a style simple and clear."

Parrington quite clearly conceived the three volumes architecturally as a massive structure rising out of Calvinistic pessimism in volume I to the aspiring peaks of romantic optimism in volume II, and then receding near the close of that volume and into the final volume III with the renewal of American pessimism in the doctrines of modern mechanistic science. (This form is suggested in III, xix.) The structure was, of course, primarily internal and literary. With an inherent sense of dramatic tension,

Parrington was able to discern in the American past a continuing series of ideals that held forth the promise of a humanitarian democracy, yet were continually counteracted by ideas that aimed to delimit and subvert that democracy. He personalized these aesthetic and intellectual ideals by creating vivid sketches of the individual writers and thinkers themselves, emphasizing their human qualities, their formative background, and their legacy. He also shaped his story (as R. W. B. Lewis and others later would theirs) as a continuing series of dialogues between men of conflicting ideologies.

Other literary qualities also give to *Main Currents* a structural coherence. The presiding tensions were cast into another guise through Parrington's skillful use of synecdoche. They became the antagonisms between the coonskin cap and the tie wig, homespun and broadcloth, the countryside and the marketplace, the wide green fields of agrarianism and the narrow cobblestone streets of the new urban industrialism. Parrington also had a remarkable instinct for locating the creative, shaping metaphor. As Harold Eby relates in his gracefully written biographical portrait introducing the posthumous final volume, the Gilded Age chapters began to take form soon after Parrington had discovered his metaphorical center or structural core in the phrase, "The Great Barbecue." The metaphor enabled Parrington to capture the essential drama and excitement of the period. And it was joined by the image of a voyage through the "main currents of American thought" that, structurally, became the book's predictable metaphor to ensure the unity of all three volumes. Parrington used the metaphor variously and often; but what is striking in this "currents" imagery is the insistent way in which liberal ideas became *the* currents, while ideas he was unfriendly to were described as "reefs," "barriers," "foundering bark," "barnacled craft . . . dragging anchor," or "moral squalls" or "chill winds."

We noticed earlier that Parrington was inclined to reserve an environmental interpretation for those ideas toward which he was unfriendly. When he warmed to his assignment, the environment and the conservative victim merged in the creative image. Increase Mather "closed the windows of his mind against the winds of new doctrine"; Timothy Dwight's mind "was closed as tight as his study windows in January"; James Russell Lowell's mind withered in "the stagnant atmosphere of [his] Elmwood study," while the doors at nearby Craigie House were "shut securely against all intrusion. The winds of doctrine and policy might rage through the land, but they did not rattle the windows of [Longfellow's] study" (I, 99, 361; II, 468, 440). By contrast, the men whom Parrington admired (when he was playing the unabashed liberal polemicist) were thinkers, and he characterized them as open-air pioneers or fearless navigators on adventurous, uncharted currents of thought, unhampered by constricting and formative pressures of environment.

The broken promise of eighteenth-century democracy was a prominent theme after volume I and was repeatedly cast into Parrington's imagery of the American garden perverted into a "pigsty." More of the earthiness of Parrington's prose grew out of imagery drawn from the barn, the dairy, the poultry house, the butchering block, the cider press, the apiary. The spirit of *Main Currents* at times was one of reverence and optimism in the promise of this native abundance in the New World environment. But more frequently, the tone became angrily sardonic, as Parrington dealt with the consolidators, the land grabbers, and the plunderers who took the harvest of this plenty and squandered it at their "great barbecue." Agrarian imagery served his purpose here, also. It reflected, in fact, the physiocratic leanings he derived from the ideas of Jefferson.

That liberal spirit of the Enlightenment provided him with another persistent pattern of images. Like Tyler, Parrington shaded (literally) his portraits to distinguish the bold men who heeded the clear light of rationality as opposed to conservative men bereft of light, benighted and often misshapen products of a dark, narrow, crooked environment. Among the creative thinkers whom he championed, Roger Williams was a "child of light" who came to America as if in the night "loosing wild foxes with firebrands to ravage the snug fields of the Presbyterian Utopia." Franklin was a man of "clear and luminous understanding," concerned that Philadelphia streets be evenly laid and well lighted. William Ellery Channing brought to the New England church "the new light—which was no other than primitive English Independency" (I, 63, 178, 106). In the enemy camp were the victims of an environment in which the clear and generous light of reason made no entry. Parrington moved from the "crooked streets of Boston" to the "crooked and diseased mind" of Cotton Mather. And in contrast to the well-lighted Philadelphia streets of the enlightened Franklin, the crooked streets of the Mathers' Boston received little more than half-light even at midday. "Though father and son walked the streets of Boston at noonday, they were only twilight figures, communing with ghosts, building with shadows" (I, 96, 109, 117).[18]

★   ★   ★

And how did such lively style and thought strike the critics in the academy and public intellectual community who reviewed the first installment of Parrington's magnum opus? The reception of volumes I and II was not unmixed. Virtually all the critics, however, realized at once that, as Carl Van Doren generously described this occasion one-half dozen years after the *CHAL,* they were witness to "an event in the history of American criticism."[19] The reviewers understood this event to be, as Parrington's main title had it, a study of American thought and, as the subtitle amplified, with American literature serving as handmaid and purveyor. To that end, reviewers praised Parrington's power and sweep as an intellectual historian, though he was nevertheless faulted for certain omissions even there. Historian Charles Beard remarked on Parrington's neglect of natural science and its influence on theology, politics, and letters; and Kenneth Murdock added education, art, and philosophy to the list. That Parrington downplayed belles lettres (or said that he did) was not seriously upsetting to the critics, though Henry Canby and several others regretted the cursory treatment of literary figures like Melville and Poe. Beard, on the other hand, praised Parrington as a critic who "has yanked Miss Beautiful Letters out of the sphere of the higher verbal hokum and fairly set her in the way that leads to contact with pulsing reality." As to his Jeffersonian bias, Helen Houston felt that it gave the volumes an effective "sense of unity," and Canby remarked that "every good history is partisan." Murdock, however, considered the liberal slant a liability that prevented Parrington's treating fairly the intelligent Tories like Thomas Hutchinson. Murdock did join with others to commend Parrington's fair reassessment of the Southern mind.

Finally, it was Parrington's style, his mastery in creating a living gallery of American writers and thinkers, that aroused the critical excitement over *Main Currents*. His influence on American letters was anticipated at once. Murdock saw in *Main Currents* a catalyst for new scholarship, including revisionist treatments of Parrington's own chapters. J. Donald Adams predicted that Parrington's "astounding gallery of American figures" would become the starting point for new biographers of these authors. And Canby wrote, "It is this book, and not the ill-proportioned 'Cambridge History of American Literature,' which should be the point of departure of every study in the developing American mind."[20]

Volume III appeared in late 1930, the year after Parrington's death, and though fragmented and incomplete, it was widely reviewed. The reasons are obvious. He had become a celebrity, winning the Pulitzer Prize in 1928 and igniting the imagination of the American academy as an heroic, free-spirited scholar in the far Northwest at work on the final installment of his massive life's work. His sudden death was correspondingly tragic and shocking to the scholarly community. In a conversation with this author in the summer of 1980, Robert Spiller vividly described the moment, still indelibly etched in his memory. In June 1929, he was on a Guggenheim Fellowship in England, studying Cooper as a critic of his time. As Spiller returned his books to the desk at the close of a day at the British Museum, standing alongside him was Parrington, on leave from Washington to complete volume III of *Main Currents*. The two men had never met, though Spiller had reviewed the first two volumes for the *Philadelphia Public Ledger* (14 May 1927)—and had singled out for praise the pages on Cooper as a social critic. The two chatted and then planned to have lunch when Parrington next returned to the museum. Within a few days, Spiller read in a London newspaper that Parrington had died suddenly of a heart attack. He was buried in the garden at his dwelling, the George Inn, Winchcombe, in Gloucestershire. That he should be laid to rest in another country makes Parrington seem all the more a mythically heroic loner in the annals of American literature study.

In late 1930, colleagues at the University of Washington, including Harold Eby, brought out Parrington's uncompleted *The Rise of Critical Realism in America,* and this fragmentary third volume gained critical attention that verged, in some cases, on hyperbole. Parrington's former colleague at Washington, V. L. O. Chittick, asserted that, far from an "incomplete skeleton," this volume was superior to its predecessors, for Parrington was here in full command of the period with which he was most familiar, and he was not hampered, as before, by the frustration of trying to consult rare primary documents. Chittick also defended Parrington's aesthetic instincts, basing the case on the old-fashioned criterion of "the faultless taste with which he reveals the essential quality of an author through quotation."

In a more balanced critique, Morris Cohen nevertheless concluded with the praise that Parrington's work ranked with Tocqueville's "great classic," and Cohen paid a final tribute to Parrington's luminosity "and the remarkable verve and felicity of expression which make this a rarely delightful book." Parrington's cross-disciplinary approach to American thought was now familiar to his critical audience, and Stanley Williams, for whom Parrington had edited *The Connecticut Wits* (1926) in Harcourt, Brace's

American Authors Series, hailed Parrington's approach to American authors as more illuminating than the belletristic lantern. Edward Wagenknecht agreed that, in Parrington's hands at least, the historical approach to American literature was successful. Cohen, however, pointed out Parrington's simplistic characterization of periods and loose handling of crucial terms, including literature itself. Because of his economic approach and bias, Parrington also, said Cohen, was not properly aware of the quality of individual genius in America's writers. He also noted, as reviewers of the earlier volumes had, Parrington's failure to render justice to various fields of intellectual history, including religion, science, art, education, and law.

Henry Commager (NYU) noticed some of these same omissions, caused by Parrington's selective angle of vision, but Commager, with other critics, considered Parrington's Jeffersonian point of view an historian's advantage. This final volume was, to Commager, an eloquent "tragedy of American thought" written out of neo-Jeffersonian despair over the triumph of a technological civilization. (In his *The American Mind,* 1950, Commager still admitted himself to be a disciple of Parrington.) Matthew Josephson also endorsed Parrington's economic approach to our literary history, "a great, luminous improvement over the unctuous and vacant work of the school of Barrett Wendell." Josephson then presented his own critique of the Gilded Age and the technological revolution, material obviously simmering in the manuscript he would soon publish as *The Robber Barons* (1934). Norman Foerster praised the unified point of view in *Main Currents,* then termed Parrington less than a modern liberal (to his credit), and then, in contrast to Josephson, delivered a lecture on behalf of the New Humanist inner life that can shore up the modern spirit against the republican–romantic failures of Rousseau and his followers. J. Donald Adams saw Parrington's declining Emersonian faith to be implicit in the way he discussed Cabell's irony, Dreiser's pity, Anderson's recoil, and Lewis's "contemptuous amusement."[21]

In virtually unanimous chorus, the reviewers of volume III praised Parrington's dramatic gift of bold characterization that, once more, brought American writers into mutual combat over the great social and humanistic issues of American liberalism. Most frequently cited were the pages on Whitman, Mark Twain, the later Adamses, and Lewis. For these strengths, Commager regarded *Main Currents* "a great piece of literature as of scholarship." Wagenknecht, looking among the literary scene rife with various ideological biases, judged *Main Currents* a superior example of critical advocacy. And Williams echoed both Commager and Wagenknecht, terming it "a great book" with a provocative success that would, in turn, inspire great books from others in the years ahead.[22]

If we can now begin, half a century later, to read *Main Currents* as a distinguished literary, as well as intellectual, history that also becomes in itself an example of literary art, Parrington seems inevitably the foremost single architect of a total American literary history our country has seen. As the corpus of our literature has become gargantuan with the product of our dozens of excellent and distinctive American novelists and poets since Parrington's day, we doubt that a single scholar ever again will match the unifying vision and brilliant execution of a Parrington. Moreover, when the multiple-authored *Literary History of the United States* appeared in 1948, more than one nostalgic reviewer recalled, in an invidious comparison, Parrington's heroic one-man effort two decades earlier. Those reviewers realized what Parrington's contemporaries already had sensed, that he stood as a culminating figure at the end of a long first century of American literature study. Equally important, Parrington did not intimidate and inhibit his literary-historian contemporaries. On the contrary, *Main Currents* immediately spawned several single-author literary histories. Four of these deserve special attention as our story continues.

Chapter 18

The Heirs of Parrington:
Four Leftist Histories during the
Great Depression

Parrington highlighted the aesthetic side of American writing, in our authors as well as his own example, sufficiently to have signaled the new critical direction that Henry Canby, in 1929, had urged for American literary histories in his review of *Reinterpretation*. Then came the Crash in October of that year, four months after Parrington's death. His liberal social and economic criticism now seemed even more incisive, not to say prophetic as well. To intellectuals and ideologues during the Depression years, any aesthetic emphasis in Parrington went largely unnoticed. In 1930, as the posthumous final pages were being printed, *Main Currents* was already on the way to creating one scholar's almost unparalleled political impact on the American intellectual community, an influence to be felt over the next twenty-five years especially in the humanistic disciplines. At the close of the decade, Bernard Smith, writing in *Books That Changed Our Minds* (1939), described the revolutionary force of *Main Currents* on his liberal consciousness in the thirties. At the end of the forties, in the third (bibliographical) volume of the profession's cooperative *Literary History of the United States* (1948), Parrington's brief commentaries on the literary figures were continuously cited among the monographs in the biography and criticism section on individual American authors. It is true, of course, that by this time the recent school of New Critics was finding relatively little of value in these commentaries, given Parrington's allegedly nonaesthetic interpretation of American literature. And intellectual historians were presently complaining that Parrington's range was too limited, his method slipshod, his treatment often melodramatic, and many of his conclusions unreliable. Even so, more than one hundred historians in 1952 named *Main Currents* their most preferred American history published between 1920 and 1935.[1]

Only the writer of a classic work could provoke these wild

swings of admiration and rebuke. Indeed, the contradictory reactions were sometimes occurring within a single heir of Parrington's achievement. Edwin Cady recalled a meeting in these same postwar years held by the Central New York American Studies Association, an occasion devoted to the legacy of Parrington. "As it warmed up," Cady remembered, "man after man in field after field rose to 'testify'—that Parrington had been a great influence upon him but that, at least in *his* field, Parrington was no longer valid." By the "deepening dusk," said Cady, "it was suddenly apparent that the testimony had covered the whole of the book, that it had been entirely repudiated, that a kind of parricide had occurred." But then came the counterstatement and inevitable tribute: "And, sure enough, in the evening session there was a kind of angry, self-answering guilt response. It left one saying (and this represents the atmosphere), 'Now he belongs to the ages.'"[2]

Parrington's immediate influence in the academy was felt in the pages of Russell Blankenship's *American Literature as an Expression of the National Mind* (1931). Having received the B.A. at the University of Missouri, Blankenship joined the faculty of Whitman College from 1923 to 1932. The catalogs show that his two-term survey of American literature began to stress social, economic, and political backgrounds after 1926—no doubt influenced by Parrington, for Blankenship was also studying for his M.A. at Washington (awarded in 1928). In 1932, he moved to Washington, taught American literature, and presently completed his dissertation on John H. Noyes (1935). After Parrington's death in the summer of 1929, Blankenship wrote the eulogy in *Nation* (previously cited) and described the forceful classroom presence of his master. In the preface of Blankenship's *American Literature,* he ascribed his view of "the inseparable union of literature and the social environment" to having read the New Critics— that is, Macy, Mencken, Brooks, Bourne, Mumford, Van Doren, Canby, and others (pp. viii–x). But his brief association with Parrington "as instructor and friend was by far the strongest and most beneficial influence" (p. x). Though Blankenship's manuscript was completed before volume III of *Main Currents* was published in 1930, he admitted his obligations to the rest of Parrington's "monumental work . . . , the originality of which is insured by the author's acquaintance with his material no less than by his daringly liberal point of view" (p. vii).

Not only did Blankenship acknowledge these debts to Parrington and others (including Tyler's history and the plethora of monographs and essays of recent years), but he candidly disclaimed any originality at all—the preface was titled an "Apology"—either in theory, documentation, or conclusions. Why then did he approach Holt with this literary history? And why did Holt publish it? Blankenship was not quite so candid in this regard. His 724 pages of literary history were, in fact, a textbook in thin disguise, one more publisher's bid for the school trade. He wrote at the easy level of the college student. Numerous biographical sketches were combined with paraphrasing of the works, while titled subdivisions and italicized topic headings were sprinkled within the chapters. And he concluded each segment with suggested readings. In a subordinate clause in the conclusion, he referred to this "guide to American literature" (p. 718). The dedication read, "To My Classes in American Literature."

Viewed as scholarship, Blankenship's volume is significant mainly as the early symptom of a new wave of socially oriented studies of American literature in the 1930s inspired by Parrington's example—and the Crash of 1929. Blankenship, however, was not so forthcoming as Parrington in asserting his liberal bias. At the beginning, Blankenship stressed the inseparable link between literature and society (p. ix) but appeared to be an impartial historian of the ideas that had surfaced in our literature as a product of American's social environment. In the sketches of American authors, however, any reader of Parrington would be aware that the estimates in *Main Currents* had been faithfully repeated.

Blankenship introduced the "historical development of the American mind" (p. 48) by describing the causal forces of geography and race. (Nowhere did he mention Taine, however, not even in the suggested readings.) Of the two, geography was the more powerful influence: "So marked is the variation of physical environment within the United States that, if this country had been settled by one homogeneous race, the inhabitants would have developed intellectually along widely different lines" (p. 3). It followed that when Blankenship moved to the nation's highly diverse racial background, he discounted the melting-pot theory of the Americanization of character and ideas. He also argued the power of acquired "racial characteristics in thinking," begun in the Old World and "unchanged by naturalization" (p. 21). And with Parrington, he repudiated the notion that "American thought is wholly of English origin," despite our language, government, and educational system. Still, after briefly touching on the separate cultural contributions of the "races," including the promise of Jewish and Negro artists, Blankenship asserted that we can, nevertheless, identify an American tradition and a genuinely American literature that has arisen from this complex diversity.

The rest of his volume was "a close study of our writers' background and of the intellectual currents that have swept through our nation" (p. 46).

To trace the development of an American intellectual tradition in our literature, Blankenship isolated four dominant forces—the "cosmopolitan spirit" (chiefly European), puritanism, the frontier, and mysticism (Edwards appeared here, along with Emerson, Whitman, the Quakers, and others). But it turns out that none of these four influences served Blankenship very well after his first two periods, "The Mind of Colonial America" and "Romanticism in America." His third, or final, period was expectably, after Parrington's design, "The Triumph of Realism," where the reigning condition was industrialism. Belatedly, Blankenship now located a fifth intellectual influence, "science" (p. 412). In short, he followed the chief contours of *Main Currents*, along with certain formative ideas we have seen in Foerster, Hubbell, and others. The result of his eclecticism was that Blankenship's study never crystallized in a history of American thought incisively controlled by a unifying point of view or by the original conviction that inspires a vigorous rhetoric.

Finally, Blankenship expressly disregarded the aesthetic definitions necessary in his putative history of American literature, presumably following what he considered to be Parrington's example. "Whether our literature is 'great' or not," Blankenship announced in the preface, "is of comparatively slight importance." More significant was that "it is profoundly expressive of the changing American mind" (p. ix). He ignored the possibility that when he deemed a literary work to be "profoundly expressive," the reader might want an explanation of such expressive power. Here is the conception of his assignment: "The first task of the historian of literature is to determine what a given writer said. The second question is to discover why he said it." Ancillary, but expendable, tasks involved influence (he did not say what kind) and critical pronouncements on truth and goodness (p. 49). Inevitably, Blankenship did acknowledge literary workmanship, and he sent down an occasional judgment of literary artistry. His laurels for "the finest literary artist among all our contemporary prose writers," it should be noted in the present consideration of the hovering ghost of Parrington, went to his mentor's "incomparable Cabell," who received ten glowing pages. The work of F. Scott Fitzgerald, on the other hand, was never mentioned.

Blankenship must have been rather disheartened by the academy's reception of his *American Literature,* though it was mixed with enough accolades to dispel any notion that the critics were henceforth to blame for his never fulfilling an early promise as a scholar (this would be his only major contribution to American literature study). The first prominent scholar to notice the book was Stanley Williams in the *Yale Review*. In an omnibus review of recent studies—Henry W. Boynton's and Spiller's books on Cooper, Rourke's *American Humor*, Canby's *Classic Americans*, and Charles Angoff's Mencken-approved *Literary History of the American People* (mercilessly dismissed)—Williams tendered twenty-one words merely describing Blankenship's work as a story of our literature, accompanied by "underlying factors." In the *New England Quarterly*, Frederic Carpenter (Harvard) sarcastically confirmed Blankenship's modest disclaimer of any originality. "It is a Babbitt among books," but it did helpfully frame, for the most part, "a composite picture of American scholarship as it is." Carpenter credited Blankenship with a commendable respect for Emerson and Thoreau and a "genuinely important and suggestive" look at transcendentalism in Eugene O'Neill. Otherwise, Blankenship's usual conclusions were "meaningless circumlocution" (Carpenter gave punishing examples) that said "absolutely nothing." After this scathing treatment, Blankenship was rewarded in the next issue of *American Literature* with the praise of Reed Smith (South Carolina), who called the book the "latest, fullest, and best of the recent revaluations of American literature." (In Williams's review of these revaluations, Blankenship had been cruelly slighted.) Though unsympathetic toward the romantics (and more so the Puritans), Blankenship was "admirable" on Emerson and Thoreau, and for *Moby-Dick*, he showed, in fact, an "over-enthusiasm." Smith quibbled with a few of the estimates of American authors, but Blankenship's judgments made his book a bold adventure: "No one who reads it will be bored."[3]

The next year, V. F. Calverton (known to his friends as George after his actual name, George Goetz) published *The Liberation of American Literature* (1932), his own version of *Main Currents* ("This book is as much a study of American culture as it is of American literature," p. xi). But his approach to the distinctly "cultural pattern" of this country, like that of other young critics of the early 1930s, was guided by an avowedly Marxist point of view: "It is only by an appreciation of the class psychologies dominant at the time, as Marx has shown, that we can understand the nature of a culture or the direction and trend of a literature" (p. xi). Calverton, therefore, wrote with an advocacy and focus that Blankenship lacked, although *The Liberation* was often dull for all that. Unlike Blankenship and Parrington, Calverton emphasized the adverse cultural influence of England almost to the exclusion of France and Germany, for he wished to stress the "colonial complex" in America, even to the end of the nineteenth century, and to understand what elements in the American environment encouraged this Anglo-Saxon class attitude in our culture and especially, regarding the arts, in our literary history. Finally, as to the definition of literature, Calverton was more aware and yet more simplistic and confusing than Parrington and Blankenship in meeting the questions of imagination and aesthetic form in a history of ideas in literature. He acknowledged that the literary imagination assumed "forms which are more elusive than economic charts and political programmes" (p. xi) and that "content and form are inseparable" (p. xii), so that the literary historian must also don the cap of the literary critic. Even so, he had "taken the aesthetic element for granted," apparently—as we splice his separate observations—because the most significant "roots of the imagination" are indistinguishable from "class-roots," and "aesthetic criticism is fundamentally social in character, and can only be significant when derived from a sound social philosophy" (p. xii). Such was the aesthetic faith of the literary Marxist. Calverton intended to supply the "secure social basis" for a literary doctrine, leaving to future critics of the Left the "analysis of the aesthetic element" that should complete and justify his criticism (p. xiii).

Calverton did not mention Parrington in the preface, and through 480 pages of text cited him only briefly in two footnotes. Since Calverton was a Johns Hopkins graduate (1921) and then founder and editor of the New York, Marxist-oriented *Modern Quarterly* (retitled *Modern Monthly*), we might assume here an instance of the Easterner's indifference to a Seattle scholar, his liberalism notwithstanding. Yet Calverton had recently contributed two pamphlets to the University of Washington Book Store Chapbook series: *The New Ground of Criticism* (1930) and *American Literature at the Crossroads* (1931). These were trial runs for the central thesis of *The Liberation*. For Parrington, Marx had been a rather secondary influence on American liberal thought. The young Calverton (b. 1900) was probably trying to avoid comparison with the formidable Parrington by taking a direct Marxian path of his own. But he was respectful enough not to assail Parrington in *Liberation*, especially in the pages where he reduced Jefferson to a sentimental exponent of *"petty bourgeoisie"* values that were lamentably outdated even in the years of his combat with the ascendant *"upper bourgeoisie"* interests of Hamilton.

Calverton's seven chapters of American literary history are of minimal value as a study of our literary periods, genres, and modes in their historical and aesthetic evolution. Indeed, we may ask why this outsider should be granted space in the history of an academic profession. He is valuable chiefly for enlightening the academy in the early 1930s on the nature of various American class attitudes central to our national life and literature. He gave to scholars and critics during the decade an historical context for the proletarian ideology that was emerging in America. Like all historical and critical formulae, Calverton's had the virtue of a simple, repetitious consistency. In his survey, American class psychology was formed early by the clash betwen petty-bourgeois and upper-bourgeois material and moral values. This struggle was disastrous for cultural excellence in America, because there was no aristocratic tradition here to leaven the lumpish bourgeoisie. After the post–Civil War triumph of upper-bourgeois industrial and finance capitalism, the world of the petty bourgeoisie was reduced to impotent protest, chaos, and despair. But some among them discovered a liberation from their anachronistic individualism by turning to the social doctrines of a proletarian brotherhood.

Calverton viewed this class conflict primarily as an outgrowth of national experience, though he acknowledged a pervasive colonial complex of cultural inferiority to England that prevailed until our decisive nationalism took hold at the turn of the last century. That earlier suffocating habit of mind had developed in New England during the eighteenth century among the upper-bourgeois "'codfish aristocracy'" that had replaced the "petty bourgeois theocracy as the dominant class" (p. 151). The petty bourgeoisie then counterattacked when their "landhungry individualists" swarmed across the Western frontier; but even here, the upper bourgeoisie enforced their will through the power of capitalist industry and finance. After the Civil War, the upper bourgeoisie virtually dominated the nation (except in the South, where the planters were replaced by the new pettybourgeois farmers and merchants). With the trust-busting and muckraking attacks on this economic dictatorship came also the similarly ineffectual efforts of radical labor organizers—in the Social Labor Party, the IWW, and the Communist Party—to develop a proletarian psychology in the work force. Calverton realistically admitted that even since the recent Crash, "the worker continues to think of himself as an individual instead of a member of a class"

(p. 374). So the liberation from America's bourgeois-individualist culture had in no way been achieved; it was, instead, an opportunity for disaffected petty-bourgeois liberals and was receiving spirited treatment in the current work of our most vital authors.

America's literature, in Calverton's estimation, was important to study as an expression of its bourgeois dialectic. Figures whom previous literary historians had viewed as rebels in the cause of an indigenous democratic literature became instead, for Calverton, advocates of an American petty-bourgeois individualism only slightly less stultifying and misguided than the pseudoaristocratic upper bourgeoisie with whom they were at odds. Calverton did appreciate many of these writers despite their unwitting service to a confused individual and national ideal. Thoreau, unlike Emerson, at least practiced his petty-bourgeois self-reliance. Hawthorne and Melville, though envisioning no solution, were sensible enough to be dissatisfied with the deplorable state of their American society. In their time, Whitman and Mark Twain were courageously progressive bourgeois writers and, were they alive in Calverton's time, might have developed, like Dreiser, a proletarian outlook. Howells, too, fought valiantly for a democratic realism, thanks to the "frontier force" of his youth, but this "would-be radical" (p. 380) never quite disentangled himself from Boston's upper-bourgeois web. Still, he helped embolden later realists and muckrakers. The muckrake journals, however, were taken over by the plutocracy, while a new group of writers and critics—Joyceans, Cabellians, and Menckenites—wrote for a culturally superior "'civilized minority'" (p. 400).

Still others spoke for a lingering bourgeois-Comstock morality (Bliss Perry, H. W. Boynton, Booth Tarkington, Henry Van Dyke, and even Hamlin Garland), and free-verse poets like Robinson, Sandburg, and Masters sang a petty-bourgeois swan song. In fiction, Anderson, Suckow, Cather, and Lewis lacked the courage and vision of a Jack London and essentially indulged in petty-bourgeois sentimentality over an agrarian past or, in the case of Lewis, in affectionate but pointless satire of a "dying class" (p. 433). Nor was the new interest in the literature of cowboys and Indians of much consequence, and among Negro writers, only Claude McKay and the recent Langston Hughes escaped a bourgeois or racial cul-de-sac and expressed a proletarian outlook.

Calverton was encouraged that in fairly recent years American writers had been entering his phase of proletarian liberation. They included novelists Dos Passos, Michael Gold, and Charles Yale Harrison, together with critics like Sidney Hook, Joseph Freeman, Newton Arvin, Granville Hicks, and Bernard Smith.

Oddly, in these closing pages, Calverton voiced an aesthetic caveat that seems incongruous after his previous inattention to questions of literary craft. Discussing his rival journal, the *New Masses,* and proletarian criticism generally, he warned that social significance in literature was not enough and that America's proletarian critics (unlike their international contemporaries) had not insisted on rigid aesthetic standards and performance. "The proletariat as well as the bourgeoisie and the aristocracy deserves good art for its inspiration," he nicely put it. The ideal critic of the future would require superior literature and then insist that "the craftsmanship must be utilized to create objects of revolutionary meaning" (p. 460).

Not the exemplar of such criticism himself (though the *Liberation* was not markedly weaker in asesthetic consideration than many of the nonideological textbook literary histories we confronted earlier), Calverton served well the proletarian cause and had even completed his homework in American literature scholarship. Though a journalist, he cited the scholarly articles of the profession's new *American Literature* as well as the basic studies of his predecessors—the Duyckincks, Tyler, Pattee, Trent, Matthews, and others. He consulted the *CHAL* and the critics in that second decade of the century, together with the 1920s studies of the frontier (Rusk, Hazard, and Dondore), the drama (Quinn), the South (Mims), French influence (Jones), plus *The Reinterpretation of American Literature* and areas recently explored by Constance Rourke, Murdock, Canby, Untermeyer, and Frank L. Mott. Nor should we overlook Calverton's own contributions beyond the pages of the *Liberation*—his primary forays into such crucial subjects as bourgeois moral repression and censorship (*Sex Expression in Literature*), the literary voice of American Blacks (*An Anthology of American Negro Literature*), and his other studies mentioned previously. In the present chronicle, we have considered many literary histories written by scholars that one need not worry about ever consulting at length. The nonprofessorial *Liberation of American Literature*, however, is required reading into the 1980s.

Calverton's critical reception in the academy (F. O. Matthiessen's review excepted) was surprisingly free of vituperative debate, perhaps because Parrington had eased the way for Leftist advocacy in literary history. Granville Hicks (Rensselaer), who was completing his own Marxist literary history, *The Great Tradition,* found Calverton's style repetitious, academic, and dull, making the recent books of Canby (*Classic Americans*) and Lewisohn (in our chapter to follow) sparkle by comparison. "But neither Lewisohn nor Canby," he added, "nor any other historian of our literature, Parrington included, has shown us so clearly why our culture has developed precisely as it has." Hicks advised the successors of Calverton's valuable and expectably ragged pioneering effort to avoid Calverton's separation of "content and craftsmanship" and give closer attention to "the attitudes, the problems and the accomplishments of particular writers." And this aesthetic dimension was precisely what Hicks tried to supply in his own literary history the next year.

Calverton's scholarship was given the imprimatur of the profession's *American Literature* by Grant C. Knight (Kentucky), author of the recent *American Literature and Culture* (like Blankenship's volume, essentially a textbook). He credited Calverton with an argument "developed with careful reasoning, adequate documentation, excellent introductory sections giving résumés of periods of our history, and in a dispassionate and crystal-clear style." Calverton's thesis, Knight concluded, was "so important that if it be correct, *The Liberation of American Literature* will hereafter be one of the landmarks in American literary criticism, worthy of a position above even the trilogy of Vernon L. Parrington." Knight then added, "Correct or not, it must be read by every teacher and by every advanced student of American literature." Calverton may have been tempted to bring out the champagne after this acclaim from the academy. If so, such celebration was a little premature. Two months later in the *New England Quarterly*, F. O. Matthiessen (Harvard) completely refuted the misguided reviewers who were touting Calverton as, in Matthiessen's words, a great "pioneering-Marxian critic." It was Calverton's singular misfortune to be taken seriously by this gifted and thorough scholar who was on the way to the highest rank among our literary critics who harbored socialist sympathies.

Though he faintly praised Calverton's view of the frontier as a shaping force and his comments on the effects of social determinism in the work of O'Neill and Jeffers, Matthiessen devoted his review mainly to an unrelieved litany of Calverton's almost grotesque shortcomings and errors. If economic power were a precondition of a national literature, so that we had only a derivative (English) literature to 1914, how did Calverton explain a Thoreau? How could the well-born Anne Bradstreet, arriving in America at age eighteen, be termed by Calverton a member of the petty-bourgeoisie with a colonial complex? How could Upton Sinclair be called our *first* literary radical, when the spirit of revolt was a hallmark of American writers from the beginning? If our bourgeois-afflicted nineteenth century produced no literature of "vigor or vivacity," then what of Whitman and Melville? Throughout, Calverton committed the errors of one who had not read enough of the literature. And he displayed a weak historical sense that he poorly disguised with jargon, clichés, and over-simplified formulations. Matthiessen concluded by offering his own prescription for the responsible Marxist criticism America urgently required, namely, a body of writing "coming to grips with the problem of what the virtues and defects of a proletarian culture in America might really be."[4]

The next year in *The Great Tradition* (1933), Granville Hicks could afford to be more casual in his Leftist approach, thanks to the forest-clearing by Calverton, to whom Hicks acknowledged he was particularly indebted, though he suspected that the *Liberation* would be "superseded by subtler and sounder studies" (pp. 296, 307). Hicks himself was subtler, for he went beyond Calverton's repetitious, limited jargon of Marxism and spoke more variedly of economic forces and social inequities. Indeed, when he spelled out America's literary "great tradition" of social criti-cism aimed toward a revolutionary–collective good, his program-matic statement was not flashed across the preface but reserved, instead, for the final half-dozen pages. Hicks was also sounder than Calverton as a literary critic and tried, like Parrington, to wed his socialistic analyses to considerations of literary art. Hicks admitted his Parringtonian debts, and we discover one of them at once in the early description of the post–Civil War era of Parrington's "great barbecue":

> Farmer and mechanic alike admired the heroes of financial battles, dreamt of speculation, and looked forward to riches. If many were pushed away from the table so luxuriously laden with the fruits of mechanical ingenuity and the gifts of nature to the nation, they knew that the table was there, and they did not despair of finding a place at it. (p. 2)

But wisely, Hicks did not emulate Parrington's richly figurative style, instead cultivating a more literal, expository power derived from his own socialist passions (and blessedly free of the Marx-ist counters of Calverton). Hicks also distanced himself from Parrington's brand of liberalism, reform, and curious sympathy for deviant ironists like Lewis or Cabell. Hicks and Parrington dif-fered, too, in their public involvement, Hicks being the activist who, in 1933, was thoroughly radicalized and in the winter of

1934–35, became a member of the Communist Party. He is crucial to our academic chronicle as the uncommon instance of a professor of American literature who, in deed as well as word, strongly influenced the climate of scholarship and criticism from a vantage both inside and outside the university campus.

Born in New Hampshire in 1901, Hicks was, after a fashion, New England to the bone all his life. In his autobiography, *Part of the Truth* (1965), he recalled his Harvard years, 1919 to 1923, with mixed sentiment but not, like Parrington, with distaste and resentment. A poor boy, he commuted from Framington and never felt close to campus life, though he moved into a dorm his junior year. What he received from Harvard was a climate congenial to critical thought and scholarship. He took Copeland's inevitable English 12 (composition), but was not an admirer of "Copey," the "arrogant little man with his derby and his umbrella and his carefully cultivated mannerisms" (p. 33). More important were Kittredge's Chaucer and Morison's American history. S. Foster Damon tutored him for an honors thesis on Blake's *Milton*. Hicks remembered only one course offering in American literature and like other budding Americanists of the time— familiar story—he educated himself privately and haphazardly. He read *Main Street, Moon Calf, Winesburg,* and *This Side of Paradise* (his generation's "declaration of independence" [p. 34]), and much more. He also advanced his noncurricular education by joining the Liberal Club and hearing various speakers from the political Left, at the same time being active in Universalist Church activities. (Both Tyler and Parrington, it will be recalled, were drawn also to religious studies.) After graduating Phi Beta Kappa and summa cum laude, Hicks chose not to pursue teaching or graduate work, but entered the Theological School for two years. In 1925, he decided that the church was ineffective in shaping social and political attitudes (pacifism, for one), and in the fall, he accepted an instructorship at Smith College to teach multiple sections of the required course in the Bible as literature. The salary was eighteen hundred dollars a year.

The three years at Smith were decisive politically and professionally. Merle Curti, Oliver Larkin, and Harry Elmer Barnes were there. But most stimulating was Newton Arvin, already more socialistic in his thinking than Hicks and more scholarly in his grasp of American literature and criticism. With Arvin, Hicks organized a public meeting in 1927 to protest Judge Thayer's denial of the last plea for Sacco and Vanzetti, and Hicks read the resolution that Governor Fuller appoint a committee to review the evidence. This would not be the last time Hicks was to know strained relations between town and gown. Also jointly with Arvin, Hicks created and taught in the year 1927–28 a course in contemporary British and American literature, which he remembered to be "the most exciting course I have ever taught" (p. 69). He did not mention if political ideology entered the shaping and conduct of the course. Neither did he record sharing with Arvin any of the excitement of *Main Currents* in 1927 or 1928, though we assume that Hicks read his Parrington then rather than later, so that *Main Currents* may have played a part in the decision Hicks made in 1928 to teach and write on American literature. To that end, he took a leave from Smith and returned to Harvard in the fall of 1928.

The graduate year at Harvard established the crowded pattern of Hicks's career. He assisted Bliss Perry, took independent research in William Ellery Channing with Kenneth Murdock, published articles in the *Mercury* and *Forum*, reviewed for *Nation* and Harry Hansen's *New York World*, met Lincoln Steffens after a speech in Boston and Sinclair Lewis at a lunch in New York, and published "Industry and the Imagination" in the *South Atlantic Quarterly*, a piece that marks the genesis of *The Great Tradition*. As that literary history came to completion in two editions over the next six years, Hicks was also engaged in stormy academic and public affairs sufficient for several professional lifetimes.

He left Harvard in 1929 with only an M.A., assuming that he could survive in academia by dint of his mounting publications. President Nielson of Smith, however, did not rehire Hicks, despite departmental support, pleading budgetary restraints. (Hicks suspected that Nielson probably had concluded that his faculty already numbered too many radicals.) But the English chairman from Rensselaer Polytechnic Institute was recruiting young faculty, and Hicks became a professor once again. At Troy, New York, the autumn of 1929 brought for him, in addition to the October crash on Wall Street, a separate academic case of shock: five sections of composition with thirty or more practical-minded students per class; mountains of papers; and an expected daily appearance on campus from nine to five, in the fashion of business America. His strategy for surviving this crushing work schedule was to take on even more work—the writing nearest his heart, and an active public life as a radical intellectual. Besides his writing for the *Nation* and the *World*, he reviewed in *Forum* and *New Freeman*, wrote articles on Hay, Herrick, and Dos Passos (in the *New Republic*), on Hemingway (*New Freeman*), and on writers of the 1920s (*Nation*). Hicks privately discovered Faulkner. And in 1931, Hicks became a manuscript scout and reader for Macmillan. (He counted his written reports over the next thirty years at more than two thousand.) And he was now becoming a name in the New York literary circles, Arvin assured him. As the Depression set in, Hicks became far more political than in his period at Smith. "Why not Communism?" he asked himself en route to Boston in the autumn of 1931 to speak on the business crisis. Lincoln Steffens in his *Autobiography* had recently been asking the question, Edmund Wilson in the *New Republic* was advocating it (but not Party membership), and Arvin had been urging Hicks to it ever since the Crash. But he had resisted. He now read *Das Kapital.* At Yaddo in late 1931, the doom of capitalism was the main subject among liberals Morris Cohen, Louis Adamic, Horace Gregory, and Malcolm Cowley. George Goetz (our V. F. Calverton), meanwhile, invited Hicks to write for *Modern Quarterly.* This pervasive political climate also excited Hicks the literary scholar to write an American literary history along the Marxian lines in which he was now being educated.

In his memoirs, Hicks stated that he began *The Great Tradition* in 1931. At the time, it was as much a pioneering of Marxian literary analysis as Calverton's, for *The Liberation* did not appear until September 1932. Because Harvard had given Hicks very little in the way of American literature, he was catching up on Howells and James in the summer of 1931. In the fall, as we have seen, he was reading *Kapital,* meeting Steffens, and discussing communism at Yaddo. Despite his crowded activities in the months ahead, he made his life all of a piece, and by the summer of 1932, he had virtually completed the rough draft of the history. He dreaded the return to Rensselaer and the teaching in the fall. But he was exhilarated by the clarity with which Marxism was enabling him to interpret the industrial revolution and its effects on American literature. He made a final revision of his book during the winter; the manuscript was accepted by Macmillan in the spring of 1933 (the non-Marxist reader was Yale's William Lyon Phelps); and in September, Macmillan gave a small party to celebrate the publication of a new literary history which, in its turn, was destined to make more literary history.

After half a century, *The Great Tradition* remains a valuable book, and rereading it in the company of the dozens of literary histories that preceded it—the school tradebooks reviewed in preceding chapters and largely written without style or historical and aesthetic method—we realize that in Hicks the academy contributed the ideal literary critic and scholar to a confused and troubled America. With Calverton, Hicks missed many refinements of American, literary, and historical analysis due to his selective Marxist formula; but like Calverton (and Parrington), he brought to his subject a unifying vision that the reader could grasp, weigh, and dispute. From that viewpoint, American literature was conditioned by American life, and the only vital tradition of our literature, furthermore, emerged after the Civil War, the most powerful literary response being shaped by the impact of the machine on nineteenth-century society. The prewar "movement" Hicks summarily treated in an opening chapter, "Heritage." Writers of the preliminary era were unable to envision a humanizing faith in an industrial civilization, though Whitman came the closest. Unfortunately, he could not fully welcome the socialism needed to counter the abuses of capitalism because his vision of the collective good was beclouded with transcendental mysticism and the "deep-seated individualism" it had engendered. But where his idealism embraced the human possibilities of technology, Whitman was "in a sense the founder of the new American literature, the literature of the industrial era" (p. 30).

After the war, the tides of American literary development were influenced by the writers' awareness of powerful economic forces at work in the urban–industrial order. Frontier individualism from the age of Emerson now became robber-baron individualism. Through the next four decades, Hicks traced a dominant contrast between the pioneering, though ineffectual, authors who entered "The Battlefield" of economic and political struggle—Mark Twain and Warner, Hay and Howells, Boyeson and Bellamy—and those who exiled themselves from the industrial present: Jewett, James, Lanier, Adams, Garland, Crane, and the aesthetes of the 1890s. The period ended in the muckraking "Years of Hope," but Norris, Herrick, Sinclair, and London were helpless to go beyond their critiques of business malfeasance because they lacked a binding hypothesis of socialistic change, of the "forces that can transform industrialism" (p. 186). Hicks conceded that a certain renaissance could be felt from 1912 to 1925, but amid all this flowering of expression, he did not discover a single novelist, poet, dramatist, or critic of this middle generation—not Dreiser, Anderson, Lewis, Sandburg, O'Neill, or Van Wyck Brooks—with a perception of the new order that must rise out of the failures of their waning petty-bourgeois class and signal an altered course of industrial capitalism.

For the years 1925 to 1929, Hicks described a variety of inchoate rebellions and feeble commitments among the newer generation. Amy Lowell died (1925) and was posthumously attacked; disaffected aesthetes ran to T. S. Eliot (and he to royalism and the church); and the New Humanists offered a different moralistic escape from problems of a society that was apparently too solidly middle class for the new generation either to accept or overthrow. Joseph Wood Krutch felt that "faith in the emergence of the masses" (p. 263) might be the only hope, but he was not able to embrace such faith, while other pessimists like Jeffers and Faulkner could not even envision the proletarian alternative. To be sure, we also had the Archibald MacLeish contingent with their "capitalist apologetics," who joined writers like Thornton Wilder to serve "a leisure-class culture" (pp. 285–86) and elsewhere were regional escapists or trivial new critics like Yvor Winters and R. P. Blackmur, whose reading of literature reminded one of the "impassioned quibbling of devotees of some game" (p. 283). But something new was also in the air in 1925, as one discovered in the pages of Dos Passos's *Manhattan Transfer.* Though he soon floundered in bewilderment and drift, Dos Passos eventually came out of his confusion to write *The 42nd Parallel* and *1919*, novels in which "all his powers of observation and understanding have been intensified" (p. 290). The precipitating event that had intervened, of course, was the Crash of 1929.

Hicks concluded his analysis of literary movements since the Civil War with a brief look at literature written since the pronounced changes in recent American life. Since literature follows life, the Depression signaled to the best younger writers the end of an era, the old period reaching back to the liberal reformers of the muckraking years. (Here, Hicks wrote in a very few pages a crisp history of twentieth-century radicalism in America.) At present, the transition was marked by Edmund Wilson's advance (in the *New Republic*) from liberalism to communism, by the new consciousness of older writers like Dreiser and Anderson, by the writings of young black authors, and by the proletarian theater of the Provincetown Players. At the close of his period analysis, Hicks voiced a Marxian optimism that these writers "belong to an intermediary stage" and "their work will be superseded in time by a genuine proletarian literature and, eventually, by the literature of a classless society" (p. 300).

When Hicks adjusted his Marxian lenses to define the American characteristics of American literary history, he achieved again a focused clarity at the expense of genuine amplitude and complexity. The American experience, as he viewed it, had been shaped from the beginning by the ideals of bourgeois individualism, and in the nineteenth century, both the industrial revolution and frontier expansion fed the misguided dreams of bourgeois prosperity. Hicks recognized that "many regional cultures" had played a role in our continental development, due to local geographic and economic conditions as well as the transplanting of Atlantic seaboard and European traditions into the West. Had an authentic and enlightened American spirit in literature crystallized from this historical experience? For Hicks, our literary expression had too often been enfeebled because too many American writers avoided the social, economic, and political actualities, preferring to escape into irrelevant religious mysticism or genteel aestheticism. Others did struggle bravely to express and criticize a failed civilization possessing no "social solidarity," but they failed to comprehend the operating forces of industrialism. They were groping for a unifying vision afforded, if they could but grasp it, by a non-American explanation: the Marxian theory of economics and class revolution.

Hicks then demonstrated as a literary historian and critic what Calverton had avoided, how the Marxist approach to American life in literature could be wedded to a judgment of literary imagination, how the timebound mind of the historian might be coupled to the timeless sensibility of the literary critic, and how significant (that is, Marxian) content achieved degrees of successful organic form here and there in American literature. The implicit question, of course, was this: Can there also be a significant literary imagination that is not wedded to Marxism?

Hicks could not wholeheartedly laud any of America's writers, since none envisioned artistically the true desperation of the historical present and the coming of a proletarian state. Along the way, however, he was generous—patronizingly at times—and even voted a socially irrelevant work like Jewett's *The Country of the Pointed Firs* a place in the American literature canon. But among writers within Hicks's liberal family who should have done better, he administered a paternal spanking—to such as Whitman, Mark Twain, and Howells. And the muckrakers, for all their well-intentioned grumbling, were ill schooled in revolutionary theory. The only books of these years that, to Hicks, "deserve to survive" were Norris's *The Octopus,* perhaps Sinclair's *The Jungle,* and (oddly) London's *Call of the Wild* (p. 204). Dreiser gave us living characters because "he shows us the forces that work through them," but his art was clumsy, in part because he "seems always to be heavily stalking some secret that constantly eludes him" (pp. 229, 231). Sherwood Anderson had "the courage to create his own idiom and his own rhythms" (p. 229), but they could not save a flawed social vision that regarded the machine as an enemy.

Only in Dos Passos did Hicks discover the full literary possibilities emanating from the "great tradition" of anti-individualist social brotherhood. This hope for American literature Hicks derived from the growing adequacy of Dos Passos's understanding of post-1929 American life. The optimism soon increased dramatically for Hicks, and two years later, he added a chapter for a revised edition of *The Great Tradition* that celebrated the growth of Marxian-informed proletarian fiction, poetry, and drama in the works of certain others: Herbst, Farrell, Halper, Cantwell, Conroy, Schneider, Newhouse, Fearing, Gregory, and above all, Michael Gold, who was "the important link between the radicalism of the war period and the revolutionary movement of the present" (p. 297). Revolutionary literature now seemed to Hicks to be aesthetically enriched with a breadth of themes, variety of expression, depth of proletarian characterization, and a closeness of texture possible only from a new political awareness, sensibility, and clarity of purpose.

✷   ✷   ✷

Hicks was generally gratified, he confessed, by the academic and intellectual-public reception of *The Great Tradition*. Lewis Mumford praised his philosophical clarity and literary taste, and his completing the work that Brooks, Beer, Parrington, and Rourke had previously offered to a readership less responsive to social change. Mumford did chide Hicks, however, for gradually narrowing his literary inquiry, Calverton-like, away from aesthetic evaluation to the political question that asked which twentieth-century literary works were the most effective instruments of revolution. Malcolm Cowley was sympathetic to Hicks's Marxism and considered his book an effective argument on behalf of the struggle; but Cowley considered Hicks too harsh with writers who failed to achieve proletarian insight (James) or those who could not fully slough off their middle-class psychology (Herrick, Norris, Sinclair) or the regionalists who could not be expected to comprehend the national ramifications of industrialism.

R. P. Blackmur (then a free-lance poet and critic), whose critical work Hicks had termed impassioned quibbling, evened the score by calling Hicks a zealot with one idea (that "economic good is paramount and can subsume . . . the other goods of society"). Hicks also displayed, said Blackmur, defective literary taste and an intolerance for writers who did not engage his predilection for a single-class society. The new leading light of the New Humanists, Norman Foerster (by then moved from North Carolina to the University of Iowa), agreed with Blackmur and then advanced his own one idea. The "'sources of the evils'" that concerned Hicks should be located "in human nature more than in social mechanisms"—the great tradition, in other words, of Aristotle rather than of Hicks's John Reed. The overriding conflict of the time, said Foerster, might be phrased as Hicks's "naturalistic collectivism" doing battle with "a humanistic or religious individualism." But Foerster's dissatisfaction was not shared by other academic compeers—F. O. Matthiessen, Stanley Williams, and Robert Spiller—who granted Hicks mainly congratulatory comment for the cogency of his historical analysis.[5]

Hicks's services to American literature study in the 1930s continued both within the academy (albeit too briefly) and without, and he aided the cause of American Marxism with unabated energy to the close of the decade. In 1933, he joined the Marxist John Reed Club of New York and in January 1934, became literary editor and contributor for the weekly *New Masses*. The following winter, Hicks became a Communist Party member. Meanwhile, he agreed to write the biography of the party's John Reed. Hicks's public activities brought him into occasional controversy, which created uneasiness among Rensselaer officials and alumni. In May 1935, President Ricketts did not renew Hicks's contract, the alleged cause being budgetary "retrenchment." But in the wake of resulting publicity, the AAUP investigated the dismissal and determined that the decision had been influenced by Hicks's "economic and social beliefs." The student newspaper defended him as "'unquestionably the most able and most interesting teacher of English literature in the Institute'" (Hicks mentioned teaching at least one American literature course, too); and, the students added, "'he is also the most impartial.'" A short time after, Hicks was saddened to see that the student staff felt it best to recant their defense of him.[6]

Hicks was, however, far from unhappy to leave the professor's world. In autumn 1935, he applied, successfully, for a Guggenheim Fellowship to write a book on contemporary British authors (published in 1939 as *Figures of Transition*). *Proletarian Literature in the United States: An Anthology,* for which he edited the section on literary criticism, appeared in 1935; so, too, did *One of Us: The Story of John Reed,* consisting of thirty Dos Passos-like commentaries with facing lithographs by Lynd Ward. In 1936, Hicks published the full-scale biography of Reed, with a dedication to Lincoln Steffens, who then proceeded to praise the book in an open letter to the *New Republic*. When Steffens died later in the year, Hicks postponed his Marxist apologia, *I Like America* (completed and published in 1938), to help Ella Winters, Steffens's wife, edit the two-volume *Letters* (1938).

In 1939, Hicks beautifully rounds out our look at Marxist historical and literary advocacy in the 1930s. He was at Harvard for the academic year as a counselor in American history, in the company of Daniel Aaron, Henry Nash Smith, F. O. Matthiessen, and others. Again, there was community unrest over an avowed Communist on the local faculty, even though Hicks, a frail-looking, light-haired man with rimless glasses, was hardly a threatening figure. In the summer, he signed, with others, a statement of faith in Russia for its unwavering opposition to fascism. Then on 22 August, he heard about the appalling Russian–German nonaggression pact. He resigned from the American Communist Party and ended his six-year relationship with the *New Masses*. When that journal refused to print his statement of resignation from the party, he sent the statement for publication in the 4 October issue of *New Republic*. As with many other American Communists and fellow travelers, he discovered at the close of the decade the close, too, of a momentous chapter in his personal and professional life and the life of the nation. His legacy in the 1930s to future generations includes, above all, a distinguished literary history, together with the invaluable biography of Reed; the experiences of a courageous professor revealed in his later autobiography; and not least, a vivid chronicle of the years 1934 to 1939 recorded in his pages for the *New Masses*.[7]

Despite Hicks's climactic farewell to Leftist activism in 1939, our story would be incomplete without briefly noticing one last event in that year, the book of another Marxist critic who reminds us that after ten years, the pages of Parrington continued to influence American liberal scholarship and criticism. This final critic was Bernard Smith, who separately published in the last year of the decade both a tribute to Parrington and *Forces of American Criticism: A Study in the History of American Literary Thought*.

Smith's professional career falls outside the academy, but his *Forces*, like Calverton's work, found mainly an academic home. Despite Smith's growing Marxist persuasion, he was a long-time editor for Alfred A. Knopf. Beyond his editorial chores, however, he managed to enjoy a modest writing career in the company of fellow Leftists. He contributed to Calverton's *Modern Monthly*, and Hicks included Smith's "Huneker and the Tribe," originally printed in *Saturday Review of Literature,* as the culminating essay in the *Proletarian Literature* collection in 1935. (It reappeared in condensed form in *Forces*.) Like Parrington, Smith was a patient scholar who has been remembered for a single work. *Forces,* in fact, was immediatley heralded, on publication, as complementary to *Main Currents.* Unlike some of his other Marxist contemporaries, Smith never disguised or minimized his debts to Parrington. Even three decades later, after Parrington had long been out of favor in the academy, Smith wrote a modest preface to a reissued *Forces* (1971), his admittedly "oversimplified Marxist approach" to intellectual and aesthetic problems in America, and recalled the earlier critical comparison with Parrington: "I was flattered then; I remain flattered" (p. viii). Again in 1939, when he coedited *Books That Changed Our Minds* with Malcolm Cowley, Smith testified to the enormous personal, as well as national, influence of *Main Currents.* For him, an essential Marxian radicalism was implicit therein, though Parrington cast his argument in the Jeffersonian-liberal references acceptable to his American readership. A pre-Depression audience in the times of Coolidge and Hoover, Parrington may have sensed, would not be receptive to the Marxist analysis.

Smith's distinction is that he was the first to write a history of American literary criticism within the spirit of the new social history and to organize it along the lines of Marxian class analysis. (Members of the profession had reason to blush that such a work had not come forth from one of their own.) The historical contours of his survey, therefore, generally coincided with the scheme of Hicks and Calverton, as well as Parrington, and Smith's pages on the first three centuries hold no surprises whatsoever. But in his final three chapters, he strenuously tested the adequacy of modern critical schools against the social, political, and moral values of his Marxist thesis. These chapters remain valuable today because Smith used his critical yardstick skillfully to make fine discriminations among the critical impressionists, socialists, Marxists, liberals, New Humanists, aesthetes, and classicists.

The exhilarating spirit of reinterpretation in American literature scholarship and criticism at the end of the 1920s (see Chapter 15) was not recorded, however, in Smith's pages. He viewed a discouraging scene wherein partisan critics of every stripe appeared variously disillusioned, desperate, or ideologically bankrupt. But with the 1930s, the time seemed ripe for a reinvigorated American criticism, and Marxism provided the catalyst.

Could it reinspire and radicalize erstwhile liberals currently exhausted or stubbornly anachronistic? Probably not. Waldo Frank, Carl Van Doren, Lewis Mumford, Henry Hazlitt, and Joseph Wood Krutch seemed no longer capable of passionate advocacy of any productive cause. Criticism of some value could be found, however, in Matthew Josephson's *The Robber Barons* (1934) and *The Politicos* (1938) and in the work of four other critics: in Michael Gold and his revivified *New Masses* (after 1928), though Gold himself was an inept thinker; in the journalism and scholarship of V. F. Calverton, though he slighted philosophy, ethics, and aesthetics in his Marxian sociology; in Malcolm Cowley's chronicle of the "esthetic nihilists" of the 1920s (*Exile's Return*, 1934), some of whom had become students of Marx; and in the somewhat unpredictable critical career of Edmund Wilson, who showed in his work of the 1930s the increasing sophistication of the best radical criticism.

In the enemy camp at the onset of the thirties, Smith's most prominent adversaries were the New Humanists' platoon of critics, including the several heirs of More and Babbitt: T. S. Eliot, Allen Tate, John Crowe Ransom, Yvor Winters, the editors of *Forum* (since 1928), Seward Collins and his *Bookman,* and occasionally the old warrior More himself; the Freudian's Ludwig Lewisohn; and the once-liberal Van Wyck Brooks, now having drifted into the nationalistic *The Flowering of New England,* a literary history barren of analysis in its "scholarly story-telling" (p. 327). To the degree that Brooks and these other figures strongly affected American literature in the academy, they do, however, command our interest in a separate chapter, Smith's estimate notwithstanding. Meanwhile, with his book, we close out the legacy of Parrington in the 1930s and an advocacy of the Leftist perspective in our literary criticism and scholarship more forceful than we are likely ever to see again in this century. [8]

Chapter 19

More Advocacy in the Thirties: Humanists, Agrarians, Freudians, and Nationalists

In a normal progress of literary criticism and scholarship, the Marxist critics might have sustained their campaign into the 1940s. But World War II profoundly affected that movement. Not only was the intellectual life of the nation disrupted by global conflict, but also the economic process of mobilization, with massive production of weapons, brought the country out of the Depression that had energized Leftist ideology. Nor did our wartime marriage of convenience with Russia obliterate the disillusioning evidence of Communist totalitarianism implicit in the 1939 pact with Germany. In short, Marxism had soon been tainted, and the legacy of Parrington diminished. Both must therefore share the pages of our history with still other ideologies that invaded the academic world with equally ardent commitment and rhetoric, at least in the early thirties. First came a renewal of the humanistic, or anti-naturalistic, campaign of Babbitt, More, Sherman, Brownell, and others that we followed in its inception several chapters ago. In his *Literature and the American College* (1908), it will be recalled, Babbitt had begun his comprehensive indictment of the naturalistic revolution. As a recent historian of the New Humanists succinctly puts it, the modern spirit rampant after the Civil War represented for Babbitt and his allies not only the apotheosis of science and romantic individualism but the wholesale decline of the American academy: "The elective system, vocationalism, the service ideal, and the German tradition all documented for the Humanists the drastic decline of the classical and humanist tradition of the old-time college and pointed to the complicity of the universities in the materialistic culture of the country." [1]

After World War I, Babbitt's own army demobilized along with the country's AEF, and Sherman, we have seen, made his separate peace with the literary moderns. Paul More had begun his Shelburne Essays in 1904 and by the sixth series (1909) was firmly joined with Babbitt in countering the influence of Rousseau by advancing the case for religious dualism. With the eleventh volume in 1921, however, More terminated the series and turned his attention away from the ills of contemporary literature, education, and democracy, leaving the field to others. He now began his volumes on the Greek Tradition and taught it (from 1919 to 1933) at Princeton. After the fourth volume in 1927, he reenlisted in the New Humanist movement, now revitalized with new blood, and assaulted the current aesthetes and realists in American literature while he offered thanks for the responsible criticism of Harvard's Babbitt, Princeton's Mather, Cincinnati's Shafer, and too few others. And he launched a new series of Shelburne Essays.[2]

Babbitt's career in the twenties was only slightly more combative than More's, the notable publication, *Democracy and Leadership,* in 1924, being a collection of Babbitt's lectures delivered at Kenyon, Stanford, and the Sorbonne in the previous four years. The subjects, predictably, were Rousseau and romanticism, democracy and standards of individualism, true and false liberalism, naturalism and free will. Then, like More, Babbitt returned to the fray several years later in the pages of *Forum,* publishing in the month after More's essay on American literature a similar tirade against the reigning literary realism of the twenties. The only surprise was the evidence that Babbitt was, in fact, reading the current American writers. He assailed the fatalism of Dreiser's *An American Tragedy,* the patternless "naturalistic realism" of Sherwood Anderson and Sinclair Lewis, the New York of "epileptic Bohemians" in Dos Passos's *Manhattan Transfer* (termed by More "an explosion in a sewer"), and the "present preposterous overestimate" of Whitman in American poetry. Like More, Babbitt reaffirmed the high office of the critic as creator of standards for writers to come. Lacking such leadership in the 1920s, criticism had become mere self-expression, as in the "gustos and disgustos" of Mencken, whose "writing is nearer to intellectual vaudeville than to serious criticism." And with More, Babbitt challenged the academy to establish cultural standards. Our universities had failed thus far, and "Mr. Mencken's attack on the 'professors' is therefore largely justified; for if the professors were performing their function properly Mr. Mencken himself would not be possible."[3]

New recruits to the New Humanism now included erstwhile bohemian socialist and Freudian, Gorham Munson. G. R. Elliott of Bowdoin was another enthusiast in this second generation of New Humanists. In *The Cycle of Modern Poetry* (1929), he scattered his praises of Babbitt and More among the footnotes. Babbitt responded, again in Henry Goddard Leach's hospitable *Forum,* with an admiring review of Elliott's humanistic categories, and closed with the anti-romantic prediction that since "the Wordsworthians in particular are strongly entrenched in American academic circles, . . . it will be surprising indeed if Professor Elliott does not hear from them."[4]

Robert Shafer also joined in the resurgence of New Humanism after the middle 1920s, his main contribution being *Christianity and Naturalism* in 1926. Joseph Wood Krutch's *The Modern Temper* (1929) more obliquely supported the movement. Though voicing the current skeptical disillusionment and doubt over twentieth-century man's tragic stature, heroic will, and the "confidence in his ability to impose upon the phenomena of life an interpretation acceptable to his desires," Krutch nevertheless came down on the side of the anti-naturalists: "We should rather die as men than live as animals" (pp. 119, 249). Among others who were playing a substantial part was Seward Collins, who succeeded John Farrar in 1928 as editor of the *Bookman.* Even Sherman, posthumously, aided the cause when colleagues at Illinois edited two volumes of *Life and Letters* (1929) that recalled his impressive early service in the movement. T. S. Eliot was sympathetic to the New Humanism in his *Criterion.* Also, he reviewed the profession's *The Reinterpretation of American Literature* (see Chapter 15) as an endeavor of latter-day humanists, "the sanest attempt to criticize and control this post-War America" that had been too greatly influenced by the anti-puritan jibes of Mencken and a "querulous" Van Wyck Brooks. Eliot regretted the provincial zeal with which living American writers were being studied without reference to their European forbears. Though colleges were being liberated from the pedantry of philologists, the present tendency was "to fly to the other extreme: no American college is without a course or two in contemporary literature, and even of contemporary American literature." (We are curious to know who presented Eliot with this misinformation.) He deemed the contributors of *Reinterpretation* to be literary historians wisely sympathetic to the New Humanism, writing under the guidance of the "brilliant" editor, Norman Foerster.[5]

Dogged rather than brilliant may be the word for Foerster. Some half-dozen years before, in *Nature in American Literature* (1923), he had described the American naturism derived from Wordsworth and Rousseau and placed it in relation to classical and Christian traditions in order to "determine in some measure in how far it has enriched man's life and in how far it has tended to imperil his self-knowledge" (p. xiii). To Foerster, Thoreau brought those two high traditions successfully into opposition with science and romanticism, Bryant imparted an Old Testament spirit to American nature, Whittier a New Testament vision, and so on. But Foerster did not indulge in any overt speechifying on behalf of the New Humanism. That would come in *American Criticism: A Study in Literary Theory from Poe to the Present* (1928). Preceding his fifth-chapter summary of twentieth-century criticism, Foerster was seldom programmatic: Poe's reason was a faculty that should have been "aided by the senses and the will" (p. 51); Emerson was too mystical to frame abiding standards; and Whitman's plausible faith in "the slumbering divinity of the average" had been ignored by modern disciples who "describe a very undivine average that generally accepts and occasionally revolts from the physical comforts and mechanical amusements provided by applied science" (p. 222). But the final chapter culminated in a virtual manifesto setting forth the aesthetic and ethical tenets of New Humanism.

In 1930, an annus mirabilis of American critical debate, Foerster reprinted this final essay from *American Criticism* as the climactic chapter in *Towards Standards: A Study of the Present Critical Movement in American Letters*. Three chapters had appeared in the *Bookman*, where Foerster had articulated the New Humanist position on impressionist and historical critics. Ultimately, neither school possessed standards that allowed "a superior vantage point" from which to assess permanent values in literature (p. 104). He prefaced the book (dedicated to Willa Cather and Robert Frost) by wishfully fudging on his title: The humanists had, in fact, already begun to supply the literary standards for the new decade, in and out of the universities; for "the central fact in American literature at the beginning of the 1930's is [quoting Harry Hansen] 'the complete bankruptcy of the naturalistic movement'" (p. ix).

Foerster's rhetoric here sounded fairly moderate in a year of impassioned articles of faith, along with boasts, refutations, and insults emanating from a variety of symposia and manifestos, public correspondence and intemperate reviews. At the center were two critical documents that summed up the New Humanists' program and the answering argument of their enemies. Early in the year, Foerster edited *Humanism and America: Essays on the Outlook of Modern Civilisation*. The reply later in the same year, *The Critique of Humanism: A Symposium*, was edited by C. Hartley Grattan. Surrounding these two publishing events were reviews and attacks on both sides. Seward Collins and his *Bookman* were labeled reactionary, nativist, and even anti-Semitic by a writer in the *New Republic,* while Babbitt, Henry S. Canby, and Carl Van Doren, on 9 May, debated humanism in Carnegie Hall, Van Doren opposing Babbitt, and Canby submitting observations pro and con. Harry Hansen, literary critic of the New York *World,* presided. Several thousand people reportedly attended. Collins on his part rallied his readers of the *Bookman* with corrective answers to the anti-humanist charges leveled by such earlier enemies as Randolph Bourne, Van Wyck Brooks, and H. L. Mencken or later antagonists Burton Rascoe, Edmund Wilson, Malcolm Cowley, and V. F. Calverton. Collins especially savaged Rascoe's chapter in the recent *Critique of Humanism.*[6]

The initial battle cry of 1930 was sent up by the authors of *Humanism and America.* Foerster prefaced the volume with an overweening sense that the decade was ushering in an era of American humanism. "More and more persons," he was convinced, "oppressed with the stale skepticism of the post-war period, are beginning to grow skeptical of that skepticism, and are looking for a new set of controlling ideas capable of restoring value to human existence" (p. vi). He defended the humanists against the naturist's charges that they were reactionary, un-American, puritanical academicians, and he reasserted the modern humanist's "working philosophy seeking to make a resolute distinction between man and nature and between man and the divine" (p. vii). He sensed that the critical young were now pursuing this same "quest of standards" (p. xvi). He dated this new quest at 1928, and the ten essays that followed were presumably a vade mecum of the principles guiding the recent movement.

Physicist Louis T. More (Paul's younger brother) argued that science and the new pseudosciences of psychology and sociology were secondary to humanistic understanding. Babbitt explained one more time how the humanist's discipline and moderation, especially if preached in the academy, would save modern literature and culture from the indiscriminate enthusiasms of naturalism, humanitarianism, and religiosity. Paul More reiterated the appeal to human experience and common sense in the combat against the twin fetishes of pure art (Croce) and pure science (Whitehead). G. R. Elliott assailed the peculiar hubris and blindness of "secular naturism" (p. 92), while T. S. Eliot, writing after his recent conversion to the Church, deemed true humanism inseparable from religion: "The need of the modern world is the discipline and training of the emotions; which neither the intellectual training of philosophy or science, nor the wisdom of

humanism, nor the negative instruction of psychology can give"
(p. 110). The essay amounted to a critique as much as a support
of the movement.

Among the other chapters, Frank Jewett Mather urged a traditional elite patronage of the arts on the part of the social aristocracy, museums, and academy, and Robert Shafer excoriated
Dreiser's naturalism in *An American Tragedy*. Harry Clark (whose
recent adulatory review of Foerster's *American Criticism* had embarrassed the editors of *American Literature*) looked to the university for leadership toward a new humanistic social imagination, promoting the ideal of Emerson's Man Thinking to mediate
between academic aesthetes and philologists. Stanley P. Chase
praised the Southern Agrarians (about whom more in a moment)
for their pursuit of "a firmly rooted literary tradition" (p. 218).
And Gorham Munson summed up the past fifteen years of American literature as less than a renaissance. Critics like Spingarn,
Brooks, and Mencken may have been justified in berating professors who were behind the times, said Munson, but these three
mediocre critics supplied no Arnoldian breadth nor any passion
for standards. The academy, in fact, boasted the only movement
of such breadth and leadership, and within it, "the best living
critics America can show" in the persons of Babbitt and More
(p. 233).

Among the variously scathing reviews that greeted the book,
Lewis Mumford singled out Munson as an "ill-trained and over-
confident" new recruit of the Humanists, though most of his
new-found friends had given the public merely catchwords here
rather than arguments, "a series of anxious negatives and timid
discriminations" rather than a new cultural challenge, so that
these writers would have been well advised to practice their
"canonical virtue—the Will to Refrain."[7] Mumford then joined
fellow reviewers C. Hartley Grattan and Henry Hazlitt in the
quickly assembled response edited by Grattan, *The Critique of
Humanism*, which appeared at the beginning of the summer
(roughly one-third of the chapters were reprints). In a prefatory
note, Grattan described the thirteen contributors as independent
and fair-minded writers, many "formerly preoccupied with es-
thetics" but here engaged in a "general search for the ideals of a
true humanism which is not that of More and Babbitt." Grattan
then led off with an essay on the necessary wedding of humanism and science, "a balance between the individual and the environment," the "causal relation between mind and body" (pp. 7,
24), and he looked for a criticism that addresses literature as a

living experience rather than perverts it into "a source of moral precepts" (p. 29).

Edmund Wilson examined the essays of Babbitt and More in *Humanism and America,* accusing them of misunderstanding the moderns as well as their favored Greeks. To Malcolm Cowley, the New Humanists had devised an incomplete system of ethics (though their aesthetic was therefore richer than the impressionists'); and more seriously, he charged that they were "reactionary professors" showing a "total disregard of social and economic realities," as if their utopian ideal were "the salvation of society through a private school system culminating in a Humanist university" (pp. 67, 74, 70). Hazlitt repeated Grattan's critique of the humanists' dualism, as did Bernard Bandler II, who had shifted allegiances after contributing to Foerster's volume. Burton Rascoe amplified Cowley's image of the cloistered professor, portraying More with "the mind of a Presbyterian Princeton professor" and Babbitt with the mentality of the "Boston Brahmin, holding a university chair, living in academic seclusion from contact with the world of today, happily engaged, like a medieval schoolman, in shadow-boxing with the ghost of Jean-Jacques Rousseau . . ." (p. 127).

Repeated among the remaining chapters were the fallacies of humanism in regard to religious authority: Allen Tate's essay, an earlier version having appeared in Eliot's *Criterion,* reiterated some of Eliot's religious objections, as did Kenneth Burke's chapter. Moralistic literary criteria of the humanists were inspected in the essays by Henry Russell Hitchcock, Jr., R. P. Blackmur, John Chamberlain, and Yvor Winters. Lewis Mumford then completed the symposium with "Towards an Organic Humanism," envisioning all of the issues—aesthetic, psychological, ethical, economic, social, and physiological—in a richly organic, harmonious, humanistic living culture enjoyed by healthy social beings: "The most complete personalities are precisely those that have assimilated the most diverse elements in their cultures and have lived least to themselves" (p. 357).

The New Humanists barely survived the year that had begun so confidently for them in Foerster's exuberant introduction to their pronunciamento. But the *Critique* of their opponents probably had little to do with the ebbing of that momentum. Reviewers of the answering volume found the arguments about as wearisome and repetitious as the humanists' previous manifesto. More injurious were simply the basic imperatives of material survival in an academy and nation at large as the Great Depression was setting in. Such practical matters had not been anticipated in the humanists' philosophy. The fate of their movement after the summer of 1930 can be traced in various events of the scholarly and critical arena, the sputterings of advocacy, counterstatement, and valediction that lingered from year to year through the 1930s. In autumn 1930, Foerster departed the Eastern university scene and transported his doctrine to Iowa, a university that invited him to develop a humanistic program cutting across the departments of classics, German, Romance languages, and English. The next year, George Santayana launched a three-pronged attack on the retreating humanists in *The Genteel Tradition at Bay,* citing their cultural enervation, their absolutism unsupported by supernatural appeals, and the moral adequacy of the naturalism they had assailed. Also in 1931, Matthew Josephson defended another bête noire of the humanists in his *Jean-Jacques Rousseau.* In 1932, Babbitt collected some final essays in *On Being Creative.* He died in 1933, a year in which the *Bookman* became the *American Review* as Seward Collins now threw his support to the Southern Agrarians. In 1934, More produced the second volume of his new Shelburne Essays; Shafer published *Paul Elmer More and American Criticism* in 1935; More's volume III appeared in 1936; and he died the next year.

In 1937, Foerster fired his next-to-last Parthian short in *The American State University: Its Relation to Democracy* (followed by *The Future of the Liberal College*). Writing from his Midwestern base in Iowa, he repeated the critique Babbitt had made against the elective courses and the "service" ideal at Harvard in "President Eliot and American Education" eight years earlier in the *Forum* (January 1929). Foerster came at his assignment well armed with historical knowledge, statistics, and humanist dogma to trace the expansion, mediocrity, and vulgarization of higher education for the masses in America, before and after 1930. In contrast to Foerster's well-informed biases, G. R. Elliott's *Humanism and Imagination* the next year was an undistinguished and out-of-date collection of his essays and reviews, the most notable ones containing his summary impressions of Babbitt, More, and Sherman. Elliott apparently believed the cause of the New Humanism to be salvageable in 1938, for he dedicated the volume to the new generation, the students he had been teaching at Wisconsin, Bowdoin, and Amherst.

★　　★　　★

Closely resembling the New Humanists' aborted resurgence was the program initiated by the Southern Agrarians in the late

1920s. Their landmark document, *I'll Take My Stand: The South and the Agrarian Tradition, by 12 Southerners* (1930) appeared in the same year as *Humanism and America*. Seven of the dozen contributors were literary men and four of these—Robert Penn Warren, Allen Tate, Donald Davidson, and John Crowe Ransom—had been educated at Vanderbilt University and become the Nashville poets who had published the *Fugitive* from 1922 to 1925. With John Gould Fletcher, Andrew Lytle (also Vanderbilt-educated), and Stark Young, they expressed in the 1930 manifesto their new economic and social concerns over the oncoming Depression and merged them with regional literary and cultural interests. In the process, they defined a Southern Agrarian opposition to modern industrial "progress" in America. Their arguments engaged some fine distinctions among the competing literary viewpoints of the new decade. Without citing Parrington, they invoked or echoed his central liberal hero Jefferson, but their Jefferson was, by contrast, the conservative Virginian who advocated an educational system that would cultivate, above all, the gifted student rather than subject an entire populace to more education than it either wished or needed. More directly, the authors challenged the industrial utopia of the Marxists. Warren, in fact, had proposed that the symposium be titled *Tracts Against Communism*.[8]

The Agrarian stand against Communist ideology dominated the group's introductory "Statement of Principles," where the American government was viewed as a non-Soviet agent of industrial control and the Marxian machine the bane rather than the salvation of the modern worker, particularly when that worker happened also to be the farmer. Industrialism warred against a world of nature "mysterious and contingent," and therefore defeated religious humanism, as well as the artistic sensibility: "Art depends, in general, like religion, on a right attitude toward nature" (pp. xxiv, xxv). And Marxism injured the "right relations of man-to-man," in that "the responsibility of men is for their own welfare and that of their neighbors; not for the hypothetical welfare of some fabulous creature called society" (pp. xxv, xxviii). In the individual essays, the writers came around to an embattled stand against the machine as the single agent most destructive of the minds and hearts of individuals in present democratic society. More positively, however, they tried to elaborate a vision of humanism that might allow a wise, resisting, vigilant growth of industrialization in the South. "We can accept the machine," said Stark Young, "but create our own attitude toward it" (p. 355). Emphases surrounding the central program for an organic regional culture and a "religious humanism" varied among the chapters, but the authors suggested in common chorus a vision of humanism presumably more ample than the positions of Babbitt, More, Foerster, and allies. Then Young, in a final essay seemingly written as a summary to the manifesto, repeated the persistent themes: resistance to industrial progress combined with a return to the earlier Anglo-Southern ideal of the elite university would lead to social excellence in the Southern Agrarian vein and avoid the country-club strivings of Northern Babbittry. This qualitative–humanistic goal would guarantee stability amid industrial growth and change. The Agrarian program implied a philosophy to be framed in the question, "What is the end of living?" (p. 358).

For all their cavils with some of the premises of the New Humanists, the Agrarians were spiritual allies of More, Foerster, Elliott, Shafer, Clark, and others, and they were soon to close ranks in common cause. Seward Collins renewed his *Bookman* in 1933 as the *American Review* and proceeded to enlist both schools in his pages over the next five years and nine volumes of that journal's lifetime. Reviews and articles on literature, education, agriculture, sociology, and religion appeared in issues consistently dominated by humanists and Agrarians. Some of these pages found their way into *Who Owns America? A New Declaration of Independence* edited by Tate in 1936 with Herbert Agar of the Louisville *Courier-Journal* (Agar an advocate of redistributing rural landholdings). The volume was a characteristic mixture of Agrarian views on the whole spectrum of regionalism. Fletcher and Young did not contribute to this second—and last—group effort to influence academic and popular opinion on the fecund powers of regionalism to enrich American life. Meanwhile, their movement, like the New Humanism, was running out of steam. Collins's *American Review* ceased publication the next year, though Davidson persisted, collecting his essays in *The Attack on Leviathan: Regionalism and Nationalism in the United States* (1938). But as one historian of the movement writes, "Agrarianism was already a dead issue in 1936." The *Southern Review* had just been inaugurated, and Tate, Warren, and Cleanth Brooks, with others, were soon contributing their talents to a new but related campaign, this time on behalf of an "aesthetic formalism," an effort that would presently revolutionize the academic study and teaching of American literature in the 1940s.[9]

✦   ✦   ✦

Two more movements in literary and cultural advocacy in the 1930s also created an invigorating influence on literary scholarship and instruction in the academy. The Freudians owned in Ludwig Lewisohn a late spokesman to reinterpret the entire American literary tradition, while Van Wyck Brooks (an erstwhile Freudian) returned from a personal crisis to renew, with others, the search for a national ethos and usable past in our literature. In the interests of concision and representative qualities, we may consider briefly the career and works of just these two literary historians, centering on Lewisohn and his *Expression in America* (1932) and Brooks with his *The Flowering of New England* (1936). Were space not a consideration, we could profitably devote additional pages to influential work by comparable figures in and out of the profession—Newton Arvin, Lewis Mumford, and even more important, Edmund Wilson. His criticism by the early 1930s had comprehended nearly the gamut of the present chapter, from humanism (including the related issues of naturalism and even symbolism) to Freud, to the nationalistic considerations that also link Wilson, through his international Marxism, to the preceding chapter as well. Ironically, his admirable versatility among modern literatures renders any single book by Wilson less illustrative here than ones by Lewisohn and Brooks.[10]

Lewisohn made his contribution to American literature study chiefly in *Expression in America,* where he was no less passionate than the Marxists, Humanists, and Agrarians in advancing his doctrine of literature and society. Eight years before, he had stated an aversion to all literary advocacy. In *The Creative Life* (1924), a volume of journalistic pieces, he wrote of the ideal critic, "No partisanship must curb his humanity, no prejudice blunt the sensitiveness of his spirit" (p. 95). The volatile Lewisohn was not likely to admit that his partisan campaign against puritan repression in American literature and life might either blunt his sensitiveness or curb his humanity. He had nursed this fierce dislike of Pauline thou-shalt-nots ever since his youth and could date his discipleship to Goethe and Freud almost as long. Born in Germany in 1883, he grew up in South Carolina where his mother tutored her precociously literary son for entry into the American high school. When he chronicled his early Americanization in *Up Stream* (1922), Lewisohn remembered how he was taunted as a foreigner and Jew and victimized by his American adolescent, puritan-induced sexual guilt. English literature became his refuge and sublimation, and after graduating from the College of Charleston (B.A., 1901), he entered the Columbia graduate school.

Disguising various persons and places in his vitriolic memoirs, he recalled an American literature seminar with Professor Brent (Trent) and friendship with fellow student Ellard (William Ellery

Leonard). After the M.A., Lewisohn was too confused about his identity to complete the doctoral dissertation. Trent rebuked him but helped him to a job with "Single, Leaf and Company" (Doubleday Page). After some half-dozen years of literary hack-work and journalism, he tried, again with Trent's help, to enter the academic life. Refused positions, as he believed, because he was Jewish, Lewisohn finally joined Leonard at Monroe (Madison, Wisconsin) and taught German for a year before moving on to Central City (Ohio State at Columbus). Over the next eight years, which spanned World War I, Lewisohn defined his quarrel with the American academy. The campus was a dismal gathering place of job-seeking students apathetic toward the humanities. Their professors were intellectually inert and craved the conservative American's moral respectability and securities of hearth and home. Lewisohn also defined his early stance as a critic: He was an economic socialist but the advocate of personal and moral individualism; in literature, he deemed himself a "liberal" on the side of "creative" protest and rebellion. His sympathies lay with Masters, Anderson, Dreiser, and Lewis rather than Stuart Sherman and Hamilton Wright Mabie.

After Ohio State, Lewisohn was drama editor of *Nation* (1919) and then its associate editor (1920–24) under Oswald Garrison Villard. His writings there, as well as for Henry Canby in the *Evening Post*, expressed his rationale of an aesthetic liberalism. These he collected in *The Creative Life*. He made it especially clear that the university professor was a primary enemy of creative expression in American literature, as well as a "hundred percenter" apologist for conservative trustees, the Republican Party, and the Main Street Babbitts of middle-class righteousness, repression, conformity, and acquisitiveness in American life. More positively, Lewisohn was fashioning a rather amorphous literary credo after Arnold, Freud, and the universal precepts of Goethe, which would guide his odyssey through American literature eight years later. Despite the national upheavals after October 1929, he proceeded to write *Expression in America*, mainly guided by the "method of knowledge associated with . . . Freud."[11]

By adhering to Freudian dogma, Lewisohn not only discovered the center for his attack against the general public enemies of healthy experience in American life and literature, but also confronted two more definable antagonists of the day—the misinformed Marxist critics and the university professors. Among the latter, his chief enemies were New Humanists More and Babbitt, though he also assailed the foolish recent revivalists of the unhealthily repressed Melville and the "dull and formal" and less-than-candid critics of Whitman. And quite uncandidly, Lewisohn regretted that he must break his "rule to remark upon no previous critics or historians of our literature" to deplore the cheap shot the late Professor Parrington directed at modern Freudian interpreters of American authors (though Lewisohn himself "gravely" doubted Van Wyck Brooks's version of a Freudian ordeal for Mark Twain [pp. 180, 218]).

How valuable has *Expression* been to scholars and critics since 1932? Many are well aware now that the book has serious weaknesses. Lewisohn's Freudian formulae led him into a slipshod, emotional, and anti-academic method of treating periods, modes, genres, themes, and individual texts. Through it all, however, he has been for scholars and teachers of American literature one of the most influential and quotable of all our literary historians, and his book therefore deserves here a few pages of serious reconsideration.

In his introduction, Lewisohn termed his study "a kind of history of literature . . . that shall limit itself to the record of essential expression of the spirit of man" (p. xxviii). He was more precise shortly after: "The whole of our modern literature is a single act of rebellion"—against puritan dualistic doctrines (p. 2), though he also noted within this single act "the story of successive moral revolutions" (p. xxxii). Through these successive periods of moral revolution or liberation, he presented his liberal-versus-conservative dialectic to define American life, character, and ideas, and their expression in our national literature. Unlike the Marxists, his oppositions were moral rather than economic, a life-affirming Goethean and Freudian spirit in combat with the ethos of puritanism.

Earlier in *The Creative Life,* Lewisohn had regarded as pedantically contrived any theory of the evolution of literary genres. To a degree, he recanted in *Expression.* He recognized a rise of fiction, drama, and essay in the modern revolt and a decline (since the earlier twentieth century) in verse. He noted Irving's creation of a popular Americanized "*genre,* the fantastic, legendary tale" (p. 46), the displacement of Hawthorne romance by the modern novel which, in turn, evolved out of a feebler sectional novel (pp. 233, 288, 293) and had reached an apogee in 1932 in the work not of Faulkner but Hemingway (pp. 520, 521). At the same time, Lewisohn dissolved certain historical distinctions of form and mode. "Naturalism or realism is a permanent mood and method of human art," he wrote, with a blithe indifference to modal definitions and historical setting and evolution. Equally anti-historical was his view of expression as the work of three "types of the poetic mind": These were the tribal spokesman or bard; the peacetime edifier, refined wordsmith and entertainer, or "artificer"; and the "creative or eternal poet." Lewisohn's historical confusion was nicely summed up in this commentary:

> Each of these types corresponds to a phase and to an epoch of human development. To a phase rather than to an epoch. For human development is evidently not uniform. Each period is thronged with survivals from former periods, and throw-backs will occur from time to time. (p. xix)

Moreover, these three figures could appear not only in the same period but also, as in the modern case of the ubiquitous artificer, within all of the literary genres or (Lewisohn's term) guises (p. xxi).

Unlike his contemporaries, Lewisohn had gained, he believed, a morally creative and definitive vision of American character that would demonstrate the beginnings, growth, and continuing blight of the Calvinistic spirit in American life and letters. Cotton Mather and Edwards best represented the absurd Manichean moral pathology of John Calvin that had formed American character and "folk-beliefs" up to the present day. This smothering Anglo-Saxon morality continued throughout the nineteenth century in the anglophile-genteel snobbery present from Washington Irving to Brander Matthews (Lewisohn's academic nemesis during the Columbia years), though the American spirit had been periodically invigorated by the cultural influence of continental immigration. From these foreign sources, a healthier American folk character originated in the Middle West, apart from the dominant Eastern gentry, especially in Lincoln's land "of freedom and of mercy, of justice and of peace" (p. 195). The modern American novel had its origins, also, in the literary treatment of the Mississippi Valley's "rude peasantry," the work of Eggleston and Howe (p. 276). (Lewisohn's emphasis here, be it noted, was on an earthy, rather than a proletarian-class, literature.) He refused to assign environmental causes to this Western American spirit and subsequent turn-of-the-century literary flowering, since he claimed that both authentic voices and mere "artificers" had sprung from identical soil. Still, this nineteenth-century spirit did not successfully liberate American life and literature in the twentieth century. Powerful genteel publishers of the time supported other sectional writers like Bret Harte, who invented the American short story, a form having, suitably for genteel readers, the "structure of a neurosis . . . an inability to face the realities of either the self or the world" (p. 284). In the schools, the transcendental revolt of Emerson and Thoreau was taught as a harmless doctrine of individualism without reference to passional acts of nonconformity and revolution. The conservative academy, servant of genteel America, also insulated itself against the liberating expressions of an authentic American folk culture.

When he turned to his office of the literary historian as literary critic, to explicate and judge individual authors and works, Lewisohn was usually consistent but also rather vaporous. He demanded that the creative artist (distinguished from the bard and artificer) forge a powerful expression of the human spirit, to achieve "the enlargement and clarification of experience" (p. x). The task of this artist was never easy, for the genteel society of puritan America was in conspiracy against the Emersonian rebel and heretic. Still, man was ever "a speaking and singing animal and he speaks and sings, whenever he is not corrupted by professors and politicians, of what stirs his heart or touches his vital interests without regard for propriety or genteel morality or decorum" (p. 100). Lewisohn's intermittent touchstone of literary "intensity, of severity, of absorption in the concrete coil of things" was by way of Goethe, however, rather than Emerson, who had been unable to plumb the depths of experience and art like the German genius. In the late chapter on modern critics, Lewisohn elaborated his literary credo in an extended digression on Goethe. (In 1949, he published a two-volume study of his German master.)

Lewisohn's critical method, then, was an impressionistic registering of Goethean passion in the works of our variously repressed authors, their national and psychological plight explainable with the aid of Freudian insight. Lewisohn's own passion and eloquence, in turn, covered up a host of deficiencies within his critical principles and style of explication. To him, the modes of realism and naturalism were interchangeable, poetry was a useful Aristotelian term to discuss prose genres, and though he made a passing try at generic definition of the novel, nouvelle, and tale, Lewisohn also defined the short form in American fiction, as we have seen, as simply "the structure of neurosis." Indeed, on one occasion, he termed the entire work of Poe, Melville, and Hawthorne "expression that has the structure of neurosis" (p. 154). Yet he insisted that they were nevertheless creative artists and therefore to be interpreted by deeply private, not national, criteria, for the pervasive repressions of American life determined and limited only the works of bards and artificers. For our literary geniuses, then, Lewisohn disjoined the aesthetic result from any historical cause. Otherwise, puritanism might be credited with providing a profound impulse for some of our most distinguished literary art. For Lewisohn, expression and repression in America were thus locked in a riddle that his Goethean and Freudian categories never quite clarified.

For his canon of American literature, Lewisohn rejected much and approved little. An unsettling intensity of expression was, expectably, his impressionistic criterion of art, but he was as inept as most of the literary historians before him to explain how that intensity or passion occurred in the literary act. At times, he casually required "form with substance" in the work he cited or quoted. Some of his canonical judgments: Emerson's "Self-Reliance" was the "most revolutionary document in modern literature" (p. 124); once, in *The Scarlet Letter*, Hawthorne dealt with "central things," with "normal guilt, with genuine passion," and he "universalized the concrete" (p. 181); *Huckleberry Finn* was "a masterpiece despite the breakdown of form in the last fourth" (p. 231); Howells once struck a "deeper and impassioned note" in his best novel, *A Modern Instance* (p. 249); and though James only observed and never shared "normal passions," Lewisohn listed eight distinguished stories (including "The Pupil" and "The Turn of the Screw") "in which frustration and tragedy spring from inherent and permanent qualities" (p. 272). By contrast, *Walden* fell short of greatness through puritan aberrations, as in the segment "Higher Laws" (p. 151); Melville, who forever "fumed and fretted over the demon in his soul," created in *Moby-Dick* only a meandering and verbose work, "fierce and broken" (pp. 186, 192); *Leaves of Grass* as a whole was disunited, "enervating . . . and unendurable" (p. 207), and Lewisohn, the spokesman of Freudian liberation, the opponent of America's repressive gentility, attacked Whitman on the most unlikely count—his noncomformist sex life:

> I, at least, range myself morally—if not aesthetically and philosophically—with those who out of a sound and necessary instinct, the instinct after all of life and its continuance, rejected the barren homosexual and his new-fangled manner of neither speech nor song and acclaimed and still acclaim Mark Twain. (p. 213)

At the turn of the present century, Lewisohn's brief roll call of excellence began with Moody's "Ode in Time of Hesitation," Norris's *McTeague* ("impassioned exactness," p. 322), and *The Education of Henry Adams,* "not only a great but a crucial book" because of Adams's treatment of sexual power (p. 347). In a trio of works, *Sister Carrie, Spoon River Anthology,* and *Babbitt,* Lewisohn praised the revolutionary theme of sexual liberation— "the terribly sore spot in American life has been and still is in the sex life of the vast majority" (p. 470)—but he questioned their longevity as literary art. On that count, he liked Hemingway for the "strong sensuous experience and power of communicating it" in *The Sun Also Rises* and the "quite beautiful . . . affirmation and not the denial of passion—passion of indignation and passion of love" in *A Farewell to Arms* (p. 519). By the same criterion, Lewisohn dismissed Stephen Crane, whose "work lacks the sap of passion" (p. 321); Herrick, who never attained a "fusing fire" (p. 468); and Sherwood Anderson, hampered by "inner censoring forces" (p. 485). In Faulkner, Lewisohn recognized passionate hatred and pain but could not abide the "needlessly intricate and essentially confused books" (p. 521). O'Neill's most satisfactory work, because "most impassioned," was *All God's Chillun Got Wings* (p. 549).

Among modern poets, Lewisohn granted highest rank, and more than eight pages of comment, to the "intensity and elevation" of his one-time classmate at Columbia, William Ellery Leonard (p. 561). Though American poets were in the vanguard of the current movement beyond naturalism and giving birth to a new poetic diction (learned from the naturalists), he regretted in Robinson an intricacy without a "fusing ardor" (p. 558), a nihilistic despair in Cummings, and in Eliot "a despair so deep that it shatters form" (p. 587). Eliot's recent Anglo-Catholic conversion replaced a "desert of despair" with an equally dismal "refuge of blank authority," so that Lewisohn could only predict for him a place "among the minor poets and characteristic phenomena of the post-war period." He reminded the naïve youth who clung to Eliot that, unlike their idol's sterile conceptions, "the creative imagination is at one with life and its procreative processes" (p. 587).

For the spirit and shock of such opinions, Lewisohn and his book received a wide reception among public and academic critics. Even some offended reviewers welcomed the vivacity and style of *Expression*. These mixed responses came from old-line liberals, academic scholars, and Marxist hard-liners. Carl Van Doren wrote in *Nation* that *Expression*, "incidentally a superb history of American literature, is primarily a moral epic of America." He welcomed Lewisohn's revised canon of American literature, a challenge to university professors who could not let go of their special interest in the New England group, probably because they had not learned yet how to teach Twain, James, or

Dickinson. To John Macy, Lewisohn's Freudian liberalism was rather anachronistic, for the battles had largely been won some years before. Macy also thought Lewisohn irresponsible for indiscriminately labeling every American evil "puritan." He was also amateurish and confused as a Freudian analyst of Melville, Hawthorne, Whitman, James, and others. Even so, Lewisohn's was clearly "a distinguished mind and a passionately honest heart," and *Expression* "wise and eloquent" for students, a far more stimulating introduction to American literature than the wearisome handbook histories of the past.

Howard M. Jones agreed with other critics that Lewisohn did not adequately understand puritanism and foreign influences. In addition, he was less than expert on Freud, and he committed foolish errors in judgment and detail. In his less crotchety and formulistic moments, though, said Jones, Lewisohn was a critic of great subtlety. Ernest Leisy considered Lewisohn weak in establishing the cultural setting of our literature. And of course, he had leaned too heavily on sexuality to test the strengths of books and authors. Still, *Expression* was an "important, challenging book." More hospitable yet was Joseph Wood Krutch. "Schoolmarms and professors have rendered the American classics rather more dusty than most," he wrote, "but Mr. Lewisohn will encourage many readers to blow that dust away." Krutch's verdict: "I know no other book on American literature more genuinely stimulating." The review was admirably positive in view of Lewisohn's qualified estimate of Krutch, though Lewisohn may have read these comments as further evidence of Krutch's growing eclecticism.

Among other reviews, the one by Granville Hicks in the *New Republic* is of greatest interest, since publication of his Marxian *Great Tradition* was imminent. To Hicks, expectably, Lewisohn's primary use of Freud did not illuminate the personal and environmental causes of literary expression in America. Lewisohn, moreover, was a befuddled half-way determinist, separating sexual experience from environment and inconsistently arguing both creative individualism and the influence of the collective culture (as in the dodge of attributing environmental pressures to the work of bards and artificers but not to "creative" writers). Hicks liked the attention to social, political, or economic influences on Mark Twain, Howells, Spingarn, or Babbitt, but Lewisohn seemed unwilling to press on to the deepest underlying causes. Why? Hicks psychoanalyzed Lewisohn: Bourgeois America had rejected this German–Jewish immigrant. He became a heretic and rebel; but he also wanted to be accepted by middle-class America. Too confused to adopt a radical social-political-economic analysis of American experience, he followed other liberals who shadow-boxed with merely symptomatic social evils of puritan America, whether past or present.[12]

Lewisohn was chiefly stung by the jibes of the Marxians, as he presently admitted in *The Permanent Horizon: A New Search for Old Truths* (1934), a book that was to be his virtual leave-taking apologia after the critical zenith of *Expression*. With his usual emotionalism, he observed the current decline of international communism at the same time that he warned against the continuing danger of its mischievous logic. Among chapters on the Marxians' fallacy of mechanistic progress and their anti-humanistic denial of the individual's moral choice in love, religion, and the arts, Lewisohn declared his loyalty to a creative, intellectual, liberal–bourgeois individualism. It included property ownership and world peace, "security, dignity, privacy, liberation from sordid care for the sake of cultural disinterestedness" (p. 31). The chapter was titled, "A Bourgeois Takes His Stand," mocking not only the jargon of his radical adversaries but perhaps also the recent manifesto of the Southern Agrarians. Like these latter, and the New Humanists, Lewisohn, too, had taken the remarkable advent of the 1930s, with its confusion and upheaval, to be his high opportunity for critical advocacy and ascension. Like them, he was departing the scene at mid-decade. The Freudianism he had championed, however, would maintain much of its explanatory force in American literary criticism and scholarship during many years to come.[13]

* * *

As it had been for the New Humanists, Southern Agrarians, and the Freudian Lewisohn, the early thirties became for Van Wyck Brooks an opportunity to tailor and promote his critical doctrines during an interim period of hesitation and doubt. Always closely identifying his personal situation with a perceived state of the nation, Brooks recalled that in 1931, when he emerged from a four-year breakdown, "a kind of murky mental weather had set in with the thirties that was unlike the clarity of the decade before."[14] That clarity of the 1920s, for Brooks, initially had been the American intellectuals' and writers' singular sense of diffidence, disillusionment, failure, and alienation. That mood was followed, after mid-decade, by the American mind's turning homeward and reembracing national values—in Parrington's *Main Currents,* Sandburg's Lincoln, and the neo-Americanism of Constance Rourke, Harold Stearns, and Edmund Wilson:

"One could scarcely maintain any longer the negative view of the twenties" (p. 507). Brooks, too, had turned from the anti-puritanism of *The Ordeal of Mark Twain* (1920) and the critical view of alienation in *The Pilgrimage of Henry James* (1925) to a positive Emersonian embracement of America.

Unhappily for Brooks, the transition from James to Emerson was also a period of "irresolution" that carried him into "a formidable nervous breakdown," a veritable "season in hell" (pp. 432, 437). Himself emotionally and intellectually separated from the cataclysmic events at the turn of the decade, Brooks yet remained a presence in the mind and work of others. In 1928, Professor T. K. Whipple (California), in *Spokesmen: Modern Writers and American Life,* acknowledged Brooks as the most influential critic of our civilization; the next year, Waldo Frank's *The Rediscovery of America* echoed Brooks's ideals of cultural community and the creative uses of our past; and in 1930, Matthew Josephson wrote *Portrait of the Artist as an American* in a spirit of sentimental alienation and despair that the neo-Emersonian Brooks would probably have read with a troubled shock of recognition, recalling that only short years before he, too, had been there. Also in 1930, the New Humanists were trying to account for Brooks, the one-time renegade student of Babbitt, in their rejuvenated program. Norman Foerster, in an otherwise fretful essay, was pleased that "both Mr. Mumford and Mr. Brooks agree with their humanist contemporaries in insisting upon the quest of a usable past, even if they disagree as to what past is usable." [15] As for Mumford, he published in 1931 *The Brown Decades: A Study of the Arts in America, 1865–1895,* which linked him to the cultural nationalism of his close friend Brooks and their ally Constance Rourke, whose folk-oriented *American Humor* also appeared in 1931.

In 1932, Brooks himself fully reentered the critical and scholarly arena with the publication of *The Life of Emerson,* the manuscript essentially completed before his collapse in 1927 and revised thereafter by Lewis Mumford. Brooks's return was heralded within the academy by Howard Mumford Jones, who incisively described the portrait of Emerson as an unstructured prose poem strongly tinged with nationalistic ardor, "an almost model case of a great personality freely developing under American conditions." Jones welcomed this radical new direction in Brooks after the American "'stench of atrophied personality'" (quoting Brooks) in his earlier portraits of Mark Twain and Henry James. A professor who was less than enthusiastic about the resurgent nationalism that had been filling the air, however, was the latter-day New Humanist Harry Clark. In the next year, he dreaded that Brooks, Parrington, Pattee, Mumford, and others had sounded the call too many years now for a naïve literary chauvinism that hearkened back to the youthful debates of the previous century. Without referring to Brooks's recent book, Clark argued that Emerson, in fact, had espoused a transcendent Americanism, one that elevated the democratic ideal into the Platonic One, the humanists' "universal mind."[16]

Not only a literary brand of nationalism was being heard after 1930. As historian Charles Alexander explains, the essence of economic planning was also infused with the national spirit (to pave the road to recovery, "Buy American"). So, too, were our radical politics, to the end that "even international Communism recognized the power of nationalism when it adopted the Popular Front strategy." Most of the American intellectuals who turned to the Left meant to emulate but not to embrace mother Russia. The impulse was essentially national.[17] Though Brooks was never to become a political activist of the radical stripe in the 1930s, least of all a Marxist, he admitted that he "had always been a socialist on the understanding that the levelling was to be not down but up" (p. 533). And he had always envisioned a supportive community of American writers, professors, and intellectuals. By the midthirties, that dream was apparently materializing: "I took part in the newly born League of American Writers, an outgrowth of the American Writers Congress of 1935 that was intended to bring intellectuals together" (p. 534). Somewhat modeled after the earlier John Reed Clubs, the league opposed fascism and war. Their ideal of community, together with the leadership of his old friend Waldo Frank, fired Brooks with a new sense of mission. He became a member of the league's National Council, and after the Second Congress in June 1937, where Newton Arvin, Granville Hicks, and Malcolm Cowley spoke (Cowley's *Exile's Return* had recently portrayed the difficulties of Americanism in the 1920s as viewed by a more engaged Cowley in 1934), Brooks was elected one of seven vice presidents, and chairman of the Connecticut branch of the league. Indeed, he had recently been, as well, the socialist candidate for the Connecticut legislature. In November 1938, he spoke at a league meeting in New Haven and urged members to discover our models of communalism not in Russia but in the American tradition of Jefferson. (The speech was reprinted in the league's *Direction* together with Granville Hicks's rejoinder that Brooks did not understand communism.) Meanwhile, Brooks was growing leery of interloping nonwriters, "political sitters-in who were taking

the League over for the communist party" (p. 535), thereby sully-
ing the purpose of a literary guild. Nor was he encouraged by the
current purge trials in Moscow. He resigned, with other members, after the Stalin–Hitler pact of August 1939.[18]

*   *   *

In 1936, Brooks made another contribution to the cause of cultural freedom and nationalism with the publication of *The Flowering of New England*. (The year after, he donated the manuscript
at a league sale—it brought eight hundred dollars—to benefit
the Spanish Loyalists). In this first of five volumes of literary-
period histories, he reaffirmed his American faith expressed in
The Life of Emerson and now presented it within the New England contexts of our first era of national literature. In his *Autobiography,* he recalled the immediate genesis of the histories. In
1931, in St. Augustine, Florida,

> in a ramshackle plantation house, under a magnolia tree covered
> with blossoms, and with mocking-birds flitting to and fro, I began to
> read for *Makers and Finders,* my focus of interest for twenty years to
> come. I had already set out to see the country I was to write about,
> and, after hundreds of nights during my illness when I heard the
> clock strike every hour, I had formed the habit of rising with the
> sun. (p. 504)

His motive, or mission, remained as before, to recover a usable
past for American literature writers and students. But the literary problem by 1932 had been exacerbated by the anglophobic
diatribes of Mencken and the haughty anglophilia of Eliot, so
that "along with the sense of the past, the sense of nationality
had also been largely effaced in the expatriate twenties." Nor had
the professors helped the cause: "It seemed to me that this literature and art had by no means been explored, although there were
teachers of them in all the universities" (pp. 512, 519).

The overstatement in the last comment illumines Brooks's
sometimes emotional treatment of historical fact. At his best,
however, he set a rigorous standard of scholarly industry and
thoroughness. His regimen beginning in 1932 was to rise at
5:30 A.M., dress ceremonially in waistcoast and tie, and assault
his reading list of some 825 books for volume I. On three-by-five
cards, he recorded paraphrases and quotations from his authors,
though he ignored chronological order. (The cards are now deposited in the University of Pennsylvania Library.) In the winter
of 1932–33, he despaired that *The Flowering of New England*

would ever emerge from his "'torture chamber.'" But he was also inspirited by this immersion in the American past and experiencing the American present during travel to Maine in summer and Florida in winter.[19] In 1934, he was again discouraged by his slow progress and wrote to Mark Howe that he didn't know "'how to use [his] thousands of notes.'" He realized that he was unable to "'think in the expository form.'"[20] Aware of his research habits, we must deem it a miracle that *Flowering* ever saw the light of 1936. But in that summer, it appeared.

Given Brooks's aversion to chronology and the expository form, we can anticipate something less than the literary historian's passion for causal analysis. For this story of earlier nineteenth-century New England (1815 to the Civil War), he made only a pass at chronological order. The chapter titles betrayed a conception that centered on separate people and places, with a blithe disregard for overlapping chapters. The continuity frequently was determined by the impressionistic logic or whim of the author. Crucial dates of works and events were often missing. Oddly, in his conclusion, Brooks referred to his "phase of American culture" as a "movement of mind," as if he had been tracing a history of ideas being cultivated by his writers in their environment. And he then proposed that the "movement . . . followed the typical pattern of the 'culture-cycle,' as Spengler convincingly described it" (p. 539). But after a page or more of vague application of Spengler to "the New England mind" ("not to press a formula too far"), Brooks abandoned the analogy in favor of an ahistorical formula of the New England flowering—it matched D. H. Lawrence's spirit of the "'living, organic, believing community'" (p. 541).

In his most impressive pages, Brooks interpreted the Americanness of his writers and works. These were, of course, the issues of literary nationalism that had always been his special domain. Though his subject was ostensibly regional—one Southern Agrarian professor, John Wade (Georgia), snidely called Brooks's Yankeedom "a thing definitely apart from the United States"—Brooks viewed his references here and in the later four volumes to be national: "It was part of my purpose to bring the sections together and create a feeling for the nation as a literary whole" (p. 515).[21] The New England character in the nineteenth century was, therefore, national in its gradual liberation from English dependencies and the absorption of native American experience. Where vestiges of the colonial did remain forty years after Bunker Hill, the Boston mind was "timid, cautious, and derivative" (p. 16), though a classical training endowed the educated of

Boston, at least, with strong character and mind. Brooks affirmed, in a mixed metaphor, that "the ferment of the rising generation might be expected to break" the literary "yoke" of Europe (p. 16). Even along the coast and the hinterland, "a fresh and more vigorous spirit was astir" (p. 47). Rather than trace the evolution of literary forms, Brooks viewed the literature as an organic flowering of New England experience and expression usually among writers of a separate bent within the shared region, though he allowed that Cambridge was distinctly a literary community and so, too, were Concord and Salem and Boston. Writers like Emerson, Longfellow, Hawthorne, and Thoreau differed, therefore, in their cultivation of the native flowers. Although Holmes declared in Europe, "'I am a Cambridge boy!'" his poems of a homely Yankee world, on the other hand, were "composed in forms that English and Scottish poets had made familiar" (p. 356).

The comment on forms turns us from Brooks's sometimes confident, sometimes tentative forays into the New England, American, and cosmopolitan spirit of the New England flowering and leads us to his aesthetic definitions of the literature. Rigorous terminology, it must be admitted at once, was exceedingly rare in Brooks. Neither did he ever learn how to analyze the literary text itself nor the aesthetic characteristics of a literary period, movement, school, mode, and genre. (In the next twenty years, he periodically groused about the jibes of his adversaries in the academy, the New Critics, who, to Brooks, dissected and worshipped technique in American authors and yet were incapable of registering intelligent responses to literary content.) And so we were advised by Brooks that Emerson ranged from artless doggerel to sublime intensity: "His work was only good when it was great" (p. 275). On Lowell: "Of all the younger writers, he was the most adroit and the most accomplished" (p. 327). Holmes's "rhymes of an hour were fresh, adroit, correct," and "no one else could have written" his longer poems (pp. 365, 367). Brooks also was able to judge the style by the man: "These poems [of Thoreau] were of a homespun kind, well-woven, but indifferently cut, like Henry's raiment, not intended to please" (p. 303).

The chapter on Hawthorne in Salem showed Brooks at his best and most characteristic, not as an orthodox literary historian and critic but a passionate pilgrim revisiting a usable past and vividly reenacting the early experiences, indoors and out, that nourished Hawthorne's genius and many of the specific pages of his fiction (see pp. 221ff.). Today, Brooks must be read, above all, for the pleasure we may derive from his narrative voice, his recreation of historical settings and people, and finally, from his distinctive literary passion. Like Parrington nine years before, Brooks won the Pulitzer Prize in part, we assume, for the quality of his own literary art. The champion of Parrington will see him as superior to Brooks not only as an historian but also as a stylist. From the tough-minded Parrington, we were entertained not only by description of his liberal New Englanders but also, unlike Brooks, by the many acidic portraits of his adversaries there, figures that to him were rather imperfect and sometimes unlovely participants in the march of historical and literary events. Accordingly, Parrington also fashioned for his livelier purposes a varied, tart, and earthy imagery. Brooks does finally coerce us, however, to admire his staying power in page after page of intense literary appreciation of his Cambridge and Boston and various points west, north, and south of that mecca, along with the populous array of New Englanders who entered, departed, and reentered his pages.

The stylistic evaluation of Brooks's *Flowering* was limited by the irony that scholarly critics shied away from quoting or overly praising his style due to an embarrassed fear that the phrases might have belonged not chiefly to Brooks but to an author whose exact words he was casually appropriating into the web of his lyrical tapestry. F. O. Matthiessen, for one, hesitated to commend Brooks's style out of suspicion that it might be, say, Holmes he were praising. (Brooks pilfered especially from Emerson and Thoreau.) Another misgiving by reviewers from within the academy was that unacknowledged quotation was a method verging on scholarly irresponsibility. Kenneth Murdock complained that necessary contexts were thereby missing for all but the most specialized readers. Austin Warren (Boston University) appreciated Brooks's apparent distaste for scholarly apparatus, but "the gain in smoothness of intersticing seems too slight to compensate for the uncertainty with which the reader is infected. Which are, which are not, the *ipsissima verba*?"

Critics from the academy were also the most severe on other rigors of the literary historian that Brooks had neglected. Henry S. Commager (New York University) regarded the style inseparable from a slack and dubious historical method, "not one of analysis but of description" in which "impressionism [was] sublimated to scholarship." Was the flowering of the New England mind caused by the influences of Europe and Harvard Yard? The South, after all, had known both. By wealth? Both New York and Philadelphia possessed it. Murdock agreed with Commager that Brooks "rarely comes to grips with the actual stuff of thought." Rather, this was literary history by way of anecdotes and impressions that, however delightful, offered us "too little on literary criticism and too much on literary lives." (Reluctantly, Commager, admired Brooks's lives, as did most of the reviewers, who differed chiefly on which set of his numerous figures he had portrayed most memorably.) Matthiessen not only questioned how Brooks's subject could be the New England mind, but also "what Mr. Brooks conceives to be the scope of literary history." One could read fifty pages of Brooks on Thoreau, but discover no analysis of the literary art in *Walden;* "a single page of graceful praise" constituted Brooks's treatment of *The Scarlet Letter* and *The House of the Seven Gables;* he rediscovered Greenough's lectures but saw no relation to Emerson's and Thoreau's notions of organic style. Clearly, Matthiessen's *American Renaissance* (1941) was germinating in these observations, as well as in others, such as his complaints that Brooks missed James's links to the Hawthorne tradition and that "there is no discussion of the nature of tragedy in this volume."

Carl Van Doren was as effusive and generous with Brooks as he had been a few years earlier with Lewisohn's literary history. Indeed, if Brooks continued his series "with the same knowledge, range, insight, precision and grace, he will have written," said Van Doren, "not only the best history of American literature, but one of the best literary histories in any language." (Dutton ignored Van Doren's conditional clause and quoted as a publisher's blurb the words beginning "not only.") But brother Mark Van Doren (Columbia) awaited the next volume of Brooks's Makers and Finders more skeptically. Brooks's youthful spirit, his unrestrained national affection for the minute item, the picturesque detail, must often weary the less exuberant of his American readers: "Where everything is so exciting, it is hard to know where to let the mind rest." Unlike Carl, Mark asked whether Brooks's method "has limitations of the sort likely to show up as defects in the completed whole." Brooks, who would become the most indomitable of all our programmatic literary historians of the thirties, continued into the next decade, and then the next, to provide more than enough evidence to answer Van Doren's suspicion.[22]

Chapter 20

American Literature in the University: Curriculum, Graduate Research, and Controversy in the Thirties

The advocacy of literary historians and critics in the 1930s had penetrated, in various ways, the halls of higher learning in America. Some of the central figures were themselves presiding in the classrooms of the academy. Blankenship moved from Whitman to the University of Washington in 1932. Hicks was at Rensselaer until his dismissal in 1935, and Foerster left North Carolina for Iowa in 1930. His fellow humanist Harry Clark was at Wisconsin. The Southern Agrarians were at Vanderbilt and Louisiana State. But these and other presences could not immediately alter the direction of study in the English departments where American literature still looked for an academic home. A new enemy of curricular expansion also loomed now—a depressed American economy. Still, higher education moved ahead modestly in an era when a sizable number of the unemployed were left with the strenuous alternative of pursuing a college degree. More than 15 percent of the nation's youth were attending college by 1940, contrasted with 4 percent in 1900. "The prosperity of the 1920's no doubt stimulated this growth," says Bernard Berelson, "but the depression of the 1930's did not retard it." On the graduate level, the growth had been more impressive: "The number of institutions giving the doctorate rose from about 50 in 1920 to nearly 100 in 1940 and the number giving the Master's from 200 to 300."[1]

In American literature, our brief survey of the campuses can begin with Duke, where the profession's journal helped to enhance the awareness of American literature elsewhere on campus. Under the guiding spirit of editor Hubbell, by 1933 Duke was offering five courses in American literature.[2] His own undergraduate course became the legendary "Hubbell's English" to students who, in years to come, regularly overflowed into three large sections. The text in 1936 and after was Hubbell's *American Life in Literature* (Harper, two volumes). At Chicago, the picture was also bright. The American faculty during the 1930s included the venerable Percy Boynton, surrounded by Napier Wilt (since 1923), F. H. O'Hara (since 1924), Walter Blair (since 1926), Fred Millett (1927–37), and Clarence Faust (since 1930). In 1938, the department gave 45 hours of American literature, including separate courses in Henry James and Franklin, or 23 percent of the total English curriculum. Penn State continued to expand the undergraduate offerings in American literature during the 1930s, despite Pattee's retirement in 1929. Nine more hours of instruction were now taught by D. K. Merrill, W. L. Werner, and A. C. Cloetingh. In 1938, 43½ hours, or 18 percent of departmental offerings, were in American literature.

In New England, Brown emerged the leader by the end of the period, finally embracing its intellectual past when Walter Bronson and Lorenzo Sears pioneered in American literary history. Students were able to draw on the local resources, also, at the John Carter Brown Library, the Harris Poetry Collection, the Athenaeum, and the Newport Historical Society Library. In 1938, 31½ hours, or 22 percent of the department courses, were American literature, including, on the graduate level, a seminar in Melville given by S. Foster Damon. At Middlebury, Reginald L. Cook brought the offerings to 24 hours in 1938, or 26 percent of the literature curriculum. Because of the popularity of American literature, registration was restricted above the survey level. There was no graduate program, but Middlebury, with Maine and Dartmouth, had instituted an undergraduate major in American literature. Elsewhere in the region, New Hampshire allowed 12 hours (25 percent) of the English curriculum to the American field. At Harvard, American literature classes were given somewhat more consistently than before. The total offerings by 1938 are hard to determine, since the university was moving into an interdisciplinary American civilization program, especially in the graduate area.

But total hours were obviously less significant than the prestige Harvard was now lending American literature through the presence of Kenneth Murdock, Howard M. Jones, Perry Miller, and W. E. Sedgwick. In a valuable article, Clarence Gohdes (Duke) wrote in 1938 pointedly commending Harvard for breaking out of the traditional curriculum in literature and modernizing "its procedure in training Ph.D.'s in English, under the aegis of Kenneth B. Murdock, to the extent of removing handicaps in the way of the student who wishes to devote himself to the study of his country's literature." In turn, Gohdes rebuked Princeton for its usual "lethargic" indifference to American literature.[3] Columbia had declined by 1938 to a mere 13 hours, or 5 percent of literature courses, in American writers. Ralph Rusk's scholarship in Emerson gave the university virtually its only continuing prominence in American literature. Neither Raymond Weaver, Mark Van Doren, nor Lionel Trilling was teaching American literature, according to students who recalled their years at Columbia in the 1930s.[4]

At Pennsylvania, Arthur Quinn had been joined by Sculley Bradley and Paul Musser, and the curriculum in American literature remained strong, though, again, we cannot always trust evidence from catalog listings: In one year (1931), twelve courses were announced, but only six apparently were given. At North Carolina, Gregory Paine and R. W. Adams were carrying on after Norman Foerster's departure. Seven American courses were offered in 1938. In the same year at South Carolina, 31½ hours of literature (32 percent) were in American authors, with a sophomore survey required for graduation. At Louisiana State, Earl Bradsher was joined in 1937 by Arlin Turner in a literature program of eight courses (20 percent) in American writers.

In the Midwest, American programs at Wisconsin, Minnesota, and Michigan had not yet gained an eminence despite the reputation of individual professors in the past, notably Tyler, Beach, and Cairns, and a younger group—Clark, McDowell, Jones, and others. Western Reserve, in fact, had the most active program after Chicago, with 30 hours (22 percent) of literature in American writers. At Iowa, when Norman Foerster became director of the School of Letters and Science in 1930, he redesigned the curriculum into a coordinated program to advance his humanist principles. English was incorporated with the departments of classics, German, and Romance languages. In 1938, seven American literature courses were offered, and the following year, Foerster brought Austin Warren (from Boston University) onto the faculty. Foerster benefited American literature itself through his departure from the Germanic model of specialized university study: In 1939, the Writer's Workshop became a creative alternative to the traditional doctorate. Though opposition to his autocratic style presently led Foerster to resign the directorship, he remained at Iowa to shape an American Civilization program.[5]

Farther west in the 1930s, the University of Washington was thriving from the momentum of two decades under Parrington. The 1930–31 catalog listings (for the following year) showed Harold Eby teaching the lower division three-quarter survey. The upper division three-quarter survey to the Civil War (9 hours) was offered by both Eby and John B. Moore, while Joseph Harrison was teaching the annual survey of literature since 1870 (9 hours). On the graduate level, extending through the year were Moore's American Literature (2 to 5 hours) and a seminar in American Literature (2 to 5 hours) offered by Eby and Harrison. By 1935, Russell Blankenship had replaced Moore and, with Eby and Harrison, was teaching the annual survey course to the Civil War, now expanded to a five-credit course per quarter. Graduate offerings, however, had apparently shrunk, with Eby giving Moore's former graduate course (five units per quarter) and Harrison the seminar (five units) but only in the autumn.[6] Down the coast, Southern California rivaled Washington with 31 hours (30 percent) of American literature and the individual prestige of one professor, Louis Wann, the specialist in late nineteenth-century literature.

The statistics presented here—frustratingly inexact, as in previous decades, but symptomatic enough—may seem to belie the earlier comment that American literature still awaited academic recognition. We must be reminded, therefore, that the schools just cited were the standard-bearers in American literature among the 119 colleges whose catalogs Lewis examined. By his calculation, the nine front runners, on the average, were offering American students only 25 percent of the English curriculum for study of the three centuries of their own literature, and the leader, New York University, gave only 36 percent in the year 1938–39. More depressing statistics show that despite the efforts of Willard Thorp, Princeton's total for that year was 2 percent (rightly deplored by Clarence Gohdes), and of its fourteen graduate courses in English, none was in American literature. At California in Berkeley, offerings in Old Irish and German Heroic Poetry equaled American literature, and the same was the case with Caedmon and Cynewulf at Illinois or Celtic literature at Nebraska.

Lewis concluded, however, that interest in American literature at the undergraduate level was nationwide, more so at public than private institutions. In 1938, Gohdes attributed some of this activity to laws in various states that required a course in American literature for education students planning to teach in the secondary schools. The mixed blessing here, for Gohdes, was that American literature was often being taught by graduates with no specialization in the subject.[7] In the academic, as distinguished from the education, area of the campus, Lewis found that American literature nationally was seldom required for the English major, or even as knowledge in the degree examinations. On some campuses where American literature was a popular elective, he supplied evidence that enrollment limits were imposed. Though Lewis neglected to say so, we assume that no such limits were authorized on courses in English literature.

If thousands of college students in America were thus continuing to graduate without having studied even a small portion of their nation's literature, the world of textbook publishing in American literature seems not to have been ailing noticeably in the 1930s. The older style of textbook history, though, was pretty much passé. Walter Taylor (Mississippi College) was one of the few professors to compete in this dwindling trade. His *History of American Letters* in 1936 (American Book Company) was enhanced with 150 pages of valuable bibliographies by Harry Hartwick. Percy Boynton, in the same year, published *Literature and American Life* (Ginn) and G. Harrison Orians (Toledo) proceeded soon after to write *A Short History of American Literature* (Crofts, 1940)—a decided slackening of what was earlier a seemingly bottomless market for commercial-minded professors. Another side of this picture, however, was the movement away from textbook histories toward the less expensive package that incorporated biography and historical background within the college anthology, a development encouraged, no doubt, by a depression-era economy. The anthology, also, was an economical detour from more expensive complete works, and it dominated the college market even when the paperback era was inaugurated after World War II.

Another economical tactic of publishers in the Depression was to reissue earlier anthologies, sometimes in slightly revised editions. Most durable was Pattee's *Century Readings* (1919) into a fourth edition in 1932. Next in longevity was Foerster's *American Poetry and Prose* (1925), which he revised for Houghton Mifflin in 1932. Shafer's *American Literature* (Doubleday Page, 1926), enjoyed a third printing in 1933. Snyder and Snyder's anthology (1927) was revised in 1935 for Macmillan in a market active enough to allow Macmillan also to risk, two years before, the five-volume *American Literature: A Period Anthology,* with Oscar Cargill the general editor. These volumes, rather strictly periodized, were edited by Robert Spiller (*The Roots of National Culture: To 1830*), Tremaine McDowell (*The Romantic Triumph: 1830–1860*), Louis Wann of Southern California (*The Rise of Realism: 1860–1888*), Cargill (*The Social Revolt: American Literature from 1888 to 1914*), and John H. Nelson of Kansas (*Contemporary Trends: Since 1914*). If a depression gamble it were, this ambitious anthology survived and was revised in 1949. Elsewhere, Harcourt, Brace published the Jones–Leisy *Major*

American Writers in 1935; Harper the Hubbell *American Life in Literature* the next year (with two hundred adoptions within twelve months); the American Book Company published the two-volume *The American Mind* (1937) of Warfel, Gabriel, and Williams—a somewhat Parringtonian collection that included para-literary documents in intellectual history; and in 1938 came the Benét and Pearson *The Oxford Anthology of American Literature*. Also in 1938, Clarence Gohdes questioned whether too many of the profession's teachers were being lured by the profits of textbook journalism to the detriment of their higher calling, when the academy had a more serious need for scholarly monographs and especially for "sound biographies" of figures like Melville, Dickinson, James, and Longfellow. Of course, the textbook anthology summoned a certain scholarship from its fashioners, but Gohdes did not find much evidence that the insights of the ALG's *Reinterpretation* at the end of the twenties had stimulated imaginative new organization and content in most of the textbooks.[8]

The decade had begun, however, with just such responsible pedagogy in a very revealing textbook, *Courses in Reading in American Literature with Bibliographies,* arranged and edited by Stanley Williams of Yale and Nelson F. Adkins of Washington Square College, NYU (Harcourt, Brace, 1930). This volume is unusually helpful to the historian of the profession. Designing their guide to supplement reading beyond the usual anthology, rather than to suggest the actual conduct of the courses, the editors corrected the dating of various literary works, so that the book was an important addendum to the *CHAL* bibliographies. The courses suggested which authors might be taught well together, though no imaginative daring was evident in the seven clusters—writers were always contemporaneous. Presumably, the courses indicated a fair consensus of the profession, for Williams and Adkins acknowledged the help of Kenneth Murdock and F. O. Matthiessen, Harry Clark, Sculley Bradley, T. O. Mabbott (Hunter), and Odell Shepard (Trinity College).

On the graduate level of the academy, one area of American literature study that registered a perceptible gain in the 1930s was the doctoral dissertation. Lewis's survey of the university curriculum seems to support the conclusion, however, that most of the American literature dissertations were the result of terminal research, taken up by doctoral candidates after a graduate-school diet of chiefly English literature offerings. In the first five years of the decade, we discover the English department at Pennsylvania the leader in completed dissertations with seventeen, followed by Chicago (thirteen), Yale (eight), North Carolina (eight), Duke (seven), Harvard (six), Iowa (six), Virginia (five), and Peabody (five). Surprisingly low, given their earlier leadership in the movement, were the totals at Columbia (four), Wisconsin (three), Penn State (two), Texas (two), Washington (two), and Brown (two). Quantity, naturally, does not mean that the dissertations or graduate students were destined to be celebrated in the profession. California at Berkeley recorded only one Ph.D., but this was Franklin Walker, writing the first book-length study of Frank Norris. Arlin Turner's study of Hawthorne distinguished Texas, Gay Wilson Allen wrote on American prosody at Wisconsin, Hugh Hetherington on Melville and Theodore Hornberger on colonial science at Michigan, while Columbia's group included Clarence Gohdes, Lyon Richardson, and Vernon Loggins. On the other hand, quality accompanied quantity among some of the more prolific departments: at Pennsylvania, Charles Glicksberg (Whitman) and William Charvat (origins of American critical thought); at Chicago, Walter Blair (Bill Nye) and Perry Miller (orthodoxy in colonial Massachusetts); at North Carolina, Walter Taylor ("Economic Unrest in American Fiction, 1880–1901"); at Yale, Randall Stewart (Hawthorne), Alexander Cowie (John Trumbull), Townsend Scudder (Emerson), and Harry Warfel (J. G. Percival); at Duke, Roy Basler (Lincoln); and at Harvard, Thomas Johnson (Edwards).[9]

In the second half of the decade, Pennsylvania's English department again led the nation, though with a drop from seventeen to thirteen dissertations. Harvard now edged Chicago for second place, twelve to ten, with six theses completed in 1936 alone. Wisconsin also rose into contention, tied with Iowa (eight) and closely followed by Michigan (seven), LSU (seven), Washington (six), and Columbia (six). Young scholars who would influence the profession either in their thesis subject or wider research or as teachers and officeholders now came from the program at Duke in the person of Ima H. Herron ("The Small Town in American Literature"); from Virginia, Richard B. Davis (F. W. Gilmer); Chicago, Clarence Faust (Edwards) and Luther Mansfield (Melville); Columbia, Charles Anderson (Melville) and Lawrance Thompson (Longfellow); Michigan, Charles C. Walcutt (naturalism); NYU, George Arms (Howells); and from Wisconsin, Allan Halline (drama), Ernest Marchand (Norris), and Robert Falk (American criticism of Shakespeare).

The quantity of doctoral dissertations in American literature during the 1930s did not prove to tough-minded advocates like Howard M. Jones that the study of our literature was therefore exuberantly healthy up and down the curriculum and had come of age in the academy. No doubt the Depression was discouraging curriculum renovation or expansion, but Jones was sensitive to a fundamental academic conservatism still being perpetuated at mid-decade. In 1935, he read a paper on "American Scholarship and American Literature" to the English Section of MLA. Why, Jones asked, had latter-day efforts to write an embracing American literary history been forestalled, even though much basic spadework was being accomplished? He traced the cause of this sputtering scholarship to the reactionary climate in the academy, where English departments were yet mired in the lingering prejudice of British over American literature. Typically, said Jones, a fifteen-person department would have, at best, a single advocate of American literature. (Lewis, in his study seven years later, painted a slightly rosier picture of 1935 than did Jones.) Although British literature was rich and important, it should not serve as the lion's body of an English-language literature of which America's product was merely the tail. Rather, American literature should be studied against the *background* of English literature. The observations by Jones, who happened also to be chairman of the ALG in this year, probably reminded older members that Arthur H. Quinn had registered the same complaints in his paper fourteen years before. In fact, a letter from Quinn, who had been unable to attend the meeting in Cincinnati, was read to the English Section audience during the discussion period led by English literature professors Marjorie Nicholson of Smith and E. H. Wright of Columbia.[10]

In a second paper in late 1935, this time to members at the National Council of Teachers of English convention at Indianapolis, Jones repeated the litany of grievances on behalf of "The Orphan Child of the Curriculum." Although the survey of British literature was usually a requirement in the sophomore year, English majors and prospective school teachers frequently graduated with no American literature in their college program. The graduate student specializing in American literature faced examinations in British literature, but American literature was not required of students writing a British thesis. English literary tradition, moreover, bore no great interest for American students whose ancestry reached back to a different mother country (Jones's deliberate echo, no doubt, of Thomas Paine's anti-British argument of 1776). Nor did a majority of American students find much that was intrinsically compelling in the writings of Jonson, Dryden, Pope, or Newman. The American tradition, broadly realized from a study of our own literature, on the other hand, could inculcate the ideals of our nation as no British literary tradition ever would and thereby humanize our society in the future. Jones's remarks presently received a second hearing through publication in the society's journal.[11]

The *Saturday Review of Literature,* perhaps responding to a renewed stimulus Jones had given to the subject, soon editorialized twice within four months on behalf of American literature in the academy. In the first editorial, Bernard DeVoto praised American literature doctoral theses for the freshness of the topics and the alliance of aesthetic and historical approaches. He also welcomed the abolishing of old philological requirements and termed them, in the second editorial, "the worst obscenity in the academic study of literature." In this second piece, Harvard was praised for envisioning an American civilization program that would encourage an enlightened study of American literature. (At DeVoto's writing, Jones had left Michigan to become a professor at Harvard.) In a curriculum that was designed to coordinate American social, economic, and political history with belles lettres, said DeVoto, American literature would no longer be the "illegitimate stepchild" in a department favoring English literature.[12]

Jones's advocacy of American literature smacked of smallminded nationalism to some—the tiresome, century-old accusation of parochialism—but it had the good effect of thus stirring a salutary debate in the months ahead. The ALG program in 1938 at Columbia was titled "Nationalism in American Literature," with papers by Frederick Carpenter (Harvard), Harry Clark (Wisconsin), Harry Warfel (Maryland), and Robert W. Bolwell (George Washington).[13] Clarence Gohdes, too, reflected in 1938 on the "recent recrudescence of nationalism." He then wryly insinuated that perhaps America's anglophiliacs would be impressed with their own nation's literature if only English universities could be persuaded to give it a serious hearing: A professorship of American literature at Oxford or Cambridge might finally "stir up intelligent American interest in the study of the national literature."[14] Representative of some responses in opposition to Jones was the argument of A. L. Strout of Texas Technological College, who came forward in the *Sewanee Review* to dispute what he viewed to be the unfortunate chauvinism both in the editor of the *Saturday Review* and in Jones, whom he termed the "evangelist of the new cult of America first." In a point-by-point refutation, Strout argued the universality of all great literature and the need for a world tradition in literature rather than nationalistic advocacy of any stripe. In a footnote, Strout divulged his own collation of forty-five college catalogs that had convinced him American literature was sufficiently represented in the English departments of the academy.[15]

Finally, John T. Flanagan, assistant professor of English at the University of Minnesota, published in the new *College English* an article, "American Literature in American Colleges." He quoted from Jones's MLA paper of 1935 and tabulated from twenty-five college catalogs the low disproportion of undergraduate and graduate courses and hours allotted to American literature; but he attested to the genuine student appetite for American writers that he had recognized at Minnesota. And this interest was being satisfied now with enrollments that reached 150 in the survey course, 25 in American drama, 30 in the novel, and 50 in the short story. But Flanagan pointed also to the persistent difficulty of gaining respectability for American literature as a scholarly subject. In too many departments, professors around the country were teaching the American courses after taking graduate work top heavy in Beowulf, Elizabethan drama, and Dryden, with only scant study in the American field. (In contrast to Flanagan's impressive undergraduate totals, we may note that the tally of dissertations at Minnesota revealed only two on American literature in the 1930s, and one in the 1920s.)[16]

In the same month, Ernest Leisy mentioned Flanagan's article in a letter to Tremaine McDowell, Flanagan's colleague at Minnesota, and informed him that he (Leisy), too, was currently campaigning on the same circuit. He was appearing with Floyd Stovall (North Texas State Teachers) at an upcoming meeting of the Texas College Teachers of English devoted to "The Place of American Literature in the Colleges," and would also give a paper, "The Significance of Recent Research in American Literature," at a conference at the University of Oklahoma.[17] So by the close of the 1930s, the argument over American literature's rightful place in the academy continued, and the 1940s began with no evidence that the debate was letting up.

Chapter 21

Journals and Other Instruments
of the New Scholarship

At the end of the 1930s, the scholar-professors of American literature, hoping to master their subject, enlighten their students, direct graduate research, and publish their own work in a tightening job market, were blessed with various instruments and avenues of new scholarship, many of which had first appeared during the decade. Among the dozens of public and scholarly journals, old and new, some were a valuable resource but hardly an opportunity to publish in unless one were a privileged insider. The profession's own *American Literature,* which enjoyed a tenth anniversary in 1939 under founding editor Jay B. Hubbell, had become the most valuable outlet for responsible scholarly essays. It also provided a record of dissertations and other research-in-progress, plus a bibliography of current articles. Not least, Hubbell drew on the best minds in the profession for authoritative reviews of the scholarly books on American literature that were now filling the shelves of university libraries. Many of these books were published by the growing number of university presses. Thirteen new ones had been established in the thirties—a striking example of intellectual seriousness during the Depression years.

In a later age of abundant paperback-reprint copies of literary works, we must strain a little to imagine the conditions that faced the scholar and teacher of American literature in the earlier years of the century. Jay B. Hubbell's experience at Duke in 1927, mentioned earlier, must have been a frustration shared by many professors, when he realized that the college library did not own a copy of *The Scarlet Letter.* But interest in American literary history was increasing in the academy and therefore among publishers attracted to the school trade, a market that would soon ensure them (and their cooperative professors) very sizable profits. The commercial impulse took on, at times, a serious scholarly purpose as well. In 1928, Howard Jones became general editor of American literary reprints for Spiral Press. He wrote to friends in the field for their suggestions of texts most needed.[1] In 1930, the

ALG was giving the Facsimile Text Society informal advice on which rare American texts were urgently required for the American scholar. Two years later, Hubbell was appointed chairman of the Committee on Selection of Books in American Literature for that society. He, too, solicited advice from ALG members on which nineteenth-century texts should be reproduced.[2]

Hubbell had already recognized that even more fundamental to the accurate study of American literature was an access to manuscripts around the country and, indeed, the creation of a finding list of these documents. How to set about making such a check list? In the week before the 1929 MLA convention in Cleveland, he discussed the matter at a meeting of the American Association of University Professors in Durham attended by Thomas P. Martin, chief of the Manuscripts Division of the Library of Congress. In Cleveland, Hubbell then conveyed to the ALG's Advisory Council his sense of urgency regarding the check list.[3] As chairman of the Executive Committee of the ALG, Robert Spiller promptly appointed Hubbell chairman of a Committee on Manuscripts Resources. Spiller also wrote to Waldo G. Leland at the American Council of Learned Societies and described the proposed check list. Could the ACLS aid them in financial support? Leland replied that the American Historical Association had appointed a Manuscripts Commission that was making a parallel effort and perhaps the two groups might cooperate in order to secure monies and also prevent duplication of work.[4]

Spiller also received assurances of cooperation from Ernest C. Richardson, consultant in bibliography to the Library of Congress and also chairman of the American Library Association Committee on Bibliography. Richardson promised to undertake an inventory of manuscript materials in American literature at the Library of Congress. He sent Spiller a four-page account, with seven numbered sections, relating the expense of cataloging such manuscript holdings, as well as listing the library's books in American literature.[5] Hubbell's committee, meanwhile, was in touch with the American Historical Association. Representatives from both organizations met in Washington on 5 April 1930. They agreed to share a card index and to worry over the budget question jointly—how much money would be needed and where it might be secured. Other efforts and correspondence from 1930 went into Hubbell's report to the ALG in December at the MLA meeting in Washington, D.C.[6]

★   ★   ★

No one had foreseen that political trouble might come into play in a matter so academically serious and colorless as the quest for essential literary manuscripts, but it presently arrived in the form of administrative interference from the MLA. After all, ALG business was MLA business. Secretary Carleton Brown told Spiller that an advisory committee for the manuscripts check list would more properly be selected by the parent MLA's Executive Council. On 25 May 1931, Brown informed Spiller that members of that advisory committee had now been determined by the Executive Council to be Arthur H. Quinn, Howard M. Jones, and Stanley T. Williams. Spiller replied: "I am sure that our Advisory Council will not be satisfied to have the election taken from them." More pointedly to Bradley, Spiller called the bureaucratic interference "a nasty mess." It was made even messier by Spiller's having referred, in his engagement with the ACLS, to the American Literature Division of the MLA. The Advisory Committee of the MLA Executive Council had met on 25 April 1931, Brown informed Spiller, and objected to *Division* as a term that "would inevitably lead to confusion" in MLA's current relations with the ACLS. An exasperated Spiller replied that the MLA Executive Council had approved ALG's reorganization plan and yet would interfere with their freedom to designate themselves as they wished. The future approval of American literature plans and proposals by MLA was supposed to be "*in principle only,*" with direct actions left in the hands of the group's members. The recent conditions were, therefore, "exceedingly unsatisfactory." Spiller did not object to the committee members named by the MLA, but rather to American literature members' lack of "immediate control at this stage." He warned that many of them were leaning toward an "American Literature Association affiliated with the Modern Language Association." At the very least, Spiller asked that before Brown sailed to England, he respond to their demand for a "more clearly defined degree of autonomy within the Association than we have enjoyed in the past." Clearly, ALG members were aspiring to a larger professional identity than was afforded in one of fourteen groups of the English Literature Section of the MLA.[7]

Several weeks later, Spiller wrote to Brown at Oxford that the ALG's Advisory Council had granted its approval of the MLA Executive Council's choice of members on the manuscripts committee. But tempers had not completely cooled elsewhere. Hubbell had been meditating in a subversive vein and wrote in a letter of commiseration to Spiller that "some of these days we shall have to organize an AM/LIT/ASSOC of our own. Probably the time isn't ripe, but it *is* coming." Meanwhile, might they infiltrate the present bureaucracy? "I wish we could manage to put a couple of American literature men on the M.L.A. Council," said

Hubbell, "but I don't know how to go about it." Spiller assumed a wait-and-see posture for the present, writing in a rather conciliatory tone to the ALG's Advisory Council that since in this case MLA was one of the affiliated bodies of the ACLS, no doubt the ALG had best allow the manuscripts project to rest in the MLA. But he also insisted that the entire episode was bad for ALG autonomy. And at the December meeting in Madison, he reiterated to the ALG Advisory Council the necessity of their directing the projects that they originated.[8]

A rapprochement of sorts between the MLA and the ALG was achieved in the next few years as they confronted a common enemy—the Great Depression. In fact, just before the Madison meeting of 1931, Quinn of the Manuscripts Check List Committee reported to Secretary Bradley that the ACLS had approved an eighty-thousand-dollar grant for five years; unfortunately, because of the Depression, no money was available. Two years later in St. Louis, Quinn's committee reported to be still without funds.[9] Even by 1940, Hubbell was still agitating on behalf of the search for American literature manuscripts. He sent Thomas Martin at the Division of Manuscripts, Library of Congress, a tentative draft of a letter to collectors and other owners of manuscripts urging them to realize how important these materials would be to scholars. He proposed that the owners provide the Library of Congress, at the least, with photostatic copies of letters, diaries, and manuscripts of books. In 1954, Roy P. Basler (bibliographer, Library of Congress) discovered Hubbell's correspondence to Martin. But Basler doubted that money would be currently available for securing manuscripts or copies of manuscripts. Nevertheless, he enclosed to Hubbell a Library of Congress brochure that appealed to Americans to preserve family papers and manuscripts. By this later date, the ALG had a new Committee on Manuscript Holdings, formed in 1951, which would achieve for scholars of the 1960s what Hubbell's committee had pioneered, but with little success, in the early 1930s.[10]

Hubbell also initiated another labor that would be absolutely basic to growing scholarship in American literature—the accumulation of bibliographical studies. Shortly after the 1930 MLA meeting in Washington, D.C., he wrote to Ernest Leisy that Cambridge University Press was currently revising the bibliographies of the *Cambridge History of English Literature*, to be published in one volume. Why shouldn't American literature scholars do the same updating for the *CHAL* lists? Duke University Press might be interested in publishing the volume. At the 1931 meeting in Madison, Spiller was appointed chairman of the

Committee on Resources for Research, and the next year, his group considered "undertaking a complete history and bibliography of American literature, on a larger scale than the present *CHAL*." Although the time had hardly arrived for a new literary history, the committee asked members to cooperate, at least, in gathering fresh bibliographies.[11]

But 1932 was the year when the Depression first made a serious impact on American campuses. The bibliography project was inevitably hurt. Hubbell suggested that the ALG persevere and look for various avenues of support. Spiller's committee might approach a publisher—Macmillan, for example. But where would the money and trained bibliographical help come from? Perhaps, said Hubbell, a large university might be able to sponsor the research. Could Rusk be asked to approach Columbia? Hubbell doubted that money could be extracted for this work from either Carnegie or Rockefeller. And even if one returned to Macmillan, it would probably request that the ALG look for an outside subsidy to aid in publication expenses. For his part, Spiller was concerned that the ALG concentrate on a long-range plan, independent of all outside interference, with "a central card catalogue at Duke during the process of accumulation, preparatory to a publication at the end of a period of years."[12]

At the ALG meeting in 1933 in St. Louis, Hubbell as interim chairman of the Committee on Resources for Research regretted to report that no definite plan for the bibliography had been worked out. But the next year, Spiller (once again the chairman) announced at the Swarthmore meeting that the project was "now concretely defined." The committee would petition a central library (a university or the Library of Congress) to serve as repository for the file cards. Scholars with work in progress on major American authors would be asked to send duplicate bibliography cards. Thus, no money would be currently needed for bibliographical services. Plans for publication would be taken up at a later date. At the next meeting, in Cincinnati (1935), it was suggested that the ALG return to the *CHAL* bibliographies, modify their form, and also bring up to date P. K. Foley's original editions of American authors.[13]

In 1938, bibliographical assistance arrived by way of a newly funded Works Progress Administration (WPA) project. In September, it began at the University of Pennsylvania, guided by Professor Edward O'Neill of the English department. Bradley wrote to Hubbell in December that the ALG should elect a committee that would be prepared to advise some fifty WPA workers. O'Neill was elected chairman of the committee and soon described the ambitious venture in *American Literature* (March 1939). Over the next three to five years, his large staff of workers planned to compile primary and secondary bibliographies on every American author, a record, it was hoped, that would be unprecedented in scope and completeness. The final card catalog might then be housed at either the University of Pennsylvania or the Library of Congress. But the project died a gradual death in the 1940s as federal money was presently redirected into national defense. After the war, the hoped-for bibliography never received adequate funding. In its place, American literature scholars received, in 1948, Thomas Johnson's monumental volume 3 of the profession's cooperative *Literary History of the United States*.[14]

This is not to say that scholars in the 1930s were seriously deprived of bibliographical instruments for research. The indefatigable Harry Clark was general editor for two series of publications issued by the American Book Company, each generously devoted to primary and secondary bibliographies. Clark's American Fiction Series included six inaccessible novels by 1939, with introductions, chronologies, and bibliographies: *Modern Chivalry* was prepared by Claude M. Newlin (Michigan State), *Ormond* by Ernest Marchand (Stanford), *Satanstoe* by Robert Spiller and Joseph P. Coppock (Hendrix), *Horse-Shoe Robinson* by Ernest Leisy, *The Yemassee* by Alexander Cowie (Wesleyan), and *Nick of the Woods* by Cecil B. Williams (De Paul). Clark's American Writers Series was more ambitious. Originally in 1933, he planned fifteen volumes of "Representative Selections, with Introduction, Bibliography, and Notes," and even thought of collecting the introductions in the form of a literary history.[15] By the end of the 1930s, seventeen volumes had appeared, followed by seven more in the 1940s. In the separate volumes, some editors aimed for completeness in the secondary bibliography, and their annotations were the product of some of the most judicious minds in the profession: Tremaine McDowell on Bryant, Robert Spiller on Cooper, Clarence Faust and Thomas Johnson on Edwards, Frederic Carpenter on Emerson, Austin Warren on Hawthorne, Henry Pochmann on Irving, Fred Pattee on Mark Twain, Floyd Stovall (North Texas State Teachers) on Whitman, and Willard Thorp (Princeton) on Melville.

Helpful bibliographies were turning up elsewhere. An article in *American Literature,* such as Herbert R. Brown's "The Great American Novel" (March 1935), was often a valuable bibliographical source. Robert Spiller and Philip C. Blackburn produced a Cooper bibliography in 1934. In his *Major American Poets* (1936), Clark included plentiful source listings, as did

Harry Hartwick in the same year for Walter F. Taylor's *A History of American Letters*. Destined to become a standard work was Lyle H. Wright's *American Fiction: 1774–1850* (1939). Contemporary bibliographies came steadily from the current periodical listings in each number of *American Literature* and the annual bibliography for American literature in *PMLA*, both of these in the 1930s the primary labor of Gregory Paine.

*   *   *

We may imagine, for the moment, the preparations of a professor of American literature in 1939 who was surveying the scholarship of the previous ten years (as recorded in *PMLA*) on the eight authors deemed by later canon-makers to be our major figures of the nineteenth century. (Writing on twentieth-century authors was still largely the province of popular magazines rather than the scholarly journal.) If we assume that this would be, as well, pedagogical planning for a graduate seminar on the major author, our professor might also be assembling the basic scholarly instruments and standard editions of an earlier day, local holdings of the university library permitting. For Emerson, these latter would include, at a minimum, George W. Cooke's *Bibliography* (1908), the *CHAL* lists, and the Centenary Edition of Emerson's *Complete Works* (1903–4) in twelve volumes, edited by son Edward Waldo, who also edited the *Journals* (1909–14) in ten volumes. Bringing the seminar bookshelf up to date through the 1930s would require G. S. Hubbell's *Concordance to the Poems* (1932), Ralph Rusk's six volumes of the *Letters* (1939), and studies by Frederic Carpenter (1930), Van Wyck Brooks (1932), and Townsend Scudder III (1936). Just over sixty articles in the thirties could be assigned if the library were well stocked with scholarly journals.

For Thoreau, the bibliography by William White (1939) was a valuable updating of Francis H. Allen's work in 1908. The twenty-volume *Writings* (1906) remained standard. For biography and criticism, the ink would hardly be dry on Henry Canby's fine book (1939), which came at the close of a rather meager decade in Thoreau studies totaling only a couple dozen scholarly articles. Poe fared much better in that department with a tally closer to one hundred. But Killis Campbell's *The Mind of Poe* (1933) was the only distinguished study among some dozen books on Poe in the 1930s. J. W. Robertson's *Bibliography* (two volumes, 1934) was the valuable new instrument for Poe studies and James A. Harrison's seventeen-volume *Complete Works* (1902) still the best edition.

Hawthorne and Melville studies form an interesting comparison in the thirties since Melville had now been recovered and finally was pulling almost even with his elder contemporary. The main addendum to primary Hawthorne—that is, to the *Complete Works* edition many years before by George P. Lathrop (1883, twelve volumes)—was Randall Stewart's edition of the *American Notebooks* (1932). No monograph had appeared for the professor in 1939 to rival Newton Arvin's *Hawthorne* (1929). Scholarly articles had accelerated in the later 1930s to bring a total for the decade to just over fifty. Essays on Melville slightly surpassed that number, however, showing that the Melville revival of the twenties had not died away. But scholarship was hampered by the absence of reliable texts of primary Melville, the sixteen-volume *Works* (1922–24) being the unsatisfactory edition students had to rely on. Lewis Mumford's *Melville* (1929) was the only recent book to stimulate critical work until the end of the 1930s. Willard Thorp's informative introduction and bibliography in the *Representative Selections* (1938), mentioned earlier, along with Stanley Geist's and Charles Anderson's books of 1939, boded well for Melville scholarship in the 1940s.

More fertile than Hawthorne and Melville in the thirties were the studies in Whitman and Mark Twain. The foundation for work on Whitman was still the ten-volume *Complete Writings* (1902), the tenth volume being Oscar Triggs's pioneering bibliography, later supplemented by Emory Holloway for the *CHAL*, and in the 1930s, by the listings already mentioned in Stovall, Hartwick, and Clark. Some eighty-four scholarly articles in the decade were preparing the ground for a larger understanding of Whitman's sources, prosody, and biography, and more than a dozen books were written to the same end, with Newton Arvin's politically slanted study of 1938 arousing the most interest. Mark Twain was beneficiary of more than twenty volumes of scholarship in the thirties but only some fifty articles. Most of the sparks were caused by Bernard DeVoto's *Mark Twain's America* (1932), a spirited and caustic refutation of Van Wyck Brooks's *The Ordeal of Mark Twain* (1920). An unrepentant Brooks answered by reissuing *The Ordeal*, in 1933, with minor revisions but the portrait of a thwarted genius intact. Less newsworthy but of more permanent value for the broad range of Twain studies was Merle Johnson's primary *Bibliography* in 1935, which supplemented his work in 1910, as did Ivan Benson's bibliography in *Mark Twain's Western Years* (1938). The best edition of Mark Twain available in 1939 was the thirty-seven-volume *Writings* (1922–25), while the two-volume *Autobiography* (1924) was being supplemented in the 1930s by various editions of Mark Twain's letters.

Finally, what were the resources in 1939 for a seminar in Henry James? A superb bibliography was at hand, LeRoy Phillips's 1930 revision of his 1906 edition. The New York edition of *The Novels and Tales* (1907–17) was available in twenty-six volumes, Percy Lubbock had edited two volumes of *Letters* in 1920, and shortly after, he also edited a thirty-five-volume London edition of James's work (1921–23). Even so, the 1930s had not been a very profitable time for James studies. Books by Cornelia Kelley (1930) and C. Hartley Grattan (1932) did not match the scope or interest of earlier studies by Beach (1918), Lubbock (1921), and Brooks (1925). The foremost event, in fact, was the special issue of the *Hound and Horn* in April/May of 1934, which included essays by noted critics and authors, including Edmund Wilson's Freudian reading of "The Turn of the Screw" and R. P. Blackmur's discussion of James's prefaces to the New York edition. (Blackmur reprinted the essay as the introduction to his edition of the prefaces in 1934, *The Art of the Novel.*) Though James excited moderate interest thereafter in portions of books and in the public journals, *PMLA* listed only four more scholarly articles by the end of the thirties. And if we discount Edwin M. Snell's brief study in 1935, no scholarly monograph on James would be written in America during the fourteen years between Kelley's *The Early Development* (1930) and F. O. Matthiessen's *The Major Phase* (1944)—fuel aplenty for those professors who, in our next chapter, would question if the profession, for all its accumulation of facts since the *CHAL,* had yet attained the maturity of scholarship and creative criticism to venture into a large-scale new literary history. [16]

The paucity of scholarly articles on James and Thoreau in the 1930s raises the question if adequate journals had been created as an outlet for American literature professors who wanted to publish new scholarship in the field. The bibliography in *PMLA* listed among the older periodicals that printed articles on American literature in the 1930s, in addition to *PMLA* itself, the *Sewanee Review* (founded in 1892), *William and Mary Quarterly* (1892), *Journal of English and German Philology* (1897), *South Atlantic Quarterly* (1902), *Modern Philology* (1903), *Papers of the Bibliographical Society of America* (1904), *Studies in Philology* (1906), *Southwest Review* (1915), *Philological Quarterly* (1922), and many of the state historical publications. Important outlets created in the thirties for American literature scholars were the *University of Toronto Quarterly* (1930),

American Scholar (1932), the *Partisan Review* (1934), *Southern Review* (1935), *Huntington Library Quarterly* (1937), *Southern Folklore Quarterly* (1937), and for Freudians, *American Imago* (1939). The list is selective, though a full lineup would still appear skimpy in the 1980s.

Three more journals for the American literature professor should receive separate mention. The *English Journal,* founded in January 1912 as the organ of the National Council of Teachers of English, began a "College Edition" in 1928 that ran until June 1939. Basic scholarship in American literature, however, was far less prominent than the glamorous lead articles commissioned from such luminaries as Louis Untermeyer, Howard M. Jones, William Lyon Phelps, Ezra Pound, Granville Hicks, Joseph W. Krutch, Lewis Mumford, Burton Rascoe, and even Theodore Dreiser. In October 1939, the College Edition became *College English*.

More hospitable to the publishing scholar was the *New England Quarterly* (*NEQ*), founded in 1928, for it became a prolific outlet for regional literary studies that were, nevertheless, closely refereed. And the editors also elected outstanding authorities to review book-length scholarship on New England writers. The *NEQ* was second only to *American Literature* as a periodical instrument for encouraging the growth of American literature studies in the 1930s. Founded the year after *NEQ, American Literature* became at once the premier journal for the entire rank and file of the profession. Its current bibliography of scholarship in the periodicals has been cited. The journal was also a research finder, listing in each issue dissertations in progress or recently completed. Even when *Microfilm Abstracts* (Ann Arbor: University Microfilms) began publication of selected thesis summaries in 1938 (the first American literature theses appeared in the 1942 volume), the profession's own journal kept the most complete and current tally of graduate research. The record also created an air of hospitality for the work of younger members about to enter the profession.

Perhaps that atmosphere seemed less cordial to the young in other pages of *American Literature*. While the journal represented the profession's scholarship in all of its geographical and historical sweep (in contrast to *NEQ*'s narrower range), for the young professor that very scope meant that competition was keen and extensive. And manuscripts were closely refereed. The same expertise was enlisted for reviewers, so that the evaluation in *American Literature* became the critical reception that usually counted the most. The young scholar could chafe under what easily appeared a form of professional tyranny in this opinion making on the part of his or her elders. In the first ten volumes, the most prominent critics were led by Robert Spiller with twenty-two reviews, followed by Fred Pattee (eighteen), Clarence Gohdes (twelve), Louise Pound (twelve), Arthur Quinn (eleven), Lewis Leary (eleven), John H. Nelson (ten), Gregory Paine (nine), Howard Jones (eight), Kenneth Murdock (eight), Walter Blair (seven), T. O. Mabbott (seven), Ralph Rusk (seven), and Austin Warren (seven). Younger professors may also have felt that these same senior members had too frequent access to the other space in the journal. In fact, many of the reviewers never published an article in *American Literature* in the thirties, and the group as a whole averaged well under one essay per issue in the first forty numbers of the journal.

Neither was operating *American Literature* the source of unlimited editorial satisfaction and pride that the younger professional might have imagined. An impromptu visit to Jay B. Hubbell's office at Duke would quickly have dispelled such an impression. At the outset, the journal was a gratifying business success by academic expectations. Of the 250 who pledged at the Toronto meeting of 1928, 125 were subscribers even before any library orders had been filled. And the initial five-year contract with Duke University seemed generous enough to ensure that the journal would maintain a high quality in these infant years. By the second year, however, all was not well. Hubbell realized that his editorial, and self-imposed secretarial, burdens were much heavier than during the *Southwest Review* years. As he told Ralph Rusk, he planned at the 1930 meeting in Washington, D.C., to ask the editors to require the ALG Advisory Council to establish an assistant editorial position and appoint to it his new colleague at Duke, Clarence Gohdes. [17]

Extra editorial assistance was not granted by the ALG. Neither was Duke providing the necessary stenographic help in 1931. Hubbell was teaching nine hours a week (after three hours of released time for *American Literature*), he told Spiller. His students totaled nearly 110, including two doctoral candidates who were completing their dissertations, three or four more candidates beginning their thesis work, and a considerable number at work on masters' theses. Hubbell was teaching scores of undergraduates without the aid of reader assistants. Few around him realized how much time was consumed in editing the profession's journal, he complained, or that scholarly projects "like the check-list and the *CHAL* bibliographies are worth the time they take." Moreover, he always made it a point to reply decently to un-

successful, would-be contributors to the journal; he never resorted to the deadly, time-saving rejection slip. [18]

That Hubbell was having trouble processing manuscript contributions was evident in the experience of Howard Jones. In the
spring of 1931, he had sent his "American Reception of George
Sand" to Hubbell. In September, he was still waiting for a response. In October, Jones complained to ALG Chairman Spiller
that Hubbell was still not acknowledging manuscripts and sent
Spiller the copy of a letter Jones had written to Hubbell after the
editor finally returned the George Sand article with no explanation, together with someone else's manuscript bearing editorial
comments. Before the December meeting in Madison, Hubbell
wrote fellow editor Cairns, who was also on the ALG Advisory
Council, about these editorial woes and said he would not be able
to get to the meeting. But it was just as well. Thoroughly over-
worked, he was thinking that he would resign as editor of *American Literature*. At the Madison meeting, Spiller outlined to the
Advisory Council the general principle that the group should
control the projects they originated. Among these, he mentioned
attending to the current difficulty with Duke's not having provided Hubbell with adequate editorial and secretarial help. [19]

These problems with Duke were presently corrected, and most
importantly, Gohdes became managing editor in 1932, with Duke
incurring the burden of his editorial salary. Within a few years,
he relieved Hubbell completely for the first six months of each
year. Also encouraging in 1932, the MLA acquiesced to Spiller's
suggestion that *American Literature* be included as a special
joint subscription, along with *PMLA,* in the dues of association
members. But for all that, 1932 was a bleak Depression year,
and *American Literature* subscriptions decreased by two hundred. The next year, Hubbell wrote Sculley Bradley (secretary of
ALG) that the journal was doing better. And with Gohdes as
managing editor (Hubbell was now chairman of the board of editors), plus a secretary supplied by the press at Duke, Hubbell's
office was in good order. He hoped for the renewal of the MLA
joint-subscription rate ($7.20) and anticipated that after the De-
pression, the group would own a truly impressive journal, expanded to more than 125 pages and receiving more review copies
of books from the publishers. Currently, *American Literature*
boasted 413 subscribers. And Duke was renewing the five-year
contract. The Depression, however, did not go away, and in 1938,
an old bugbear—MLA interference—returned. Hubbell told
Bradley before the annual meeting at Columbia that he had just
read in the last *PMLA* that the Executive Committee was discon-

tinuing the joint-subscription rate for *American Literature,* apparently because the ALG did not own the journal. Yet other publications, Hubbell noted, were sent to MLA members at a reduced cost. Bradley promised to look into it. The result: In the May 1938 issue of *American Literature* (p. 227), Hubbell was pleased to announce that the MLA executive members had voted to extend the joint-subscription rate for *PMLA* and *American Literature* (still at $7.50 a year) through 1940. [20]

The journal correspondence (on file at the Hubbell Center at Duke) shows that Hubbell was faced with far more than business headaches, and not least were the multiple decisions regarding editorial policy on the screening and content of articles. Always looking for mature scholarship, Hubbell ran into the danger of cronyism and the apparent professional aggrandizement of editorial board members who wished to publish their own work in the journal. In the third year, Cairns told Hubbell that the editors should institute a clear policy that they would not print their own scholarship. Yet Cairns had a manuscript on Swinburne and America and would like to offer *American Literature* the first look. Hubbell was not only adamant that the pages of the journal be open to the ripened scholarship of the editors but wanted a policy that explicitly allowed the editors to write for *American Literature.* As to Cairns's Swinburne, Hubbell was not only receptive, but said he would not embarrass the other editors (or Cairns) by sending it out for an editorial judgment. The lead article in the May 1931 issue was Cairns's "Swinburne's Opinion of Whitman." [21]

The early policy has been mentioned that opposed articles on living authors or pedagogy and emphasized American literary history. *American Literature* was also to be, as the subtitle indicated, a magazine of criticism. After the first issue, Stanley Williams wrote Hubbell that the contents were good, but the journal could profit from papers "of pure criticism." Hubbell agreed, but they were not coming in. Would Williams write one? Williams said he would try. (But none ever appeared.) Given the restriction on contemporary authors, it was inevitable that some of the nineteenth-century figures would be overly represented in a short time. By 1934, Pattee told Hubbell that the saturation point was arriving for both Poe and Whitman. (In six years, twenty-four articles and notes had appeared on Poe and seventeen on Whitman.) Another objection regarding content was raised by Kenneth Murdock (who knew that Pattee agreed) and came after Hubbell reserved space for an obituary on Parrington in 1929. In the future, who would be chosen to receive an obit?

Who would not merit one? When Cairns died in 1932, Hubbell decided to write one. Murdock reiterated that the selective tribute created problems of favoritism and precedent. But the memorial notice appeared in the November 1932 issue, as did another in March 1938 on the death of Killis Campbell, written by Floyd Stovall and Tremaine McDowell. [22]

American Literature was inevitably monitored by the alert young and old who were watchful of politics in many guises. But ALG members were still a like-minded guild, for the skirmishes that had united them against the larger MLA during more than a decade were far from over. Their sense of embattled neglect within the parent organization continued to rankle as it bound them together. At the Swarthmore meeting at Christmas of 1934, someone raised the earlier issue that American literature was underrepresented on the inner councils of MLA—specifically the Executive Council. The result had been scant or tardy attention to matters important to the ALG. Separate representation on the council for the ALG, it was felt, seemed just in view of the problems unique to the group. Chairman Stanley Williams was asked to appoint a committee to confer with the new secretary of MLA, Percy Long (Carleton Brown resigned at the 1934 meeting at Swarthmore), regarding obligatory representation by the ALG. To promote their status, newly elected chairman of the ALG, Howard Jones, prepared the speech in 1935 (discussed in the preceding chapter), which he delivered to the English section of MLA at the Cincinnati meeting in December. But first, he wrote to Hubbell for information (supplementing that already received from Spiller and Bradley) on the ALG's earlier treatment within the MLA. Among the disagreeable facts on hand, Jones himself mentioned these: (1) 1,405 articles had appeared in *PMLA,* and a mere 29 were on American literature; (2) no president of MLA had been elected with a scholarly speciality in American literature; and (3) no presidential address had ever focused on American literature. [23]

In his paper, Jones prefaced these charges, as we have seen, with a brief review of the perennial slighting of American literature study in the nation's English departments. This campus attitude, he alleged, had inevitably insinuated itself into the professional society. In his conclusion, Jones proposed not a change in the MLA constitution but, instead, a change of heart among the preponderance of anglophiles in the membership. The paper was printed in *American Literature* and subsequently issued as a pamphlet by the American Book Company. [24] Secretary Long, shortly after the meeting, sent Jones a copy of a reply he had read at an English section meeting. The report was titled, "The Official Record of the Association with Respect to American Literature: *A Statement by the Secretary.*" Long spoke to the alleged failure to give "American literary history its due share of attention" within the MLA. He refuted the allegation by noting the following: (1) Among the twelve books published under MLA sanction was Professor Krapp's two-volume *English Language in America;* (2) the ALG was privileged within MLA to have its own journal; (3) *PMLA*'s record of acceptances for American literature articles showed that, in the past nine years, only forty had been submitted and, of these, twenty-two had been accepted; (4) at the 1935 meeting in Cincinnati, American literature showed an attendance of 138, or a mere 3 percent of the MLA membership in good standing; and (5) even so, this tiny fraction had been accorded favored status among the many groups within the MLA. Long's figure of 3 percent was arrived at carelessly if not deviously. The ALG program had an actual audience of 151 (small difference), but among 1,400 MLA members *in attendance*, this amounted to 11 percent. The other 2,300, or 60 percent of members in good standing, had not traveled to Cinicinnati. [25]

Jones, meanwhile, set out to publicize the cause of the ALG even more widely and offered his paper to the *Saturday Review of Literature*. That journal declined publication, perhaps to avoid giving offense to a majority readership within the MLA. If so, *Saturday Review* discovered new courage at the end of the year and featured the ALG in an editorial just before the December 1936 meeting in Richmond. The writer of that editorial, Bernard DeVoto, predicted that ALG meetings would be the "most vigorous" at the upcoming convention. He remarked on the growth of the group during the past ten years and judged their journal more interesting than *PMLA* and its articles superior in eliciting broadly literary values. Overall, the American literature scholars were "now doing the most humane and most valuable research that the M.L.A. can show," said the editorial. [26]

Secretary Long was previously correct, of course, in his assessment of the disproportionate influence in the MLA enjoyed by the comparatively fewer members of the ALG. But the membership was increasing in the thirties. This growth brought not only notions of increased power within the MLA, but also internal problems of democracy for the group. An ALG elite was already visible in the twenties, and at the annual meeting in New Haven in 1932, one call for a new democracy came in the resolution that *American Literature* was to publish in each May issue the two new members proposed for the Advisory Council by the Nominating Committee. All members, in fact, were to be free to mail in their own nominations. Then the two with the most nominations on these ballots were to be added to the two choices of the Nominating Committee, and all four were to be named in the November *American Literature*.[27]

Still, a glance at the ALG programs during the rest of the 1930s, as recorded in *PMLA*, discloses that the group was yet dominated by a select group of senior members. If the annual professional meeting, with the papers and offices, be viewed as another "instrument" of American literature scholarship, access to its benefits did not extend quite so far as some could wish. One senior professor, Emory Holloway of Queens College, confirmed that impression in a letter to Hubbell after the 1939 meeting in New Orleans: "There *is* a feeling that a few persons run the Group, including the programs." On the other hand, the seniors did not always have their way in the activities of the ALG. In *American Literature,* for example, despite his hospitality to Cairns's unrefereed Swinburne–Whitman article eight years before, Hubbell in 1939 told advisory editor Fred Pattee that his manuscript on Constance Fenimore Woolson had been rejected. But Hubbell had done an editorial favor for his old friend to ease the shock. He had persuaded *South Atlantic Quarterly* to take the article. The incident nicely illustrates a small truth to close these middle chapters on professional politics and scholarship: Even the most eminent member of the ALG could not win them all; but at the worst, he might be able, with a little help from his friends, to settle for second best.[28]

Killis Campbell (1872–1937)
(*Photograph Collection, Barker Texas History Center, The General Libraries, University of Texas at Austin*)

Joseph W. Beach (1880–1957)
(*University of Minnesota, University Archives*)

Norman Foerster (1887–1972)
(*North Carolina Collection, University of North Carolina Library at Chapel Hill*)

Vernon L. Parrington (1871–1929)
(*Pacific Northwest Collection, University of Washington Libraries*)

Arthur H. Quinn (1875–1960)
(*University of Pennsylvania Archives*)

George F. Whicher (1889–1954)
(*Amherst College Archives*)

Jay B. Hubbell (1885–1979)
(*Jay B. Hubbell Center, William R. Perkins Library, Duke University*)

Clarence Gohdes (1901–)
(*Jay B. Hubbell Center, William R. Perkins Library, Duke University*)

Ernest E. Leisy (1887–1968)
(*University Archives, Southern Methodist University*)

Louise Pound (1872–1958)
(*University Archives, University of Nebraska–Lincoln*)

Harry H. Clark (1901–1971)
(*From the Collection of the University of Wisconsin–Madison Archives*)

Granville Hicks (1901–1982)
(*George Arents Research Library, Syracuse University*)

Tremaine McDowell (1893–1959)
(*University of Minnesota, University
Archives*)

Kenneth Murdock (1895–1975)
(*Harvard University Archives*)

Sculley Bradley (1897–)
(*Duke University Archives*)

Book Three Maturity

The *Literary History of the
United States* and the Academy
in Wartime (1939–1948)

Chapter 22

The Profession Plans a New Literary History

After a decade of abundant and varied scholarship that had been encouraged by the instruments of new scholarship and stimulated by the bold formulations of Leftists, Freudians, humanists, Agrarians, nationalists, and others, the inevitable next stage was the making of a cooperative new literary history that might emerge with an overarching perspective on the bewildering variety of all this scholarly production. Major authors had been reassessed in distinguished new monographs, many of them controversial—Arvin's Hawthorne and Whitman, Brooks's Emerson, Canby's Thoreau, Mumford's Melville, and DeVoto's Mark Twain. Arthur H. Quinn had sketched a history of American fiction and Gay Wilson Allen a survey of American prosody. On the shorter haul, Gregory Paine, bibliographer for *American Literature*, counted 365 scholarly articles on American literature in more than one hundred journals during the final year of the decade alone.

Taking a longer view, we have seen that the dust hardly had settled after the reception of the final volumes of the *CHAL* in 1921 when Jay B. Hubbell sensed that a reinterpretation of American literature was already warranted. His plans culminated in the summer of 1926 during the discussion with Norman Foerster that led to the new pioneering essays of *The Reinterpretation of American Literature* in 1928. In the autumn of 1926, Chairman Hubbell was planning, as well, the final touches for the upcoming ALG meeting in Cambridge. He wanted Howard Jones on the program and hoped that the ALG could be persuaded to decrease the call for pedagogical papers. However popular their range, they ended up being merely "scattering and superficial." Hubbell wanted the group to point their program papers, instead, toward the scholarship that "will actually help to work up the field—pave the way for a satisfactory history of American literature to be written a generation from now."[1]

The idea of a new literary history seems never to have been absent from Hubbell's mind thereafter. Before the annual meeting in Madison in 1931, he repeated to his fellow editors of *American*

Literature his recent suggestion to Chairman Robert Spiller and Secretary Sculley Bradley—that the ALG should now discuss the possibility and advisability "of the Group's undertaking a comprehensive history of American literature."[2] At the meeting, the Advisory Council of ALG approved in principle a new history of American literature and appointed a Committee on Resources for Research, with Spiller as chairman, but also suggested that a subcommittee might be designated to chart a specific course for the new history. Before the meeting in 1932, Hubbell wrote to Spiller's committee members, urging that they assume the function of such a subcommittee and begin to "consider concretely the form and scope of the needed work, to investigate the possibility of beginning in the near future a joint bibliography of the subject, and to prepare a report for the next meeting." Preliminary considerations would include the expertise of possible contributors, the form of the text, and negotiations with a publisher—perhaps Macmillan. Spiller replied that he envisioned an initial period of five years devoted to bibliography, in a format different from that of the *CHAL,* before the text of a new history could even be contemplated. The minutes of the ALG meeting at Yale the next month (December 1932) mentioned Spiller's report for the Committee on Resources for Research. Its deliberations during the year included "undertaking a complete history and bibliography of American literature, on a larger scale than the present CHAL," though the committee (agreeing with what Spiller had said privately to Hubbell) felt the time was not ripe for authoring the text and urged cooperative preliminary work on the bibliography.[3]

At the meeting in Swarthmore two years later, Spiller's committee proposed that a central library be located for the beginning of this ambitious bibliography. At the same meeting, Spiller read "The Task of the Historian of American Literature," which he also published in the *Sewanee Review.* He described the current state of American literature studies and concluded that the profession was not yet prepared to replace "the illogical and now almost obsolete *Cambridge History of American Literature.*" Parrington's work in *Main Currents* should be viewed as a "prerequisite to the new literary history," an admirable labor in the continuing transitional period of critical, historical, and textual groundwork. Spiller identified areas of ignorance requiring scholarly illumination before the comprehensive new history could be undertaken. Our knowledge of European influences remained scanty, he wrote, as did the relationships between national culture and literature, and the specific influences on individual writers. While Foerster had developed the valuable concept of a romantic movement, we as yet but dimly realized the genesis of American romanticism in the post-Revolutionary forerunners of Emerson and, earlier, in the colonial figures who championed a liberation of spirit and conscience in the New World. We must see the movement as it extended beyond a merely New England expression, and all these considerations must stimulate new monographs that reassess the individual writers. We were similarly deficient in explorations of realism and naturalism as literary modes and movements and continued to conceive our literary development, instead, around wars or the shifts in our political history. Our genre historians, likewise, had suffered from this scarcity of sophisticated and widely ranging inquiry. In short, Spiller concluded, we cannot expect to launch a new literary history for a good while: "We must be patient."[4]

By the 1938 meeting in New York, the ALG Advisory Council apparently felt it had been patient long enough. Member Henry Canby moved that a committee be created to inquire if a new cooperative literary history might not soon be feasible. Spiller was appointed chairman of the committee, with Easterners Bradley, Canby, Ralph Rusk, Stanley Williams, and Californian T. K. Whipple. Spiller went to work at once. At the New York convention, he talked with members who were working on aspects of literary history. Committee member Whipple had proposed to a publisher a history since 1870. Alexander Cowie was at work on his history of the American novel (it finally appeared in 1948 in Harry Clark's American Writers Series). Shortly thereafter, Spiller discovered that Bradley was also projecting a literary history since 1870 and was currently trying to write a history of American poetry for the same period. (Neither was ever published.) And Clark was acting on his earlier scheme. He was now selecting introductions from his American Writers Series volumes, he said, to shape a literary history that promised to have great appeal to a publisher.[5]

Spiller called the first meeting of his Committee on a Cooperative Literary History for 25 March 1939, at 10 A.M., in the Columbia University Faculty Club. He also wrote to Carl Van Doren, asking him to join the committee as an "informal advisor," so that they might profit from his *CHAL* experience—how it was organized and financed, who bore the risk, how payment was arranged for editors and contributors. "I infer from *Three Worlds*," Spiller wrote, "that you have reason to know more than a little about that classic." Van Doren, however, was away on a lecture tour at the time. He subsequently replied both with information

and advice. The time seemed ripe for a new history, said Van
Doren, it should necessarily be cooperative and planned along
lines different from the *CHAL*. As to the financing of the *CHAL*,
he recalled that Putnam had paid the main editors $250 each per
volume (with III and IV considered one volume) and contributors received roughly $5.00 a page. (The correct figures were
$187.50 and $2.50, respectively. See Chapter 2 above.)[6]

The agenda for the March 1939 meeting at Columbia (attended by all members but the ailing Whipple, who died not long
after) included eight items: (1) Should a multivolume history be
attempted *now*? (2) How should opinions be solicited from ALG
members? (3) Should they project a history of five volumes? ten?
twenty? How should contributors be determined? Or the editorial board? (4) What point of view toward literary history should
they assume: (a) that literary history lies within cultural history?
(b) that an aesthetic emphasis should determine periods, forms,
movements, and major writers? And how much space should be
reserved for background material (for example, higher education, growth of periodicals, the role of the frontier)? (5) What
should be the arrangements for publication? For pay to the contributors? (6) Should a bibliography accompany each volume, as
in the *CHAL*? Or be a separate volume? Or be entirely omitted?
(7) What suggestions should be prepared for the executive members of the ALG at the December 1939 meeting? (8) What should
be the next steps and meetings of this committee?

After discussion, Canby moved that the ALG try now to undertake a new history. Spiller suggested that the committee poll ALG
members regarding the type of history to be written. But first, a
selected number of members should be consulted. To that end,
he prepared a memorandum listing these format possibilities:
(1) a compilation of chapter essays, after the fashion of the *CHAL;*
(2) a series of individual volumes, as in the Yale Chronicles; (3) a
multivolume history, with an editor-in-chief for each volume; or
(4) a history of whatever format with a single editor-in-chief.[7]
This last suggestion for a single editor came from Canby, who
repeated the notion in the *Saturday Review of Literature* in August. The ostensible occasion was a recent issuing of Parrington's
Main Currents in one volume. Canby then mentioned that the
American group of the MLA was sponsoring a new cooperative
history—not quite the case as yet, of course; and he was coyly
silent on his own role. Was there a new Parrington on the horizon, he then asked, possessing the required vision and leadership
of an editor-in-chief?[8]

After his mailing, Spiller received suggestions from forty-eight selected members. Fifteen favored separately authored chapters, though not in a random grouping as in the *CHAL*. Thirteen preferred an editor of each volume. Many pointedly opposed a single master editor. Among those with comments on bibliography, no consensus was apparent. Particular responses to the four format options from around the profession included the following: Theodore Hornberger (Texas) preferred option 3. How could one editor (option 4) coordinate many authors? There should be a bibliography per volume, as in the History of American Life series (edited by Schlesinger and Fox for Macmillan, 1929–). Randall Stewart (Brown) felt that an editor-in-chief would undercut the autonomy of individual contributors and create a procrustean history. A single style and interpretation should not be attempted. Thomas Johnson (Lawrenceville School) preferred option 4 but felt that requisite bibliography and research in American literature would not be achieved for the writing of a cooperative history until 1950. Howard M. Jones (Harvard) also felt that any type of cooperative history would be premature because too few of our American literature scholars had the necessary range of historical vision and grasp of historical facts.[9] Newton Arvin (Smith), like Stewart, doubted that a history written in cooperative fashion could also attain critical freshness.

Henry Pochmann (Wisconsin) preferred option 3. Norman Foerster (Iowa) preferred option 1 and then option 2, as did Frank L. Mott (Iowa). Alexander Cowie (Wesleyan) would combine options 1 and 3. Floyd Stovall (North Texas State Teachers College) preferred option 4 and then option 3.

Walter F. Taylor (Mississippi College) preferred some modification of option 1. As to option 4, it would be impossible for the ALG to agree on a single editor-in-chief. Sculley Bradley (Pennsylvania) said no to options 3 and 4, and questioned if American literary scholarship were yet adequate to produce a literary history (thus agreeing with Johnson and Jones). Finally, Harry Clark (Wisconsin) suggested a fifth possibility—a twenty-volume history, with a clear aesthetic distinction (which the *CHAL* lacked) provided by DeQuincey's literature of knowledge and literature of power.

Two publishers were immediately attracted to a large new literary history. Edward Hodnett, advisory editor at Columbia University Press, wrote to Spiller in January 1939 and then reiterated the interest shortly before the March meeting of the committee at Columbia. Following the meeting, Macmillan wrote to Spiller about prospective arrangements as publisher. Spiller replied that the committee had no power to enter into an agreement. It was merely a fact-finding body at present and would report its deliberations at the December meeting in New Orleans. He added, however, that no commitment had been made in any form with any publisher. Macmillan's Theodore Purdy, Jr., continued through the summer to remind Spiller of their interest in the venture. In August, Canby told Spiller that Bennett Cerf of Random House was also interested. A few days before the December meeting in New Orleans, George Brett of Macmillan gave Spiller a firm offer. They would advance ten thousand dollars together with an additional ten thousand dollars for editorial expenses. The proposed history would run to twelve volumes in the format of Rusk's current edition of Emerson's letters (Columbia University Press, 1939), with approximately five hundred pages per volume, or 215,000 words. Two of the twelve volumes would be bibliographical; cost: sixty dollars a set, with final delivery date of 1 January 1946. [10]

The New Orleans meeting in 1939 was prepared by Chairman Hubbell, who invited Gregory Paine to read a paper on research in American literature accomplished since the *CHAL*. Hubbell asked Walter Taylor to relate social history to literary history. Hubbell then intended Spiller to serve as commentator. But he later decided that Spiller would be more effective as the authoritative reporter for the Committee on a Cooperative Literary History. In late October, Napier Wilt (Chicago) advised Spiller to get his committee report to members of the ALG before the New Orleans meeting so that a reasoned discussion could take place. "I rather expect the plan, whatever it is, will come in for quite a bit of criticism," Wilt warned Spiller, "and I suggest that one member of your committee be formally appointed to defend the plan." Wilt's letter was, for Spiller, a tip-off of trouble to come—from Harry Clark, Yvor Winters, and others. [11]

Spiller's committee held a last meeting in November 1939 to prepare their report to the ALG at the December convention in New Orleans. Spiller then wrote to members that they might strengthen their hand at this crucial moment by asking Howard M. Jones to come aboard. The committee agreed. As Spiller knew, Jones was currently working with Kenneth Murdock and Perry Miller on the early stages of a history of American literature in the colonial period, to which an ALG-authorized history might form a multivolume sequel. Jones replied to the invitation by questioning if being on both projects just then might not place him in an uneasy position. And was this ALG committee planning to become the editorial board of a new history? Spiller told Jones that the future role of the committee would be discussed in New Orleans. Meanwhile, Spiller wished to tell Wilt at New Orleans that Jones was on the committee. Four days later, Spiller then had second thoughts, agreed with Jones that the two histories presented a certain awkwardness for him, and suggested they reconsider his role after the upcoming meeting.[12]

✱   ✱   ✱

In retrospect, the New Orleans meeting of 1939 looms as one of the decisive moments in the history of American literature studies. What became the *Literary History of the United States* was, in effect, born there, even though its ultimate fate was to be an enterprise officially separated from the group. In the program, after an opening session on Melville, 135 members gathered to hear a consideration of "Problems and Methods in Literary History." Taylor's paper was titled "Toward a Reinterpretation of the Gilded Age" and Paine's, "The Progress of American Literary Scholarship." But of more central concern was the awaited report by Spiller's committee. In an atmosphere of considerable tension, as he remembered it, Spiller presented an account of the two New York meetings of 25 March and 24 November, together with the solicited opinions of ALG members and the committee's own consensus on the four options for a literary history. He noted that the committee favored the fourth, or Canby, plan of a single editor-in-chief responsible for an overall conception, with a small editorial board to help shape the materials provided by experts in the field (that is, ALG members together with others in special cases). The present committee would serve as a board of directors overseeing the project. The history would run to a maximum of a dozen or so volumes, including special studies, bibliography, and notes. The committee would contract with an established publisher for a delivery date some time after five years of planning and composition.[13]

The report was accepted in what, outwardly, appeared to be a spirit encouraging forward movement on the cooperative history. But inevitable questions of ALG supervision and editorial control surfaced almost at once to aggrieve Spiller's committee. For the moment, Spiller, Bradley, Canby, Rusk, and Williams were reappointed by Chairman-elect Wilt, and the committee was then enlarged with new members Jones, Hubbell, Percy Boynton, and Louis B. Wright (Huntington Library), "with power to sign a contract and arrange the mechanical details of publication and to provide machinery for selecting a permanent editorial board, which shall determine the approach and methods to be employed in the history." One session in the 1940 meeting in Cambridge (and Boston) would consider problems in writing a literary history. [14]

After the 1939 meeting in New Orleans came some crowded and decisive months. Chairman Wilt wrote to ALG secretary, Tremaine McDowell, early in the next year and suggested that the recommendations in the report of Spiller's committee should either be voted on at once by the Advisory Council or they should delay action until the December meeting in Cambridge. McDowell then wrote to the Advisory Council members, enclosing the Spiller report and raising the issue of a council response. Should the council vote now? Conduct a discussion by mail and then vote? Meet before December? Or vote in December?

McDowell received replies from Clark, George Whicher (Amherst), Stovall, Leisy, Leon Howard (Northwestern), Harry Warfel (Maryland), and Louise Pound (Nebraska). Among the more pointed responses, Stovall questioned in what fashion Spiller's proposed board of directors of the history were to work with the publisher and ALG, and just how an editorial board for the project would be chosen. Howard counseled delay of the history and referred to Spiller's article in the *Sewanee Review* five years before that advised patience; and Warfel also thought the history premature. Wilt next wrote to McDowell that the Advisory Council of the ALG should probably have control of a cooperative history, superseding Spiller's board of directors. Or perhaps joint control could be achieved: Spiller's committee might elect four of its members to a governing board and the Advisory Council elect the other members.

McDowell then summed up and variously quoted the responses from ALG members and mailed them to the council, together with a copy of the letter from Wilt. He also asked members who were prepared to vote now to send their official reactions to the report of Spiller's committee. After McDowell received the returns from his mailing, he wrote to Spiller, emphasizing the council's objection to Spiller's committee's serving as the permanent board of directors. Spiller then consulted with his committee by mail and replied that it agreed with the council and that the American Council of Learned Societies had agreed to sponsor a joint meeting of his committee and the Advisory Council. Spiller suggested the week of 9 September 1940, in New York, since Clark and Warfel would already be in the city for the program of the English Institute. (The meeting failed to materialize, but Spiller attended the institute and was enthusiastic over the papers touching literary history.) [15]

Spiller's committee was faced with further difficulties in 1940 when, within its own ranks, certain members—Jones, Hubbell, and Wright—now felt (as had the Advisory Council's Leon Howard and Harry Warfel) that a new history was premature, that the profession was, in fact, ten years away from writing such a multivolume study. Furthermore, Jones, joining Hubbell, objected to an editor-in-chief, as well as Wilt's compromise proposal for a governing board. So the 1940 Christmas meeting promised to deliver a few more sparks among professors with increasingly proprietary concerns over the ALG's high-prestige new enterprise. Years later, Spiller recalled that his committee's upcoming report was mailed to ALG members in October. Several weeks before the meeting, Secretary McDowell also circulated the report to the Advisory Council in order to call special attention to the deletion of the committee's previously assumed position as a governing board for the history. And he took the liberty to urge the council to see the benefit of moving the literary history onward with as much dispatch as possible—this despite the counsel of delay we have seen by members on both the council and Spiller's committee. [16]

At the Cambridge meeting in December 1940, the Spiller report was never delivered. A model of order and completeness, it first summed up the report of the previous year: (1) In five to ten years after inception, the group would have a ten-volume history and a one- to three-volume supplementary history with a like number of bibliographical volumes, to a completed opus of twelve to sixteen volumes; (2) the venture would be controlled by a small editorial board; and (3) a contract would be sought among established publishers. Spiller noted that there were no committee meetings in 1940, due to the geographical spread of the membership, but business had been achieved through correspondence. He listed the work accomplished in six categories: (1) One foundation was considering a grant of twenty-five to fifty thousand dollars to allow one-year leaves for ten to twenty scholars over the five- to ten-year period needed to write the history. (2) The Library of Congress had volunteered space to serve as headquarters and a central location for periodic meetings. (3) To secure a close working partnership between the editors and the bibliographical staff, the WPA Bibliography of American Literature at the University of Pennsylvania might be moved to central quarters at the Library of Congress. (4) Editorial expenses were estimated in six figures. Sources for this money would be sought after a contract was signed. (5) Five publishers were interested. Two had made tentative proposals, one of whom had offered a ten-thousand-dollar subsidy. Both assumed that sales would cover the costs of contributor honoraria, production, and distribution and also realized that a completion date would be a fair number of years into the future. (6) The proposed next step was to meet with the ACLS and report to the group at the December 1941 meeting (in Indianapolis). Spiller concluded that the cooperative history was feasible in three ways. As a work of literature, it would succeed, in spite of many hands, through editorial control of underlying principles and theory. Academically, it would be a valid updating of the *CHAL* if there were no hurry to meet a publisher's deadline. And financially, potential support seemed to be there—from interested parties like Macmillan, Yale, Columbia, Carnegie and Rockefeller Foundations, and the ACLS.[17]

Why was the report of Spiller's Committee on a Cooperative History never presented for consideration and debate by the group at the Cambridge meeting? Spiller remembered that his committee "had little difficulty in reading the handwriting on the wall" after they perused the upcoming papers by Louis B. Wright, Harry Clark, and Yvor Winters (Stanford) published in *American Literature* the month before the meeting. The committee called "a hasty conference in a nearby restaurant" and then "agreed to accept the inevitable and empowered its Chairman to withdraw its proposal and to move instead for a new Committee to explore the resources in American libraries and collections."[18] The committee then met with the Advisory Council and presented the substitute motion. The committee was thanked for its year's work and then discharged. The council agreed to appoint a new committee of five for one year who would look into necessary research and further plans of procedure; petition ACLS to provide expenses for a preliminary conference; and be empowered, as individuals, to appoint a committee for personal help. To maintain some continuity and ensure a regional democracy, the council made the following nominations (not to be announced until accepted):

For Chairman: *first choice,* Robert Spiller (Swarthmore); *alternate,* Gregory Paine (North Carolina). For East Coast Member: *first choice,* Robert Spiller or Sculley Bradley (Pennsylvania); *alternate,* Oscar Cargill (NYU). For Southwest Member: *first choice,* Ernest Leisy (SMU); *alternate,* Theodore Hornberger (Texas). For Pacific Coast Member: *first choice,* Louis B. Wright (Huntington Library); *alternate,* Dixon Wecter (UCLA). For Southeast Member: *first choice,* Gregory Paine (North Carolina); *alternate,* Charles Anderson (Johns Hopkins). For Midwest Member: *first choice,* G. Harrison Orians (Toledo); *alternate,* Walter Blair (Chicago).[19]

The following day, an audience of 225 attended the program on "Problems and Aims in American Literary History." Wright's paper, "Toward a New History of American Literature," argued for a broadly cultural approach to the history and a comprehensive grasp of literary activity reaching different audiences of a given period. Such a history would require a goodly amount of original, as well as corrective, scholarship. After our bibliographical inventory of what we know, we should look to the graduate schools for the pioneering young scholars who would help explore the unknown materials and backgrounds that could then be synthesized in a new literary history. As commentator on Wright's paper, Jones noted that a cooperative literary history would require, beyond adequate bibliographical knowledge, a well-informed philosophy and scholarship. In his opinion, this generation of scholars was not so equipped, at least at present.

Harry Clark's paper, "Suggestions Concerning a History of American Literature," elaborated his theory of an American literary history based on DeQuincey's literature of knowledge and literature of power—expressed in his previous response to Spiller's opinion survey and a part of his paper in September for the English Institute.[20] Clark posed the leading questions of European and indigenous interplay; historical development of forms and ideas; and the evaluative, universal judgment of the literary product. He was more optimistic than Wright that the scholarship was at hand for a vast updating of the *CHAL.* Unlike Jones, Clark believed that an embracing philosophy of literary history, one that would reconcile political and belletristic aspects of our literature, was available if we turned to the formula in DeQuincey's double view of literature. Appropriate criteria of scholarship and judgment would be devoted to each category. Clarence H. Faust (Chicago) responded that neither DeQuincey's nor any other single theory could encompass the multiple problems of selection and interpretation in an American literary history.

Yvor Winters argued, in "On the Possibility of a Co-operative History of American Literature," that the enterprise was hampered by the profession's relatively uncritical acceptance of Parrington's simplistic umbrella of Jeffersonianism and also by the historical ignorance usual in our single-author specialists. Willard Thorp responded especially to the first charge, observing that Parrington's biased approach to an American literary history posed no danger nor did his neglect of form for substance. We had all been forewarned. In the general discussion after all three papers, secretary McDowell detected a common expression of the need for "any good revision, even a temporary one," of the *CHAL*. McDowell did not feel, then or later, that an ALG majority was disposed to an indefinite postponement of the history. But Spiller recalled years later that the "general tenor . . . was negative" in the program discussion of 1940. Members seemed generally in agreement that necessary scholarship was not yet ripe for an ALG cooperative literary history. [21]

The year of decision about a literary history for the ALG became 1941. Spiller's new Committee on Materials of American Literary History assigned itself three areas of survey: (1) universities granting a Ph.D. in American literature, (2) manuscripts and printed sources for an American literary history, and (3) the state of existing scholarship. By the December meeting in Indianapolis, the first two investigations had not been completed. The third was scheduled by the committee and Chairman Wilt as the topic of part two of the annual program and titled, "The Present State of Scholarship in American Literary History." At the meeting, the historical field, from colonial times to 1914, had been divided among six panels. Each panel, led by a member of the committee, appraised the available and the needed scholarship in the given historical time frame. All of the discussion groups considered six categories of inquiry: (1) general histories and histories of ideas, (2) histories of literary types, (3) bibliographies and critical editions, (4) biographies and critical estimates, (5) regional studies and studies of social agencies, and (6) international cultural influences.

The first panel, "Literature of the Colonies—to about 1790," was organized during the year by chairman Louis B. Wright, but in his absence at Indianapolis, the panel was chaired by Leon Howard. Participants were Clarence Faust and Lyon Richardson (Western Reserve). Nineteen members attended the session. The second panel, on "Literature of the New Nation (to about 1830)," was chaired by Gregory Paine, with contributions by Oral Coad (New Jersey College for Women), Milton Ellis (Maine), George Hastings (Arkansas), Henry Pochmann (Wisconsin), and Charles Manning (Centre College, Kentucky). Attendance at this session was twenty-three. Spiller chaired "The Literature of the Mid-Century: The North," with papers by Gay Wilson Allen (Bowling Green), Alexander Cowie, Willard Thorp, and Frederick Tolles (Cambridge, Massachusetts). The audience numbered thirty-five.

The fourth panel, supplementary to Spiller's, was "Literature of the Mid-Century: The Old and New South," chaired by Ernest

Leisy. Contributors were Guy Cardwell (Tulane), Edd Parks (Georgia), John Eidson (Georgia), and Spigg Howard (no academic address). Attendance was twenty-nine. Panel number five was "The Literature of National Expansion," chaired by G. Harrison Orians, with B. A. Botkin (Library of Congress), Fred Lorch (Iowa State), Franklin Walker (Oregon), and Mentor L. Williams (Michigan) participating. Fifteen members attended. Drawing the largest audience (forty-seven) was the panel on "The Literature of the Whole Nation—1870 to 1915," with Sculley Bradley as chairman. Oscar Cargill, Harry Clark, Harry Warfel, Louis Wann (USC), Fred Millett (Wesleyan), Allan Halline (Bucknell), and George Howgate (Wilmington College, Ohio) were panelists. [22]

No groundswell of enthusiasm for an official literary history emerged from this well-organized meeting in Indianapolis. On the other hand, it is not clear that the discussions convinced an ALG majority that the profession was indeed too immature to undertake a cooperative history. In 1942, Spiller's Committee on Materials of American Literary History conducted its continuing survey of scholarly resources and activity. At the end of the year, the committee compiled an ample report but to relatively little purpose. Milton Ellis was elected chairman of the ALG for 1942, with Alexander Cowie the secretary, but the New York meeting in 1942 and the 1943 convention were canceled due to transportation difficulties attending World War II. Tremaine McDowell, the previous secretary, wrote to the Advisory Council in 1943 explaining that the findings of Spiller's committee, recently reported, had not been made public because of various disagreements on their substance, the inability of contributors to devote needed time on the writing, and Macmillan's declining to publish the results as a manual (because of the war). McDowell appointed Spiller, Warfel, and Secretary-elect Cowie to be custodians. The pages were entrusted to Spiller's college library at Swarthmore. [23]

The larger story of 1942 is Spiller's action, urged and supported by Canby and others, to keep the projected literary history alive by steering it into unofficial channels, to establish an independent editorial board, and return to Macmillan for further negotiations. "I hope you will keep clear of the skirts of the American Literature Group," Stanley Williams wrote to Spiller in early 1943, "After all, they had their chance." McDowell wrote to ALG members, also in early 1943, briefly summarizing, and justifying, this private break with the group. After the disagreements perceived at the Boston meeting in 1940, the direction had slowly and inevitably moved toward "a briefer interpretative history in two or three volumes written by a few hands, designed as a synthesis for the general reader as well as the scholar" and managed now as a private enterprise. McDowell then revealed the names of the four editors and three associates at work on the history: Spiller, Thorp, Canby, Johnson, Jones, Williams, and Wecter. In a subsequent mailing to the Advisory Council of the ALG, however, McDowell submitted his personal view that the majority of ALG members may well have regarded the profession mature enough 2½ years before to sponsor an undelayed literary history. [24]

Chapter 23

The Cooperative History Goes Independent: Organization and Theory (1942–1943)

After the meeting at Cambridge in Christmas 1940, when the Committee on a Cooperative History withdrew its report to the ALG during what appeared to be an adversely critical spirit in the program papers and among the group, Henry Canby wrote to Spiller about a new approach to this scholarly venture. Canby already dreaded the prospect that an ALG history, if written, would be another *CHAL* miscellany "turned over to an opposition [of ALG members] which (frankly and confidentially) I think contains a high proportion of mediocrities." He was anxious to go a different route and proposed to Spiller a get-together in May 1941, at Canby's place in Killingworth, Connecticut, with invitations going to Howard Jones and Stanley Williams. The next month, Canby reported to Spiller that Williams was keenly interested. But Spiller himself had been having his doubts, since he was chairman of the new ALG Committee on Materials of American Literary History that was presumably working toward a future history authorized by the group. He recalled: "I did not see how I could honestly serve two masters: the Group in its research project and a private team writing an interpretive synthesis." He then resolved the conflict, as he told Canby, by seeing the independent history as a less definitive interpretation centering on the major writers and their cultural backgrounds. And so in late spring 1941, a conference of four—Canby, Spiller, Williams, and Jones (Willard Thorp and Thomas Johnson were not in the picture yet nor was Dixon Wecter)—met to discuss the work that would develop privately in the following year on the *Literary History of the United States* (hereafter, the *LHUS*). Not one of them at that time, however, volunteered to take the primary initiative.[1]

The group did not meet again in 1941, but Spiller and Canby renewed their plans in the autumn for this somewhat modest, multiple-authored history, and Macmillan repeated the offer of advanced royalties (but not the subsidy) previously extended for an ALG-sponsored history. After the December convention of the MLA in Indianapolis, Canby wrote to Spiller eager to know exactly what had developed at the meeting. To Spiller, the most important occurrence was an encounter at his hotel with Willard Thorp of Princeton, who agreed to become Spiller's coeditor of this independent history. Canby seems not to have known of this new editor-to-be, however, until March 1942, when he wrote to Spiller that he welcomed the interest expressed by "Thorpe" [*sic*]. Shortly thereafter, Thorp wrote to "Mr. Canby" that he and Spiller had been talking about "this matter of a new history of American Literature." The discussions were becoming more than casual. At a lunch with Thorp at the Nassau Club in Princeton on 2 June 1942, Spiller recalls that they "laid out the essential guidelines for the new and now living project. . . . Perhaps the most important item was a decision to take the bus (this was wartime) down to nearby Lawrenceville and ask Tom Johnson to be our bibliographer. After a half-hour talk in his home, he said, 'I have never before made so important a decision so quickly, but I agree.'"[2]

Spiller elaborated their "essential guidelines" in a working proposal, "*In re* The History of American Literature," stipulating that he and Thorp would bring together a 450,000-word literary history, to be finished in 1944. It would be in one volume, from 1,000 to 1,200 pages, including text, bibliography, notes, and index. Canby would serve on the editorial board, with a 10 percent share of the royalties for his advice and editorial work. Jones and Williams would serve as advisory editors for the manuscript and perhaps as contributors but would have no voting power. One hundred to two hundred dollars would be paid for these editorial services. Because tentative, the plan for the editorial board might be altered to embrace a larger geographical spread to the South and West, to include perhaps Charles Anderson (Johns Hopkins), Tremaine McDowell or Joseph Warren Beach (Minnesota), George Stewart (California), or others. A bibliographer might also be added to the board, working in cooperation with the WPA bibliographical project at the University of Pennsylvania to compile two hundred to three hundred pages of selected listings. This person (Thomas C. Pollock of NYU perhaps, or Ernest Leisy of SMU) would receive 10 to 20 percent of the royalties. (Almost at once after drafting this working proposal, dated 2 June 1942, Spiller and Thorp had found their bibliographer in Thomas Johnson.) Spiller noted that Macmillan had offered ten thousand dollars in advance royalties for a literary history. Should the editors talk further—with Houghton Mifflin? With other publishers?

From the advance on royalties, they could pay contributors two cents a word, with an added three cents after royalties of ten thousand dollars. The editorial board would be empowered to reject manuscripts or edit them according to the general pattern and thematic structure of the entire history. The chief contributors would be Spiller and Thorp, each writing roughly one-fourth of the text. The advisory editors would have second choice thereafter in selecting their own possible contributions. To gain relief from teaching burdens, the board would seek a grant from Rockefeller or Carnegie to the sum of ten thousand dollars. From the grant, Spiller and Thorp would receive twenty-five hundred dollars each (half-time teaching), as would the bibliographer, leaving twenty-five hundred dollars for miscellaneous expenses.

Though this sketch would be modified in the subsequent planning of the *LHUS*, Spiller had provided the group with a firm basis from which to work. In July 1942, Johnson officially accepted the offer to join an informal editorial board. At the same time, Spiller invited Williams and Jones to come onto the board as advisory editors. Williams readily accepted his role in what Spiller announced as a two-year undertaking. Jones was tentative: The book on colonial literature he was coediting with Perry Miller and Kenneth Murdock was bogged down, since Miller had gone into the Army, and Jones was not hitting it off too well with Murdock. Several months later, Dixon Wecter agreed to join as an associate, and the editorial group that would engineer the *LHUS* to its completion over the next five years was essentially formed. [3]

On 1 August 1942, Spiller, Thorp, and Johnson met in Princeton to discuss an early outline for the *LHUS*. Johnson became the recording secretary and treasurer and would thenceforth issue copies of the minutes of meetings and other communications to Thorp and Spiller for their corrections before circulating them to the other editors. Letters and important documents would be sent to the three contributing editors only on approval of the four chief editors. Because they were conveniently close geographically—Spiller at Swarthmore, Thorp at Princeton, Johnson at Lawrenceville School, and Canby in New York City—the four editors easily made a quorum for some nineteen two-day meetings in the crucial three years to follow. The board members worked in close cooperation, clearly knowing their editorial duties (Canby's related chiefly to business details of publishing, including permissions). The agenda of the meetings ranged from financial matters, including applications for grants, to discussing potential contributors, shifting conceptions of the history, and final duties during the reading of manuscripts. [4]

In rapid and efficient order, then, the *LHUS* became a private enterprise in 1942. Four business matters concerned the main editors in the summer and following months: (1) foundation support, (2) relief from campus professorial duties, (3) legalization of their "corporation," and (4) a suitable contract with a publisher. Canby wrote to Spiller in late July 1942 that Philip Jessup at Carnegie was agreeable to diverting some of the funds proposed to go toward the war effort and assigning it to the *LHUS*. Spiller replied that he would draw up the budget for a grant of thirty thousand dollars. And Canby replied, meanwhile, that Carnegie funds had, in fact, been made available. [5]

In August 1942, Lawrenceville granted Johnson a half-time teaching and committee load for the next two years, presumably the term for completing the *LHUS*. To facilitate Johnson's bibliography, Princeton allowed him headquarters in a Princeton library cubicle, together with a library page who would double as a typist. Johnson came to learn, however, that compiling a selective bibliography for the literary history would be a lengthy, piecemeal job stretching far beyond this two-year period. Blessedly, in April 1944, near the end of this two-year relief at Lawrenceville, Johnson received a Rockefeller grant. Spiller, meanwhile, was seeking from Swarthmore's President Nason a leave patently overdue. In August 1942, it was granted, covering the anticipated period for completing and publishing the *LHUS*: full salary during the spring semester of 1943 and the subsequent two years at one-half pay. Later in 1943, both Spiller and Thorp received Rockefeller grants (five thousand dollars each). [6]

Late in 1942, the four chief editors understood the wisdom of incorporating as a business, of becoming a legal partnership. As a private nonprofit corporation (for tax purposes), Spiller was designated president, Thorp vice president, and Johnson treasurer. In November 1942, the informal partnership was legally drawn up. It was signed by the parties in January 1943. With the board legally prepared to conduct its business, members ironed out the contract with Macmillan. In October 1942, the publisher had sent Spiller a draft of the contract. Financial terms were as follows: advance: $10,000; royalties: 15 percent domestic, 5 percent foreign; sale of rights to book club or organization: 50 percent; English edition: 50 percent; and editors' proportional shares: Spiller, 35 percent; Thorp, 30 percent; Johnson, 25 percent; Canby, 10 percent. The contract was signed and mailed by Macmillan on 20 January 1943.

The corporation had a dual identity, of course, for it was also a policy-making committee of scholars. As such, the four officially defined their editorial responsibilities: chairman: Spiller, editor-in-chief and main welder of the ideology; vice-chairman: Thorp, chiefly responsible on matters of scholarly accuracy; secretary: Johnson, bibliographer, with responsibility for notes at policy meetings, circulation of minutes; and adviser: Canby, the role of elder statesman. The document merely confirmed the previous understanding and especially the role Spiller had taken for himself months earlier. In July 1942, after the editorial board (excepting Wecter) was officially designated, Spiller had written to his colleagues that the urgent next step was to sketch and outline the history. Mainly, they should "review critically the literature of the mid-nineteenth century and of the present in the light of its causal antecedents and backgrounds." The former period could be satisfactorily treated through the major authors, but the past thirty years called for groupings—by schools or types. These two areas conceived, they could then consider intellectual, economic, and political forces, the problems of literary production, and the minor writers. From the design of this preliminary outline, they could then decide on chapter assignments for the entire history with as little overlapping as possible. By the end of August 1942, Spiller had drafted an exploratory "Statement to Contributors."[7]

In the weeks and months to follow, the conception and outlining were discussed, revised, and generally agreed to in various exchanges among the editors. Through it all, Spiller's original sense of a cresting of the history at the end of two flourishing periods—the midnineteenth century and the 1930s—remained the dynamic principle of the larger historical form of the *LHUS*. The theory of romantic cycles appeared in his correspondence with Canby early in 1941. Spiller had proposed two introductory, formative questions regarding the "proposed survey history of American literature." First was the aesthetic question of what great literature is and who the great American writers are (Spiller figured that they numbered somewhere from six to twelve). Second was the definition of what is American—the issue of nationalism amid our heterogeneous races, languages, customs, traditions, and occupations. Spiller discovered the answer to both questions in a romantic formula applied to American backgrounds and writers. In his theory, "only a romantic movement can create great literature," though within such a welling-up of expression must come also "a degree of control through self-criticism." Both the creativity and the critical discipline were present in America from 1830 to 1870. But developing also were "disruptive forces of national experience" that were "undermining the structure." After 1870, "the whole process was being repeated in terms of the larger nation. By about 1910, this second romantic movement was learning its own discipline through the development of a critical movement." In view of this dual unfolding of a cyclical history, Spiller asserted in 1941 that we were probably living in "the great day of American literature."[8]

The panel discussions at the 1941 MLA meeting in Indianapolis the following Christmas (see Chapter 22) may also have sharpened Spiller's awareness of how some of the best minds in the ALG (and potential contributors to a new literary history) viewed their nation's literature and scholarship. More important, however, were some conceptual obligations he had already incurred, going all the way back to fellow scholars of the 1920s. As he subsequently wrote to Norman Foerster, whom he first met in 1923, that scholar's *"Four Major Factors"* (puritanism, the frontier, romanticism, and realism) greatly influenced the basic structure of the *LHUS*. They combined with Foerster's phrase "European culture and American environment" to govern much of the argument of the entire *LHUS*. The first five parts recapitulated Foerster's "frontier spirit" through the Puritan tradition to the rise and fall of the first romantic movement; and subsequent chapters traced that same frontier spirit through the rise and fall of the realistic movement.[9] The two romantic cycles, however, were Spiller's original conception.

In 1942, then, Spiller and fellow editors were drafting in one paper, and again in another, the blueprint and working instructions for a new history. Thanks to Spiller's complete and extensive record, we can follow the conceptual process in close and fascinating detail. Continuing into late summer, he was giving special care to the intellectual-background essays and wrote a four-page sketch, "Introductory Chapters on the History of American Thought" (12 September 1942). These chapters would be united by an overarching theme and four recurring themes. The dominant idea was that American literary expression grew out of European thought and experience (chiefly British) continuously assimilated in the new world until the total nation was settled and a distinctive culture formed. The stages of this development were "importation, modification, fertilization, and dynamic return." The four themes that recurred "with a fair degree of consistency" were (1) the revolt against authority in religion and philosophy, (2) the revolt against authority in government, (3) the illusion of infinite resources, and (4) the skepticism of scientific inquiry.

These conceptual pages gave Spiller a basis for the larger treatment of five general principles, together with a six-page provisional outline, both of which he prepared for editorial scrutiny at the beginning of 1943. The first principle repeated the concept of a transplanted European culture, as "two principal cycles" developed from settlements east and west of the Alleghenies. The second principle stated the purpose of literary history, "to provide the historical context for the critical judgment of masterpieces, the works of major authors, and the chief currents of popular taste in writing." And Spiller now reiterated that the shape of that history in America emerged from two phases or cycles, the one culminating with the major writers of 1830–1870 and the second with the resurging expression in modern times. The second principle led to the third and finer principle of the history's organization, with consideration of sections and chapters on (1) thought: the evolution of the American mind; (2) instruments of culture; (3) major authors, minor contributors to literary forms, and regional aesthetics; and (4) summary assessment of period taste and literary achievement. The fourth principle asserted the four recurring themes, drafted in the previous document, that unified the intellectual background chapters. The fifth principle posited a freely critical but not doctrinaire spirit for contributors, though the critical focus on contemporary literature would be the "forms or movements rather than major authors because the relative importance of contemporary authors is difficult to determine even tentatively."

Next came a provisional outline, dated 1 January 1943, the product of discussion and revision in the preceding months. The editors anticipated a history in two parts containing five sections each, and subdivided into sixty-one chapters. Subsequently revised at least nine times, even to March 1946, this early outline in its main contours remained surprisingly intact in the eighty-one chapters of the published *LHUS:*

Outline (1 January 1943)	LHUS (final version)
Book I. The Literature of the New Nation (1607–1890)	
Section I. The Colonies: Importation and Adaptation (to 1760) (7 chaps.)	Part I. The Colonies . . . importation and adaptation (8 chaps.)
Section II. The Republic: Adaptation and Fertilization (1760–1820) (5 chaps.)	Part II. The Republic . . . inquiry and limitation (7 chaps.)
Section III. The Nation: Fertilization and Dynamic Return (1820–1850) (7 chaps.)	Part III. The Democracy . . . the meaning of independence (8 chaps.)

Outline (1 January 1943)	*LHUS* (final version)
Section IV. High Noon (1830–1870) (6 chaps.)	Part IV. Literary Fulfillment (6 chaps.)
Section V. The Civilized East: Refinement and Success (1850–1890) (7 chaps.)	Part V. Crisis . . . conflict, refinement, success (8 chaps.)
Book II. The Literature of the Whole Nation (1775–1945)	
Section I. The Opening of the Frontiers: West and South (1775–1880) (6 chaps.)	Part VI. Expansion . . . new perspectives (10 chaps.)
Section II. Sectionalism and Local Color (1860–1890) (5 chaps.)	Part VII. The Sections . . . tradition and experiment (9 chaps.)
Section III. Making of Modern American Literature (1870–1890) (7 chaps.)	Part VIII. The Continental Nation . . . disillusion, reform, definition (9 chaps.)
Section IV. Coming of Age of American Literature (1900–1920) (5 chaps.)	Part IX. The United States . . . confidence and criticism (8 chaps.)
Section V. Literature in the United States (1920–1945) (6 chaps.)	Part X. A World Literature (8 chaps.)

Throughout 1943, the editors refined the outline, guiding themes, and rationale of the history. Dixon Wecter responded to the outline of 1 January, calling the two-cycle theory a happy formulation. He foresaw difficulties with the introductory linking chapters, however, and especially with overlap in Spiller's four recurring themes. Spiller answered Wecter's misgivings when he fashioned a revised outline on 16 January, and appended a page with further suggestions for the framing chapters on historical backgrounds. They were to be related as closely as possible to the literature itself. The instruments chapters should deal with external conditions that affected both literary content and creation of audiences, and this discussion should lead to summary essays on taste. The decline of the East should be clearly followed by sectional writings, and the division date should be clarified, "making our two cycles more nearly two phases." And the history should emphasize Southern culture and European relationships. He hoped that he had "explained if not justified" these chapters to Wecter's satisfaction, Spiller wrote in a letter to Williams, and continued, "There is a danger that a literary history may exist in an aesthetic vacuum or fall into the genre of social and intellectual history (like Parrington's). These chapters will, we hope, provide just enough contact with the American mind and scene to set us free for full exercise of our critical faculties on the literature."[10]

Williams, on his part, never quarreled with the outline as it went through the various revisions, including a change to four books rather than two, with an epilogue symposium for the period 1940 to 1945 (in a version contemplated in 2–3 February 1945), and ultimately to the ten parts that stand in the final version. Williams concerned himself, instead, with names of likely contributors to the various chapters. Canby suggested only minor changes in the 16 January revised outline, citing problems of overlap between sections III (1820–50) and IV (1830–70); questioning the title, "The Civilized East" of section V, as though the East, previous to 1850, were uncivilized; and looking for greater clarification of how our literary regionalism formed in relation to the continental nation.[11]

If Thorp harbored some reservations on Spiller's conception, they do not appear in the record. He worked with Spiller to establish the content of individual chapters and determine the cooperative assignments of the two chief editors. Among the techniques they should design together, Spiller suggested the need for preliminary indexes of American authors and their works that would be discussed in the chapters treating criticism, thought, taste, and instruments of culture.[12] In the overall division of responsibilities, each of the ten parts should have a supervising editor, and they proposed the following assignments: Spiller for parts II, III, VII, and VIII; Thorp for IV–VI and X; and Canby for I, IX, and before it was scrapped, the proposed epilogue.

The member of the team least enthusiastic with Spiller's conceptual plan was Jones. To him, the divisions in Spiller's outline of 1 January 1943, were unclear not only in distinguishing the sectional and the national, but also in determining which authors were representative of each. He felt Spiller was aiming at too great an inclusiveness. And he did not feel Spiller's two cycles to be really distinct and sequential. After a week and more of reflection, Jones wrote again and this time caustically dismissed "the unworkable concept of two simultaneous cycles of American literature—surely, if you will back off and look at it, one of the oddest notions about literary history yet to be invented!" Strongly suspect, too, were the four forces in Spiller's original conception. Jones had deliberately not examined the revised outlines of 16 January and 2–3 February, so as not to be "swayed by them." Instead, he enclosed an outline of his own, without cycles, in seven parts.

Jones proposed the following divisions and their main characteristics:

   I. The Colonial Period (1492–1739): Literature of exploration, discovery, and explanation of the New World.
   II. American Eighteenth Century (1739–1776): Literature of ideas, the Americanization of European thought.
   III. Nationalization of Letters (1776–1836): Politics in literature, belles lettres, local versus national literature.
   IV. Romantic Triumph (The American Renaissance) (1836–1865): Dynamic nature, regionalism of East, South, and West.
   V. American Silver Age (1865–1890): Cosmopolitanism versus realism, sociological and economic forces override earlier politics and philosophy, democratizing of literature as culture becomes pedagogical.
   VI. Literature of Imperial Republic (1890–1919): Revives elements of part III, plus literature with humanitarian purpose.
   VII. American Literature Comes of Age (1919–): New criticism, techniques, and psychology; polarizing of conservative and radical positions in politics and culture.

Jones also stressed, more than the *LHUS* outline, the literature of travel, political and social controversy, autobiography, popular religion, and historical writing.[13]

Spiller responded that while Jones's organization appeared to depart from the lines developing in the *LHUS* plan, the two basically agreed in their total conception of our literary history. Spiller then reported to the other editors that he had met with Jones, and while they were cordial, Jones was adamantly opposed to the two-cycle theory. Or as Spiller rather gently put it, "He does not stress the evolutionary basis for literary development as much as we do." Also, Jones had warned against assuming that Beardian economic and political history could be viewed as intellectual history. Despite the ideas arising therefrom, such history is distinguished by its factual basis. Spiller revised section VII, the post–Civil War period, in May (perhaps influenced by Jones's prodding). But when Spiller presently sent the revised outline to Jones, the reply came back that it was unsatisfactorily timid for the years after 1865. (This era became, in the not-so-timid title and treatment of Jones's book in 1971, *The Age of Energy*.)[14]

Shortly thereafter, Jones asked to be dropped from the enterprise because, he said, his graduate school and other duties at Harvard were very heavy. Spiller pleaded with him to stay on. The editorial group, he said, profited from the "Jonesean salt—or is it acid?" That criticism had already caused them to rethink the theoretical bases of American literary history. In view of Jones's withering criticism of the double-cycle theory, the request speaks highly for Spiller's tolerance, a personal quality that had enabled him, in countless ways and at various stages, to keep the history from going under. Not that Jones was deemed indispensable. Spiller wrote to Canby in August 1943 that if Jones went off the board, they might ask Carl Van Doren. Also, Tremaine McDowell would be a good replacement and would help remove any stigma of the board's appearing to represent an Eastern establishment. Several weeks later, in fact, the editors did invite Van Doren to become an associate. Van Doren replied that thirty years before, he had freely given himself to the *CHAL* on behalf of our infant literary history; but currently he was too busy to enter the editorial service once again. Jones ultimately stayed. But the cycle theory stayed as well.[15]

Chapter 24

The Editors in Profile (1943)

The four editors and their three associates formed an *LHUS* team of scholar-teachers whose careers to 1943, if recounted in elaborate detail, would bear on virtually every important phase of American literature study since the *CHAL*. Their guiding spirit, Robert E. Spiller, was born in Philadelphia, son of a Virginia father who had moved to that city to study medicine at the University of Pennsylvania. Spiller received his B.A. there in 1917 and then served in World War I "in the hills of Southern France, winning the war for Democracy by pounding a typewriter in the Headquarters office."[1] After the war, he returned to Pennsylvania as a graduate student of English literature and an instructor in the English department (1920–21). In 1921, he received an M.A. and completed course work for his doctorate.

Spiller became an instructor of English at nearby Swarthmore in 1921 while hoping, after writing the doctoral dissertation, to become a university professor. But as he recalled many years later, "I went to Swarthmore for two years before going on to a university, but it was so exciting that the two years stretched to twenty-four" before he returned to his alma mater in 1945 after Arthur H. Quinn retired. Indeed, it was Quinn in the early 1920s who caused the decisive turn in Spiller's scholarly life. As a student, Spiller had developed a passion for the English romantic poets, and

> I wasted a year trying to shape my own speculations about the political mysticism of William Blake into acceptable form [for a dissertation], and then another year working on an uncongenial topic in Middle English drama [at the suggestion of Albert Baugh]. Finally, in desperation, I turned to Professor Arthur Hobson Quinn, most of whose survey courses in American literary types I had taken, and asked him for a topic. He suggested that the history of the travel essay in America "had not been done." "Where do I begin?" I asked, thinking of Irving, Emerson, and Henry James. "Begin at the beginning," he advised.

With the energy and brilliance of an intelligent young man in a hurry, Spiller soon had the Ph.D. (1924) and his first published

book, *The American in England During the First Half Century
of Independence* (1926). A Guggenheim fellowship quickly followed, and Spiller was off to Europe to widen his expertise especially in Cooper as "a social and political critic of comparative
cultures rather than merely the writer of romances of the wilderness, the Indians, and the sea. To set this matter straight became
my main scholarly activity for a decade." Spiller became a biographer, editor, and bibliographer, and produced five books on
Cooper between 1930 and 1936.

There were related areas for Spiller to explore and conquer in
the profession. Though undergraduate literature at Swarthmore
was typically weighted toward the English writers, he managed
an occasional seminar in American literature. And in time, the
school boasted one of the strongest humanities programs in the
country under Spiller's chairmanship. Outside the campus, he
earned the friendship and respect of professional colleagues in
the American Literature Group of the MLA, most of them his seniors. He was only twenty-four and without a Ph.D. when he
served as acting secretary of the group at its third meeting in
1923, his mentor Quinn presiding. In 1930 and 1931, he became
chairman of the group and in 1932, was elected to the Advisory
Council. He remained on that body during two three-year terms.
Also through these crucial years, he served on the Committee on
Publications en route to the founding of *American Literature* in
1929, the Committee on Resources for Research, and climactically, the Committee on a Cooperative Literary History. When
the last-named was disbanded in 1940, Spiller also chaired its replacement, the Committee on Materials of American Literary
History. He was an advisory editor of *American Literature* from
its maiden issue in 1929 to 1931 and then a member of the editorial board for the rest of the decade.

The man from undergraduate Swarthmore, as previously
noted, was the most prolific reviewer for the profession's journal
during its first decade (and from 1940 to 1943, he added thirteen
more reviews). In these reviews, and others elsewhere, Spiller
was advancing on his most important scholarly field, the theory
of American literary history. Some of the landmark volumes he
thoroughly pondered and then reviewed over the course of twenty
years were Lawrence's *Studies in Classic American Literature*,
Parrington's *Main Currents in American Thought*, *The Reinterpretation of American Literature*, Jones's *America and French
Culture*, Foerster's *Towards Standards*, Rourke's *American Humor* and *The Roots of American Culture*, Canby's *Classic Americans*, Hicks's *The Great Tradition*, Cowley's *Exile's Return*,

Brooks's *The Flowering of New England* and *New England: Indian Summer,* Matthiessen's *American Renaissance,* and Kazin's *On Native Grounds.*[2] Spiller's learning in these critiques and his other scholarship came to be recognized and rewarded in the years before the *LHUS* with summer professorships at ranking universities: Harvard (1930), Columbia (1931 and 1937), University of Southern California (1933), and Michigan (1936).

✱   ✱   ✱

Willard Thorp was Spiller's junior by three years, but he made a much tardier pilgrimage from English to American literature scholarship. He grew up in Sidney, New York, where his prep-school literature, as he wrote later in a brief memoir, "was the standard one that still persists in many places"—a drama of Shakespeare each year, plus *Silas Marner, Ivanhoe,* and so on.[3] He recalled studying only one American work, Lowell's *The Vision of Sir Launfal.* His education in American literature—again the familiar story—came through undirected reading in the local library. When he matriculated at Hamilton College in the class of 1920, the English department's curriculum was the British writers. "Where was American literature? No course; no explanation of *why* there was no course."

Thorp went on to Harvard for an M.A., and was now determined to study his own nation's literature, only to discover that Chester Noyes Greenough offered the single course, a year-long survey that met three times a week. (The reader was young Kenneth Murdock.) Thorp gained permission to audit, but after one term—they had arrived only to Benjamin Franklin by February in the classroom of "the frostiest lecturer I have ever listened to"—he stopped attending. Later in the year, he began a three-year teaching apprenticeship at Smith College as an assistant professor of English and public speaking. In 1924, he returned to graduate school, this time Princeton, and wrote his doctoral thesis on Elizabethan drama under Thomas M. Parrott. Too modest to say so in his reminiscences, Thorp was clearly an outstanding student, receiving his Ph.D. in 1926 and becoming at once a member of the Princeton faculty. This remained his lifetime academic address. He published four books in the next ten years, all on English literature.

And how did Thorp become a convert to American literature? Colleagues and friends piqued his curiosity about books like Mark Twain's *Pudd'nhead Wilson* or Van Wyck Brooks's *The Pilgrimage of Henry James,* and he read them for pleasure. In the mid-1930s, one of his old classmates from Princeton, Austin

Warren, was asked by Harry Clark to suggest someone for the Melville volume in Clark's American Writers Series. Warren suggested Thorp, and "Harry took me sight unseen." A large man with an enthusiasm for scholarly research and an extraordinary talent for organization, Thorp plunged in, as he would time and again in the years to come, to "work up" an area of the American field into which he had arrived so belatedly. Moreover, as we discovered in a previous chapter, work on Melville in the midthirties was similarly behind the times:

> There was almost everything to be done. Every time I came away from the New York Public Library or a call on the Metcalfs up in Cambridge, I had a discovery, or more than one in my brief-case. Into those three wonderful years I packed all my years of neglect of my native literature.

After the Melville book (1938), Thorp became active in the affairs of the American Literature Group. At the MLA meeting at Cambridge in 1940, he was a discussion leader at the symposium on problems and aims of American literary history and was elected to a three-year term on the Advisory Council. The next year, he gave a paper for Spiller's panel on "The Literature of the Mid-Century: The North." By then, Spiller had recognized in Thorp the ideal coeditor of a new American literary history. Years later, Spiller praised Thorp's complementary abilities and interests, as well as the wide learning in American literature that he had amassed in so short a time:

> Whereas I was most concerned with the philosophy and structure of the whole, he was interested in the specific problem, the specific chapter, the specific author, the perfection of detail. He could have written any chapter in the book, but he left the organizing of the overall history primarily to me. He was the most informed and perceptive of us all in designing special chapters and in suggesting contributors. [4]

Thorp brought his organizational abilities to bear, as well, on teaching American literature at Princeton and developing the national American Studies movement. In 1940, he and Lawrance Thompson fashioned "American Literature, 1800–1870," the first graduate course in American literature ever to be offered at Princeton. Thorp recognized, too, the need for an undergraduate text in American literature that would serve the intellectual breadth he required to properly study American literature. In

1941, with Princeton colleague Carlos Baker and historian Merle Curti (Columbia), Thorp published *American Issues,* a two-volume anthology subtitled *The Literary Record* and *The Social Record,* respectively. The same year, he was appointed to the ALG Committee on Curricula in American Civilization, and in the next decade, he served as president of the American Studies Association. If he had come to American literature study, in his words, as "a convert, not a founder," he helped to direct that subject into the interdisciplinary paths of the new American studies with the pioneering vision of a veritable founder.

★　★　★

Thomas Johnson was not the foremost bibliographer on the American literature scene when Spiller and Thorp drove down from Princeton to nearby Lawrenceville School in 1942 and persuaded him to join the editorial board in that capacity. But Johnson had more than modest credentials and was, in addition, the foremost scholar of New England literature among all the contributors. He was, in fact, a New Englander by birth and training, though he departed down the Atlantic coast for a professional career. Having graduated from Williams College in the class of 1926, he pursued graduate studies, perhaps inevitably, at Harvard. In the years before he received the doctorate (his dissertation in 1932 was "Jonathan Edwards as a Man of Letters") he taught at Rutgers and Williams.

After his graduate work, Johnson coedited a pair of distinguished books. The first was on Edwards, with Clarence Faust (Chicago), in Harry Clark's American Writers Series (1935); the second, with Perry Miller (Harvard), *The Puritans,* also in a Harry Clark venture with American Book Company titled American Literature Series, ranged far beyond Edwards to become the classic source book and anthology on the period. (It was reissued twenty-five years later with revised bibliographies—still a standard book for the period.) For the first time, Johnson's widely ranging scholarship and bibliographical knowledge of the early period was displayed. But in 1939, he made a far greater splash in American literature studies. It was he who introduced the scholarly world to the verses of Edward Taylor, four hundred pages of manuscripts that had lain over two centuries in Yale University archives. (Perry Miller, speaking at the University of Washington in the early 1960s, remarked that the casual ignoring of these manuscripts over so many years was what Harvard men had come to understand as "scholarship at Yale.") Beyond the revelation of Taylor's poetic genius, Johnson showed in *The Poetical Works of Edward Taylor* the meticulous attention to the smallest essential detail that distinguishes the bibliographical scholar.

Johnson the bibliographer stepped forward more prominently the next year with the *Printed Writings of Jonathan Edwards*. At Lawrenceville School in New Jersey since 1937, he clearly thrived on the alternation between prep-school instruction and the intense concentration demanded of textual and bibliographical scholarship.[5] In 1942, he became the bibliographer for the ALG, succeeding Gregory Payne and Raymond Adams, and prepared the American listings for *PMLA* until he was relieved five years later by Lewis Leary. His achievements as an educator during the war, and as an outstanding authority on Emily Dickinson in the next decade, await telling in later pages.

Henry Seidel Canby was senior member of the board, in both age and editorial experience. Already approaching his middle sixties when the history was under way, his most productive years were behind him. But he had lost none of his ardor for a national literature that would both mirror and inspire the special qualities of being an American in a country unique to Western civilization. As a cultural critic, he often had asked not if an American book were artistically excellent but, instead, what good result it would have on our nation and its literature. He served the intellectual and literary life of America more than six decades until his death in 1961.

Born in 1878 in Wilmington, Delaware, Canby graduated from Yale in 1899 and the next year began his long, and only, teaching career at his alma mater (he took a Ph.D. in 1905). Though he is remembered as an influential editor and taste shaper, his earliest profession was in the classroom. Canby was a publishing pedagogue, and by 1913, he had written three textbook histories of the short story in English and two texts on composition. Two years later in *College Sons and College Fathers* (a sexist title for which he apologized), Canby assessed college education from many perspectives, in and out of campus, though his strongest emotions rested with the mission of the underpaid English professor to stimulate even mediocre students and hope to realize, amid our huge commercial civilization, Whitman's dream of an audience for a great national literature.

Canby memorialized his early years at Yale again in *Alma Mater* (1936). But university life did not contain all of his energies, and in 1911, he began his double life of professor and journalist. He assisted Wilbur Cross in founding and editing the *Yale Review,* acquiring thereby "my first peeps through the ivory wall, my first professional contacts with contemporary American literature, of which we scholars in English then knew little."[6] After serving in World War I as a liaison officer for the British Ministry of Information, Canby returned to establish far broader "contacts with contemporary literature" when he became, in 1920, the first editor of the *Literary Review* of the *New York Evening Post.* In that service, he was still the teacher, and his domain now was the "education of the reading American mind," as he termed it in his descriptive and informal, but not formulistic, *Definitions* (1922 and 1924), collections of his articles over the four-year term on the *Literary Review.*

When the *Post* was sold to the inhospitable Cyrus Curtis, Canby and his brilliant staff of the *Review,* William Rose Benét, Amy Loveman, and Christopher Morley, began the *Saturday Review of Literature,* with Canby becoming vice president to its publisher, Henry R. Luce. For a dozen years as editor, and even beyond, when he relaxed into chairman of the board, Canby reviewed the major works of American literature scholarship and every creative writer of large or modest reputation. He studied and reviewed literary historians Parrington, Calverton, Angoff, Brooks, and Smith, as well as Beer's *Mauve Decade,* Foerster's editions of the *Reinterpretation of American Literature* and *Humanism and America,* More's *On Being Human,* Sherman's posthumous *Life and Letters,* and scholarly works on Increase Mather, Emerson, Thoreau, both Alcotts, Whitman, Bret Harte, and Mark Twain. Of the living belletristic authors, Canby's list was so inclusive that a roll call becomes pointless. His response to these members of a "Brief Golden Age" was unfailingly sympathetic—except for an occasional complaint that some were creating "art for science's sake."

Beyond his largely amiable criticism, Canby was a serious scholar and aspired, in the 1920s, to write a history of American literature. Pressures of his editorial life at the *Saturday Review,* together with a new office in 1926 as chairman of the board of editors for the new Book-of-the-Month Club, made it impossible for him to accomplish the herculean and sustained research of literary history. *Classic Americans* (1931) was the most ambitious attempt, an extended essay on "The Colonial Background," followed by chapters on his eight major authors before the Civil War. Two of them, Thoreau and Whitman, inspired Canby to a dozen more years of serious literary research. When the two books appeared, he earned a new reputation as a subtle, thorough, and at times, boldly speculative biographer. In the years just before the *LHUS* was conceived, Spiller read the *Thoreau* (1939) in manuscript, and Howard Jones gave it a mixed review. So, too, did F. O. Matthiessen, whose own Thoreau in *American Renaissance* two years later was a figure considerably less mild and polite. But Canby's full-scale portrait was the best the American scholars would read until Walter Harding gathered subsequent evidence for his biography in the mid-1960s. Similarly, Canby's *Walt Whitman* (1943), though less than the final and complete biography Willard Thorp termed it in his review (*Saturday Review of Literature*, 13 November 1943), was to endure for scholars and general readers until Gay W. Allen in *The Solitary Singer* (1955) updated Whitman in the light of modern critical and biographical discoveries.

Canby, then, possessed scholarly, critical, and professional experience, together with publishing and literary connections over the entire span of years since the *CHAL* and even before. His range of talents seemed to Spiller ideal for the purposes of the *LHUS*. Canby was also totally committed to the professional goals of the ALG. He had been an MLA member since early in his career, serving one year as a program chairman in contemporary literature. In 1936, he was voted to a three-year term on the Advisory Council of the ALG. In 1940, he became a member of Spiller's Committee on a Cooperative Literary History and then a prime mover of the *LHUS* as a private enterprise. In that history, he coauthored "Creating an Audience" with Malcolm Cowley, and Cowley regretted that Canby was too modest to allow them to bestow enough credit in the chapter "to Canby himself, or to the team he assembled in 1920 [Benét, Loveman, and Morley], or to the magazine they founded in 1924, for helping to create and hold together that essential audience."[7]

✦   ✦   ✦

At Yale, Canby enjoyed the scholarly company and support of Stanley T. Williams, the senior among the three *LHUS* associates. (In these chapters, we shall refer to them from time to time merely as fellow editors.) Williams was born in 1888, the son of an educator in Meriden, Connecticut. Like Canby, Williams became a thorough man of Yale, receiving his undergraduate and graduate degrees there (Ph.D., 1915) and then promptly earning a lifelong tenure on the Yale faculty. It was interrupted only by service in the first world war. In the 1920s, he turned his interest away from the English Victorian period (his *Studies in Victorian Literature* appeared in 1923) when he inherited the American literature course from William Lyon Phelps. Though Williams soon cultivated the entire history of American literature, in the 1930s, he concentrated on Irving and Hawthorne. In the forties, he was chairman of the English department and directed a record number of dissertations on Melville. One of these graduate students was Nathalia Wright, who later described Williams's special manner and talent as a professor:

> In person Professor Williams was tall and imposing in appearance. His class room manner was dignified and appropriate more to the lecture system than to discussion. Yet he wrote new notes for his lectures each time he delivered them. He was always open to new ideas and more than willing to help serious students. His style in lecturing, writing, and conversing was formal yet sympathetic, always stimulating, and often humorous. [8]

Unlike Spiller and Johnson, who produced impressive scholarly studies while teaching on the undergraduate and secondary levels, Williams more traditionally coordinated the scholarly life with the teaching responsibilities of a university professor. His first books on American literature were geared below the rigors of the advanced classroom. The heavily illustrated *American Spirit in Letters* (1926) and the *Courses of Reading in American Literature with Bibliographies* (1930, with Nelson Adkins) have been mentioned in previous chapters. Similar in pedagogical purpose was his concise *American Literature* (1933) and the textbook anthology *The American Mind* (1937), which he coedited with Harry Warfel (Maryland) and historian Ralph Gabriel (Yale). Williams also worked for Harcourt, Brace from 1925 to 1929 as general editor of The American Authors Series, which included, notably, Parrington's edition of *The Connecticut Wits* (1926) and Hubbell's *Swallow Barn* by J. P. Kennedy (1929). Among the rest of Williams's twenty-eight books, authored or edited, he was best known by 1943 as a towering figure in Irving studies. In his American Authors Series, he edited the Knickerbocker *History* (1927, with Tremaine McDowell). By 1937, he had also edited seven volumes of journals, notes, and letters of Irving and compiled (with Mary A. Edge) *A Bibliography of the Writings of Washington Irving* (1936), all of this scholarship preparing him to become the preeminent authority on Irving and his times in *The Life of Washington Irving* (1935, two volumes). Williams's celebrity as an American literature scholar brought him invitations to review scores of books (more than a hundred throughout his career).

Williams was, finally, one of the distinguished activists in the profession. He was an advisory editor of *American Literature* at its birth and member of the editorial board for a dozen years, beginning in 1938. In 1929, he was elected to the ALG Advisory Council and served as chairman of the group in 1933 and 1934. Along with Canby, for whom Williams reviewed scholarly books in the *Saturday Review,* he had been an enthusiastic member of Spiller's Committee on a Cooperative Literary History. Williams was an inevitable candidate for the editorial team of the *LHUS.*

★   ★   ★

Howard Mumford Jones represented Harvard on the *LHUS* board. Remarkably, Jones rose to the height of the profession in modern times without taking a Ph.D. His career, as he seemed to realize when he wrote his autobiography, was in its way the stuff of American legend.[9] Born in 1892 in Saginaw, Michigan, Jones was destined by heredity and experience to know the native land of which he would write so extensively, never more so than in his great trilogy of works after retirement. His family had seventeenth-century New England origins, but his parents promptly modernized their only child, taking him to Chicago to witness at first hand, from a baby carriage, the Columbian Exposition of 1893. The family moved to Milwaukee and then to LaCrosse, Wisconsin, several years later. Like many another American literature scholar, Jones received his early education in that subject through self-indulgent trips to the local town library. In high school, he accepted his four years of Latin, but his heart belonged to American history and the debating team. He was also an efficient typist, a skill that rewarded him with a summer job as secretary to Hamlin Garland, who kept a summer home in nearby West Salem. After two years at the State Normal School in town, Jones entered the University of Wisconsin in the class of 1914.

At Wisconsin in the LaFollette era, Jones found many a progressive on the faculty and, as an English major, discovered his liking for literary regionalism. But neither ideology was present in his American literature class taught by Norman Foerster. Jones remembered that readings for the course came from W. B. Cairns's "dull, if accurate" recent textbook of literary history and Foerster's own anthology.[10] More stimulating were the long walks around Lake Mendota with William Ellery Leonard, a "striking personality" on the faculty. No doubt the hospitable Leonard had recognized an equally striking personality in his young hiking companion. At graduate exercises in 1914, Jones was the class orator. And with scarcely taking a next breath, he received the M.A. the following year at the University of Chicago, where

John M. Manly taught him the "Introduction to Graduate Study"; Charles R. Baskerville, British drama; and Robert M. Lovett, the course in Milton. Not American literature, nor even English, became Jones's thesis area. Already cosmopolitan in his learning, he translated Heine's "The North Sea," with a critical introduction. It became his first book in 1916.

Also in 1915, at the University of Chicago, Jones started his teaching career as a composition instructor. (With American involvement in the European war being debated, he joined the First Illinois Cavalry but was discharged for bad eyesight.) Thereafter, for nine years, he experienced a succession of dark times. After a year at Texas, where Killis Campbell and L. M. Payne taught American literature, the university faced a budget crisis, and Jones moved to the University of Montana for two years. That interval was marked by a brief, unfortunate marriage and an experience in provincial wartime bigotry among the anti-German, anti-socialist denizens of Missoula. Nor was Montana a place for the professor still without a Ph.D. So Jones accepted a new offer at Texas, since the former governor had been impeached and the education climate improved. As an associate professor of comparative literature, Jones now began to ponder "the slow adaptation of Old World assumptions to a New World setting," thereby enlarging his earlier regional–national ideas into an international context. His thesis subject thus defined, he took a year's leave in 1924, returned to Chicago, and wrote his dissertation. But at examination time, he was told to complete more course work. The demand seemed ludicrous, and he withdrew from doctoral studies forever. Furthermore, he enjoyed the wicked pleasure of seeing his dissertation, revised as *America and French Culture,* published by North Carolina in 1927.

North Carolina, indeed, now became Jones's destination. The University of Texas had abolished his department and professorship while Jones was away. He filed a grievance with the American Association of University Professors, but then his former department head at Texas, James F. Royster, who had departed for North Carolina, offered Jones a position as associate professor, and he dropped the grievance at Texas. At North Carolina, Jones enjoyed, for a first time, his colleagues in the British department (English, not American, literature was his subject), but when the Crash of 1929 forced the school to reduce salaries, Jones accepted an offer from Michigan.

At Michigan, from 1930 to 1936, Jones became a teacher of American literature, though he also taught the English romantics and, in 1932, received a Guggenheim fellowship to write a book on Thomas Moore (published in 1937). More important, however, was his sustained work now in the American field: *The Life of Moses Coit Tyler* (1933) was succeeded by an excellent textbook anthology, *Major American Writers*, with Ernest Leisy (1935). Not that Jones was only then becoming a student of American literature. In the twenties, he had written articles and reviews, edited the poetry of Poe (1929), contributed "The European Background" to *The Reinterpretation of American Literature* (1928), and indeed, as early as 1918, had been assistant editor for Percy Boynton's *American Poetry*. Now in the 1930s, Jones also contributed the "Longfellow" to John Macy's *American Writers on American Literature* (1931), several entries in the *Dictionary of American Biography,* and even during his Guggenheim year, Jones was at the Huntington Library reading not only Thomas Moore but also documents of colonial and Revolutionary America. This research, he recalled, "unconsciously prepared me to deal with such of my future Harvard colleagues as Kenneth Ballard Murdock, F. O. Matthiessen, and Perry Miller, who, like the Cratchit children, were steeped to their very eyebrows in New England writing."[11]

Harvard, in fact, was presently his next, and final, stop as a professor. To the astonishment of his Michigan colleagues and himself, Jones in the spring of 1936 received an invitation to participate in the Harvard tercentenary, to be the recipient of an honorary Litt.D., and to become Professor of English at a salary of ten thousand dollars. The invitation, on reflection, should not have been so astonishing when the sum of Jones's contributions to the profession had been tallied up, as they obviously had been at Harvard. Besides his scholarship, he had served as an advisory editor of *American Literature* and been active in the ALG as a member of the Advisory Council. In 1935, and now again in 1936, he was chairman of the group. Jones had championed the drive for a higher status of Americanists within the British-oriented MLA, as well as a more sensible balance of American literature courses in the curricula of the academy. He carried this advocacy into the opinion-making journals, where he also reviewed American literature in the making—from Hemingway, Faulkner, and Dos Passos to Lewis, Sandburg, and Cather. (Jones's own early creative work included three plays, a half-dozen short stories, and a score of poems.) Before and into his years at Harvard, Jones wrote constantly his penetrating and fearfully candid reviews of the American criticism or scholarship of Babbitt, Brooks, Eliot, Foerster, Lewisohn, Kazin, Murdock, and *LHUS* coeditors Canby and Williams. In Canby's *Saturday Review* alone, Jones contributed more than one hundred reviews by 1943. Active in the ALG program at Cambridge in 1940 on "Problems and Aims in American Literary History," he was a prized addition to the Spiller team, though he was never to be excessively thrilled as a participant. In *The Theory of American Literature* (1948) and its later "Postscript" chapter (1965), he entered a generally unenthusiastic few paragraphs on the planning and execution of the *LHUS*. In his autobiography thirty years after the event, the experience was not mentioned at all.

✱   ✱   ✱

Dixon Wecter, the third associate, was the *LHUS* man in the West. His was a version of the regional balancing act that Illinois's Stuart Sherman had performed with the *CHAL*. Like Sherman, Wecter was destined to play a minor part in most of the editorial decisions. "Dixon was a helpful occasional voice from the West," Spiller said later on, "but was little involved." [12] Born in Houston in 1906, Wecter took his B.A. at Baylor in 1925. For his graduate work, however, he was soon on his way east, first to Yale for the M.A. (1925) and thence to Oxford as a Rhodes Scholar and eventually for the doctorate (1936). The occasional voice from the West for the *LHUS*, ironically, was the most Europeanized in education among all of the editors. Wecter returned to the West for a career as a university professor of English, first at the University of Denver (1933–34) and Colorado (1934–39) and then UCLA (1939–49). In 1943, he also became an associate in research at the Huntington Library, a tribute to his achievement in several scholarly books.

That scholarship made Wecter peculiarly valuable to his fellow editors. *The Saga of American Society* (1937, with an acknowledgment to Jones) and *The Hero in America* (1941) were distinctly social, with only scant literary, history, but they fitted Wecter for the historical background chapters he was presently asked to contribute. As a modern authority on Mark Twain, however, he was only beginning to make an impression. In 1946, he was named literary editor of the Mark Twain estate and had projected a multivolume biography when he died in 1950.

In the profession, Wecter joined MLA in 1935 but did not participate actively in the meetings. His name surfaced in the ALG after the Cambridge meeting in 1940 when the Advisory Council dismissed, with thanks, Spiller's Committee on a Cooperative History. When the new five-person Committee on

Materials for American Literary History (eventually to be chaired by Spiller) was being contemplated, Wecter was suggested as the Pacific Coast alternate if Louis B. Wright (Huntington Library) should decline. Wright accepted, but Wecter was remembered by Spiller and his fellow editors when they rounded out their seven-man team.

Chapter 25

Screening the Contributors—
and Early Contributions (1943–1944)

In early 1943, the editors had conceived, revised, and more or less agreed on the contents and historical rationale of the *LHUS*. The next stage was an editorial screening of the profession to select the ideal contributors to the new literary history. But first, as we have seen, the editors assumed the right to preempt their own subject matter, to assert their droits des seigneurs. Spiller and Thorp had been prepared initially to write one-half of the work themselves. In February 1943, Jones, for all his unhappiness with Spiller's conception, was serious about participating in the writing. He requested the chapter on Irving and Cooper, which logically should go to Spiller or Williams, and Spiller concurred. Eventually, Jones passed the assignment on to Williams who, after the agony and failure of attempted concision, accomplished the task in two separate chapters. Jones ended up writing "The European Background," which introduces the history, an essay for which no scholar was more fit. This would be his only chapter. His greater contribution came in tough-minded editorial critiques of the other chapters. Williams finally wrote three more chapters—on Hawthorne (chap. 27), Lanier and Dickinson (chap. 55), and Robinson (chap. 69). [1]

Dixon Wecter contributed chapter 56 on Mark Twain, together with background essays for parts V–VII. He also contracted in late 1943 to write the chapter on the Cambridge poetic ascendancy (later titled "The New England Triumverate: Longfellow, Holmes, Lowell," chap. 35) and promised to deliver it by 1 June 1944. Earlier, the editors had trouble locating a suitable scholar for the subject. Wecter himself soon bowed out. Jones suggested that Spiller try to find a young scholar with a fresh view on these poets. Wecter solicited Leon Howard, but Howard declined with the excuse that writing the chapter would not be "decent," since he was one of the ALG members who had strongly argued that a new literary history was premature. Clarence Faust (Chicago) also declined. Finally, Odell Shepard (Trinity College, Connecticut) was persuaded. [2]

Although intensive editorial criticism would come in 1945, board members produced their own earliest drafts for editorial scrutiny in 1943. And they were by no means uncritical of each other's work. On 29 and 30 June 1943, members assembled at Killingworth, Connecticut, for a critical session. Canby served as a guinea pig and read his version of the introduction—material that was criticized, revised, and finally written by the board-at-large. (Canby also wrote the chapter on Whitman, plus passages to beef up chapter 44 on "Humor" by Cornell's Harold W. Thompson.) At the same meeting, Williams read a draft of his Hawthorne chapter. The result was greeted, or rather, blistered with criticism. On 14–16 September 1943, the group met again, this time at Swarthmore, to hear Spiller's chapter on Henry Adams and Thorp's on Stedman and others. In the final reckoning, Spiller wrote four chapters, including Emerson, parts of three more, and the thematic and narrative continuity between other chapters. Thorp wrote four chapters, including the Melville, and part of a fifth. Johnson managed chapter 6 on Jonathan Edwards (his thesis subject in 1932 at Harvard) in addition to his colossal chores as bibliographer of volume III. In all, the editors and associates accounted for more than one-quarter of the history—nineteen complete and parts of five more of the eighty-one chapters.

An equally formidable assignment for the editors in 1943 was selecting scholars around the nation best qualified to write the many chapters that remained. A standard form was devised, "Confidential Report on Possible Contributors," that included the academic address, the reason for choosing the professor, field or fields of expertise, his or her types of ideas and nature of his or her literature judgments (historical or critical), scholarly style and particular audience appeal, and availability.

Willard Thorp was especially diligent in this homework and not reluctant to offer candid and sometimes tart opinions of the profession's worthies as he sifted the lists of possible assignees. Spiller insisted that they select people because they had something to say rather than because they had already said. In this connection, he was especially concerned over the need to eliminate tactfully, on account of age, certain men of knowledge, experience, and scholarly achievement. Perhaps, he told Thorp, the older generation of scholars could be acknowledged as an honorary group, after listing editors and associates and contributors, and be labeled "consultants." But Spiller worried, "Is this too cumbersome, weak-kneed, opportunist, etc.?" Williams agreed with Spiller's judgment to exclude certain scholars as diplomatically as possible. Spiller later wrote to Thorp suggesting a prefatory word on the "old guard"—Quinn, Boynton, Pattee, Foerster, Hubbell, and a few others. The preface did, in fact, cite these and other elderly noncontributors who had advanced important scholarship since the *CHAL*.[3]

On 22 and 23 May 1943, the board met in Princeton to agree on a sizable list of contributors. In June, invitations went out for the first half of the history (parts I to V).[4] Further invitations were sent during the summer. One notable acceptance was from Carl Van Doren, who agreed to write six thousand words on Franklin.[5] Also, a number of refusals were coming back. Carl's brother Mark Van Doren declined the chapter (no. 79) on modern poetry (finally written by F. O. Matthiessen); Carl Becker (Cornell) the chapter (no. 22) on Southern backgrounds from 1760 to 1820 (ultimately written by John D. Wade of Georgia); Norman Foerster of Iowa the introductory chapter (no. 24) to part IV, 1820–1850 (it went to David Bowers of Princeton); and Frederick Lewis Allen on the instruments of culture, either in 1910 to 1925 or 1925 to 1940—chapters that later were carefully designed and rescheduled. Others who declined in the weeks and months to follow included Edmund Wilson, Van Wyck Brooks, T. S. Eliot, Foster Damon (Brown), Edward Tinker (NYU), Alfred Kazin, Robert Penn Warren of Minnesota (twice), Charles Anderson (Johns Hopkins), Newton Arvin of Smith (twice), Henry Pringle (Columbia), Norman Holmes Pearson of Yale (twice), and Clarence Gohdes. Harry Clark received a late invitation to write chapter 11 on the pamphlets of the American Revolution but refused on the interesting grounds that he planned to review the *LHUS*. The review, if written, never appeared.

Scholars who accepted invitations were given an identical set of materials. In addition to the complete outline of the history, they received an assignment sheet contract and were on the mailing list for the successive editorial memoranda. Those mailings would keep the contributors abreast of editorial conferences, set down the rules for preparing and submitting the manuscript, and follow the progress of work completed. Through every stage—from conception and composition to editorial scrutiny of manuscripts and suggested revisions—the editors and contributors were clearly avoiding much of the haphazard planning and execution implicit in the pages of the *CHAL*.

Also in 1943, the editors had grown more realistic about deadlines for the composition and publication of the proposed history. As the board was forming the previous July, Spiller had written Williams that he hoped to have the manuscript ready, probably for Macmillan, "in about two years." It would be a single volume of 500,000 words with perhaps two hundred pages of selected bibliography. Spiller had since learned that delays would occur in soliciting, and resoliciting, contributors for the many additional chapters of the burgeoning outline and text of the history. The editors were promptly readying their own drafts of various chapters in 1943 and, as noted already, had met for trial sessions of editorial criticism. By September, Spiller had sent to Wecter in California Williams's chapters on Hawthorne and Dickinson–Lanier, Canby's revised introduction, and Spiller's own chapter on Henry Adams. A little belatedly, the editors established a conceptual point of view in a six-page guide to all editors and contributors, which went out to invited participants on 10 December, 1943, together with a form that asked when each manuscript would be completed. Any promise would not be legally binding. The suggested dates, significantly, ran well into the future: from an imminent 1 January or 1 June 1944, to 1 January or 1 June 1945, to 1 January or 1 June 1946! The anticipated publication was now announced as autumn 1946. [6]

During the first year, the history, then, had become a realizable, if unpredictably massive, venture. Rockefeller had expressed its confidence in September 1943 with grants of five thousand dollars each to Spiller and Thorp. Johnson, on half-time duties at Lawrenceville for two years, beginning in the fall of 1942, remained to be accommodated with a grant, and Canby was monitoring it in New York. On 15 April 1944, Johnson wrote to Canby that Rockefeller had come through. Princeton supplemented Thorp's Rockefeller grant, enabling him to be free on full salary from November 1944 to February 1945 and from July to October 1945. After his leave at full salary from Swarthmore in spring 1943, Spiller continued to be supported at one-half salary, supplemented by the Rockefeller grant, from autumn 1943 to 1945. (In autumn 1945, he departed Swarthmore for his alma mater, the University of Pennsylvania.) Additional funding came from the American Philosophical Society (APS). [7]

Financial arrangements for some of the other participants were not, at least in the beginning, overly munificent. Malcolm Cowley understandably complained to Spiller that the one cent per word for contributors, to be paid *after* the war, was a "fabulously low rate." Spiller proceeded to exert his influence in several directions. Macmillan was persuaded to exhibit the true spirit of the Christmas season in 1943 and generously supplied all contributors with a ten-dollar advance. Shortly thereafter, the publisher advanced fifteen thousand dollars for expenses in preparing the manuscript. With this sum, together with an ACLS grant of one thousand dollars for editor-and-contributor meetings, the *LHUS* almost at once became solvent. Contributors' pay was increased by two cents a word, payable at or before publication. And associates would receive four hundred rather than two hundred dollars. "What a guy Spiller is!" Johnson wrote to Canby in admiration of Spiller's persuasive powers, once more, in the field of grantsmanship and high finance.[8] Finally, to confirm that they were indeed engaged in a credible enterprise, the board adopted an official letterhead: "The Literary History of the United States (in preparation)" with all seven names duly listed. For heady accomplishment with relatively minor headaches, 1943 had been a banner year and the momentum into 1944 was well nigh irreversible.

Into 1944, the editors could see the contours of the history being realized. Some last chapters were solicited, while certain earlier ones were resolicited. The procedure was rigorous and called for scrupulous and sensitive judgments. As Williams wrote to Spiller, he felt it a duty to be frank about the credentials of his colleagues as scholars. But he hoped also to avoid the petty temptation of some leading members in the profession (he named one) to deliver "indiscriminate, ruthless, and often superficial judgments of colleagues." Issuing late invitations also created problems of diplomacy for the editors. A scholar belatedly solicited could easily feel offended and reject the invitation. By 1944, Randall Stewart (Brown), for example, had not been asked. Spiller suggested that Wecter approach Stewart gingerly. Because Williams wanted the Hawthorne chapter, Stewart initially had been out of the picture. (But Williams had also urged that Stewart's name be placed on the list of alternate contributors.) It was well into 1944 before Stewart was asked to write chapter 20, eventually titled "Diversity and Innovation in the Middle States." He declined, offering the reason that Scott-Foresman wanted to push the Blair–Hornberger–Stewart anthology into wartime production rather than postpone it for the duration. (Even so, the two-volume anthology, *The Literature of the United States,* did not appear until 1946.) Spiller discussed replacements with Thorp: Norman Holmes Pearson or even Stewart's coeditor Theodore Hornberger (Texas). (The suggestion of Hornberger implies that there must have been some doubt that Stewart had given a legitimate excuse.) Spiller thought of doing the chapter himself if it could not soon be assigned, but he would then be unable to work up properly the treatment of the critics (chap. 68, "The Battle of the Books"). The assignment on the middle states presently went to Luther S. Mansfield of Williams College, a visiting professor at Swarthmore from 1944 to 1945. [9]

Chapters on single authors had been easy to assign; in fact, the editors preempted most of them. But multiple-author assignments offered some difficulty. Thorp suggested Willa Cather as a possible writer of the chapter "Western Record and Romance" (53), mindful that the editors must allow her to have her way. The chapter was eventually written by Wallace Stegner (Stanford). The editors had solicited Robert Penn Warren to write the companion chapter on the East and South, though Spiller doubted that Warren could be persuaded. Spiller asked Carlos Baker (Princeton) if he would be willing to step in if Warren defaulted. What Warren had been invited to write were six thousand words on local color in the East and South, from 1870 to 1890; the chapter was to be called "Literary Exploration: The Old America." When Warren declined, Baker wrote the chapter (52), later retitled "Delineation of Life and Character." [10]

Perhaps no segment gave the editors more aggravation than a proposed epilogue for the history. Initially, it was conceived as a symposium on the current state of American literature, to be written by several hands, such as Edmund Wilson, T. S. Eliot, Van Wyck Brooks, and James T. Farrell. Wilson's reply came in a printed postcard naming the types of invitations he systematically refused. This was one of them. Thorp tried to "swallow [his] anger," he told Spiller; and perhaps Christian Gauss (dean of the college) could persuade the old Princetonian Wilson. Or if Eliot accepted, perhaps Wilson might. But Eliot declined. So, too, did Brooks. And the editors decided in mid-1944 to table the epilogue. In January 1945, it was officially abandoned. They elected to replace it with a couple of closing chapters, one on American literature abroad, which Clarence Gohdes was invited to write. The second chapter might go, say, to Malcolm Cowley or a foreign writer, such as Philippe Soupault or W. H. Auden. (Auden by then was teaching jointly at Swarthmore and Bryn Mawr.) But the editors then decided not to solicit a second chapter after all. Several weeks later, they changed their minds and agreed to place the first as a closing discussion to part V (chap. 37, "Heard from the New World," and written by Harold Blodgett of Union College). The second, appearing as a final chapter 81, "American Books Abroad," was contributed not by Gohdes but Cowley. [11]

As 1944 gave way to 1945, the editors were prepared to criticize pages now completed rather than worry about screening scholars to write additional chapters. Only minor problems of soliciting remained. Carl Sandburg had reported nothing on the Lincoln chapter, but Spiller noted a hopeful sign: Sandburg had cashed the advance check from Macmillan. If he should not come through, they could ask Everett Hunt of Swarthmore to extend "The Orators" (chap. 33) to include Lincoln. If R. P. Blackmur (Princeton) could not move ahead on Henry James (he was also trying to complete his book on Henry Adams), they might ask F. O. Matthiessen. Cowley had not reported on his earlier assignment, "How Writers Lived" (chap. 75), but Spiller was certain of Cowley's delivering. Bernard DeVoto had withdrawn from chapter 45 ("Western Chroniclers and Literary Pioneers"). Wecter was a possible replacement, though Spiller felt Wecter had shown in chapters already submitted that he "can't handle the larger issues of intellectual history with any freedom or scope." Spiller suggested Henry Nash Smith (Texas) instead, partly because Smith's thinking was in harmony with Spiller's cyclical theory of American literary history. Smith wrote the chapter. [12]

With most of the authors at work on their chapters in 1944, the editors scheduled a number of conferences to discuss mutual approaches, procedures, and coordination of closely related chapters. On 4–5 March, they arranged a large meeting in New York with editors and contributors, together with representatives from foundations and the Book-of-the-Month Club. Among other matters of scholarly business, they agreed that it would be useful to editorial planning if contributors submitted a preliminary, ample precis of their proposed chapter content. On 4 April, Johnson, Thorp, and Spiller held an "interim business meeting" at Johnson's Lawrenceville and decided that editorial criticism of chapters was to be coherently summarized, by either Spiller or Thorp, and then sent to contributors for their revisions. Spiller agreed to write these summaries. Later in the year, two meetings brought together contributors whose closely linked chapters needed careful welding. On 7–8 October, Spiller assembled his fellow contributors to part IV. In another conference, he brought together Ralph Gabriel (Yale), Henry Commager (Columbia), and Allan Nevins (Columbia) in New York to establish agreement on the content of their introductory chapters to parts VIII, IX, and X, respectively. Commager questioned how three historians could share the years 1890 to 1940. Spiller tried to describe the common ground and special content of the Commager and Gabriel chapters. For Nevins's part, "What any historian does with the period from 1930 to the present is his own business." [13]

In an end-of-year memorandum to contributors, the editorial

board summed up the activity through 1944. In the past six months, four conferences between editors and contributors had brought no major changes in policy, conception, or outline. Some details had been clarified or elaborated, and a very few chapters added or rearranged. This editorial mailing, both in form and explanation, must have assured contributing members of the profession that they were engaged in a superbly well-organized operation. Under "Present Status," they learned that twenty-one of the projected seventy-nine chapters were in and that the editors hoped to see half of the book in first draft by early 1945. Contributors were urged to produce chapters promptly, since the main editors (Spiller and Thorp) would be on Rockefeller leaves in the winter and spring, and the bibliographer (Johnson) in the following year. "Submission of Manuscripts" called for at least two copies "on thinnest possible paper" (to save postage), one to circulate among editors and associates and the second to serve as either an insurance copy or to be sent to contributors with related chapters. All the authors were apprised of the "Principles of Organization," including the five types of chapters within the ten parts of the history: intellectual backgrounds, instruments of culture, major figures, minor authors, and summaries. Chapters on minor figures had been given special consideration, organized by regions (for example, Southern colonial literature) or literary forms (contemporary fiction) or literary groups and movements (the Stedman school, and so forth) or homogeneous subliterature (American language). The editors had also devised "Principles of Selection of Material," including lists of authors suggested for each contributor. Under "Method and Style," minimal footnotes were suggested. Prepublication of chapters was allowed, with permission of the editors and Macmillan, and was even anticipated in order to advertise the history (money to go to the author). And so, 1945 was expected to be an abundant year in composition, editorial criticism, and revision.

Meanwhile, the country had been mobilized and engaged in a global war for more than three years, with casualties in excess of 300,000 dead and 500,000 wounded by the close of 1944. The wartime travails of the nation, both at home and abroad, had pervasive consequences for the academy and the profession. The years of national upheaval partly interrupted humanistic learning, but they also stimulated the serious, life-enhancing quest for permanent aesthetic and historical values in our country's literature. Those effects, indispensable to our story, are interpreted in the wartime chapter that follows.

Chapter 26

American Literature and the Academy during World War II (1939–1945)

The editors of the *LHUS* launched their history and carried it through gestation and fulfillment under circumstances remarkably similar to the making of the *CHAL*. Both were initiated in a period of nationalistic sentiment and progressive thought that was succeeded by the heightened self-awareness and patriotic emotion that course through a nation in wartime. Lastly, both cooperative histories were completed and gained a final assessment three years into the postwar era.

Among the editors, Spiller, who was in his middle forties, did not reenter military service. As he explained it,

> The period 1939–1944 had been one of unrest and change for me as for many others, but not altogether for the same reasons. Swarthmore, being a Quaker college, was relatively undisturbed by the war. . . .
> By this time I had become a Quaker myself and I felt it my calling to keep the aims of idealism alive at home rather than to take an active part in the war.

He wrote, for example, "Higher Education and the War" to assess the impact on college curricula and enrollments after the Selective Service Act of September 1940 and the declaration of war following Pearl Harbor. Repeating President Roosevelt's challenge that our colleges should help preserve the culture that our soldiers were fighting for, Spiller did not lose the opportunity to champion the study of American literature and to praise universities like Princeton for recently announcing an interdisciplinary American civilization program (Willard Thorp was director). "The study of American culture," Spiller concluded, "must become the center and the guiding principle of our entire scheme of liberal education from the earliest grades to the most abstruse levels of graduate research." [1]

Though Canby was an advanced sixty-three after Pearl Harbor, he served in a capacity similar to his earlier work for the British during World War I, acting as a consultant to the U.S. Office of

War Information. Thomas Johnson, son of an army general, was
in his early forties and did not seek active duty. But he gathered
two collections of essays to edify the young men at his Lawrenceville School and American youth at large. His subtitles made
unmistakable the pedagogical currency of the volumes: *Men
of Tomorrow: Nine Leaders Discuss the Problems of American
Youth* (1942) and *Return to Freedom: The Affairs of Our Time
and Their Impact upon Youth* (1944). He was persuasive in soliciting some of the most prominent writers in the nation to contribute: Samuel E. Morison, Reinhold Niehbuhr, Pearl Buck,
Herbert Agar, Jacques Barzun, and even our old friend of the
CHAL, John Erskine. Just after the war, Johnson enlisted fellow
editors Canby and Thorp, plus Malcolm Cowley, Christian Gauss,
and others, for still another volume of essays of inspiration and
guidance: *A Man's Reach: Some Choices Facing Youth Today*
(1947). Many of these contributors had participated in the
"Lawrenceville Forum Lectures" chaired by Johnson. [2]

Stanley Williams had been a second lieutenant in the Army
Signal Corps in World War I, but now was approaching his middle
fifties. Jones reached his fiftieth birthday in April 1942, but he
took an active role on the home front. Harvard had joined the
many universities that had turned much of their campuses over
to college programs for U.S. military units, and because naval intelligence classes and strategic research were being conducted at
Harvard, the Yard was deemed a logical target of German bombs.
Jones became assistant chief of the Harvard Auxiliary Police,
composed of six companies of aging volunteers who drilled on
weeknights in Memorial Hall and subsequently patrolled the
war-darkened streets of Cambridge. After this rather comical
tour of duty, Jones helped educate German prisoners of war con-
fined at Fort Kearny in Rhode Island. He fashioned a course in
American history and "in a vague way, supervised the learning of
English."[3] Meanwhile, his fellow associate, Dixon Wecter, like
Spiller and Johnson, promoted national purpose and idealism
through his writings. In *Our Soldiers Speak, 1775–1918* (1943,
with William Matthews), Wecter recalled the quiet patriotism
and courage of common soldiers in earlier American wars. In
1944, he wrote *When Johnny Comes Marching Home,* preparing
his countrymen for the difficulties of readjustment to postwar
America by recounting the aftermath of three previous wars; and
in the same vein, he contributed "Education and the Soldier's
Return" to Johnson's *Return to Freedom,* also published in 1944.

Willard Thorp was also active during the war on the domestic
front, most importantly, as Spiller had noted, by guiding the

new American studies at Princeton. Thorp was also immersed in public debate over the political and social obligations of writers and members of the academy in peace and war. The polemics were touched off by Archibald MacLeish, who had become Librarian of Congress in 1939 and soon gathered to himself the robes of cultural spokesman for the Roosevelt Administration. His speeches were published as pamphlets by the U.S. Printing Office. In 1940, he wrote in the *Nation* a piece titled "The Irresponsibles." There he warned that posterity will ask why our intellectuals and writers of the prewar decade merely watched from their ivory-tower isolation while books were being destroyed and writers and scholars were exiled or imprisoned and murdered in various countries abroad. "Why did the scholars and the writers of our generation in America fail to oppose those forces while they could—while there was still time and still place to oppose them with the arms of scholarship and writing?" The question was rhetorical, and MacLeish had the response prepared. In the America of 1940 and earlier, totalitarian oppression was unopposed because we no longer propagated the responsible "man of letters," that individual who was earlier committed to the past as a scholar and the present as a writer, "a man who admitted a responsibility for the survival and vitality of the common and accumulated experience of the mind." A modern-day Milton, Voltaire, or Bartholomew de las Casas would already have spoken up to thwart "the revolution of the gangs" of fascist Germany, Russia, and Spain. Our scholarship and writing today were no doubt excellent, said MacLeish, but also irresponsible because disengaged. The scholar was scientific and neutral, and the aridity of the usual Ph.D. dissertation became, therefore, the "perfect image of his world."[4]

Thorp and others immediately responded, either in support, clarification, or annoyed refutation of MacLeish. Thorp presented two more reasons why members of the academy "feel themselves justified in their irresponsibility—which they designate by such sanctified terms as 'scholarly aloofness,' 'dispassionateness,' and 'devotion to permanent values.'" First of all, the American university, especially if private, is run not by professors but almost totally by trustees, so that the scholar easily rationalizes his retreat to "ultimate truth." Secondly, the roadmarks to academic success, from graduate student to rising professor, are clearly marked, and they allow no detour from the prescribed activities of "the graduate seminar, the Ph.D. oral, the published article, the monograph, the paper read at the meeting of the learned society." Passionate social commitment is not part of the academic game and even scholarly advocacy is frowned on: One is tacitly forbidden to pass judgment on even the chosen figure of his scholarly lifetime.[5]

Among other members of the academy who were roused by MacLeish and are also intimately part of our chronicle of American literature study, Perry Miller of Harvard sided rather closely with both MacLeish and Thorp. To Miller, the American scholar-professors of 1940 invoked the hard-won victory earned in the nineteenth century to pursue the truth objectively; but even here, their deeper objectives were job security, promotion, and practical comforts. Amid these ivory-tower materialists masquerading as dispassionate scholars were "the few with broader vision," but they "are met by their colleagues with spoken or implied rebukes for having deserted the citadel of the fraternity, their precious freedom from partisanship."[6] Miller's admirable championing of the partisan intellectual's wider vision, an echo of Emerson's scholar as a man of action, must have carried a strange ring, however, to some of his Harvard colleagues who were anything but disengaged, albeit too far toward the radical left to be responsible in MacLeish's and Miller's sense. One of them was then-Communist Richard Schlatter, a committed radical at Harvard who viewed Miller himself as staid and conservative: "This combining of thinking and acting did not affect all individuals equally—Perry Miller was never much of an activist—but it affected the whole institution and thus, indirectly, all its members. Everyone was aware of the question, 'knowledge for what?'"[7]

On his part, Miller viewed himself as a vigorous, broad-visioned, anti-Soviet interventionist while these left-wing internationalists, opposers of the so-called "imperialist war," were naïve isolationists. Leo Marx, a student in the Harvard class of 1941, recalled that Miller "was an ardent interventionist who was likely to bait me mercilessly when I walked into his room."[8] Miller presently served in Europe during World War II. As a former major, he returned to Harvard in 1946 to renew a career brilliantly begun before the war. His stunning critical appreciation of the Puritans in *The New England Mind* (1939) can best be understood in the context of his later postwar studies.

Joining Thorp and Miller in the same issue of *Nation* were others who supported and elaborated on MacLeish's comments on academic irresponsibility. Kenneth Murdock felt the more serious rift to have occurred in the scholar-professor's failure to discover and impart to students the humane values out of the past that should guide our next generation of citizens. (Murdock's friend and colleague, the politically radical F. O. Matthiessen, was making his partisan commitments known to students and general public, as we presently shall discover, but he did not reply to MacLeish's charges.) Waldo Frank, unlike Murdock, believed that our scholars and writers had pursued humanistic values but had never learned enough to relate the parts to the whole (echoing Miller's "broader vision"). Their new religion, an empirical rationalism, had prevented such a synthesis.

This qualified consensus with MacLeish did not last in the light of further reflection. The following week, Robert E. Mathews (Ohio State) spoke for those who wondered if MacLeish had paused long enough in framing his thesis to account for the rather widespread activism easily visible within the academy in the work of groups like the American Civil Liberties Union, the American Federation of Teachers, and the American Association of University Professors. Political conscience in the academy was manifest in those organizations, and if the voices were not quite comparable to Milton or Voltaire, perhaps MacLeish could lend his eloquence in that direction and provide some positive leadership. Two weeks later, John Gould Fletcher wrote less temperately to refute MacLeish's "falsehoods" by injecting some corrective history. The dissociated scholar could be dated all the way back to the sixteenth century, but the humanistic question of his "direct action" in his society was a bogus issue. Civilization and culture, Fletcher the Southern Agrarian affirmed, "can only be defended against destruction by upholding in one's work a given tradition or by adding something to it." Finally, Morton Zabel (Loyola) wrote an extened, two-part critique in which he assailed MacLeish's long-time acrobatics and alternations on the subject of pure versus committed writing and criticism. Then, too, said Zabel, there was the example of MacLeish's flaccid and essentially irresponsible poetic imagination patterned, over a total career, after other poets and dependent on echoes of their work. [9]

* * *

MacLeish had an eminent ally in Van Wyck Brooks, who interpreted "The Irresponsibles" as support for his own campaign for healthy-minded authors expressing affirmative nationalism in our literature. MacLeish had asserted, said Brooks, "the free will of the writer, too long forgotten in a world that has been drugged by fatalism." In his autobiography, Brooks dated some of this malaise more precisely to the liberal writer's fatalistic disillusionment after the Stalin–Hitler pact some nine months earlier: "The whole idea of progress through collective effort disappeared from the general mind of writers." As to the Brooks–MacLeish credo of literary nationalism, the fallout from Brooks's *The Flowering of New England* (1936) had piqued American literature professors sufficiently so that in 1938, the program of the ALG at Columbia had been given over to "Nationalism in American Literature," with papers by Professors Harry Clark (Wisconsin), Frederic Carpenter (Harvard), Harry Warfel (Maryland), and Robert Bolwell (George Washington). The next year, F. W. Dupee, a *Partisan Review* editor presently to become a Jamesean specialist at Columbia, assessed "The Americanism of Van Wyck Brooks" and found it wanting in aesthetic and intellectual criteria. For all his eloquent championing of the American artist, Brooks had permitted "the spiritual New Englander in him to absorb the modern critic, the visionary to consume the skeptic."[10]

In 1940, Dupee's spiritual New Englander brought forth *New England: Indian Summer*. Again, Brooks was praised in the academy for his verve and creative talents and abused for the laxity of his historical and literary analysis. He seems not to have resented these misgivings of the academy, and in fact, he had acceded to friendly proddings after the *Flowering* that he should make his sources known to the reader. In *Indian Summer,* he had supplied an original version of footnote documentation by unleashing (in tiny print) a torrent of asides and addenda. The areas in which he was hypersensitive, though, included his nationalist sympathies and the aesthetic component (or lack of it) in his social approach to literature. Theodore Morrison (Harvard) and Morton Zabel (who presently assailed MacLeish's version of Americanism) scored Brooks on these two counts, and Brooks recorded their charges, especially, of soft-headed nostalgia and sentimental nationalism. Years later, they surfaced in the pages of an angry rebuttal in Brooks's autobiography.[11]

In fact, Brooks in 1940 was aware that his career had reached a new crisis, characteristically matching the national crisis, and he embarked on his own critical assessment, and justification, of Van Wyck Brooks, which he bracketed with the current state of the nation, the literary community, and the academy. Besides his cheering, in June, MacLeish's assault on irresponsibles among writers and professors, Brooks favored American intervention not long after, and months before Pearl Harbor he called for "an immediate declaration of war."[12] Something more self-assertive was also brewing, and it began to appear after the reception of *Indian Summer.* Early in 1941, he became a contributing editor of the *New Republic,* and in its pages from February to August, he published an autobiographical series of nine "Opinions of Oliver Allston." These were charming, desultory essays on the progress of Brooks's own convictions and predilections: his passion for the literary life, not as a scholar but (echoing MacLeish) a man of letters; his mild irritation with professional critics; and his casual philosophy of politics, society, human nature, and American life. These Brooksian musings were familiar enough and excited no animus in the academic and literary community. He was riding the crest of public favor and more than lukewarm academic approval. In an article for *College English* in April, Professor Dayton Kohler (Virginia Polytechnic) praised the critical patriotism of Brooks's lifelong search for a usable past, and regarded the two New England volumes judicious "literary histories which make clear the strengths and weaknesses of a cultural tradition we are trying to save today." Beyond their inspiriting value in the midst of the current war, said Kohler, "these point to a new literary nationalism which may revitalize for all time the resources of American literature for the writer and the scholar."[13]

But in late summer 1941, Brooks's mellow apologia took a combative and sour turn. He published a pamphlet, *On Literature Today* (Dutton), in which he cast off the Allston persona and angrily quarreled with the life-despairing authors of literary modernism, from Eliot, Pound, Joyce, and Mencken to Hemingway, O'Neill, and Dreiser, along with the professors who, for example, mistook the dead-bones New England of an O'Neill as an accurate and honest vision. Only Frost, Sandburg, and friend Lewis Mumford explicitly were saved from Brooks's grim condemnation. Then on 10 September, he spoke at Columbia University on "Primary Literature and Coterie Literature," and published in the *Yale Review* during the same month his observations on the earlier creators of a "primary literature" who favored the life drive and espoused the great values of courage, justice, mercy, honor, and love—Dante, Milton, Tolstoy, Hugo, Dickens, Goethe, Ibsen; and in America, Emerson and Whitman. The next month, these inflammatory observations were published as chapters 17–19 of *The Opinions of Oliver Allston*.

Dwight Macdonald, meanwhile, had been preparing an impassioned diatribe against Brooks's speech at Columbia, and it soon appeared in his *Partisan Review*. To Macdonald, Brooks's prescription for an affirmative content in modern American literature recalled the Moscow trials a few years before when the "specific cultural values of Stalinism" were enforced. And Brooks's speech also supported the "cultural counter-revolution opened by Archibald MacLeish's attack on the 'irresponsibles'" the year before, a coercive, official movement, said Macdonald, to enforce "the swing behind the government in the war crisis." Brooks, that is, had become "our leading mouthpiece for totalitarian cultural values" that opposed the "free inquiry and criticism" of Joyce, Eliot, and James, tough-minded critics who exposed "the overmastering reality of our age: the decomposition of the bourgeois synthesis in all fields."[14]

The *Partisan* solicited responses to the "Brooks-MacLeish Thesis," and they appeared in the next issue. Among them, William Carlos Williams was saddened to see what had become of the once-adventurous critic in Brooks; Henry Miller professed surprise that this silly man was still alive; and Louise Bogan accused Brooks of being a nationalistic moralist "on behalf of an official literature" who had little conception of how the artist creates. Allen Tate endorsed Macdonald's critique but balked at the antibourgeois values he imputed to modern authors. Theirs was instead, said Tate, a vision of evil that went beyond capitalism; and Macdonald himself appeared guilty, like Brooks, of approving a political stance in his favored authors. James T. Farrell agreed with Macdonald's analogy between Brooks's cultural nationalism and the Moscow trials, but he shared Brooks's animosity toward the literary and critical vision of T. S. Eliot. For his part, Eliot responded with weariness over hearing, once again, the charges of coterie elitism and undemocratic negativism directed against him and others.[15]

The Opinions of Oliver Allston (1941) reaped for Brooks his habitual share of accolades and adverse comment, the latter becoming more charges to be quoted with grim amusement in his *Autobiography* ("'the leading patriot of American culture,'" "'a narrow and embittered old gentleman,'" and so forth). But he had endured his earlier "season in hell." He now moved indomitably from the self-assessment, therapy, and catharsis of *The Opinions of Oliver Allston,* surely one of his most provocative and important books, to writing his third volume of our literature's makers and finders.

With *The World of Washington Irving* (1944), however, Brooks decisively fell from grace in the American academy. His previous histories had been reviewed respectfully enough by academic critics, for Brooks's industry, daring, and enthusiasm could only be welcomed in a profession still sensitive to the neglect and alleged immaturity of American literature studies. But the four years between *New England: Indian Summer* and *The World of Washington Irving* were a period of heightened and sophisticated scrutiny of American literary history, first in the ALG program sessions and then among the editors and contributors to the *LHUS*. When Robert Spiller, Stanley Williams, Malcolm Cowley, Arthur H. Quinn, and Robert G. Davis (Smith College) completed their analysis of *The World of Washington Irving,* Brooks would become an author more often studied in order to be corrected, parodied, or warned against. His literary enthusiasms kept him popular, however, among a vast middle-brow book club audience.[16]

*   *   *

The most important scholarly critique of *The World of Washington Irving* was written by F. O. Matthiessen. As in the previous books on New England, Matthiessen noted, Brooks had failed to analyze literary works and ideas, neglected chronology, and preferred anecdotal rather than probing biography. "Parrington, disciplined as he was by Sainte-Beuve and Taine," by contrast, "could give us in a dozen pages a more comprehensive and telling estimate of an author's intellectual significance than Brooks can often do in four or five times the space." Brooks was neither a social nor intellectual nor literary historian, nor was he a critic; rather, he was a "lyric poet manqué." He had written on Poe without learning that "like Poe, he must be concerned with the first principles of the arts with which he is dealing." On the tragic side of Poe's mind, Brooks was, however, more perceptive than he had been eight years before on Hawthorne, probably because Poe's tragedy was closer to the surface. Still, Brooks preferred not to dwell on "'the haunted mind'" of Poe or Brown or Freneau, nor to adopt Arnold's objective "seeing the object as it really is" and expose the "complex and warring forces that make up human life at any period." Amid the warring forces set loose in 1944, Brooks apparently meant to provide a bracer of nationalistic self-confidence. If so, said Matthiessen, "he may be right, although it could be argued that we will emerge from this war the most confident of all countries in the superiority of our ways, and that what we need more is an astringent antidote to shake us out of any complacent and fatuous dream of 'the American century.'" Matthiessen remembered that the younger Brooks, on the other hand, had been an incisive cultural critic and his books had encouraged not the sense of defeat and futility (as Bernard DeVoto had distorted the Brooksian legacy from the 1920s) but "a challenge for reinvigoration" among the idealistic youth of Matthiessen's generation.[17]

Like nearly all of his other criticism, Matthiessen's review of Brooks was the self-expression of the total man. We hear the youthful student and professor of the twenties, as well as the committed teacher, scholar-critic, and social activist of the thirties and on into World War II. After spending much of his boyhood in the Illinois mansion of his paternal grandfather, a German immigrant who became a multimillionaire, Matthiessen had gone to prep school in Tarrytown, New York, and then become an undergraduate at Yale (class of 1923). There, he had been the model student, active in literary journalism, a member of religious and political clubs, and an outstanding scholar. He was named class orator and awarded a Rhodes scholarship on graduating. The Yale classrooms, however, did not prepare him to become a specialist in American literature: "Literature at Yale had still meant English literature," he wrote in a late memoir. His topic for the B.Litt. thesis at Oxford (1925) was "Oliver Goldsmith as Essayist and Critic." But the attitude of the English toward America made him defensive, and he began to read American authors: "Whitman was my first big experience, particularly the *Children of Adam* and *Calamus* poems, which helped me to begin to trust the body." (Just before, he had confessed to his new friend, the painter Russell Cheney, that he was homosexual. They became lifetime companions, but Matthiessen was reticent about his sexual life and, as teacher and critic, apparently never broached homosexuality in Whitman or James.) He first read *Walden* during a trip up the Rhine and *Moby-Dick* after returning to America.

He commenced graduate work at Harvard in 1925, received an M.A. the next year, and completed a Ph.D. in 1927. Kenneth Murdock's early American historiography was Matthiessen's only class in American literature. His most challenging teacher was Irving Babbitt ("he forced me to fight for my tastes"). Hoping to write a dissertation on Whitman, Matthiessen was advised that too much had already been done; his thesis, revised and published after four years, became *Translation: An Elizabethan Art* (1931). With Ph.D. in hand, Matthiessen returned to Yale to begin a teaching career at his alma mater, and during a two-year apprenticeship, he wrote his first book, the rather impressionistic *Sarah Orne Jewett* (1929). (His mother was a distant relative of Jewett.)[18] Before moving to Harvard in the fall of 1929, Matthiessen was reading extensively in other American writers and had begun to formulate the scholarly method and outlook that would characterize the work of his maturity. In the *Yale Review*, he reviewed jointly *The Reinterpretation of American Literature* and Norman Foerster's *American Criticism*. "It is time for the history of American literature to be re-written," proclaimed the twenty-seven-year-old Matthiessen, and while its "new historian must take into account every side of American culture . . . he must remember that his real quarry is aesthetic values." He appreciated Foerster's treatment of the critical Poe, Whitman, and Emerson but challenged Foerster's prescriptive humanism for the twentieth century (the dogma Matthiessen was expert on after his recent classroom hours under Irving Babbitt). The critical standards America should possess would best be derived from our own creative relation to works of the past and from the demands of "our own environment." The critical labors of T. S. Eliot or Edmund Wilson, Matthiessen concluded, "although more uncertain and experimental, seem far more fertile than those of Mr. Foerster."[19]

In the fall of 1929, Matthiessen accepted an instructorship at Harvard, largely because of the undergraduate honors field in history and literature, an expanding legacy of Barrett Wendell that centered on close student–professor tutorials and offered the freedom for Matthiessen to elect his own subject areas. During this first year, he fell into the exhilarating and productive, but frequently exhausting and dangerous, pattern of his future academic life. The tutorials drained his energy, and he doubted that his students (Van Wyck Brooks, Jr., was one) were responding to his pedagogical style. In addition, he was preparing lectures for a first teaching of his English literature courses and was asked to offer a half-year course in American literature in the South and West, which he titled "American Literature Outside New England." He was required, as well, to take on certain administrative assignments in the near future—senior tutor at the new Eliot House (where he received a suite of rooms) and chairman of the tutors in history and literature. As a scholar, he was living mainly on promise and was promoted to assistant professor. He had attracted some attention outside Harvard with the book on Jewett and his few book reviews; was asked by Edmund Wilson to review Newton Arvin's *Hawthorne* for the *New Republic;* and within months after the second year began, Matthiessen received an invitation from W. E. Norton to write an American literary history "'from the new social and historical angle' since 'American literature has become a stepchild of the English Literature Departments.'"[20]

Receiving the letter from Norton may be viewed as one of the most decisive events in Matthiessen's scholarly life. For the next ten years and more, he shaped the ideas that would become *American Renaissance* and integrated them into his professional and public life. His conception of literary art as experience organically derived from and expressing humane and democratic values became translated into a philosophy of his own professorial and social engagement in American life both in and out of the academy. He was trying to achieve an organic unity of his responsibilities as a professor, scholarly critic, and a Christian Socialist dedicated to radical change in American capitalistic society.

It is regrettable that so few students write memorial descriptions of their most noted American literature professors as they held forth in the classroom. But truth to tell, the majority of good college and university professors share a remarkable sameness of classroom manner. They eschew outlandish appearance and strained histrionics in favor of the sympathetic and articulate search for meaning in the literature at hand. Matthiessen, however, was distinctive and memorable enough to warrant here a brief description of his style as a teacher. Former students have remembered "Matty" in the classroom to be intensely absorbed in human and social values expressed by his writers, with an equal concern to communicate their passions to the students. To reach and touch the individual student, Matthiessen championed the tutorial. Early in his career at Harvard, he scheduled conferences on Saturday to talk and meet personally with students in regular classes as well. In the 1940s, he attracted the brightest graduate students at the same time that his undergraduate classes were large and yet personal. Kenneth Lynn (Johns Hopkins), who wrote his bachelor's thesis on Melville with Matthiessen, has remembered the course in Shakespeare during his sophomore year in 1942. Friends had recommended Matthiessen.

> At the outset I was not impressed. A short, stocky man, largely bald-headed, and wearing rimless glasses, he looked to me like a grocer. His voice was hardly more commanding than his physical presence: it had a metallic quality, and went up and down the scale in a kind of singsong that I found annoying. Apparently the only hand gesture in his repertoire was sudden downward motion, thumb-side down, palm open, followed by a lateral movement in the direction toward which the palm faced. That hand gesture, however, turned out to be symbolic of what I most loved about his teaching. For the downward part of the gesture was a cutting motion, as if he were trying to force his way to the axis of reality, and the sideward part was a revelatory motion, like the pushing aside of a curtain, which was always accompanied by fresh insights into the meaning of existence.

Matthiessen was not a theatrical teacher whom students took as "an experience," as the American-campus term today has it.

John Rackliffe explained, "His lectures lacked the rhetorical al-
lure and the sure-fire emotional appeal which often make a
teacher popular. He offered the student other qualities: honesty,
intelligence, solidity, subtlety, and delicacy of perception." But
the complex and emotional Matthiessen occasionally had his
powerful moments of bad temper. Lynn again:

> He was lecturing on *Hamlet,* and had not finished what he wanted
> to say when the bell sounded. A student sitting to Matthiessen's left
> at once arose and began moving toward the aisle. Suddenly Mat-
> thiessen swerved, stabbed his right index finger straight at the
> student, and yelled at the top of his lungs, "Will you sit down!" For
> approximately the next two minutes, he was out of control. He had
> poured his whole being into this course, he raged, and we would not
> even extend him the courtesy of hearing him out. Finally, he calmed
> down and said he was sorry for yelling, but before dismissing the
> class he cried out as if in pain, "Hamlet had a temper, too."[21]

Other students of Matthiessen in the 1940s confirmed some of
Lynn's impressions. Leo Marx (then at Minnesota) recalled a
class period on Dreiser that began on a low, almost shy and embarrassed, note until Matthiessen warmed to the experience of
poverty and alienation in Dreiser. At that moment, the voice
changed, urgent hand gestures began, and Matthiessen moved
to the front of his desk to erase any barriers to his close rapport
with the students. Like Irving Babbitt, whose conservative prejudices had challenged him as a student, Matthiessen was a teacher
who let his biases show. But he did not recruit students to become partisan disciples. His concern for them was genuinely human and intellectual. Richard Wilbur, one of these students, put
the matter concisely: "He knew more students, I think, and cared
more about them, than any teacher of his time at Harvard."[22]

Matthiessen was prepared to accompany his students into
battle after the United States entered World War II. After several
visits to the recruiting office, he was rejected by the marines for
being one-half inch too short. He was still subject to the draft but
was classified 4-H. J. H. Summers, his student and a conscientious objector during the war, heard Matthiessen "hope that he
could get into some special program concerned with drama production or education for the troops."[23] However, Matthiessen remained at Harvard and, like Spiller at Swarthmore, dedicated
himself to keeping the humanities alive in wartime, "and though
it won't be easy to be part of [President Conant's] rapidly disappearing university, still there I can fight, if only a rear-guard action, for the values I really believe in." Restless and looking for

"steady new work" to wage his battle on the home front, Matthiessen launched a course on Henry James in the spring of 1943, "though I waver back and forth continually in the degree of my interest in him." He instinctively preferred Melville and Shakespeare.[24] Meanwhile, Matthiessen directed his writing to such topics as the danger—he had observed its coming on under Conant's leadership at Harvard—that scientific and mechanistic views were undermining the modes of value and truth in the arts, religion, and philosophy. Reviewing a symposium on *Liberal Education Reexamined,* Matthiessen praised small colleges like Spiller's Swarthmore and the tutorial system at Harvard for creating an "interplay of minds between teachers and students" and educating future leaders in the ideals of community. But he worried that freedom, as the term was bandied about in wartime, might lead to a postwar laissez faire individualism with small sense of the individual's obligations and interrelations in a democratic society, particularly within "a decaying and confused era of capitalism such as this country will still be living in."[25]

Later in 1944, when his *Henry James: The Major Phase* appeared, Matthiessen made the prefatory clarifications of his scholarly and critical stance. He was countering Van Wyck Brooks and Parrington, who had scolded James for his deracination but ignored his artistry and moral seriousness. More important at the moment, however, Matthiessen the teacher acknowledged

> a group of Harvard undergraduates who, during the tense winters of '42 and '43, kept insisting that until they were needed by the Army, they meant to continue to get the best education they could. Wiser than many of their elders, they refused to be distracted from primary values. When I said, half meaning it, that a book on Henry James was to be my overaged contribution to the war effort, they urged me to be serious. They believed that in a total war the preservation of art and thought should be a leading aim. They persuaded me to continue to believe it. (p. xvi)

The dedication "For My Instigators, Especially J.C.L. P.T.R. H.W.S." referred not to critics of James but to a leader of the radical Student Union, another leader of the student's aid-to-Britain movement, and a student pacifist.[26]

Early in 1945, Matthiessen became sufficiently discouraged with Conant's Harvard that he threatened to resign. The "'community of scholars,' scholars who were concerned with scholarship in relation to living in the contemporary world," as he had envisioned Harvard during the 1930s, had been destroyed by administrative assaults on his humanistic area of Harvard Yard. Matthiessen's ideal of a community of scholars may ring oddly when we realize that he disdained the MLA and therefore community with its ALG membership. He frequently used "academic" in a pejorative manner, but he did believe in cooperative scholarship, as Kenneth Murdock learned when they edited Henry James's *Notebooks* (1947).[27] And Matthiessen wrote the chapter on Poe for the *LHUS*. Still, when Robert Spiller invited him in 1941 to participate in Indianapolis in one of the discussion groups assessing current knowledge in American literary history, Matthiessen declined. Excerpts from his letter to Spiller, dated 15 September 1941, expose the unlovely side of the profession (as Matthiessen saw it) at the same time that he clearly revealed the social activism that he continuously required in his life as a professor:

Dear Spiller,

I was very glad to have your letter. I am afraid that I must appear to many as hopelessly intransigent and perfectionist in my attitude toward the M. L. A., but the standards engendered by its existence have long seemed to me productive of more harm than good. And I have felt no vital function performed by the annual meetings where far too many unrelated papers are read with no opportunity for adequate discussion. Your projected group for this year sounds potentially far more fruitful, and if I hadn't already made some engagements for that week in New York, I might be tempted to try again. . . .

It's not that I'm negligent of the possibilities of group action. For instance I've been willing to sit through five day sessions of the national convention of the Teachers Union, since beyond the boredom of the protracted parliamentary proceedings there emerged real struggles and issues, real controversy and discussion on major questions for educators and I could come away with the sense I had become a more integral part of an important social movement. But from my contacts with the M. L. A. I have had the sense that most of the papers were delivered for pure professionalism, i.e., either to gain jobs or to show off. At least no atmosphere was created that challenged my thought either as a teacher or a writer.[28]

Bernard Bowron (Minnesota), at Harvard in the forties, knew that to Matthiessen, the scholar-critic's life was a calling and to that serious end, Matthiessen gradually shaped a private credo that came to full expression in *American Renaissance*. His approach to literature combined radical social thought, a conviction that the most significant literature withstood the most rigorous aesthetic analysis, and a view of man that was essentially tragic.

He came to grief in the instances where he wanted to admire a writer unreservedly while it was obvious that one or more of these criteria were imperfectly realized. He was powerfully affected by T. S. Eliot, who came to Harvard as Charles Eliot Norton Professor in 1932. Eliot reinforced the lessons in literary form that Matthiessen had learned after I. A. Richard's visit to Harvard in 1929, and Eliot also strengthened Matthiessen's religious and tragic sense of man. Matthiessen became the ideal American critic to write *The Achievement of T. S. Eliot* (1935). But the socialist in Matthiessen kept a discreet and presumably embarrassed silence on Eliot's conservative royalism. Politically, Matthiessen was closer to the liberalism of Brooks and Parrington or the Marxism of Calverton and Hicks, but Matthiessen lamented their frequent insensitivity to literary form. Edmund Wilson, in that twin regard, was more congenial, and in his Eliot book, Matthiessen acknowledged Wilson's importance.[29]

Matthiessen's insistence on aesthetic principles is the more remarkable when we know the intensity with which he sympathized with Leftist social thought and action. His political consciousness was lively enough by 1932 so that he briefly joined the Socialist Party and voted for Norman Thomas. Up to that time, he had cast a Yale undergraduate's straw vote for Harding, joined the Labour Club at Oxford, and voted for Smith in 1928. By 1935, Matthiessen had merged political and professorial interests and helped form the radical Harvard Teachers Union. The years from 1936 to 1941 at Harvard were unprecedented in the academy for the political awareness of faculty and students. Reunited in a symposium at Hobart and William Smith Colleges in 1975, Harvard men recalled those years and the central role that Matthiessen played. Harry Levin (Harvard), a student in Matthiessen's first course in 1929, recruited him for the Harvard Teachers Union, which numbered 150 members at its peak—junior faculty and graduate students but few senior professors. Matthiessen was the most celebrated professor, serving as the group's first vice president. In 1940, he became president. But the next year, the union under Matthiessen's leadership came to an end. The war played an unexpected role, the main trouble beginning at a meeting on 22 May 1940 chaired by Matthiessen. The issue seemed minor enough, a vote to give five dollars to the anti-war chest of the radical Student Union. But the Teachers Union was split on the question of American intervention, and the vote was dangerously close, 34 to 33 in favor of the donation. Defections and resignations followed. Indeed, Matthiessen was himself a pacifist in 1940, for he regarded the English and French, after their response to the Spanish Civil War and at Munich, too unreliable to support as allies. As president of the crumbling Teachers Union, he did try in the coming year to shun national and international issues. In the spring of 1941, with intervention increasingly imminent and the Teachers Union fatally weakened, Matthiessen's friends gave him a testimonial dinner. The occasion was the publication of *American Renaissance,* but it was also felt that the evening, in Leo Marx's words, also "appropriately marked the end of that tumultuous era" of social activism within the academy.[30]

While Matthiessen was spending a part of his prodigious energies to fulfill his ideal of the socially engaged professor, he was reserving another part for his closely related work as a scholar. This period of social activism from 1936 to 1941 had also been a time of intensive scholarship—the difficult, crucial years of the making of *American Renaissance.* By the summer of 1936, he was reading completed segments of the book to critical friends. An early riser, he always went promptly to his writing desk (even in Europe) and worked until lunch. This unflagging industry had brought him, by the summer of 1938, to "the most difficult phase" of the writing, and in the fall, he began a year's leave from Harvard to finish the book. But then near-tragedy struck. Accustomed to the pressure of his crowded university life, "the readjustment to leisure was hard," he wrote in a journal diagnosis of his insomnia and nervousness. In December 1938, he had consulted a doctor in Boston. He then entered a sanitarium in Waverly, Massachusetts, there to remain until mid-January. Further analyzing his collapse, he recalled an overnight stay at Kenneth Murdock's when he had awakened to a climactic fantasy of self-doubt and suicide wherein

> it would be better if I jumped out the window. And during the succeeding week at Kittery I was recurrently filled with the desire to kill myself. Why? . . . Because my talent was less than I thought? Because, on the first onset, I couldn't write the book I wanted? Such reasons seem preposterous to anyone reasonable, and certainly they do to me as I sit here this evening.[31]

The experience, of course, was to be eerily duplicated much later, in 1950. Again on leave, this time to complete the book on Dreiser, and consumed by self-doubt, disappointment, and loneliness, he made his tragic leap from the window of a Boston hotel.

On 13 January 1939, his doctor suggested that Matthiessen take up residence in Boston and after a month, return to the book. The next fall, he was again keeping a full schedule at Harvard, which meant a busy round of pedagogical and political activities, along with the early-morning sessions at his writing desk. The next year, he delivered the 1,006 pages of typescript to Norton, only to have the manuscript rejected as being too long and expensive. Matthiessen then submitted it to Houghton Mifflin, who judged the 300,000 words too dense with detail. Finally in late autumn 1940, Oxford University Press accepted, with the proviso that Matthiessen subsidize one-third of the costs, amounting to $1,000. (Later, he also paid $348.04 in author corrections in the proofs.) In March 1941, he was reading page proofs, relieved that he and Oxford had finally agreed on a title. Possibilities had included *Man in the Open Air, From East to West, Literature for Democracy, American Masterwork,* and *The Great Age in American Literature. American Renaissance* was Harry Levin's suggestion in late 1940, and Matthiessen argued with Oxford as to its fitness: This was a period of "creative ripeness" paralleling England's, and Melville himself so deemed it in his analogies to the Elizabethan age. Only at the last minute did Matthiessen alter the words "Language and Art" in the subtitle to "Art and Expression [in the Age of Emerson and Whitman]."[32]

He phrased the preface with equal care, stating his method and credo so eloquently that many of the reviewers paused to quote from the opening pages at length. Above all, he sounded a note unprecedented in American literary histories, that he would be concentrating on the major works of his authors and also would be "evaluating their fusions of form and content" (p. vii). Elsewhere, he reiterated the primacy of his aesthetic approach. His literary period was shaped by Emerson's "theory of expression" (influenced by Coleridge), which Thoreau built on, Whitman extended, and Hawthorne and Melville reacted against in its "philosophical assumptions" (p. xii). Matthiessen also hoped to shed aesthetic light on literary modes of allegory, symbolism, and myth. For the individual works, "most of the criticism of our past masters has been perfunctorily tacked onto biographies" (p. xi), but he would give them close analyses, with generous instances from the text itself. (In practice, he also invoked the principle of aesthetic tension espoused by the new textual critics, as well as Eliot's objective correlative and dissociation of thought and feeling.)

Matthiessen did admit to a historical aim, "to place these works both within their age and in ours" (p. vii), and while he would try to determine the authors' debts and aims, he also invited readers to understand the work in the light of their own experiences. Eight themes would give internal structure to the history (though the primary approach, he insisted, would still be to examine diction and rhetoric, for "an artist's use of language is the most sensitive index to cultural history" [p. xv]). These eight themes would be the relation of the individual to society (with tragic implications), the nature of good and evil (and the tragic implications), the transcendentalist's word one with the thing, the tradition of oratory, the poet as seer, the photographer and painter as seer, the symbolic fusing of appearance and reality, and the "organic union between labor and culture" (pp. xiv–xv). In this last regard, Matthiessen observed that his five authors "wrote literature for democracy," and their scholar should therefore obey a similarly binding democratic purpose.

Contradictions and weaknesses in Matthiessen's procedure would be charged aplenty by critics in the after years. Those who first reviewed *American Renaissance,* however, were deeply impressed by his strengths as a literary historian and critic. George S. Hellman, a member of the old *CHAL* team, commended this "significant volume" largely for the multiplicity of themes and the most extended discussion of *Moby-Dick* in American criticism and scholarship. Stanley Williams praised the Melville pages and liked much of the Hawthorne, as well, in what was "probably the most firmly fibred book ever written on a substantial period of American literature." Robert Spiller wrote two reviews, beginning the first on a note of wartime urgency: "In an era of crisis, a people naturally turns to its historians and critics and prophets for reassurance of its faith in its own destiny." Matthiessen was all three, and he had written "the most profound work of literary criticism on historical principles by any modern American with the possible exception of Lowes's 'Road to Xanadu.'" Spiller's more academic review was in *American Literature,* where he argued that Matthiessen had created a method for other special studies and for an ultimate literary history of the United States. That method lay in his "emphasis upon masterworks as the primary material of literary history; the ability to remain on the plane of art and culture while giving full weight to the causal significance of social and intellectual forces; and the sense of pattern in past events."

There were adverse comments also, and many seem remarkably astute, coming years before Matthiessen's achievement was being reassessed from the perspective of time. Some of these first critics registered minor but telling complaints about his style. Clifton Fadiman noticed that Matthiessen was "virtually devoid of humor," and many a reader in the profession must have concurred. (Hawthorne's irony directed at the Emersonians, we now recognize, was totally missed in Matthiessen's discussion of sin and evil.) Elsewhere, his frequent and far-ranging literary connections, from Shakespeare and the seventeenth-century metaphysical and baroque writers in James, Eliot, and Hopkins led Williams to ask if Matthiessen kept readers "on these divergent bridlepaths too long"; and Spiller agreed that Matthiessen's references were "somewhat eclectic and fortuitous, the product of Mr. Matthiessen's own intellectual equipment than of inevitable and organic relationship to the main study."

The most serious criticism was directed at the tensions and contradictions in Matthiessen's ideal of a democratic culture. Spiller, however, was convinced that Matthiessen had demonstrated how "we have created a native myth of the democratic man, capable of all the range of experience of truth and error, good and evil, of the traditional heroic man, and that American literature has at least once explored and expressed the eternal verities of that myth." Spiller reaffirmed the immediate wartime benefit of the book: "In a time of crisis this is the sort of assurance that we need." Granville Hicks disagreed. Matthiessen was confusing and evasive in his stance on Christianity, democracy, Melvillean evil, and Emersonian goodness. Hicks put the case incisively: "Having rejected so much that logically belongs with Greenough's democratic ardor, and having accepted so much that logically belongs with Eliot's royalism, he ought not to be surprised if we find his passion for democracy something of a paradox." Hicks echoed Spiller's note of urgency but felt that Matthiessen's politics and literary interpretations were too vague and indecisive in these times, for "events are forcing these philosophical problems upon us and demanding decisions. Clarity becomes a major obligation."[33]

Alfred Kazin also reviewed *American Renaissance,* and his remarks are interesting for biographical as well as critical reasons. *On Native Grounds* came out the next year and was twice reviewed by Matthiessen. He and Kazin became colleagues and friends some years later at the six-week Salzburg Seminar for American Studies in 1947, where Kazin recognized Matthiessen as the unassuming leader whose camaraderie with students and faculty bespoke the very essence of this international gathering. But Kazin also believed Matthiessen to be politically naïve in his inability to recognize that postwar Communist societies were contemptuous of individual freedom.[34] In Kazin's review of *American Renaissance* in 1941, he was struck by the daring of Matthiessen's pioneering attempt, "based upon every possible resource in modern scholarship and criticism, to study our representative nineteenth-century classics as works of art." His only weakness was an aspect of his formidable knowledge and scope: The diversity of his materials, the shifting focus onto and away from the five figures, the extensive quotation, and the strong influence of Eliot had left Matthiessen seemingly "lacking in critical personality and authority." But Kazin detected no minor contradictions between Matthiessen's treatment of human evil and the hope for a humanely created socialistic order. Indeed, the spirit of democratic fraternalism (following Louis Sullivan), Kazin believed, had given Matthiessen an outlook of great "acuteness and flexibility," so that we might now understand how his five literary geniuses had lived within, and given creative expression to, "the democratic imagination" of America.[35]

Politically, Kazin himself in the thirties, and just after, had never been more than a bleachers intellectual-radical, a routine and detached Socialist. "I was not worshipful of ideologists," he recalled in his autobiography.[36] A native New Yorker, he was surrounded in his youth by Marxist and socialistic journalists, intellectuals, and authors. Like Whitman earlier in New York, Kazin was both in and out of the game. He worked his way through CCNY (class of 1935) and Columbia (M.A., 1938) by writing precocious reviews for the *New Republic, Scribner's*, and the Sunday newspapers. One of these reviews was a critique of Matthiessen's *The Achievement of T. S. Eliot* (1935), which the twenty-year-old Kazin judged faulty "in trying to draw too many parallels" but also abundant in "careful analyses and insights."[37] In the review of *American Renaissance* six years later, when politics should now have been at issue, Kazin did not realize any incongruity in the liberal Matthiessen's admiration for the ultraconservative Eliot, even though it did occur to Kazin privately to wonder how classmate Francis Corcoran in 1937 could reconcile his Catholicism with Communist Party membership. (That incongruity, to be more precise, Kazin noted in memoirs he wrote thirty years later.)

Kazin, then, was not, like Matthiessen, given to agonizing over the duties of the radical intellectual as a man of action. In 1938, with a master's degree from Columbia in hand, Kazin happily isolated himself in the "great sun-filled reading room of the New York Public Library, reading toward the first chapters of a book [he] had begun, at the instigation of Carl Van Doren, on modern

American writing" (p. 133). In the fall, he was also teaching English romantic poets on Monday evenings at a branch of CCNY, grading papers, and writing reviews. Over the next four years, he was frequently at the library when it opened and, except for luncheon and dinner interruptions, enjoyed its famous literary riches—and the motley Depression crowd of Communists and unemployed—until the 10 P.M. closing. In the summer of 1940, he lived in a cottage in Provincetown where he "worked at a huge dining table" and felt the joy of seeing the book falling into shape (p. 150). With the help of a Guggenheim fellowship (and later, a Carnegie grant), he was supplementing his earnings as a critic. In that role, he received a special stimulus that summer from reading *New England: Indian Summer,* Brooks's period overlapping Kazin's work in progress. In his review, Kazin was surprisingly mellow, praising the book as the most serious study of the writers after the Civil War since Mumford's *The Brown Decades,* both works with which Kazin was now in competition. (Mumford he felt as a greater influence.) "It is true," he allowed, "that there is something disquieting in Brooks's prevailing sweetness, the unceasing effort to charm, the vague radiance of his prose," but Kazin appreciated that Brooks had pursued the "actual complex of manners and culture" without riding "some convenient thesis."[38]

After another summer of work, this time at the Yaddo Writers Colony, with completed sections appearing in five academic and popular journals, Kazin finished his "wildly ambitious literary and intellectual history." It was published in late October 1942, with acknowledgments to Carl Van Doren, Henry Canby, and Newton Arvin for criticism of early drafts, and to Oscar Cargill for scholarly reading of the galleys. Five years of work had ended, though more to the consternation than relief of the twenty-seven-year-old author:

> As the reviews began to come in, the sudden invitations, the florid compliments and passionate attacks, I would take any train to Washington to lose myself in the commotion of war. I was desperate to get overseas. I could not bear so much examination, the loss of my old solitude when I had had the whole long day to read and write in.[39]

Neither the compliments nor the attacks were notably florid or passionate in most of the reviews from the academy. Rather, the reception of *On Native Grounds* was appreciative, well-informed, and judicious. Four of the critics would soon be members of the *LHUS* team. Robert Spiller found some fault with Kazin's "sophisticated irony" and "overwrought style" but acclaimed the book "a serious and successful essay in genuine literary history." Howard M. Jones judged Kazin "sensitive, sympathetic, and informed," and Gordon Haight (Yale) liked the Parringtonian range in Kazin that was supplemented by aesthetic judgments, though James and Dreiser deserved more space. F. O. Matthiessen added other important writers who were slighted (Twain, Eliot, Lardner), but expectably, he approved the intersection of aesthetic values with moral history, the painful alienation from native grounds in certain authors, and the resulting "sense of tragedy" that issued in "'a clutching violence.'"[40]

The larger response to *On Native Grounds* within the academy is less easily described, but this acclaim from noted professors must have broadly affected other scholarly opinion at the time. Was the book accurately assessed? After the war and into the fifties, as knowledge about Kazin's authors and the uses of criticism enjoyed virtually quantum leaps, his reading did not seem so prodigious, and his deficiencies were more obvious. (To many a beleaguered graduate student after the war, however, Kazin's dazzling assaults on Hemingway, Faulkner, and a host of critical elders made him a model of cockiness and youthful daring.) He underrated Howells's literary passion, bandied "reality" and "realism" and "naturalism" and "tragedy" about with no clear and consistent definitions, and he missed the complexities of periodizing the three mini-eras of his half-century. Most aggravating were the soaring generalities unsupported by close explication, or the breezy and pompous overwriting that frequently formed a smokescreen to disguise the limits of a critical sensibility not yet matured. Examples:

[On Stephen Crane] He accepted the world always, hating it always, plotting his way through it alone with a contempt close to pain. (p. 68)

[On Parrington] Reality! In the obsession with that conception Parrington betrayed the fact that, like all his generation, he was only an apprentice to reality. . . . To think of Parrington in his time and place, given the spirit of the age that supported him and the traditions that composed him, is to think of a mind that performed a notable service but was not notable in itself, one that was militant, occasionally moving, and significantly narrow. (p. 164)

[On Thomas Wolfe] The failure and triumph went hand in hand to the end, the nonsense and grandeur; and more than he knew—was not this his distinction?—they were his alone. (p. 484)

✱   ✱   ✱

One chapter in *On Native Grounds,* "Criticism at the Poles," drew sharp reactions for its significant rebuke of a recent new movement in literary explication and pedagogy, namely the New Criticism. Lionel Trilling (Columbia) wondered if Kazin's omission of poets had not distorted the essential sanity, creative growth, and wise inwardness of modern American literature, attributes we scarcely heard in "Anderson's quasi-religious whine, Dreiser's sourness, Hemingway's brag, Faulkner's rant." And because the New Critics "have helped remind us what poetry is," Kazin might have treated them more charitably. But for Haight, Kazin's attacks on the preciosity of the New Critics included "many things that have long needed saying."[41]

Far more impassioned, however, was the case for the defense from one of its own. Cleanth Brooks (Louisiana State) wrote a slashing criticism of Kazin as a faddish New York critic capitalizing, like Van Wyck Brooks, on the nationalist fever of a country at war. But Brooks presently settled down to the real business of his review, an answering argument for the New Critics whom Kazin had attacked while embracing the other Brooks as an ally. The year before, in *The Opinions of Oliver Allston,* Van Wyck Brooks had linked the "coterie-writers" to the dilettantish "school of coterie-critics." Quoting mainly from John Crowe Ransom's *The New Criticism* (1941), Brooks's persona Allston ridiculed I. A. Richards, T. S. Eliot, Ivor [*sic*] Winters, R. P. Blackmur, Ransom, and Cleanth Brooks as trivial critics without values who analyzed poetry with the same mechanistic and scientific zeal as our depressing novelists had been portraying modern man in his environment. Brooks-Allston dreaded the impact of this criticism in the academy among misguided professors

> who theorized, as he [Allston] said, *in vacuo.* It was not only that they wrote exclusively in relation to pupils, but that they wrote of literature without reference to feeling; and this was because they did not possess feeling, however they explained the matter otherwise.[42]

Kazin had repeated essentially this charge that Cleanth Brooks and his school were given over to critical preciosity, isolated textual analysis, and an antiseptic formalism (this last feature reinforcing, for the Southern Agrarians in their midst, the sacred ideal of form amid the anarchy of an industrial democracy possessed of no "sense of race and community and the soil" [p. 428]). Brooks alleged in his review that Kazin had in fact gone to the same school of "careful 'textual examination'" in his astute pages, for example, on the meretricious art and sentimentality of John

Steinbeck. Regarding Kazin's and Van Wyck Brooks's fear that the New Critics were infecting the academy: "I can assure him personally that the new formalists have next to no influence in the universities."[43]

Cleanth Brooks's disclaimer of influence by 1943 carried an excess of either modesty or disingenuousness. In 1936, with John T. Purser and Robert Penn Warren (both at LSU with Brooks), he had edited *An Approach to Literature,* which had gone to a second edition in three years. Even more influential was the revolutionary *Understanding Poetry* (1938), where American and British poems were organized according to common aesthetic properties rather than by chronology or author or didactic subject matter. In a prolonged "Letter to the Teacher" in that volume, the editors explained that the poem should be studied as an end in itself and "even if the interest is in the poem as a historical or ethical document, there is a prior consideration: one must grasp the poem as a literary construct before it can offer any real illumination as a document" (p. xi). Elsewhere in the letter, as well as in the introductions, explications, and exercises for each section (and a final glossary), the editors sprinkled the pages with criteria for their method of analysis and judgment. Professors and students now owned a critical vocabulary and method that insisted on the awareness of the poem's structure, paradox, irony, unity, ambiguity, complexity of attitude, together with the functions of imagery and symbolism, dramatization of theme, and the organic relationship among the elements. *Understanding Poetry* was, of course, largely a summary of the critical diction and principles drawn from a host of predecessors. Brooks and Warren were presenting to members of the academy a short course in I. A. Richards's *Principles of Literary Criticism* (1924) and *Practical Criticism* (1929), William Empson's *Seven Types of Ambiguity* (1929), T. S. Eliot's *Selected Essays* (1932), Allen Tate's *Reactionary Essays* (1936), John Crowe Ransom's essays being collected in *The World's Body* (1938), and Warren's recent article on irony in Ransom's poetry. The foreground included Brooks's own published essays, as well, which were presently collected, with others, in *Modern Poetry and the Tradition* (1939). As we realized in a previous chapter, embracement of tradition, including classical control and form (as opposed to romantic feeling and free form), links the New Criticism also with Southern Agrarian ideals and the earlier New Humanism of Babbitt and More.

Brooks and Warren were not content to rest their textbook labors on these two books from the thirties. In 1943, while Brooks was discounting major influence in the academy, they were already awaiting the royalties on a third text, *Understanding Fiction*, dedicated to Southern Agrarian Donald Davidson. Now they applied the New Critical method specifically to teaching fiction (fifteen, or slightly fewer than half, of the selections were from American literature). As in *Understanding Poetry*, the literature was arranged by internal features of the genre rather than by chronology. Again, selections were preceded by a long, indoctrinating "Letter to the Teacher." Once more, the letter, along with the editors' interpretations and glossary, referred to irony, paradox, total structure, drama versus exposition, and the "organic relation existing among the elements." This time, the elements included such techniques as focus of narration, aesthetic distance, setting, characterization, and plot construction. Symptomatic of Brooks's annoyance over charges that New Critics were indifferent to the content of great literature, he and Warren asserted and reiterated that the formalists' approach did not ignore the idea in a literary work; rather, they pursued, above all, the "vital and functional relationship between the idea and the other elements in that structure—plot, style, character, and the like" (p. xv).

The New Critics also purveyed their message through various journals that were happy to publish these eminent professor-critics: the *Virginia Quarterly Review, Yale Review, Sewanee Review, Saturday Review of Literature,* and even the politically slanted *Partisan Review*. Most importantly, they edited two excellent journals of their own, Brooks and Warren's *Southern Review* (1935–41) and Ransom's *Kenyon Review* (founded in 1938). (*The Explicator,* established in 1942 by Mary Washington College professors George Arms, John Kirby, Louis Locke, and Edwin Whitesell, encouraged close reading also, but the authors usually published items that were not guided, in most cases, by other New Critical requisites.) In the autumn of 1940, the two journals published in consecutive parts "Literature and the Professors: A Symposium." The *Southern Review* introduced the series with this comment: "The lag between modern criticism and the current methods of teaching literature in most colleges and universities has from time to time occasioned comment." The forum would permit an extended discussion, the participants in this first issue being Ransom (Kenyon), Tate (Princeton), Joe Horrell (North Carolina), Wright Thomas (Wisconsin), and Harry Levin (Harvard). Ransom invited professors to come out from behind the academic barriers of historical scholarship and adopt a speculative or critical attitude "tough, scientific, and aloof from the literary 'illusion' which it examines"; Tate chided professors who indulged in safe and pseudo-scientific research without bringing a critical intelligence into play; and Horrell, recently liberated from a graduate education in secondary readings, urged fellow professors to "let the literature intervene" in their graduate and undergraduate classrooms. Thomas had tested his graduate students as critics of an anonymous poem (his own) and discovered that they could only recite historical principles and comment in a vapid jargon, and Levin stressed our responsibility to the present over an allegiance to the past.

The symposium continued in Ransom's *Kenyon Review* with participants Cleanth Brooks (LSU), Sidney Cox (Dartmouth), Arthur Mizener (Wells), Hade Saunders (pseudonym of a graduate student in a Midwest university), and Lionel Trilling (Columbia), who presently would rebuke Kazin for his flippant pages on the New Critics. Brooks refused to condone the modern English department for "the stupid, or trifling, or plainly muddle-headed books, articles, dissertations, and theses which its machinery commits it to turn out," and he blamed this dreary condition on the professors. They had failed to bring their intelligence and taste to bear on an ultimate reading of the inner structure of the literary work itself. Cox, too, asked for imaginative teaching to replace the practice of current pedagogues "who have only a pedlar's pack of assorted facts about books and authors, their categories, times and influences, with critics' conflicting appraisals." Mizener added that because professors defaulted on their critical duties, "the serious evaluation of literature is carried on outside our universities by talented amateurs who are, as no one is more acutely aware than they, without adequate learning." Saunders noticed that, like his professors, fellow graduate students had virtually no creative taste. These budding teachers were "unable to give a rational personal opinion of Cummings or MacLeish," but "such is the state of English that they will be able to camouflage this weakness with a barrage of historical chit-chat." Trilling invoked Matthew Arnold's notion that literature is "a civilizing agent," and charged fellow professors to blend aesthetic and historical methods by approaching the work itself with the responsive intelligence of a historical imagination.[44]

Another journal, the profession's pedagogical *College English,* allows further glimpses at the influence that the New Critics were enjoying in the academy. Indeed, George Gullette (Toledo) promptly replied therein to the symposium in the *Kenyon* and *Southern Review.* He welcomed a challenge to the grinding dullness of the historical survey course, but the New Critics had overestimated the sophistication of the average sophomore.

Martin Schockley and Charles C. Walcutt (Oklahoma), on the other hand, had reorganized their American literature curriculum from the sophomore level to graduate work by abandoning the historical, geographical, and bibliographical backgrounds except as they might illuminate the close reading of texts. They had ended the lecture system, too, in favor of classroom discussion of selected literary works of fewer authors. Edd W. Parks (Georgia), who enjoyed close ties with the *Southern Review,* agreed that the "most rewarding and valid" approach to literature was to see the "particular poem as a poem, the novel as a novel," but like Gullette, he observed that such teaching was only successful with students of high intelligence and strong knowledge of backgrounds. He pointed out that even a professional close reader like Ransom (in *The World's Body*) had exposed his puzzlements with Milton's technique in "Lycidas." Parks proposed the inevitable compromise in his twin conclusions: "The work of art has many meanings, and aesthetic appreciation is not enough," and "to make use of literature as intellectual history does not require any disregard of critical standards." David Daiches (Chicago) reported that his department had revised the master's program in English so that the first year centered on specific works in American and English literature, with the student aided by a required course in practical criticism. Literary-history backgrounds were then introduced in the second year, becoming the culmination rather than starting point in the student's education in literature.[45]

And so the debate continued. Into 1944, R. W. Short (Sweet Briar College) rejected the patchwork changes being fashioned here and there by history-oriented professors—new surveys, interdisciplinary offerings, honors sections, student theses, and the like. To Short, "their aim has been to preserve the roots of their establishment," whereas the radical escape from dry-as-dust historicism was available in the "well-known textbook of poetry" by Brooks and Warren. Short proposed that *Understanding Poetry* be adopted throughout the undergraduate curriculum, from freshman English to the most advanced classes. Wallace C. Brown (University of Kansas City) also rebelled against traditional literary history, where the importance of Poe was argued by the scholar who then was unable to analyze and evaluate the poetry as poetry. Brown named the new formalists "our best critics today" and then launched into a comparative analysis, New-Critical style, between Poe's "Annabel Lee" and, to his mind, the superior "To Helen." His criteria were unity, structural integrity, ambiguity, complexity and anti-romantic objectivity. But the New

Critics were not without their detractors in these months. Darrel Abel (Purdue) wrote an essentially pro-romantic counterstatement, alleging that in the criticism of Tate, Ransom, and Cleanth Brooks, the "tendency is their effort to define poetry as intellectual exercise and to deny that its value consists in its appeal to the feelings." Reading these charges, Brooks returned to the lists to defend himself with the same arguments he had garnered against the jibes of Van Wyck Brooks and Alfred Kazin. In the best New-Critical manner, he began with the concrete example (an explication of "Tears, Idle Tears," the treatment anticipated in the loaded questions on the poem in *Understanding Poetry*) and advanced to the general statement: Modern criticism is concerned with structure more centrally than feelings and message "not because it accepts the conventional, sterile division of poetry into 'form' and 'content,' but because it realizes that the way that a thing is said determines what is said."[46]

In the meantime, a movement that would enrich the understanding of "what is said" in American literature had been gaining favor in the academy. Usually termed American Civilization or American Studies, the curriculum joined American literature not to the English literary backgrounds but to related courses in American culture offered in other departments of the humanities. Such cross-disciplinary study was, of course, implicit in the American and historical aspects of our literary scholarship ever since Moses Coit Tyler's literary histories and central to many of the textbook histories that flowed from professorial pens thereafter. Practitioners of the New History after World War I encouraged a broader cultural approach to history, and Parrington's *Main Currents* in 1927 forcefully returned Americans to the wide range of documents that explained our cultural past and illuminated the present. Matthiessen at the close of the 1920s, it will be remembered, favored Harvard over Yale as an academic residence because of the tutorials that integrated literature with history. But two years after Matthiessen left, Yale then introduced a course in "American Thought and Civilization," taught by Stanley Williams and Ralph Gabriel, and in the next year began a graduate program in the field. The first interdisciplinary Ph.D. was awarded in 1933 at Yale to A. Whitney Griswold, who had written "The American Cult of Success." Harvard began its program in 1936, the American civilization faculty of Kenneth Murdock and Perry Miller made even more formidable by the appointment of Howard Jones. Matthiessen, however, showed little interest in the doctoral program, as recalled by Henry Nash Smith, who received its first Ph.D. in 1940.

Still, Matthiessen may have been the most important pioneer of American Studies, for it was he, in 1941 with *American Renaissance,* who opened the way to the subtle exploration of symbolism and myth in American cultural documents. To make those materials accessible, three publishers brought out anthologies especially fitted to the broad new curriculum that acted, too, as a spur to the study of American literature. The American Book Company issued *The American Mind* (two volumes), edited in 1937 by Yale innovators Williams and Gabriel (with Harry Warfel of Maryland); and in 1941, Lippincott published *American Issues,* edited in two volumes by Princeton's Willard Thorp and Carlos Baker, with Merle Curti (Columbia) handling the historical selections. Three years later, Crofts brought out *America in Literature,* edited by Tremaine McDowell (Minnesota). By the early 1940s, these texts served a sizable number of institutions that had been devising interdisciplinary programs in American civilization on both undergraduate and graduate levels.

This new field received its first substantial recognition in the profession during the ALG meeting in Indianapolis in 1941. A Committee on Curricula in American Civilization was appointed, with members Willard Thorp, Luther Mansfield (Williams), and Clarence Faust (Chicago) as chairman. The MLA did not hold an annual meeting during the war years of 1942 and 1943, but the ALG committee proceeded to survey seventy-six institutions, many of which had initiated courses and majors in American civilization, and among those who had not, close to thirty reported their intention to begin. Early in 1944, the committee was able to publicize its findings in the Sunday edition of the *New York Times.* As American participation in the war continued, the programs grew in popularity, reflecting in many cases, no doubt, the rising spirit of nationalism. A partial list of colleges with wartime interdisciplinary curricula for undergraduates included Princeton, Minnesota, Ohio State, Northwestern, Maryland, Cincinnati, Kansas City, Wells, Barnard, Colby, Vassar, Hollins, Brooklyn, Howard, Oregon State, Wyoming, Scripps, and Temple. Graduate programs were now under way at Pennsylvania, New York University, New Mexico, Brown, Maryland, and Minnesota.[47]

At the ALG meeting in 1945 in Chicago, members gathered to hear papers on "The American Civilization, or Culture, Program." Participants included committee members Thorp and Mansfield. Thorp reported on "The Adoption of the Program in

Colleges and Universities," while Mansfield described "The Benefits from the Study of American History." Other speakers represented schools that had instituted the program: Guy A. Cardwell (Maryland), "The Imperfect Training of American Literature Students"; Ernest Leisy (Southern Methodist), "The Benefits from the Study of American Political Science, Philosophy, and Economics"; Tremaine McDowell (Minnesota), "American Studies and the Humanities"; and Henry Pochmann (Wisconsin), "The Relation of American Studies to European Literature." An audience of 190 attended the program.[48] The following year, with Thorp now chairman of the ALG, American civilization studies received further impetus as part of the "Report to the ALG of the MLA on the Teaching of American Literature," prepared by John Hite (Princeton), who had assembled data from one hundred colleges and universities. (Hite's report has been cited in previous chapters.)

The National Council of Teachers of English, too, had formed its Committee on the College Study of American Literature and Culture, with William G. Crane (CCNY) as chairman. In 1948, it published *American Literature in the College Curriculum,* the survey this time comprehending more than seven hundred colleges and universities. Some sixty were offering undergraduate programs in American studies, and about fifteen were granting advanced degrees. Schools besides Crane's that were represented on the committee were New Mexico (George Arms), Chicago (Walter Blair), Pennsylvania (Sculley Bradley), California at Berkeley (Frederic Carpenter), Rutgers (Rudolf Kirk), Southern Methodist (Ernest Leisy), James Ormond Wilson Teachers College (John S. Lewis, Jr., who summarized his thesis—NYU, 1941—for "Part I: Historical Summary to 1939"), Minnesota (Tremaine McDowell), North Texas State Teachers (Floyd Stovall), Princeton (Willard Thorp), Washington and Jefferson (Charles C. Walcutt), Pennsylvania Military College (Harry Warfel), and Pennsylvania State (William Werner). One of the most important results from the report was that part III, "The Growth of American Civilization Programs," gave Tremaine McDowell much of the invaluable data for his *American Studies,* also published in 1948. With McDowell's book, the movement now possessed a history. The following year, his University of Minnesota sponsored *American Quarterly,* a journal officially designed to publish articles and reviews on scholarship in American civilization. And in 1951, the profession itself owned an official title, the American Studies Association.[49]

*   *   *

While American civilization advocates were directing American literature into a closer partnership with American cultural history, and the New Critics were pulling the two fields farther apart, a third group comprised the familiar antagonists of before: the anglophiles and Americanists in the standard English department. The 1940s opened with the proponents of American literature continuing to wonder that so many of their teaching colleagues in the academy remained colonialists in their deference to England. Leonard Koester (Louisville) reported that visiting educators from abroad admired our departments named after the various foreign cultures, and then asked if they might visit the American department to understand how we organized and presented our own literature and culture. They were directed, instead, to the English department. There, a course in American literature might appear at the end of the departmental curriculum, "with perhaps one in American culture—open to Seniors and graduates." Koester proposed that we strike the word *English* from the departmental office door, replace it with *American,* and revise the curriculum so that English literature served as a background to the primary study of American authors. Floyd Stovall confirmed Koester's conclusions by examining the catalogs of some seventy colleges, private and public. Of those that offered American literature at all, it rated no more than 20 percent of the literature courses in English departments, and these offerings were usually elective surveys at the junior level. The more largely attended, because required, sophomore survey was devoted to English literature.[50]

These common objections did not influence Dean William C. DeVane of Yale. He proposed in 1941 a revision of the university's English major but gave no importance to American literature. His article incensed Amos L. Herold (Tulsa), who replied that American prose should enter courses at the freshman level and English literature should cease to monopolize the sophomore course. He repeated what Koester and Stovall had observed, that few students elected the later courses devoted to American authors (Herold's estimate was 10 to 20 percent). Yet American literature was intrinsically more important and interesting. Herold quoted from students who made comparative evaluations of American and English authors grouped together in one of his courses. Franklin had far greater appeal to the students than Dr. Johnson, Thoreau than Swift, and Whitman than Tennyson and Browning.[51]

Through the final three years of the war, American literature in the academy seems to have made some modest advance over the

state of the discipline as Stovall and the others had rather gloomily viewed it. Any progress at all had to be impressive when we
recall that these were also the years when the navy, army, and air
force were occupying English department classrooms and many
professors were teaching practical communication skills to inductees. To what degree literature professors were renovating the
literature curriculum at this time to increase the American offerings can be partly inferred by an end-of-the-war study undertaken by the same NCTE committee that surveyed the American
civilization programs in the academy. The data for its conclusions
were derived mainly from four sources: a questionnaire mailed
to 692 institutions in May 1945 (678 responded); a second questionnaire to 450 institutions in May 1946, regarding the special approach and method of instruction (250 of the 339 replies
were useful); supplementary letters to individual professors; and
an examination of 703 catalogs for 1947 to 1948. These last-
mentioned announcements probably reflected the programs
developed, though not fully executed, late in the war. Many institutions, the committee concluded, "have indicated their interest in the last two years in expanding their work in American
literature, but most of them have been too busy caring for the influx of veterans and other students to be able to make many additions to their curriculums."[52]

The committee conscientiously weighed statistics that, at first
glance, seemingly argued that vast gains had already been accomplished for American literature in the undergraduate curriculum.
Of the 711 universities and colleges listed in the *Educational Directory* for 1946–47, only 9 or 10 failed to offer courses in American literature. On the other hand, only 30 required American
literature for graduation and 24 percent required it for English
majors. Elective courses in American authors were, two-thirds of
the time, mixed with English literature. The usual course was
the survey, customarily offered through two semesters and totaling four to six hours of credit. In ninety syllabi of these survey
courses mailed to the committee, Emerson, Hawthorne, and
Whitman appeared in more than seventy, followed by Poe (sixty-
two), Mark Twain (fifty-seven), Thoreau (fifty-six), and Melville
(fifty-two). Four out of five professors teaching the survey mixed
discussion with their lecture, their predominant emphasis being
on literary history, though 39 percent gave secondary consideration to aesthetic values. Only 5 percent followed the aesthetic approach alone.

Apart from the survey course, American writers appeared
most frequently during 1945–46 in the mixed (with English)

course on modern drama, with aesthetic appreciation rather than literary history the usual approach. Closely following in popularity among colleges responding to the questionnaire of May 1946 were mixed courses in contemporary poetry (23 percent) and contemporary fiction (17 percent). The most popular elective in strictly American literature was the fiction course, offered by 19 percent of the institutions. Various other electives—American genres, modes, periods, and regions (especially New England and the South)—were given by fewer than 10 percent of the colleges and universities. The most frequent single-author courses were on Whitman, Emerson, Poe, or Mark Twain.

Such was the apparent state of American literature study in undergraduate programs around the country by the close of World War II. To the degree that the statistics were accurate, how much optimism could they inspire in members of the profession? In the parent English department, American literature clearly remained in a rather dismal minority state. Throughout the nation, Middlebury College continued to be the only institution that valued our authors highly enough to form a separate department of American literature.

In advanced study, however, and in postdoctoral scholarship, American literature research had maintained much of the vitality and growing maturity of the late thirties, though it fell off inevitably at the height of the war from 1943 to 1945. In 1940, approximately fifty-two American literature dissertations were completed in the nation's English departments, over 25 percent more than in the previous year. Some 140 additional graduate students completed their work in the next three years. But in 1944 and 1945, annual totals dropped to fewer than thirty. The university English departments most productive in Ph.D.s in American literature from 1940 to 1945 were Iowa (nineteen), NYU (sixteen), Pennsylvania (fourteen), Chicago (fourteen), Yale (fourteen), Wisconsin (thirteen), Ohio State (thirteen), and Vanderbilt (thirteen). Emerson, Melville, and Mark Twain, respectively, received the most single-author dissertations. The literary–historical approach was still dominant in the graduate schools, as we infer from the many dissertations on general topics and fewer than 10 percent on authors whose reputations had been established in the twentieth century. Noteworthy, too, during the war years was the number of individuals completing their graduate work who were to become rising members of the profession. Prominent among this new generation who soon contributed significantly to postwar scholarship were Edwin Cady and Russel Nye (Ph.D.'s received at Wisconsin), Edgar Branch and

Ernest Sandeen (Iowa), William Gibson, John Gerber, and Ernest Samuels (Chicago), Lewis Leary (Columbia), Edward Davidson, Merton Sealts, Tyrus Hillway, Harrison Hayford, and Norman Pearson (Yale), Carl Bode (Northwestern), Frederick Hoffman and Hyatt Waggoner (Ohio State), Stephen Whicher (Harvard), and Roy Pearce (Johns Hopkins).[53]

In 1944, Bernard DeVoto hailed "the maturity of American literature," especially at his alma mater, Harvard, where practicing poets and novelists were visible on the faculty, along with outstanding scholars of the day, including Matthiessen and Jones.[54] DeVoto was not close enough to the academy, however, to realize that this development had also been arrested by the distractions and dislocations of the war. The most important books were completed before the serious impact of American intervention. Besides the works of Van Wyck Brooks, Matthiessen, Kazin, the New Critics, and the *LHUS* editors, Fred B. Millett (Wesleyan) added to the store of basic bibliographical and biographical knowledge in *Contemporary American Authors* (1940). The next year, Joseph W. Beach (Minnesota), in *American Fiction, 1920–1940*, acknowledged his bibliographical debts to Millett while anticipating Kazin's book of the following year. Sharing the limelight with Matthiessen and Beach in 1941 was Oscar Cargill (NYU) with *Intellectual America: Ideas on the March*, a convenient, if cumbersome, treatment of ideological backgrounds to American literature. In 1942, besides Kazin's *On Native Grounds*, American scholars were greeted with *The Economic Novel in America* by Walter F. Taylor (from Mississippi College; Taylor acknowledged his thesis director of long ago at North Carolina, Howard Jones). Also in 1942 came Constance Rourke's posthumous *The Roots of American Culture*, edited, with a preface, by Van Wyck Brooks. The most important works for American literature study to appear thereafter were *Social Darwinism in American Thought* (1944) by Richard Hofstadter (Maryland) and *Freudianism and the Literary Mind* (1945) by Frederick Hoffman (Ohio State).

Scholarly articles in American literature had proliferated before American intervention but then declined perceptibly in the published totals of 1944, 1945, and 1946. Listings in the *PMLA* bibliography of books and articles during those years contrast vividly with publications for 1941, 1942, and 1943, when seventeenth- and eighteenth-century studies had totaled 149 items but now only 108. Scholarly work treating the literature from 1800 to 1870 fell from 324 entries to 226, and 1870 to 1900 from 178 items to 122. Twentieth-century studies fell less drastically from 147 entires to 112. Such statistics, properly examined, always call forth various conclusions and require distinctions between quantity and quality. But obviously World War II curbed the growth of American literature scholarship. Then came an unprecedented explosion of postwar studies, and the lost ground was rapidly recovered. After a decade, publications in 1955 exceeded those of 1945 by 500 percent.

Among the scholarly articles and reviews published during the war years, the most authoritative usually appeared, once again, in *American Literature*. The profession's journal, despite a growing reputation for old-fogey historical scholarship, was also faring handsomely as an economic venture: In December 1943, Jay B. Hubbell reported a profit of $984.84! But he was visited with headaches, too. Professors grieved over their treatment in a review, or tried to avoid adverse criticism by suggesting to Hubbell ideal reviewers, or presented themselves as the fit reviewer of a recent book. Others urged that Hubbell welcome more essays in criticism or on contemporary authors or publish the fledging efforts of a favorite graduate student.[55] Hubbell's mail was never light in manuscripts. He required three rejections of a submission before returning it. The rejected author then had many other outlets. Besides the older journals, fourteen newer ones founded in the war years were hospitable in part or exclusively to American literature.[56]

*   *   *

Hubbell experienced another gratifying profit in the war years when his two-volume anthology textbook, *American Life in Literature* (1936), was selected by the U.S. Armed Forces Institute (USAFI) for the home-study program it had begun in 1941. (In the first ten years, the USAFI counted almost two million enrollments from servicemen pursuing higher education.) In the year 1944–45, Hubbell gained royalties on fifty thousand sets of his text purchased by the government from Harper.[57] The more famous partnership between the government and the academy came, of course, in 1942 when the army, navy, and air forces organized college training programs in cooperation with some five hundred colleges and universities. When the draft age was lowered to eighteen in December 1942, these campuses, and especially the all-male institutions, faced a severe decrease in incoming freshmen. Such institutions heartily welcomed the influx of 300,000 servicemen, most of them aged seventeen to nineteen. Dartmouth, for example, greeted 1,993 naval trainees on 1 July 1943. The group comprised four-fifths of the campus population. Although the military students in most colleges were

taught separately, Hobart–Smith in 1943 combined their naval
V-12 and civilian undergraduates. In this student body, 393 trainees joined fifty Hobart men and 175 Smith women in a camaraderie that extended beyond the classroom to a school spirit in
intercollegiate sports and on-campus social life. On the other
hand, at the 223 institutions that had begun to educate the army,
rather than the navy, inductees were not so fortunate. When the
1943 draft quota fell short by 200,000 men, the War Department,
on 18 February 1944, ordered 100,000 members of the Army
Specialized Training Program (ASTP) to line duty.

To what extent was teaching American literature a part of
these wartime college programs? Unfortunately, the subject was
virtually ignored. Army courses were devoted almost totally to
technical knowledge, with a single English course designed to
teach communication skills—a nonhumanistic emphasis that
promptly drew the criticism of President Dodds of Princeton.
The navy, in principle, stressed that its students were to be given
a college education appropriate to officers and gentlemen, with a
curriculum centered on traditional core subjects in the liberal
arts. They included, however, little more than American history
and psychology. Those who went through the standard naval
V-12 program received no course in literature, either American
or British. As in the army program, basic communication skills
were taught.[58]

Although the academic curriculum of the armed forces during
the war was heavily tilted toward technical training, the emphasis away from the humanities seemed to various observers only a
practical and temporary necessity. "This is a technician's war,"
was the good-humored concession of G. H. Estabrooks, professor
of psychology at Colgate who had rapidly transformed himself
into an instructor of physics for navy men, at least half a dozen
of whom were far his superior in the subject. Henry Canby, by
contrast, took a longer philosophical view and worried that the
humanities were now, and had been for some time, seriously neglected. Prewar and wartime "technology has outrun its human
controls." Sadly, literature professors themselves, over the past
twenty-five years, had increasingly aped the scientific pursuit of
fact and overlooked the humanistic insights and tastes and aspirations that they should have been communicating as teachers
and writers. Newton Arvin observed, in a similar vein, that over
these same twenty-five years, American literature study had
been invaded by a spirit of practical ambition and a corporate
business mentality. The profession was imbued with practices
after the industrial model: Observe the inner councils of the

ALG, with its officers and various committees, and members vying in a concerted scramble to gain publishing royalties in the school book trade. The scholar-professor had now become a sales manager with his or her own narrow field or territory. Most of the products were "little more than dismal monuments to unlearned specialization, bibliographical diligence, and ponderous insensitiveness to the real needs of the youthful mind."[59]

Others were more hopeful about the humanities, American literature study, and the military experience in the academy during the war. Emory Holloway, who had written the Whitman chapter of the *CHAL* during World War I, dispensed with his usual syllabus at Queens College after Pearl Harbor and charged his students to relate their directed readings to the theme of "democratic life as reflected in the slow growth of American literature." The result was an in-class book authored by the students, with annotated bibliographies for each chapter. Richard F. Miller, who taught in the college military program in 1943 and 1944, discovered that American democratic life itself became a present reality at Washington State when men of different social classes and races and regional accents learned to respect each other and affirm not only an American but world ideal of peace and brotherhood. Finally, F. O. Matthiessen, who could easily applaud Arvin's cynical estimate of professional politicking in the academy, was looking, instead, like Miller, to the fine egalitarian spirit nurtured by the army and navy college programs. These educational opportunities, Matthiessen was certain, had given to intelligent youth of lesser means the chance to enjoy what would be understood as a birthright under socialism. Writing in January 1944, he hoped that the government would grant similar educational aid to veterans after the war. Five months later, President Roosevelt signed the Serviceman's Readjustment Aid Act to fulfill the wish expressed by Matthiessen. Furthermore, many of those among the fifteen million veterans who began or completed their college careers under this "G.I. Bill of Rights" helped accelerate the serious study of American literature on a scale undreamed of in previous decades. The quantity, quality, and variety of this scholarship, into and throughout the 1950s, must be viewed, in large degree, as a legacy of the G.I. Bill.[60]

Chapter 27

The *LHUS:* Shaping the Text (1945–1948)

In another part of the academy, as the nation moved into the fourth year of war, the editors of the *LHUS* were judging incoming manuscripts from contributors, and their subsequent revisions, in an effort to shape an eventual eighty-one chapters into a literary history coherent in substance and, as far as possible, harmonious in style. The ramshackle effect in much of the *CHAL* had been due to an absence of unifying theory and editorial vision, and those shortcomings had been on Spiller's mind from the outset. As the history was mushrooming into a team undertaking of fifty-five collaborators, Jones reminded Spiller that historical and critical unity would be nearly impossible. Spiller acknowledged that editors must be tolerant of individual approaches; but he was also confident that diverging viewpoints could be minimized through editorial communication with the authors at various stages from conception to composition to revision. During an editorial meeting in Princeton, in late 1943, the board had proposed that after each manuscript went the critical rounds, it should return to the subeditor of the section for a digest of the criticism. Then it would go to Spiller for a final comment and be returned to the author for revision. But as noted previously, the board agreed some months later that Spiller should write all the critical summaries. Thorp would try to ensure factual accuracy in the chapters, but the bibliographical correctness, it was agreed, would be solely Johnson's responsibility. Later on, Wecter was designated special critic "on coordination and transition," to avoid an overlap of the general connecting chapters in the various sections.[1]

Because authors completed chapter assignments in the ten sections at different times, editorial readings of chapters, naturally, were not completed in consecutive order. Even so, this crucial phase of the *LHUS* can best be reviewed by discussing chapter submissions in their historical sequence. The responses by editors and authors in so many chapters were bound to be, at times, a little harsh and, in fact, too much so to be closely reproduced here. Thus, our summary account only suggests, as politely as possible, the lively nature of the editorial activity and many of the exacting judgments.

The editors and associates submitted their criticism on a form attached to each incoming chapter. The page was headed first draft and indicated section, chapter, title, contributor, and date received, as well as the editorial routing before the criticism came to Spiller. Critical comments were initialed by each editor. Spiller then wrote a diplomatic summary and sent it to the author, usually managing an initial compliment ("a remarkable job") before advising needed changes that had been suggested, here and there, by some of the seven editorial critics. Thorp red-penciled the places where he wanted authors to double-check their accuracy. After the authors had complied with revisions, the manuscripts usually went to just the main editors, then were routed to Thorp who again made a test for accuracy, then to Johnson who skimmed off the suggested bibliographical data, and then to the typist.

Jones sent his manuscript of chapter 1, "The European Background," accompanied by a note terming his assignment, because of its scope, impossible in such limited space—a complaint that soon became familiar as other collaborators responded. Jones invited Spiller to toss the chapter in a waste heap if it would not go *as is*. He could not envision an alternative approach to his subject. When Jones received the editorial suggestion to revise in order to give a clearer American emphasis leading into the next chapter on "Colonial Literary Culture" by Louis B. Wright, Jones disdained the request. On publication, however, the closing paragraph stressed that English settlers "developed colonial education, colonial books, colonial publishing, colonial literary art" (I, 15). Spiller obviously had linked the chapters himself. In addition to chapter 2, Louis Wright was the author of chapter 4, "Writers of the South." Both received scorching criticism, a private editorial verdict being that chapter 2 was dull even after revision. When Spiller sent Wright the critical summary of chapter 4, Wright was so incensed that Spiller wrote to ask Jones if he would take the assignment if Wright resigned. However, as it turned out, Wright calmed down and revised the chapter.[2]

Randolph G. Adams, librarian at the Clements Library at the University of Michigan, delivered his chapter 3, "Reports and Chronicles," with a note repeating the grievance already voiced by Jones, that he had been asked to be inclusive and concise. The editors' criticism, however, was in a different vein; they found the chapter stylistically inferior. It needed freshness, an awareness of the interests of the general audience who would be reading the *LHUS,* and a more positive attitude toward those Puritan writings that did not have the appeal enjoyed by belles lettres. Not without protest, Adams revised even to a fifth draft.

Problems of conception and compression plagued authors of section II as well. Jones, in particular, considered Spiller's instruments chapter 10 ("The Making of the Man of Letters") far too drawn out and belabored, especially with regard to his concept of literary nationalism. Chapter 11, "The War of the Pamphlets," by John Harvey Powell, generally pleased all the editors except Jones, who charged that Powell failed to frame the great issues of the Revolution. Powell complained that he was being asked, in revising, to compress his chapter and yet supply more data. But he revised to a second and then a third draft.[3] Alexander Cowie had rough going with his chapter 14, "The Beginnings of Fiction and Drama," among all the editors but Johnson. Jones considered it obvious, dull, and timid. Spiller softened the request to Cowie for revision by informing him, first of all, that he had received "a chorus of mild approval" from the readers. In the eventual revision, some of Cowie's sentences were moved to Spiller's instruments chapter 10 on the early man of letters in America ("with passages by Alexander Cowie").

Section III, "The Democracy," became a relatively easy cluster of chapters for the editors to approve. Tremaine McDowell's lead chapter (16) and his treatment of Bryant and his early New England contemporaries (21) gave no trouble, nor did Williams's Irving and Cooper after he divided his discussion into two chapters.[4] Spiller's instruments chapter 17 ("Art in the Market Place") was another matter, as he extracted and fused to his own account various passages from Odell Shepard's chapter on New England (chap. 35), Luther S. Mansfield's on the middle states (chap. 20), and John D. Wade's on the South (chap. 22). Indeed, Wade's chapter ultimately received a rewriting at the hands of Thorp. F. O. Matthiessen's essay on Poe (chap. 23), which completes section III, called for no basic revision. Not a recognized specialist on Poe, Matthiessen was not an amateur, either. In Spiller's words,

[W]e learned through one of his graduate students that Matthiessen had wished to include Poe in his *American Renaissance* but found later that he did not fit into the scheme of the book. Because Poe at that time seemed to need the kind of fresh perspective that we thought Matthiessen might supply, we chose him in preference to the more thoroughly informed Quinn or Mabbott.

After reading the chapter, some of the editors, however, missed the usual Matthiessen touch of brilliance and subtlety, "the kind of fresh perspective" that, it had been hoped, he might bring to the *LHUS*. To Jones, the essay by his Harvard colleague was satisfactorily balanced and (deadly term) "workmanlike."[5]

According to Spiller's romantic-cycle theory, section IV, "Literary Fulfillment," represented the initial cresting of American literature. Of the six chapters, four were written by the editorial staff, joined by David Bowers (Princeton) and Townsend Scudder (Swarthmore). The lead chapter by Bowers ("Democratic Vistas") generally pleased all the editors except Jones, who considered it "inadequate as a setting" for this eventful stage of the history. Bowers became a World War II casualty in the summer of 1945, and Spiller revised the beginning and ending of this chapter, as he would others, "to tie the book together and to emphasize dominant themes" (II, 1393). He also removed philosophical jargon and, wherever it appeared, the term romanticism. For his own chapter on Emerson (25), Spiller asked for and received a long critique from Stephen Whicher (Swarthmore) that raised such objections as (1) the absence of pre-Darwinism and (2) an overvaluation of the later *Conduct of Life*. Smaller revisions of the sixty-page manuscript were suggested, in the margins, by Johnson and Thorp. Townsend Scudder's original draft of his Thoreau (chap. 26) was, to all the readers, unorthodox, too heavily biographical, and "impressionistic." He reduced the biography in favor of a critical emphasis even more impressionistic. But Spiller, in a letter to Canby, admitted that they were all aware when they selected "Towny" that his scholarly-critical manner leaned toward impressionism.[6]

Elsewhere in section IV, Williams's Hawthorne (chap. 27) had a checkered career. Begun in early 1943, he offered his earliest drafts at the editorial roasting that June, rewrote it, received more editorial criticism, and finally, after removing not merely original sentences but entire paragraphs, submitted a fifth revision two years later. Thorp's Melville and Canby's Whitman fared much better, though Thorp received a mixed reception that points to the healthy critical spirit of any good editorial board. Johnson praised the "brilliant analysis and focus" of the chapter. But Jones called the essay "vastly and badly overwritten" and, symptomatic of the Melville revival, uncritical of the writer's obvious defects. (Thorp's book in 1938, previously cited, was a recent contribution to the revival.) It would be easy here to descend into spicy inference and impute (unfairly) to Jones a small-minded vindictiveness: Not long before, Thorp had reviewed

Jones's *Ideas in America* and, to the displeasure of his fellow editor, Thorp regarded only five of the thirteen reprinted pieces to be timely and valuable. Spiller sent to Thorp a summary of criticism of the Melville chapter, along with a comment characteristically diplomatic: "This fine chapter could stand as is, but will of course profit by styling, cutting, and sharpening."[7]

Section V, "Crisis," completed Spiller's first cycle. Chapter assignments here were difficult to make, and the book as a unit was late in being framed. Wecter's "A House Divided and Rejoined" led off these eight chapters, which filled out the contours of the midcentury after the five single-author chapters of section IV. Trouble with Wecter's essay surfaced at once. Jones termed it "pretty flat stuff," the case of a contributor's writing a chapter but not having a chapter to write. When Wecter returned to the United States in early 1946 after nine months of teaching in Australia, he promised to revise and, in fact, to rewrite the chapter from scratch. Eric Goldman gave his Princeton colleague Thorp a plan of the chapter on "The Historians" at the beginning of 1945. But the written chapter seemed to Jones less carefully assembled. He viewed it as messy, pedestrian, deficient as both history and criticism, and inferior to the corresponding treatment in the *CHAL* (by John S. Bassett).[8]

Section V continued with "The Orators" by Harold Harding (Cornell) and Everett Hunt (Swarthmore), a manuscript that read like an undergraduate exercise according to the demanding and caustic Jones, who had unmistakably become the counterpart of W. P. Trent, the sharp-minded editor and critic of the *CHAL* who had saved many of those pages from scholarly disgrace. The entire board, in fact, agreed with Jones and unanimously voted for a rewrite. Finally, Thorp coauthored the chapter and received from Harding and Hunt approval of his revision. "Literature and Conflict" by George Whicher (Amherst) was a chapter also less than compelling, according to Jones, and the others complained that it was tediously cluttered with names and titles. (Whicher and Carl Van Doren were the only contributors to both the *CHAL* and *LHUS*.) The next chapter, on Longfellow, Holmes, and Lowell, as noted earlier, went several times in search of an author. The *CHAL* editors, too, it will be recalled, had trouble locating a twentieth-century Longfellow man. Odell Shepard finally obliged. His chapter was criticized mainly for its omissions. Thorp wanted a consideration of Holmes's novels, and Jones asked for comment on the elderly Lowell's Arnoldian influence on the 1880s and 1890s.

Henry Nash Smith (Texas) wrote "Minority Report: The Tradition of the Old South" as a late addition to section V. Designed to give fuller treatment of the romance literature of the mid-decades, the chapter was also intended to be a background for the later emergence of the Southern Agrarians. Should one of these living "Fugitives" have written the chapter? The editors agreed that a member of that group would not be objective enough. Like Smith's other chapters, this one was judged superior, and Spiller even planned to use the initial chapter-linking paragraphs virtually as Smith had revised them—clear evidence, again, of Smith's sympathy with Spiller's conception of American literary history. Harold Blodgett's "Heard from the New World" (chap. 37) was, like Smith's, a late assignment after the epilogue-symposium chapters were ruled out. Blodgett's essay was meant to parallel in midcourse the companion chapter, "American Books Abroad," by Cowley, which ends final section X. Jones missed any reference to Balzac's fondness for the new world's Cooper but otherwise regarded Blodgett's pages to be of higher quality than most of the accumulating manuscript.

The chapters drafted for section VI, "Expansion," varied in reception from almost unqualified praise—for Henry Smith's "The Widening of Horizons," Mencken's "The American Language," and "Folklore" by Arthur P. Hudson (North Carolina)—to a verdict that "The Mingling of Tongues" by Henry A. Pochmann (Wisconsin), with the assistance of Joseph Rossi (Wisconsin) and "others," required a thorough rewriting. The chapter was too long and dense even after revision. (The subject—plural cultures and the melting pot—was originally planned as two chapters.) A ghostwriter was brought in, at a fee of one hundred dollars, to reshape the essay. This turns out to have been Margaret F. (Mrs. Willard) Thorp, who thus became one of the anonymous "others" in the table of authors.[9] Also in need of fairly drastic assistance was Harold W. Thompson (Cornell) and his chapter 44, "Humor." Johnson insisted that it be completely rewritten, and Canby finally coauthored the chapter; the table of authors this time specifically acknowledges, parenthetically, the help of "passages by Henry Seidel Canby." In the responses to remaining chapters of section VI, Jones's again were the most vitriolic and perhaps, too, the most incisive. He considered "The West as Seen from the East" by George R. Stewart (California) to be sophomoric. He called for a stronger literary emphasis in both "Abraham Lincoln" by Sandburg and "The Indian Heritage" by Stith Thompson (Indiana). Spiller included in his summary editorial comment to Thompson an extra bit of revealing editorial policy: "We have made a rule of thumb for the entire work that we should avoid the

discussion of critical controversies and the mention of critics."
At least, he added, such polemics were meant to be reduced to a
minimum.

Next came the seventh grouping, chapters 48–56 on "The Sections" after the Civil War. Predictable difficulties of overlap were
now discovered among the various regional figures. His fellow
editors agreed with Spiller, however, that Thorp's "Defenders of
Ideality" (Stedman, Stoddard, Aldrich, and so forth) was a model
chapter for other contributors to imitate. "Delineation of Life and
Character [in East and South]" was Carlos Baker's vexing assignment after Robert Penn Warren had refused it, and Baker chafed
under the demands to compress a plethora of works and authors.
In addition, Baker's chapter intersected George Whicher's prewar
"Literature and Conflict" (chap. 34), Wallace Stegner's "Western
Record and Romance" (chap. 53), and "Realism Defined:
William Dean Howells" (chap. 54) by Gordon Haight (Yale). Consequently, the editors sent Baker the completed drafts of these
chapters to blend with his own. In the process, Baker came
to realize fully the miseries of coordinating a massive literary
history: He was wrestling with the difficulties of even an agreed-
on terminology (for example, realism), the perplexities of literary influence, and the chronological weaving of varied threads
throughout an entire literary period or movement.[10] The final
three chapters of section VII treated, more or less separately, the
career of Howells by Haight, of Lanier and Dickinson by Williams,
and of Mark Twain by Wecter. To Haight, unfortunately, fell the
responsibility of establishing the conceptual aura of realism in a
chapter also discussing the extended career of Howells and De
Forest. Success in such a task was scarcely to be hoped for, and,
in the editorial fallout, Haight received the greatest sympathy
from Jones. Of the two other chapters, Wecter had little difficulty
with Mark Twain. Such was not the case for Williams writing on
Lanier and Dickinson. He began the chapter in July 1943 and
rewrote it for an editorial critique in December of that year. In
April 1944, Williams received editorial commentary asking him
to revise his imagistic style, cut not only "tortuous sentences" but
entire paragraphs, and emphasize both regional and experi-
mental (aesthetic) aspects of the two poets.

Such was a part of the culminating activity for editors and associates of the *LHUS* as they suggested revisions and at times
rewrote paragraphs and even chapters of the best scholars in the
profession. Three sections remained to be put into shape for the
printer in 1946 and 1947. As related earlier, the editors arranged
various conferences to bind into continuity the related back-

ground chapters. Gabriel, Commager, and Nevins, before writing the introductions, respectively, to sections VIII, IX, and X, had met with Spiller in late 1944 to discuss and agree on the content of their chapters. At the same time, Spiller had sent Canby's chapter 72, "Fiction Sums Up a Century," to Maxwell Geismar who was continuing the fictional account in chapter 77, "A Cycle of Fiction." Canby termed his chapter the most difficult writing he had ever attempted, in part because the editors had realized to their chagrin that they had forgotten to include Edith Wharton in their sketch of the contents. Though he held a low opinion of her writing, Canby struggled to accommodate Wharton in his chapter.[11]

R. P. Blackmur (Princeton) on Henry James and Williams on Edwin Arlington Robinson created separate difficulties. Blackmur was dilatory, explaining that he was "lost in the fog of Adams"—the book that would remain unfinished even at his death in 1965. What Blackmur did produce arrived in January 1946 in a style that was the most idiosyncratic of all the contributors—gnarled and confusing, said the editors. Confusing, too, was the structure of his chapter. He altered the organization satisfactorily in his revision but left to Spiller the labor of editing the style—for clarity, pace, and, to some degree, uniformity with the rest of the history. Blackmur pleaded only that Spiller not "alter the tone," and that he send along in the mail as speedily as possible the contributor's check: Blackmur was involved in an expensive drilling for water on his farm in Maine.[12] Williams's essay on Robinson was his fifth for the history. He began in August 1943, then revised and sent it to the editors in late autumn. The chapter was returned in April 1944, with directions to revise further. Wecter had judged Williams's "methods of psychological and esthetic analysis" appropriate to Hawthorne and Emily Dickinson, but not to Robinson. The consensus was that Williams should try to emphasize Robinson's relation to the currents of later nineteenth-century thought and that he shorten the chapter in the process (the continuing expansion–contraction dilemma experienced by other contributors).[13]

Perhaps the foremost headache the editors suffered in these closing chapters came from their decision to enlist celebrated contributors outside the academy to give a contemporary luster and authority to the modern period. That few were able to oblige may have turned out to be a disguised blessing. If Blackmur's style presented problems, how could the editors have merged into stylistic or critical harmony the writing of Edmund Wilson, T. S. Eliot, Van Wyck Brooks, and others? Of those writers in the public arena who joined the venture, H. L. Mencken wrote an essay (chap. 40) on "The American Language" that was surprisingly harmonious with the rest of the history. But Sandburg's chapter on Lincoln, after being agonizingly tardy, was exceedingly slight as literary history. Malcolm Cowley became quite irascible after reading criticism of his essay on the twentieth-century audience. Canby, who was writing a closely related chapter, arranged to lunch with Spiller and Cowley. The result was Spiller's merging the two essays into chapter 67, "Creating an Audience," a Cowley–Canby partnership to the complete satisfaction, at least, of Canby.[14]

Novelist and critic James T. Farrell cordially accepted an invitation to be part of the *LHUS*. The ups and downs of his participation comprise a brief history of their own. In late 1943, Spiller had written Farrell that the editors were planning an epilogue with chapters by Farrell, Archibald MacLeish, T. S. Eliot, and Edmund Wilson. Farrell replied that he would be willing to write a chapter. The epilogue was still in the offing when the editors held an early conference with various contributors in March 1944 at the Harvard Club in New York, a meeting highlighted by Farrell's unexpected appearance at the same time that the vice squad was patrolling the streets to remove *Studs Lonigan* from the bookstores. By early 1945, the editors had not been able to persuade the authors of an epilogue, aside from Farrell, to write a chapter and so had decided to abandon the notion of this symposium. Meanwhile, however, the chapter on Dreiser was in trouble. Among the trio of likely experts—Newton Arvin, F. O. Matthiessen, and Alfred Kazin—the editors had selected Kazin in December 1943, only to learn now in January 1945 that he meant to go to Europe and would not be able to finish the chapter. Spiller then proposed that Farrell be asked.[15]

Farrell agreed once again to join the *LHUS* team. But interpretive disagreements on Dreiser arose at once. According to Spiller's second cycle, American literature in Dreiser's time was working its way out of the valley of postwar realism, moving toward a new cyclical ascent into the 1930s, and Dreiser had played the role of a twentieth-century transitional writer. Farrell could not regard Dreiser as transitional. True, Dreiser was an important historical figure, but he was not clearly influenced by what came before. And whom was he transitional to? F. Scott Fitzgerald? And was the theory of transition supposed to suggest progress? By May 1946, Spiller had read Farrell's draft of the chapter and suggested that he rewrite it. Short of that, would Farrell agree to Spiller's coauthoring the chapter? Farrell suggested that Spiller try to per-

suade Matthiessen, instead, to write the chapter. Spiller obliged.
But Matthiessen declined, out of respect, he said, to Farrell's fitness for the job. (Matthiessen was currently sketching his own
book on Dreiser.) Farrell then wrote to Matthiessen and offered
to send the present draft of the Dreiser chapter as a spur to
Matthiessen's reconsideration of the invitation. And on the same
day, Farrell wrote to Spiller that if Matthiessen remained adamant, Spiller could rewrite the chapter and say that he had
drawn on Farrell's essay (which Farrell had now given to the
Chicago Review). Spiller replied that Matthiessen had said he
would not be at leisure to write the chapter within the year. The
history was racing by now toward a deadline with Macmillan. So
Farrell agreed that Spiller could acknowledge that he had based
the chapter on Farrell's article and give Farrell two-thirds of the
contributor's pay—by then three cents a word for the four thousand words. Less the ten-dollar advance, Farrell was then paid
seventy dollars. When we compare the Farrell article to Spiller's
version, the terms seem fair enough. Not only did Spiller cast the
introductory portion into a literary–historical context, but he
trimmed the Dreiserian prolixity from Farrell's style.[16]

★   ★   ★

No less than in their reading and criticism of original drafts, the
editors felt their share of pressures and woes when authors' revised chapters began to pour in—or, in some cases, failed to appear as the deadline with Macmillan approached. 1 January 1946
had been the deadline for first drafts, and Spiller encountered
various frustrations when even these manuscripts failed to arrive on time. In mid-January, more than twenty chapters were
not yet in hand. The board agreed in March that Spiller should be
empowered to make a 1 May 1946 deadline on all first drafts (the
date that had previously been set for revised chapters) and that
tardy contributors should be faced with the possibility of their
late chapters not being used, their contracts being broken, and
other contributors commissioned. By August, Spiller was plagued
with aggravations from every variety of contributor. Some had
promised their revised chapters but were beyond the deadline,
others were awaiting criticism of a tardy first draft, and still
others had not yet written a first draft. In a letter to Thorp, Spiller
listed twenty-six chapters that were yet to receive a final editorial
reading. Still, when he met with Macmillan in late October 1946,
Spiller agreed to a projected publication date of late 1947.[17]

Early in 1947, Thorp was sending edited chapters along to
Spiller while others were still being revised and proofread by

the authors. Some contributors expressed their gratitude. Merle Curti appreciated revisions of style (which the editors, in fact, had been hesitant to make). Walter Taylor liked Spiller's connecting sentence at the close of his chapter 60 on turn-of-the-century fiction, and Harry Levin suggested only a few verbal changes "in your otherwise admirable introductory paragraph" in his "The Discovery of Bohemia" (chap. 64). Malcolm Cowley, however, was prickly about suggested revisions of his chapter 67.[18]

The tardiest chapters came from Morton Zabel (Loyola of Chicago), who was writing "Summary in Criticism" (chap. 80); from Harold Blodgett, whose "Heard from the New World" (chap. 37), it will be recalled, was a late solicitation; and "Speculative Thinkers" (chap. 76) by Brand Blanshard (from Swarthmore to Yale in 1945). Of these, Spiller termed Zabel's "the toughest case—with the possible exception of Farrell." Three years before, when Cowley learned that he might be sharing section X with Zabel, he warned that Zabel would likely deify the Southern critics and slam Van Wyck Brooks. The problem was averted by having Spiller treat Brooks in the earlier chapter 68, "The Battle of the Books." Then a different worry came in the form of Zabel's exasperating delays in delivering his manuscript. (From 1944 to 1946, he was visiting professor at the University of Brazil.) Finally, Spiller pried a first draft from him in February 1947.[19]

Early in March 1947, Spiller wrote to George Brett at Macmillan that only one chapter was out on editorial rounds, he had now prepared nine of the ten sections, and hoped to deliver the manuscript, with all corrections by the authors, on or before 1 April. The late chapter turns out to have been Blanshard's. The following day, Spiller returned it to Blanshard with editorial corrections and asked for the return copy by 15 March. On the previous day after he had talked with Brett, Spiller also wrote a memorandum suggesting that it might be profitable for the associates, along with the editors, to read the final draft as he had fashioned it. The Macmillan editor would be grooming the manuscript between 1 April and 15 May. Spiller asked his editorial team, therefore, to indicate which week each of them could reserve for this final reading. (Revised chapters had not generally been sent to the associates.) Jones immediately replied that he could see no sense, at that late date, in having all of the editors read (or essentially *re*read) the entire manuscript. Spiller concurred, and the revised manuscript circulated among only the main editors. The subsequent authorized manuscript for the book became the official copy after this edited version of the authors' revised chapters was then typed and reedited by both the publisher and the *LHUS* editors. Although this copy was then given a final retyping before printing, galley proofs were read against the previously typed (authorized manuscript) copy, with its inked reeditings, in order to spot any errors in the galleys that might have crept in during the final retyping.[20]

Thomas Johnson's bibliographical labors had taken their own course, though much of his work depended on the cooperation of the other contributors. In spring 1943, style sheets were designed as a guide to bibliographical form and footnote documentation. Almost at once, Johnson and Spiller were debating alternative methods of compiling bibliography, including a possible request that all contributors keep a set of three-by-five cards for a bibliography of their chapters. For the final form, Johnson preferred a separate bibliographical essay to accompany the historical text rather than the pattern of chapter bibliographies adopted in the *CHAL*. (As in that earlier history, though, *LHUS* eliminated in-text footnotes.) After chapter assignments had been confirmed, Johnson sent a form letter to each contributor, asking for a list of studies pertinent to the chapter, with annotations on their merit and the location of recommended editions. Supplied with this information, Johnson then, Spiller felt, should design individual-author bibliographies as well as the general bibliographical essay on culture, movements, and influences. Johnson's chief bibliographical concern, which arose during the writing of his own chapter on Edwards, was the problem of selectivity. Most of that worry was alleviated in mid-1945 when Macmillan decided that the bibliography, as Johnson had hoped, should stand as a separate volume. Johnson was elated. Through most of 1946, he continued to write the general bibliographical essay and compile the single-author bibliographies, aided by the references supplied by chapter contributors. In late November, Spiller wrote Macmillan that Johnson had his manuscript ready and wanted a conference with the publishers to determine format and design.[21]

The hard work was virtually completed and the book in press by June 1947. The final making of the *LHUS* was mainly routine, even to the publisher's warning to enter all late revisions in the manuscript before galleys were set. Copy editing the manuscript was completed in the summer of 1947. Galley sheets by the hundreds were mailed to and fro among publisher and editors through the final months of the year, and soon the editors were reading early page proofs simultaneously with late galleys. In June 1948, index copy went to Macmillan, who returned proofs in August, along with a proposed dust jacket. The book cover suggested by

Macmillan was to be red. That color was stoutly opposed by Spiller, and the cover was changed to navy blue.[22]

On 8 November 1948, Thorp was examining his printed copy of the *LHUS,* just arrived from Macmillan. With his exacting eye, he noticed wobbly left-hand margins in volume I, page 42 and following, plus inconsistent spacing at the top and bottom of several pages. Even so, he wrote to Spiller in a spirit of fulfillment that no doubt was shared, in varying degrees at this late date, by all of the other editors—though some may not have concurred in his final wish:

> Such fun we have had! And what a wonderful editor, guide, task-master, Spiller is. . . . You seemed to feel that the answers were there and that they would come out, if we would only keep talking and thinking. Working with you & Tom & Henry has been one of the happiest experiences of my life. I wish we were beginning all over again.

Chapter 28

Reception of the *LHUS:*
Summary Estimate of the Profession

The critical reception of the *LHUS* marks an important chapter in American literary scholarship. For various members of the academy who reviewed it, this cooperative work of the 1940s was an index of the distance they had journeyed as a distinctive profession. This historical awareness led some to reflect on the early years of American literary consciousness but particularly to track the course from the *CHAL* through the Parrington late 1920s to the return of Van Wyck Brooks in the thirties and on to the *LHUS*. Many had also read the pronouncements made by fellow reviewers, whether out of wariness of their own assignment or due to a sense of critical history in the making. The reviews, therefore, can be profitably arranged in their own historical sequence. It is also interesting to see, here and there, how Spiller, in particular, reacted to the reception of this gigantic effort, which, as it turned out, was perhaps the last truly comprehensive literary history the profession will ever undertake.

The critique by the profession began with Norman Holmes Pearson's review in the *Saturday Review of Literature,* then edited by Norman Cousins, with Canby the chairman of the editorial board. Before writing it, Yale's Pearson (who had been courted as a contributor) had asked Spiller for information on the editorial intentions of the *LHUS*. Pearson opened the review by establishing the historical significance of the history and congratulating the editors for now challenging English departments in the American academy who, for years, had slighted American literature. The new history was a welcome replacement of the *CHAL,* a cooperative effort that had lacked "autocratic editorial bravery." Pearson also ranked the *LHUS* above Parrington's *Main Currents*, despite his "brilliant idiosyncracy." Pearson went on to praise the fine chapters on individual authors but considered the essays on multiple authors and cultural milieus even more important. The literary-period conception of pre–Civil War diversity and postwar homogeneity, in particular, would very likely influence theory in literary histories to come. Pearson also approved

the new regional emphases that countered the recent overstatement of Western influence on American literature, as well as the
long-time exaggeration of New England's influence on the colonial and national literatures. For once, full play had been given to
writers of the South and the middle states, the latter due, perhaps, to the editors' allegiance to their own area. Beyond the regional and international influences on our literature, Pearson
predicted that the *LHUS* would induce future historians to
downplay British influence and discover that literatures in other
than the English tongue have contributed strongly to American
"'united'" states literature.[1]

Perry Miller (Harvard) was more critical. Pointedly lauding the
bibliographical sections of volume III as the "most exciting portion of the enterprise," and which could, fortunately, be purchased
separately, he prepared the reader for a distinctly qualified review
of the text. Many individual chapters were "admirably written"—
Adrienne Koch's "adjectival circumlocution" on the Revolution's
philosophical statesmen was an obvious exception. But the overall effect, said Miller, "is curiously muffled . . . [with] a lack of
emphasis that nearly engulfs the whole undertaking in monotony." As ALG members had done earlier, Miller questioned if the
venture was not premature, representing as it did "the consolidation of a discipline that rapidly—one might even say too rapidly—
arrived at maturity." Indeed, he went on to ask if the concept
"'history of literature' is any longer viable or even feasible . . .
whether there really can exist a history of literature instead of the
history of something (or many somethings) with which literature
is concerned, especially in the present intellectual situation."
The *LHUS* might be seen, in a sense, to mark the end of an era,
but it offered little in the way of orientation to the future. Perhaps
it could serve as a stimulus to future definitions, discoveries, and
rediscoveries.[2]

Historian Arthur Schlesinger, Jr. (Harvard), capsulized his dissatisfaction with the *LHUS* and all cooperative histories. Perhaps
thinking of Parrington, he wrote: "The fact is that it is only the
individual vision which can be communicated with intensity to
other individuals; and all the resources of bureaucracy are no
substitute." The sins of collectivity and forgettable writing in the
CHAL were repeated here, even though the *LHUS*, with its
"streamlined apparatus of principles, outlines, and conferences,"
had "replaced the laissez faire collaboration of the Cambridge
History." The strong editorial hand, to Schlesinger, had brought
an "emphasis on moderation" and tended "depressingly to dull
uniformity . . . prevailing monotony." It also failed to relate the-

ology, philosophy, and social history to literary creation. But these weaknesses were partly offset by the strong chapters from Mencken, Commager, Wecter (Mark Twain), Spiller (Henry Adams), and some few others, including the controversial Blackmur on Henry James—a good essay, said Schlesinger, though atrociously written. He foresaw the bibliographical volume III, not the textual chapters, as becoming the more enduring achievement of the *LHUS*.[3]

The spring of 1949 brought the *LHUS* more discouraging reviews from within the academy. Oscar Cargill (NYU) in *College English* announced at the outset that this publishing event was less significant than the appearance of the *CHAL*, because American literature study thirty years later was firmly established. He singled out a number of the general essays as superior but praised almost none of the chapters on individual authors. Treatments of Emerson (Spiller), Whitman (Canby), and Twain (Wecter) were "flatly disappointing"; the chapter on James (Blackmur) was obscurantist; Lanier and Dickinson (Williams) were an "unhappy bedding"; the Poe suffered from Matthiessen's lack of critical sympathy; and so on. Cargill was provisional even in his praise: Editorial control had allowed a general stylistic integrity, but the overarching conception prevented freedom and brilliance to come through in the criticism. The chapters on Melville (Thorp) and Adams (Spiller) were among the best, and perhaps so because these author-editors were "less conscious of the restraints since they were self-imposed." The bibliographies were "incontestably valuable . . . (despite their poor indexing)."[4]

Jay B. Hubbell's critique in the *Yale Review* carried the weight of one of the profession's foremost pioneers who had championed a new cooperative history since the middle twenties, though he had not been asked to contribute to the *LHUS*. (Why Hubbell and other elderly scholars were passed over, but acknowledged in the preface, was explained in Chapter 25.) The historical perspective of an insider makes Hubbell's remarks valuable. He viewed the *LHUS* as a welcome advance over the *CHAL*, largely due to its "careful planning," though a monotonous style also resulted from this editorial control. He praised favorite chapters—Jones's opener, Krutch on O'Neill, and William Charvat (Ohio State) on "The People's Patronage"—along with the "well-planned" volume III, whose bibliographies were clearly indebted to scholarly journals since 1915. So spoke the founding editor of *American Literature*. In the text, however, Hubbell saw evidence that scholarship in American literature had not sufficiently come of age. The history was weak on "writers and general topics on which little research has been done" (including Hubbell's own speciality, the literature of the South). Where the scholarship had been impressive, the editors had solicited distinguished members of the profession to communicate it, to be sure, but many lacked authority in their particular areas of assignment. Where were the outstanding experts on Emerson, Hawthorne, Melville, Poe, and Whitman? And where were the younger scholars, lately trained in psychological criticism, the New Criticism, and the correlation of literature with the other arts? These questions led Hubbell to recall the crucial meeting of the ALG in Cambridge in 1940 when the profession withheld endorsement of the new literary history. Whether the decision was correct or not, one effect was now clear: "If the group had officially undertaken the task, assuredly most of the distinguished scholars who have no part in the present work could have been induced to contribute."[5]

In *Harper's,* Jacques Barzun (Columbia) began his review favorably enough with an estimate of future influence: "It is more than likely that the middle-aged citizen of 1980 will spontaneously echo the opinions of the present Big Four." Nor should this effect on literary taste be too baneful, for the scholarship was "thorough, many-sided, and truly written for the general reader." But Barzun then reflected on the main failure of the *LHUS*. One sensed no passion for literature itself in these pages. Barzun's model here was George Saintsbury, a critic often prejudiced but always passionate, and never perfunctory. Barzun complained, too, that the enormous compression of such a history enabled none of our great figures—Blackmur's James excepted—to emerge with any clarity and gradation among the shapers of our literature. Responding to this review, as well as Hubbell's, Spiller wrote to the sympathetic Pearson, "We are in a period right now when the disaffected are having their day and the *LHUS* is suffering from an amazing amount of vitriol which is being poured on its head."[6]

In addition to Barzun's and Hubbell's comments, Spiller was aware of a recent adverse review by Henry A. Myers (Cornell) in the *Quarterly Journal of Speech.* Pearson was preparing to respond to the review, he told Spiller on 16 April 1949, and he enclosed his proposed remarks. Myers had criticized the *LHUS* on two bases: uncertainty of definition and lack of coherence. The definitions of literature, American literature, and literary history in the "Address to the Reader" were "so flabby as to be well-nigh worthless" and led to an uncertainty in scope and emphasis. With an eye to his specialized journal readers, Myers singled out and welcomed American oratory (which had been treated by

Harding, Hunt, and Thorp) as "an aspect immensely more deserving of explicit and separate treatment" than obscure subjects
like "The Indian Heritage" (by Stith Thompson of Indiana).
Shortcomings in coherence involved poor writing but more important was the "lack of a consistent point of view and a standard
of values" in this bureaucratic collaboration. As Schlesinger had,
Myers quoted in his review the disparaging remarks in Cowley's
chapter treating modern corporate journalism and script writing, and Myers turned them on the editors of the *LHUS*. With
other reviewers, he also pointed more favorably to Parrington who,
like Tyler, achieved coherence of style and judgment through one-
man authorship.[7]

In his rebuttal to Myers in the same journal, Pearson defended
the scope of the *LHUS* as consistent with its rationale and praised
the contributors as an eminent group who "characteristically represent the contemporary academic opinion of American literature." They had described the terrain on which we could now go
forward "singly, in groups, and as a group." Myers replied by
charging that Pearson had not refuted the main arguments relating to definition and coherence. Furthermore, Myers refused to
believe that this history presented the official or orthodox view
within the American literature establishment. Instead, we received in the Emerson of Spiller, the Melville of Thorp, and so on,
perhaps the representative viewpoint of "a respectable segment"
of American literature scholars. Myers noted, finally, that Pearson
stood out as the single reviewer of the *LHUS* who seemed, for
whatever reasons, disposed to be altogether favorable. The rebuke indicated that Myers, too, had been keeping an eye on how
fellow critics were assessing the *LHUS*.[8]

If Spiller had felt reviews in the spring to be unseasonably
early and "annoying flies of summer," the mature variety appeared
in a summer review for the American Studies Association's recently christened *American Quarterly*.[9] The trio of critics were
Daniel Aaron of Smith College (vol. I), Leslie Fiedler of Montana
State (vol. II), and R. A. Miller of Indiana (vol. III). The reviewers
were familiar with the critical consensus up to then: The *LHUS*
had impressively assembled information not available to the
CHAL; it was somewhat disappointing as literary criticism; and
the bibliography volume was the most praiseworthy. Aaron argued that the prized coherence of the *LHUS* was external and
rationalized rather than intrinsic. Chapters on major and minor
writers showed very little critical audacity. Each followed a
lugubrious pattern of introduction, pertinent biography, chronological description of works (with minimal judgments and no re-

interpretation), and a final estimate. The historical–cultural chapters were, fortunately, less regimented, and the reader could even acquire some new knowledge in Charvat's "Literature as Business," Blodgett's "Heard from the New World," and Henry Smith's "The Tradition of the Old South." Perhaps, Aaron concluded, the first volume would provide, at least, the "impetus for a richer and more searching examination of the American literary past."

More severe was Fiedler's critique of "the most ambitious and least rewarding" volume II. Only Blackmur succeeded in escaping "the prevailing *American Literature–PMLA* style." Critical judgment on contemporary literature was either absent, foolish (as in Maxwell Geismar's praise of Steinbeck and Wolfe), or a confusion of literary taste with social or moral approval. Examples included Thorp's high regard for Sandburg but Geismar's reservations on Farrell and Wright. Also, in failing to grapple with the rift between "mass civilization and minority culture," or in glossing over the split between the artist and his or her middlebrow, liberal, optimistic reading audience, the *LHUS* had fashioned a spuriously happy ending to volume II.

Miller, too, was far less cordial than earlier reviewers when he assessed the much-admired bibliography. He reserved strongest plaudits for the 207 individual-author listings, with special approval of the information therein that pointed the scholar to definitive and best editions. In the main, however, this third volume was very complicated to use, since it was seemingly organized to complement, in some unknown manner, the first two volumes. Partially a history itself, volume III was also, at times, an overlapping of the main historical text. The "Guide to Resources" was neither sufficiently detailed nor current, rendering it inferior to sources elsewhere that provided information on manuscript collections. Where the essay treated themes and movements, it had ignored American social history altogether. (Schlesinger had called attention to this deficiency in the history proper.)[10]

Rene Wellek's critical review, also in the summer of 1949, was equally significant on other grounds. Not persuaded by the American literary–cultural assumptions and definitions generally accepted within the profession, the multilingual coauthor of the recent *Theory of Literature* (1948, with Austin Warren) was particularly unhappy over weaknesses in literary methodology. "The most serious deficiency of these volumes," said Wellek, "is the failure to provide a continuous and coherent history of poetic styles, prose-genres, devices, and techniques—in short, a history of literature as art." His demands for such a history were patently rhetorical and visionary. The *LHUS* team did have at their disposal scores of earlier histories deficient in literature as art. But such works, in their aesthetic lapses, could not then yield a corrective method for the close treatment of metrics, prose styles, genres, and techniques—in English, American English, and indeed all other pertinent languages—together with indirect revelations of how to demonstrate evolution in a "continuous and coherent history." Nor are there even today exemplary studies in these difficult areas sufficient to guide the shapers of a new American literary history. Perhaps in the next century, literary scholars will have become expert in the learning and method necessary to meet Wellek's stated and implicit requirements for a linguistic and aesthetic history of American literature.[11]

The more official estimate of the *LHUS*, in *American Literature*, did not appear until January 1950, after much of the air had cleared. Hubbell had solicited a review from Ralph Rusk (Columbia) more than two years before. (Like Hubbell, Rusk was one of the uninvited whose work had, however, been honored in the acknowledgment prefatory to volume I.) Hubbell wanted a critic, he had said, with no axe to grind but who would not condone "serious errors." Rusk had been tempted, but declined because of the press of his current work on Emerson. A year later, at publication of *LHUS*, Hubbell sought out Rusk again and coaxed him with the lament that most of the able reviewers had either contributed to the *LHUS* or were campus colleagues of the contributors. Rusk agreed, then asked for a delay, and finally delivered the review in September 1949.

Four months later, *LHUS* was noticed in the pages of the profession's own journal with a hospitality that was, at best, lukewarm. The essay on Rusk's man Emerson by Spiller was judged uneven, marred by either errors or misleading clichés, such as Emerson's alleged optimism. Rusk also charged that Thorp had exaggerated Melville's achievement and Matthiessen T. S. Eliot's. On Poe, Matthiessen was better. Blackmur's essay on James was an instance of pure criticism in danger of dissolving into the same mist as James's own rarefied thought and convoluted style. The bibliography volume was the "most valuable part of the work" but was marred by errors obvious enough to the specialist. Rusk concluded that the writing of American literary history in the future would probably be devoted to separate period histories—a surprisingly accurate prophecy—and that they would be "designed to serve mainly as handy guides to criticism and biography." Eventually, sectional boundaries might evaporate in favor of an international perspective on our literature.[12]

One last belated review was written by Hubbell's colleague at Duke, Clarence Gohdes, himself at work on *The Literature of the American People* (1951) with Arthur Quinn, Kenneth Murdock, and George Whicher. Gohdes mainly reaffirmed the essence of earlier praise and blame, noting that amid the uneven quality ("a few of the contributors, as well as one editor, took their obligations lightly") appeared some valuable chapters in literary history. Those on Mark Twain (Wecter) and Henry Adams (Spiller) were among the best essays to date. The chapters on American literature abroad by Blodgett and Cowley were "as good short accounts of the subject as are available." (This is the area, we recall, to which Spiller had invited Gohdes to contribute.) And Gohdes joined in the chorus of acclaim for the bibliography, "at once an introduction to the historiography of American literature, a guide to investigation in all things American, a companion to the essays in the first two volumes, and an independent 'factual' history." He singled out for special rebuke Bowers's "inadequate" introduction to transcendentalism and Blackmur's "unfortunate essay on Henry James [which] will at one and the same time confound the 'general reader' and make any sensible Jamesian laugh." As to the intelligent general reader whom the editors hoped to capture, Gohdes predicted that "few will transfer allegiance from the more palatable impressionism of Van Wyck Brooks." The *LHUS* would stand, nevertheless, as an influential "monument to the critical taste of its generation." Gohdes then returned, in memory, to the momentous ALG meeting a decade before: "The group of specialists in American literature affiliated with the Modern Language Association lost an unusual opportunity to improve the status of their intellectual province when they refused to endorse this work as originally projected."[13]

✱   ✱   ✱

Our long story climaxes, then, with the reception of the *LHUS*. In a number of respects, this cooperative history may be viewed as the foremost event in American literature studies. It embodied twenty-five years and more of professional self-consciousness— and over 150 years of an American literary self-awareness. Even though the American Literature Group of the MLA in 1941 appeared to have reached a consensus that scholarship was not even yet fully seasoned for a large-scale assessment of our literary history, the editorial board of the *LHUS,* without official sanction, soon recruited a team that essentially represented the profession. As the venture progressed under Spiller's masterly direction, so, too, did interest in American literature studies both within the academy and among publishers, book clubs, and foundations.

Perhaps the final magnitude of this enterprise even had a slightly menacing effect on would-be literary historians. The output of such an impressive army of scholars and critics, together with expenditures by Rockefeller, Macmillan, ACLS, APS, and various universities of the contributors, brought about the sense of an ending. A huge scholarly undertaking such as this could not soon be duplicated or surpassed. The prefatory encouragement that every generation must write its own literary history may even appear disingenuous if not faintly cynical. The next generation, in fact, witnessed the mildly corrected and updated edition of 1953 (after sales of ten thousand copies), the bibliographical supplement by Richard M. Ludwig in 1959, and the further bibliographical additions of the third (1963) and fourth (1974) editions, with their postscript chapters. That writing a full-scale literary history, with very few exceptions, soon became a lost art in these years cannot, of course, be directly blamed on the continuing presence of the *LHUS*. The profession was moving in various directions after 1948, indeed after 1945, as we shall notice in the Epilogue.

The historical text of the original *LHUS* remains today essentially unrevised. An assessment now can, therefore, regard the value and significance of the history from an interesting dual perspective, first in 1948 and then at the present time. The growing maturity of the profession in 1948 was writ large not only in the pages of the *LHUS*, but in the accumulated story of their inception, gestation, and reception. The American literature scholars in the 1920s and 1930s had generally been united within the ALG, though not without the expected family bickerings in a youthful profession. By the annual meetings of 1940 and 1941, the family had grown closer to maturity. Members were capable of candid self-criticism. Perhaps here and there, we also detect a less salutary taint of mistrust and jealous rivalry. After a war came and went, the new generation of graduate students, no less than their prewar professors who felt a vested interest in the *LHUS*, greeted the new history with the sense of now belonging to a profession with a confirmed identity and the critical success of a cooperative scholarly labor achieved in three formidable volumes. Yet such was the nature of the profession that at the very moment when it seemed to be bound more closely together, older members began at once to question the achievement of the *LHUS*, while younger members were dispersing into scholarly pastures new. Not only were questions being raised if the *LHUS* were the best horizontal summation of what was known in the discipline; but the time had also come for a more vertical approach to our literature and within the interdisciplinary American Studies movement, a pursuit both vertical and diagonal.

From the perspective of our later time, as American literature studies have vastly accelerated into other reaches of interpretive theory, textual sophistication, historical scholarship, and practical criticism, what permanent value can we assign the *LHUS*? The chapters on individual authors are still cited in present-day scholarship and criticism. Into the 1970s, Spiller was pleased with this durability and amused to discover that he had become "a mythical author-editor, 'Spiller et al.'"

> [A]nd now, when I meet new people—often those who owe their Ph.D.'s to good cramming sessions with this book—the faces momentarily expose their surprise that I am a real human being and not merely a name on the library shelf. But there seems to be no doubt in their minds that the book itself is very much alive as the major work in its field throughout the world.[14]

Few will want to quarrel with Spiller's evaluation in the final sentence. These authoritative volumes have met no competitor since midcentury as they have made their way into private and public libraries throughout this country and the major libraries in Europe and Asia. Through foreign sales and translations, together with free distribution by the United States Information Agency, the history fashioned by Spiller et al. is still distinguished as "the major work in its field throughout the world." As to the cramming sessions it continues to precipitate among graduate students, what recommendations and caveats might we hear a professor in the 1980s offer to his or her aspiring M.A. and Ph.D. students who are about to spend their days and nights with the *LHUS*?

The historical backgrounds can be recommended as among the most rewarding chapters in the *LHUS*, not least because our literature students today know so little history. These essays, because compact, carry generalizations that are not, of course, amply supported when we feel quarrelsome over a point of historical controversy. (Some are also in need of updating.) Of permanent value are the convenient primary bibliographies of the 207 authors, collected in the second half of volume III in 1948. The bibliography of secondary scholarship and criticism is less useful; nor are the supplementary portions in later editions competitive with the numerous and more complete rival essays and listings of secondary bibliography over the past three decades (beginning with the ALG's own *Eight American Authors* in 1956).

There are very few chapters that do not repay a careful reading. Thomas Johnson, in his chapter on Edwards, accounted well enough for the philosophy but was weak on Edwards's literary craft. Franklin's "genius for terse clarity and his delicate ear for cadence" were neatly explicated by Carl Van Doren in one of the best introductory essays still to be found on the literary Franklin. Qualifying his admiration for Irving with misgivings over that writer's indolent romanticism, Stanley Williams had trouble making up his mind how great the claims for Irving's permanence should be. But this chapter, too, is well worth reading today, far more than Williams's superficial and dated essay on Cooper. Tremaine McDowell's pages on Bryant in chapter 21 ("In New England") remain sound, but Matthiessen's on Poe seem markedly old-fashioned. He termed Poe's heroes "isolated, dreamy, and introspective" (I, 330). And he discussed *Eureka* apart from any aesthetic and cosmic connections to those earlier heroes, though it is hardly fair to rebuke him for not anticipating Richard Wilbur's work in the late 1950s. More to the point, Matthiessen was here given a second chance to interpret Poe as a fellow artist and thinker in the company of the five figures of *American Renaissance* (1941) but was not able to pull together the related strands between Poe and that celebrated quintet of light and dark romantics.

In section IV, "Literary Fulfillment," Spiller's first cycle of American literary achievement peaked in a constellation of six chapters. David Bowers ("Democratic Vistas") framed the period with an obvious borrowing from Matthiessen's thesis, namely, "the reorientation of literature under the influence of New England transcendentalism" (I, 346), and compressed the chief origins and tenets of that philosophy. Bowers overstated, however, the liberation of the major writers from their non-American sources. Spiller then interpreted the phases in Emerson's career in an essay that has not been surpassed as an incisive introductory and summary treatment of the much-abused sage of Concord. By contrast, Townsend Scudder's chapter on Thoreau was merely a summary ramble of truisms. On Hawthorne, Williams at least attempted to read the separate works conscientiously. His Hawthorne lived aloof in Concord, boldly speculating on the moral distempers of the Puritan mind and defining their essence through the frame of symbolism and the texture of style. The chapter should be read in the company of Matthiessen's version of Hawthorne, as well as Erskine's in the *CHAL*. Thorp on Melville remains a dependable overview, but many of his observations on the fiction, especially after *Pierre*, easily date this chapter as pre-1950. Canby's essay on Whitman was reliable enough, though he missed the structural importance of symphonic form that Whitman claimed for *Leaves of Grass*. As a result, Canby described Whitman's effort to construct a "cathedral" in the continuing editions as succeeding "only in imitating an American World's Fair" (I, 486). Similarly breezy and inaccurate was the assertion that "not one particle of evidence that he was homosexual" had ever been discovered (I, 484)—though by today, this has become a tired, indeed almost a dead, issue in Whitman studies.

In volume II, Sandburg's 8½ pages on Lincoln came off the top of the poet's shaggy head. On American discovery of Europe after 1850 to the end of the century ("Pilgrim's Return"), Thorp considered Charles Eliot Norton's interest in European art to be narrow, his religious prejudice unabated ("a lifelong hatred of Catholic institutions," II, 830), and his account of the cathedral at Orvieto less important than DeForest's notes on the punishing "cures" offered at Divonne. All of these are dubious judgments. Thorp was better on the question posed for Emerson, Hawthorne, Howells, Jarves, James, and Mark Twain: What is the American writer after midcentury to do about Europe? Carlos Baker's chapter on Eastern and Southern regionalism stands as testimony to the frustration of the literary historian who hopes to analyze both the history and literary excellence of many interrelated works and writers. The reader is left with a series of unsupported judgments. Jewett's stories were "works of art, and of a high order." Though a finer artist than all but Jewett, Freeman used local idioms and customs "for high-lighting and never for substance." The reader senses Murfree's literary power to be derived from "an authoritative knowledge," and Harris, too, exudes authority from a "close knowledge . . ." (II, 847, 851, 852). Kate Chopin was rated an impulsive and untidy artist, and Baker did not mention *The Awakening* (its recovery would come two decades later). He also grappled with terminology, so that Freeman encompassed "a larger measure of modern realism" than Jewett because Freeman stressed "the caging of environment, the captivity of circumstance" (II, 848). That blurring of realism with naturalism could not have eased the problem of definition for Gordon Haight in "Realism Defined: William Dean Howells," a facile and misleading sketch of Howells's career that mined the old clichés about the alleged prudishness and capitulation to an American plutocracy until the reading of Tolstoy, of course, worked a profound social change of heart.

Following Haight is Williams's chapter on Lanier and Dickinson, "Experiments in Poetry," in which Lanier fares better than Dickinson. (In the fourth edition, the new coeditor, William M. Gibson, rewrote completely the section on Dickinson.) Dixon Wecter's chapter 56 was a favorite with several contemporary reviewers, but the progress in Mark Twain scholarship since 1948 has rendered this chronological sketch of very little biographical or critical interest for readers today, though they might well heed Wecter on the chivalrous Twain's Victorian fear of sex. Blackmur's chapter on James was stylistically tidied by Spiller, but it is still difficult to fathom the discussion on the international theme, the social conflict attending aesthetic vocation, and the pilgrim in search of moral truth within European social conventions. Sometimes the reader's effort is rewarded, as when Blackmur disentangles James's response to human and destructive social forms as well as to "the passionate heroism of true vocation." These subjects gain ultimate expression in the characters' difficult, shifting encounters with good and evil in the Jamesean "dramatized fairy tale" (II, 1049, 1053).

In the chapter on turn-of-the-century fiction, Spiller crisply establishes the terms of Zola's naturalism and then discusses Garland and London satisfactorily. Spiller's pages on Crane and Norris suffer from attempts to identify the authors with their various characters, for no apparent purpose except that an aesthetic advantage appears to be gained in Crane's work where such identifications are presumably absent, as in the Western, Mexican, and Cuban tales. There "Crane achieves that instantaneous balance between reality and imagination which makes for great art" (II, 1024). Equally unsubstantiated are the assertions that with the reappearance of *Maggie* in 1896, "modern American fiction was born," or that the close of *The Red Badge of Courage* "strikes at deeper levels of reality than does Maggie's suicide" (II, 1022, 1023). By contrast, Spiller's essay on Henry Adams remains, with his earlier chapter on Emerson, virtually immune to criticism, a small masterpiece of its kind in lucid and concise explication.

Finally, there is Williams's interpretation of Robinson—a misguided portrait of the poet as a solitary aesthete and questioner in the great New England tradition. That Robinson illuminated the social history of the time, not unlike Dreiser or Sherwood Anderson, is not obvious to a reader of this chapter. Matthiessen was more acute and reliable in his pages on Pound and Eliot, though not on Hart Crane. And Zabel's "Summary in Criticism" since 1925 was, quite literally, produced in summary haste as he touched perfunctorily the several positions that emerged after the critical rebellion of 1915 to 1925, including humanism, Marxism, a mildly returning aestheticism in Pound and Eliot, and so on. The critical movement in the mid-1940s, according to Zabel, was "toward assimilation and synthesis, an attempted compromise of methods, an effort to strike a reasonable balance . . ." (II, 1373). And he (or Spiller) concluded:

> Now, perhaps, the moment had arrived for a more difficult task than is possible to sectarians, extremists, or insurgents; namely, the undertaking of a whole view of literature which admits the possible benefits of diverse intellectual and critical disciplines but insists on keeping the central integrity of literature intact, and holds in view the unity of art with the total sum of human experience and its moral values. (II, 1373)

Perhaps one meaning arising, or descending, from this cloud of rhetoric was that the *LHUS*, with its brigade of scholars and critics, had in fact spearheaded the drive toward assimilation, compromise, and synthesis while affirming the integrity of literary art and the organic unity of art and life.

Such synthesis and common purpose would appear unlikely from the corps of contributors, assuredly a less-than-homogeneous band, ranging from older-generation impressionists with peremptory judgments and little talent for explication, to interdisciplinary cultural historians, to moderate Leftist and Freudian apostates of the 1930s, to several devotees of a struggling new formalism. That the *LHUS* was able to emerge at the end with a semblance of unified tone, style, and vision could be largely credited to the firm editorial hand of Robert Spiller. In 1974, the year of the fourth edition, he looked back on the mixed reviews of the maiden volumes and regarded as "perhaps the most perceptive" Pearson's awareness of the "historical perspective and balance."[15] Spiller's satisfaction was justified. The *LHUS* had mainly triumphed where the *CHAL* had failed. This success was owing, first, to Spiller's editorial stitchery, the fitting together of chapter beginnings and endings in thematic continuity, a process that also brought, as well, a fairly sustained effect of stylistic uniformity. (Leslie Fiedler's complaint that this style was rather drearily redolent of *PMLA* and *American Literature* pedantry is not warranted. The history was, and remains, remarkably lucid and read-able for a cooperative work so extensive and scholarly.)

A more profound continuity was afforded by Spiller's two con-trolling concepts of American literary creation and history. First was the theory that our significant national literature had un-folded through the organic expression of American life closely experienced by our major writers in their time. Secondly, the longer historical pattern of this expression of our life in literature could also be described organically, this time in the metaphor of cyclical birth, growth, flowering, and decline. Indeed, American literary history had undergone a pair of cycles, one cresting in the renaissance of the romantic 1850s, and the other approach-ing completion during the 1920s. This cyclical theory helped Spiller ensure a fair degree of coherence and forward movement to the nearly seven dozen chapters of the *LHUS*. To develop the organic view of literature and life, the editors carefully assigned historical chapters on American culture, including the instru-ments of culture, and arranged them strategically among the chapters on belles lettres. Authors of these background chapters were fairly mindful that the ultimate history here should be liter-ary, while transitional paragraphs between chapters helped pro-mote the organic connections of history and literature. In order to alert readers of the second edition to the unifying organic prin-ciple, the editors revised the typography of the contents table so that titles of the historical background chapters were distin-guished by italics. In a prefatory comment, the editors further underlined their literary–historical axiom:

> The view of literature as the aesthetic expression of the general cul-ture of a people in a given time and place was, from the start, an axiom in the thinking of the editors and their associates. Rejecting the theory that history of any kind is merely a chronological record of objective facts, they adopted an organic view of literature as the record of human experience and of its history as the portrait of a people, designed from the curves of its cultural cycles and the colors of its rich and unique life. (I, ix)

The reference to cultural cycles seems rather offhand, and we recall that Jones had forcefully rejected Spiller's cyclical theory in the planning stages of the *LHUS*. In the preface of the first edi-tion, the editors did not call attention to Spiller's double cycle of American literary history, and the reviewers, strangely enough, were silent, whether in admiration or suspicion of the theory, although we might assume that it provided an inevitable focus for critical debate. No critic so much as posed the standard challenges: Does the cycle account not only for resemblances but also the differences within the turn of the wheel? And does the cycle account for the main features of historical development *between* the turns of the wheel? In the text itself, Spiller's theory did not explicitly emerge when the history entered the first climax in section IV, the "Fulfillment" of the New England flowering. But neither was it too subtle to have been missed. Presumably, the New England histories of Van Wyck Brooks and F. O. Matthiessen had made believers of even the most sophisticated critic.

The development of the second cycle was something new, yet no reviewer questioned it. Why? Spiller, we discover, had now sewn the chapters more firmly together with the cyclical pattern to argue a trough period that was succeeded by a second renaissance. Connecting paragraphs of strategic chapters after section IV, that is, were clearly linked to advance the history and illustrate the two-cycle theory, or vice versa. Harold Blodgett in "Heard from the New World," posed his central issue—how the rest of the world now saw us—within the frame of "a cycle of literature, coincident with the rise of a Romantic Movement and deriving its chief inspiration from the matured civilization of the Atlantic seaboard," a first cycle of our literary history just completed at the Civil War (I, 618). The next chapter, Henry Nash Smith's "The Widening of Horizons," reiterated that "American literature to the end of the Civil War, the literature of the First Republic, presents a pattern of growth, maturity, and decline" (II, 639). In the postwar era, the art of Henry James and Mark Twain belonged to "an age of transition rather than of fulfillment" (Smith, "The Second Discovery of America," II, 789). In Thorp's postwar "Defenders of Ideality," the ideals of the prewar renaissance survived but without "their familiar bearings," so that for writers like Twain, Howells, and others, "the issue was sharply drawn: if one wished to write, one must choose to defend the older order or throw in one's lot with the new. There was no easy blending of ideality with reality in these uncertain times" (II, 809).

Appropriately, Spiller himself introduced the second cycle in "The Battle of the Books." He dated the new watershed of American literature at roughly 1910. Crucial issues were now being properly raised, and "the intellectual and social ferment of these years take shape as a critical movement concerned with literary theory in and for itself." Spiller closed the chapter by cautiously tracing the preparatory, formative criticism that slightly pointed toward the new cycle of the 1920s. In the two preceding decades, however, "the two great tasks of redefining the American cultural tradition and of developing a systematic literary criticism had scarcely begun" (II, 1135, 1156). With the opening and closing of Canby's "Fiction Sums Up a Century," we read a similar effort to define the intercycle trough and the turn of a new wheel. The fictioneers of the early twentieth century were historical victims in a time of pause: "They were prewar in inspiration or in their sense of fundamental values, and were summary, not icono-clastic, in their artistic purposes." But something new happened for writers in the electric twenties, for they were experiencing both a culmination of an old era (the Second Republic between the civil and first world wars) and the innovative excitement of a new. The promise of renaissance was strengthened, too, by "an aware and receptive audience" (II, 1208, 1236).

Unhappily, the authors of the climactic modern chapters under section X, "A World Literature"—Geismar on fiction, Krutch on drama, and Matthiessen on poetry—did not accommodate the second cycle very well. Geismar viewed Dos Passos's *USA* as increasingly despairing, with *The Big Money,* like Hemingway's *To Have and Have Not,* "a sort of apotheosis of state horrors" and the characters socially benighted. In Faulkner, "the cultural pattern of isolation, of revolt, and of denial, the heritage of the American twenties lasting over and fully forming the American novelists of the 1930's reached an extreme." The provincial Gants of Thomas Wolfe were no less stalemated, while the Leftist dog-mas of politically oriented writers rendered the masses into little more than an aesthetic abstraction (II, 1303, 1306, 1310, 1313).

To Krutch, dramatists like Anderson and Stallings, Howard and Lawson, were historically discontinuous with any American tradition, but he worked up some enthusiasm over the experi-mental theater of the 1920s and 1930s and, less convincingly, the hits of the early 1940s by Thornton Wilder, Ellen Chase, and William Saroyan. Matthiessen, however, heralded no poetic ar-rival of a second American renaissance. The political and eco-nomic interests of the thirties were more effectively expressed in fiction and drama, he felt. Amid poets like Williams and Stevens, or Phelps Putnam and Howard Baker, only T. S. Eliot (predictably in the light of Matthiessen's recent study) achieved any eminence as he wrote fully distinguished poetic meditations under the ad-vancing shadows of the coming war. These chapters, in short, did not quite lead the closing section of the *LHUS* toward the high noon of a second literary flowering in America.

In the second edition (1953), Spiller and Thorp coauthored a

"Postscript" chapter, conceived in order "to round out the account of the second literary 'renaissance'" (I, x). But Spiller had in mind a larger and more effective justification of his two-cycle theory of American literary history, and it appeared two years later as *The Cycle of American Literature: An Essay in Historical Criticism* (1955). Spiller now enjoyed the luxury of greater space to defend, in particular, his debatable second cycle on the eve of World War I: "Literature is likely to come into its own at such moments in history because only in times of fulfillment is life's tragedy safely confronted. Emerson ushered in the first American renaissance by his call for introspection in an epoch of achieved nationality" (p. 212). This second renaissance was heralded by the mature introspection and various but appropriate literary forms of Dreiser and Frost; and it blossomed in the moral and artistic creations of Fitzgerald, Wolfe, and Hemingway. This second flowering, aided by the "creative tensions" of naturalism and symbolism, received its critical rationale especially from the comprehensive vision of Edmund Wilson.

In an adventurous final chapter, Spiller corralled various other moderns who brought the second renaissance to an artistic peak in the 1930s that he, though not his contributors to the *LHUS* climactic pages, deeply realized. The presiding genius was Faulkner, not Steinbeck, despite their social, moral, and primitive similarities: "It was Faulkner's great period as it was the richest period in America's literary history." But every rise has a fall, and Spiller in 1955 viewed the fading of the second renaissance. No fresh impulse was yet forthcoming in the postwar years. A conservative temper presided, the older writers were now teaching on university faculties, and younger writers were content to ape the verses of Eliot or the prose of Hemingway. In place of romantic rebels, we heard young voices that "seemed to be calling for values, standards, and security rather than for further upheaval and change" (pp. 301, 303).

In the third-edition postscript of *LHUS* (1963), Spiller reiterated (with Thorp) that the second renaissance had come and gone. Where the romantic energies had not been played out, they were being successfully stifled by the dogmas of the New Critics. Even so, "the times seemed ready, by 1960, for new forces and new directions," at least in fiction (pp. 1410, 1405). In short, Spiller and Thorp were satisfied that the *LHUS* of 1948 could stand as a unified and completed treatment of American literary history for some time to come. And indeed we can view those volumes in their own right as a culminating literary event, a fitting climax to this biography of a profession. An era of defining our country's three centuries of literary history, begun with the pioneering summary volumes of the *CHAL* and surviving two world wars, may have been drawing to a close. But in a nation ever on the move, postwar scholars were pouring onto the campuses of the academy in unprecedented numbers. The profession itself was ready to entertain "new forces and new directions" for American literary scholarship at midcentury.

F. O. Matthiessen (1902–1950)
(*Harvard University Archives*)

Cleanth Brooks (1906–)
(*Louisiana State University Photograph*)

Robert Penn Warren (1905–)
(*Louisiana State University Photograph*)

Henry Nash Smith (1906–)
(*University of Minnesota, University
Archives*)

Robert E. Spiller (1896–)
(*Courtesy of Mr. Spiller*)

Willard Thorp (1899–)
(*University Archives, Princeton*)

Henry S. Canby (1878–1961)
(*Yale University Library*)

Thomas H. Johnson (1902–)
(*Lawrenceville School Archives*)

Stanley T. Williams (1888-1956)
(*Yale University Library*)

Howard M. Jones (1892–1980)
(*Harvard University Archives*)

Dixon Wecter (1906–1950)
(*Copyright 1945 by Associated Students UCLA*)

Postwar Epilogue

New Directions in a Thriving Profession

The ink was not dry on galley proofs for the *LHUS* when Harry Clark, chairman-elect of the ALG, planned to feature in the program at Christmas 1948 a session on "Explanations for the Major Transitions in American Literary History." With other noncontributors to the Spiller enterprise, Clark was already embarked on a course of reinterpretation in what must have appeared to the *LHUS* team as unseemly haste. While the earliest reviews were just reaching the streets, fully six hundred of the four thousand MLA members who had gathered in New York elected to hear Clarence Faust (Stanford), Leon Howard (Northwestern), Merrill Heiser (Iowa), G. H. Orians (Toledo), Perry Miller (Harvard), Floyd Stovall (North Texas Teachers College), and Robert Falk (Rutgers) speculate on the rise and decline of various periods and modes in American literary history. If one intention had been to anticipate a postmortem for the *LHUS*, to be succeeded by a new flurry of literary histories, the next decades did not turn out that way. The Quinn–Murdock–Gohdes–Whicher history (1951) was already nearing completion. In 1954, Clark published an edition of the program papers of 1948, titled *Transitions in American Literature History* (Alexander Kern of Iowa replacing Perry Miller on the transcendentalists). Six years later, Leon Howard's *Literature and the American Tradition* was the next American literary history. Through the 1960s and 1970s, senior American literature scholars resembled their colleagues in history who, as John Higham has observed, "very largely lost interest in comprehensive themes and overarching generalizations."[1] The *LHUS* was still unchallenged after a fourth edition in the 1970s. But at the present writing, a new generation's *CHAL* and a one-volume Columbia history are actively under way.

Early in the fifties, the postwar scholars who had scrutinized the *LHUS* were aware that contributors had not dramatically reinterpreted American works and authors. In the main, they had consolidated, summarized, and brought into focus the bulk of what was currently known in the field by the midforties. Did such knowledge argue, at last, that the profession by then had, indeed, arrived at maturity? If so, the postwar generation was prepared to extend that knowledge into new ventures, though more limited in scope, at least for the present. "Everything remains to be done, or done again," was the motto of the exuberant postwar scholar and the forward-looking among his or her mentors. Returning from the war, one sensed that the world, and America, were no longer the same. American literature had begun to mean, as never before, the expression of diverse minorities and regions, as well as the experience of a nation disabused of much innocence and living under the burden of internal tensions and the dread of nuclear holocaust. In literary scholarship and criticism, these recognitions and pressures helped create a veritable age of energy. The G. I. Bill brought thousands of war veterans, many of them ambitious literary scholars, into the universities and graduate schools. Together with professors from the previous generation of the *LHUS*, they engaged in a cross-fertilization of life experiences and literary intelligence to produce revivals or revisions of older authors and a new critical appreciation of contemporary writers. In traditional and newly founded journals, in commercial and university presses, the intellectual energy of these postwar scholars, old and young, soon culminated in an eruption of articles and books unprecedented in American literature studies.

Within this new ferment was also an awareness of tradition and continuity. The *LHUS* editors again showed the way in various activities of the profession. Spiller and Thorp each served as president of the American Studies Association in the 1950s, the decade when American literature was the most important among the integrated disciplines of American Studies, both in curricula and publications. In 1951, the American Studies Association's infant journal, *American Quarterly,* moved from Minnesota to Spiller's Pennsylvania. Johnson became the foremost authority on Emily Dickinson, Thorp wrote a history of twentieth-century American writing, and Williams completed the two-volume *Spanish Background of American Literature* the year before his death in 1956. Both Spiller and Thorp were closely associated with other professional undertakings during the period. When the ALG sponsored a review of research and criticism, *Eight American Authors* (1956), Spiller wrote the bibliography essay on Henry James and Thorp on Whitman. (Williams, who originally proposed the volume, wrote the Melville chapter.) The epochal production of standard Editions of American Authors, initiated in 1962 and centered in the MLA, with William Gibson director, had an origin in the ALG Committee on Definitive Editions in 1947 to 1948, with Thorp as chairman; and he became a member of the first Executive Committee for the Editions in 1963. Textual scholarship came of age in these editions of nineteenth-century authors, aided with generous funding by the new National Endowment for the Humanities and resources from various university presses. In the 1960s, the editions included Mark Twain (University of California Press), Crane (Virginia), Howells (Indiana), Irving (Wisconsin), Melville (Northwestern), Thoreau (Princeton), Hawthorne (Ohio State), and Whitman (NYU). Harvard published the Emerson volumes both before and after the center was established, and Spiller was present at the heart of the venture. In the 1970s, eleven more editions were under way, one of them Cooper's novels and his gleanings in Europe. Spiller the textual editor again was there.

Of the remaining portion of the *LHUS* team, Dixon Wecter died in the summer of 1950 at the age of forty-five in the midst of his significant work on Mark Twain. Henry Canby wrote a final book, *Turn West, Turn East* (on Mark Twain and Henry James), in 1951; resigned from his long service with the Book-of-the-Month Club in 1955; and died six years later at age eighty-two. Just after the war, Jones published a generally reliable survey of some of the changing concepts that have guided American literature scholarship, *The Theory of American Literature* (1948). Until his retirement from Harvard in 1962 at age seventy, Jones was active in every aspect of professional life, and even beyond 1962, he continued to add to his considerable laurels. He won the Pulitzer Prize for *O Strange New World* (1964) and the following year served as president of the MLA. In that office, he enjoyed the power of influencing the association to revise its regulations so that, among other changes, the ALG, whose status in the parent organization he had argued for so vehemently back in the 1930s, rose in 1966 to the full respect of its new title, the American Literature Section. In the 1970s, Jones completed his trilogy of American cultural history with *Revolution and Romanticism* (1974) and *The Age of Energy* (1971). He died in 1980 at the age of eighty-eight, to be survived, at this writing, by the all-but-indestructible Johnson, Thorp, and Spiller.

For some other figures in our previous story, the postwar years were not so kind. Van Wyck Brooks completed his Makers and Finders series with volumes 4 and 5, *The Times of Melville and Whitman* (1947) and *The Confident Years: 1885–1915* (1952), respectively, and lived to write on American writers and artists in Italy as well as a late book on Howells. He continued his counter-attack on the ascendant New Critics for their undue attention to literary craft to the neglect of content and feeling. But for years before his death in 1963, Brooks's highly personalized works had ceased to be cited even for their content by postwar scholars (while professors Cleanth Brooks and Robert Penn Warren had now become respected students of American literature). Meanwhile, Alfred Kazin contributed his critical and editorial skills to the postwar assessments of Fitzgerald and Dreiser, but he was too often pegged in the academy as the once brilliant and promising author of *On Native Grounds*. F. O. Matthiessen, his study of Dreiser all but complete in 1950, committed suicide that year in the midst of rising cold war antagonisms. In 1944, he had awaited the return of G.I.'s to the campuses, expecting them to renew the social commitment they had displayed at Harvard in 1939 and 1940 and to "insist that after the war we must develop democratic cultural values as well as the society to support them."[2] But he must have noticed by 1950 that the war-weary veterans had returned with little taste for radical politics. Beneficiaries of capitalist largesse under the G.I. Bill, they quickly became the traditional professor's ideal student, the industrious bookworm, serious and mature and motivated, but the bookworm nevertheless. Very few, we suspect, had voted in 1948 for Henry Wallace, Matthiessen's candidate.

This studious atmosphere lingered into the sixties until the conflict in Vietnam awakened the academy to the political and social realities of a "military–industrial complex," what Matthiessen would have understood as the "decaying and confused era of capitalism" he had anticipated in 1944. (He would have been gratified by the revolt of the radical young at the MLA convention of 1968, and the ostensible democratizing of participation in the programs and other MLA governance thereafter.) During those two postwar decades of academic seriousness, important works of scholarship and criticism multiplied to a degree impossible to describe adequately in brief space. Period histories abounded. Perry Miller dominated the colonial studies and then continued into the earlier nineteenth century of New England and New York. Studies in the romantic period also came from Harry Levin, R. W. B. Lewis, and Joel Porte. The later nineteenth century was illuminated in the work of Charles Walcutt, Robert Falk, Donald Pizer, Warner Berthoff, Jay Martin, Harold Kolb, and Larzer Ziff. Genre studies were equally plentiful: in poetry, Roy Pearce, M. L. Rosenthal, and Hyatt Waggoner; in fiction, Alexander Cowie, Maxwell Geismar, Richard Chase, Leslie Fiedler, and A. N. Kaul.

In studies of single authors, twentieth-century figures were, for the first time, paid serious and sustained attention, while earlier writers finally attained something close to a sophisticated evaluation of their achievement. Spurring this scholarship were the single-author bibliographies splendidly assembled in the *LHUS* (volume III). Important, too, were Matthiessen's probing chapters earlier in *American Renaissance,* where he helped define the moral and aesthetic worlds of Emerson and Thoreau, the separation of head and heart in Hawthorne, the Shakespearean cast of Melville's tragic view, and the organic principle in Whitman's democratic verses. Kazin, too, stimulated a serious new interest in writers like Fitzgerald, Hemingway, and Faulkner through the incisive, quotable, and at times outrageous critiques in *On Native Grounds.* Postwar scholars who spearheaded these modern appraisals were Gay W. Allen (Whitman), George Arms, William Gibson, and Edwin Cady (Howells), Carlos Baker and Philip Young (Hemingway), Donald Pizer (Garland and Norris), Irving Howe (Anderson and Faulkner), Arthur Mizener (Fitzgerald), Lawrance Thompson (Frost), Emery Neff (Robinson), Peter Lisca (Steinbeck), Edward Davidson (Poe), Ralph Rusk and Sherman Paul (Emerson), Randall Stewart (Hawthorne), Walter Harding (Thoreau), Richard Chase and Leon Howard (Melville), Edgar Branch, Walter Blair, Louis Budd, and Henry Nash Smith (Mark Twain), Leon Edel (James), Ernest Samuels (Henry Adams), James Beard (Cooper), and John Berryman (Stephen Crane). Among these scholars, many guided the profession after the war as chairmen of the ALG: Stewart, Howard, Allen, Blair, Waggoner, and Smith.

Much of this scholarship was more strongly laced with analytical criticism than in the prewar years, and that fusion was strengthened by the so-called symbol-and-myth school in American Studies, some of the group being heirs of Matthiessen: Henry N. Smith, Leo Marx, John W. Ward, R. W. B. Lewis, and Alan Trachtenberg. Other critical explanations of the literary text embraced one or, eclectically, several approaches, from the New Criticism and Northrup Frye's categories to the varieties of imported existentialism and covert biases of racism and sexism. The Freudian approach was still in, but Marxist criteria were mainly out. The contradictions of naturalism within American— and the New Humanists'—freedom of the will still attracted a share of scholarly critics. Over the horizon beyond the sixties, a gathering smorgasbord of interpretive theories awaited the professor alert to movements and fads—semiotics, grammatology,

audience response, structuralism, deconstruction, a newly seasoned Freud and Marx, and more.

Some of these approaches after World War II had resulted in
first books growing out of the professor's revised dissertations,
usually published by some of the fifty thriving university presses.
Such publication, however, became more difficult as graduate
schools grew in size and number. Expansion and competition
were accelerating in all academic fields. In 1940, for example,
100 institutions granted the doctorate and 300 the master's; the
figures in 1958 were, respectively, 175 and 569. During the same
interval, recipients of both degrees had trebled.[3] In American
literature alone, James Woodress counted the annual number of
dissertations from 1948 to 1955 at roughly 100 per year, increasing to 135 per year thereafter to 1961. Put another way, more dissertations had been written in these postwar years than in the
entire period from the first dissertation in 1891 until 1948. What
percentage of the owners of these new Ph.D.'s became publishing
scholars in American literature? A computer expert may one day
correlate the *PMLA* bibliographies with Woodress's dissertation
authors during these years and provide an answer. In the 1960s
and after, Twayne publishers came to the rescue of many a young
untenured professor by soliciting the dissertation for their prolific
United States Authors Series, which was soon running to hundreds of monographs.

Dissertations could also be published piecemeal, and the postwar years brought a harvest of new journals to accommodate articles produced by new professors living under the injunction to
publish or perish. (Statistics on manuscripts submitted and rejected in 1961 and 1965 by dozens of these journals were tabulated in *PMLA*, November 1966.) In addition to scores of new
magazines that invited criticism and scholarship in American
and other literatures, a sizable number were created to encourage strictly American literature research in limited areas: *Early
American Literature, Emerson Society Quarterly, American
Transcendental Quarterly, American Literary Realism, Studies
in American Fiction, Studies in American Humor, Western American Literature, New England Folklore,* and so on. Single authors
gave the focus to many a journal, quarterly, review, or newsletter,
and most of them were able to survive. They commemorated
writers like Dreiser, Dickinson, Faulkner, Fitzgerald, Hemingway, Frederic, Higginson, Stephen Crane, Stevens, Tennessee
Williams, Flannery O'Connor, Hawthorne, London, Pound (*Pai-
deuma*), Poe, Lewis, Steinbeck, Thoreau, Eliot, and Whitman.

Rare was the university that now failed to sponsor a periodical that printed American literature scholarship. At Duke, meanwhile, *American Literature* remained the leading journal for scholarship in the traditional vein of literary history, its articles thoroughly refereed, the reviews judicious, and the notices of current dissertations and articles a constant record of the profession's vitality. After Jay B. Hubbell retired in 1954, the editorial reins were firmly handled, consecutively, by Clarence Gohdes, Arlin Turner, and in the 1970s, by Edwin Cady.

Intimidated by this flood of publications, how could the scholar now hope to keep up in the field? James Woodress fully realized this frustration when he returned from Europe in the early sixties after only one year's absence and was confronted with fifteen hundred new American literature items in the *PMLA* bibliography. The remedy he proposed to the Advisory Council of the ALG, and soon edited with the cooperation of American literature colleagues and ALG sponsorship, was *American Literary Scholarship: An Annual* (Duke University Press). Beginning with the year's work in 1963, these annual essays, written by experts on various literary periods and figures, soon became the most useful, because critical, bibliography of American literature studies. The profession was here benefited by a review and evaluation of scholarly articles that were merely listed in the *PMLA* bibliography. The growth of American literature scholarship since 1963 is easily reflected in the annual expansion of the *ALS*: Essays in the first volume numbered 224 pages, compared to 593 pages in 1980. (The first bibliography essay in *PMLA*, by Norman Foerster, covered the scholarship of 1922 in six pages.)

Indeed, the vast quantity and range of scholarly publication in the modern academy have rendered bibliography a major necessity and resource, a special field in itself. Among the indispensable volumes have been Woodress's ALG-supported *Dissertations in American Literature* (1957 and updated in 1962 and 1968); *Sixteen Modern American Authors* (edited by Jackson Bryer, 1969), the 624 pages chiefly a record of postwar attention to these major twentieth-century writers; and *Fifteen American Authors before 1900* (edited by Robert Rees and Earl Harbert, 1971), which supplemented *Eight American Authors* (1956), itself revised and updated in 1971 (edited by Woodress). More recently, G. K. Hall, Scarecrow Press, Shoe String Press, and other publishers have been issuing a wide variety of reference guides, bibliographies, and check lists of criticism and scholarship. Most spectacular of all has been Joseph Blanck's primary *Bibliography of American Literature,* the first volume published in 1955. Blanck's work was conveniently accompanied five years later by the primary sources listed in *American Literary Manuscripts* (Joseph Jones et al., for the ALG).

✻ ✻ ✻

In the postwar classrooms, American literature generally continued to play a subordinate role within the entrenched curriculum and examinations for the degrees in "English." But the superior vitality of the American offerings was increasingly recognized by students and then by the textbook publishers, who soon enjoyed a brisk new market, with an enthusiastic assist from American literature professors willing to share in the profits. Inexpensive paperbacks radically altered the teaching of American literature. Publishers like Rinehart, Viking, Norton, Scribner, and Houghton Mifflin enabled students in the 1950s and after to purchase their own copies of classic novels and an author's selected shorter works. With these texts in hand, students could be guided in a close reading rather than being forced to listen to lectures in the prewar fashion when such works had been expensive and therefore, as textbooks, in short supply.

Even more influential and lucrative for both publisher and professor have been the successful anthologies used in popular survey courses. A number of older volumes, to be sure, had remained in print even into the early 1960s, usually after undergoing one or more revisions. These included collections edited by Pattee (Century, 1919), Foerster (Houghton Mifflin, 1925), Cargill et al. (Macmillan, 1933), Jones and Leisy (Harcourt, Brace, 1935), Hubbell (Harper, 1936), Benét and Pearson (Oxford, 1938), and Thorp, Curti, and Baker (Lippincott, 1941). Since World War II, however, these anthologies have met furious competition. Some of the most prominent rivals have been Blair, Hornberger, and Stewart (Scott, Foresman, 1946), Bradley, Beatty, and Long (Norton, 1956), and Perry Miller et al. (Harcourt, Brace, 1962). These textbook anthologies, which would soon meet another wave of competitors in the 1970s, reflected almost totally the progress of American literature scholars and professors since the war. Introductory essays combined literary history with critical awareness (and Blair, Hornberger, and Stewart even removed their background interchapters in 1964 to fashion a separate volume, *American Literature: A Brief History*). In the Miller anthology, Richard Wilbur helped redirect Poe studies with an introduction that underscored the strategic importance of *Eureka*. Also in keeping with the times were helpful and extensive bibliographies that accompanied selections of each author. These anthologies, rigidly selective but running into multiple volumes, reminded one that the field of American literature, after three and one-half centuries, had grown very fertile indeed. And when students from the postwar baby boom swelled enrollments and faculties in the academy during the Vietnam era and then lined up to purchase these generous collections, the riches of American literature were unmistakably flowing in many new directions.

Appendix

Leaders of the American Literature Group (1921–1948)

The chief sources here have been *PMLA, American Literature* (*AL*), and the Archives of the ALG, Memorial Library, University of Wisconsin.

I have not indicated the occasions when another member substituted for an elected chairman or secretary–treasurer who was absent from the annual meeting. Multiple terms of a secretary–treasurer or bibliographer are noted in the initial year only. Academic addresses that did not change are mentioned only once. At the Cleveland meeting of 1929, the Nominating Committee presented the names of a six-person Advisory Council (hereafter, AC), paired to serve three years, two years, and one year respectively (see Chapter 13). Thereafter, two new members were nominated annually for a three-year term. When the plan of organization (again, see Chapter 13) was refined after 1929, the AC held considerable power. It ratified the Nominating Committee's choice of the ALG chairman and other officers, and the outgoing chairman selected the new Nominating Committee, which presented the next slate of leaders to the AC. At the New Haven meeting of 1932, the group approved a bylaw to allow a degree of mail-ballot democracy by publishing in the annual May issue of *AL* the names of the Nominating Committee's new pair of candidates for the AC as well as the two leading candidates among any mail-in nominations (see Chapter 21).

The board of editors (hereafter, BE) for *AL* was originally formed in 1928 through an ad hoc Committee on Publications. Thenceforth, new members were to be nominated by the AC, although the Nominating Committee actually assumed this task in 1929, the proposed names then being ratified by the AC. The BE selected the members of their Advisory Board (see Chapter 16). These members, too numerous over the years to be listed here, are indicated in the quarterly issues of the journal. Many of the names given in the present compilation were to reappear regularly on the *AL* Advisory Board as well as on important committees and annual programs of the ALG, thereby keeping alive the argument of self-perpetuating elitism within the group. Jay B. Hubbell was permanent editor-in-chief of *AL* after 1928, and his Duke colleague Clarence Gohdes (beginning in 1932) was annually reelected by the AC as managing editor.

1921   Annual meeting of the Modern Language Association was held in Baltimore. Killis Campbell (Texas), chairman; Francis A. Litz (Johns Hopkins), secretary–treasurer.

1922   Philadelphia. Arthur Quinn (Pennsylvania), chairman.

1923   Ann Arbor. Percy Boynton (Chicago), chairman; Norman Foerster (North Carolina), bibliographer for *PMLA*.

1924   New York City. Fred Pattee (Penn State), chairman; Ernest Leisy (Southern Methodist), new secretary–treasurer.

1925   Chicago. Jay Hubbell (Southern Methodist), chairman.

1926   Cambridge. Jay Hubbell, chairman.

1927   Louisville. Kenneth Murdock (Harvard), chairman; Robert Spiller (Swarthmore), new secretary–treasurer; Gregory Paine (North Carolina), new bibliographer.

1928   Toronto. Kenneth Murdock, chairman; Sculley Bradley (Pennsylvania), new secretary–treasurer; Norman Foerster, new bibliographer.

1929   Cleveland. Kenneth Murdock, chairman; Ernest Leisy, new bibliographer. AC: Sculley Bradley, W. B. Cairns (Wisconsin), Janette Harrrington (Senior High School, Little Rock, Arkansas), T. O. Mabbott (Hunter), Gregory Paine, Ralph Rusk (Columbia), and Norman Foerster, chairman. BE: W. B. Cairns, Kenneth Murdock, Fred Pattee (Rollins College), and Ralph Rusk.

1930   Washington, D.C. Robert Spiller, chairman. AC: Gregory Paine and Arthur Quinn, three years; W. B. Cairns and Kenneth Murdock, two years; Milton Ellis (Maine) and Stanley Williams (Yale), one year. BE: Same as 1929.

1931   Madison. Robert Spiller, chairman. AC: Howard Jones (Michigan) and Ralph Rusk join Paine and Quinn, Cairns and Murdock. BE: Same as 1930.

1932   New Haven. Ralph Rusk, chairman. AC: T. O. Mabbott and Robert Spiller join Ellis (for Rusk) and Jones, Paine and Quinn. BE: Robert Spiller joins Cairns, Murdock, and Rusk.

1933   St. Louis. Stanley Williams, chairman. AC: Percy Boynton and Tremaine McDowell (Minnesota) join Mabbott and Spiller, Ellis and Jones. BE: Killis Campbell joins Murdock, Rusk, and Spiller.

1934   Swarthmore. Stanley Williams, chairman. AC: Norman Foerster (Iowa) and T. K. Whipple (California) join Boynton and McDowell, Mabbott and Spiller. BE: Same as 1933.

1935   Cincinnati. Howard Jones, chairman. AC: T. O. Mabbott and Robert Spiller reelected to join Foerster and Whipple, Boynton and McDowell. BE: Same as 1934.

1936   Richmond and Williamsburg. Howard Jones (Harvard), chairman. AC: Henry Canby (Yale) and Thomas Pollock (Ohio State) join Mabbott and Spiller, Foerster and Whipple. BE: Norman Foerster joins Murdock, Rusk, and Spiller.

1937   Chicago. Sculley Bradley, chairman; Tremaine McDowell, new secretary–treasurer; AC: Norman Foerster and Henry Pochmann (Mississippi State) join Canby and Pollock, Mabbott and Spiller. BE: Same as 1936.

1938   New York City. Sculley Bradley, chairman; Gregory Paine, new bibliographer. AC: Harry Clark (Wisconsin) and Ernest Leisy join Foerster and Pochmann, Canby and Pollock. BE: Stanley Williams joins Foerster, Rusk, and Spiller.

1939   New Orleans. Jay Hubbell, chairman. AC: Floyd Stovall (North Texas State Teachers) and Harry Warfel (Maryland) join Clark and Leisy, Foerster and Pochmann. BE: Murdock joins Foerster, Spiller, and Williams.

1940   Cambridge and Boston. Napier Wilt (Chicago), chairman. AC: Louise Pound (Nebraska) and George Whicher (Amherst) join Stovall and Warfel, Clark and Leisy. BE: Emory Holloway (Queens) and Austin Warren (Iowa) join Murdock and Williams.

1941   Indianapolis. Napier Wilt, chairman. AC: Leon Howard (Northwestern) and Willard Thorp (Princeton) join Pound and Whicher, Stovall and Warfel. BE: Same as 1940.

1942   Annual meeting canceled due to World War II restrictions on travel. Milton Ellis, chairman; Alexander Cowie (Wesleyan), new secretary–treasurer. AC: Perry Miller (Harvard) and Louis Wright (Huntington Library) join Howard and Thorp, Pound and Whicher. BE: Same as 1941.

1943   Wartime meeting canceled. Tremaine McDowell, chairman; Thomas Johnson (Lawrenceville School), new bibliographer. AC: Sculley Bradley and Walter Taylor (Mississippi College) join Miller and Wright, Howard and Thorp. BE: Walter Blair (Chicago) and Harry Clark join Murdock and Williams.

1944   New York City. Louise Pound, chairman. AC: Theodore Hornberger (Texas) and Randall Stewart (Brown) join

Bradley and Taylor, Foerster (for Miller in the Army) and Wright. BE: Same as 1943.

1945 Chicago. Gregory Paine, chairman. AC: Walter Blair and Oral Coad (New Jersey College for Women) join Hornberger and Stewart, Bradley and Taylor. BE: Same as 1944.

1946 Washington, D.C. Willard Thorp, chairman; Allan Halline (Bucknell), new secretary–treasurer. AC: Clarence Gohdes (Duke) and Dixon Wecter (Huntington Library) join Blair and Coad, Hornberger and Stewart. BE: Same as 1945.

1947 Detroit. Perry Miller, chairman. AC: Roy Basler (George Peabody College) and Henry Pochmann join Gohdes and Wecter, Blair and Coad. BE: Same as 1946.

1948 New York City. Harry Clark, chairman; Lewis Leary (Duke), new bibliographer. AC: Charles Anderson (Johns Hopkins) and Fred Millett (Wesleyan) join Basler and Pochmann, Gohdes and Wecter. BE: Same as 1947.

Notes

The following short titles and abbreviations are used in the notes:

Persons

SB	E. Sculley Bradley
HC	Henry S. Canby
JE	John Erskine
NF	Norman Foerster
JH	Jay B. Hubbell
TJ	Thomas H. Johnson
HJ	Howard Mumford Jones
TM	Tremaine McDowell
FOM	F. O. Matthiessen
KM	Kenneth Murdock
VP	Vernon Louis Parrington
FP	Fred L. Pattee
SS	Stuart P. Sherman
RS	Robert E. Spiller
WT	Willard Thorp
WPT	William P. Trent
MT	Moses Coit Tyler
VD	Carl Van Doren
DW	Dixon Wecter
BW	Barrett Wendell
SW	Stanley T. Williams

Articles and Books

"Curriculum"	Fred L. Pattee, "American Literature in the College Curriculum," *Educational Review* 67 (May 1924): 266–72.
LL-SPS	Jacob Zeitlin and Homer Woodridge, eds., *Life and Letters of Stuart P. Sherman* (1929), 2 vols.
MCP	John Erskine, *The Memory of Certain Persons* (1947).
RW	Perry Miller, *The Raven and the Whale: The War of Wits and Words in the Era of Poe and Melville* (1956).
SSW	Jay B. Hubbell, *South and Southwest: Literary Essays and Reminiscences* (1965).
TW	Carl Van Doren, *Three Worlds* (1936).
Woodress	James Woodress, ed., *Dissertations in American Literature 1891–1955, with Supplement 1956–1961* (1962).

Unpublished Manuscripts

Bibb	Evelyn R. Bibb, "Anthologies of American Literature, 1787–1964" (diss., Columbia University, 1965).
Hall	Lark Hall, "Vernon Louis Parrington: The Genesis and Design of 'Main Currents in American Thought'" (diss., Case Western Reserve, 1979).
Hassold	Ernest C. Hassold, "American Literary History before the Civil War" (diss., University of Chicago, 1933).
Hite	John Hite (Princeton), "Report to the American Literature Group of the Modern Language Association on the Teaching of American Literature," Dec. 1947, 24 pp. mimeographed, in ALG-UW (see Manuscript Collections). Hite surveyed some one hundred colleges and universities.
Lewis	John S. Lewis, Jr., "The History of Instruction in American Literature in Colleges and Universities of the United States, 1827–1939" (diss., New York University, 1941).
Walker	Franklin T. Walker, "William Peterfield Trent: A Critical Biography" (diss., Peabody College for Teachers, 1943).

Manuscript Collections

ALG-UW	Archives of the American Literature Group of the Modern Language Association, Memorial Library, University of Wisconsin. In eight boxes, much of the history of the ALG is suggested within programs, reports, minutes, and correspondence. (In 1986, this collection was moved to the Jay B. Hubbell Center at Duke—JBH-DU below.)
CC-CU	Columbiana Collection, Low Memorial Library, Columbia University. Folders of photographs and news clippings pertaining to John Erskine, Brander Matthews, W. P. Trent, Carl Van Doren, and George Woodberry were especially useful in this study.
JBH-DU	Jay B. Hubbell Center for American Literary Historiography, Perkins Library, Duke University. This is a growing collection of papers and correspondence related to group enterprises in American literature scholarship (including the journal *American Literature*), as well as manuscripts, classroom notes, and biographical sketches of noted American literature professors.
LHUS-UP	*Literary History of the United States* Archives, Special Collections, Van Pelt Library, University of Pennsylvania. Includes twenty-nine boxes of correspondence, procedural papers, manuscripts, and proofs that record a step-by-step history of the *LHUS*.

CVD-PU   Carl Van Doren Papers, Rare Book Room, Firestone Library, Princeton University. The boxing of the collection is described differently in a card catalog, in a volume titled LITMSS, VII, and in a bound checklist. The checklist is the most convenient of the three and indicates thirty-eight boxes in nine categories (writings, correspondence, pictures, and so forth). Box 13 contains the twelve journals, 1910–16, that I have chiefly consulted.

Periodicals

AL   *American Literature*
AtM   *Atlantic Monthly*
CE   *College English*
Na   *Nation*
NEQ   *New England Quarterly*
NR   *New Republic*
NYHTB   *New York Hearld Tribune Books*
NYTBR   *New York Times Book Review*
NAR   *North American Review*
PMLA   *Publications of the Modern Language Association*
PR   *Partisan Review*
SRL   *Saturday Review of Literature*
SR   *Sewanee Review*
TLS   London *Times Literary Supplement*
YR   *Yale Review*

Introduction

1. *The Teacher and American Literature: Papers Presented at the 1964 Convention of the National Council of Teachers of English* (1965), vi.
2. *PMLA* 84 (Sept. 1969): 1232–33.
3. "Something Is Happening But You Don't Know What It Is, Do You, Mr. Jones?" *PMLA* 85 (May 1970): 417–22. The title is a protest lyric by Bob Dylan.
4. Kenneth Lynn reported in 1965 that the fifteen-year effort (1955–70) to triple the number of college professors was becoming "an awesome task" and the research division of the National Education Association had recently admitted only limited success in persuading young men and women to enter various fields of college teaching—including "English"—where "demand has far outrun supply." See Lynn and the editors of *Daedalus*, eds., *The Professions in America* (1965), ix, xii.
5. *History: Professional Scholarship in America* (1965), 5. Because American literature in the academy has a history and fate essentially different from that of American history as Higham reveals it, my study is organized differently from his. But I recommend his lucid and informative book to those who wish to see my story in a larger setting. Important, too, is Burton J. Bledstein's critique of the

middle-class psychology that guides academic professionalism, an analysis that coincides at various points with Ohmann's book. See *The Culture of Professionalism: The Middle Class and the Development of Higher Education in America* (1976). For a corrective statement that professions also ensure valuable standards of performance and promote the excellence Americans need and expect, see Thomas L. Haskell's review of Bledstein in *New York Review of Books* 24 (13 Dec. 1977): 28–33.

6. Peter Loewenberg, in *Decoding the Past* (1983), acidly addresses this particular issue of American identity: "Academic life in America has many pseudo-Englishmen, crypto-Frenchmen, and quasi-Italians. The desire to disassociate oneself from one's own personal and collective past will have as a correlate an inability to tolerate a depth experience in the present" (p. 76). He also gives examples that illuminate my brief references to Oedipal and sibling anxieties and antagonisms in the profession, during graduate school and after.

7. That we need this bracing of the spirit more than ever is obvious on many of the nation's campuses. As this book goes to press, U.S. Department of Education Secretary William J. Bennett has announced that five recent surveys of graduation requirements in the academy show that 72 percent of colleges and universities do not require the study of American literature (and American history). See "Bennett Accuses Colleges of Lax Admission, Graduation Rules," *Los Angeles Times*, 29 Jan. 1986, 16.

Chapter 1. Prelude: Origins of the CHAL

1. *MCP*, 242.
2. *TW*, 108.
3. 22 Mar. 1913. Unless indicated otherwise, all of this autobiographical information is drawn from CVD-PU.
4. In *LL-SPS*, I, 258. VD added a minor, though revealing, fact many years later in a letter to Franklin T. Walker, who was writing a biography of WPT. In the original proposal to WPT for an American literary history based on the *CHEL* model, Putnam had asked that Brander Matthews be chosen as coeditor. But WPT and Matthews had been disputing bitterly over the prewar political unrest and national rivalries in Europe (about which, more later). Matthews, therefore, did not join his Columbia colleagues as an editor, although he was invited to contribute chapter 23 on "Writers of Familiar Verse"—Holmes, Lowell, and others. See Walker, 327–28, 354.
5. Walker, 330, 333.
6. Unless indicated otherwise, my summary of WPT's career is drawn from Walker.
7. For further data on WPT's activities with the journal, see esp. "Ten Years of the Sewanee Review: A Retrospect," *SR* 10 (Oct. 1902): 477–92, by WPT's successor, John B. Henneman; and Alice L. Tur-

ner, *A Study of the Content of the Sewanee Review, with Historical Introduction* (1931), 1–11, and passim.

8. "Mr. Brander Matthews as a Critic," *SR* 3 (May 1895): 273–84.
9. "American Literature," *Dial* 28 (1 May 1900): 334–40.
10. JH to Walker, 21 Jan. 1941, in Walker, 268.
11. "The Teaching of Literature in College," *Na* 87 (3 Sept. 1908): 204. In this article, JE also urged professors to focus on the aesthetic experience rather than on biographical and historical backgrounds. He recalled in his memoirs that the suggestion had brought abusive mail from teachers, critics, publishers, and even novelists (*MCP*, 183). For more on JE's early career, see classmate Melville Cane's "John Erskine: An Appreciation," *Columbia Library Columns* 7 (Nov. 1957): 4–12. Excerpts from JE's letters to Cane are printed on pp. 13–17.
12. JE explained this joint authorship in a letter to Walker, 10 July 1942, in Walker, 294.
13. *Many Minds* (1924), 72. I am also summarizing *LL-SPS*.
14. *The Autobiography of Mark Van Doren* (1958), 65, 67.
15. *MCP*, 242.
16. *TW*, 76–78.
17. *TW*, 97–98; *Many Minds*, 203.
18. Once more, my biographical data, unless otherwise noted, are taken from CVD-PU.
19. SS to VD, 24 Jan. 1915, *LL-SPS*, I, 260. This letter is dated 1914, but SS refers to VD's recent bibliographical piece on Brown in *Na*, and it did not appear until 14 Jan. 1915. I have therefore corrected the date for the new year.
20. *TW*, 195.

Chapter 2. Organizing the CHAL *Team*

1. *LL-SPS*, I, 258.
2. *TW*, 108.
3. *TW*, 108; Walker, chap. 11, passim.
4. SS to VD, 13 Jan. 1914, in *LL-SPS*, I, 260.
5. SS to VD, 31 Jan. 1914, in *LL-SPS*, I, 261–63.
6. Letter lent by Mims to Walker, who quotes it on 332–33.
7. U.S. postcard, WPT to VD, 24 June 1914, in CVD-PU (as is all other correspondence in this chap. unless noted otherwise).
8. WPT to VD, 26 Sept. 1914.
9. *MCP*, 243.
10. Ibid. News clippings in CC-CU record Woodberry's difficulties at Columbia beginning in 1902 when Pres. Butler refused to accept private donations to support Woodberry's funded professorship in comparative literature. Students and young alumni, among others, rallied unsuccessfully to Woodberry's defense.
11. *MCP*, 84, 112, 141, and 246.
12. SS to VD, 3 Dec. 1914, in *LL-SPS*, I, 264.

13. WPT to VD, 8 Sept. 1914.
14. These letters are in the Parrington Papers, now in the custody of VP's grandson, Dr. Stevens Parrington Tucker. Hall viewed these letters and recorded their contents in her dissertation, 163, 193n. VD recalled this relationship twelve years later in his review of volumes I and II of *Main Currents* in *Century* (June 1927).
15. Undated letter in Walker, 334n. In a letter to Chittick on 27 May 1919, VD wrote, "I wish I'd had you do the ["Early Humorists"] chapter for the C.H.A.L. instead of that [illegible] Will Howe." The assignment might have given Chittick's career a boost. He was unable to find a publisher for his *Haliburton* until 1936.
16. Reprinted in *Memories of a Publisher* (1915) in the "Appendix: The European War, 1914–1915" with other of Putnam's anti-German letters to the New York *Evening Post, Tribune,* and *Times*. The final letter, to the London *Times* (20 Nov. 1915), affirmed Putnam's, and America's, support of England. In CC-CU, the WPT folder includes a bound copy of his poem in the private printing.
17. Walker, 299–302.
18. WPT to VD, 9 Sept. 1915.
19. Leonard "to the General Editors of *The Cambridge History of Am. Lit.,*" 6 May 1915; JE to VD, 8 and 9 July, 25 Aug. 1915; WPT to VD, 17 Aug. 1915.
20. WPT to VD, 9 and 14 Sept. 1915.
21. JE to VD, 16 Sept. 1915; and SS to VD, 30 Oct. 1915, in *LL-SPS*, I, 263–64.
22. Riley to VD, 11 Aug., 14 Oct., and 1 Dec. 1915.
23. Postcard to VD, 16 Mar. 1916.
24. WPT to VD, 13 June 1916.
25. JE to VD, 26 June, 6 and 22 Aug., and 7 Sept. 1916.
26. Riley to VD, 23 July 1916; G. H. Putnam to VD, 3 Aug.; Leonard to VD, 30 Aug., 6 and 8 Sept. 1916. Trent's correcting Putnam on Irving was, no doubt, personally delicious, but it points to more than spiteful pendantry of the moment. Over the next five years, Trent edited six volumes of Irving's journals, three of them (1919) with George Hellman.
27. WPT to VD, 21 Feb. 1917; G. H. Putnam to VD, 19 Oct. 1917.
28. Leonard to VD, 8 May 1917; and VD to WPT, 29 June 1917.
29. Putnam to VD, 5 Nov. 1917.

Chapter 3. Preface to Volume I: Trailblazers in the Nationalist Era of Samuel Knapp

1. Richard B. Davis and Ben H. McClary, eds., *Lectures on American Literature: with Remarks on Some Passages of American History* (1961), 30. Page numbers hereafter will appear in my text.
2. It is to Knapp's scholarly credit, however, that Moses Coit Tyler's masterly portraits of colonial figures (see Chapter 6) were indebted to Knapp's *Biographical Sketches of Eminent Lawyers, Statesmen, and Men of Letters* (1821).

3. Davis and McClary, *Lectures,* iii–iv.
4. Goodrich, *Recollections of a Lifetime, or Men and Things I have Seen* (1857), II, 279, 320–21, and 380–89.
5. See Lewis, chap. 1.
6. Bibb, 38–40.
7. Lewis, 19–22; Hite, 1.
8. Bibb, 50.
9. Vol. 30 (Jan. 1820): 79. In context, the remark comes within a plausibly argued but nonetheless condescending plea for a more fitting modesty from "Jonathan," in the wake of Smith's having reviewed a rather drab nonliterary work, *Statistical Annals of the United States of America* by Adam Seybert (1818).
10. We now have more knowledge of the actual British response to American literature in these early years. A recent count tallies 450 American publications noticed, and presumably read, by British critics (especially on Irving and Cooper) from 1798 to 1826. See William S. Ward, "American Authors and British Reviewers: A Bibliography," *AL* 30 (Mar. 1977): 1–21.
11. "American Literature," in *The Works of Fisher Ames* (1809), 458–72. The volume was compiled by "a number of his friends" the year after Ames's death.
12. *On the Development of American Literature from 1815 to 1833, with Especial Reference to Periodicals* (1898), 36.
13. "On the Dangers and Duties of Men of Letters," *Monthly Anthology* 7 (Sept. 1809): 145–58.
14. "An Address Delivered to the Phi Beta Kappa Society, at their Anniversary Meeting at Cambridge," *NAR* 2 (Nov. 1815): 13–32.
15. "Essay on American Language and Literature," *NAR* 1 (Sept. 1815): 307–14; and "Reflections on the Literary Delinquency of America," 2 (Nov. 1815): 33–43.
16. "On Models in Literature," *NAR* 3 (July 1816): 202–9. E. T. Channing was editor of the *Review* in 1818 with cousin R. H. Dana; the following year, Channing became the influential Boylston Professor of Rhetoric and Oratory (1819–51) at Harvard.
17. "An Address Pronounced before the Society of Phi Beta Kappa," *NAR* 3 (Sept. 1816): 289–305.
18. "An Essay on American Poetry," *NAR* 7 (July 1818): 198–211. The essay was reprinted as "Early American Verse" in Parke Godwin, ed., *Prose Writings of William Cullen Bryant* (1884), I, 45–56.
19. *The Sketch Book* was published by Irving in New York, the first five installments appearing as volume I in 1819 and the final two as a second volume in 1820. The book was reprinted in London in 1820 by John Miller (vol. I) and John Murray (vol. II).
20. "National Literature," *Salmagundi: 2nd Series* (1835), II, 265–72. This revised edition is the accessible version today.
21. *NAR* 12 (Apr. 1821): 466–88.
22. *Essays on Various Subjects of Taste, Morals, and National Policy* (1822), 141–66.

23. *A Discourse Concerning the Influence of America on the Mind* (1823), 19.
24. The speech is reprinted in Joseph L. Blau, ed., *American Philosophic Addresses, 1700–1900* (1946), 64–93.
25. See John C. McCloskey, "The Campaign of Periodicals after the War of 1812 for National American Literature," *PMLA* 50 (Mar. 1935): 262–73.
26. Quoted from Neal's autobiography in Fred L. Pattee's edition of Neal's *American Writers* (1937), 16. I am following Pattee in the summary that follows.
27. In *The Complete Writings of James Russell Lowell* (1904), XII, 55.
28. See Godwin, ed., *Prose Writings,* I, 24–35.
29. The manuscript was published for a first time in *Every Other Saturday* 1 (12 Apr. 1884): 116–17.
30. The *Notions* were published in two volumes in 1828 in both London (Henry Colburn) and Philadelphia (Carey, Lea and Carey). My pages refer to the Colburn printing.
31. Robert E. Spiller, *Fenimore Cooper: Critic of His Times* (1931), 127. RS adds that some forty such notions-of-the-American books had been published in England since 1800 and their popularity was yet to peak. In 1830 to 1835, twenty-five more were "written by all classes of men and women, from ex-barbers to clergymen, and reviewed at length and with enthusiasm by the leading journals of England."
32. For a more extensive if not always clearly organized treatment of this subject, see Benjamin T. Spencer, *The Quest for Nationality: An American Literary Campaign* (1957).
33. *An American Dictionary of the English Language* (1828), 2 vols., and *Dissertations* (1789).
34. "American Literature," reprinted in Edwin H. Cady and Harry H. Clark, eds., *Whittier on Writers and Writing* (1950), 24–26.
35. Untitled review, *The Christian Examiner* 36 (Jan. 1830), 269–95. In *The Works of William E. Channing* (1841–43), I, 243–80, the essay is titled "Remarks on National Literature."

Chapter 4. Rufus W. Griswold and the Collectors' Marketplace

1. *The Complete Writings,* XII, 37.
2. *Recollections,* II, 382.
3. In addition to my own inspection of the *Columbian,* I have profited from William J. Free, *The Columbian Magazine and American Literary Nationalism* (1968). Also useful are Earl L. Bradsher, *Mathew Carey: Editor, Author, Publisher* (1912); David Kaser, *Messrs. Carey & Lea of Philadelphia: A Study in the History of the Booktrade* (1957); H. Milton Ellis, *Joseph Dennie and His Circle: A Study in American Literature from 1792 to 1812* (1915); and, of course, Frank L. Mott, *A History of American Magazines* (1938), vol. I (1741–1850).

4. *Recollections,* II, 291.
5. *NAR* 29 (Oct. 1829): 487–96.
6. *Recollections,* II, 289. Goodrich's memory is faulty when he recalls that the review of Kettell appeared in Walsh's Philadelphia newspaper, the *National Gazette.* It is found, instead, in his new *American Quarterly Review* 6 (Sept. 1829): 240–62.
7. *Recollections,* II, 259–64. Ralph Thompson's *American Literary Annuals and Gift Books, 1825–1865* (1936) has been reprinted (1967). The 469 annotated works in his "Catalog" (pp. 102–63) have been microfilmed by Research Publications, Inc. (1966), which has also published *Indices* to Thompson's list and the microfilms, compiled by E. Bruce Kirkham and John W. Fink (1975). The most reliable and succinct account of *Godey's* is in Mott, *A History of American Magazines,* I, 580–94.
8. H. M. Griswold, *Passages from the Correspondence and Other Papers of Rufus W. Griswold* (1898), 167–72, 204–6.
9. *RW,* 195.
10. *Passages from the Correspondence,* 223–24. Hassold, 93n–94n, conveniently summarizes the reviews of *Prose Writers.*
11. *The Literary World* 1 (20 Mar. 1847): 149–51.

Chapter 5. The Duyckincks among the Young Americans, the Knickerbockers, and Others

1. John Stafford, *The Literary Criticism of "Young America": A Study of the Relationship of Politics and Literature 1837–1850* (1952), 82.
2. *RW,* 12.
3. These ramblings are collected in his *Knick-Knacks from an Editor's Table* (1852).
4. Reprinted in *Prose Writings of William Cullen Bryant,* II, 389–90, cited previously.
5. "Critical Notices," *Southern Literary Messenger* 2 (Apr. 1836): 326–36. Poe was editor of the *Messenger* from Dec. 1835 to Jan. 1837.
6. The *Graham's* review appeared in June 1842 and the *Miscellany* in Nov. Sources for the quotations in this paragraph are most conveniently discovered in James A. Harrison, ed., *The Complete Works of Edgar Allan Poe* (1902), XI, 124–26, 147–160; XV, 32.
7. In Philadelphia *Saturday Museum* of 28 Jan. 1843, reprinted in *Complete Works,* XI, 220–43. Modern Poe critics agree that this review is not his; or at best, he had merely a small hand in it.
8. See *Complete Works,* XI, 157.
9. The full story of Poe's journalistic friends and foes is recounted in Sidney P. Moss, *Poe's Literary Battles* (1963).
10. The literati sketches cited are in *Godey's Lady's Book* (vol. 32, 1846) as follows: Briggs (May, pp. 199–200), Clark (Sept., p. 132), Hoffman (Oct., pp. 157–58; the passage on Clark is on p. 158), and Duyckinck (July, pp. 15–16). The entire series appears in vol. 15 of the *Complete Works* (1902).

11. Mary C. Oliphant, Alfred T. Odell, and T. C. Eaves, eds., *The Letters of William Gilmore Simms* (1953), II, 70, 107, 115, 131, 225, and 582.

12. C. Hugh Holman, ed., *Views and Reviews in American Literature, History, and Fiction,* first series (1962), 7–28. Simms was responding here to one more of the perennial Phi Beta Kappa addresses on the subject, this time Alexander Meek's "Americanism in Literature" delivered at the University of Georgia on 8 Aug. 1844.

13. The overall reception is summarized in Holman, xxx–xxxii.

14. "American Literature: Its Position in the Present Time, and Prospects for the Future" in *Papers on Literature and Art* (1846), reprinted in Mason Wade, ed., *The Writings of Margaret Fuller* (1941), 358–88.

15. The opinion is cited from an unpublished diary of 1843 in the Duyckinck papers, New York Public Library, by Stafford, 32.

16. Quoted by Miller, *RW,* 243. The sketch of Poe appeared in *Graham's* 27 (Feb. 1845): 49–53.

17. *The Complete Writings* (1904), XII, 1–87.

18. Quoted in Stafford, 2.

19. "German Writers: Heinrich Heine," *Graham's* 20 (Mar. 1842): 134.

20. See Samuel Longfellow, ed., *The Works of Henry Wadsworth Longfellow* (1886–91), VIII, 366–68.

21. *NAR* 69 (July 1849): 196–215; Miller, *RW,* 265, 256.

22. Quoted in Miller, *RW,* 89.

23. See *Literary World* 7 (17, 24 Aug. 1850): 125–27, 145–47. The air of rural Massachusetts further to the east in the early 1850s was also circulating intimations of American literary genius closely tied to our climate and landscape. In his journal of 2 Feb. 1852, Thoreau recorded his own sense of the matter: "We shall be more imaginative; we shall be clearer, as our sky, bluer, fresher; broader and more comprehensive in our understanding, like our plains; our intellect on a grander scale, like our thunder and lightning, our rivers and our lakes, and mountains and forests." Rephrased, the notation appeared in "Walking" ten years later.

24. See the preface to the *Cyclopaedia* (1855), vii, ix. Though Jared Sparks's *Library of American Biography* (25 vols., 1834–47) was not mentioned in the preface, the Duyckincks acknowledged Sparks and his work in II, 165–67.

25. *RW,* 329.

26. *NAR* 82 (Apr. 1856): 324.

Chapter 6. Moses Coit Tyler and the Rise of American Literary History

1. *A History of American Literature, 1607–1765,* 131, 393. Hereafter, *HAL.* My text is the generally available reissue of the two-volume 1878 work in one volume (1949).

2. See Howard M. Jones, *The Life of Moses Coit Tyler* (1933), 47. Hereafter, HJ. This valuable biography is based on a dissertation at

Michigan by Thomas E. Casady that Jones prepared for publication after this young scholar's premature death. Jones also wrote the sketch of Tyler in *The Dictionary of American Biography* (1936). Tyler's daughter, Jessica Tyler Austin, selected valuable primary documents in her *Moses Coit Tyler, 1835–1900: Selections from His Letters and Diaries* (1911). Hereafter, Austin. More correspondence and papers are deposited in the Bentley Historical Library, University of Michigan.

3. *Autobiography* (1905), I, 26–29.

4. Austin, 24–66; HJ, 49–115.

5. Norman Foerster's sustained critique, *The American State University: Its Relation to Democracy* (1937), will be discussed in chap. 19.

6. Lewis, 58–76. Gilder's speech, "The Colleges and American Literature," is in *The Critic* 12 (2 July 1977): 1.

7. Lewis, 95–96. HJ, p. 127, also assumes this "first" for Hart.

8. Lewis, 95; Hite, 3. Hart's *Manual* has been reproduced by Johnson Reprint Corporation (1965). In his introduction, Eberhard Olsen seems unaware of MT's review and credits E. P. Whipple, in his centennial sketch for *Harper's* (cited below in note 19), for writing the first scholarly or critical notice of Hart's book (p. vi).

9. *The Christian Union* 7 (5 Mar. 1873): 188; Lowell, "On a Certain Condescension in Foreigners," *AtM* 23 (Jan. 1869): 82–94.

10. "Underwood's American Literature," *The Christian Union* 7 (25 June 1873): 504. MT's account of his months of "dreary labor" with Morley's *Manual* is in Austin, 103–7.

11. "Curriculum," 269.

12. HJ, 156, 157.

13. Preface to *HAL,* xvi.

14. Bibb, 155, 152. A number of these early books are fortunately accessible to literary scholars today through microfilm distribution.

15. Nichol expanded his essay for Scottish publication as *American Literature: An Historical Sketch, 1620–1880* (1882). I resist the temptation to discuss this foreign view of American writers because Nichol seems not to have made much impact on American scholarship.

16. *Athenaeum,* no. 375 (3 Jan. 1835): 9–13; 377 (17 Jan. 1835): 52–55; 380 (7 Feb. 1835): 105–7; 382 (21 Feb. 1835): 147–50.

17. Flint's sketches are in the following numbers of the *Athenaeum* for 1835: 401 (4 July): 511–12; 402 (11 July): 526–27; 405 (1 Aug.): 584–86; 407 (15 Aug.): 624–25; 409 (29 Aug.): 666–68; 411 (12 Sept.): 696–98; 412 (19 Sept.): 714–16; 416 (17 Oct.): 782–83; 417 (24 Oct.): 802–3; 418 (31 Oct.): 817–19; and 419 (7 Nov.): 831–32. To these early essays by Flint and Willis can be added two sketches in American literary history in 1837, one by the Rev. Royal Robbins as an addendum to Robert Chambers's *History of the English Language and Literature* (1837), and the other by Judge Henry St. George Tucker (president of the Supreme Court of Virginia), "Discourse on American Literature," an address full of Emer-

sonian optimism, to the Lyceum at Charlottesville, Va., on Dec. 1837, reprinted in Thomas W. White's *Southern Literary Messenger* 4 (Feb. 1838): 81–88. I am indebted to Hassold, 69, for locating these essays of Robbins and Tucker.

18. Tuckerman himself, with thirty-nine other writers, was soon sketched in still another quasi-history before MT. The unsigned series, "American Authors," ran in the *Christian Intelligencer* from 8 May 1856 to 28 May 1857. Obviously, editors of the *Intelligencer* felt that the Duyckincks' *Cyclopaedia*, which appeared scarcely a half year earlier, had not sated the American reader's appetite for more sketches. (I am grateful to Professor Hershel Parker for calling my attention to these columns.)

19. Two substantial and judicious essays on American literary history that may have goaded MT's competitive spirit were by lecturer-critic E. P. Whipple: "The First Century of the Republic" and "American Literature" in *Harper's Monthly* 52 (Feb. and Mar. 1876): 401–20, 514–33. They were collected in his posthumous *American Literature and Other Papers* with an introductory note by John G. Whittier (1887).

20. Austin, 95–102; HJ, 175–87. MT corrected various errors when Putnam produced the editions of 1879, 1881, and 1897.

21. FP writes that when MT went to Cornell, "he insisted that his title should be 'Professor of American History and Literature,' and while he offered no courses bearing the name American Literature, he announced at the start that in all his courses he intended to 'use American literature as a means of illustrating the several periods of American history.'" See "Curriculum," 269.

22. Austin, 42–43. In 1889, Tyler briefly considered writing a series of historical novels, beginning in Gov. Berkeley's time (Austin, p. 235). MT's great successor Parrington did write an unfinished novel, we discover in Chapter 17 below.

23. The reviewer in *AtM* quoted felicitous touches but was also wearied by "a little excess of picturesque phrase." Still, he praised Tyler's enthusiastic and critical spirit. So did the critic for *Scribner's*, but he complained that Tyler maintained a high pitch so constantly as to render some of his enthusiasms ineffective. A. R. McDonough wrote in *NAR* that Tyler's style "deserves praise for clearness and dignity, though its use of epithets is sometimes a little hasardé." See *AtM* 43 (Mar. 1879): 405–7; *Scribner's* 17 (Mar. 1879): 757–58; and *NAR* 128 (Apr. 1879): 444–45.

24. In his review for *Na* 28 (2 Jan. 1879): 16–17, Thomas W. Higginson considered MT's advocacy of Roger Williams injudicious but called the rest of the book "truly admirable both in design and in general execution" and with other critics, enjoyed the fresh and vigorous style.

Chapter 7. Charles F. Richardson and the Ferment of the Eighties

1. Volume I appeared in early 1887; volume II followed in early 1889. Page references will be given in my text.
2. Lowes, "The Modern Language Association and Humane Scholarship," *PMLA* 48 (Supplement, 1933): 1399–1408.
3. See especially J. Churton Collins, *The Study of English Literature: A Plea for Its Recognition and Organization at the Universities* (1891). For Trilling, see "Literature and Power," *Kenyon Review* 2 (Autumn 1940): 434. The year after Arnold's address, Columbia's George P. Marsh delivered "An Apology for the Study of English," a prewar plea that our universities institute a new curriculum in English language and literature guided by the "general philological science" currently applied to classical languages. See Theodore W. Dwight and George P. Marsh, *Inaugural Addresses* (1859), 59–93.
4. For general postwar background, see C. Alphonso Smith, "The Work of the Modern Language Association of America," *PMLA* 14 (1899): 240–56. This was Smith's Presidential Address to the Central Division of the MLA in Omaha, Dec. 1898. Also helpful is Frank Aydelotte (professor of English at Massachusetts Institute of Technology), "The History of English as a College Subject in the United States," in *The Oxford Stamp and Other Essays* (1917), 174–98, and Nelson A. Crawford, "American University Presses," *American Mercury* 18 (Oct. 1929): 210–14.
5. *PMLA* 3 (1887): 238–44, li–liii.
6. *History: Professional Scholarship in America,* 37.
7. Other regional affiliates of MLA were slow to form: the South Atlantic in 1928, South Central in 1940, Rocky Mountain in 1947, Midwest in 1960, and Northeast in 1971.
8. "American Classics in School," *AtM* 60 (July 1887): 85–91.
9. *PMLA* 5 (1890): 5–22.
10. Lewis, 110, 119–20.
11. Lewis, 110; FP, *The First Century of American Literature, 1770–1870* (1935), v.
12. FP, "Curriculum," 269; Lewis, 116, 114, 119; Hite, 4.
13. Lewis, 111–20; FP, "Curriculum," 269; Hite, 3–4.
14. Austin, 235.
15. The archives of Baker Library at Dartmouth have preserved three boxes of Richardson papers and memorabilia. Folders 5 and 6 of box 3 contain photographs and newspaper clippings, including President Nichols's remarks in the *Boston Post,* 9 Oct. 1913.
16. Pattee, *The First Century,* v.
17. Reviews cited are in *Na* 44 (24 Feb. 1887): 172; *Dial* 7 (Feb. 1887): 343–45; and *AtM* 59 (June 1887): 847–49. Bibb names George Woodberry the *Na* reviewer (p. 192).
18. See *Na* 48 (17 Jan. 1889): iii.
19. *Na* 48 (14 Feb. 1889): 143–44; and Edward P. Anderson, *Dial* 9 (Jan. 1889): 235–37.
20. Diary entry, 3 Jan. 1889, in Austin, 235.

Chapter 8. Barrett Wendell in a Turn-of-the-Century Harvest

1. For Howells's alternative title, see *NAR* 172 (Apr. 1901): 628. Years later, Howells apologized for the "very abominable spirit" of the review and BW graciously understood. See Howells to BW, 11 Sept. 1914, and BW to Howells, 13 Sept. 1914, in Mildred Howells, ed., *Life in Letters of William Dean Howells* (1928), II, 336–37. Pattee's comment is in "Call for a Literary Historian," *American Mercury* 2 (June 1924): 134.
2. In his *Barrett Wendell* (1975), Robert T. Self speculates, on the other hand, that because BW's literary history was received "merely as the conservative, anglophile, provincial history of New England literature," he may have "helped to solidify the professional attitude against American literature in the universities" (p. 10).
3. *Critical Woodcuts* (1926), 254–55.
4. *Barrett Wendell and His Letters* (1924), 39–40.
5. "Barrett Wendell," *American Mercury* 5 (Aug. 1925): 448–55.
6. See William R. Castle, Jr., "Barrett Wendell—Teacher," in *Essays in Memory of Barrett Wendell, by His Assistants* (1924, reissued 1967), 5, 8, 9; the chapter "Teacher of the Fine Arts at Harvard" in my *Charles Eliot Norton* (1959); and Santayana, *Persons and Places: The Middle Span* (1945), 170–72.
7. In *Penn State Yankee* (posthumously published, 1953), 268, and quoted in James J. Martine, *Fred Lewis Pattee and American Literature* (1973), 58.
8. See Lewis, 133–53.
9. Whitman, "Have We a National Literature?" *NAR* 152 (Mar. 1891): 332–38; Torrey, "The Demand for an American Literature," *AtM* 79 (Apr. 1897): 569–73; Mabie, "American Literature and American Nationality," *Forum* 26 (Jan. 1899): 633–40; Johnston, "The True American Spirit in Literature," *AtM* 84 (July 1899): 29–35; Moore, "Tendencies of American Literature in the Closing Quarter of the Century," *Dial* 29 (1 Nov. 1900): 295–97; Triggs, "A Century of American Poetry," *Forum* 30 (Jan. 1901): 630–40.
10. "The Study of American Literature in Colleges," *Andover Review* 18 (July–Dec. 1892): 154–62.
11. See Lewis, 159. But he reports that in a letter of 11 July 1939, Arthur H. Quinn wrote that he gave the "first purely graduate course in American literature" in 1905 at Pennsylvania. It was titled "Forms and Movements in American Literature" (p. 199n).
12. Woodress, 66, 30, 72, and 19.
13. Bibb, 263.
14. *Graduate Education in the United States* (1960), 14, 16. See, too, George Santayana's critical reminiscence of Harvard in this transitional era, "The Academic Environment," *Character and Opinion in the United States* (1920), chap. 2.
15. Shepherd, "English Philology and English Literature in American Universities" and "The Teaching of Literature Once More," *SR* 1

(Feb. 1893): 153–60; and 2 (Nov. 1893): 105–14; Henneman, "The Study of English in the South," *SR* 2 (Feb. 1894): 180–97, and "English in the Southern Universities," Payne, 163–66; McKellar, "College English," *SR* 5 (Oct. 1897): 479–85.

16. For a fuller discussion of this publishing for the school market, see Bibb, chap. 5. She lists and discusses forty-one books in all the three categories in the years from 1890 to 1912. (My own reading of most of these volumes occupied a long summer, but the bulk of those copious notes, and others on the contemporary reviews of these books, must now be relinquished to a future study.) Another useful work is Burt L. Dunmire's "The Development of American Literature Textbooks Used in the United States from 1870 to 1952" (diss., Univ. of Pittsburgh, 1954), a study of books at the secondary level. He reported that before 1930, only two of his sixty-six texts were written by high school English teachers; from 1930 to 1952, however, one-third were so authored (p. 25).

17. "Curriculum," 268; and Martine, 13.

18. Ibid., 269.

19. This genetic history is condensed from the diaries in Austin, 105–287.

20. "Moses Coit Tyler," *Annual Report of the American Historical Association* 1 (1901): 189–95. For the mixed reception of the *LHAR*, see Herbert L. Osgood, *Political Science Quarterly* 13 (Mar. 1898): 41–59; Charles K. Adams, *AtM* 82 (Aug. 1898): 174–89; and four reviews by Paul Leicester Ford: *Na* 64 (10 June 1897): 438–39, and 66 (3 Mar. 1898): 171–72; *American Historical Review* 2 (July 1897): 738–40, and 3 (Jan. 1898): 375–77.

21. Howe, *Barrett Wendell and His Letters*, 136.

22. Ibid., 112–13.

23. And after he had written this wistful tribute to the age of Emerson, BW soon wrote to William James, longing for the truly confident certainties of an even earlier time: "I love the memory of Cotton Mather; and should be happier in a world that hadn't been graced by Channing or Emerson or ———." (25 Oct. 1900, in Mark A. De Wolfe Howe, ed., "A Packet of Wendell-James Letters," *Scribner's Magazine* 84 [Dec. 1928]: 677–78.)

24. In his textbook version for the schools, *A History of Literature in America* (in collaboration with Chester Noyes Greenough, 1904), BW permitted some capsule impressions of James, Howells, Norris, Wharton, and Bret Harte, together with an extended discussion of Mark Twain as both an indigenous humorist and a careful artist.

25. Castle, *Essays in Memory of Barrett Wendell*, 4–10.

26. See the *Dial* 29 (10 Dec. 1900): 485–87, probably written by editor William M. Payne, who signed the very similar review in *AtM* 87 (Mar. 1901): 411–18; Gates, "Impressionism and Appreciation," *AtM* 86 (July 1900): 73–84, reprinted as the final essay in his *Studies and Appreciations* (1900); and Gates, *The Critic* 38 (4 Apr. 1901): 341–44.

27. See WPT's posthumous tribute, "Moses Coit Tyler," *Forum* 31 (Aug. 1901): 750–58.

Chapter 9. The CHAL (Volume I) Appears

1. *Boston Evening Transcript,* 17 Nov. 1917, part III, 8, and 8 Dec. part III, 8; *NYTBR,* 25 Nov. 1917, 497; Putnam to VD, 27 Nov. 1917, in CVD-PU.
2. *Outlook* 117 (19 Dec. 1917): 653; *Dial* 63 (20 Dec. 1917): 646; the *Literary Digest* 56 (12 Jan. 1918): 34–35; the *American Review of Reviews,* 57 (Feb. 1918): 216; and the *Springfield Republican,* 2 Dec. 1917, 19.
3. *Na* 106 (14 Feb. 1918): 183–85; Leonard to VD, 12 May 1918, in CVD-PU. The *Nation* index identifying anonymous contributors, compiled by Daniel C. Haskell (1963), extends only through 1917.
4. *Times Literary Supplement,* 23 May 1918, 237–38.

Chapter 10. And Then Volume II

1. WPT to VD, 25 Aug. 1917. All correspondence in this chapter is in CVD-PU.
2. JE to VD, 10 Sept. 1917.
3. U.S. postal card, WPT to VD, 14 Sept. 1917. Concerning WPT's comment on Moses's race, VD annotated his correspondence to advise future scholars that WPT joked about Jews only with VD and was not anti-Semitic.
4. WPT to VD, 7, 14 Aug. 1918.
5. Martine, 13. And see "Two Text-Books," *Na* 63 (27 Aug. 1896): 163–64. The reviewer (C. M. Colby) complained that Pattee urged the epithet immortal on too many American authors but then slighted Holmes and Higginson.
6. *Penn State Yankee,* 271, quoted in Martine, 64.
7. *Literary Digest* 60 (8 Mar. 1919): 42; *The Outlook* 121 (2 Apr. 1919): 580–81.
8. Vol. 66 (19 Apr. 1919): 428.
9. *American Historical Review* 24 (July 1919): 702–4.
10. Vol. 109 (30 Aug. 1919): 309–10.
11. *Spectator* 122 (26 Apr. 1919): 529–30; *New Statesman* 13 (26 Apr. 1919): 97–98.
12. *The Athenaeum,* no. 4643 (25 Apr. 1919): 236–37. The review owed more than a little to Eliot's recent "The Hawthorne Aspect," in the *Little Review* 5 (Aug. 1918): 48–53.

Chapter 11. Interim: Some Insurgent Critics versus "the Professors"

1. NF's comments are in *Toward Standards* (1930), 42–44.
2. FP, "Curriculum," 272. This "consciousness" may have been only

a myopic nationalism heedless of new international obligations, Agnes Repplier suggested in "Americanism," *AtM* 117 (Mar. 1916): 289–97. She detected in this chauvinism a hangover of the literary nationalism rekindled by the centennial of 1876. But Pattee countered this argument in another article where he viewed the teaching of post–Civil War authors, especially the nationally minded ones, as particularly beneficial during World War I. See "Americanism through American Literature," *Educational Review* 57 (Apr. 1919): 271–76.

3. Lewis, 238–42; Hite, 22–23.

4. Lewis, 218. Perry's *The American Mind* (1912) showed how seriously he was probing the native traits, Emersonian and otherwise, in our literature.

5. Wesley First, ed., *University on the Heights* (1969), 182; JH, *SSW,* 22.

6. FP, "Curriculum," 271; Martine, 51; Lewis, 199n, 225, 228.

7. FP, ibid.; Hite, 6, 8, 17, 23; JH, *SSW,* 23.

8. Lewis, 218, 226; Hite, 5, 9; DeVoto, "The Maturity of American Literature," *SRL* 27 (5 Aug. 1944): 15.

9. Lewis, 224; Hite, 13. The Univ. of Washington data come from my own inspection of the catalogs. Professor George Arms, Univ. of New Mexico, wrote some of this information on Armes to me on 7 Nov. 1977 as he described this distant and rather quirky relative ("as you gather, the connection doesn't overwhelm me").

10. See Woodress. I have not included the few theses written on American literature in departments other than English.

11. Mae J. Evans, "How Much Work Is Done in American Literature in the High Schools, and by What Methods?" *School Review* 11 (Oct. 1903): 647–49.

12. Berdan, "American Literature and the High Schools," *Arena* 29 (Apr. 1903): 337–44; Pierce, "A Survey of Contemporary American Literature," *Arena* 38 (Dec. 1907): 619–25.

13. Tucker, "What is Wrong with American Literature?" *South Atlantic Quarterly* 14 (Jan. 1915): 47–52; Peckman, "Lopsided Realism," ibid. 15 (July 1916): 276–81; Björkman "An Open Letter to President Wilson on Behalf of American Literature," *Century* 87 (Apr. 1914): 887–89.

14. Wager, "Democracy and Literature," *AtM* 116 (Oct. 1915): 479–86; Gerould, "The Extirpation of Culture," ibid., 445–55; Boynton, "American Neglect of American Literature," *Na* 102 (4 May 1916): 478–80. An earlier article that stressed the obligation of professors to reverse the decline of our modern literature by developing a discriminating taste in their students was George F. Parker's "Some American Literary Needs," *SR* 18 (Jan. 1910): 1–22.

15. The honors school of English at Oxford and at Cambridge is treated in an interesting context by Alvin B. Kernan, *The Imaginary Library* (1982), 92, 94–95. See also Dexter, *A History of Education in the United States* (1904); Thwing, *A History of Higher Educa-*

tion in America (1906); and Cook, *The Higher Study of English* (1906).

16. Bourne, *NR* 6 (1 Apr. 1916): 245–47; Mather, "University Teaching of English," *Na* 83 (8 Nov. 1906): 387.

17. The lecture at Columbia, 9 Mar. 1910, was published by the university in 1911 (35 pp.) and reappeared in *Creative Criticism: Essays on the Unity of Genius and Taste* (1911).

18. Spingarn's review was in the *Journal of Philosophy, Psychology, and Scientific Methods* 10 (4 Dec. 1913): 693–96. For Babbitt's reply, see ibid. 11 (9 Apr. 1914): 215–18.

19. *Dial* 64 (11 Apr. 1918): 337–41.

20. *Van Wyck Brooks: An Autobiography*, with a foreword by John Hall Wheelock and introduction by Malcolm Cowley (1965), 111–23, 157. This is a three-in-one volume that includes Brooks's previous volumes of autobiography: the pre-1920s *Scenes and Portraits* (1954), the 1920s of *Days of the Phoenix* (1957), and subsequently *From the Shadow of the Mountain* (1957).

21. See 4, 24, 34. Subsequent pages will be indicated in parentheses after the quotations.

22. See Ernest Gruening's sketch of Macy in the *Dictionary of American Biography* (1933), XII, 177–78.

23. *TW*, 167.

24. *History of a Literary Radical and Other Papers*, with an introduction by Van Wyck Brooks (1920), 26–30, 64–66. This portrait of "The Professor" originally appeared in *NR* 13 (10 July 1915): 257–58.

25. "Suggestions for Teachers of American Literature," *Educational Review* 21 (Jan. 1901): 12–14.

26. "Our Cultural Humility," *AtM* 114 (Oct. 1914): 505–7.

27. Originally in *AtM* of July 1916, titled "Trans-National America," the comments and quotations can be found in *History of a Literary Radical*, 260–65. For a counterstatement that immigrants should recognize their national obligation and identity, see Agnes Repplier's "Americanism" in the Mar. 1916 issue of *AtM*, cited previously.

28. Mencken foolishly berated Pattee (a professor "somewhere in Pennsylvania") for stupidity in his *A History of American Literature since 1870* (1915): "From end to end of his fat tome I am unable to find the slightest mention of Dreiser" (p. 134). Had Mencken read the front end of Pattee's pioneering history, he would have known why Dreiser would not be there. Pattee elected to consider only the writers whose distinctive work appeared before 1892.

29. Mencken to FP, 2 June 1924, in Martine, 114.

30. The review, "H. G. Wells and the Victorians," *Na* 100 (20 May 1915): 558–61, was reprinted as "The Utopian Naturalism of H. G. Wells" with the subheading "(Before the War)"; it was then followed by an addendum, "(Since the War)." The wartime quotation here is in *On Contemporary Literature* (1917), 75. Other page numbers appear in my text.

31. Years later, after Mencken reviewed (favorably) VD's autobiography, *Three Worlds,* he wrote to VD that it was SS's slurs against the innocently nonpolitical Dreiser rather than himself that chiefly angered Mencken and that SS had no evidence against Dreiser for such pro-Germanic accusations. (Mencken to VD, 1 Sept. 1936, in CVD-PU.)

32. "Beautifying American Literature," *Na* 105 (29 Nov. 1917): 593–94. SS was sufficiently pumped with chauvinistic war fever that two days after this review appeared, he delivered a tirade, not so well known, against Mencken, Nietzsche, et al. This paper to the National Council of Teachers of English, titled "America and Allied Ideals," was then issued as pamphlet 12 in the War Information Series (Wash., D.C.: Committee on Public Information, 1918).

33. Mencken may have been deliberately inaccurate in suggesting that Brownell was on the Amherst faculty; he did arrive on two occasions to receive an honorary doctorate from the college. Mencken noted on p. 130 that Sherman was born in Iowa, and he persisted in giving Iowa as Sherman's academic address, apparently a demeaning tactic like his previously locating Pattee obscurely "somewhere in Pennsylvania."

34. Written under the pseudonym Search-Light, "A Kind Man," *New Yorker* 1 (24 Oct. 1925): 11–12.

35. For the fullest, or at least the most intimate, understanding of Frank's early success and perplexing later decline, see Alan Trachtenberg, ed., *Memoirs of Waldo Frank,* with an introduction by Lewis Mumford (1973).

36. Why, asked Frank in a footnote, had Frost been honored in England before his own country recognized him, as was the case, too, with Whitman, Dreiser, Masters, and Anderson? "There is really no mystery in all this," he replied. "England has no repressive and pervasive academies to make her deaf . . . [when] the unregenerate American utterance is heard" (p. 159n). Obviously, Frank was not acquainted with Oxford and Cambridge.

37. Elliott, "New Poetry and New America," *Na* 107 (30 Nov. 1918): 652–54.

38. George Santayana's stimulating British lectures on American character during this second decade of the century, though nonliterary, nicely complemented the young insurgents in his arguing that our intellectual life and philosophical opinions were rooted in the academic timidity of a genteel tradition. See especially the last three chapters of *Character and Opinion in the United States* (1920).

39. When *CHAL* vols. III and IV appeared in 1921, Mencken again welcomed the vastly assembled materials although they, too, awaited the illumination of an interpretive and critical intelligence. See the *Smart Set* 65 (June 1921): 138–41.

Chapter 12. The CHAL *Completed*

1. 28 June 1919. Again, all correspondence is in CVD-PU unless indicated otherwise.
2. WPT to VD, 11 July and 30 Aug. 1920. VD's comment appears on the second letter.
3. Noted by VD on WPT's letter of 4 Apr. 1921.
4. WPT to VD, 18 June 1921.
5. This cursory and somewhat belittling view of popular minor figures should not have surprised readers of Boynton's recent *A History of American Literature* (1919), which he organized not by periods—except the colonial—but largely in chapters on major authors. Subordinate figures had been assiduously weeded out.
6. The critical responses in the preceding paragraphs appeared chronologically as follows: Chew, *Na* 112 (13 Apr. 1921): 552–53; Macy, *NR* 27 (8 June 1921): 52–53; Bronson, *American Historical Review* 26 (July 1921): 812–13; HC, *Literary Review* (of the N.Y. *Evening Post*), 23 July 1921, 4; Phelps, *NYTBR,* 4 Sept. 1921, 16, 24; and NF, *Freeman* 4 (28 Dec. 1921): 380–81. One of the first reviews, again in the *Boston Evening Transcript* (12 Mar. 1921, Part III, 7), though merely descriptive, made a prophetic suggestion: VD should amplify his "Later Novel" chapter and write an extended study of the American novel. In fact, his genre history was imminent. For Mencken's review, see Chap. 11, n. 39. British reception was strangely indifferent this time, and when the *TLS* finally reviewed the volumes on 8 Dec. 1921 (p. 806), the result was essentially the critic's own appreciation of Howells, Twain, and James, with no judgment of the success or demerits of the completed history. Such indifference appears to have been reciprocated by scholars of American literature in the early 1920s, who were caring less and less what English critics had to say about our books and authors.
7. Riley to VD, 28 Feb., 23 July, and 8 Aug. 1918; 8 Jan., 27 Mar., and 7 Nov. 1920. All personal correspondence cited on this episode is in CVD-PU.
8. "Stop Sale of Book Deriding Mrs. Eddy," *New York Times,* 19 Apr. 1921, 5, 12.
9. Riley to VD, 22 May 1921; VD to Riley, 1 June 1921.
10. WPT to VD, 18 June 1921.
11. "Correspondence: Professor Riley's Article on Christian Science," *NR* 27 (22 June 1921): 14.
12. In "Correspondence": Grabo, 27 (29 June 1921): 143, and Cohen (20 July): 220.
13. Riley to VD, 26 July 1921; "Correspondence: Mr. Riley and the Christian Scientists," *NR* 28 (7 Sept. 1921): 49.

Chapter 13. A New Era: The Profession Establishes a Political Voice

1. "Americanism through American Literature," *Educational Review* 57 (Apr. 1919): 271–76.
2. "Tradition and Freedom," *Na* 111 (8 Dec. 1920): 651–52. Pertinent also is Lewisohn's "America in Europe," *SRL* 1 (9 May 1925): 737–38.
3. "A Question of Honesty," *Freeman* 2 (2 Feb. 1921), 486–87.
4. *TW*, 108.
5. Walker, 318–476. Lewisohn's comments appeared in a letter to Walker, 4 Oct. 1941, 427.
6. The quotations appeared in Helena H. Smith, "Professor's Progress," *New Yorker* 3 (10 Dec. 1927): 29; and William S. Knockerbocker, "John Erskine," *SR* 35 (Apr.–June 1927): 167. See also *JE's MCP*, 341–45, and *My Life as a Teacher* (1948), 165–75.
7. But as the anonymous critic in *Freeman* had recently puzzled, in "Professor Sherman's Tradition," how could SS extol the traditional moral roots of America at the same time that he celebrated the uprooters—Franklin, Emerson, Thoreau, and Mark Twain? See *Freeman* 2 (27 Oct. 1920): 152.
8. *The Genius of America* (1923), 218, 219, 230.
9. *Critical Woodcuts* (1926), xii–xiii, 11, 242.
10. *The Main Stream* (1927), 143–44.
11. *TW*, 171, 144, 149.
12. *TW*, 196.
13. The copy of RS's letter is dated 3 Mar. 1939 and the secretary's reply 8 Mar. 1939. Both are in LHUS-UP.
14. *TW*, 195–96.
15. Manly's address is in the appendix of *PMLA* 36 (1921): xlvi–lx. See also JH to Robert Falk, 26 Mar. 1954, in ALG-UW, and *SSW*, 24. In 1929, Fred B. Millett (Chicago) expanded the Manly and Rickert volume from 188 to 378 pp. and supplied an "Introduction to Contemporary American Literature" (pp. 3–99).
16. Appendix of *PMLA* 37 (1922): xxx–xxxi.
17. "Proceedings," *PMLA* 38 (1923): xxviii.
18. JH to Falk, 26 Mar. 1954, ALG-UW; *SSW*, 24–26. Martine, 106–7, provides the title of FP's paper and notes that it became the published "American Literature in the College Curriculum" and "The Old Professor of English: An Autopsy" (p. 124n). RS's report in *PMLA* 39 (1924), xxxix, merely referred to a paper.
19. RS to JH, 25 Nov. 1927, in JBH-DU.
20. Leisy mimeographed memorandum to ALG, 6 Mar. 1927, and Leisy to JH, 20 May 1927, in JBH-DU.
21. Berelson, *Graduate Education in the United States,* 28–29.
22. Snyder to JH, 2 Jan. 1927; Leisy to *JH,* 22 Jan. 1927. Both in ALG-UW.
23. Minutes of both sessions are in ALG-UW.
24. Ibid.

25. As this last sentence indicates, I shall frequently resort to last names as they become familiar in the chapters that follow, and familiar academic addresses will generally not be repeated.

Chapter 14. American Literature in the University: Study and Debate in the 1920s

1. Lewis, 252.
2. In a conversation on 14 June 1977, Durham, North Carolina.
3. Lewis, 270–71, 278–82; Hite, 11.
4. Lewis, 258–64.
5. See Samuel E. Morison, *The Development of Harvard University* (1930), 101.
6. Leisy, "Materials for Investigations in American Literature," *Studies in Philology* 23 (Jan. 1926): 90–115, and 24 (July 1927): 480–83; Leisy and JH, "Doctoral Dissertations in American Literature," *AL* 4 (Jan. 1933): 419–65; Leary, "Doctoral Dissertations in American Literature, 1933–1948," *AL* 20 (May 1948): 169–230; Woodress, passim.
7. *History: Professional Scholarship in America*, 60.
8. Quoted by Berelson, *Graduate Education in the United States*, 18, 19.
9. *SSW*, 30.
10. This report is in *JBH-DU*.
11. KM to RS, 6 Jan. 1928, and the minutes of the Toronto meeting are in ALG-UW.
12. *Autobiography*, 257.
13. *NAR* 209 (June 1919): 781–85. On the pseudonym, see Lewis, 283.
14. *Educational Review* 69 (June 1922): 7–15.
15. *YR* 12 (Apr. 1923): 469–75; and *Points of View* (1924), 80–85.
16. "Curriculum," 272.
17. "American Literature in Colleges and Universities," *School and Society* 23 (27 Feb. 1926): 307–9.
18. *SR* (Apr. 1927): 206–15.
19. HC, *SRL* 3 (8 Jan. 1927): 493, 499; and JH to Leisy, 18 Jan. 1927, in ALG-UW.
20. *American Mercury* 13 (Mar. 1928): 328–31.

Chapter 15. The Reinterpretation of American Literature *(1928)*: *Professional Scholarship after the* CHAL

1. See *PMLA* 38 (1923): 19–25, and 41 (1926): 23, 28.
2. NF explained the ALG paper to Robert Falk, 6 Mar. 1954. In the *PMLA* "Proceedings," 41 (1926): v, the fourth number of the program of English XII in 1925 was given, however, as "The Present State of American Literary History," a discussion led by NF. He attested to a rewriting in a letter to JH, 22 Jan. 1926. For the article,

see *SRL* 2 (3 Apr. 1926): 677–79. All correspondence in this chapter, unless noted otherwise, is in ALG-UW.

3. JH to NF, 14 Jan. and NF to JH, 22 Jan. 1926. JH enlarged on some of these ideas in "The Decay of the Provinces," *SR* 35 (Oct. 1927): 473–87.

4. NF to JH, 21 Jan. 1926.

5. JH to HJ, 16 Oct. 1926.

6. NF to JH, 7 Jan. 1927.

7. NF to JH, 23 Apr. and KM to JH, 5 May 1927.

8. NF to JH, 23 Apr. and Leisy to JH, 28 May 1927. In his review of Parrington's posthumous volume III of *Main Currents in American Thought*, titled *The Beginnings of Critical Realism in America*, NF wrote that VP agreed to write the chapter on realism for the *Reinterpretation* in the year of his Pulitzer, or 1928, and NF realized that the chapter was "virtually an outline of Professor Parrington's third volume." See *SRL* 7 (4 Apr. 1931): 705.

9. Brown to NF, 3 Jan. 1928 and NF to Falk, 6 Mar. 1954. The late substitution of Clark is discussed in NF's report to contributors, 18 Aug. 1928, in JBH-DU. Clark's apology to JH for the hurried writing that brought added labor to JH while reading proofs with Paine—NF had departed for Europe in late 1928—appeared in Clark to JH, 3 Oct. 1928, in JBH-DU.

10. On xi. The full title reads *The Reinterpretation of American Literature: Some contributions toward the understanding of its historical development*, edited by Norman Foerster for the American Literature Group of the Modern Language Association. Other page numbers appear in my text.

11. See *PMLA* 39 (1924): 239–53; Kaufman, *Modern Language Notes* 40 (Apr. 1925): 193–204.

Chapter 16. American Literature *(1929): The Profession Has a Journal*

1. NF to JH, 30 Dec. 1924, in ALG-UW.

2. Pound to JH, 17 Nov. and 18 Dec. 1925; NF to JH, 24 Dec. 1925. All in ALG-UW.

3. Pound to JH, 20 Nov. 1926; Campbell to JH, 20 Jan. 1927. In ALG-UW.

4. Campbell to JH, 6 Dec. 1927; *SSW*, 29–30; KM to JH, 28 Nov. 1927; SW to JH, 23 May 1927. All primary documents in the rest of this chapter are in JBH-DU unless otherwise noted.

5. *SSW*, 27–28; SW to JH, 23 July 1927; FP to JH, 15 Nov. 1927; RS to JH, 25 Nov. 1927; Leisy to JH, 29 Nov. 1927.

6. SW to JH, 9 Dec. 1927. In *SSW* (p. 30), JH referred to a letter received from Prof. Theodore Zender of Brown (recent Yale dissertation on Joel Barlow) who had mentioned to his colleagues that an American literature journal might well be sponsored at Brown.

7. RS's memorandum and the letter to JH are both dated 22 Jan. 1928.
8. RS to JH, 5 Feb. 1928; Soule to RS, 10 Feb. 1928; Rusk to KM (carbon copy sent to RS), 29 Jan. 1928.
9. *SSW*, 31–33.
10. Flowers to RS, 16 Feb. 1928, reprinted in *SSW*, 31; RS to Damon, 18 Feb.; RS to Flowers, 20 Feb.; RS to Committee on Publications, 20 Feb.; JH to RS, 21 Feb.; RS to JH (telegram), 24 Feb.; JH to Rusk, 21 Feb.; Rusk to JH, 24 Feb. 1928.
11. RS to JH, 3 Mar. 1928 (regarding the previous day's meeting of the committee), and RS's memorandum and final report to the ALG as chairman, Committee on Publications of the group, 15 Mar. 1928.
12. JH to RS, 23 May and RS to JH, 29 May 1928.
13. JH to Harry H. Clark, 4 Jan. 1929; RS to JH, 28 Feb. 1928; KM to JH, 6 Mar. 1928; Rusk to JH, 7 Apr. 1928.
14. RS's final report of the Committee on Publications, 15 Mar. 1928; "The New American Literature Journal," read to the ALG by JH, Dec. 1928. See also *SSW*, 33–34.
15. KM to JH, 23 June; Cairns to JH, 30 June; TM to JH, 19 Oct. 1928. See also *SSW*, 35.
16. JH's memorandum to editors, 6 Dec. 1928; TM to JH, 8 Dec. 1928 and 18 Feb. 1929; Leisy to JH, 15 Jan. 1928; "The New American Literature Journal," read by JH to the ALG, Dec. 1928.
17. Leisy to JH, 15 Jan.; RS to JH, 28 Feb.; FP to JH, 8 Mar. 1928.
18. Leisy to JH, 15 Nov. 1927; FP to JH, 8 Mar. 1928. FP also wanted "letters to the editor," he told JH on 31 Dec. 1928, an idea that obviously went unheeded.
19. FP to JH, 8 Mar. 1928; KM to JH, 26 Oct. 1928; SB (secretary of ALG) to JH, 5 Jan. 1929.
20. KM to JH, 17 May 1929; JH to KM, 26 June; JH to Leisy, 29 June; TM to JH, 6 Sept.; JH to Mabbott, 1 Nov.; Mabbott to JH, 11 Nov.; JH to Cairns, 29 Jan. 1930.
21. JH, "The New American Literature Journal"; FP to JH, 14 Mar. 1929; Rusk to JH, 19 Apr. 1929.
22. Documents cited include Cairns, "Comment on the Clark–Foerster Review," 26 Jan. 1929; JH to Clark, 4 Jan. 1929; NF to JH, 12 Jan. and 16 Jan. 1929; KM to JH, 22 Jan. 1929; FP to JH, 2 Feb. 1929.
23. Cairns to JH, 18 Oct. 1929; Cargill to JH, 4 Jan. 1937.
24. Paine to JH, 27 Aug. 1929. The review appeared in *AL* 1 (Nov. 1929): 327–30.
25. Cairns to JH, 22 Feb. 1931. The review was in *AL* 3 (Mar. 1931): 102–3.
26. JH to FP, 1 Dec. 1931; FP to JH, 16 Jan. 1932. Millett's review of *The New American Literature* appeared in *AL* 3 (Nov. 1931): 323–26.
27. Pochman to JH, 8 Feb. 1934 and 1 Dec. 1935. The two reviews are in *AL* 7 (Mar. 1935): 106–8, and 8 (May 1936): 217–23.
28. HJ to JH, 9 Jan. 1937. The review is in *AL* 9 (Mar. 1937): 97–98.
29. Clark to JH, 6 May 1934 and 8 Nov. 1936; Gohdes to Clark, 15 Feb. 1950.

30. Cairns to JH, 17 Oct. 1930; JH to Cairns, 16 Sept. 1931; FP to JH, 16 Jan. 1932.
31. KM to JH, 27 Jan. 1933; HJ to JH, 12 Feb. 1939.

Chapter 17. Parrington's Main Currents in American Thought *(1927–1930)*

1. "Parrington, Mr. Smith, and Reality," *PR* 8 (Jan.–Feb. 1940): 24–40.
2. The basic document on VP's early life and career is an autobiographical sketch (c. 50 pp.) in 1918, which his grandson, Stevens Parrington Tucker, is preparing for publication along with other unpublished diaries, correspondence, and writings. I am indebted to two scholars who have inspected the personal sketch: Richard Hofstadter in *The Progressive Historians: Turner, Beard, Parrington* (1968) and Hall in her doctoral thesis (1979). Because Hall provides page numbers for her quotations, and seems to have examined this document with the greater care, I am following her account. I have also consulted materials at the University of Washington Libraries: the Harold Eby Papers, the V.L.O. Chittick Papers, and the VP items in the Pacific Northwest Collection.
3. Hofstadter says that VP's parents "strained their resources" to send him east for these two years (p. 363). James L. Colwell, "The Populist Image of Vernon Louis Parrington," *Mississippi Valley Historical Review* 49 (June 1962): 58, writes, however, that VP's father had acquired a modest financial cushion. Hall gives the scholarship figure, but she does not mention where the money came from (p. 75).
4. Hall, 77–79, 119. This diary and others will be published by Tucker.
5. Hall, 81–92.
6. Hall, 93–96, 123.
7. My synoptic discussion of VP's teaching at Washington comes from Hall, 137–47, and my own examination of the university catalogs and the VP materials in the archives of the University of Washington Libraries.
8. Blankenship remarked on VP's classroom manner, also, in an obituary article, "Vernon Louis Parrington," *Na* 129 (7 Aug. 1929): 141–42.
9. This information is in the archives of the University of Washington Libraries.
10. In the "English Studies" section of the *Washington Alumnus* 5 (17 Nov. 1911): 12, the notes on faculty research mentioned that VP was at work on a history of American literature in two volumes, and that volume 1 was completed.
11. Mr. Tucker is readying for publication the early manuscript and several drafts of *Main Currents,* along with other unpublished writings that will aid our understanding of VP's development, not the least being portions of an autobiographical novel, "Stuart Forbes: Stoic."
12. For this publishing information, I am indebted to the Parrington

Papers and Eby Papers at the University of Washington, and to Hall (169–71).

13. The quotation is in an unpublished letter to Elias T. Arnesen, 17 Nov. 1924, cited by Hofstadter, 377n.

14. *The Theory of American Literature* (1948), 141–42.

15. Quoted by Vernon Parrington, Jr., "Vernon Parrington's View: Economics and Criticism," *Pacific Northwest Quarterly* 44 (July 1953): 99.

16. All future pagination to *Main Currents* will be indicated in parentheses in my text, the quotations taken from the original Harcourt, Brace edition of 1927 (vols. I and II) and 1930 (vol. III). The present quotation is in I, iii.

17. Robert Skotheim first analyzed Parrington's inconsistent explanation of how environment affected ideas in the new world. See Robert A. Skotheim and Kermit Vanderbilt, "Vernon Louis Parrington: The Mind and Art of a Historian of Ideas," *Pacific Northwest Quarterly* 53 (Summer 1962): 100–13.

18. For a fuller discussion of Parrington's literary art, see Skotheim and Vanderbilt, 104–111.

19. *Century* 114 (June 1927): 254. See also VD's review in *NYHTB*, 1 May 1927, 5.

20. Reviews mentioned in this representative survey are Adams, *NYHTB*, 1 May 1927, 3; Beard, *Na* 124 (18 May 1927): 560, 562; HC, *SRL* 3 (25 June 1927): 925–26; Houston, *The Independent* 119 (22 Oct. 1927): 412; and KM, *YR* 17 (Jan. 1928): 382–84. Other reviews are listed in Hall, 485–87. Hofstadter, 490–91, briefly discussed the reception of *Main Currents* and then presented valuable data on the sales of various editions as a measure of continuing influence. To mid-1967, 304,000 volumes had been sold; and sales on the thirty-fifth-anniversary year (1962) alone equaled the total figure of the first decade. Within these totals, volume III had sold slightly less well, partly because it was not included in the paperback editions between 1955 and 1963.

21. For an interpretation of Parrington's late pessimism, wistful despair, and rallying hope, especially in "A Chapter in American Liberalism," which closes volume III, see Skotheim and Vanderbilt, 112–13.

22. Reviews mentioned here, in nearly chronological order, are Adams, *NYTBR,* 9 Nov. 1930, 14; Josephson, *Na* 131 (3 Dec. 1930): 615–16; Cohen, *NR* 65 (28 Jan. 1931): 303–4; Commager, *The Symposium* 2 (Jan. 1931): 122–28; Chittick, *AL* 2 (Jan. 1931): 442–46; NF, *SRL* 7 (4 Apr. 1931): 705–6; Wagenknecht, *Virginia Quarterly Review* 7 (Apr. 1931): 301–4; and SW, *NEQ* 4 (Apr. 1931): 352–54.

Chapter 18. The Heirs of Parrington: Four Leftist Histories during the Great Depression

1. John W. Caughey, "Historians' Choice: Results of a Poll on Recently Published American History and Biography," *Mississippi Valley*

Historical Review 39 (1952): 289–302. But in the same year, John Higham summarized the case against VP in "The Rise of American Intellectual History," *American Historical Review* 61 (1952): 460–61.

2. Letter to me, 12 Sept. 1962.
3. See SW, *YR* 21 (Dec. 1931): 432; Carpenter, *NEQ* 5 (Jan. 1932): 179–80; Smith, *AL* 4 (Mar. 1932): 78–82. In *SRL* 8 (1 Aug. 1931): 27 and *NR* 69 (25 Nov. 1931): 52, the book was moderately praised.
4. The reviews cited are Hicks, *NR* 72 (7 Sept. 1932): 104–5; Knight, *AL* 4 (Jan. 1933): 407–9; FOM, *NEQ* 6 (Mar. 1933): 190–95. Two other incisive reviews were by HC, *SRL* 9 (7 Sept. 1932): 101–2; and John Chamberlain, *Na* 135 (7 Dec. 1932): 571–72.
5. See Mumford, *SRL* 10 (23 Dec. 1933): 370; Cowley, *NR* 76 (8 Nov. 1933): 368–69; Blackmur, *Hound and Horn* 7 (Jan.–Mar. 1934): 351–55; NF, *American Review* 2 (Nov. 1933): 107–11; FOM, *Atlantic Bookshelf* (Dec. 1933): n. pag.; SW, *YR* 23 (Winter 1934): 417; RS, *AL* 6 (Nov. 1934): 358–61, and reprinted with an introductory comment in his *Milestones in American Literary History* (1977), 35–38.
6. *Part of the Truth*, 130–32.
7. These writings are now accessible in Jack A. Robbins, ed., *Granville Hicks in the New Masses* (1974). For an account of the group who founded the *New Masses* in 1926 with Joseph Freeman after the failure of *The Liberator* (1918–24), which had succeeded the original *The Masses* (1911–18), see Freeman's *An American Testament* (1936).
8. Most of the reviewers tolerated, even praised, Smith's ideological approach to American criticism (Lionel Trilling a major exception) while they were rather predictably disappointed with his aesthetic delinquency. See HC, *SRL* 20 (30 Sept. 1939): 8; Albert Guerard, *NYHTB*, 1 Oct. 1939, 4; Peter M. Jack, *NYTBR*, 15 Oct. 1939, 2, 32; Trilling, *PR* 7 (Jan.–Feb. 1940): 24–40; and Austin Warren, *AL* 12 (Jan. 1941): 504–8. Trilling later recast this review essay ("Parrington, Mr. Smith, and Reality") with a 1946 review of Dreiser's *The Bulwark*, for the memorable chapter, "Reality in America," in *The Liberal Imagination* (1950).

Chapter 19. More Advocacy in the Thirties: Humanists, Agrarians, Freudians, and Nationalists

1. J. David Hoeveler, Jr., *The New Humanism: A Critique of Modern America, 1900–1940* (1977), 4.
2. See "The Modern Current in American Literature," *Forum* 79 (Jan. 1928): 127–36, reprinted with slight revisions as "Modern Currents in American Literature" in *The Demon of the Absolute*, New Shelburne Essays, vol. I (1928), 53–76.
3. "The Critic and American Life," *Forum* 79 (Feb. 1928): 161–76, reprinted in *On Being Creative and Other Essays* (1932), 201–34.

4. See *Forum* 82 (Oct. 1929): xviii, xx, xxii, xxiv. Less susceptible to Babbitt's current rhetoric was Alfred Kreymborg. In *Our Singing Strength: An Outline of American Poetry (1620–1930)* (1929), he repudiated the standards of "objective criticism" being acclaimed by "confident people" and supported the impressionistic criticism that Babbitt was ridiculing. For Kreymborg, "the subconscious temper of the beholder colors the thing beheld" (p. 2); and he quoted approvingly Poe's creative pact between poet and reader (and critic).

5. See *Times Literary Supplement*, 10 Jan. 1929, 24.

6. Alter Brody, "Humanism and Intolerance," *NR* 61 (29 Jan. 1930): 278; "Babbitt Debates New Humanism Here," *NYT,* 10 May 1930, 4; and Collins, "Criticism in America: I. The Origins of a Myth, II. The Revival of the Anti-Humanist Myth, and III. The End of the Anti-Humanist Myth," *Bookman* 71 (June 1930): 241–56, 353–64; (July 1930): 400–15; 72 (Oct. 1930): 145–64, 209–28. And see Hoeveler, *The New Humanism,* 24–26.

7. *NR* 62 (26 Mar. 1930): 162.

8. Louis D. Rubin, Jr., "Introduction" to the Harper Torchbook edition (1962), xvii. Future page numbers in my text refer to this available newer edition.

9. Malcolm Bradbury, *The Fugitives: A Critical Account* (1958), 107.

10. D. H. Lawrence's remarkable essays on Cooper, Poe, Hawthorne, Melville, and Whitman in *Studies in Classic American Literature* (1923) must also be passed by in the present study, since they were apparently considered outré by earlier American scholars. Nearly all the authors of monographs on these figures in the 1920s and 1930s, and even Lewisohn himself, omitted mention of Lawrence's Freudian commentaries. Not until F. O. Matthiessen drew liberally on Lawrence's insights in *American Renaissance* (1941) did scholars begin to accept them. Unfortunately, Matthiessen never mentioned the title of Lawrence's book. Two years later, Edmund Wilson printed the entire *Studies* in his *The Shock of Recognition* and thus prepared the way for Lawrence's lively influence on American literature studies after World War II.

11. *Expression in America* (1932), vii. All page numbers hereafter are in parentheses in the text. Apparently out of a commercial motive, the book was retitled *The Story of American Literature* in later printings.

12. Reviews cited are VD, *Na* 134 (13 Apr. 1932): 429–30; Macy, *SRL* 8 (12 Mar. 1932): 583–84; HJ, *YR* 21 (Summer 1932): 836–39; Leisy, *AL* 5 (Mar. 1934): 285–86; Krutch, *NYHTB,* 13 Mar. 1932, 1; and Hicks, *NR* 70 (13 Apr. 1932): 240–41. For a New Humanist perspective on Lewisohn's "nonsense, and often offensive nonsense," see Dorothea Brande, *The American Review* 2 (Dec. 1933): 189–98.

13. On Freud and American literature, before and after Lewisohn's *Expression,* the standard account is Frederick J. Hoffman's *Freudian-*

ism and the Literary Mind (1945), enlarged in a second edition of 1957.

14. *An Autobiography* (1965), 451. Other page numbers occur in my text.
15. "The Literary Prophets," *Bookman* 72 (Sept. 1930): 35–44.
16. HJ, *Virginia Quarterly Review* 8 (July 1932): 439–42; Clark, "Nationalism in American Literature," *University of Toronto Quarterly* 2 (July 1933): 492–519.
17. *Nationalism in American Thought, 1930–1945* (1969), ix, 6, 11, 13.
18. For a good, brief treatment of Brooks's political activity, see Raymond Nelson, *Van Wyck Brooks: A Writer's Life* (1981), 214–28.
19. Nelson, 210–12.
20. William Wasserstrom, *Van Wyck Brooks* (1968), 40.
21. For Wade, see *Southern Review* 2 (Spring 1937): 807.
22. In chronological sequence, the reviews cited are VD, *NYHTB,* 16 Aug. 1936, 1–2; Commager, *NYTBR,* 23 Aug. 1936, 1, 15; Mark Van Doren, *YR* 26 (Sept. 1936): 168–70; FOM, *NEQ* 9 (Dec. 1936): 701–9; Warren, *The American Review* 8 (Dec. 1936): 245–49; and KM, *AL* 8 (May 1937): 465–67. Three additional reviews verged on the ecstatic: R. P. Blackmur, *Na* 143 (22 Aug. 1936): 218–19; HC, *SRL* 14 (22 Aug. 1936): 3–4, 15; and Malcolm Cowley, *NR* 88 (26 Aug. 1936): 79–80.

Chapter 20. American Literature in the University: Curriculum, Graduate Research, and Controversy in the Thirties

1. *Graduate Education in the United States,* 25–26.
2. Unless otherwise indicated, my information comes from Lewis, 260ff.
3. Gohdes, "The Study of American Literature in the United States," *English Studies* 20 (1938): 63.
4. See again Wesley First, ed., *University on the Heights* (1969).
5. See Hoeveler, *The New Humanism,* 120–22.
6. Data in the Northwest Collection, University of Washington Libraries.
7. "The Study of American Literature in the United States," 64.
8. Ibid., 64, 66.
9. This information was arranged without benefit of a computer from the data in Woodress.
10. See secretary's notes in *PMLA* 50 (1935): 1354. HJ's remarks were soon published in *AL* 8 (May 1936): 115–24.
11. *English Journal* (college edition) 25 (May 1936): 376–88. Three years later, the college edition became the separate journal, *College English.*
12. "The American Scholar" and "Enlightened Research," *SRL* 15 (26 Dec. 1936): 8, 14, and 15 (10 Apr. 1937): 8.
13. Bolwell's paper, subsequently printed in *AL* 10 (Jan. 1939): 405–16, was obvious and perfunctory, but the footnotes contained a helpful bibliography.

14. "The Study of American Literature in the United States," 65, 66.
15. "Culture and Cult," *SR* 47 (Jan.–Mar. 1939): 96–105. For more of the debate, see C. R. Heck, "The 'American Way' in College," *Harvard Educational Review* 8 (Mar. 1938): 228–36.
16. *CE* 1 (Mar. 1940): 513–19; and Woodress, passim.
17. Leisy to TM, 21 Mar. 1940, in ALG-UW. Leisy's paper in May 1940 at Oklahoma appeared in *CE* 2 (Nov. 1940): 115–24.

Chapter 21. Journals and Other Instruments of the New Scholarship

1. HJ to JH, 5 Sept. 1928, JBH-DU.
2. In ALG-UW is a list of texts proposed by ALG members. See also JH to Emory Holloway, 19 Nov. 1932, in JBH-DU.
3. Conversation with me at Duke, 14 June 1977. JH to RS, 26 Feb. 1930, calls attention to the error in the 1929 minutes by Secretary SB in which Gregory Paine was named the originator of the check list proposal (JBH-DU).
4. RS to Leland, 9 Feb. 1930, and Leland to RS, 24 Feb., in ALG-UW. The ACLS was founded in 1919.
5. Richardson to RS, 26 Feb. 1930, ALG-UW.
6. Records are in ALG-UW.
7. Correspondence is in ALG-UW: Brown to RS, 25 May 1931; RS to Brown, 1 June 1931; RS to SB, 3 June 1931; Brown to RS, 5 May 1931; RS to Brown, 3 June 1931.
8. In ALG-UW: RS to Brown, 29 July 1931; JH to RS, 21 Sept. 1931; RS to ALG Advisory Council, 1 Oct. 1931; and ALG minutes of 28 Dec. 1931.
9. Quinn to SB, 22 Dec. 1931 and ALG minutes, 29 Dec. 1933; both in ALG-UW. See also JH, *SSW* (p. 26), on the aborted check list efforts due to the Depression.
10. JH to Martin, 6 Mar. 1940, and Basler to JH, 26 Aug. 1954, are in JBH-DU. *American Literary Manuscripts* (1960) was the work of ALG members Ernest Marchand (San Diego State), H. Dan Piper (Cal Tech), J. Albert Robbins (Indiana), Herman E. Spivey (Tennessee), and Joseph Jones, Chairman (Texas).
11. JH to Leisy, 9 Jan. 1931, JBH-DU. ALG minutes at the Yale meeting, 29 Dec. 1932, are in ALG-UW.
12. JH to Committee on Resources for Research (Nelson, KM, SW, and RS), 14 Nov. 1932; JH to SW and SB, 12 Dec. 1933; RS to SB, 24 Dec. 1933. All in ALG-UW.
13. Minutes of these three ALG meetings are in ALG-UW. The full title of Foley's work is *American Authors, 1795–1895: A Bibliography of First and Notable Editions Chronologically Arranged with Notes* (1897).
14. SB to JH, 9 Dec. 1938, is in JBH-DU.
15. Clark to JH, 29 Apr. 1933, JBH-DU.
16. A further item on James in the 1930s should be mentioned not for its own particular value, which is relatively minor, but for the sig-

nificance of the total enterprise of which it was a part. This was VD's sketch of James in the *Dictionary of American Biography (DAB)*, the first of several dictionaries to appear in the 1930s, not only on American authors, but also on American linguistics and the American theater. The *DAB* was edited by Allen Johnson and later by Dumas Malone and sponsored by the ACLS (twenty-one volumes, 1928–44). Volume I in 1928 was reviewed in the first issue of *AL* the next year by W. B. Cairns, who termed the initial publication "almost an epoch-making event" for the profession, a new instrument of biographical scholarship to complement the *CHAL, Who's Who in America,* and nineteenth-century reference works by Kettell, Griswold, Duyckinck, Allibone, Stedman, and others.

17. *SSW,* 35; JH conversation with me, 14 June 1977; JH to Rusk, 11 Nov. 1930, JBH-DU.
18. JH to RS, 23 Feb. 1931, ALG-UW; *SSW,* 45.
19. HJ to JH, 18 Sept. 1931 and JH to Cairns, 21 Dec. 1931 are in JBH-DU. HJ to RS, 14 Oct. 1931 and the minutes of the Advisory Council, 28 Dec. 1931 are in ALG-UW.
20. ALG minutes at Yale, 29 Dec. 1932 and JH to SB, 18 Dec. 1933 are in ALG-UW. JH to SB, 6 Dec. 1938 and SB to JH, 9 Dec. 1938 are in JBH-DU.
21. Cairns to JH, 10 Jan. 1931 and JH to Cairns, 13 Jan. 1931 in JBH-DU.
22. SW to JH, 11 Apr. 1929; JH to SW, 17 Apr. 1929; SW to JH, 19 Apr. 1929; FP to JH, 12 Dec. 1934; KM to JH, 2 July 1929 and 20 Aug. 1932. All are in JBH-DU.
23. JH to RS, 21 Sept. 1931 and ALG notes of the Swarthmore meeting are in ALG-UW. HJ to JH, 14 Aug. 1935 is in JBH-DU.
24. HJ stipulated to *AL* that the reprint was not to be used as advertising bait by American Book Company to boost their series (the American Writers Series was being edited by Harry Clark). See HJ to Gohdes, 20 Apr. 1936, in JBH-DU. Ironically, HJ, with S. I. Hayakawa, subsequently edited the volume on Holmes (1939) in Clark's series.
25. Copy of Long's reply is in ALG-UW. My figures come from "Proceedings," *PMLA* 50 (1935): 1328, 1343, and 1362.
26. "The American Scholar," *SRL* 15 (26 Dec. 1936): 8.
27. SB to JH, 20 Mar. 1933, in JBH-DU.
28. Holloway to JH, 26 Jan. 1940; JH to FP, 1 Feb. 1939; both are in JBH-DU. FP's "Constance Fenimore Woolson and the South" appeared in *South Atlantic Quarterly* 38 (Apr. 1939): 130–41. For a roster of the leaders of the ALG from 1921 to 1948, see the Appendix.

Chapter 22. The Profession Plans a New Literary History

1. JH to HJ, 16 Oct. 1926, ALG-UW.
2. Letter of 15 Dec. 1931, JBH-DU.

3. JH to the committee, 14 Nov. 1932; RS to JH, 16 Nov. 1932; minutes dated 29 Dec. 1932. All are in ALG-UW.
4. *SR* 43 (Jan. 1935): 70–79.
5. SB to RS, 30 Jan. 1939; Clark to RS, 16 Mar. 1939. This and all subsequent correspondence in the present chapter, unless noted otherwise, are in LHUS-UP.
6. RS to VD, 3 Mar. and VD to RS, 15 Mar. 1939.
7. The agenda, minutes of the meeting, and memorandum are in LHUS-UP. The Yale "Chronicles of America Series" (1919) were edited by Allen Johnson, assisted by Gerhard R. Lomer and Charles W. Jefferys.
8. "Wanted—A History," *SRL* 20 (19 Aug. 1939): 8–9.
9. The letter from HJ (20 May 1939) is in ALG-UW.
10. Hodnett to RS, 31 Jan. and 23 Mar. 1939; correspondence with Macmillan in Apr. is in ALG-UW; HC to RS, 22 Aug. 1939; Brett to RS, 22 Nov. 1939.
11. JH to RS, 16 Oct. 1939; Wilt to RS, 27 Oct. 1939, and RS's conversation with me, 6 June 1977, in Philadelphia.
12. Memorandum to the committee, 27 Nov. 1939 and various replies are in LHUS-UP, as are HJ to RS, 9 Dec. 1939, and RS to HJ, 12 Dec. and 16 Dec. 1939.
13. RS's notes for this report are in LHUS-UP.
14. These minutes are in ALG-UW.
15. Wilt to TM, 1 Mar. and 18 Apr. 1940; TM to Advisory Council, 5 Mar. and 18 Apr. 1940; TM to RS, 19 May 1940; RS to TM, 19 June 1940. All, plus responses from council members, are in ALG-UW.
16. HJ to JH, 7 Nov. 1940, in JBH-DU; RS, "History of a History: A Study in Cooperative Scholarship," *PMLA* 89 (May 1974): 608; TM to Advisory Council, 4 Dec. 1940, in ALG-UW.
17. The report is in ALG-UW. In this same file bearing the ALG minutes of 1940 is an eleven-page carbon of a paper by RS, titled "Literary History and Cooperative Scholarship," in which he placed the committee report in historical perspective, summarizing the achievements of American literature scholarship since the *CHAL*. He then stressed that in canvassing opinion among the group during the past year, his committee had discovered that the majority of the members wanted to see editorial control over the multiplicity of contributor chapters, a unity of conception that would ensure a common agreement regarding environmental and evolutionary causes and effects, including the influences of local American conditions and European backgrounds. Contributors would be granted freedom of treatment within the framework of these causative forces. In "History of a History," RS admitted to a faltering memory but believed that this essay, which was neither published in advance with the other program papers (in *AL*) nor read to the group, "may have been circulated to the membership in mimeographed form" (p. 608).
18. "History of a History," 608.
19. Advisory Council minutes, ALG-UW.

20. See *English Institute Annual* for 1940 (1941), 115–29.
21. Minutes of the program are in ALG-UW. Remarks of RS are a covering note, dated 28 Sept. 1971, on the offer from Macmillan, previously cited, which was given as a letter by Brett to RS at the New Orleans meeting, 22 Dec. 1939 (in LHUS-UP). The papers of Wright, Clark, and Winters are in *AL* 12 (Nov. 1940): 283–305.
22. A copy of mimeographed notes sent to panelists is at JBH-DU. Minutes, including the figures on attendance, are in ALG-UW. In the proceedings of the meeting, published in *PMLA* 56 (1941): 1384–85, minor discrepancies appeared. The second panel attendance was given as twenty-one, the main titles of panels three and four became "Mid-Century Renaissance," and several participants were not mentioned.
23. A copy of the report is on file, along with TM's communications to the Advisory Council on 30 July 1943 and 28 Dec. 1944, in ALG-UW.
24. SW to RS, 14 Feb. 1943. TM to ALG, 12 Mar. 1943, and to Advisory Council, 30 July 1943, are in ALG-UW.

Chapter 23. The Cooperative History Goes Independent: Organization and Theory (1942–1943)

1. HC to RS, 6 Jan. and 24 Feb. 1941; RS to HC, 9 Feb. 1941. Unless noted otherwise, all documents on the making of the new literary history are in LHUS-UP. RS's recollections of the spring of 1941 and the house party at Killingworth are vividly gathered in his "History of a History," 610.
2. HC to RS, 20 Jan. and 27 Mar. 1942; WT to HC, 8 Apr. 1942. See also RS's "History of a History," 610.
3. WT to RS, 8 July 1942; RS to TJ, 11 July and TJ to RS, 13 July 1942; RS to SW, 11 July and SW to RS, 14 July 1942; RS to HJ, 11 July and HJ to RS, 16 July 1942; RS to DW, 27 Oct. and DW to RS, 6 Nov. 1942.
4. On the Princeton meeting, RS to HC, 2 Aug. 1942; on mailings, RS to TJ, 16 Aug. 1942. In LHUS-UP, box 6 contains Editorial Policy and Plans, an orderly file of board meetings, with the agenda and minutes numbered and dated.
5. HC to RS, 29 July and 11 Aug. 1942; RS to HC, 2 Aug. 1942. The grant application is dated 15 Sept. 1942.
6. TJ to RS, 11 Aug. and RS to TJ (copy to WT), 14 Aug. 1942. On 23 Jan. 1943, RS wrote to WT (copy to TJ) that he was prepared to devote full time to the *LHUS*.
7. RS to fellow editors, 21 July 1941; RS to WT, 10 Aug. 1941.
8. RS to HC, 9 Feb. 1941. RS formulated these ideas in "Blueprints for American Literary History" in the same year at the centennial at Fordham. He reprinted the paper in *Pennsylvania Literary Review* 8 (1957): 3–10 and in *The Third Dimension* (1965), 26–36.
9. RS to NF, 11 Nov. 1966, in ALG-UW.

10. DW to RS, 12 Jan. 1943 and RS to SW, 18 Jan. 1943.
11. HC to RS, 5 Mar. 1943.
12. RS to WT, 23 Jan. 1943.
13. HJ to RS, 31 Jan. and 10 Feb. 1943.
14. RS to HJ, 13 Feb. 1943; RS to HC and TJ, 20 Feb. 1943; RS to SW, 25 May 1943; and HJ to RS, 14 June 1943.
15. RS to HJ, 30 July 1943; RS to HC, 11 Aug. 1943; RS to VD, 16 Sept. and VD to RS, 20 Sept. 1943.

Chapter 24. The Editors in Profile (1943)

1. "How I Discovered America without Really Trying" (An address before the Franklin Inn Club of Philadelphia, Fri., 26 Sept. 1980), 3. This autobiographical sketch of 18 pp., which is based on headnotes to the essays that RS reprinted in *Late Harvest* (1981), is in JBH-DU. In the pages that follow, I rely on more of this memoir for information and quotations, together with data derived from *PMLA* and *AL* that have been valuable, too, for the rest of the chapter. For RS, I also draw on reminiscences he has shared with me since June 1977. I have also derived basic facts on all seven men from *Who's Who in America*.
2. Robert H. Walker and Robert F. Lucid understood that most of these, and other, reviews were an important record of RS's theoretical meditations on literary history, leading to the *LHUS*, and persuaded him to gather them, with headnotes, for the collection *Milestones in American Literary History* (1977).
3. The four-page memoir, "A Convert; Not a Founder," is in JBH-DU.
4. *Milestones in American Literary History*, 105.
5. TJ's fondness for Lawrenceville is documented in his correspondence in the school archives of the John Dixon Library.
6. *American Memoir* (1947), 253.
7. "Dr. Canby and His Team," *SRL* 47 (29 Aug. 1964): 54–55, 177. This was the fortieth-anniversary issue.
8. "Stanley Thomas Williams," a three-page typescript, dated 1982, in JBH-DU. See also *The National Cyclopaedia of American Biography* 46 (1963): 249–50.
9. In addition to *Howard Mumford Jones: An Autobiography* (1979), see "A Bibliography of Howard Mumford Jones" in the festschrift *Aspects of American Poetry*, ed. by Richard M. Ludwig (1962), 303–35.
10. Jones's memory of such a collection may be faulty, since NF's first American literature anthology, *Chief American Prose Writers*, did not appear until 1916. Perhaps Cairns's *Selections from Early American Writers, 1607–1800* (1909) was Jones's text.
11. *Autobiography*, 162.
12. Letter to me, 2 Aug. 1982.

Chapter 25. Screening the Contributors—and Early Contributions
(1943–1944)

1. HJ to RS, 28 Feb. and RS to HJ, 25 May 1943. All documents in this chapter are in LHUS-UP.
2. DW to RS, 20 Mar. and 9 Aug. 1944; HJ to RS, 15 July 1944. In 1960, Howard published his own history, *Literature and the American Tradition.*
3. RS to SW, 19 Jan. 1943; RS to WT, 10 Feb. 1943; SW to RS, 2 June 1943; RS to WT, 23 May 1945.
4. RS to HC, 22 June 1943.
5. RS to VD, 22 July and VD to RS, 26 July 1943.
6. RS to SW, 11 July 1942; RS to DW, 18 Sept. 1943; and TJ's minutes of the editorial meeting, 19 Dec. 1943.
7. RS to DW, 18 Sept. 1943; HC to RS, 4 Feb. 1944; TJ to HC, 15 Apr. 1944; WT to RS, 25 Aug. 1944.
8. Cowley to RS, 22 Dec. 1943; RS to DW, 19 Apr. 1944; and TJ to HC, 15 Apr. 1944. In his role as treasurer of the *LHUS* corporation, TJ also told HC, he now planned to use $14,000 of the Macmillan advance to buy short-term government notes in $1,000 units. But in a memorandum dated 4 May 1944, he informed the board that he had deposited in the bank in Princeton one $10,000 U.S. Treasury Note and three $1,000 notes.
9. SW to RS, 9 Jan. 1944; RS to DW, 25 Jan. 1944; SW to RS, 6 June 1943; Stewart to RS, 28 Dec. 1944; RS to WT, 9 Jan. 1945.
10. WT to RS, 25 Jan. 1944; RS to Baker, 20 Mar. and Baker to RS, 23 Mar. and 4 May 1944; RS to Baker, 15 Feb. 1947.
11. Memoranda of meetings on 10–12 June 1944 and 13–14 Jan. 1945; WT to RS, 1 Feb. 1944; memorandum by RS to editors, 13 Feb. 1945; and RS to Blodgett, 3 and 13 Apr. 1945.
12. RS to editors (but not associates), 13 Feb. 1945; RS to HC, 27 Feb. 1945.
13. RS to HC, 23 Jan. and 4 Apr. 1944; RS to David Bowers, 26 Sept. 1944; Memorandum on Introductory "Thought" Chapters, 20 Oct. 1944.

Chapter 26. American Literature and the Academy during
World War II (1939–1945)

1. "How I Discovered America," 10; *Journal of Higher Education* 13 (June 1942): 287–97.
2. Information on the lecture series is in the Johnson Papers, archives of the John Dixon Library, Lawrenceville School.
3. *Autobiography,* 218.
4. "The Irresponsibles," *Na* 150 (18 May 1940): 618–23. Also issued as a pamphlet (1940) for one dollar.
5. Correspondence in "On 'The Irresponsibles,'" *Na* 150 (1 June 1940): 681.

6. Ibid.
7. "On Being a Communist at Harvard," *PR* 44 (Number 4, 1977): 613. *Knowledge for What?* was, of course, the title of Robert S. Lynd's recent book (1939).
8. John Lydenberg, ed., *A Symposium on Political Activism and the Academic Conscience: The Harvard Experience, 1936–1941* (Geneva, N.Y.: Hobart and William Smith Colleges, 5 and 6 Dec. 1975), 33.
9. Mathews, *Na* 150 (8 June 1940): 718; Fletcher, *Na* 150 (22 June 1940): 766, 768; Zabel, "The Poet on Capitol Hill," *PR* 8 (Jan.–Feb. 1941): 2–19, and Mar.–Apr. 1941): 128–45.
10. Brooks, *Na* 150 (8 June 1940): 718, and *Autobiography,* 536; Dupee, *PR* 6 (Summer 1939): 69–85.
11. Morrison, *NEQ* 13 (Dec. 1940): 719–23; and Zabel, *Na* 141 (17 Aug. 1940): 137–38.
12. "Correspondence," *NR* 105 (1 Sept. 1941): 280.
13. "Van Wyck Brooks: Traditionally American," *CE* 2 (Apr. 1941): 629–39.
14. "Kulturbolschewismus Is Here," *PR* 8 (Nov.–Dec. 1941): 442–51.
15. "On the 'Brooks–MacLeish Thesis,'" *PR* 9 (Jan.–Feb. 1942): 38–47; T. S. Eliot, "A Letter to the Editors," (Mar.–Apr. 1942): 115–16.
16. See RS, *SRL* 27 (14 Oct. 1944): 24–26; SW, *YR* 34 (Winter 1945): 346–48; Cowley, *NR* 111 (9 Oct. 1944): 463, 465; Quinn, *AL* 16 (May 1945): 348–52; and Davis, *Na* 159 (7 Oct. 1944): 411–12.
17. *NYTBR,* 1 Oct. 1944, 1, 20.
18. FOM never gave a sketch to *Who's Who in America.* Biographical information has accumulated in various sources. After his death, 1 Apr. 1950, colleagues and friends contributed reminiscences and biographical essays to a special issue of the *Monthly Review* 2 (Oct. 1950), which were then gathered into a cloth-bound *F. O. Matthiessen (1902–1950): A Collective Portrait,* edited by Paul M. Sweezy and Leo Huberman (1950), with an added biographical sketch by Sweezy (pp. ix–xii). Hereafter, this volume will be cited as *Collective Portrait.* George A. White, "Ideology and Literature: *American Renaissance* and F. O. Matthiessen," *Tri-Quarterly* 23/24 (Winter/Spring 1972): 430–500, includes significant data, while vital statistics appear in Joseph H. Summers and U. T. Miller Summers, "Francis Otto Matthiessen," *Dictionary of American Biography,* supplement 4, 1946–1950 (1974), 559–61. Giles B. Gunn's *F. O. Matthiessen: The Critical Achievement* (1975) laces critical analysis with the chronological thread of FOM's life. For autobiography, especially on FOM's political and educational opinions, see the journal of later 1947, *From the Heart of Europe* (1948). Recently, Louis Hyde, FOM's classmate at Yale, has edited *Rat & the Devil: Journal Letters of F. O. Matthiessen and Russell Cheney* (1978), an invaluable record of a twenty-year friendship in which FOM describes the progress of his reading and writing, together with his

teaching duties and personal relations at Harvard. It will be cited hereafter as *Journal Letters*.

19. *YR* 18 (Mar. 1929): 603–5.
20. The letter, dated 17 Dec. 1930, is in the FOM collection at Yale and cited by Hyde, *Journal Letters*, 225. Other information in this paragraph has also been drawn from Hyde.
21. "F. O. Matthiessen," *American Scholar* 46 (Winter 1976): 86–88. For Rackliffe, see *Collective Portrait*, 245.
22. Marx, "The Teacher," and Wilbur, "Statements by Friends and Associates," in *Collective Portrait*, 37–41, 145.
23. *Collective Portrait*, 142.
24. *Journal Letters*, 271, 274, 277.
25. "The Humanities in War Time," *The 1943 Harvard Album*, 33–37, and "Education After the War," *NR* 110 (24 Jan. 1944): 121–22.
26. Paul M. Sweezy, "Labor and Political Activities," *Collective Portrait*, 68.
27. J. H. Summers and KM, *Cooperative Portrait*, 143 and 129–30, respectively.
28. *Milestones in American Literary History*, 54.
29. Besides Bowron's "The Making of an American Scholar," *Collective Portrait*, 44–54, FOM's development is helpfully discussed in White, "Ideology and Literature," and Gunn, *F. O. Matthiessen*, 3–67.
30. Sweezy and Marx, *Collective Portrait*, 61–68 and 41, respectively.
31. *Journal Letters*, 246.
32. Details of the composition of *American Renaissance* are derived here from White, "Ideology and Literature," and Hyde, *Journal Letters*, passim.
33. Reviewers cited are Hellman, *NYTBR*, 15 June 1941, 4; Fadiman, *New Yorker* 17 (7 June 1941): 74, 76; SW, *YR* 31 (Autumn 1941): 200–2; RS, *SRL* 24 (14 June 1941): 6 and *AL* 13 (Jan. 1942): 432–35; and Hicks, *NEQ* 14 (Sept. 1941): 556–66.
34. *Collective Portrait*, 282–83.
35. *NYHTB*, 13 July 1941, 3.
36. *Starting Out in the Thirties* (1965), 4. Biographical data on the making of *On Native Grounds* is drawn from this book; page numbers appear in my text.
37. *NR* 85 (15 Jan. 1936): 290–91.
38. *PR* 7 (Sept.–Oct. 1940): 402–4.
39. *New York Jew* (1978), 6, 20. Kazin was not drafted, but after serving as contributing editor for *NR* and *Fortune*, he went in 1945 on a Rockefeller fellowship to study the popular education movement in the trade unions and armed forces in England.
40. RS, *AL* 15 (Nov. 1943): 303–5; HJ, *SRL* 25 (25 Oct. 1942): 5–6; Haight, *YR* 15 (Mar. 1943): 620–22; FOM, *NEQ* 16 (June 1943): 326–28 and "Criticism and Fiction," *Journal of the History of Ideas* 4 (June 1943): 368–73.
41. Trilling, *Na* 155 (7 Nov. 1942): 483–84; Haight, *YR* 15 (Mar. 1943): 621.

42. *The Opinions of Oliver Allston,* 246.

43. *SR* 51 (Jan. 1943): 52–61.

44. "Literature and the Professors: A Symposium," *Southern Review* 6 (Autumn 1940): 225–69; and *Kenyon Review* 2 (Autumn 1940): 403–42.

45. See Gullette, "The Professor and His Critics," *CE* 2 (May 1941): 776–85; Schockley and Walcutt, "The American Literature Curriculum at the University of Oklahoma," *CE* 1 (May 1940): 679–85; Parks, "Literature as Intellectual History," *CE* 3 (Mar. 1942): 574–76; and Daiches, "The New Program for the A.M. Degree in English at the University of Chicago," *CE* 4 (Nov. 1942): 121–26.

46. Short, "The Dilemma Presented by Historical Scholarship," *CE* 5 (Jan. 1944): 214–18; Brown, "The English Professor's Dilemma," *CE* 5 (Apr. 1944): 379–85; Abel, "Intellectual Criticism," *American Scholar* 12 (Autumn 1943): 414–28; and Brooks, "The New Criticism: A Brief for the Defense," *American Scholar* 13 (Summer 1944): 285–95.

47. "Courses in American Civilization," *New York Times,* 16 Jan. 1944, E9; *American Literature in the College Curriculum* (1948), 32–49.

48. "Proceedings," *PMLA* 60 (1945): 1377.

49. A recent bibliographical essay that complements my synoptic account is Philip Gleason's "World War II and the Development of American Studies," *American Quarterly* 36 (1984): 343–58.

50. Koester, "Where is the American Department?" *Journal of Higher Education* 11 (Mar. 1940): 135–37; Stovall, "What Price American Literature?: American Scholar and American Literature," *SR* 49 (Oct.–Dec. 1941): 469–75.

51. DeVane, "The English Major," *CE* 3 (Oct. 1941): 47–52; and Herold, "'The English Major' Reconsidered," *CE* 4 (Dec. 1942): 174–78.

52. *American Literature in the College Curriculum,* 22. My remaining data come from pp. 23–31 of this report.

53. Information in this paragraph was derived from the listings in Woodress.

54. DeVoto, "The Maturity of American Literature," *SRL* 27 (5 Aug. 1944): 14–18.

55. JH to Alexander Cowie, 9 Dec. 1943, ALG-UW; and miscellaneous editorial correspondence, JBH-DU.

56. See Donna Gerstenberger and George Hendrick, eds., *Directory of Periodicals* (1959).

57. Bibb, 380.

58. The most concise but also detailed background and survey of military programs in the academy during World War II is "The American College in Wartime," printed in three parts by *Publisher's Weekly* 144 (13 Nov. 1943): 1862–68; (27 Nov. 1943): 2014–21; and (11 Dec. 1943): 2166–71. "Hobart under V-12" appeared in *Newsweek* 22 (2 Aug. 1943): 72, one of several journalistic feature articles that described the military experience on American campuses. For the

ASTP debâcle, two informative articles are "Bomb for the Colleges," *Newsweek* 23 (28 Feb. 1944): 90; and Robert G. Hawley, "The Army Quits the Colleges," *Harper's* 188 (Apr. 1944): 419–25.

59. Estabrooks, "Campus Revolution," *Saturday Evening Post* 216 (18 Sept. 1943): 14–15, 74, 77; HC, "The American Scholar and the War," *SRL* 26 (13 Jan. 1943): 10, 21, prepared for the MLA meeting in 1942, which was "not held on account of restriction on travel"; and Arvin, "Report from the Academy: *The Professor as Manager,*" *PR* 12 (Spring 1945): 275–78.

60. Holloway, "The American Tradition and the Future," *CE* 4 (Apr. 1943): 417–22; Miller, "Some Unexpected Results of College Military Programs," *CE* 5 (May 1945): 444–48; and FOM, "Education after the War," *NR* 110 (24 Jan. 1944): 121–22.

Chapter 27. The LHUS: *Shaping the Text (1945–1948)*

1. RS to HJ, 13 Mar. 1944; minutes of the meeting of 13–14 Nov. 1943; RS to TJ, 10 Apr. 1945; and RS to DW, 1 Feb. 1946. All correspondence in this chapter is in LHUS-UP.

2. HJ to RS, 24 Dec. 1945; RS to HJ, 13 and 26 June 1946. The editorial critiques are in boxes 8–15, LHUS-UP.

3. Powell to RS, 3 Mar. 1946.

4. In a letter to RS on 22 June 1945, SW gave a timetable summary of his five chapters for the *LHUS*. On the Irving and Cooper, he had begun composition in Oct. 1943, sent the manuscript to the editors in Apr. 1944, and agreed to separate the authors into two chapters in June 1944. By June 1945, he was satisfied that he had shaped the Cooper chapter to a proper length.

5. RS's comment is in "The History of a History," 612.

6. RS to Bowers, 21 Mar. 1945 and to Mrs. Bowers, 5 Sept. 1945; RS to HC, 27 Feb. 1945.

7. SW to RS, 22 June 1945. The date of WT's composing the Melville chapter is indicated in a letter to RS on 10 Sept. 1945: He was preparing to write the essay while on vacation in Sewanee. His review of HJ is in *NEQ* 18 (Mar. 1945): 110–12. He wrote shortly thereafter to RS that HJ was unhappy with this reception, "but I have appeased him" (26 Apr. 1945).

8. DW to RS, 11 Jan. 1946; WT to RS, 31 Jan. 1945.

9. RS to Margaret Thorp, 11 Mar. 1946 and Margaret Thorp to RS, 16 Mar. 1946.

10. Baker to RS, 17 Dec. 1945; Baker to WT (copy to RS), 27 Feb. 1946.

11. Geismar's response appears in RS to HC, 5 Dec. 1944. HC's response is in a letter to RS, 15 Dec. 1944.

12. RS to Blackmur, 22 Oct. 1945, 14 Mar. 1946, and 31 Aug. 1946; Blackmur to RS, 19 Nov. 1945 and 5 Jan., 13 Mar., 28 July, and 4 Sept. 1946. See also RS, "The History of a History," 614, 616.

13. DW to RS, 7 Dec. 1943; SW to RS, 22 June 1945.

14. RS to HC, 8 and 29 Nov. 1946.
15. RS to Farrell, 21 Nov. 1943; Farrell to RS, 17 Dec. 1943; RS to HJ, 13 Mar. 1944; HC to RS, 29 Dec. 1943; RS to Farrell, 16 Jan. 1945.
16. Farrell to RS, 14 Feb. 1945, 22 May, and 8 Aug. 1946; RS to Farrell, 14 May, 26 July, 5 Aug., and 20 Aug. 1946; Farrell to FOM, 8 Aug. 1946. Farrell's essay on Dreiser appeared in the *Chicago Review* 1 (Summer 1946): 127–44.
17. RS to WT, 5 Aug. 1946; RS to HC and TJ, 24 Oct. 1946.
18. Curti to RS, 8 Mar. 1947; Taylor to RS, 1 Mar. 1947; Levin to RS, 13 Mar. 1947; and Cowley to RS, 3 Mar. 1947.
19. Cowley to RS, 9 Apr. 1944. Spiller's comments on Zabel are dated 23 Feb. 1947 in box 20, LHUS-UP.
20. RS to Brett, 4 Mar. 1947; RS to Blanshard, 5 Mar. 1947; memorandum of 4 Mar. 1947; HJ to RS, 10 Mar. 1947; and RS, "History of a History," 614. The authorized manuscript, with inked-in revisions, is in boxes 19 and 20, LHUS-UP. A note on a piece of cardboard in box 19 explains the stages of the manuscript described in the present paragraph.
21. RS to TJ, 20 May 1943; TJ to contributors, 22 Mar. 1944; RS to TJ, 20 Apr. 1945; RS to HC, 22 May 1945; TJ to RS, 2 May 1946; and RS to Brett, 25 Nov. 1946. The typed manuscript of the bibliography volume is in box 21, LHUS-UP.
22. Brett to TJ, 25 Aug. 1947; RS to WT, 19 June 1948; WT to RS, 29 June 1948, and RS to WT, 10 Aug. 1948. Uncorrected page proofs and a carbon copy of the index are in boxes 22 and 23, LHUS-UP.

Chapter 28. Reception of the LHUS: *Summary Estimate of the Profession*

1. *SRL* 31 (27 Nov. 1948): 9–10, 33. During a conversation on 6 June 1977, RS described Pearson's preparation for the review. By an absurd error, among the pictures of the editorial board, *SRL* mistakenly produced one of economist and government official Willard Long Thorp.
2. *NYTBR*, 5 Dec. 1948, 4, 47.
3. *Na* 168 (22 Jan. 1949): 103–4.
4. *CE* 10 (Mar. 1949): 353–54.
5. *YR* 38 (Spring 1949): 558–61.
6. RS to Pearson, 20 Apr. 1949, LHUS-UP. Barzun's review is in *Harper's* 198 (Mar. 1949): 108–12.
7. *Quarterly Journal of Speech* 35 (Apr. 1949): 242–49.
8. Pearson, "A Review of a Review," and Myers, "The Reviewer's Reply," in *Quarterly Journal of Speech* 35 (Oct. 1949): 354–57.
9. The phrase is in RS to Pearson, 20 Apr. 1949, LHUS-UP.
10. *American Quarterly* 1 (Summer 1949): 169–83.
11. *Kenyon Review* 11 (Summer 1949): 500–6.
12. *AL* 21 (Jan. 1950): 489–92. Correspondence mentioned is in JBH-DU: JH to Rusk, 29 Sept. 1947; Rusk to JH, 3 Oct. 1947; JH to

Rusk, 12 Nov. 1948; Rusk to JH, 15 Nov. 1948; Gohdes to Rusk, 21 Jan. and 13 Sept. 1949. In LHUS-UP, box 27, Rusk's review is filed with a note attached by the perhaps battle-weary RS: "I don't recall—and objectively so—a review so basically filled with *no, not, un-, mis-,* and solid paragraphs of summary negatives. Gee! What an unhappy guy!"

13. *Modern Language Notes* 65 (Apr. 1950): 258–61. Other reviews, many on file in LHUS-UP, include in chronological order: *Kirkus* 16 (15 Aug. 1948): 430; H. W. Hart, *Library Journal* 73 (15 Sept. 1948): 1276; Emmett Dedmon, *Chicago Sun,* 28 Nov. 1948, 9; Lloyd Morris, *New York Herald Tribune Weekly,* 28 Nov. 1948, 1; *New Yorker* 24 (4 Dec. 1948): 181; Ernest Leisy, *Dallas Morning News,* 5 Dec. 1948; *Springfield Republican,* 5 Dec. 1948, 12; Edward Wagenknecht, *Chicago Sun Tribune,* 5 Dec. 1948; Eleanor Tilton, *Philadelphia Enquirer,* 12 Dec. 1948; *Time* 52 (13 Dec. 1948): 118 ("What a reader misses here is what he finds in Vernon Louis Parrington's *Main Currents in American Thought:* one mind in command of a subject, sometimes pulling a boner but more often arousing excitement and curiosity, and always leaving on the reader the sharp stamp of an original point of view"); George Mayberry, *NR* 119 (27 Dec. 1948): 25–26; C. J. Rolo, *AtM* 183 (Jan. 1949): 88; Roy Hillbrook, *Current History* 16 (Jan. 1949): 31; George Snell, *San Francisco Chronicle,* 9 Jan. 1949, 10; *Booklist* 45 (15 Jan. 1949): 175; James van Zandt, *Churchman* 163 (15 Jan. 1949): 31; W. E. Garrison, *Christian Century* 66 (16 Feb. 1949): 207–8; Marcus Cunliffe, *School and Society* 70 (23 July 1949): 57–58; *Times Literary Supplement,* 29 July 1949, 481–82; Henry W. Sams, *Journal of Higher Education* 21 (Jan. 1950): 50–52; and Harry R. Warfel, *Modern Language Quarterly* 12 (Mar. 1951): 114–15.
14. "The History of a History," 602.
15. Ibid.

Postwar Epilogue: New Directions in a Thriving Profession

1. "Epilogue: A Time of Troubles," in a 1983 reprinting of *History: Professional Scholarship in America* (1965), 238.
2. "Education After the War," *NR* 110 (24 Jan. 1944): 122.
3. Berelson, *Graduate Education in the United States,* 32, 35.

Index

NOTE: This index does not record all the pages in which names of the countless American literary figures appear and reappear in the book. If writers have been discussed or mentioned in the text as critics, editors, literary historians, or teachers, they are entered here.